Hearing Voices

The Histories, Causes and Meani_ _
Verbal Hallucinations

The meanings and causes of hearing voices that others cannot hear (auditory verbal hallucinations, in psychiatric parlance) have been debated for thousands of years. Voice-hearing has been both revered and condemned, understood as a symptom of disease as well as a source of otherworldly communication. Those hearing voices have been viewed as mystics, potential psychiatric patients or simply just people with unusual experiences, and have been beatified, esteemed or accepted, as well as drugged, burnt or gassed. This book travels from voice-hearing in the ancient world through to contemporary experience, examining how power, politics, gender, medicine and religion have shaped the meaning of hearing voices. Who hears voices today, what these voices are like and their potential impact are comprehensively examined. Cutting-edge neuroscience is integrated with current psychological theories to consider what may cause voices and the future of research in voice-hearing is explored.

SIMON MCCARTHY-JONES is a Postdoctoral Fellow at Macquarie University's Centre for Cognitive Science, in Sydney, Australia.

Hearing Voices

The Histories, Causes and Meanings
of Auditory Verbal Hallucinations

Simon McCarthy-Jones

CAMBRIDGE
UNIVERSITY PRESS

CAMBRIDGE
UNIVERSITY PRESS

The Edinburgh Building, Cambridge CB2 8RU, UK

Published in the United States of America by Cambridge University Press, New York

Cambridge University Press is part of the University of Cambridge.

It furthers the University's mission by disseminating knowledge in the pursuit of education, learning and research at the highest international levels of excellence.

www.cambridge.org
Information on this title: www.cambridge.org/9781107682016

© Simon McCarthy-Jones 2012

First published 2012
First paperback edition 2013

A catalogue record for this publication is available from the British Library

Library of Congress Cataloguing in Publication data

McCarthy-Jones, Simon, 1978–
    Hearing voices : the histories, causes, and meanings of auditory verbal hallucinations / Simon McCarthy-Jones.
        p. ; cm.
    Includes bibliographical references and index.
    ISBN 978-1-107-00722-2 (Hardback)
    I. Title.
[DNLM: 1. Hallucinations–history.   2. Hallucinations–psychology.
3. Auditory Perception–physiology.   4. Hallucinations–etiology.   5. Mental
Disorders–history.   6. Public Opinion–history. WM 204]
    616.89–dc23

                                                                                    2011035576

ISBN 978-1-107-00722-2 Hardback
ISBN 978-1-107-68201-6 Paperback

For those whose voices have not been heard (yet)
With gratitude to my wife, whose love creates me

Contents

Figures

Tables

Text boxes

Introduction

'If you go to New South Wales', observed Aldous Huxley, 'you will see marsupials hopping about the countryside. If you go to the antipodes of the mind, you will encounter all sorts of creatures at least as odd as kangaroos ... Strange psychological creatures leading an autonomous existence according to the laws of their own being' (Huxley, 1972, p. 85). One such species of strange creature is the voices heard sporadically by many, and frequently by a few, which other people cannot hear. Such experiences form the topic of this book.

How can we define somewhat more precisely the topic that it is focused on?[1] In the language of the contemporary mind sciences (e.g. psychology, psychiatry) this book is about auditory verbal hallucinations (AVHs). As has been remarked before, it is surprisingly difficult to come to a satisfactory definition of AVHs (Aleman & Larøi, 2008). David's (2004) general definition of a hallucination can be adapted to create a definition of an AVH as: 'Hearing speech in the absence of corresponding external stimulation of the ear, with a sufficient sense of reality to resemble a veridical perception, over which the subject does not feel s/he has direct and voluntary control, and which occurs in the awake state.' Yet this definition is insufficient for a number of reasons. One problem is that it only covers a subset of experiences involving hearing voices. In practice, AVH is used as a blanket term to cover a range of experiences which can range from hearing a clear voice coming from the external world when there is none there (which may lead you to go and look behind the sofa to see if someone's there) through to inaudible, soundless voices located within one's own head, and experiences that are more 'thought-like' than voice-like (Bleuler, 1950; Moritz & Larøi, 2008). Some have argued that the latter are pseudo-hallucinations (or pseudo-AVHs in this case). However, the distinction between hallucinations and pseudo-hallucinations has been argued to be of limited use

---

[1] An important issue in this book will be who constitutes this 'we' that does the defining and deciding.

1

(Bentall, 2003; Copolov, Trauer & Mackinnon, 2004). Indeed, Berrios & Dening (1996) describe the concept as a way for psychiatrists to 'call into question the genuineness of some true hallucinatory experiences that do not fit into a pre-conceived psychiatric diagnosis' (p. 761). The full spectrum of voice-hearing experiences will be classed as part of the family of AVHs here. The phenomenology of AVHs will be examined in Part II of this book, but it is clear from this initial pass that we are talking about a range of experiences with a family resemblance to each other (Wittgenstein, 1953), which may elude a single definition.

A different road may be trodden by considering Wittgenstein's famous maxim that we 'Don't ask for the meaning, ask for the use' (Fann, 1971, p. 68). This suggests that we can best establish the meaning of a term not by defining it, but by examining how it is used (ibid.). How, then, is the term AVH used? Sarbin (1967) has argued that the use of the term hallucination is 'pejorative, coterminous with madness, lunacy, and schizophrenia' (p. 379). Thus, AVH is not a neutral term, but the sediment of a battle which has hardened, turned to stone, and taken on the appearance of eternity. As we will see in Chapter 2, its contemporary meaning as a medical symptom was forged in the furnace of the English Civil War. Medicine at this time became a weapon of war, an axe to be wielded by a church–state motivated by the need to invalidate the claim of people to have meaningful, religious communications with the divine. The pejorative connotation of the term 'hallucination' has led to service-user-led organisations (such as the Hearing Voices Movement) advocating the use of the more neutral terms 'hearing voices' and 'voice-hearing'. This reflects the fact that the term AVH is one which has been created by a professional class who do not typically have the experience themselves, and which is rejected by those who do. As such, it is a colonial term (see Chapters 3, 12; Dillon & May, 2002).

A simple definition also cannot give us a feel for the wider consequences of hearing voices. Whilst many people will hear voices sporadically (Chapter 6) with little impact on their lives, for those who hear voices frequently, the experience is about more than just hearing a voice; it is about the changes in them and their world that it leads to, whether this be positive or negative.[2] After and during such extensive voice-hearing experiences, the world changes for the individual. It is not an abstract experience which one can learn about by just examining the

---

[2] As we will see in Chapter 5, negative experiences of voices are problematic due to the basic human needs that are often impaired by not being able to cope with them. Yet hearing voices is also about benevolent voices, spirit guides and meaningful insights. Hearing voices is many things.

> **Box I.1: Ten questions regarding hearing voices**
>
> 1. What are the phenomenologies of hearing voices, and how do they vary?
> 2. What are the meanings of hearing voices?
> 3. What are the proximal biological and psychological causes of hearing voices?
> 4. What are the distal biological, psychological and social causes of hearing voices?
> 5. How can we develop histories of hearing voices?
> 6. Why do voices often co-occur with other specific experiences (e.g. delusions)?
> 7. What makes some voices distressing, and how can distressed people recover?
> 8. How could (and should) voices be prevented from occurring in the first place?
> 9. How do power, interest and politics affect voice-hearing and voice-hearers?
> 10. What do voices tell us about the nature of self, thought and consciousness?

properties of the voice. It is a lived experience (Chapter 5) and an experience lived, in most of the Western world, in hostile territory. Throughout this book I will vary my use of the terms hearing voices and AVHs, depending on the context they are being discussed in, but the issues raised here over terminology should be kept in mind.[3]

What is an appropriate answer to the enigmatic experience that is hearing voices? This very much depends on which question we are interested in, and who 'we' are. I can only speak for myself, but I propose that there are at least ten key questions which need to be answered (see Box I.1). In order to start to address these questions (and they will not all be covered here), this book will focus on four key areas: (1) the histories of hearing voices, (2) the phenomenologies of hearing voices (i.e. what is the experience like?), (3) the causes of hearing voices and (4) the meanings of hearing voices. Of course, these are not neat, isolated questions, and they will interact with each other

---

[3] Elsewhere, to reflect the dark past (and present) of the term, I proposed that we refer to hallucinations as ~~hallucinations~~, in order to force us to keep these pejorative and historical factors in mind (Jones, 2010b; McCarthy-Jones, 2011a). Over hundreds of pages, though, this is not the most aesthetic approach, and would undoubtedly cause my own personal civil war with my proofreaders, so I will not employ it here.

For example, by examining a history of hearing voices in Part I, we will see how fluid/stable the phenomenology of voices has been across diverse times and cultures, how different meanings have been given to the experience (and what drives these changes in meanings) and encounter historical figures' theories of what causes voices. I use the term 'histories' in the title of this book to reflect that in addition to creating a history of hearing voices across the sweep of the centuries, I also wish to stress how the personal history of a voice-hearer is key to understanding their experiences (Chapter 11). By examining the phenomenology of hearing voices in Part II we will see what voices are like today, how properties of voices encourage specific meanings and establish what neuropsychological models need to be able to explain. By examining the causes of hearing voices in Part III, in a biopsychosocial way, we will have to square our answer with the results of an examination of the meanings people give to the experience. For example, how does a neural understanding of voices impact upon religious and spiritual interpretations of voices? We may imagine these four key areas as each sitting on a corner of a square, linked by a line to each other, illustrating their inter-relatedness. This joined-up approach based in history, phenomenology, causation and meaning seems to me to be a sensible way to understand hearing voices, or indeed, any human experience.

This approach will need input, at a minimum, from disciplines such as psychiatry, psychology, philosophy, sociology, anthropology, biology, neurology, history, theology, medical humanities and English studies and, crucially, from both voice-hearers and non-voice-hearers. If I was pushed to name such an approach, I might reach for the slightly pretentious term 'synergistic disciplinary pluralism' (SDP). I must disappoint you from the start, though, by telling you that I am not qualified to undertake this task. However, I salvage my self-esteem by suggesting that no one person is likely to be qualified to undertake such a project on their own. Hence, this book should be seen as a provisional start for a greater project – an interdisciplinary study of hearing voices to be undertaken jointly by a team of experts-by-training (including members from at least all of the disciplines above) and experts-by-experience (voice-hearers themselves).[4] Thus, I see this book as something which will be followed by a more comprehensive project, but hope that it still has value in itself.

I am trained as a research psychologist and am not a clinician. My own personal experiences of hearing voices have been limited to occasional voice-hearing experiences as I have been on the verge of falling asleep.

---

[4] The two are, of course, not mutually exclusive.

I thus claim no profound insights from first-hand experience. However, I have had the privilege of having been able to research this area for many years, to talk with people from all over the world about their experiences of hearing voices (some of whom have been given psychiatric diagnoses, others who have not), and to discuss hearing voices with colleagues from a range of disciplines. Any errors in this book are, of course, mine, not theirs.

I hope all of this has not put you off reading this book. It is my hope that you will be able to take something useful from it, and that perhaps in return you too can come to be involved in the journey to better explain and understand the experience of hearing voices, whatever your experiences, training or background.

Structure of this book

Part I of the book creates a history of hearing voices. I try to avoid a Whiggish account, i.e. a narrative which is one of inevitable, continual progress from ignorant superstition to a culmination today in our biomedical accounts of AVHs. As will be seen in Part I, there have always existed, side-by-side, two jostling discourses of hearing voices: the biomedical, pathological story and the spiritual or otherwise meaningful story. These discourses have been used as tools at various times by various people to achieve invariant aims: control and power, be this the Church trying to discipline its flock, or the voice-hearer trying to regain control and power over the meaning of their own experiences which were taken from them. Of course, some discourses span both these accounts, with St Thomas Aquinas, for example, in his account of voice-hearing, searching for the angels that moved the humours. A future work may wish to examine these different discourses separately and in greater detail.

Part II will look at the phenomenology of hearing voices today. This will first examine the phenomenology of voices in a psychiatric context, the lived experience of hearing voices in those diagnosed with a psychotic disorder, and start to think about how one may recover. We will then go outside of voice-hearing diagnosed as a mental disorder to examine voice-hearing and religion, and the varied cross-cultural voice-hearing experiences. Next we will examine voice-hearing in the general population (adult and child) and in what have been termed 'healthy voice-hearers' (Moritz & Larøi, 2008, p. 104)[5] – individuals with extensive and

---

[5] The terminology is something of a minefield here. I will use the term 'healthy voice-hearer' in this book to refer to someone who frequently hears voices, copes with them, and is able to live their life. This is not meant to imply that there are 'unhealthy

complex AVHs who cope well with their experiences and do not seek psychiatric help. The question will be addressed as to what differentiates those with voices who have become psychiatric patients to healthy voice-hearers. In this part of the book I will also make a distinction between two types of voices, which I will term Type 1 and Type 2 AVHs, and which I will suggest may have different causes and require different therapeutic approaches.

Part III will then look at the causes of hearing voices. It will first examine the neuroscience of hearing voices, then relate these findings to (neuro-)cognitive models of such experiences. Next we will go 'beyond the brain' to look out at the world and consider psychosocial causes of hearing voices.

Part IV will then consider the meanings of hearing voices, and examine the clashing paradigms that sometimes occur between two very different ways of understanding the hearing voices experience. The new 'Maastricht approach' to hearing voices, which has emerged out of the Hearing Voices Movement, will also be examined here. I will then pull these strands together in the Conclusion, where I will put forward what I think is a useful model of hearing voices, and what new aspects need to be considered.

It is worth stating at the outset what this book will not look at in any significant detail, lest you be flicking through this Introduction in a bookshop wondering if this book is for you. First, as the book's focus is on voice-hearing experiences that spontaneously occur, voices which are intentionally induced (e.g. in trance states or through ingestion of psychedelics) will not be examined. There is a fascinating literature on the invocation of voices through rite, ritual and drugs, from Ancient Sumeria and Egypt to today (e.g. Bourguignon, 1970), and such experiences may inform both our understanding of the causal mechanisms underlying voices, and cultural analyses of the meaning of hearing voices in society. However, this lies outside the scope of the book. Second, as it is auditory verbal experiences that will be focused on, non-verbal auditory hallucinations will not be examined. Thus musical hallucinations, noises, other sounds, and to everyone's disappointment, the intriguingly named 'exploding head syndrome', in which one hears an explosion, roar or ringing noise deep inside the head within an hour or two of falling

---

voice-hearers' who have some form of disease, but rather that there are some people who have voice-hearing experiences which they cannot cope with, and that this causes them distress and impairs their life. The opposite of a healthy voice-hearer would hence be a distressed voice-hearer (and not an unhealthy voice-hearer). The terminology is not ideal.

asleep (Blom, 2010), will not be examined. Again, although such experiences may inform our understanding of AVHs (as, indeed, may hallucinations in other modalities), they are also outside the scope of this book. Third, although hearing voices on the border of sleep will be examined briefly, the main focus of the book will be on voices occurring whilst individuals are fully awake. Finally, although treatments for AVHs will be covered, the main focus of the book is on the histories, causes, meanings and phenomenologies of AVHs. These caveats aside, we can now head back 7,000 years to Sumeria, hopefully safe in the knowledge of where we are going. Onwards!

A history of hearing voices

Introduction to Part I

An attempt to track the experience of hearing voices through the course of history is laden with a number of potential pitfalls. First, can we really apply our contemporary concept of auditory verbal hallucinations (AVHs) to people and societies that pre-date it, and who would not have understood their experiences in this way (Leudar & Sharrock, 2003)? This retrospective approach is problematic for the contemporary psychiatric concept of the AVH, as it is open to the accusation that it treats it as having an objective ontological existence, being 'out there, independently of the psychiatric discourses and practices that attempt to define and to treat it' (Borch-Jacobsen, 2001, p. 20). Instead, Borch-Jacobsen has proposed that the 'history of psychiatry and/or madness should ideally be the history of those complex interactions that give rise, through feedback, amplification and crystallization, to new psychiatric concepts' (p. 28). Whilst I will endeavour to follow Borch-Jacobsen's recommendation, it is notable that this part of the book is not, however, a history of madness. Instead it is the development of a history of hearing voices; how the experience has been understood, how it became synonymous with madness, and how people have tried to liberate it from madness.

1   From Ancient Mesopotamia to the pre-Reformation world

The earliest voices

Hearing voices in ancient times

Although language in *Homo sapiens* is estimated to have evolved around 50,000 years ago, the first writings appeared only around 5,000 years ago (Harley, 2010), in the cradle of civilisation, Ancient Mesopotamia.[1] In the lower half of Mesopotamia at this time lived the Sumerians. In addition to being credited with inventing the wheel, the plough, the first city states (Noble *et al.*, 2008), and even history itself (Kramer, 1971) the Sumerians also developed what is thought to be the first writing, cuneiform (*c*.3000 BC). Cuneiform documents were created by impressing signs with a cut reed onto clay tablets. The individual strokes that made up the signs were wedge shaped, thus giving rise to the name cuneiform (lit. 'wedge shaped'). The oldest written Mesopotamian medical text is a therapeutic manual written in Sumerian dating from the Ur III period (2112–2004 BC), which contains instructions for treating skin problems in patients, but no diagnoses (Scurlock & Anderson, 2005). The Sumerian city states of southern Mesopotamia were eventually united with their northern neighbours in Akkad to form Babylonia, centred at Babylon, near modern Baghdad. The Assyrian kingdom formed further north, near what is now Mosul. By the time of the Old Babylonian period (1894–1595 BC) Mesopotamian medical texts, written in Akkadian, a Semitic language, began to include descriptions of signs, symptoms and diagnoses, along with treatment details. By the Middle Assyrian and Babylonian periods (1430–1050 BC) there was enough knowledge to create diagnostic and prognostic handbooks. The most detailed Babylonian medical text we have is the *Diagnostic/Prognostic Handbook*, which consists of forty cuneiform tablets compiled by the physician Esagil-kin-apli (*c*.1050 BC). The first two tablets of this

---

[1] Literally meaning the 'land between two rivers', the rivers in question being the Tigris and Euphrates.

handbook deal with ominous signs the physician might encounter on the way to see the patient, with the following tablets dealing with specific illnesses such as bodily aches, fevers, infectious diseases and skin lesions. Although the Babylonians understood that many medical conditions had natural causes, other conditions (e.g. epilepsy) were viewed as being the result of supernatural causes, such as being 'seized' by a god or ghost (Scurlock & Anderson, 2005). These were still to be treated medically, however.

The context for hearing voices at this time was one where the reality of ghosts (spirits of the dead) and demons was accepted. Specifically auditory encounters with these entities are hard to pin down, however. In terms of human spirits, at death a spirit (Sumerian = 'gidim', Akkadian = 'etemmu') separated from the body (Scurlock, 1995). This spirit was intangible, though potentially visible and audible (Baumgarten, Assmann & Strosmsa, 1998). It could return to persecute the living, even entering the victim through their ears (Black & Green, 1992). The reason for this persecution was that ghosts continued to require periodic offerings of food and water even after death. If they received their offerings, they could be turned to for help, for example, by taking the family's troubles away with them when they returned to the Netherworld after one of their periodic visits. If, on the contrary, they failed to receive their accustomed offerings from their living relatives, or if the family to which they belonged had died out leaving them with nobody to care for them, they returned from the Netherworld in a very bad mood to afflict the living. Some ghosts, like the people they once were, could be difficult, or just plain greedy. Seeing a ghost was, in this context, not a good thing (Scurlock, 2006). If you saw *and heard* a ghost this was a particularly bad thing, as it indicated that the ghost had noticed you (Finkel, personal communication). Indeed, hearing voices (in particular angry or mournful voices) was taken as bad sign, not necessarily in the sense of being a bad omen, but as a sign to the ancient physician that something was very wrong with the patient (Scurlock, personal communication).

A range of scholars have attempted to translate the experiences recorded in medical cuneiform tablets into contemporary medical parlance, yet reports of hearing voices remain elusive. For example, Scurlock & Anderson (2005) offer the translation of one cuneiform medical passage as 'If a mournful cry [*ikkillu*] cries out to him and he continually answers it [and] when it cries out to him, he says: "Who are you?" a muttillu-bird has touched him' (p. 380). Yet it is very unlikely that this mournful cry is actually human speech. The key word, *ikkillu*, means a loud cry or din. It could be taken that the person is hearing a noise like that of a muttillu bird. However, a second instance where this same *ikkillu* experience is referred to is stated as being caused by 'the rabisu of the wastes'. As a rabisu is a type of Babylonian demon (lit. 'the croucher', who would lie in wait for you) this suggests it is not a bird sound, but a humanoid cry – although we still cannot pin this down as being actual speech, particularly since the demon is described as having the face of a goat or being in the form of a goat (Scurlock, personal communication). What may be more relevant to voice-hearing is what ancient physicians referred to as 'confusion of self', such as that found in Scurlock & Anderson (2005, §16.92): 'he can see the illness that afflicts him, he talks with it and continually changes his self' (Scurlock, personal communication).

Kinnier Wilson (1965) claims to identify a description of a voice-hearing experience in the Maqlu series of tablets, which discuss witchcraft. In a discussion of the types of fellow persecutors witches would have, Kinnier Wilson argues that one of these persecutors, a bel-egirri was 'probably not seen at all, being doubtless that "voice" which may issue short commands or comments, sometimes feared, sometimes respected, in auditory hallucinations' (p. 294). However, his conclusion does not appear to be 'doubtless'. The noun 'bel' literally means owner of a certain characteristic or property, and the compound bel-egirri can be translated broadly as a slanderer who gives you a negative reputation. Thus, a bel-egirri could be seen as a Lord of Slander (much like Beelzebub means 'Lord of the Flies'). However, the preceding types of witches' colleagues discussed in this passage included bel-lemutti and bel-dababi. As these are specific terms for people who would be involved in a legal process, it is unclear whether the reference to these terms means there are real people out there who are persecuting the patient, or whether these are hallucinatory voices. In fact, it appears more likely that these are not auditory hallucinations (Finkel, personal communication; Scurlock, personal communication). It thus appears that Kinnier Wilson's desire to find psychiatric symptoms in Babylon may have coloured his reading of this text.

In Ancient Egypt, communication with the dead was used to help restore mental balance (Weckowicz & Liebel-Weckowicz, 1990). As in Ancient Mesopotamia, the main method for this communication was through incubation of dreams, particularly by sleeping in certain temples, during so-called 'temple sleep' (Okasha & Okasha, 2000). There is an extensive literature on such dream incubation, but next to no literature, to my knowledge, on voice-hearing experiences in clear consciousness. The closest suggestion of such an experience I can find comes from one of the surviving Egyptian medical papyri, the Ebers Papyrus (*c*.1550 BC). In this, 'mental illness' is discussed in a section on disease of the heart. The Egyptians appear to have assigned to the heart the functions we now know are performed by the brain, such as movement control, decision making and hearing (ibid.). In this section, one passage reads: 'As to "raving through something entering from above" this means that his mind raves through something entering from above' (Ebbell, 1937, p. 118). It is possible, given the context of this passage, which is preceded by a passage appearing to relate to depression, and followed by a passage on forgetfulness, that it is some form of psychological experience, and possibly a form of hallucination. However, this remains speculative. Hence, there remains much work to be done to better understand how and if voice-hearing was occurring at this time, and how it was understood.

The theory of Julian Jaynes

The lack of clear evidence of hearing voices in Ancient Mesopotamia and Egypt, equivalent to the experiences reported by individuals today, could be seen to lend some support to one of the most radical theories in the field of voice-hearing which is relevant to this era. In 1976, Julian Jaynes published his book, *The Origin of Consciousness in the Breakdown of the Bicameral Mind,* a book which Richard Dawkins has argued to be 'one of those books that is either complete rubbish or a work of consummate genius, nothing in between' (Dawkins, 2007, p. 392). In this book Jaynes argues that in the bicameral period, a term which he uses to refer to the period 9000–1000 BC (Jaynes, 1986), all humans automatically heard voices when 'anything that could not be dealt with on the basis of habit, any conflict between work and fatigue, between attack and flight, any choice between whom to obey or what to do, anything that required any decision at all was sufficient to cause an auditory hallucination [i.e. hearing voices]' (Jaynes, 2000, p. 93). In this period, Jaynes argues, the brain is bicameral (literally 'two-chambered'), with the left hemisphere of the brain involved in normal human speech production – 'the language of man' – and the right hemisphere producing 'the language of the gods' (p. 104). In novel decision-making situations of the type above, Jaynes argues that speech is generated via excitation of Wernicke's area in the right temporal lobe of the brain, and then passed via the anterior commissure into the auditory areas of the left temporal lobe. Experientially, this resulted in people hearing the voice of 'a god' telling them what to do. For a variety of reasons (including social disorganisation, overpopulation and writing replacing the oral/auditory mode of command giving) around the end of the second millennium BC (a date of 1400 BC is given for when this breakdown occurred in Ancient

Mesopotamia by Jaynes, 1986) this bicameral mind broke down, self-consciousness arose and the voices of the gods were replaced by the verbal inner speech we have today.

The popularity of Jaynes' theory has led to the formation of its own society (www.julianjaynes.org). Although having a society is no indication of a theory's truth, Jaynes' work has received approving mention in recent years in a letter to the *Lancet* (Olin, 1999), and has been argued to be consistent with the neuroimaging evidence from studies of voices (Sher, 2000). Others have been less impressed. For example, Aleman (2001) has argued that Jaynes' theory is not consistent with the neuroimaging evidence, and that research on AVHs should focus on more 'down-to-earth' hypotheses (p. 64). Nevertheless, the theory deserves some critical consideration. Although Jaynes' work produces four separate hypotheses, only two will be considered in this book. The first, a neurological model which proposes that hearing voices is caused by activation in the right hemisphere, which then is transmitted to the left hemisphere, will be examined in Chapter 8. The second hypothesis, that before around 1200 BC hearing voices was the norm, is examined here.

Jaynes (2000) musters evidence from a range of sources for his theory. One key argument is that in the *Iliad* (developed around 1230 BC), characters such as Agamemnon and Achilles do not have conscious thoughts. Instead, their actions begin 'not in conscious plans, reasons, and motives; they are in the actions and speeches of gods' (p. 72). Who were these gods? Jaynes argues they were 'voices whose speech and directions could be as distinctly heard by the *Iliadic* heroes as voices are heard by certain epileptic and schizophrenic [*sic*.] patients, or just as Joan of Arc heard her voices' (pp. 73–4). This argument is weakened by Cavanna *et al.*'s (2007) observation that the *Iliad* as a whole is not always consistent with Jaynes' proposal. They note that 'crucial decisions, such as Hector's decision to take on Achilles, do not seem to be inspired by anything other than the heroes' conscious volition' (p. 13). Yet they do note that the *Iliad* does lack a single word for consciousness and even mind, whereas later Greek writers such as Euripides and Aeschylus have a complex mental vocabulary very like our own.

I am not in a position to evaluate the arguments based on the *Iliad*, however, after having been fortunate enough to converse with leading Ancient Mesopotamian scholars,[2] I am able to offer a view based on Jaynes' evidence in this area. First, Jaynes (2000) makes much of a

---

[2] Dr Irving Finkel, Ancient Mesopotamian (i.e. Sumerian, Babylonian and Assyrian) script, languages and cultures specialist at the British Museum, London; Dr JoAnn Scurlock, Oriental Institute, University of Chicago.

carving of a stone altar made about 1230 BC for the king of Assyria, Tukulti-Ninurta I. In this carving, Jaynes claims that the king is kneeling before an empty throne, where normally in previous carvings a god would have been shown. As Jaynes puts it, 'No scene before in history ever indicates an absent god. The bicameral mind had broken down' (p. 223). However, first it is an altar, and not a throne the king is kneeling in front of, and more importantly, the altar is in fact *not* empty, but has on it what is either a clay tablet with a stylus, or a hinged writing board; if this symbol has been correctly understood, this will be a symbol of the god Nabu, the god of writing, who was a major god in the Assyrian pantheon (Finkel, personal communication).

Jaynes also uses excerpts from Mesopotamian poetry to support his claim that the voices of the gods vanished around this time. To support this argument Jaynes cites the first lines in the poem *Ludlul Bel Nemeqi*, which run: 'My god has forsaken me and disappeared, My goddess has failed me and keeps at a distance, The good angel who walked beside me has departed' (Jaynes, 1986, p. 12). The poem Jaynes refers to, known in English as the *Poem of the Righteous Sufferer* (Lambert, 1963), is a lament for the physical and social problems the Righteous Sufferer was under-going. However, it is clear that he has only metaphorically lost his god, i.e. bad things were happening to him, and that Jaynes is reading this poetic language too literally. For example, later in the poem when things begin to improve for the Righteous Sufferer, we read that the god Marduk 'pulled me from the Hubur river ... he took my hand' (ibid., p. 59). Most of us would not conclude from this that Marduk literally went around pulling people from rivers. Occam's Razor would hence suggest a metaphorical interpretation is the accurate one.

Jaynes also argues that when bicameral voices were still heard in Mesopotamia, rituals such as *mis-pi* (mouth washing) and *pit-pi* (opening of the mouth) were performed on statues as aids to the production of literal hallucinated voices (see Jaynes, 2000, p. 182). However, such rituals were actually done to allow the god to enter the statue in order to receive the offerings people made to him, and not in order to allow the god literally to speak (Scurlock, personal communication). In fact, in Ancient Mesopotamia the main method of communication with the gods was through dreams and the interpretation of omens. There is *absolutely no evidence* that people routinely heard the voices of the gods (Finkel, Scurlock, personal communications).

Jaynes further claims that reading in the third millennium BC may have been a matter of literally hearing the cuneiform, and notes that the word used for hearing in this context is GIŠ-TUG-PI. In fact, most specialists in this area state that cuneiform is likely to have been read aloud and certainly not heard as an auditory hallucination (Finkel, Scurlock, personal communications). Furthermore, GIŠ-TUG-PI means 'understanding', not hearing (Scurlock, personal communication). Jaynes' argument that because people believed in gods they could only have done so because they heard their voices, also does not stand up to scrutiny. Very few people in the West base their own personal faith on their own experiences of voice-hearing.[3] There is hence no good evidence at all that before the end of the second millennium all people were voice-hearers.

In conclusion, we have little evidence of voice-hearing in the Ancient World. However, this is likely due to us not having sufficient records to examine. There is no evidence for Jaynes' theory that a breakdown in a bicameral mind was occurring around 1200 BC, or that people in Ancient Mesopotamia routinely heard voices before this time. However, as we will see in Chapter 8, Jaynes' proposal that AVHs may have a source in right hemisphere activation appears to have better neuroscientific support.

Ancient Greece and Rome

Dodds (1951) has argued that the most common type of hallucination in Ancient Greece, whilst awake, was a vision of a god or hearing a divine voice which 'commands or forbids the performance of certain acts' (p. 116). He notes that this type of voice is consistent with one of the five-fold types of dreams later noted by Calcidius, a fourth-century Christian. Calcidius noted five types of dreams, one of which was when a '*spectaculum*: a *caelestis potestas* [*heavenly/godly coercive power*] revealed itself to one who is awake and orders or prohibits something' (Reddoch, 2010, p. 78). Dodds allows that such reports may have been influenced by 'literary tradition in creating a stereotype form' (p. 117), but still concludes that 'experiences of this kind had once been fairly frequent' (ibid.). It is worth noting here that, as we will see in Chapter 4, voices issuing commands are the most common type heard in psychiatric populations today, allowing us to see a continuity in voice-hearing stretching back across the millennia.

The rise of Classical Greece in the fifth century BC and the philosophies of Socrates, Plato and Aristotle resulted in new ideas about voice-hearing. Aristotle (384–322 BC) had two theories of how hearing voices could occur. The first was based on internally arising voice-traces being

---

[3] Although see Chapter 6 for some exceptions to this rule.

mistaken for external voices. For Aristotle, perceiving objects led to physical changes which left traces of the perception – 'phantasms' – behind. He argued such phantasms enabled the faculty of imagination, and could be mistaken for external perceptions. He wrote that 'even when the external object of perception has departed, the impressions it has made persist, and are themselves objects of perception: and let us assume, besides, that we are easily deceived respecting the operations of sense-perception when we are excited by emotion' (Aristotle, 1984, p. 732). In illustrating how such hallucinations could occur, he achieved the impressive feat of making something clearer by employing hypothetical salty frogs. If frogs were placed at the bottom of a barrel with salt on their heads to weigh them down, as the salt dissolved, the frog would rise. Likewise, Aristotle argued, phantasms could rise from the depths of the soul to the surface when we went to sleep (as blood left the sensory organs and returned to the heart), or it could also happen when we were awake, through movement of blood.

A second way which Aristotle believed phantasms arose was based on misinterpretations of experiences from the world. For example, 'persons in the delirium of fever sometimes think they see animals on their chamber walls, an illusion arising from the faint resemblance to animals of the markings thereon when put together in patterns; and this sometimes corresponds with the emotional states of the sufferers, in such a way that, if the latter be not very ill, they know well enough that it is an illusion; but if the illness is more severe they actually move according to the appearances' (ibid.). Aristotle grounds this account in what the person expects to hear, but also in the emotions they are currently experiencing, which predispose them to see things (or hear things) through expectation (Leighton, 1982). In terms of the relationship between such experiences and illness, Aristotle saw voices as being a more severe sign of illness if people acted upon them (ibid.).

Without an example of voices at this time, this is all somewhat dry and abstract, so let us turn to the most famous example of voice-hearing in Ancient Greece, Socrates (469–399 BC). Acknowledged as being the founder of Western philosophy, his works today survive most famously through the writings of his pupil, Plato (428–348 BC). Plato tells us that Socrates heard a voice, which started in his childhood, and which 'always deters me from the course of action I was intending to engage in, but it never gives me positive advice' (Plato, as cited in Long, 2009, p. 64). In contrast, Xenophon reports Socrates as saying that his voice did tell him what to do (Leudar & Thomas, 2000). In either case, we can follow Long's (2009) speculation that 'we might do well ... in supposing that the sign [voice] manifested itself to Socrates in moments when he found himself seriously divided over the right course of action to follow' (p. 70).[4]

The issue of Socrates' voice was raised at his trial. Why should this be? It appears that the reason his voice was problematic was due to the jealousy and suspicion of others. Socrates lived in a polytheistic society, where gods were thought to be able to communicate with humanity. However, this process was effectively regulated so that priests, necromancers and oracles could experience voices, but 'ordinary persons ... did not hear or expect to hear the voice of a divinity' (Long, 2009, p. 63). Thus, as McPherran (1993) has argued, because Socrates was able to hear a divine voice without having to go to the temple, and hence had a great intimacy with a god, this produced envy, hatred and slander in other people. Similarly, Van Riel (2005) also argues it was the fact that *only he* could hear the voice that aroused the ire of other Athenians. Furthermore, legalistically, Socrates seems to have been the first person in Athens to have been charged with the crime of introducing new divinities, with McPherran (1993) arguing that the problem with this was that his voice had not been 'licensed by the state' (p. 133) or gone through the normal process of introducing a new god.[5] Another problem was that there was no way for others to verify the veracity and wisdom of Socrates' internal voice (ibid.). Hence, people could have been concerned that the voice was that of a god that wished to harm Athens, or that it was simply a delusion of Socrates. My overall reading of this instance of voice-hearing is that Socrates' voice disturbed the powers that be due to its making him 'special', giving him potential influence and power, creating a perceived threat to an establishment which did not have access to such an experience. As a threat to power, Socrates had to be dealt with.

It is interesting to examine how others in antiquity tried to explain the cause of Socrates' voice. Plutarch (AD 46–120) famously explored Socrates' voice in his work, *De Geio Socrates* (*The sign of Socrates*). Plutarch (1878) wrote, with parallels to Aristotle, that when we have dreams we are able to hear voices, as we are undisturbed and quiet, but when awake we are 'a hurry of tumultuous passions and distracting business' (p. 404). Socrates' mind, because it was 'pure, free from passion, and mixing itself with the body no more than necessity required [and] was easy to be moved' (ibid.), allowed him to hear a voice. Indeed,

---

[4] This involvement of voices at a moment of decision making concurs with Jaynes' account of voice-hearing.
[5] We will see such non-State-sanctioned voice-hearing causing problems for the voice-hearer throughout history.

Plutarch proposes that 'the speeches of the Daemon, sound only to those who are of a quieter temper and sedate mind, and such as we call holy and divine men' (p. 406). It is notable that here, hearing voices is being seen as a sign of positive personal characteristics rather than a diseased or imbalanced mind/body. Like Plutarch, Calcidius also suggested that Socrates' voice came to him as he was a chaste, clean and intelligent soul (Russell, 2010).

Plutarch also had a protagonist put forward another account (indebted to Plato). In this account each person has a measure of reason. Their 'reason' could be integrated into the body in varying degrees. Some people 'plunge themselves into the body' (p. 410), making their reason corrupted by passion and appetite, and leading to irrationality. For others a 'purer part' of the soul, 'the mind', remains without the body, being like a string that puppeteers the part of the soul in the body. The mind is called by the more perceptive person 'a Daemon'. This Daemon could wander, find out information and then impart it back to the individual in the form of a prophetic voice.

Medical explanations of voices were also available at this time. It is thought that the Greek scholar Alcmaeon was one of the first people to experiment directly with the brain (in animals), attempting to find its auditory and visual channels. Alcmaeon believed that the origin of diseases was a disturbance in the interaction between bodily fluids and the brain (Angst & Marneros, 2001). Medical explanations really came to the fore through Hippocrates' (460–370 BC), his fellow Greek physicians', and later the Roman physician Galen's (AD 129–199) development and use of the medical theory of the four humours. The humoural theory acted as a way for a physician to define a professional area, which excluded other practitioners, and which also functioned to provide a non-shameful basis of explanation, i.e. disease was not punishment from the Gods (Simon, 2008). The brain was placed at the centre of this model. Hippocrates wrote that 'Men ought to know that from the brain, and from the brain only, arise our pleasures, joys, laughter, and jests, as well as our sorrows, pains, griefs and tears' (Hippocrates, as cited in Porter, 2002). Similarly, Galen was later to write: 'Do not go to the gods ... but go and take instruction on the subject from an anatomist' (Galen, as cited in Peterson, 1982).

In addition to biology, Hippocrates and his colleagues still stressed the relevance of a person's biography and the social environment in the development of mental disease. However, a solely biological account of experiences such as hearing voices proved seductive. The Roman physician, Aurelius Cornelius Celsus (second century AD), was an important translator of Greek physicians' writing into Latin. In Celsus's classification, hallucinations (presumably including voices) could occur in *phrenesis*, an acute delirium arising with a fever; in *melancholia*, which was of longer duration and occurred in the absence of fever; or in a third class of madness (*quod robusti corporis esse consuevit*) which comes on seemingly without cause (O'Brien, 1924). In a slightly mysterious distinction, Celsus distinguishes between hallucinations of a gloomy and of a cheerful nature.[6] Whilst black bile was the cause of the former, white bile was the cause of the latter (ibid.). In most cases hallucinations, including voice-hearing, were thought to have a biological basis resulting from an excess of black bile. Quite what black bile is remains unclear, but it is thought that it was believed to be a black liquid whose effects were physically seen when stools, blood or skin turned darker (Porter, 2002). Black bile was thought to cause hallucinations and voice-hearing through its negative effects on imagination and reason (Sarbin & Juhasz, 1967). This led to a primarily physical treatment of such maladies, with hallucinations, due to their presumed cause in an excess of black bile, being treated by purging through use of hellebore (O'Brien, 1924). Hellebore was not a pleasant drug (*plus ça change*) and could lead to convulsions and death.

After Athens was sacked in 86 BC, the Roman Empire became dominant, and the source of intellectual power shifted from Athens to Alexandria. Platonism was revived in Alexandria by neo-Platonists, the most prominent being Plotinus, and became highly influential upon Christian thought. The reality of the experience of hearing voices remained well known. For example, Cicero noted that the experience of hallucinations was implacably real at the time (O'Brien, 1924). In Ancient Rome there was the belief that after death people's souls became spirits. The philosopher Plotinus (204–70), according to St Augustine (354–430), believed that the good spirits of men became '*lares*' and the bad spirits of men became '*lemures* (larvae)'. If it was unclear whether a spirit was good or bad, these were referred to as '*manes*'. Other writers referred to the *manes* as good spirits, however. Good spirits were honoured under the official title of the *Di Parentes* in the festival of the Parentalia. *Lemures* (the noxious spirits) were propitiated in the festival of the Lemuria (Thaniel, 1973). At the Parentalia or Feralia on 18 and 21 February, living descendants shared a meal with the benevolent spirits of their ancestors (*manes*). There was hence a socially acceptable framework for people hearing voices in which to frame their experiences.

---

[6] This may parallel the positive and negative voices heard today – see Chapter 4.

> **Box 1.1: The root of the term 'hallucination'**
>
> The most thorough analysis of the historical roots of the term
> 'hallucination' has been performed by Rojcewicz & Rojcewicz
> (1997). They note that the term 'hallucination' derives from the
> Latin verb *alucinari* or *hallucinari* ('to wander in mind, to talk idly,
> to rave'). *Alucinari*, they argue, is a verb dating from classical times,
> used by philosophers such as Cicero and Seneca, yet is a relatively
> rare term. They observe that in classical Latin it is not documented
> prior to Cicero (106–43 BC), nor after Columella (*c.*AD 60).
> However, they note that Aulus Gellius (*c.*AD 160) reports that
> *alucinari* is derived from a Greek term meaning 'to be distraught, to
> be uneasy, to have no rest'.
>
> Rojcewicz & Rojcewicz (1997) also describe Straus's (1958)
> work examining the relation between the basic human experience
> of hearing and its intrinsic connection to carrying out orders.
> Straus notes that hearing is a fundamentally passive experience. As
> he puts it, 'In hearing I am a receiver; the tones come at me and
> compel me'. Straus observes that in many languages, the words
> 'hearing' and 'obedience' derive from the same root. In German,
> hören (hearing) is connected with gehorchen (obeying), just as the
> Greek term 'I hear' is related to the Greek term 'I obey'. Rojcewicz &
> Rojcewicz also note that the Latin *oboedire* (to obey) comes from
> *ob-audire* (to listen from below), from *audire* (to hear). The Russian
> and Hebrew words for hearing and obeying are similarly related,
> they note. In English, too, 'to listen to' can mean 'to obey'.
> It is therefore unsurprising that Straus comes to the conclusion
> that, in hearing, obedience is foreshadowed. This is particularly
> interesting, given the high prevalence of voices which issue
> commands today (see Chapter 4).

Judaeo-Christianity 'a new kind of miraculous voice' (Philo Judaeus)

The Old Testament

The inclusion of a range of voice-hearing experiences in the books of the
Old Testament firmly established hearing voices as a potentially divine
experience, and validated it as a way that God could contact humanity.[7]
Prophets such as Isaiah, Jeremiah and Ezekiel experienced voices without having to resort to techniques employed by 'lesser' prophets to attain
trance states, such as dances, music, intoxicating drinks or self-injuring

---

[7] I am not concerned here with the veracity of these stories, but rather the influence they
had on how people understood hearing voices.

frenzies (Lewis, 1978). Ezekiel heard the voice of God more times than any other prophet, a total of ninety-three (Stein, 2010). This included hearing God's voice giving him commands to eat a scroll: 'he said unto me, Son of man, cause thy belly to eat, and fill thy bowels with this roll [i.e. a scroll] that I give thee. Then did I eat [it]; and it was in my mouth as honey for sweetness' (Ezekiel 3:3), and to cut his hair: 'son of man, take thee a sharp knife, take thee a barber's razor, and cause [it] to pass upon thine head and upon thy beard: then take thee balances to weigh, and divide the [hair]' (Ezekiel 5:1). Additionally, as is well known, in the Old Testament God speaks to Moses from the burning bush[8] and dictates the Ten Commandments to him (Exodus 23). He speaks to Balaam, directly, and through his donkey (Numbers 22), as well as to the Israelites from a fire,[9] to Job,[10] and famously to Elijah,[11] including the fabled 'still small voice'[12] (1 Kings 19:12).

Philo Judaeus of Alexandria (AD 20–50), a Jewish scholar, tried to explain how God spoke to Moses. Philo (c.AD 50/2011) wrote: 'Did he then do so, uttering himself some kind of voice? Away! let not such an idea ever enter your mind; for God is not like a man, in need of a mouth, and of a tongue, and of a windpipe'. Instead, Philo proposed that God created 'an invisible sound to be created in the air', 'fashioned the air and stretched it out and changed it into a kind of flaming fire, and so sounded forth so loud and articulate a voice like a breath passing through a trumpet' and that God 'breathing forth vigorously, aroused and excited a new kind of miraculous voice', but that this sound implanted itself 'in the soul of each individual another hearing much superior to that which exists through the medium of the ears'. For the next two thousand years, such theological attempts to create a mechanistic account of voice-hearing that linked the natural and supernatural would continue to be problematic.

The New Testament and early Christianity

In the New Testament, voice-hearing continued to signify supernatural communications. Divine voice-hearing experiences are found both during the lifetime of Jesus, as well as in the early Church. At Jesus's baptism, we are told: 'And there came a voice from heaven, [saying],

---

[8] 'God called unto him out of the midst of the bush, and said, "Moses, Moses"' (Exodus 3:4).

[9] 'And the Lord spake unto you out of the midst of the fire: ye heard the voice of the words, but saw no similitude; only ye heard a voice' (Deuteronomy 4:12).

[10] 'Then answered the Lord unto Job out of the whirlwind' (Job 40:6).

[11] 'Behold, there came a voice unto him, and said, "What doest thou here, Elijah?"' (1 Kings 19:13).

[12] Although different scholars use different translations of this 'still small voice' passage.

Thou art my beloved Son, in whom I am well pleased' (Mark 1:11). It could be argued that one of the most critical effects of Christ and Christianity on voice-hearing in later years was how it changed the meaning of events in the inner world. Before the time of Christ, a sin was something you did, but Christ now taught that: 'Ye have heard it said by them of old time; Thou shalt not commit adultery: But I say unto you, that whosoever looketh on a woman to lust after her hath committed adultery with her already in his heart' (Matthew 5:27).[13] Thus, thoughts themselves became suspect, were given a moral character, and had to be vigorously monitored. You were now morally responsible for what happened in your head.[14] The binding of the inner world had begun.

In the third and fourth centuries we find voice-hearing in the Desert Fathers. These were Christian ascetics who abandoned rural or city life to live a life of prayer, solitude and fasting in the deserts of Egypt. The most famous of these was St Anthony (c.250–356) who, troubled by lust, took to the desert to remove himself from temptation. In the raging silence of the desert, under conditions of fasting and introspection, the monks would sometimes hear voices. In Anthanasius's (296–373) *Life of Anthony* we find reports of St Anthony hearing the voices of demons: 'Very often also without appearing they imitate the music of harp and voice, and recall the words of Scripture ... They arouse us from our sleep to prayers; and this constantly, hardly allowing us to sleep at all. At another time they assume the appearance of monks and feign the speech of holy men, that by their similarity they may deceive and thus drag their victims where they will' (Anthanasius, 1994, p. 203). However, such voices were to be ignored, 'no heed must be paid them even if they arouse to prayer, even if they counsel us not to eat at all even though they seem to accuse and cast shame upon us for those things which once they allowed ... they may carry off the simple to despair; and that they may say the discipline is useless, and make men loathe the solitary life as a trouble and burden' (ibid.). Elsewhere we are told that St Anthony, after having had an illness removed by God, asked God why he had taken so long to do it, and then 'a voice came to him, "Antony, I was here, but I waited to see thy fight; wherefore since thou hast endured, and hast not been worsted, I will ever be a succour to thee, and will make thy name known everywhere"' (ibid., p. 199). Thus, although voice-hearing experiences were not seen as signs of illness, they were

---

[13] I suspect this idea was not entirely new with Jesus, and probably has a complex back-history, but it acts as a good symbolic turning point.

[14] As we will see in Chapter 12, guilt and shame appear to be key emotions in voice-hearing, and this development can only have encouraged such emotions.

nevertheless treated with suspicion, with the devil being ever-present. Later desert monks such as Evagrius (345–99), who created a taxonomy of eight tempting thoughts, *logismoi*, which were later to become the seven deadly sins, wrote of voices as personifications of concepts, rather than voices of demons per se. Thus, writing on the demon of sexual immorality, Evagrius states that this demon would contaminate the soul, making it 'speak certain words and hear them, as if the thing were actually there to be seen' (Evagrius, n.d., a, 8). Evagrius also notes that demons could 'use external things to produce fantasies, such as the sound of waves heard at sea' (Evagrius, n.d., b, 4), presumably meaning that voices could occur when listening to unpatterned noises such as that of the wind.

A writer who was to be highly influential in topographies of voices in the Christian era was St Augustine (354–450). Augustine had a tripartite model of Man, in which man consisted of spirit, soul and body. The soul (Hebrew: *nephesh*, Greek: *psuche* 'living, thinking being'), was a living thing created by God, equipped with reason and designed to rule the body. The spirit (Hebrew: *ne shamah* 'wind', Greek: *pneuma* 'breeze') was the deepest part of us which communes with God, our 'inner man' (Eph. 3:16). Hence, a model of self was used at this time which was open to divine (or demonic) intrusions. St Augustine's (1982) influential distinction between three possible types of visions (corporeal, spiritual and imaginative) was also applicable to voice-hearing experiences, or 'locutions' as they were referred to at the time. *Corporeal locutions* were so called because they are 'perceived through the body and presented to the sense of the body' (ibid., p. 186). Underhill (1911) was later to refer to this as 'the exterior voice, which appears to be speaking externally to the subject and to be heard by the outward ear' (p. 328). Such voices are actually heard by the ear, just like natural speech. *Imaginative locutions* were not heard in this way, but were more interior. These were understood by Augustine as being caused by memories 'or fictitious images, fashioned by the power of thought' (Augustine, 1982, p. 186). Underhill refers to such voices as a 'distinct interior voice' (Underhill, 1911), which speaks in clear words but is recognised as being inside the mind. Finally, in *spiritual/intellectual locutions* there was no sound or voice at all. A voice is heard, but without any sound or words. A voice is imprinted into the spirit, not in a sensory way, but in a direct intellectual way (Finnis, 1998). Underhill refers to this as an 'inarticulate voice' (1911) which leaves more of an impression than definite words.

Christianity assigned these three types of voices different spiritual values. Intellectual voices were the most desirable. Imaginative voices, 'distinct interior words', were often treated with suspicion by the Church authorities because, as they were so precise, they were hard to resist (Obermeier & Kennison, 1997). Finally, voices heard by the exterior ear were actively regarded with 'suspicion and dislike' (Underhill, 1911, p. 277). Greater status was given to individuals who predominantly saw visions ('visionaries'), as compared to individuals who only heard voices, and for whom there was no equivalent term, such as 'vocieary' (Obermeier & Kennison, 1997). This was in part based on the idea that the eyes are the window to the soul, making it the desired form of divine communication (Riehle, 1977, as cited in Obermeier & Kennison, 1997).

As we will see, individuals in the Christian tradition who heard voices (and who were often classified as mystics) nearly always caused problems for the Church. As Jones (1969, as cited in Obermeier & Kennison, 1997) notes, 'To the Church as an institution, the mystic is a maverick. He is a nonconformist and a troublemaker; he upsets efficiently functioning procedures; he rejects the authority of the institution whenever it conflicts with his private vision. The weight of numbers and of persons, traditions, convenience, decency, and respectability count for him as nothing in comparison with his inner conviction ... with such individualists the Church has a simple alternative: It can either canonize them or expel them as heretics. It cannot ignore them' (p. 152).

After the fall of the Roman Empire in AD 476, medicine became based not on first-hand observation, with the dissection of bodies being forbidden, but upon memorisation of the teachings of Hippocrates and Galen (Peterson, 1982). Brain anatomy was not to advance until the Renaissance in the sixteenth century, with the work of Andreas Vesalius. In the twelfth century there began to be a shift in the concept of possession, from the idea of possession of the body which manifested in physical occurrences (e.g. pains), to spiritual possession in which demons could cause voices (Sluhovsky, 2007). This concept was applied to the first medieval mystic, Hildegard of Bingen (1098–1179) who, although having voices and visions which were authenticated by the Church as being divine in origin, was a key example of the new understanding that possession could occur in a spiritual/psychological way, with no bodily signs (ibid.). Hildegard experienced a mix of voices and visions. For example, she reports that 'I heard the voice from Heaven saying to Me, Speak therefore of these wonders ... Again I heard a voice from Heaven saying to me, Cry out and write!' (Hildegard of Bingen, as cited in King-Lenzmeier, 2001, p. 27). Elsewhere she reports that 'When I was sixty-one years old ... I heard a voice from Heaven saying to me ... Speak and write, therefore, now according to Me and not according to yourself' (p. 52). Hildegard is clear that these experiences happened to her when she was wide awake: 'I hear these things not with the bodily ears, nor the thoughts of my mind … but entirely within my soul, with my external eyes open, so that I never suffer a lapse into ecstasy, but I see them fully conscious by day or night' (Hildegard of Bingen, as cited in Flanagan, 1998, p. 188). Possibly more interesting than her experiences themselves was the fact that Hildegard was a *woman* voice-hearer, and hence had to work harder to gain acceptance of her experiences than a man would have. She was forced to justify her prophetic mission as a woman by arguing that God could no longer rely on corrupt men and had turned to communicating with frail women such as herself (Elliott, 2002). The acceptance of Hildegard's voices and visions as authentic was due to her positioning herself as a humble woman treading on forbidden ground (hence protecting her from the criticism of the patriarchal Church hierarchy), getting male scribes to write down her reports of her experiences, writing in the language of the Church (Latin) and getting her experiences endorsed by one of the most prominent experts on mysticism of the time, Bernard of Clairvaux (Obermeier & Kennison, 1997). The use of scribes impacts upon the extent to which we hear Hildegard's own voice, with her third scribe in particular appearing not to be willing to write down what Hildegard said in her own idiosyncratic style, instead altering her words (Staley, 1994). As we will note in Chapter 12, robbing the voice-hearer of their voice and colonisation of their experience continues today.

In late medieval and early modern Europe, women's accounts of voice-hearing start to appear, with the authorities finding it hard to silence their accounts of hearing divine voices (Sluhovsky, 2007). At this time women were still considered to be weaker than men, being thought to be more prone to 'contaminations' and 'impressions', to have a more active imagination and a weaker intellect, all of which made them more susceptible to spirits (ibid.). As we will see later, whereas women who exhibited forms of 'spiritual uniqueness' in the late medieval period were able to become prophetesses, visionaries, divine guides and saints, by the early sixteenth century the Church's anxieties led them to be viewed as witches, victims of possession or fakes (ibid.).

St Thomas Aquinas

A century after Hildegard's experiences, the state of the understanding of voice-hearing can be found through an examination of the most prominent theologian and thinker of the time, St Thomas Aquinas (1225–74).[15]

---

[15] For a more detailed account of the relationship between Aquinas and hearing voices, see McCarthy-Jones (2011a).

Aquinas had a sophisticated and wide-ranging understanding of voice-hearing. He was aware that voice-hearing could occur due to purely natural reasons, such as through the use of herbs, or through natural and spontaneous physiological changes, stating that 'imaginative apparitions are sometimes caused in us by the local movement of animal spirits and humors' (Aquinas, *Summa Theologica* (henceforth *ST*), Ia q. 111 a. 3). Consistent with Aristotle, St Thomas argued that the same humoural activity associated with dreaming may occur when awake, writing that 'the commotion of the spirits and humors may be so great that such appearances may even occur to those who are awake, as is seen in mad people [*phreneticis*], and the like' (*ST*, Ia q. 111 a. 3). He was clear that the source of such 'madness' was a disease of the body. In what he termed 'abstraction from the senses' (*ST*, IIa IIae q. 173 a. 3), things created in the imagination could be taken for real. People who experienced 'naturally occurring' hallucinations, as opposed to those with a divine supernatural source, Aquinas noted, may still have laid claim to be, or thought themselves, prophets. However, he argued that such individuals were 'foolish and mad ... not true but false prophets ... they speak a vision of their own heart, and not out of the mouth of the Lord' (*ST*, IIa IIae q. 171 a. 1). Aquinas was also aware that particular states were conducive to hallucinations with natural causes. For example, he noted that 'When the soul is withdrawn from corporeal things, it becomes more adapted to receive the influence of spiritual substances, and also is more inclined to receive the subtle motions which take place in the human imagination through the impression of natural causes, whereas it is hindered from receiving them while occupied with sensible things' (*ST*, IIa IIae q. 172 a. 1).

A key point to stress here is that the Christian Church, before, after and during the Middle Ages, *did not automatically think you were possessed, or were being spoken to by God or the Devil if you heard voices.* Yet, many today continue to think that they did. Thus Rowe (2000) writes: 'The Christian Church taught that a person in a psychosis was possessed by the devil or evil spirits which had to be driven out' (p. xi). Similarly, Kendall (2001) claims that 'medieval theologians like Thomas Aquinas attributed hallucinations and insanity to demons and other supernatural influences' (p. 490), and does not note Aquinas's naturalistic and materialist explanations.

In terms of supernatural causes for hearing voices, Aquinas was, of course, open to this explanation, as he believed that for man's salvation 'certain truths which exceed human reason' had to be communicated to us by divine revelation (*ST*, Ia q. 1 a. 1). Hearing voices was one way of receiving such divine revelation. Aquinas most clearly addresses voices with a supernatural source in his discussion of prophetic knowledge. He states that 'prophets know things that are far removed from man's knowledge' and that 'they may be said to take their name from φανός, "apparition", because things appear to them from afar' (*ST*, IIa IIae q. 171 a. 1). Prophetic experiences, in Aquinas's view, hence allowed people to see and hear divine things. As Philo had been, Aquinas was also keen to understand exactly how God could communicate with us. His primary theory was that angels could induce voices by moving 'the spirits and humors from within' (*ST*, Ia q. 111 a. 4). Voices with demonic origins were discernible from such experiences. For example, Aquinas argued that 'demons reveal what they know to men, not by enlightening the intellect, but by an imaginary vision, or even by audible speech; and in this way this prophecy differs from true prophecy' (*ST*, IIa IIae q. 172 a. 5). Furthermore, 'the devil sometimes utters what is false, the Holy Ghost never' (ibid.). He also noted how hallucinations with a demonic source could mix truth and lies, approvingly quoting St Bede's wise words that 'no teaching is so false that it never mingles truth with falsehood' (ibid.).

The meaning of someone hearing voices from a divine supernatural source could vary, according to Aquinas. Being the direct recipient of voices did not necessarily make one a prophet. The key to being labelled a prophet was not hearing voices per se, but being able to correctly interpret such experiences.[16] The ability to interpret the meaning of such experiences was said to occur through the bestowing of a divine prophetic light (*lumen propheticum*) on the individual. In fact, Aquinas argued, one could be termed a prophet by simply interpreting others' hallucinations, without having them oneself, as in the case of Joseph's interpretation of Pharaoh's dream (*ST*, IIa IIae q. 173 a. 2). However, if one both had the hallucination oneself, and was able to correctly interpret it, then one was a more excellent prophet than one who simply interpreted another's hallucination (*ST*, IIa IIae q. 173 a. 2). Such a prophet, in Aquinas's phrasing, both lifts the veil of darkness (i.e. has a perceptual experience) and removes the veil of ignorance (i.e. correctly interprets it). It is in this way we can understand, says Aquinas, biblical passages such as Job 12:22, where it states: 'He discovereth great things out of darkness' (*ST*, IIa IIae q. 171 a. 1).

---

[16] The idea that there is a 'right way' to interpret voices continues to the present day. At this time the Church had the authority to pronounce, but by the nineteenth century psychiatry had the power, and the voice-hearer's own voice (i.e. their explanation of their experience) was still submerged, like a cry under water.

Aquinas considered the argument that just as some people find it hard to learn mathematics, maybe some people find it harder than others to experience divine voices. However, he rejected this argument and argued that there was no predisposition or type of person for whom experiencing divine voices was more likely. Nevertheless, Aquinas did note that certain types of lifestyle made it more probable. He argued that 'prophecy requires the mind to be raised very high in order to contemplate spiritual things, and this is hindered by strong passions, and the inordinate pursuit of external things' (*ST*, IIa IIae q. 172 a. 4). He hints that leading a solitary life is thought to be more conducive to such experiences, 'lest worldly employment should be a hindrance to the gift of prophecy' (ibid.). Furthermore, he states that 'God's gifts are not always bestowed on those who are simply the best, but sometimes are vouchsafed to those who are best as regards the receiving of this or that gift" (ibid.). Yet he also argues that 'a natural indisposition ... [can be] removed by the Divine power' (*ST*, IIa IIae q. 172 a. 3). Nevertheless, the Church at this time was clearly very careful as to in whom it sanctioned voice-hearing, and also careful to hold the trump card that it was the Church, not the voice-hearer, who had the ultimate say over what their experience meant.

The fourteenth century: women, voices and politics
'You will not be overcome' (Julian of Norwich)

Aquinas's work, especially his *Summa Theologica*, can be seen as the pinnacle of scholasticism, the rigorous use of argumentation and reason to establish theological truths. However, many reacted against the desiccation of this approach by reintroducing the ideas of a personal relation with Christ and the piety born of emotion (Saunders, 2005), resulting in a prominent mysticism. Emotion and introspection were at the core of this approach (and as we will see in Part III, such factors appear to play a key role in hearing voices) and many such mystics experienced voices and visions. Furthermore, in the century following Aquinas's death, three big events in fourteenth-century Europe occurred: the Hundred Years War (1337–1453), the Black Death (peaking around 1350) and the Great Schism (1378–1417). This led to a vacuum in institutional authority (Elliott, 2002), which provided a new space for people to speak out about what they thought their voices meant. Particularly important was the event known as the Great Schism. Since the early fourteenth century the papacy had resided in Avignon, not Rome. However, in the late fourteenth century, Pope Gregory XI (1336–78) was persuaded by a number of female visionaries and voice-hearers to move the papacy back to Rome. The first of these was St Birgitta of Sweden (1303–73). St Birgitta experienced a range of visions, had voices which spoke to her during these visions, and believed that she was 'God's mouthpiece' (p. 39). During prayer she 'heard the voice' (p. 40) of the Virgin Mary, who advised Gregory to return to Rome (Blumenfeld-Kosinski, 2006). Whilst Gregory was deliberating, St Birgitta died. At this point, St Catherine of Siena (1347–80) stepped in, advising and managing to get Gregory to move the papacy back to Rome. Catherine's authority drew much on visions and voices she had experienced, which dated back to her first vision of Christ when she was a child. Although Gregory moved the papacy back to Rome, his death in 1378 shortly afterwards led to the Great Schism (also called the Western Schism, to differentiate it from an earlier schism in 1054) as the newly appointed pope in Rome, Urban VI, was challenged by a rival pope, Clement VII, who established himself in Avignon. This crisis of authority led to what Blumenfeld-Kosinski (2006) has described as 'an unprecedented visionary activity, a phenomenon one could call mystical activism' (p. 34). For example, Constance de Rabastens in the years 1384–6 argued for the Roman pope's authority, based on her visions. In addition to her visions she also had prominent voice-hearing experiences, with Blumenfeld-Kosinski (ibid.) noting that for Constance, 'most specifically political communications from Christ are of an auditory nature' (p. 155).

Such female voice-hearing and the authority this gave women in their interactions with male-dominated religion and politics did not go down well in many quarters. Jean Gerson, writing in retrospect, argued that Pope Gregory XI had been 'seduced' by female visionaries into making the decision to return to Rome, and blamed St Birgitta and St Catherine for causing the Great Schism (Blumenfeld-Kosinski, 2006). Indeed, both St Birgitta and St Catherine and their status as divinely inspired visionaries were attacked by political opponents (Schussler, 2009).

The Great Schism was widely perceived to be a satanic means to increase confusion, making the need to discern between divine and demonic voices more pressing. Also around this period, lay people were acting as spiritual guides for clergy, which posed another threat to the Church. Two key figures in the discernment literature at this time were Henry of Langenstein (1325–97) and his pupil, Jean Gerson (1363–1429). Langenstein was interested in the discernment of spiritual experiences, such as hearing voices, and argued that a key way to discern spirits was to assess if a person's behaviour was moderate. Immoderate and vain behaviour was linked to immoral people (Sluhovsky, 2007). Similarly, Gerson argued regarding St Birgitta's visions that only people who conducted themselves 'prudently and cautiously' could have true visions and voices. There was intense suspicion of unsupervised and interiorised spiritual experiences. In this way, spirits and voices were not discerned, people were.

Gerson was famous for his attempt to apply discernment criteria to the voice-hearing experience of Joan of Arc (1412–31). In fact, more generally, Gerson worked 'with particular zeal to disqualify women altogether as appropriate arbiters of spiritual matters' (Elliott, 2002, p. 29). Joan's voices are described in Box 1.2. The fact that Joan had voices which seemed external to her put her in an awkward position straight away because, as noted above, these were the lowest form of divine communication, and viewed with the most suspicion. In contrast to Hildegard of Bingen, Joan did not try to get Church approval and authentication of her voices, and her voices spoke in French (the language of the people), not Latin (the language of the Church) (Obermeier & Kennison, 1997). As Obermeier & Kennison wryly note, 'Visions – carefully orchestrated and sanctioned – can help Hildegard to authorial power, but voices – naively employed – can send Joan to the stake' (p. 155).

Interestingly, Obermeier & Kennison (1997) suggest that Joan, despite her descriptions of seeing the visual form of people such as St Michael, may not have actually seen them at all, with this being something she felt obliged to state at her trial. Indeed, when 'Asked how she knew whether the apparition was man or woman, she answered she knew for certain, she recognized them by their voices [*cognoscit eas ad voces ipsarum*]' (Barrett, as cited in Obermeier & Kennison, 1997, p. 147).[17]

The existence of popular, lay mystical experiences and claims of contact with the divine threatened Gerson, who was an academic and wished to have authority over these issues. As he put it, 'Are men who are quite learned, both in ability and training, to be kept from speaking about such matters because they are schoolmen?' (Elliott, 2002).[18] Women were already barred from universities and Gerson wanted to take over as the expert on mysticism (experiences which he did not have himself). He had his own framework for how voice-hearers should

---

[17] In a contemporary explanation for Joan's experiences, d'Orsi & Tinuper (2006) argue that Joan's voices resulted from a genetically inherited form of epilepsy. They suggest that as Joan sealed her letters with wax, we may be able to find one of her hairs caught in one of these seals, and test for the genes associated with this form of epilepsy.

[18] Irrespective of what position one takes on the potential for supernatural voices to exist, if anyone was able to stop 'schoolmen' from speaking on such matters, then we would have a genuine miracle on our hands.

Box 1.2: The voices of Joan of Arc

Most of what we know about Joan of Arc's voices comes from her trial documents. Whether a document of condemnation is the most trustworthy of sources is, of course, highly debatable. Nevertheless, we are told Joan 'declared that at the age of thirteen she had a voice from God to help her and guide her. And the first time she was much afraid. And this voice came towards noon, in summer, in her father's garden: and the said Jeanne had [not] fasted on the preceding day. She heard the voice on her right, in the direction of the church; and she seldom heard it without a light ... She said that if she was in a wood she easily heard the voices come to her. It seemed to her a worthy voice, and she believed it was sent from God; when she heard the voice a third time she knew that it was the voice of an angel. She said also that this voice always protected her well'. Joan further added that 'This voice comes from God; I believe I do not tell you everything about it; and I am more afraid of failing the voices by saying what is displeasing to them, than of answering you'.

Her trial transcript records that 'before the siege of Orleans, and since then, they have spoken to her every day, often calling her Jeanne the Maid, daughter of God'. Joan is also reported to have said 'that there is not a day when she does not hear this voice; and she has much need of it'. The voice also appears to have forbidden her to say certain things at the trial. At one point in the trial transcript: 'Asked whether the voice had forbidden her to answer everything she was asked, she said: "I will not answer you that. I have revelations concerning the king which I shall not tell you." Asked again if that had been forbidden her [by the voice], she replied: "Believe me, it was not men who forbade me"'. She did not always do what the voices told her, for example, 'Asked if ever she did anything contrary to their command and will, she answered that she did what she could and knew, to the best of her power. And as for her leap from the tower at Beaurevoir, she did it against their bidding'. We can see clear parallels with Socrates' daemon here in the way the voice advises/commands on the performance of actions.

In her trial transcript, Joan notes that there is 'a saying among little children, "Men are sometimes hanged for telling the truth"'. Women, it would seem, are burnt for the same. Joan died in flames, burnt at the stake in May 1431, aged only nineteen. We can only hope that she returned to the light that she saw.

understand their voices, writing that: 'If such extraordinary revelations should happen to come to a person, then he should reject them with holy, humble, and diffident modesty. Such a person should think of such matters as resulting from an injury done to the imagination and should worry about being ill in the same way that insane, manic, or depressive people are' (Gerson, 1998, p. 339). This act of mental colonialism ripped the meaning of the experience from the hands of the voice-hearer. It is hence quite clear that lay and female claims to hear voices acted as a powerful threat to the authority of the hierarchical male society. Fire could not be far away.

Other notable voice-hearers at this time were two female mystics, Julian of Norwich (1342–1416) and Margery Kempe (1373–1438). Both lived in an era when there was a tradition for the devout Christian to withdraw into themselves, to visualise Christ and to speak to him (Hirsh, 1989). Julian of Norwich's work, *Revelations of Divine Love*, is notable for being one of the first books ever written by a woman in the English language. In this, Julian reports how God, 'without voice and without opening of lips, formed in my soul this saying: With this the fiend is overcome' (Julian of Norwich, 1977, p. 201). She reports this experience again later, stating that 'our Lord very humbly revealed words to me, without voice and without opening of lips, as he had done before, and said very seriously: Know it well, it was no hallucination'[19] (p. 314). In her last voice-hearing experience she stirringly notes that: 'He did not say: You will not be troubled, you will not be belaboured, you will not be disquieted; but he said: You will not be overcome' (p. 98).

Margery Kempe's 'spiritual autobiography', written in the third person, is the first time in which voice-hearing and visionary experiences are set down in narrative form in English. In addition to experiencing a range of visions, Margery reports how she 'heard with her bodily ears such sounds and melodies that she could not well hear what a man said to her at that time, unless he spoke louder. These sounds and melodies had she heard nearly every day for the term of twenty-five years … especially when she was in devout prayer' (Peterson, 1982, p. 14). She records both God and Jesus sometimes speaking to her. For example, Margery states that Jesus said to her, 'Margery, my daughter, what do you say to my father in response to these words that he speaks to you?' (MacAvoy, 2003, p. 71). A number of concurrent signs were used to validate this divine origin. For example, both Margery and her male

---

[19] The term she uses is 'raving', which the translator translates as the modern term 'hallucination', see Julian of Norwich (1977).

scribe who wrote down her experiences were 'blessed with the gift of tears' (Staley, 1994, p. 35). Her use of a male scribe (or series of scribes), like Hildegard of Bingen (though not Julian of Norwich), also acted as an important way of validating her claims. As Staley notes, without a scribe she would merely be 'a woman of forty-something (that age, thought of as postmenopausal and thus less "female", in which so many medieval woman say they began to write), who sits down to record a series of visions and adventures that occurred some years before' (p. 36) which would weaken her authority. Margery has also been argued to use 'the voice of God as a screen for the social criticism inherent in many of her descriptions' (ibid.), and was able to do this by drawing on the recog- nised format of the holy woman who renounces early social and sexual roles (Staley, 1994) and the genre of female sacred biography (MacAvoy, 2003). In terms of causes, Hirsh (1989) notes that the most common location in which Margery would hear the voice was the silence of a church or oratory, suggesting potential proximal causes to us. In terms of distal causes, Margery dates the onset of these experiences to her giving birth (see Chapter 4 for similar experiences today).

The fifteenth century: mechanical devils

Given the prominence that women were now having, and the threats this posed to the male establishment, we may not be surprised that it was at this point in history where we see the emergence of the persecution of women in the witchcraft craze of the fifteenth century. This madness did no favours for people who heard voices, especially women. The craze was driven by Pope Innocent VIII's commissioning of two Dominican monks, Fathers Kramer and Sprenger, to investigate the phenomenon of witchcraft, which resulted in the publication of the book known as the *Malleus Maleficarum* (Latin for 'the hammer of witches'). This work, in addition to giving descriptions of how to interrogate and determine whether someone was a witch, also touched specifically on voice-hearing, attempting to explain how the devil talked to witches. Kramer & Sprenger (1486/2000) argued that 'devils have no lungs or tongue ... therefore they cannot truly and properly speak ... [therefore] they pro- duce, not voices, but sounds which have some likeness to voices, and send them articulately through the outside air to the ears of the hearer' (p. 110). In addition to these voices with an external locus, like St Thomas Aquinas and the Christian tradition they argued for an internal locus of demonic voices, too. Here, they drew on St Thomas's and Avicenna's concept of the inner senses, which included common sense, imagination, fancy, thought and memory. Kramer & Sprenger argued that it was fancy that was the treasury or repository of ideas received through the senses, with memory having no such perceptual nature. They observed that dreams occurred through 'natural local motion caused by the flow of the blood to the first and inmost seat of their faculties of perception ... an intrinsic local motion in the head and cells of the brain' (p. 50). This motion could also be caused by devils when individuals were awake, with such beings able to 'stir up and excite the inner perceptions and humours, so that ideas retained in the repositories of their minds are drawn out and made apparent to the faculties of fancy and imagination, so that such men imagine these things to be true'. This they termed 'interior temptation' (ibid.). The devils may have been supernatural entities, but they worked through natural causes. Like the discernment literature in the previous century, one of the main aims of demonology was to establish whether experiences such as voices had supernatural or natural origins (Clark, 1999). Yet, a threat to orthodox demonology was that 'demonic' experiences could be explained as being naturalistic hallucinations (ibid.). Such arguments were taken up by a number of thinkers in the sixteenth century as a major shift in the conception of human nature was taking place.

Chapter 1: summary of key points

- We have little good evidence of voice-hearing before the time of Ancient Greece, most likely due to a lack of records.
- Hearing voices in Ancient Mesopotamia, particularly angry or mournful ones, appears likely to have been regarded as a bad sign.
- No evidence was found for Julian Jaynes' hypothesised bicameral mind and its subsequent breakdown in Ancient Mesopotamia.
- The Christian Church, before, after and during the Middle Ages, did not automatically assume someone was possessed, or being spoken to by God or the Devil, if they heard voices.
- Christian thinkers had both naturalistic and supernatural explanations for voices, with biology being involved in both types of accounts.
- In St Augustine's influential distinction, externally located voices (corporeal locutions) and internally located voices (imaginative locutions) were thought more likely to be from demonic forces than voices heard but without any sound or words (spiritual/intellectual locutions) which were more likely to be divine.
- Women who heard voices and attempted to claim religious authority on the basis of these met with great resistance from the patriarchal religious establishment.

- In both Classical Antiquity and early Christianity, the potential for voice-hearing to be seen as a sign of divine favour led to power (in the later case, the Church) mobilising against voice-hearers to keep a tight rein on the meaning of voice-hearing.
- However, the Church was about to lose it's grip . . .

2   Political voices: religion, medicine and hearing voices

The sixteenth century: Reformation, liberation, contemplation[1]

It has been argued that during the sixteenth century the very nature of self and subjective experience began to change (Elias, 1991), with the phenomenon of 'psychologisation' starting to be seen (Elias, 1970). Elias argues that in sixteenth-century court life there began to be an increasing awareness that people had an 'interiority' in contrast to their appearance. People increasingly understand themselves as what Elias (1991, p. 28) terms *Homo clausus* (enclosed, locked people), characterised by an attitude of 'being alone, with an inner "true" self, a pure "I" and an outward costume'. This new form of self-consciousness was linked to growing commercialisation, the rise of courts and urban classes, the increasing power of man over nature, and the transition from an external conscience dependent on authority to a more autonomous individual conscience. Just as nature was more closely examined by thought and observation, so people themselves came under the glare of this lens. Unlike their medieval predecessors, people from the Renaissance onwards were more able to see themselves from a distance. We may speculate that someone with a view of their self as being locked up inside them would be more likely to see mental intrusions as threatening, leading to negative perceptions of the voice-hearing experience. At this time we also see the beginning of the development of personal characteristics the West values, namely self-control and control of circumstances (Watters, 2010). Tellingly, Watters notes that 'When humans do not assume they have complete control of their experience, they do not so deeply fear those who appear to have lost it' (p. 159). Voices were hence unlikely to be greeted by such a society.

---

[1] Although Sarbin and Juhasz (1967) state that the first use of the term 'hallucination' in English occurred in this century (1572) in an English translation of Ludwig Lavater's book *De spectris, lemuribus et magnis atque insolitis fragoribus* [*Of ghostes and spirites walking by nyght*], the term does not actually appear in this work (Rojcewicz & Rojcewicz, 1997).

During the Italian Renaissance there were significant advances in anatomy and the understanding of the human body. It was at this time that Andrea Vesalius (1514–64), produced *De Humani Corpis Fabrica* (*On the fabric of the human body*), a beautiful and revolutionary study of the human body.[2] In addition to a better understanding of anatomy, there was also a shift away from accepting the authority of past medical authorities (e.g. Galen, Hippocrates) and towards a culture of observation. Vesalius stressed that students should not accept the teachings of existing authorities, but should explore the human body for themselves based on their own observations. This opened the door to more medical interpretations of voices. Indeed, the sixteenth century saw a number of Renaissance physicians react against the *Malleus Maleficarum* by proposing naturalistic explanations of events previously claimed to have supernatural origins. In 1515, Andrea Alciati argued that witches were more in need of purification by the purging drug hellebore than by fire (Midelfort, 1999). However, the most influential of such arguments was given by Johann Weyer (1515–88) in his 1563 work, *De prestigiis daemonum et incantationibus ac venefiis* (*On demonic manifestations, incantations and magicians*). In this he argued that witches were simply suffering from hallucinations resulting from melancholy (a disease with a physical cause), and were not in fact affected by the devil. Due to this, Weyer is often lauded today as the father of psychiatry, and portrayed as the voice of sane medical science in a superstitious time. This is, of course, an oversimplification, as Weyer still accepted that demonic possession and influence was possible (ibid.). Indeed, most thinkers at this time seemed to co-exist within both natural and supernatural frameworks. La Loyer, in his 1586 work, *Quatre livres des spectres*, although coming down on the side of the reality of spirits, did at least in its debate suggest that this was an open question (Clark, 1999). Other leading contemporary physicians, such as Felix Platter (1536–1614), also argued that both supernatural and natural causes of mental disease were possible (Weckowicz & Liebel-Weckowicz, 1990). Platter did, though, state that blasphemous hallucinations (presumably including hearing demonic voices) were signs of possession. Indeed, the phenomenology of many voices lent themselves to demonic interpretations, especially those which told the voice-hearer to hurt themselves.[3] For example, in a case from Germany in 1579, it is reported that a man's wife 'ran outside under the

---

[2] Although Johnson (1978) has stated that Vesalius was the first person to use the term 'hallucination' in a medical setting, this argument seems to rest on a mistranslation (Rojcewicz & Rojcewicz, 1997).

[3] These are still an exceedingly common form of AVHs today, see Chapter 4.

impression that something was telling her to drown herself' (Midelfort, 1999, p. 310). Consulting the original German, it is clear that this 'something' was a spoken voice.

The Reformation

If the physicians were unsure of what hearing voices represented, theologians were having an even worse time of it. On 31 October 1517, Martin Luther nailed his *Ninety-Five Theses on the Power and Efficacy of Indulgences* to the door of Wittenberg Cathedral, heralding the start of the Protestant Reformation. This triggered a series of upheavals, and ultimately led to a radical change in how voice-hearing was understood. The Reformation began with a series of protests against the doctrines and practices of the Catholic Church by a number of reformers in addition to Luther, such as John Calvin and Ulrich Zwingli. The invention of the printing press in the 1540s and the subsequent printing, by Gutenberg and others, of bibles, from the 1550s onwards, in local tongues rather than Latin, enabled more of the public to have access to the text of the bible (Ward, 2006). This led to people questioning traditional church interpretations of Scripture. Although one of Luther's tenets was 'sola scripture' – a basis of Christianity not in authoritarian pronouncements, but in Scripture itself, this was complicated by the fact that the meaning of Scripture is not transparent and clear. As the fundamental heart of Protestantism was effectively that anyone could err in their interpretation of Scripture (ibid.), this theology enabled a space for people to develop their own interpretations of Scripture and their own experiences. One problematic manifestation of this was that soon after the start of the Reformation, Luther was faced with the problem of individuals taking his proposed individual relationship with God to the extreme. He was faced with 'erroneous doctrines' proclaimed by prophets who popped up claiming to hear the voice of God directly, unmediated by Scripture. Luther referred to these individuals as '*Schwarmers*' – taken from the terms for stirred-up bees (Heyd, 1995). These individual claims to access religious truth through direct divine revelation was a threat to the authority of ministers and to the principle of sola scripture (ibid.). The way that Luther dealt with this was to insist that such spirits be judged by their accordance with Scripture (ibid.). You could hear from God, but if it contradicted Scripture, it wasn't God speaking.

Luther also faced, and resisted, the medicalisation of voices heard in a religious context. He observed that doctors, when confronted with 'divine voices', would 'dispute and . . . draw conclusions about the nature of the constitution of the blood or the whole body' (Luther, as cited in Midelfort, 1999, p. 91). Luther observed that people were 'taught by doctors ... [to] say that one's complexion or melancholy is to blame, or the heavenly planets, or they invent some other natural cause' (ibid.). Whereas in Chapter 1 we saw Jean Gerson attempting to colonise voice-hearing from a religious point of view, now we see medicine attempting to colonise the religious discourse. Voice-hearers were again being forced to speak in someone else's words. In contrast to a medical approach, Luther argued that divine voices and visions were 'not melancholy dreams that have no bearing on reality' (ibid.), and expressed concern that people were not paying full attention to the signs that God was sending.

In England, changes in the perception of voice-hearing were also occasioned by the changing position of the Anglican Church on possession and exorcism. In the last decades of the 1500s, individuals such as William Weston (an English Jesuit priest) and John Darrell (a Puritan minister) claimed to perform successful exorcisms (Walker, 1983). Exorcism had been used by Christ and the Apostles to validate early Christianity, but since the Reformation exorcisms had begun to be used by one denomination of Christians as propaganda against another (ibid.). A campaign was mounted by the Anglican Church to discredit such exorcisms, which took the form of works such as the Anglican Bishop Harsnett's work, *A Discovery of the Fradulent Practices of John Darrell* (1599), and the Puritans John Deacon & John Walker's 1601 work, *Dialogical Discourses of Spirits and Devils*. In their book, Deacon and Walker argued that possession- and miracle-type events were neither delusions, nor naturalistically explainable, but the work of the devil – hence enabling them to link the diabolic to the Catholic religion (Walker, 1983). In contrast, the Anglicans argued that the age of supernatural intervention per se had ceased (ibid.). The Anglican doctrine of the cessation of miracles made it possible 'for a pious Christian to live in a world entirely devoid of any supernatural occurrences' (ibid., p. 73). However, by denying the reality of possession and witchcraft, the Anglican Church was forced into adopting medical views of such experiences, as proposed by individuals such as the physician Edward Jorden. Similarly, as with Dutch and German physicians, the English physician Harsnett used melancholy to account for belief in diabolic activity, referring to the old adage *cerebrum Melancholicum est sedes daemonum* (a melancholic brain is the seat of demons) (Walker, 1983). In the case of possession, the English physician was expected to take into account the patient's whole being, including whether they had a natural disease or not. Key diagnoses for voice-hearers were epilepsy, hysteria or melancholy, which it was known could produce persistent hallucinations (ibid., p. 10). The danger here, of course, was that medicine had the potential to act as a universal religious acid (to adapt Dennett's, 1995, phrase) burning its way through all religious experiences including voice-hearing ones.

The sixteenth-century Spanish mystics: discerning voice-hearers

In addition to the humanist medicalisation of voices and the issues the Protestant Reformation had raised surrounding voices, the Catholic Church in Europe was at this time producing a number of influential mystics who wrote on hearing voices. In particular, in Spain the writings of St Teresa of Avila (1515–82) and St John of the Cross (1542–91) were to prove influential. St Teresa and St John were both members of the Catholic Order of Our Lady of Mount Carmel, founded in the twelfth century on Mount Carmel, a site long regarded as a sanctuary and where Pythagoras is reputed to have meditated (Brenan, 1975). This Order is characterised by prayer, silence, meditation and contemplation. By undertaking such practices St Teresa and St John can be argued, like the early Desert Hermits, to have taken a highly experimental approach to the interior life (Maitland, 2008). For the Desert Hermits, 'silence emerged as an effective instrument for inducing profound experiences' (ibid., p. 203), and this appears to have been the case for St Teresa and St John who both had personal experiences of voice-hearing (e.g. Box 2.1).[4]

St Teresa, after entering the Carmelite convent of the Incarnation at Avila aged 20, against her father's wishes (Cangas et al., 2008), and following a long period of illness, began the intense practice of mental prayer (Zimmerman, 1912). This involved withdrawal from external stimuli, entrance into contemplative meditation, and was followed by her voice-hearing experiences as well as visions, trances, raptures and a 'state of union' with God (Brenan, 1975). When she was aged 52, she first met the 25-year-old man known to the world today as St John of the Cross. Whilst still a youth, words allegedly came to St John which seemed to be spoken by God, saying, 'Thou shalt serve me, in an Order whose former perfection thou shalt help to restore' (Peers, 1943, p. 15). St John particularly identified with individuals in the Bible, such as

---

[4] For a contextualised account of St Teresa and her experiences, see Cangas et al. (2008). For a detailed topography of St John of the Cross's classification of hallucinations, see Jones (2009).

Box 2.1: St Teresa's voice-hearing experiences

St Teresa (2008, pp. 181–97) reports that since the time 'when our Lord granted me that grace' hearing voices had, for her, been 'an ordinary occurrence'. The words of the voices, she said, were 'very distinctly formed; but by the bodily ear they are not heard. They are, however, much more clearly understood than they would be if they were heard by the ear.' The voices had to be listened to. As she noted, 'when we wish not to hear anything in this world, we can stop our ear, or give attention to something else', whereas, in contrast, from the voice of God 'there is no escape, for in spite of ourselves we must listen'. Of her voices she writes that 'many of them are reproaches. He sends them when I fall into imperfections. They are enough to destroy a soul. They correct me ... [and give] both counsel and relief. There are others which bring my former sins into remembrance ... Some are warnings against certain dangers to myself or others; many of them are prophecies of future things, three or four years before hand; and all of them have been fulfilled ... Here, then, are so many reasons for believing that they come from God, as make it impossible, I believe, for anybody to mistake them.'

St Teresa also had to acknowledge the status that society afforded her as a woman. She wrote that the safest thing to do was to tell one's confessor everything one is experiencing and 'obey him'. As she genuflects, 'I do so; and if I did not, I should have no peace. Nor is it right that we women, who are unlearned, should have any'. The parallel of this to the relationship between the contemporary voice-hearer and mental health professional is striking. Indeed, the voice-hearer's struggle for their own voice parallels that of the woman's struggle for a voice throughout much of history.

Moses, David, Jeremiah, Paul and John, due to the concrete personal experiences they reported (Kavanaugh & Rodriguez, 1991). Given this, it is unsurprising that, starting from his and St Teresa's own experiences, he embarked on a programme of empirical mysticism, exploring this realm in a theological context (Zimmerman, 1910). Indeed, it has been argued that 'nothing but his own deep and varied experience could have made him what he may well be termed – the greatest psychologist in the history of mysticism' (St John of the Cross, 1943, p. xl).

Both St Teresa and St John wrote extensively on hearing voices. However, the presence of the Inquisition in Spain at this time made the dangers of being perceived as being misguided or heretical very salient. At this time, unlike *Monty Python*, everyone expected the Spanish

Inquisition. Furthermore, naturalistic accounts of hallucinations put forward in previous centuries by theologians such as Oresme, Langenstein and Gerson had raised questions about the validity of hallucinations arising from contemplative states (Fogleman, 2009). For example, Langenstein argued that excessive contemplation was likely to harm the body's sensory faculties, leading to physically or bodily induced false visions, which were hateful to God (ibid.). Oresme (c.1320–82) in his work, *De causis mirabilium*, argued that although divine and demonic intrusions were possible, most were probably the products of sensory malfunctions, and could be traced back to natural causes (Clark, 1999). In evaluating the value of voices heard due to contemplative prayer, it was the character of the person having the experience that was claimed to be important. For example, Oresme described truly divine visions as coming to 'men of sober and peaceful life, whose souls are like clear and shining mirrors, clean from worldly thoughts' (Fogleman, 2009, p. 17). We see a parallel with the positive personal characteristics of Socrates that were deemed to be why he heard a voice (Chapter 1). Once again, though, we see here a way to ensure that any voices heard by potentially subversive individuals could be discounted as being non-divine.

St John (1943) introduced the first major new classification of voice-hearing since St Augustine, creating three types of supernatural hearing voices experiences. These he referred to as successive, formal and substantive locutions. *Successive locutions* occur when absorbed in meditation, when the person 'by means of its reasoning discovers things which it knew not with respect to the subject of its reflections, so that it seems not to be doing this itself, but rather it seems that another person is supplying the reasoning within its mind or answering its questions or teaching' (1943, p. 209). He says that in this state the soul 'is reasoning with itself and answering itself as though it were two persons convening together; and in some ways this is really so … and thus it utters them to itself as though to a third person'. *Formal locutions*, which may be experienced both in and out of meditative states, are termed this by St John as they are 'communicated to the spirit formally by a third person, the spirit itself playing no part in this' (p. 215). Whereas successive locutions come when a person is thinking on a topic, and are related to it, formal locutions may come out of the blue, such as when the person is 'far from thinking of the subject of what is being said to it' (p. 216). Such words may be clearly formed or not, and there may be only one word, or many. Furthermore, they 'are apt to be continuous, either instructing the soul or discussing something with it' (ibid.). St John notes that in such experiences 'it is just as though one person were speaking with another' (ibid.). He draws on the authority of the Bible here, citing the examples of Daniel (Daniel 9:22), who had an angel speak within him and give him instructions, and Moses (Exodus 3:10) who was commanded by God to go to and deliver his people from pharaoh.[5]

Finally, *substantive locutions* differ from formal locutions, in that they 'produce vivid and substantial effects upon the soul, whereas words which are merely formal do not' (p. 219). Indeed, he claims that 'they are of such moment and price that they are life and virtue and incomparable good to the soul; for one of these words works greater good within the soul than all that the soul itself has done throughout its life' (ibid.). St John gives the example of a person in a state of great fear suddenly hearing God saying to them 'Fear thou not' (ibid.) and that this made them feel 'great fortitude and tranquillity' (ibid.).

In line with Christian teachings, both St John and St Teresa believed hearing voices could have a number of sources, being variously God, the devil or one's own imagination. Regarding this latter category, St John discussed voices occurring in a natural context, but without using a medical model, preferring instead a self-talk model. He wrote about how he was 'appalled at what happens in these days – namely, when some soul with the very smallest experience of meditation, if it be conscious of certain locutions of this kind in some state of recollection, at once christens them all as coming from God, and assumes that this is the case, saying: "God said to me . . ."; "God answered me . . ."; whereas it is not so at all, but, as we have said, it is for the most part *they who are saying these things to themselves*' (p. 210, emphasis added).[6]

As with theological writers in the previous century, St Teresa and St John were concerned to give guidelines to help people discern the source of a voice they heard, and not to be seen to be encouraging heretical voice-hearing. As such, St Teresa (2007) advised, as Martin Luther had, that unless the voice 'agrees with the Scriptures, take no more notice of it than you would if it came from the devil himself' (p. 84). She also argued that the location the voice was heard from, 'whether they come from within, from above or from without, has nothing to do with their coming from God' (ibid.). In order to identify genuine supernatural communications, St Teresa first argued that such

---

[5] We are told that Moses showed 'such great repugnance that He had to command him three times to do it and to perform signs for him' (St John, 1943, p. 216), possibly suggesting that such locutions have the potential to be repetitive and insistent. However, the aim of such quotes to report phenomenological accuracy is obviously questionable.

[6] Many psychological models today offer a similar explanation, see Chapter 9.

locutions are heard clearly (not like something half-heard in a dream), and so clearly that the phrasing can be noted, including any speech errors such as omission of syllables. Second, genuine locutions come unexpectedly, sometimes even during the middle of a conversation. Third, they refer to things that 'one never thought would or could happen, so that the imagination cannot possibly have invented them' (p. 101). Fourth, they 'contain a world of meaning such as the understanding alone could never put rapidly into human language' (ibid.). Fifth, not only can words be heard, but more is understood than merely what the words say. Sixth, if the locutions are genuine they cannot be ignored (which imagined voices can). Instead, 'we have no ears which we can stop, nor have we the power to refrain from thought' (p. 102).

Once a voice had been discerned as genuine (i.e. having a supernatural source), it then needed to be further discerned as to whether the source was divine or demonic. St Teresa (2007) set out a number of characteristics which she believed indicated they came from God. The most important, was 'the sense of power and authority which they [the words] bear with them' (p. 97). She gives the example of a troubled person hearing the phrase 'Be not troubled' (ibid.), with this being enough to calm them. A second characteristic was that 'a great tranquillity dwells in the soul' (p. 98), and a third that the words 'do not vanish from the memory for a very long time: some, indeed, never vanish at all' (ibid.). Furthermore, such words, if referring to the future, are felt to have a complete certainty. St John (1943) adds the more traditional discernment criteria that the more completely exterior and corporeal voices are, the less likely they are to be from God. He also believed external and corporeal experiences communicated less 'than would be the case if the same things were more interior and spiritual' (p. 103). St Teresa also echoes St John's criteria, arguing that locutions from the devil are pronounced very clearly, can be easily understood, do not leave room for confusion, leave the soul in turmoil and restlessness and encourage pride. From the Church's point of view, a vague voice-hearing experience was likely to be more desirable, as it could be interpreted in many ways by the Church, whereas a clear simple voice reported by a voice-hearer left less wiggle room for the Church to impose its own interpretation.

A particularly important consequence of St Teresa's writings was that she explicitly embraced the emerging medical interpretations of the voices that were in the air at the time, writing of how voices may be divine/demonic or sickness-based. For example, she noted that: 'Sometimes – often, indeed – this [hearing voices] may be a fancy, especially in persons who are melancholy – I mean are affected by

> **Box 2.2: Voice-hearing in the sixteenth century in a Jewish context**
>
> Joseph Caro (1488–1575) was the greatest Jewish legal scholar of his time. He was also a voice-hearer. Lewis (1978) describes how Caro was the recipient of messages from a spirit guide (a Maggid) who made bold statements and claimed unquestionable authority. Caro recorded these statements in a diary for fifty years. Examples of what the voices said include: 'I speak through your mouth, not in a dream but as a man talks to a fellow man ... I address you while your eyes are wide open, and your utterances are loud' (p. 14). The voice, reports Lewis, advised Caro that if he was puzzled by a particularly hard problem in Talmudic exegesis, he should focus on the problem, and wish to be helped by the Maggid, who would then give him the answer. The voice most often occurred on the Sabbath, would take account of whether other people were present and comment on the political situation. The voice also told him 'You are considered very eminent and lofty and sublime by the Holy One, Blessed be He, and the prophets, the tannaim, amoraim, geonim and codifiers in Heaven. Whatever you do, God will crown with success' (ibid.). Interestingly, on one occasion the Maggid declared to him 'I am the echo of your thoughts' (ibid.).

real melancholy – or have feeble imaginations' (p. 96). Of such people, wrote Teresa, 'no notice should be taken ... One should listen to them as one would to sick persons ... One should humour such people so as not to distress then further. If one tells them they are suffering from melancholy, there will be no end of it' (p. 97). Further, unless the voice agreed with the Scriptures, they should take no notice of it as it may 'in fact, come only from your weak imagination' (ibid.). Although labelling some of her nuns as sick (*enferma*) meant Teresa was able to save them from the Spanish Inquisition, this further opened the door to a medical discourse on hearing voices (Sarbin & Juhasz, 1967).

The seventeenth century: the medicalisation of voices by religion

At the start of the seventeenth century, belief in the natural and the supernatural co-existed uneasily. The traditional medieval and Renaissance view, that man existed at the point of convergence of the natural and supernatural worlds, still allowed hearing voices to be explained by either of these approaches (MacDonald, 1983). At this time although encounters with angels and spirits were rare, they were not by themselves seen as signs of mental abnormality (ibid.). MacDonald reviewed 2,483 cases treated by the physician Rev. Richard Napier (1559–1634) in the early seventeenth century, and found 5.1 per cent of his patients reported hallucinations, although we are not told what percentage heard voices. Twenty-eight of his patients reported Satan had appeared to them, either visibly or as a disembodied voice, urging them to commit suicide.[7] Patients reported hearing voices telling them that they would burn and be damned, and that they should hurt themselves or others, and in one case to 'kiss my arse' (p. 202).[8] Napier, himself a licensed physician, was said to have spoken to Raphael, the Archangel of healing, in order to work out the best way to treat patients (Porter, 1987). It was this ability, rather than any medical expertise, that was the basis of his being granted a licence to treat patients (Furdell, 2002).

Yet at this time John Locke's (1632–1704) writings, were making disorders of perception (such as hearing voices) prominent signs of madness (MacDonald, 1983). Following Locke, explanations for all phenomena, including religion and religious experiences, had to be rational (Porter, 2002). This led to the seventeenth and eighteenth centuries gradually moving from a view of madness being associated with 'animality' (p. 148) – violent, bestial actions associated with animals – to being associated with unreason (Foucault, 2006). Advances in physical science and anatomy further prompted the ruling elite to embrace secular explanations for mental disorder and to repudiate magical and religious methods of treatment (MacDonald, 1983). Humanistic physicians battled to secure a monopoly over the care of the insane, and to take power away from clerical doctors, astrologers, wizards and apothecaries (ibid.).

It was in the seventeenth century, particularly in England, that there was a violent clash between personal-spiritual interpretations of voices, and medical accounts, resulting in the victory of the latter, and a major medicalisation of hearing voices. Yet it was the Anglican Church, not the physicians, that led the charge for the medicalisation of voices in order to maintain its power and authority. The Thirty Years War, the English Revolution and a general crisis all over Europe, were accompanied by an upsurge of millenarian movements, the spread of radical religious sects and frequent voice-hearing experiences and pronouncements (Heyd, 1995). When the 'world turned upside down' (Hill, 1991) in

---

[7] A very common experience today, be in it the context of psychosis, combat veterans with PTSD (Chapter 4), or healthy individuals (Chapter 7).

[8] Again, as we will see in Chapter 4, these are also common presentations to physicians today.

seventeenth-century England due to the English Civil War (1642–51) and the beheading of Charles I in 1649 by the Parliamentarians, the ensuing Interregnum ('between reigns') period where a fragile English republic existed until Charles II ascended to the throne in 1660, resulted in a crisis of authority (Heyd, 1995). During this Interregnum, preachers such as Richard Overton put forth the view, originally put forward by Luther, that each man was his own 'King, Priest and Prophet' with natural rights and duties to speak, preach and rule in the community (Witte, 2007, p. 1541). As we have seen, Luther's protests seeded revolutionary ideas in sixteenth-century Europe which challenged not only the traditional authority of the clergy over laity, but eventually all traditional authority structures – rulers over subjects, husband over wives, parents over children and masters over servants (Witte, 2007). This led to a number of religious 'Dissenters' creating their own churches, and splitting from the established Anglican church, the Church of England. The Church of England was hence faced with a problem of authority, with individuals claiming direct inspiration, power and authority from God. Such individuals were referred to as 'enthusiasts'. A definition of enthusiasts from 1646 defines them as 'fanatical men, who either feign or presume to have God's breath and inspiration, and whether by diabolical, melancholic or voluntary illusions, deceive themselves and others that such inspiration should be assigned to divine revelation' (Heyd, 1995, p. 19).

One example of a new religious movement arising in the Civil War period was the Religious Society of Friends (or 'Quakers'). This movement's founder, George Fox (1624–91) experienced during his youth something of a spiritual crisis: 'I fasted much, walked abroad in solitary places many days, and often took out my bible, and sat in hollow trees and lonesome places until night came on' (Fox, 1808, p. 90). He considered joining with other dissenting movements, but found himself unable to, for example, rejecting one group as they claimed 'women have no souls' (p. 89). Soon afterwards Fox reports that 'when all my hope in them [priests] and in all men were gone, so that I had nothing outwardly to help me, nor could tell me what to do; then, I heard a voice which said "There is one, even Christ Jesus, that can speak to thy condition". When I heard it, my heart did leap for joy' (p. 91). Fox then began to preach publicly, and attracted a following that became known as 'Friends'. Fox's advice was to listen for the voice of God, 'a still voice that speaks to us ... that is not be heard in the noises and hurries of the mind, but is distinctly understood in a retired frame' (p. 51). For following his beliefs he was jailed a number of times, although he was later able to personally persuade Oliver Cromwell that he was not a threat. Responses by physicians to Fox at the time included that the voices and other experiences claimed by his followers were the 'stronger impulses of a warm brain' (Dr Nicolas Robinson, as cited in Porter, 2002, p. 30).

Another example of a voice-hearing-inspired enthusiast movement was the wonderfully named Muggletonians. In 1661, John Reeve published a book called *Divine Looking Glass Or the Third and Last Testament of Our Lord Jesus Christ* (Reeve, 1661/2003). In this he first argued that hearing voices from God was a key part of what it was to be a religious figure, stating that 'Wherefore can any man upon this earth that counts himself ... to be a true prophet, apostle, minister, preacher ... without a voice of distinct words to the hearing of the ear from the everliving God?' (p. 108). He then describes his own voice-hearing experience: 'by voice of words spoken unto me, by his eternal spirit three mornings together, to the hearing of the ear as a man speaks to his friend' (p. 93). After introducing the passage from Revelation 11:3, in which God says 'I will give power to my two witnesses, and they will prophesy', he then stated that God told him 'he had chosen me as his last messenger for a great work unto this bloody unbelieving world' (ibid.). Reeve then explained how this was applicable to him and his friend, Muggleton, as the voice said that 'he had given me understanding above all the men in the world ... and had given me Lodowick Muggleton to be my mouth' (ibid.). The Muggletonians were born.

Women were also still claiming to hear the voice of God. For example, Lady Eleanor Davies (1590–1652) claimed to be a prophetess and to hear the voice of God, a 'heavenly voyce' (Feroli, 2006, p. 40). This 'voyce' told her a range of things, such as 'There is nineteen years & a halfe to the daye of judgement' (p. 52). This voice was used by her to attempt to make political suggestions, including prophesying the fall of Charles I. As with female voice-hearers we met earlier (e.g. Joan of Arc, Hildegard of Bingen), gender was a significant factor here. Lady Eleanor had to explain why God has spoken to her, a woman, a member of the 'weaker sex', and suggested that this was due to the stubbornness and stupidity of men in the current generation (Feroli, 2006).[9] Feroli suggests that as a woman, Lady Eleanor had to link her voice to a heavenly source rather than a product of her own brain, in order to have any authority. Given what we have seen from earlier centuries in terms of the outcomes of interactions of voice-hearing women with politics, we

---

[9] Some would say this was an overly optimistic view of earlier men.

should not be surprised that this did not turn out well. Lady Eleanor was sent to the famous mental asylum, Bethlem (Porter, 1987).[10]

The enthusiasts and other groups with 'socially subversive political ideas' horrified the ruling elite, who developed a deep animosity towards any religious group which claimed authority based on direct revelation through voice-hearing (MacDonald, 1983, p. 225). The tactic the Church of England used to mount an attack on the enthusiasts was to declare the voices and visions of radical dissenters to be insane delusions based on false perceptions and diseased imaginings (ibid.). Enthusiasm was proclaimed as a sign of illness, with both old humeral physiological explanations (based around this being caused by an excess of black bile), as well as newer neurological explanations[11] being used to account for it. As was the case with George Fox, enthusiasts who claimed to have direct revelatory experiences were therefore written off as 'melancholic', and mentally sick. The medicalisation of this debate can be seen to be part of the process of medical marginalisation of nonconformists generally in this period, as argued for by Foucault (Heyd, 1995). Heyd argues that 'In designating religions eccentrics and non-conformists as "mentally sick", the critics of enthusiasm imperceptibly redefined religious orthodoxy in medical terms of health and mental balance' (p. 10). This led to the Church of England becoming the champion of secular interpretations of mental illness, asserting that voices and visions were naturally caused, with bishops talking of 'noisome fumes ... vapouring up to the brain ... [cause people to] strongly persuade themselves, that the devil assaileth their minds' (MacDonald, 1983, p. 207). Anglican arguments thus encouraged the public to regard enthusiasts as being sick in mind (MacDonald, 1983). Examples used to this end were cases such as that of the enthusiast, Thomas Schucker, from 1526. After delivering an excited 'Anabaptist' sermon the previous day, Thomas required his younger brother to kneel before him, and asked for a sword. While reassuring his parents that he would not do anything but what God the Father commanded him – he proceeded to cut off his brother's head.[12] This was cited as a case of enthusiasts being involved in patently immoral acts, discrediting the idea that these were divine inspiration (Heyd, 1995).

[10] For those of you thoroughly depressed by the burning and incarceration of female voice-hearers, and in need of an immediate tonic, skip to Box 3.3 in Chapter 3. You'll feel a lot better.

[11] It was in this period that Thomas Willis, an Anglican Royalist, coined the term 'neurologie' (Porter, 2002).

[12] See Chapter 12 for contemporary research on the relationship between command AVHs and violence.

The fact that the alternative religious movements (the dissenters) had attempted to heal the mad, also led the orthodox elite to abandon religious therapy for madness until the early nineteenth century (MacDonald, 1983), leaving a gap for medical psychology to become the only acceptable alternative. Indeed, the failure of demonological explanations of hearing voices to help establish social order (Porter, 2002) combined with the Anglican Church's antipathy to religious therapy (exorcisms, etc.) encouraged the orthodox elite to regard mental disorders from a secular perspective. Scientific theories and medical treatment were the only ones which were seen as religiously neutral, and hence avoided disapproval from established clergy (MacDonald, 1983).

The Church already had allies in the fight to medicalise hearing voices. This can be most clearly seen in the work of an Oxford scholar, Robert Burton (1577–1640). Burton not only advocated a medical account of hallucinations, but railed violently against religious explanations. Heyd (1995) has argued that the use Burton made of the medical tradition for the purpose of creating religious controversy was 'momentous', infusing his medical conception of melancholy into his controversy with Catholics and enthusiasts. Burton (1621/1821) argued that people's 'corrupt phantasie [imagination] makes them see and hear that which indeed is neither heard nor seen' and that 'As they that drink wine think all runs round, when it is their own brain: so is it with these men' (p. 311). He explains this in the medical terminology of 'Corrupt vapours mounting from the body to the head' (p. 312). Burton cites an example of 'a woman, that still supposed she heard the devil call her, and speaking to her' (p. 314), which he claims 'proceed most part from a corrupt imagination' (p. 315). He also cited the old proverb that 'as the fool thinketh, so the bell clinketh' (p. 314), suggesting that people may hear what they want to, but potentially being based on a real external stimulus being misinterpreted.[13] Going beyond these general critiques, Burton aided the Anglican attack on the dissenting clergy, declaring they suffered from a mental disease which he termed 'religious melancholy' (MacDonald, 1983, p. 223). Burton pushed for an account where the 'knavish imposters of juglers, exorcists, mass-priests and mountebanks ... can counterfeit the voices of all birds and bruit beasts almost, all tones and tunes of men, and speak within their throats, as if

---

[13] Shakespeare writes in *Much Ado About Nothing* (Act 3, Scene 2) that 'he hath a heart as sound as a bell, and his tongue is the clapper, for what his heart thinks his tongue speaks'. Is what a heart thinks what the head hears? We will return to this in Chapter 11 when we examine the hypervigilance model of AVHs.

they spoke afar off, that they make their auditors believe they hear spirits' (p. 314). Such arguments had previously been put forward by Reginald Scot (1538–99), who argued that Pope Boniface VIII 'counterfetted a voice through a cane reed, as though it had come from heaven, persuading him to yeeld up his authoritie of popeship' (Scot, 1584, p. 270). Yet Burton went much further, referring to papists as 'stupid, ignorant and blind', and Anabaptists as 'rude, illiterate, capricious, base fellows', with such individuals being 'blind idiots, and superstitious asses' (Burton, 1621/1859, p. 384). Charming. He also argued that 'never any visions, phantasms, apparitions, enthusiasms, prophets, any revelations, but immoderate fasting, bad diet, sickness, melancholy, solitariness, or some such things were the precedent causes' (p. 388). Indeed, solitariness, he argues, is a key cause of hearing things.[14]

Descartes (1596–1650) also put forward a neurological account which could be used to explain hearing voices, as explained by Dennett (1991). Descartes used the analogy of the bell-pull, which used to be used to communicate between rooms before the invention of intercoms. A wire would run from, say, a handle in an attic room to a bell in a basement room. If someone pulled the chain in the attic, that would cause the bell in the basement to ring. But if someone in the middle of the house pulled the wire, the person in the basement would 'hallucinate' a bell in the attic. Thus Descartes' account allowed that any activation in the brain in the pathways between the ear and the centre of consciousness could result in hearing voices that were not there (ibid.).

Such naturalistic arguments did not take off in the general population immediately. First, the Church's naturalistic arguments were only partially accepted by the educated classes because they could see this could lead to the questioning of God (MacDonald, 1983). Second, the general population continued to believe in demonology and witchcraft in the seventeenth century because they offered a comprehensible framework for them to cope with and understand forces that threatened their body and mind (ibid.). The largest part of the population, men and women without property, did not have their minds changed, argues MacDonald, as 'the abandonment of the old, semimagical view of the world was impossible without a vast transformation in the material lives and educational standards of the whole society' (p. 217). Most importantly, medicine was not actually any good at curing mental problems. Its brutal physical means made many people think that religious methods were actually better (ibid.). Francis Bacon himself noted that since the

---

[14] See Hoffman's (2007) account of voice-hearing in Chapter 11 for a contemporary echo of this.

Greeks, medicine had moved 'rather in circle than in progression ... I find much iteration, but small addition' (Bacon, 1605/2002, p. 211).

As a result of this collision between religion and medicine, we see a number of autobiographical accounts of individuals hearing voices in a religious context at this time that also utilise a biological conception of the voices into their account of the experience. One interesting example is that of George Trosse (1631–1713). Trosse was a Presbyterian minister, and had spent time in jail for participating in an illegal religious gathering (Peterson, 1982). In his memoir, *The Life of the Reverend Mr George Trosse*, he reflects on a number of experiences from earlier in his life, including episodes of voice-hearing. At first, Trosse thought he was hearing the voice of God: 'I was thus walking up and down, hurried with these worldly disquieting Thoughts, I perceiv'd a *Voice*, (*I heard plainly*) saying unto me, *Who art thou?* Which knowing it could be the Voice of *no Mortal*, I concluded was the *Voice of God*' (p. 29). However, as the voice began to give strange commands, Trosse's view of the voice changed. He describes how 'I was praying upon my Knees, I heard a Voice, as I fancy'd, as it were just behind me, saying, *Yet more humble; Yet more humble* ... undoubtedly concluding it came from God, I endeavour'd to comply with it' (ibid.). Yet the voice continued to command him to kneel on his bare knees, then take off all his clothes. When this still wasn't good enough for the voice, he put his head in a hole in the wood of the floor to more fully prostrate himself. He then records that 'standing up before the Window, I either heard a Voice, which bid me, or had a strong Impulse, which excited me, to cut off my Hair; to which I reply'd, I have no Scissors. It was then hinted, that a knife would do it; but I answer'd I have none. Had I one, I verily believe, this Voice would have gone from my Hair to my Throat, and have commanded me to cut it: For I have all Reason to conclude, that the Voice was the Voice of Satan' (p. 27). At this point he comes to the conclusion that 'pretending the Worship of God, I fell, in effect, to the Worshipping of the Devil'. He then notes that 'many of the Quakers formerly were deluded by such Voices ... which they mistook for the Holy Spirit of God ... I verily believe that those many Visions and Voices among the Papists ... came from the same Author, or Cause, viz. A crack'd Brain, impos'd upon by a deceitful and lying Devil' (p. 30). This 'crack'd Brain' approach was soon to become dominant.

The eighteenth century: meaning out, medicine in

The momentum of the medical conception of hearing voices continued, and by the middle of the eighteenth century the prevailing view among

> **Box 2.3: A voice-hearer in the eighteenth century: William Cowper**
>
> William Cowper (1731–1800) was an English poet and hymnist. The onset of his voices was preceded by a range of acts by Cowper which he perceived as sins, including wishing that a clerk in the House of Lords would die so that Cowper could have his job (Peterson, 1982). The clerk did indeed die. Although Cowper was offered the job, it then came to light that the appointment was contested and he would have to face scrutiny in public. Distressed by this prospect Cowper, unsuccessfully, attempted suicide by hanging. After tying a rope to the ceiling and kicking away the chair under him, he recalls that 'While I hung there, I distinctly heard a voice say three times, "*Tis over!*"' (p. 66).
>
> After this event, though, Cowper continued to hear the voices: 'Satan piled me closely with horrible visions, and more horrible voices. My ears rang with the sound of torments' (p. 65). Cowper found a cure after reading the Bible led to his conversion to Christianity. His doctor, at first worried by this turn to religion, eventually accepted it after seeing its positive effects on Cowper. In the end Cowper came to see his experiences not as an accidental sickness of the mind, but due to God's chastisement through satanic possession.

the educated elite was that 'people who claimed to have divine inspirations of devilish afflictions were insane' (MacDonald, 1983, p. 170). The content of hearing voices which had previously been 'culturally integrated and semantically pregnant, i.e., their content was believed to carry a message for the individual or the world' (Berrios, 2002, p. 35) was now largely lost as a consequence of this medicalisation (ibid.). In this century an influential text was William Battie's (1758) *Treatise on Madness*. Battie argued that a man is 'properly mad' if he is 'fully and unalterably persuaded of the existence or of the appearance of any thing, which either does not exist or does not actually appear to him, and who behaves according to such erroneous persuasion' (p. 6). He thought that voices could be caused by an endogenous (i.e. 'proceeding from within') disturbance of the nerves in the brain. This he termed original madness, which he believed 'neither follows nor accompanies any accident, which may justly be deemed its external and remoter cause' (p. 59). He proposed that hereditary causes may be involved in such cases. This madness, he thought, was 'not removable by any method' (p. 61). In contrast, he viewed 'consequential madness' as resulting from a disturbance in nerves caused by an event in the external world, and being amenable to cure.

Events such as fever, epilepsy, childbirth, passions of joy and anger, were all potential causes of consequential madness, as they resulted in spasms of the neck, forcing blood back up into the 'minutest vessels of the brain' (p. 53). Overwork by philosophers could lead them to become 'infirm and shattered' and could be said to have 'cracked their brains' (p. 57). Gluttony and idleness were also potential causes, due to their not resulting in 'due propulsion of the fluids' (p. 58). Here he points the finger at 'St Anthony and the lazy monks his followers, [and] the extasies of sendentary and cholorotic Nuns' (ibid.). Treatment was possible by simply addressing these causes. Yet still, MacDonald (1983) argues that at the same time, the poor and much of the public did not take this view, and this resulted in 'the creation of two, often antagonistic, mental outlooks, each with a different interpretation of insanity' (p. 172).

An example of how voices were understood in the eighteenth century can be seen in the case of Emanuel Swedenborg (1688–1772), who experienced extensive voices and visions (see Jones & Fernyhough, 2008a, for a fuller discussion). Those who met and knew Swedenborg had a charitable and non-stigmatising view of his experiences, and agreed that he was of sound judgement (Toksvig, 1948). Many of those who levelled charges of insanity against Swedenborg before meeting him seemed subsequently to have had second thoughts (ibid.). In addition to his demonstrated rationality in everyday life, Swedenborg's high social standing, combined with his failure overtly to cross the line from religious into political prophecy (Ingram, 1998), may also have played a role in his generally sympathetic treatment. Others who did cross into political prophecy, such as the English preacher Richard Brothers, who in 1795 prophesied the fall of the monarchy, were rapidly institutionalised (ibid.). As Brothers wryly noted, 'I and the world happened to have a slight difference of opinion; the world said I was mad, and I said the world was mad. I was outvoted, and here I am' (Brothers, as cited in Johnstone, 2000, p. 222).

Swedenborg was acutely aware that he may have been thought of as mad, writing of individuals who 'persuaded others that I was insane' (Swedenborg, 1883, n. 2772). For example, in 1770 the early Methodist, John Wesley, wrote that Swedenborg 'is one of the most ingenious, lively, entertaining madmen that ever set pen to paper' (Wesley, 1986/ 1770, p. 216). Yet the most influential commentator, in terms of cementing a particular view of Swedenborg, was his contemporary Immanuel Kant. Kant (2002/1766) wrote that he did not believe that Swedenborg had simply invented his experiences, and found the 'coherent delusion of the senses' to be a 'remarkable phenomenon' (p. 50). Despite this measured tone, certain passages of Kant's work are more critical of Swedenborg. For example, Kant states that he would not blame the reader if he dismissed characters such as Swedenborg as 'candidates for the hospital' (p. 35). Importantly, Kant also introduced the distinction between the raw experiences (e.g. hearing voices) Swedenborg had, which Kant termed 'deludedness of the senses' (p. 50), and the rationalisations, elaborations and interpretations Swedenborg made from these (i.e. that he was hearing Abraham's voice), which he termed 'deludedness of the reason' (ibid.). This can be seen to relate to previous distinctions that had been made. For example, Foucault (2006) notes: 'Under the influence of Locke many doctors sought the origin of madness in a problem of the senses. If one saw devils and heard voices, this could not be the fault of the soul – the soul did nothing more than receive what the senses provided' (p. 210). However, others argued the contrary. For example, Boissier de Sauvages (1706–67) argued that a cross-eyed person who sees double is not mad, but anyone who sees double and believes that he is seeing objects is insane. This was hence a problem of the soul, not the eye (Foucault, 2006). Such distinctions created a space which separated the experience of voice-hearing from the explanations people gave for it, and opened the way to the concept of hallucinations in the sane.

Chapter 2: summary of key points

- The new sense of self that began to develop from the sixteenth century onwards in the West was antithetical to the experience of hearing voices.
- The Reformation in the sixteenth century, and the emerging power vacuums in Europe, gave voice-hearers a chance to raise their voices and claim their own meanings.
- The sixteenth-century Spanish mystics developed a detailed phenomenological analysis of voices.
- In England, the advent of enthusiasts who heard divine voices and claimed religious authority on the basis of this, resulted in the Anglican Church unleashing medicine on voice-hearers.
- Voice-hearing lost its richer meaning and the medicalisation and pathologisation of the experience became dominant.
- Whereas Classical Antiquity had argued voices occurred in sedate, chaste and intelligent souls, now physicians such as William Battie argued they resulted from factors such as gluttony and idleness.
- Whereas the educated elite accepted medical theories, the lay population remained less convinced, partly due to medicine's lack of efficacy in helping those distressed by hearing voices.

3 From the birth of psychiatry to the present day

The nineteenth century: psychiatry, neurology and spiritualism

The Industrial Revolution in the eighteenth and nineteenth centuries, and the rise of capitalism, were to have a number of impacts on voice-hearers. First, there had to be a second reformation. This took the form of a 'reformation of character', with people having to internalise the capitalist ethic and to discipline themselves – control had to come from within (Scull, 1981). Capitalists had to 'make such machines of men as cannot err' (Wedgwood, as cited in ibid., p. 73) and economic and physical threats were not enough to achieve this; people had to discipline themselves. Starting from childhood, children had to become their own slave-drivers (Scull, 1981). This led to a 'peculiar and mystifying ... form of compulsion to labor for another' (Dobb, as cited in ibid., p. 74). Hence, voices were now even more unsettling than ever, as they undermined the self-disciplined model of man. The whispers of voices could drown out the booming voice of the marketplace. Second, society required its poorest people to focus on working for wages. The mad, including those driven to social and occupational impairment by voices, could hence no longer be tolerated (Scull, 1981). In the image of the newly developed industrial machines, the mad, whom voice-hearers were often numbered among, were now seen as 'defective human mechanisms', which had to be repaired, so that they could go and function in the marketplace (ibid., p. 115).[1] This motivation gave the rise to the asylum system and the presence of large numbers of patients in the same place. This enabled a class of physicians to observe a large number of patients and apply the prevailing medical techniques to them. The psychiatrist was born. This term was first used by the German physician, Johann Christian Reil, in 1808, and was created by joining 'psyche'

---

[1] We will see a similar argument by Warner, relating mental health to the need for labour, later in this chapter.

(soul/mind) with '-iatry', from the Greek *iatros*, meaning physician (Marneros, 2008). Reil emphasised that people who were mentally ill should not be treated by experts of other disciplines (such as philosophy, psychology or theology), but by this new type of doctor, the psychiatrist (ibid.).

If you were a voice-hearer and in distress, a new option had arisen for you at the end of the eighteenth century: moral treatment. At this time treatments had not advanced much since Ancient Greece, being a range of bodily assaults including bleeding, purging and blistering. The mad person was still predominantly seen as bestial, and treated accordingly, even if they were royalty (Warner, 1985). However, the combination of the prevailing Enlightenment ideas, with specific local factors such as the spirit and freedom of the French Revolution, political reforms and, in England, the bourgeois ideal of the family (ibid.) opened the door to a new form of treating the mentally ill. The death of the Quaker Hannah Mills in appalling conditions in the York Asylum in 1790 resulted in a fellow Quaker, William Tuke (1732–1822) and his colleagues setting up a new place for the treatment of the mentally ill. The resulting York Retreat opened in 1796 and introduced a new form of therapy, 'moral treatment'. This basically involved a regular Victorian regime of work, piety and moderation in a bright, clean and friendly, family-like atmosphere where patients would wear their best clothes (Johnstone, 2000). The view of the mad person was now that of someone not entirely devoid of reason. As one visitor wrote in the visitors book at the York Retreat, 'one regards them, it seems, like children who have too much energy, and who put it to dangerous uses' (Warner, 1985, p. 111).

Whilst conventional histories described the positive aspects of the Retreat, others have argued that this was more moral management than moral treatment (Hubert, 2002). The most extensive critique has come from Foucault. Although Tuke is considered to be a liberator of the mad, the truth, claims Foucault (2006), was something quite different. Foucault argues that: 'A religious and moral milieu was imposed from without, so that madness, without ever being cured, had a restraint placed on it' (p. 483). The use of religion had the aim, argues Foucault, 'to constitute a milieu in which, far from being protected, he was maintained in a state of perpetual unease, constantly threatened by Law and Guilt' (ibid.). Work was stressed, as it was superior to physical coercion in creating regular hours, employing attention, removing liberty and fixing people in a system of responsibility. More useful still, claims Foucault, was the gaze of others, which Tuke termed 'the desire of esteem' (p. 486). Evening events where people wore their best clothes exposed people to the evaluative gaze of others – 'the madman was invited to turn himself into an object for the eyes of reasonable reason' (p. 487). Such 'Surveillance and Judgement' (p. 488) culminated in self-restraint where the mad were confined by work and the gaze of others in a 'universe of Judgement' (p. 487). 'Something was born here', states Foucault, 'which was not repression but authority' (p. 488).

Tuke's approach presented a challenge for the development of psychiatry, because he was a layman claiming authority to treat the 'mentally ill'. Indeed, Tuke was explicit that he did not think a professional class was required to treat patients, arguing that the previous abuses of patients had resulted from 'the mystery with which many of those who have had the management of the insane have constantly endeavoured to envelope it' (Tuke, as cited in Scull, 1979, p. 142).[2] Tuke's failure to professionalise and jargonise his discipline, of course left it open to attack from psychiatry, which could claim new medical remedies to cure madness. Indeed, the start of the nineteenth century was characterised by the emerging discipline of psychiatry attempting (and succeeding) to establish its authority to treat mental disorders by fully wrestling this authority away from retreats and treatments given by religious figures. Treatment of women became contentious, with Jules Ferry (1870, as cited in Goldstein, 2001) arguing that 'women must belong to science or else they will belong to the church' (p. 374), and by medicalising women's distress, this meant they consulted a physician rather than a priest, keeping them away from the Church (Goldstein, 2001). Indeed, Schmidt (2002) has argued that medical psychiatry was created precisely in order to contain politically delusions of religious fervour. This struggle of psychiatry to wrestle away power from the Church is most clearly seen in France, at the birth of psychiatry.

In 1801 Philippe Pinel proposed that, for non-organic madness, moral treatment was needed. In his understanding, this meant working with the intellect and emotions of patients, rather than the traditional methods of bleeding and purging of the body (Goldstein, 2001).[3] Yet the roots of Pinel's idea for moral treatment drew on (some may say, 'appropriated') existing work with mental patients by charlatans (uncertified practitioners).[4] For example, the Catholic Brothers set up a number of hospitals specifically for the insane, where the monks were

---

[2] See the Soteria project (Chapter 12) for a contemporary instantiation of non-professionalised treatment.

[3] Let us not romanticise this approach, though – see Foucault (2006), Goldstein (2001), for a review of Pinel's harsher methods and techniques.

[4] Notably, both Pinel and his favourite pupil, Esquirol (Porter, 2002), had received religious training earlier in life. Esquirol had been in a seminary and Pinel had received minor orders (Goldstein, 2001).

to be courteous and gentle to the patients, and where there were regular and constant visits from staff, in a one-to-one situation (Goldstein, 2001). The Christian philosophy of love for one's fellow man was conducive to this approach, and Christian treatments did not aim at suppressing pain, but rather at helping the person to cope by aiding hope and courage (ibid.).[5] In the 1820s and 1830s, individuals like Xavier Tissot were actively fighting for a religious version of moral treatment over a medical version (ibid.). Yet by stressing the physical aspects of mental disorder, physicians were able to achieve power. In contrast to Pinel's view that some mental disorders were not associated with neural changes, Esquirol, who had attended Comte's lectures (and, indeed, Comte had been a patient of Esquirol's), took a materialist, empirically based position (ibid.). He wanted to link insanity to brain changes, rather than try to work with a Platonic idea of a disease which could be seen in specific symptoms. For him a disease was equated to a specific brain lesion. This materialist emphasis is seen in the French physician Broussais's criticism of Pinel for being 'too stingy with the blood of lunatics' (Goldstein, 2001, p. 264). In England, as Scull (2006) has noted, early psychiatrists were also motivated to insist on purely physical causes and to reject moral treatment, as this was the only way to avoid the suggestion that the clergyman rather than the physician was the right person to treat insanity.

Returning to hearing voices specifically, it was around this time, in 1817, that Esquirol subsumed the experiences of hearing voices, seeing visions and similar experiences in other sensory modalities into the common term 'hallucination'. This term distinguished such experiences from illusions or delusions, which had previously been referred to under the general heading of hallucination. Esquirol wrote that 'if a man has the intimate conviction of actually perceiving a sensation for which there is no external object, he is in a hallucinated state: he is a visionary' (Esquirol, as cited in Berrios, 2002, p. 37). He believed that 'the functional alterations, brain mechanisms and the clinical context' involved in hearing voices was 'the same as in visions' and hence argued a generic term for this category of experiences was needed. 'I propose the word hallucination', wrote Esquirol (ibid.). His approach firmly moved hearing voices from being an experience that may tell us something about the world (i.e. potentially with theological/spiritual value) to being medical symptoms (Berrios, 1990).

---

[5] See Chapter 6 for explicit Christian-centred therapy today, and Chapter 12 for a compassion-focused approach to voices.

Esquirol (1845) described a range of voice-hearing experiences, noting that a voice-hearer 'hears persons address him, asks questions, replies, holds a continued conversation; distinguishes very clearly reproaches, abuse, threats and commands which are addressed to him ... He hears also celestial harmonies; the songs of birds, a convert of voices, and this, when no voice is near, and a profound silence reigns around' (p. 105). What did Esquirol think these voices were? He proposed that 'the pretended sensations of the hallucinated are images and ideas reproduced by the memory, associated by the imagination, and personified by habit. He dreams, whilst fully awake' (p. 107). The proto-psychiatrist Baillarger (1809–90) also took a similar view, arguing that hallucinations resulted from a failure to control one's memory/fantasies, and drew parallels to a schoolchild who, let loose to run at recess, brings back ideas, images and memories that that were found without our aid and never requested (Goldstein, 2001).

In Baillarger's view, it was a failure of the 'moi' to act as a break on the imagination which could be excited by 'le physique' (ibid.). Insanity was hence a failure of the will to control the faculties, with the will being unable to cope with experiences arising from cerebral overexcitation (ibid.). Like the Christian writers before him (e.g. St Augustine, St John of the Cross), Baillarger observed that whilst some voices were externally located, others seemed to come from 'the interior of the soul', and hence he introduced the term 'psychosensory' to describe the former (i.e. corporeal locutions) and 'psychic hallucinations' for the latter (i.e. imaginative locutions) (Baillarger, 1846, as cited in Graham & Stephens, 1994, p. 96). Consistent with these French ideas, the Scottish physician, Samuel Hibbert (1782–1848), also argued that voices resulted from the recall of forgotten memories. For example, he cites approvingly Hartley's earlier contention that hallucinations are 'common ideas of the memory, recalled in a system so irritated, that they act nearly with the same force as the objects of immediate sensation, for which they are mistaken' (Hibbert, 1824, p. 326).

But what triggered such events in the first place? Esquirol (1845) argued that 'we cannot conceive of the existence of this symptom, but in supposing the brain to be acted on by some cause. The brain may be set in action by a sudden and violent commotion, by a strong mental conflict, or by vehement passion' (p. 108). The content of voices, he noted, were either associated with the normal events of the person's life or 'ally themselves to the nature of the cause that has kindled up the excitement of the brain' (p. 109).[6] Who did Esquirol think heard voices

---

[6] See Chapter 11 for modern studies of traumatic/stressful life events preceding onset of AVHs.

Box 3.1: Voices at the birth of psychiatry in France

Esquirol (1845, pp. 94–5) gives a number of examples of
individuals hearing voices. He describes one case of a gentleman
who was head of a large German city whose inhabitants
attacked the French army, resulting in disorder in the city. The
gentleman felt himself liable for this and cut his throat with a razor.
Upon recovering, he heard voices 'that accuse him … [that] are
continually repeating in his ear that he has betrayed his trust – that
he is dishonoured, and that he can do nothing better than destroy
himself'. Esquirol suggests that an apt name for the voices would
be 'babblers', and the gentleman agrees. One of these voices
'borrows the Russian idiom'. This voice tells him to 'Slay thyself;
thou canst not survive thy disgrace'. Another voice he hears,
though, is 'that of a lady, who calls upon him to take courage, and
entertain confidence'. The gentleman responds to his voices. 'He
questions and replies, provokes, challenges, and becomes angry,
while addressing those persons who he believes are speaking to
him'. Esquirol also notes that 'Aside from this, he reasons with
perfect propriety, and all his intellectual faculties preserve their
wonted integrity. He participates in conversation with the same
degree of spirit, intelligence and readiness, as before his sickness.'
Esquirol notes that in this gentleman 'If the conversation interest
him, he no longer heard voices. If it languishes, he hears them'.

   In 1844, shortly after the death of Esquirol, the proto-psychiatrist
Baillarger presented a paper which included a summation of
what voices were observed to be like at this time. He noted that 'the
most frequent and complicated hallucinations affect hearing:
invisible interlocutors address the patient in the third person, so
that he is the passive listener in a conversation; the number of
voices varies, they come from all directions, and can even be heard
in one ear. Sometimes the voice is heard in the head, or throat or
chest; the insane-deaf is more prone to hear voices' (Baillarger,
as cited in Berrios, 2002, p. 39). We will return to voice-hearing in
the deaf in Chapter 4.

and what did he think the experience mean? First, insanity in his view
was characterised by hallucinations such as hearing voices. Such voices
may be heard in the context of delirium in conditions such as 'mania,
lypemania, monomania, ecstasy, catalepsy, hysteria and febrile delirium'
(ibid.). Yet they may also occur also in the absence of delirium, as can be
seen from the example in Box 3.1, with Esquirol being clear that people
could hear voices and still function well, and reason, even if they were
still 'sick'. For example, he cites the case of a gentleman whose 'malady

had been characterized by hallucinations of hearing, although perfectly restored to reason, experiences still the same hallucinations ... It persisted for four months' (p. 64). Although Esquirol noted that hearing voices was 'most frequently the lot of feeble minds', he added that 'men the most remarkable for their strength of understanding, the depth of their reason, and their vigor of thought, are not always free from this symptom' (p. 110).

The French Société Médico-Psychologique debate on the meaning of voices

Esquirol's observation that both the 'feeble' and the 'great' could hear voices laid the ground for a debate amongst the French proto-psychiatrists about the meaning of hearing voices. This debate, which stretched over three decades from approximately the 1830s onwards, culminated in the 1855 debate at the Société Médico-Psychologique. During this debate, a range of views were proposed. At one extreme existed views such as those of Leuret, who argued that hearing voices was inherently pathological, and an indisputable sign of madness (James, 1995). In contrast, Brierre de Boismont, a Roman Catholic doctor, was placed in an awkward position by his colleagues' arguments that hearing voices was a sign of madness. Their approach implied that the Christian prophets, and more recent religious figures such as Joan of Arc, who had experienced hearing voices and seeing visions, were insane. The need for a category of hallucinations co-existing with sanity was, for de Boismont, crucial, as otherwise, he notes, 'we are compelled to admit that eminent men ... must be placed in the Pandemonium of the insane, if the diseased hallucination is the only form that can be recognised' (de Boismont, 1860, p. 369). Hence, he argued that the opinion that turns celebrated men 'into hallucinated lunatics, must be rejected, and reason permitted to claim these great men as their own' (p. 370).

In order to achieve this aim, de Boismont (1860) noted that it was true that the 'majority of the insane are subject to hallucinations; but it is equally certain, that they may occur by themselves' (p. 261). From this flowed his argument that hallucinations were not necessarily a 'sign of insanity' (p. xiv), and that they may co-exist with sanity. One influential case in supporting this thesis was the oft-cited case of a German bookseller, Nicolai, who in 1799 experienced a number of visual hallucinations of a known deceased acquaintance, as well as other unknown figures. Nicolai was able to deal effectively with the continuance of these hallucinations, to the point where he came only to experience mild anxiety when they spoke to him. Upon seeking medical assistance, he

**Box 3.2: Voices at the birth of psychiatry in
Great Britain**

Hibbert (1824) provides an example of a voice-hearing experience
in the case of a four-year-old girl who rested her feet upon a
Bible. The girl reported that she then 'heard a voice at my ear say
"Put the book where you found it … the voice repeated the
mandate, that I should do it immediately"' (p. 106). Hibbert
comments that 'the voice … can only be regarded as a renovated
feeling of the mind, resulting from some prior remonstrances
that she might have incurred from her protectors' when she previously mistreated the Bible. Hibbert also noted the role of other
factors in hearing voices as well; in particular, expectation. Here he
cites the example of Coleridge, who noted the possibility that the
'babbling of a brook will appear for a moment the voice of a friend
for whom we are waiting, calling out our own name' (p. 363).
Hibbert also confronted the question of hearing voices as genuine
omens. He notes the report of Boswell that a trusted friend
reported to him that 'walking home one evening at Kilmarnock, he
heard himself called from a wood, by the voice of a brother who
had gone to America; and the next packet brought an account of
that brother's death' (p. 174). To balance this, Hibbert also noted
that Dr Johnson reported distinctly hearing his mother call his
name, 'Sam' (he was in Oxford, she in Litchfield at the time), but
that in this case 'nothing ensued' (p. 175), thus underlining that
Boswell's example was a coincidence and that voices had no real
supernatural power.

came to receive a diagnosis not of insanity, but 'hallucinations compatible with reason' (Berrios, 2002, p. 36). De Boismont (1860) subdivided
the category of 'hallucinations co-existing with sanity' (p. 34) which he
argued for, into hallucinations corrected by the judgement, and those
not. This distinction arose from de Boismont's division of hallucinations
into 'two distinct elements, the sensible idea and the mental conception'
(p. 259). The sensible idea referred to the raw experience (i.e. the
hearing of the voice), whereas the mental conception referred to how the
experience was understood. This can be seen to build on Kant's distinction, mentioned in Chapter 2. In hallucinations corrected by the judgement, individuals 'correctly regarded their hallucinations as the offspring of
the imagination, or as arising from the unhealthy state of the body' (p. 74).
In hallucinations not corrected by judgement, individuals' explanations
were 'led by their belief in the supernatural', yet they 'gave no evidence of a
disordered intellect' (ibid.). De Boismont (1860) claimed that the prominent religious figures of the past fell into this latter category.

De Boismont (1860) also noted the importance of context, arguing that historical figures' interpretations of their hallucinations belonged to 'society and not the individual' (p. 363). His contemporary, Lélut, also admitted the possibility that there could be 'more or less continual, chronic hallucinations, considered by the hallucinators as real sensations, which are nevertheless compatible with an apparently whole set of reason, and which allow the individual who suffers them, not only to manage to continue to live with his fellow men, but even to bring to his conduct and the management of his interests all the soundness of judgement which is desirable' (Lélut, as cited in James, 1995, p. 91). Lélut concluded that figures such as Swedenborg, whom we met in Chapter 2, 'were not mad, but they were hallucinators, hallucinators as no longer exist, nor can exist, hallucinators whose visions were the visions of reason' (ibid., p. 92). He recognised that such historical figures had 'hallucinations in a religious and reforming mode which was fostered by the spirit of the age' (p. 91) and that this spirit of the age, 'incapable of understanding such a form of madness, obliged the hallucinator and his witnesses to believe in the reality of his false perceptions' (ibid.).

The nineteenth century also saw the birth of the method of 'médecine retrospective' (Littre, 1860, p. 103). This involved attempts to reinterpret, in the light of contemporary medical knowledge, the experiences of influential religious and philosophical figures such as Socrates, Moses and Saint Teresa of Avila, whose experiences had previously been predominantly situated in a religious discourse (James, 1995). Such an undertaking acted simultaneously to undermine religious accounts of voice-hearing by replacing them with a 'correct' account, and solidify the status of current psychiatric theories. This approach and its contemporary instantiations will be returned to in Chapter 12.

Voices and sanity in England

The sanity–insanity debate was also evident in England. The agnostic and materialist English psychiatrist, Henry Maudsley, had the explicit aim to promote science over religion (Leudar & Sharrock, 2003), and a flavour of his views can be achieved by considering his writings on the voices of visions of Swedenborg. Maudsley concluded that 'though he [Swedenborg] was insane, he was capable of taking care of himself sufficiently well, and of managing his affairs with prudence' (Maudsley, 1969, p. 434). This view appears to be in line with the French proto-psychiatrists' concept of Swedenborg's hallucinations co-existing with sanity, except that Maudsley saw Swedenborg's hallucinations as being intrinsically constitutive of insanity. This seemingly paradoxical conclusion becomes clearer when we note that, although Maudsley was aware of the existence of hallucinations co-existing with sanity, he proposed that this concept only applied to hypnagogic and hypnopompic hallucinations (those occurring on the borders of sleep) (Leudar & Thomas, 2000). Hallucinations such as Swedenborg's, occurring in clear consciousness, were understood by Maudsley as being pathological and indicative of mental illness. Given Maudsley's conclusion that Swedenborg was 'capable of taking care of himself sufficiently well, and of managing his affairs with prudence', it is somewhat troubling that he added that 'had he [Swedenborg] lived at the present day in England it is very doubtful whether he would have been left in undisturbed possession of his freedom and his property' (ibid.). Maudsley's hypothetical scenario was soon to be tested, though, and not found in his favour (see Box 3.3). Indeed, whether a person hearing voices was insane, and whether this required a custodial sentence was an issue that psychiatry did not wish to be scrutinised because, as Owen (1989) puts it, the medical profession was displeased with examination of issues that highlighted 'the inadequacies of mental science' (p. 164).

The work of Francis Galton also noted the existence of voices in the sane. Galton (1907/2011) noted, for example, the case of a woman, apparently in vigorous health, who 'told me that during some past months she had been plagued by voices. The words were at first simple nonsense; then the word "pray" was frequently repeated; this was followed by some more or less coherent sentences of little import, and finally the voices left her' (p. 121). From this Galton concluded that: 'In short, the familiar hallucinations of the insane are to be met with far more frequently than is commonly supposed, among people moving in society and in good working health' (ibid.). Galton observed that not only did voices occur in the general population, but that they also occurred in a number of 'great men' (p. 126).[7] In order to account for this, Galton argued that these occurred due to the loneliness of greatness.[8] He writes that 'The hallucinations of great men may be accounted for in part by their sharing a tendency which we have seen to be not uncommon in the human race, and which, if it happens to be natural to them, is liable to be developed in their overwrought brains by the isolation of their lives ... a great philosopher who explores ways of thought far ahead of his contemporaries must have an inner world in which he passes long and solitary hours. Great men may be even

---

[7] Medlicott (1958) was later to refer to such figures as 'The Great Hallucinated'.
[8] See Chapter 10 for Hoffman's contemporary theory of AVHs involving loneliness and isolation.

Box 3.3: The indomitable Georgina Weldon

Georgina Weldon (1837–1914) was her own woman. A renowned soprano, spiritualist, advocate of female suffrage and a woman who liked to dress 'rationally', her behaviour caused discomfort to her husband, Henry, from whom she was separated and receiving £1,000 a year in maintenance (Owen, 1989). In 1878 Henry therefore approached the psychiatrist, Dr Lyttleton Stuart Forbes Winslow (1844–1913), who agreed to supply the two required physicians to certify Georgina insane, and to incarcerate her in one of his asylums for around £500 a year (ibid.). They did not count on the spirit of Mrs Weldon, however, who escaped (in a 'pair of wonderful old slippers') before they could lock her up, and then managed to get herself declared sane by a magistrate.

Writing in the *British Medical Journal* a year later, Forbes Winslow (1879, p. 128) tried to justify his actions, and one of the cornerstones of his argument was that Mrs Weldon must have been mad because she heard voices. He noted, she 'firmly believed that, whilst in a convent in Paris, she had heard a miraculous voice which summoned her to London'. He went on to write: 'I will ask you whether you consider an individual who labours under "auricular delirium" [hearing voices], and who obeys an imaginary voice, of sound or of unsound mind. Have you not met with, in your experience, persons who, whilst under this morbid idea, have committed acts of a most serious character? I have at the present moment under my care a gentleman whose only delusion is that he is addressed by an imaginary voice; but, in consequence of this hallucination, he has made four attempts to destroy himself. I maintain that "auricular delirium" is one of the most unfavourable symptoms that exists in mental disorder' (ibid.).

Forbes Winslow argued that in the hallucinations of the insane, 'those of hearing appear to be decidedly the most common', noting this opinion is 'endorsed by all authorities on the subject'. By this logic, if one of his patients was found eating bamboo shoots, he would be at risk of being mistaken by Forbes Winslow for a panda, because of foods eaten by pandas, bamboo is decidedly the most common. This opinion is also endorsed by all authorities on the subject. Unfortunately for Forbes Winslow, the only authority that counted regarding the meaning of Mrs Weldon's voice-hearing experience was the law. Once the 1882 Married Women's Property Act was had passed, Mrs Weldon was legally able to sue Forbes Winslow. She taught herself law, represented herself in court, and won (Owen, 1989).

indebted to touches of madness for their greatness' (p. 127). In terms of the use of such experiences, Galton concluded that many 'voices were meaningless or absurd; and that there was not the slightest ground for accrediting the majority of them to any exalted or external source' (p. 264).

By the mid-nineteenth century in England, clear and bold statements were being made as to the causes of voices and insanity. An Editorial in the *Journal of Mental Science* (which was later to become the *British Journal of Psychiatry*) stated that insanity was purely a disease of the brain (Scull, 1979), bringing us back full circle to Hippocrates and Galen. The Editorial also stated that the physician was now the responsible guardian of the lunatic and should ever remain so (ibid.). A key catalyst to a shift to a neurological approach to voices, in the second half of the nineteenth century, was the influential paper published by the Italian psychiatrist Tamburini (1881/1990). He first argued against the 'peripheral' model of hearing voices, advocated by those such as Erasmus Darwin, in which voices were caused by peripheral irritation of sensory organs. Then the 'intellectualistic' model, subscribed to by figures such as Esquirol, Lelut, de Boismont and Maudsley, in which hearing voices results from a disturbance of imagination and memory resulting in thoughts being changed into sensations, was dismissed. Instead, he put forward his own neuroanatomical theory. In this model, hearing voices resulted from irritation (spontaneous activity) in cortical centres where auditory sensory impressions became perceptions. This led Tamburini to propose a search for 'the brain centres for hallucinations' and to make the suggestion that hearing voices was perhaps associated with irritation in the fourth cerebral ventricle, the posterior ganglia of the thalamus, or areas of the cortex itself, specifically the temporoparietal/superior temporal gyrus. As we will see in Chapter 8, this latter suggestion was spot on.

Tamburini's neurological approach to hearing voices was eagerly taken up by other researchers. For example, a significant figure in French psychiatry at the time wrote that, 'As far as the localization of hallucinations is concerned I accept Tamburini's theory that relates hallucinations to the excitation of certain parts of grey matter in the brain' (Chaslin, as cited in Berrios, 1990, p. 147). Similarly, in an 1883 edition of the *British Medical Journal*, an author noted that 'Some day it might be possible to say during life what layer of grey matter was altered in a case of insanity, or what hallucinations were accompanied by hyperaemic spots on the cortex; but this would probably not take place for some time' (Bevan Lewis, 1883, p. 628). The result of Tamburini's approach was to move the debate away from the meaning of hearing voices, which had been the focus of the earlier 1855 debate (sanity vs insanity) and towards the neurological mechanisms underlying the experience (Berrios, 1990). As Tamburini suggested that voices were the result of random activity in a specific part of the brain, this meant the content and meaning of voices was sidelined. If, post-Esquirol, voices were in any way semantically pregnant, Tamburini's work effectively aborted them. This approach, although leading to some benefits, still has devastating effects on voice-hearers and their understanding of their experiences today (as we will see in Chapters 11 and 12).

An alternative discourse: the spiritualist movement

In the general population around this time, a very different discourse was arising regarding voices, which assigned meaning and value to the content of voices. In mid-nineteenth century America, the spiritualist movement began. Individuals, such as the Fox sisters and Andrew Jackson Davies in America, claimed to have mediumship and clairaudience ('clear hearing') abilities which they demonstrated through seances by 'communicating' with the dead. We have already seen in Box 3.3 how hearing voices in such contexts could be viewed. The causes for the birth of this movement are complex and multifaceted. Carroll (1997) argues that in part it was caused by the twin impacts of Enlightenment thinking, which encouraged a rational and scientific approach to God, and Romanticism, which stressed subjective experience. This led to a denial of the existence (or knowability) of a spirit realm, a shift from external/ empirical to internal/intuitive sources of religious experience, and a transformation from a religious and social order based on deference and hierarchy to one based on personal experience, spiritual equality and individualism, and a diminishing of respect for professional clergy (ibid.). As this happened at a time when the competitive market economy was developing (leading to increased materialism and uncertainty), the revolutionary generation of Americans were dying off (leading to a loss of connection to the past), and existing clergy and churches were perceived to be ineffective in helping people deal with the resulting uneasiness and change, it all culminated in an openness of many to spiritualism (ibid.). Yet, many rejected the claims of the spiritualists. 'What would I have said six years ago' wrote one New York lawyer and classical scholar 'to anybody who predicted that before the enlightened nineteenth century was ended hundreds of thousands of people in this country would believe themselves able to communicate with the ghosts of their grandfathers?' (p. 1). The spiritualist phenomenon was to influence not only the meaning of hearing voices, but also theories of their causation. Demonstrations of automatic writing facilitated the drawing of a parallel between automatic speech and hearing voices. Thus, in 1897 Edmund Parish proposed that AVHs were a form of automatic speech (Gould, 1948).[9]

The claims of the spiritualists were investigated by the Society for Psychical Research (SPR), founded in London in 1882, resulting in the first large-scale systematic study of the prevalence of voice-hearing. The SPR performed a survey of 17,000 normal participants, termed the *Report on the Census of Hallucinations* (Sidgwick *et al.*, 1894, p. 33) and found that 2.9 per cent of people reported having experienced hearing voices.[10]

In addition to spiritualist discourses resisting a pathological, brain disease model of hearing voices, the medicalisation of voices and their pathologisation was also resisted by prominent thinkers such as William James. James was a truly remarkable thinker. One can have the kernel of an idea today and then consult James' work to see it fully and eloquently elaborated in something written over a century ago.[11] At the time of James' writing, hallucinations such as hearing voices were one of the main legal criteria for judging someone insane (Rubin, 2000). In his work, *The Varieties of Religious Experience*, published in 1902, James argued for alternatives to the biomedical ways of understanding religious voice-hearing experiences. James (1902/1960) famously noted that what he termed medical materialism 'finishes up Saint Paul by calling his vision on the road to Damascus a discharging lesion of the occipital cortex, he being an epileptic', 'snuffs out Saint Teresa as an hysteric, [and] Saint Francis of Assisi as an hereditary degenerate'. He claimed such an approach was simple-minded, and argued that experiences such as hallucinations should be dealt with not by 'superficial medical talk', but by an inquiry into 'their fruits for life' (p. 398). Drawing on Socrates' experiences and the findings of the SPR (1894), James noted that 'Even if by this demon [of Socrates] were really meant hallucinations of hearing, we know now that one in eight or ten of the population has had such an experience and that for insanity we must resort to other tests than these' (James, as cited in Rubin, 2000, p. 197). In concluding his thoughts on whether hearing voices and other such phenomena are pathological or not, James argued that 'There is no purely objective standard of sound health. Any peculiarity that is of use to a man is a

---

[9] See Chapter 9 for contemporary inner speech-based models of AVHs, and the Conclusion for Sommer & Diederen's (2009) use of the concept of automatic right hemisphere speech.

[10] See Chapter 7 for further details and contemporary studies.

[11] This gets irritating after the third time it happens.

point of soundness in him' (p. 198). He noted certain people's uses of medical terms as being 'merely as an artifice for giving objective authority to their personal dislikes ... The medical terms become mere appreciative clubs to knock a man down with' (p. 199). Instead, James counselled, 'A certain tolerance, a certain sympathy, a certain respect, and above all a certain lack of fear, seem to be the best attitude we can carry in our dealing with these regions of human nature' (ibid., p. 199). Wise words.

In summary, although Tony James (1995) has argued that it was during the nineteenth century that, for the first time, medicine claimed as part of its domain experiences that had traditionally fallen under the authority of the Church, we can see this instead as a consolidation of the power given to medical accounts of the experiences by establishment religions, such as the Anglican Church in the mid-1600s. The rise of the neurological model was accompanied by the decline in a framework in which the content of voices had anything meaningful to say about the world. This latter framework was a threat to the power of the established religions, and offensive to materialism. Only voice-hearers were left thinking their voices might have some meaning other than that of a biological illness. And who was going to listen to them?

The twentieth century

The birth of schizophrenia

At the dawn of the twentieth century it was commonplace for hallucinations still to be seen as pathological and indicative of mental illness (Leudar & Thomas, 2000), and the psychiatric framework remained the dominant method of understanding them. Inspired by Maudsley, psychiatry limited the phenomena conceptualised as 'hallucinations of the sane' to hypnagogic and hypnopompic hallucinations, and the neurology of Tamburini led to a lack of focus on the content of voices. Perhaps most importantly for voice-hearers, the start of the twentieth century saw the introduction of the influential concept of schizophrenia.

In 1887, Emil Kraepelin (1856–1926) made an influential argument that was to shape the twentieth-century's approach to mental illness. He argued there were three forms of psychosis: dementia praecox (senility in the young), manic depression and paranoia, each of which had distinct symptom patterns, anatomical pathologies and causes (Bentall, 2003). In his 1896 work, *Dementia Praecox and Paraphrenia*, Kraepelin (1919) named hearing voices as a 'symptom peculiarly characteristic of dementia praecox' (p. 7). He observed that 'They are almost never wanting in the acute and subacute forms of the disease. Often enough they accompany the whole course of the disease; but more frequently they gradually disappear, to reappear more distinctly from time to time in the last stages' (ibid.). Kraepelin noted that 'These most extraordinary disorders, quite foreign to healthy experience, are at first usually kept secret by the patient, so that one only hears something about them when they have already existed for a long time' (p. 13). He reported that 'Many patients feel themselves very much troubled by telephony, they stop their ears, "do not like such treatment by voices". One patient begged that "the blessed nonsense should be taken away". Others regard themselves as specially privileged. "I hear from a distance; not everyone can do that" said a patient' (ibid.). Kraepelin was a masterful observer of symptoms and his writings on what voices were like form the most complete and detailed description which had been made up to that point in history. We will see his detailed phenomenological descriptions of voices in Chapter 4. Yet it is worth noting here that when giving reports of the voices heard by patients with dementia praecox, Kraepelin often reports that, apart from hearing voices, patients were 'otherwise thoroughly clear and intelligent' (p. 11).

Following Tamburini's example, Kraepelin focused on biological causes of this 'disorder', arguing that 'we must probably interpret [AVHs] as irritative phenomena in the temporal lobe' (p. 219). He hired Alois Alzheimer (1864–1919) to find brain changes associated with dementia praecox, but none were found (Lieberman, Stroup & Perkins, 2006). In addition to neurological models, Kraepelin was also open to psychological explanation, noting that in some cases the voices could 'give expression to, what the patient feels in himself' (p. 49) and that 'thinking, feeling, and acting have lost the unity and especially that permanent inner dependence on the essence of the psychic personality, which provides the healthy human being with the feeling of inner freedom' (p. 52). Such experiences could, in his view, often arise following changes in personality in youth, especially in 'vagrants and criminals' (p. 227).

In 1911, Eugene Bleuler proposed that dementia praecox be replaced by the term 'schizophrenia', as he found that the experiences associated with dementia praecox were not limited to the young or people he considered 'demented' (Bleuler, 1950, p. 7). Somewhat ironically (given the misunderstandings in the lay public of what schizophrenia means, i.e. 'split personality'), Bleuler explicitly introduced this term to 'give the disease a new name, less apt to be misunderstood' (p. 8). In his view, AVHs were a secondary or accessory symptom of schizophrenia, i.e. they resulted from psychological changes occurring in response to the primary symptoms directly caused by the illness. As such, Bleuler implied that the content of hearing voices might be understood through psychological approaches (WHO, 1973), with the content being unique to the individual person. Indeed, around this time we see an emphasis on psychological approaches to voice-hearing. Bleuler noted that voices in patients with schizophrenia 'are the means by which the megalomaniac realizes his wishes, the religiously preoccupied achieves his communication with God and the Angels; the depressed are threatened by catastrophe; the persecuted cursed day and night' (p. 97). Notably, Bleuler, influenced by Freud and based on his own clinical experience, reached for a psychological understanding of voices in schizophrenia in contrast to the biological approach which was to be dominant by the end of the century. He argued that hearing voices in schizophrenia was 'precipitated by psychic occurrences' (p. 387), arguing against Kraepelin's idea that AVHs were caused by excitation of sensory centres which did not, in Bleuler's view, 'do sufficient justice to the fact that hallucinations express entire strivings' (p. 389). Instead, Bleuler argued that behind voices are 'wishes and fears, strivings and their obstacles' (p. 392) and that they express 'thoughts, fears and drives' (p. 388). In fact, Bleuler went as far to argue that 'In part (possibly entirely) the overt symptomatology certainly represents the expression of a more or less unsuccessful attempt to find a way out of an intolerable situation' (p. 460).

Psychoanalysis, mysticism and meaning

Despite the psychiatric paradigm, at the start of the twentieth century there still existed many with a commitment to mysticism, which is best seen in Evelyn Underhill's influential book, *Mysticism* (Underhill, 1911). In this work, Underhill asked the age-old question as to whether hearing voices 'represent merely the dreams and fancies, the old digested percepts of the visionary, objectivized and presented to his surface-mind in a concrete form; or, are they ever representations – symbolic, if you like – of some fact, force, or personality, some "triumphing spiritual power", external to himself?' (p. 322). Underhill answered that hearing voices 'may be either of these two things: and that pathology and religion have both been over-hasty in their eagerness to snatch at these phenomena for their own purposes' (ibid.). Underhill notes that some may be 'morbid hallucinations: some even symptoms of insanity', but that in her view 'there are some, experienced by minds of great power and richness, which are crucial for those who have them. These bring wisdom to the simple and ignorant, sudden calm to those who were tormented by doubts ... Arrive at moments of indecision, bringing with them authoritative commands or counsels opposed to the inclination of the self' (p. 323). The question then arises as to how we distinguish between the two, the classic discernment question which we have seen stretches back over the centuries. Underhill effectively gives the same answer as William James did – a pragmatic answer, 'their life-enhancing quality' (p. 323).

The openness of those of a mystical bent to the potential meaning-fulness of voices was shared, albeit in different ways, by the emerging psychoanalysts. In 1900, one of Bleuler's appointments to his staff was a young doctor called Carl Gustav Jung (1875–1961), who introduced a discussion group on psychoanalysis into the hospital (Bentall, 2003). Psychoanalysis had been born in 1890s Vienna from the work of Freud. Although Bleuler's initial enthusiasm for psychoanalysis, or more accurately, his enthusiasm for Freud's 'all-or-nothing' approach to it, faded (ibid.), psychoanalysis was nevertheless to provide an influential account of voice-hearing. The rise of psychoanalysis in the twentieth century shifted attention back to the potential meaning-fulness of the content of voices, and away from their neurology. After the First World War, and an epidemic of shell-shock and other psychiatric problems, there was an increasing awareness that mental disorders could have roots in environmental events, opening up the arena of psychological models and interventions, making society fertile for psychoanalysis (Scull, 2006). Box 3.4 gives an example of voice-hearing in this pre-psychoanalytic, environmentally-focused context.

Freud (1856–1939), the creator of psychoanalysis, was, argues John Irving (2011), 'a novelist with a scientific background. He just didn't know he was a novelist'. Freud's stories were to become highly influen-tial. Freud himself had voice-hearing experiences. He recorded how 'During the days when I was living alone in a foreign city – I was a young man at the time – I quite often heard my name suddenly called by an un-mistakable and beloved voice' (Freud, 1901/1958, p. 261). Although Freud was originally neurologically-orientated, when his idol, the neurologist Charcot, put forth the proposal that ideas them-selves could cause bodily symptoms, Freud correspondingly also moved from neurological-based models of mental disorder to psycho-logical causes based in the person's mental life (Webster, 1996). For Freud, the development of the ego normally occurred under pressure from the real world, with the ego remaining loyal to external percep-tual reality (Eigen, 2005). However, Freud believed that if there was a failure of reality testing by the ego of the person, then hearing voices could result.

Box 3.4: Hearing voices in a First World War private

An interesting case of hearing voices relating to the First World War is given by R. G. Rows, M.D. (Temporary Major) in the *British Medical Journal* (Rows, 1916). This is interesting as a case study of how voices were understood as a psychological phenomenon at this time, and how they could be successfully treated as such.

The patient was a 31-year-old private, who was admitted into hospital hearing voices. He heard the voices of his brother, elder sister and brother in-law, telling him what to do and what not to do. Rows enquired about the patient's past and found that five years ago he had slept with a prostitute, his 'first and only offence in sexual matters'. At first he was not disturbed by this, but later he thought he could 'detect a strangeness in the behaviour of his family, as if they knew of his misdeed'. It was then that he began to hear voices like those of his brothers and sisters coming from the wall. At the outbreak of the war he enlisted and was sent to fight in France, but his voices distracted him so that he couldn't perform his military duties, and he was invalided and sent to hospital.

Rows treated the patient 'by the usual manner employed here, namely, by seeking the cause of his mental disturbance'. This was identified as the affair with the prostitute and in his previous drinking. Rows explained to the patient that 'the basis of his trouble was really the repetition of the memory of these incidents, together with the unpleasant emotional feeling associated with them, which had produced in him a self-reproach'. By 'persistent reasoning and persuasion week by week' the patient's voices disappeared.

What sort of material, according to Freud, was the ego incorrectly identifying as a real experience? He initially believed that hallucinations resulted from forgotten traumatic experiences from childhood which returned and forced themselves into consciousness. Thus, he argued that in AVHs, 'something that has been experienced in infancy and then forgotten re-emerges – something that the child has seen or heard at a time when he could hardly speak and that now forces its way into consciousness, probably distorted and displaced owing to the operation of forces that are opposed to its re-emergence' (Freud, 1937, as cited in Blom, 2010). These traumatic experiences, argued Freud, had their roots in actual experiences of childhood sexual abuse. This formed the basis for his so-called 'seduction theory' (Masson, 2003). There was, indeed, an awareness of the extent of childhood sexual abuse at this time. Tardieu (1860, as cited in Hobbs, Hanks & Wynne, 2004) had reviewed 11,576 cases of people accused of rape or attempted rape and found that almost 80 per cent of victims were children, mostly girls

4–12 years old. Freud himself had probably seen an autopsy of a child killed during an act of sexual abuse (Shalev, Yehuda & McFarlane, 2000), and owned a book by Tardieu, which discussed the sexual abuse of children (Masson, 2003). However, soon after Tardieu's death, Fournier argued that children were faking sexual abuse to extort respectable men (Hobbs, Hanks & Wynne, 2004), and Freud also changed his mind. This may have been partly due to problems arising from accusing his client's parents of incestual abuse (Webster, 1996), as well as the reactions of his colleagues (Shalev, Yehuda & McFarlane, 2000). In his renunciation letter he wrote that 'such widespread perversion against children was not very probable' (Freud, 1897, as cited in ibid.). His revised theory was that voices were fantasies or wish fulfilments, recreating things which have been lost or destroyed earlier (Eigen, 2005). For Freud 'wishing ends with hallucination' (ibid., p. 41). As Webster (1996) notes, 'it is undeniably the case that Freud's repudiation of his seduction theory has repeatedly led to real instances of sexual abuse being overlooked or denied by psychoanalysts intent on treating memories as fantasies' (p. 212). As we will see in Chapter 11, the high prevalence of childhood sexual abuse in those with AVHs means that Freud's influential change of mind has likely had catastrophic effects. Indeed, Masson has argued that Freud's focus on 'an internal stage on which actors performed invented dramas for an invisible audience of their own creation' came at the cost of a shift away from 'an actual world of sadness, misery, and cruelty' (Masson, 2003, p. 144).[12] Notably, although psychoanalysis was a talking cure working with meaning, it was still not the meaning of voice-hearing for the voice-hearer themselves. Psychoanalysis introduced an entirely new set of jargonised terms for the voice-hearer to learn, to explain their experiences within, and again colonised the voice-hearing experience.

Although Freud appears not to have had contact with many patients who heard voices, Jung not only had patients with such experiences (Box 3.5), but also appears to have had them himself. Jung argued that the 'biology, anatomy and physiology' of schizophrenia 'have had all the attention they want' with little to show for it, and also observed the tendency for medical psychology to know 'far too little ... of anything outside the medical department' (Jung, 1960, p. 249). In contrast, Jung argued for a need to focus on the psychology of voices, and their content. As a result of his work with such patients, Jung reports that he came to realise that 'hallucinations contain a germ of meaning' and that 'a personality, a life history, a pattern of hopes and desires' lie behind

---

[12] Masson's point regarding a shift away from 'an actual world of sadness, misery, and cruelty' remains a relevant critique of many contemporary approaches to AVHs, too.

such experiences (Jung, 1963, p. 127). He thus concluded that, in schizophrenia, there was 'no symptom which could be described as psychologically groundless and meaningless' (Jung, 1960, p. 178). What did Jung think caused voices? He rejected the idea that AVHs should be reduced to 'a disease of the brain cells', which he claimed was 'superficial and unwarranted' (p. 206). Instead, like Aristotle, he linked the mechanism underlying voices to dreams, but he also argued that they were caused by the content of repressed complexes (unconscious thoughts and feelings) which is able to 'force itself across the threshold of consciousness' (ibid.). He claimed that if a conscious attitude of an individual was too one-sided, then a 'counter-irritant' would arise to try and create a correcting balance.[13] This could form the basis of a hearing voice experience. Rather than take a pathological illness view, he intimated that the emergence of such voices should be 'the beginning of a healing process' (p. 208) which would re-establish balance. For example, he argued that if an isolated individual begins to hear strange voices, then these drive him into making contact with his surroundings. This, he noted restored the balance, but to the detriment of the individual (ibid.). As a result of this, Jung believed that voices could be treated and cured by psychological means.

The influence of psychoanalysis began to fade as the century progressed, though, with many writers today dismissing it as 'only a historical curiosity of the 20th century, like animal magnetism and phrenology' (Noll, 2007, p. 39). Whilst many would argue that this was a case of the baby being thrown out with the bathwater, in reality the shower curtains were also stolen and the bathroom set on fire. However, despite psychoanalysis being a four-letter word to many in the mind sciences today, the ideas of Jung in particular can be seen to be at the heart of many of the ideas in the Hearing Voices Movement today (see below).

In addition to writers such as Freud and Jung, the German psychiatrist and philosopher, Karl Jaspers, also thought that voices were meaningful experiences. Jaspers made the distinction between understanding mental 'symptoms', such as hearing voices, and explaining them. Symptoms were understandable if they could be seen to arise meaningfully from the patient's personality and life history. Some symptoms, in Jaspers' view, such as delusions, could not be understood, however well one knew the patient; they were un-understandable (Bentall, 2003). However, hallucinations such as hearing voices, he

---

[13] This shares much with dialogic approaches to inner speech and AVHs today, see Chapter 9.

Box 3.5: Jung and hearing voices

What sort of voices did Jung encounter? He reports one patient who referred to her voices as 'invisible telephones' (1960, p. 99), which would interact with the patient. For example, when Jung was attempting to get the patient to freely associate a word, 'the telephone called out "The doctor should not bother himself with these things"' (p. 149). Jung noted how the voice 'has the character of an ironically commenting spectator who seems to be thoroughly convinced of the futility of these pathological fancies and mocks the patient's assertions in a superior tone'.

Jung was clear to link voices to events in the patient's life. For example, he reports the case of a girl who was seduced when her fiancé was away, a fact which she hid from him. Ten years later she started hearing voices which talked of her secret, and which forced her to confess to her husband. He notes that 'many patients state that the "sin register" is read out in all its details, or that the voices "know everything" and "put them through it"' (Jung, 1960, p. 90). Although Jung's concept of the collective unconscious stated that hallucinations and delusions were informed by more than just the individual's own history, instead being influenced by universal archetypes, he tends to apply such analyses to visions rather than voices. Voices are thus left to be examined in relation to the individual's own personal history.

How did Jung 'treat' voices? Jung (1963, pp. 126–7; 1960, p. 248) reports that one of his patients 'heard voices which were distributed throughout her entire body'. The patient designated a voice which she heard in the middle of the thorax as being 'God's voice'. This voice was 'reasonable and helpful'. 'We must rely on that voice', Jung said to her. This voice of God, noted Jung, 'made very sensible remarks, and with its aid I managed very well with the patient' (1960, p. 248). Once this voice said, 'Let him test you on the Bible!' Jung reacted by assigning the patient passages of the Bible to memorise, on which he then tested her once a fortnight. For seven years. Jung notes that as a result, 'her attention was kept alert, so that she did not sink deeper into the disintegrating dream'. As a result, 'after some six years the voices which had formerly been everywhere had retired to the left half of her body, while the right half was completely free of them'. Jung also tailored his terminology to the patient, finding that explaining it in theological terms was helpful.

argued, were understandable: 'the contents of hallucinations ... are not completely accidental but to some extent have meaningful connections, and are significant of experience in the form of commands, wish-fulfilments, teasing and ridicule, agonies and revelations' (Jaspers, 1962, p. 410).

Jaspers was also responsible for the influential distinction between the form of a voice (e.g. classifying someone hearing a voice saying 'he's picking up the toast' as a third person AVH) and the content of the voice. According to Jaspers, 'Form must be kept distinct from content which may change from time to time, e.g., the fact of a hallucination is to be distinguished from its content' (p. 58). Bracken and Thomas (2005) argue that for Jaspers the content of the symptom was 'very much of secondary importance' (p. 10), and indeed, Jaspers did write that 'from the phenomenological point of view it is only the form that interests us' (p. 59). However, he also wrote that 'the psychologist who looks for meaning will find content essential and the form at times unimportant' (ibid.). Jaspers noted with scepticism the theory of Wernicke that hearing voices could occur through either direct neurological means, 'direct irritation' (p. 536), or through sejunction (an act of disjoining). Whilst normally consciousness is a unitary experience where many simultaneous psychophysical processes are knitted together, sejunction is a breakdown of this unity (Cutting & Shepherd, 1987) leaving fragments which can be experienced as voices. This troubled Jaspers, as to him it 'looked for an absolute without meaning, a product of brain processes' (1962, p. 546).

Many other theorists put forward models of AVHs during this time in addition to purely psychoanalytic and neurological models, yet many were clearly indebted to the ideas of Freud. A particularly interesting theory which departs from the psychoanalytic flavour of the age is that of Morton Prince. Prince argued that AVHs were the emergence of subconscious verbal images (i.e. sounds of words used in subconscious inarticulate thoughts or internal speech) into consciousness (Prince, 1922). In one study Prince reports trying to objectively tap into subconscious thought by recording a patient's automatic writing. He covered a patient's hand with a cloth and found that the patient reported hearing a voice saying 'I smell cigarettes' at the same time as she wrote this. The patient denied knowing what she had written, claiming she herself only found out once the cloth was removed and the writing revealed. Elsewhere (McDougall, 1927) actually offers the result of an interesting experiment (or thought experiment, it is not clear to me which) to support this argument. In this, an individual is hypnotised and told he will hear a word (i.e. hallucinate) when he returns to his normal state. After he has returned to normal consciousness, hallucinated and then is put back under hypnosis, the hypnotised subject reports that at the time of the hallucination he was thinking of the word. Going beyond subconscious thought per se, Prince then works with the idea of two personalities existing in the same person. If person A is the normal consciousness state, then AVHs emerge when the subpersonality, personality B, thinks a word, which A then experiences as an AVH. For Prince, then, AVHs are what a secondary personality (a co-conscious process) thinks, and which the primary personality hears as a result. McDougall (ibid.) notes that it is impossible to prove conclusively that any personality other than oneself thinks consciously, and also questions how many AVHs such an account can explain. Notably in the process of his discussions, McDougall seems to split AVHs into two categories: (1) Reproductive AVHs, which are memories of previous voices coming into consciousness, and (2) Prince's AVHs, which are the reflection in a person's consciousness of thoughts thought by a secondary consciousness.[14]

Holocaust

In 1929, Franz Kallmann was undertaking work on the genetics of schizophrenia with the German Research Institute for Psychiatry in Munich. This work was eventually published as a book in 1938. As Kallmann's work on patients diagnosed with schizophrenia is replete with examples of hearing voices (see Kallmann, 1938, pp. 165–78) it is relevant to our history of voice-hearing. In the introduction to his book, Kallmann talks of the 'menace to public health constituted by the traits and unchecked propagation of schizophrenia symptom-carriers' (p. xiii). 'Although', he argued, 'it is the primary duty of medicine to care for the weak and the diseased, the obligation to protect biologically sound families has become of major importance' (ibid.). Indeed, everyone, thought Kallmann, 'would be much happier without those numerous adventurers, fanatics and pseudo-saviors of the world who are found again and again to come from the schizophrenic genotype' (ibid.). On the final page of his work he hopes that 'we may arrive, in the not too distant future, at a *complete solution* of the problems dealing with the complex relations between the phenotypical manifestation of the schizophrenia trait' (p. 272, emphasis added). It is only a short step from this to what happened in the 1930s and 1940s in Germany. Kallman's Ph.D. supervisor was the physician Ernst Rudin, who worked at the German Research Institute of Psychiatry in Munich, and who, in 1933, served with Heinrich Himmler on a committee which drafted legislation enabling the compulsory sterilisation of psychiatric patients (Bentall, 2009). Ironically, Kallmann himself had to flee Germany (writing his book in New York) as he was half Jewish (ibid.).

---

[14] This echoes the distinction I make in Chapter 7 between Type 1 and Type 2 AVHs.

The deeds of the Nazis defy adequate verbal description. Their crimes were unspeakable acts which must be spoken of. The systematic mass murder of people who were not 'desirable members' of their society (Meyer-Lindenberg, 1991), such as Jews, gypsies and people with mental health problems (including voice-hearers), was an atrocity which language is inadequate to describe. The Nazis first applied the term 'unworthiness' to the 'incurably mentally ill and disabled' and then to all members of society they considered undesirable (ibid.). In what has been called the greatest criminal act in the history of psychiatry, the Nazis are estimated to have killed between 100,000 and 137,500 patients with schizophrenia, based on the idea that it was an inherited genetic disease (Fuller-Torrey & Yolken, 2010). If we estimate that the prevalence of voices in those diagnosed with schizophrenia at the time was 50 per cent,[15] then this means that at least 50,000 voice-hearers were murdered, either by being led into rooms designed to look like showers, gassed and then burnt in crematoria, or by shooting, starvation, or lethal injection.[16] Many more were sterilised, the youngest of whom was a two-year-old girl (Meyer-Lindenberg, 1991). Only 20 per cent of all psychiatric in-patients of the time survived (ibid.). Strous (2010) asks how it was that 'so many (senior and junior) psychiatrists, many with phenomenal international reputations, participated in and even initiated much of the genocide against mentally ill individuals?' (p. 209). He wryly notes that 'The German code of medical ethics already as early as 1931 was known to be one of the strictest and most advanced in the world ... We now know how much difference it made' (ibid.). To attempt to explain this, Meyer-Lindenberg (1991)[17] notes that during the first two years of the Nazi regime, 1,200 university professors were removed from office (412 from medical faculties, 61 of whom were professors of neuropsychiatry). In 1934, Rudolph Hess set up a commission to assess the reliability of professors. Important posts were reserved for so-called 'reliable doctors'. Some psychiatrists fought bravely against this, such as Dr John Karl Friedrich Rittmeister, who tried to oppose the Nazi ideas. He and his wife hid Jewish citizens in Berlin, and he wrote publicly of the tortures and atrocities he saw around him. In return for his bravery he was executed by guillotine on

---

[15] Although estimates of voice-hearing in schizophrenia today are much higher than 50%, the diagnostic criteria have changed. In a 1931 study of 1,408 patients with schizophrenia, just over 50% experienced auditory hallucinations (Bowman & Raymond, 1931).

[16] And this does not take into account any Jews and gypsies who heard voices in the absence of any distress.

[17] The information below is taken from Meyer-Lindenberg (1991).

13 May 1943. Dr Karsten Jasperson, Head of the Psychiatric Department in Bethel, repeatedly refused to aid and abet such murder, wrote to Hitler to protest, and alerted the Cardinal of Munster, Count von Galen, to the murder of psychiatric patients. Von Galen openly denounced these murders in a famous 1941 sermon. As a result, the Nazis proclaimed that Christianity and National Socialism were incompatible, writing that 'It is clear that Christian churches try to keep alive even creatures unworthy of life' (p. 10). After the war, Meyer-Lindenberg observes, a number of papers on what had happened to psychiatric patients at this time were not published, as Kurt Schneider, whom we will meet later, and Karl Jaspers, whom we met earlier, were 'reluctant' (p. 11).

The Diagnostic and Statistical Manual of Mental Disorders

Soldiers returning from the Second World War were reporting a number of complaints, and this generated the need for a clear classification system to understand these problems. In an attempt to create clearly defined and reliable psychiatric diagnoses, the first edition of the bible of psychiatry, the *Diagnostic and Statistical Manual of Mental Disorders* (DSM) was published by the American Psychiatric Association in 1952 (DSM-I, APA, 1952). At this mid-century point, the meaning of voices was still debated within psychiatry. Many key psychiatric figures (e.g. Menninger) maintained that voices in 'normal' people were rare and that when they did occur they were typically signs of psychosis. Yet others (e.g. Will, Lhermitte, Smythies) continued to note that voices occurred in the sane, with some again influenced, like the French proto-psychiatrists, by the presence of famous historical figures who had experienced voices (Medlicott, 1958). In the DSM-I, hearing voices was not specifically referred to, with the more general term 'hallucination' being used. Hallucinations were part of the clinical descriptions given in DSM-I in diagnoses including 'schizophrenic reaction', 'psychotic depressive reaction', organic brain syndromes and alcoholic hallucinosis. The use of the term 'reaction' reflected the influence of Adolf Meyer's work, which proposed that mental disorders represented reactions of the personality to psychological, social and biological factors (APA, 1994). In later versions of the DSM, the term 'reaction' was removed, ostensibly to 'be neutral with respect to theories of etiology' (ibid., p. xvii). In the DSM-II (APA, 1968) hearing voices is only mentioned once, and this is in relation to 'other alcoholic hallucinosis' in which it is noted that 'accusatory or threatening auditory hallucinations in a state of relatively clear consciousness' may occur (p. 25). Hallucinations per se remained associated with psychotic disorders such as schizophrenia. However, that AVHs were primarily linked with schizophrenia in psychiatrists' eyes at this time was shown in a classic study by Rosenhan (1973a), whose meaning is still debated today. In this study, Rosenhan and eight other individuals, after each calling different hospitals for an appointment, presented complaining that they had been hearing voices. In fact, they were just feigning such voices. When they were asked what the voices said, they stated that they were often unclear, but as far as they could tell they said 'empty', 'hollow' and 'thud', and nothing else. They also reported that voices were unfamiliar and were of the same sex as themselves. All except one were diagnosed with schizophrenia, and they were all admitted to wards. Rosenhan (1973b) later argued that a key problem was not that the psychiatrists believed the pseudopatients, nor that they were admitted to a psychiatric hospital. Instead, as Rosenhan put it, the problem was 'the diagnostic leap that was made between the single presenting symptom, hallucinations, and the diagnosis schizophrenia (or in one case, manic-depressive psychosis). Had the pseudopatients been diagnosed "hallucinating", there would have been no further need to examine the diagnosis issue. The diagnosis of hallucinations implies only that: no more. The presence of hallucinations does not itself define the presence of schizophrenia. And schizophrenia may or may not include hallucinations' (p. 366). Rosenhan (1973a) also noted that when hallucinations have a clear cause (drugs, hypnagogia) then these are attributed to the surrounding behaviours themselves. However, 'when the stimuli to my hallucinations are unknown, that is called craziness, or schizophrenia – as if that inference were somehow as illuminating as the others' (p. 254).

It was in the landmark publication of DSM-III in 1980 (DSM-III, APA, 1980) that hearing voices first came to be specifically mentioned in relation to the psychotic disorders (schizophrenia and affective disorder). Two new innovations were introduced. First, whether the emotional tone of the voice was consistent with that of the voice-hearer is seen as being diagnostically relevant. Second, the form of voices is seen as being of diagnostic relevance. In terms of schizophrenia, DSM-III explains that hallucinations are common in the schizophrenic disorders, but that 'by far the most common are auditory [hallucinations], frequently involving voices the individual perceives as coming from outside the head. The voices may be familiar, and often make insulting statements. The voices may be single or multiple. Voices speaking directly to the individual or commenting on his or her ongoing behaviour are particularly characteristic. Command hallucinations may be obeyed, at times creating danger for the individual or others' (pp. 182–3). The content of voices is then introduced as being significant in two ways. First, one of the named diagnostic criteria for a schizophrenic disorder is 'auditory hallucinations on several occasions with content of more than one or two words, having no apparent relation to depression or elation' (p. 188). Thus affect-incongruent voices are seen to be associated with schizophrenia. In contrast, if the effect of the AVH is congruent with the voice-hearer's own mood, this is seen to be consistent with an affective disorder. For example, the DSM-III explains that in a manic episode 'God's voice may be heard explaining that the individual has a special mission' (p. 207), and that a major depressive episode 'may involve voices that berate the individual for his or her shortcomings or sins' (p. 211). Voice content is also relevant for a diagnostic purposes in a second way, with 'hallucinations with persecutory or grandiose content' (p. 191) being a diagnostic criterion for 'paranoid-type schizophrenia'.

In addition to the content, the form of voices is introduced as being of diagnostic significance. Specifically, certain forms of AVHs are named as a diagnostic criteria for a schizophrenic disorder, namely 'auditory hallucinations in which either a voice keeps up a running commentary on the individual's behavior or thoughts, or two or more voices converse with each other' (p. 188). These criteria came from the work of Kurt Schneider. Earlier in the century, Schneider (1959) had laid out a range of what he termed first rank symptoms (FRSs), which he thought were of special diagnostic importance for schizophrenia. These were 'voices conversing with one another, and voices that keep up a running commentary' (p. 96). An example of this first type of voice that Schneider gives is a patient diagnosed with schizophrenia who 'heard his own voice, day and night, like a dialogue, one voice always arguing against the other' (p. 97). Mellor (1970) gives a later example of such voices, citing the case of a patient who heard one roughly spoken voice saying 'G.T. [the patient's name] is a bloody paradox' and another higher in pitch then saying 'He is that, he should be locked up' (p. 16). Schneider's second type of voice, a running commentary, was illustrated by him in the case of a woman diagnosed with schizophrenia who heard a voice say, whenever she wanted to eat, 'Now she is eating, here she is munching again' or when she patted her dog she heard, 'What is she up to now, fondling the dog?' (p. 97). Mellor gives an example of a woman who would hear a voice which would go on and on in a monotone saying 'She is peeling potatoes, got hold of the peeler, she does not want that potato, she is putting it back, because she thinks it had a knobble like a penis, she had a dirty mind, she is peeling potatoes, now she is washing them' (ibid.). It was Schneider's voice-hearing criteria that came to be used in the DSM-III as sufficient experiences (when accompanied by social and occupational impairment) for a diagnosis of schizophrenia.

The DSM-III also discusses AVHs in relation to a number of other diagnoses. As with the DSM-II (APA, 1968) AVHs are specifically noted to occur in alcoholic hallucinosis. The DSM-III observes that 'The voices may address the individual directly, but more often they discuss him or her in the third person ... The actions of the individual are practically never the result of the hallucinations commanding the individual to act in a certain way, but rather are motivated by the desire to avoid disgrace, injury, or other consequences of what the voices threaten' (p. 135). Multiple personality disorder is also noted in regard to AVHs, with it being stated that 'One or more of the personalities may be aware of hearing or having heard the voice(s) of one or more of the other personalities or may report having talked with or engaged in activities with one or more of the other personalities' (p. 257). If an individual heard voices, and none of the above diagnoses were appropriate, then the diagnosis of 'atypical psychosis' in which, for example, 'persistent auditory hallucinations' are 'the only disturbance' (p. 203) could be employed.

Currently, the latest version of the DSM – DSM-IV-TR (APA, 2000) – does not differ in many regards to how DSM-III treated voices. However, a number of changes are noteworthy. First, of the three types of voices which were of diagnostic significance for schizophrenia in DSM-III (voices meeting Schneider's FRS criteria, voices of a grandiose or persecutory nature and mood-incongruent voices), DSM-IV-TR specifically mentions only voices meeting Schneider's FRS criteria in relation to schizophrenia. Broadly speaking, if an individual has AVHs which 'consist of a voice keeping up a running commentary on the person's behavior or thoughts, or two or more voices conversing with each other', which are present for a significant portion of time during a one-month period, which cause social/occupational dysfunction, and when there are signs of disturbance for at least six months, then this is sufficient for a diagnosis of schizophrenia. Other types of AVHs are only symptomatic of schizophrenia if accompanied by other symptoms (e.g. delusions). The stipulation that AVHs need to be accompanied by social/occupational dysfunction allows (in theory) that AVHs in themselves are not pathological. By the logic of the DSM-IV-TR, two individuals could have exactly the same voice-hearing experience; if one of them has social/occupational impairment, s/he then has a mental disorder, if the other does not, s/he does not have a mental disorder. The question then becomes, following Rosenhan (1973a), as to whether psychiatry in practice accepts that voice-hearing per se is not pathological, or whether in the real world the mere experiencing of AVHs is seen as pathological. I am sure many voice-hearers will have an opinion on this based on their experiences.

It is also worth noting that DSM-IV-TR explicitly acknowledges that cultural factors need to be considered. It states that 'visual or auditory hallucinations with a religious content may be a normal part of religious experience (e.g., seeing the Virgin Mary or hearing God's voice)' (p. 306). Furthermore, following the work of Lukoff, Lu & Turner (1992), the DSM-IV-TR also has a classification of 'Religious or Spiritual Problem'.[18]

Psychology and the complaint-based approach to hearing voices

In parallel to the changes in psychiatry over the twentieth century, changes in psychology were also occurring. The shift from the hegemony of psychoanalysis to the dominance of behaviourism had little lasting impact on the theory as to what caused voices (although, see Burns, Heiby & Tharp, 1983), but the associated change in treatment had a significant impact both on voice-hearers and on the electricity consumption of America. However, in the 1960s writers such as R.D. Laing once again raised the eternal dichotomy of whether the content of voices was meaningful or meaningless – arguing that experiences in schizophrenia, such as hearing voices, were 'much more socially intelligible than has come to be supposed by most psychiatrists' (Laing & Esterson, 1964, p. 13). For example, Laing & Esterson reported the example of a woman, Ruby, who was admitted to hospital because she heard voices outside her head calling her 'slut', 'dirty' and 'prostitute', and with 'delusional' beliefs. In a series of interviews with Ruby and her family, Laing & Esterson found that six months before hospital admission she had fallen pregnant. Her family, upon finding out, 'while trying to pump hot soapy water into her uterus, told her ... what a fool she was, what a slut she was' (p. 121). In interviews, the family told them 'with vehemence and intensity, that she was a slut and no better than a prostitute' (ibid.). Ruby had eventually miscarried at four months.

In the post-war years, violence remained a popular treatment for voices (among those doing the treatment, anyway). Bucher & Fabricatore (1970) attempted to get a person with voices to give himself

---

[18] See Chapter 6 for contemporary religious and cross-cultural perspectives on voice-hearing experiences.

an electric shock whenever he heard them. In the long term, this was unsuccessful. Bennett & Cesarman (1953) applied Walter Freeman's technique of transorbital lobotomy to people with voices. This involved placing an ice-pick-like instrument under the upper eyelid, which was driven with a mallet through the bone and into the brain. This was then wiggled round to cut the connections between the frontal cortex and the thalamus. In Bennett & Cesarman's study, this did not stop the voices. The patient may not have had a broken brain beforehand (cf. Andreasen, 1985), but they damn well did afterwards. Shorter (1997) refers to this period in psychiatry as 'The Lobotomy Adventure' (p. 225), which brings to mind a picture of happy patients and 'surgeons' skipping through flowery meadows having jolly larks together. Suffice to say, 'adventure' is not the word I would use.

The treatment of voices was radically changed by both the introduction of antipsychotic medications in the 1950s (Chapter 8), as well as a move to community-based treatments.[19] The new antipsychotic medication undoubtedly brought relief to some voice-hearers,[20] and this led to a resurgence in the medical model of voice-hearing. Yet, the cognitive revolution in the 1970s, arising out of the development of the digital computer in the Second World War (Slade & Bentall, 1988) led to an explosion of information processing theories for the causes of voices (see Chapters 9 and 10), as well as a greater interest in the possibility of talking therapies. The decade of the brain (the 1990s) led to a focus on the neural instantiation of such theories and the development of cognitive neuropsychiatric approaches to voices.[21] However, of great significance for how voice-hearing was understood was that psychology started to move away from psychiatric diagnoses and towards a focus on voices in their own right – the so-called 'complaint-based approach', and this is worth examining.

In Spitzer's (1975) critique of Rosenhan's (1973a) study, he argued that a diagnosis of the participants in the study with schizophrenia was correct, based on the nature of the experience and 'the desire to enter a psychiatric hospital, from which it is reasonable to conclude that the symptom is a source of significant distress' (p. 446). Spitzer indignantly asked, 'Does he [Rosenhan] believe that there are real patients with the single symptom of auditory hallucinations who are misdiagnosed as schizophrenic when they actually have some other condition? If so, what is the nature of that condition?' (p. 446). Spitzer notes three types of

[19] See Warner (1985) and Shotter (1997) for contrasting discussions of the events occurring around this time.
[20] Although see Appendix A.   [21] Discussed in Chapter 8.

AVHs and the conditions he believed they were associated with (which was to be influential in the design of DSM-III):

(a) Hallucinations of voices accusing the patient of sin when associated with depressed effect, diurnal mood variation, loss of appetite and insomnia (psychotic depression).
(b) Hallucinations of God's voice issuing commandments, associated with euphoric effect, psychomotor excitement and accelerated and disconnected speech (mania).
(c) Hallucinations, difficulty thinking clearly, lack of emotion and incoherent speech (schizophrenia).

Spitzer then claimed that each condition responded to specific treatments (electroconvulsive therapy, lithium and major tranquillisers, respectively). Is this claim true, though? Bentall (2003) argues that only one study has ever actually tested this. Johnstone *et al.* (1988), in a double-blind trial, randomly allocated 120 patients with a range of psychotic diagnoses, symptoms of which included hallucinations, delusions and abnormal mood, either to receive treatment of an antipsychotic (pimozide), lithium carbonate (an anti-mania drug), both or neither. At the end of the study it was found that pimozide improved hallucinations and delusions, regardless of the patient's diagnosis. The implications of this study were that drug response was specific to symptoms, not diagnoses, and hence that research and clinical treatments should focus on the experience of hearing voices in itself (Bentall, 2003).

In 1986, Jacqueline Persons suggested that efforts to understand the psychological processes underlying experiences such as AVHs would be 'more successful if the phenomena themselves are studied directly than if diagnostic categories (e.g., schizophrenia) are studied' (Persons, 1986, p. 1252). This approach, she argued, had a number of benefits, for example, a researcher interested in the causes of hallucinations wanting to compare the performance of patients with and without hallucinations would not need to assign psychiatric diagnoses to patients, but just to compare individuals with and without hallucinations. Around the same time, Slade & Bentall (1988) also argued that: 'Hallucinations should be studied in their own right, rather than as part of larger psychiatric syndromes' (p. 56), an approach which was also influentially argued for by Frith (1992). This approach, which focused not on diagnoses, but specific experiences such as hearing voices, was developed in detail and implemented by Bentall (2006), who termed this a complaint-orientated approach (carefully avoiding the term 'symptom'). Bentall argued for 'abandoning psychiatric diagnoses altogether' (p. 224), in particular noting the problems with the reliability and validity of the diagnosis of schizophrenia (Bentall, 2006; Boyle, 2002). Instead, Bentall proposed attempting to explain the 'actual complaints that patients bring to the clinic, such as hallucinations ... This strategy assumes that, once these complaints have each been explained in turn, there will be no "schizophrenia" or "bipolar disorder" leftover to account for' (p. 224). We will see the processes that Bentall has argued to underlie AVHs in Part III of this book. In setting out his complaint-based account, Bentall noted the work of the Dutch social psychiatrist Marius Romme, who since the 1980s has argued that voice-hearers are more in need of emancipation than cure (Chapter 12). The work of Romme, and the ensuing Hearing Voices Movement, led to a significant shift in how voices were understood in the last decades of the twentieth century, and how they are seen today.

The Hearing Voices Movement: science is the belief in the ignorance of experts (Richard Feynman)

Experiences in the mental health system by voice-hearers have always led them to propose reform. John Thomas Percival (1803–76), the son of the only British prime minister to be assassinated (Spencer Percival), was a voice-hearer. Percival noted that 'To the voices I heard ... I surrendered up my judgement ... fearing I should be disobeying the word of God, if I did not do so' (Peterson, 1982, p. 101). After being kept in an asylum for three years, Percival started the Alleged Lunatics' Friend Society (Porter, 1987). Percival complained of his treatment not being explained to him, of not being consulted or trusted, being lied to, being denied pen and paper, his letters opened, and being treated 'as if I were a piece of furniture' (Percival, as cited in Porter, 1987, p. 272). Percival argued that the greatest part of the violence that occurs in lunatic asylums 'is to be attributed to the conduct of those who are dealing with the disease, not the disease itself' (ibid., p. 273).[22] This pressure group campaigned for the civil rights of people labelled as lunatics. Similarly, the founder of the Mental Hygiene movement in the United States, Clifford Beers (1876–1943), was also a voice-hearer. In his memoir, *A Mind That Found Itself*, he describes his voice-hearing experiences: 'Certain hallucinations of hearing, or "false voices", added to my torture. Within my range of hearing, but beyond the reach of my understanding, there was a hellish vocal hum. Now and then I would recognize the subdued voice of a friend; now and then I would hear the

---

[22] See Chapter 5 for similar complaints today.

voices of some I believed were not friends. All these referred to me and uttered what I could not clearly distinguish, but knew must be imprecations [spoken curses]' (Beers, 1908, p. 23). He reports witnessing acts of brutality when he was a patient in a mental institution: 'I became well acquainted with two jovial and witty Irishmen. One was a hodcarrier, and a strapping fellow ... He irritated the attendants by persistently doing certain trivial things after they had been forbidden. The attendants made no allowance for his condition of mind ... He was physically powerful, and they determined to cow him ... I was an ear witness. It was committed behind a closed door; and I heard the dull thuds of the blows, and I heard the cries for mercy until there was no breath left in the man with which he could beg even for his life. For days that wrecked Hercules dragged himself about the ward moaning pitifully' (p. 172). After this he determined to improve psychiatry and mental health treatments.

By the time of the 1980s, the movements of post-colonialism and postmodernism, noted by Arthur Frank in his book, *The Wounded Storyteller* (Frank, 1995), created trends that allowed the voice-hearer's own voice to be heard.[23] Frank notes Talcott Parson's observation that a core social expectation of being sick is surrendering oneself to the care of a physician. Thus, when a voice-hearer tells their story, this will be moulded by the expectations of what is to be told, and what counts as the story that the doctor wants to hear (ibid.). Applying Frank's concepts, we can see that up to this point the modern experience of voice-hearing had been dominated by the technical expertise of psychiatry. This had led to psychiatry becoming 'the spokesperson' for voice-hearing, taking it over 'just as political and economic colonialism took over geographic areas' (p. 6). But Frank notes how postmodernity causes this to change. What is different in postmodern times, he argues, is that people feel a need for a voice they can recognise as their own: 'Postmodern times are when the capacity for telling one's own story is reclaimed' (p. 7). Now, he notes, 'Those who have been the objects of others' reports are now telling their own stories. As they do so, they define the ethic of our times: an ethic of voice, affording each a right to speak her own truth, in her own words' (p. xiii). Thus, voice-hearers begin to tell their truths (see Chapter 12).

Against this background of post-colonialism and postmodernism, the Hearing Voices Movement was born from the specific interaction between a Dutch psychiatrist, Marius Romme, and his voice-hearing

---

[23] See also Bracken & Thomas (2005).

patient, Patsy Hague.[24] In addition to the cultural factors discussed above, the movement's roots can be seen also to be located in wider social factors. The increased biologisation of mental illness and the psychiatric industry's marketing of antipsychotic medication, as we have seen, led to a predominantly medical model of mental illness. This left no space for voice-hearers to make sense of their experiences, and no-one to listen to them. The internet also made it easier for people to communicate across the world and for the Hearing Voices Movement to become international and to grow rapidly. The number of patients who had been moved out of in-patient care and into the community also made it possible for a voice-hearing community to develop to a much larger degree than if all voice-hearers had been locked in small wards. All of these factors, and surely many others, made the interactions between Romme and Hague able to grow into something revolutionary.

Hague had come to Romme complaining of hearing voices. She had a diagnosis of schizophrenia, had been prescribed antipsychotics which had not helped the voices, and had been hospitalised. She had been thinking and speaking more about suicide, and the only positive she could find was Julian Jaynes' (2000) work on the bicameral mind. She found it reassuring that voice-hearing may once have been a normal way of making decisions. As Hague herself later wrote, 'Those of us who still hear voices are therefore probably living in the wrong century' (Romme & Escher, 1993, p. 198). Romme thought other voice-hearers might find it useful to hear Hague's views on this, and started setting up meetings. He was struck by the eagerness with which Hague and other voice-hearers recognised each others' experiences. Romme also noted the powerlessness of these voice-hearers to cope with their voices, and so appeared on a Dutch television programme to appeal for voice-hearers to contact him. Four hundred and fifty voice-hearers replied, of which one hundred and fifty said they had found ways to cope with their voices. Romme sent out a questionnaire asking about their experiences, invited respondents who could cope for an interview, and selected twenty people who coped and could explain their experiences well. These twenty people became the speakers at the first voice-hearing conference in Utrecht, Holland, on 31 October 1987, attended by three hundred and sixty voice-hearers. Among other things, this conference revealed that in addition to the voices heard by people in the psychiatric system, many people in the general population heard voices, found

---

[24] See James (2001) for a more comprehensive account of the development of the Hearing Voices Movement.

them useful or beneficial, and felt no need to contact psychiatry about these experiences (Romme & Escher, 1993).

At later conferences, Romme argued that hearing-voices groups, where voice-hearers could come together and talk about their experiences, coping strategies and the meaning of their voices, 'need to be established in each country, where people [who hear voices] can talk together about hearing voices ... to offer the hearers of voices an organization through which they can *emancipate* themselves' (Baker, 1989, p. 29, emphasis added). Following this, there was an explosion of hearing-voices groups and networks across the world, aided by the work of INTERVOICE,[25] the International Community for Hearing Voices. The national voice-hearing movements in each country were (and still are) driven by passionate and knowledgeable experts by experience and/or experts by training. Today in England alone there are over one hundred and eighty hearing-voices groups, which Dillon & May (2002) argue are places which assume that voice-hearers have inherent expertise and wisdom about their lives, and allow a safe and democratic place for them to tell their own stories, discover their own truths and explore ways forward. In practice, what occurs in hearing-voices groups can vary widely, depending in part on the knowledge of the facilitator or originator of the group, from groups where voice-hearers discuss coping strategies, to groups where they actively explore both the life events that may have been associated with onset of their voices and the specific triggers of their voices at the current time. Whilst the former are still greatly valued and appreciated by attendees, and provide a place of refuge and safety in a world which does not understand, they can have a slight air of hopelessness about them to the external observer, with an attitude of 'just getting by' dominating, rather than active exploration of the roots of voices, and a reclaiming of one's life.

The effects of the Hearing Voices Movement have been profound in many ways. First, it has empowered many voice-hearers, allowing them to cope better with their experiences, and it is not hyperbole to say it has saved people's lives.[26] It has also resulted in a number of voice-hearers moving from the positions of psychiatric patients without hope of recovery, to being professional researchers, advocates or writers. It is now common to refer to such individuals as 'experts by experience', and to non-voice-hearing experts (e.g. researchers or mental health professionals who don't hear voices), as 'experts by training'.[27] Second, it has put

---

[25] See www.intervoiceonline.org.   [26] Many voice-hearers have said this to me.

[27] I myself find the term 'expert by experience' somewhat condescending, as it does not reflect the fact that in addition to their own experiences many such individuals

forward a new model of the causes of hearing voices which views them as relating to traumatic events in the individual's life, with the content of the voices being meaningful (much as Bleuler and Jung argued), and rejects a narrow biomedical paradigm which views voices as the random productions of a diseased brain (see Romme *et al.*, 2009). What differentiates this work from previous historical theories of hearing voices is that the theories of voices that have been developed, to a large degree, have been developed in direct partnerships with voice-hearers themselves. We will see the quantitative research evidence base for a causal role of trauma in Chapter 11. Outside of the research literature, many have been convinced by hearing and reading the personal narratives that individuals, trained in the way of the Hearing Voice Movement, have written of their lives, that these offer good evidence for a causal role of traumatic events. Because Romme and colleagues view the content of the voices as a 'code' or a metaphorical expression of such emotional crises (ibid.), treatment involves listening to the voices, understanding the emotional crises they reflect, and working with these. Hence, medication is initially seen as useful in reducing anxiety, but then as often impairing the ability of individuals to work with their voices. Yet 'treatment' is not really the right word here. Romme (personal communication) argues that voices are a common human variation, not necessarily pathological in themselves, and that it is a failure to cope with them that leads to illness. As such, he argues that voice-hearing needs an emancipation process, drawing a parallel with the struggle over homosexuality. Romme argues that just as people who are homosexual need to accept that this is the way they are (and that it is neither theirs nor psychiatry's job to change this), so people who hear voices need to accept that the voices are real, and a natural human variation which they should be allowed to experience without persecution or being forced to change into non-voice-hearers (just as homosexual individuals used to be attempted to be cured into heterosexuality). Finally, this movement has led to a resurgence in the alternative meanings of the voice-hearing experience, and the creation of a space where these accounts are accepted.

At present many of the tenets of the movement, which are reflected in what is known as the Maastricht approach (see Chapter 12), have tentatively been accepted by some in the mental health system. This is in large part due to educational work performed by prominent voice-hearers themselves, and their allies, including the provision of specific

are as familiar (if not more familiar) with the academic research literature than many 'experts by training'.

training for mental health professionals, conference presentations, as well as the publication of many prominent books (e.g. Coleman & Smith, 1997; Hornstein, 2009; Romme & Escher, 1993; Romme *et al.*, 2009). However, a somewhat uneasy relationship currently exists between psychiatry and the movement, partly due to many in psychiatry believing voices to be a brain disease typically associated with schizophrenia (rather than an understandable reaction to trauma, as proposed by many in the movement), partly due to the debate over the scientific validity of the concept of schizophrenia itself, and partly due to professional interests being threatened. How the relations between the two will evolve remains to be seen.

Next on our voice-hearing journey we will attempt to answer the question as to what voices people hear today are like. The short answer, as we will see, is that they are pretty much the same as they have always been ...

Chapter 3: summary of key points

- In Chapter 2 we saw how religion, in the seventeenth century, had begun to willingly transfer power to psychiatry vis-à-vis hearing voices, in order to medicalise religious dissenters' experiences of voice-hearing.
- At the start of the nineteenth century, this transfer was completed, with psychiatry assuming full authority over the voice-hearing discourse. Notably the first psychiatric treatments were born out of the Church's techniques for helping voice-hearers.
- Yet mysticism and spiritualism still allowed some voice-hearers to make their own sense of their experiences, outside of a biomedical paradigm.
- Around 50,000 voice-hearers were killed in the Holocaust.
- World wars led to emphasis on the environmental causes of voices, and psychoanalysis brought back the concept that the content of voices was meaningful (although this was the psychoanalyst's meaning, rather than the voice-hearer's).
- The development of antipsychotic medications reaffirmed a biomedical view of AVHs as an endogenous brain disease, and the diagnosis of schizophrenia became synonymous with voice-hearing and a loss of hope.
- The *Diagnostic and Statistical Manual of Mental Disorder* defined how voices related to pathology.
- The concept of sane voice-hearers was debated in mid-nineteenth-century France, but had to wait until the postmodernist, post-colonialist discourses of the twentieth century became prominent before voice-hearers'

were offered an opportunity to emancipate themselves on a large scale, through the Hearing Voices Movement.

- Most in the Hearing Voices Movement highlight trauma as a cause of many voices, assume the meaningfulness of the content of voices, and work directly with the voices themselves to reduce the voice-hearer's distress (see also Chapter 12).
- How relations between the Hearing Voices Movement and psychiatry will evolve in the future remains unclear.

Part II
The phenomenology and lived experience of hearing voices

Introduction to Part II

Part I of this book, in addition to reviewing a history of hearing voices, has hopefully given a flavour (particularly through the discussion of historical figures' voice-hearing experiences) of what voice-hearing is like. Part II will be dedicated to deepening this understanding.

In Chapter 4 we will examine the phenomenology of hearing voices in individuals who have received psychiatric diagnoses as per the *Diagnostic and Statistical Manual of Mental Disorders* (DSM), as well as voice-hearing in other medical conditions. Phenomenology, although a term used in many ways, will be taken here to refer to the systematic study of experience. It will be found that although the prevalence of voices differs between diagnostic categories, there are more similarities than differences in the phenomenology of the voices across diagnoses.

In Chapter 5 we will then turn to the lived experience of hearing voices in individuals with the psychiatric diagnosis most linked with hearing voices: psychosis. This chapter will also start to examine how recovery may be achieved and what it means to recover.

Chapters 6 and 7 will then examine voice-hearing outside of the DSM. After observing that clinicians must be sensitive to religious and cultural factors in making a diagnosis, Chapter 6 will examine voice-hearing that would not be classified as a mental disorder by the DSM, specifically that relating to contemporary religion, as well as in other societies throughout the world.

In Chapter 7 we will then examine another category of voice-hearing not covered by the DSM: voices which do not cause distress and/or social and occupational impairment. This will involve examining the prevalence and phenomenology of AVHs in individuals in the general population (where such experiences are generally infrequent and fleeting), as well as in healthy voice-hearers, who hear extensive and complex voices which are phenomenologically (and, incidentally, neurologically) very much like those found in individuals with a diagnosis of psychosis, but without the associated distress or impairment. This will lead us to reconsider the meaning of voice-hearing and its relation to illness, which will then be taken up later in Part IV.

One aim of Part II is to try to communicate what voices are like; however, this is hard to do on paper. A much better insight can be gained by a technique employed by trainers of the Hearing Voices Movement. In this you sit and try to have a conversation with another person (perhaps pretending you are in an interview, or having a chat in the pub). Whilst you do this, a third person stands with their mouth close to your ear and quietly says the type of things that voices say. By taking part in this simple experiment you soon get a feeling for what it might be like to hear voices continually, and how hard it is to function normally unless you can find some form of effective coping mechanism.

4   The phenomenology of hearing voices in people with psychiatric diagnoses

What are the voices that people hear actually like? People who seek help from mental health professionals for their voices can attract a number of different psychiatric diagnoses, depending on what other experiences they also present with. As such, we will examine the prevalence and phenomenology of voices in each of the major diagnostic categories in which voice-hearers may be found. Why should we care about establishing the phenomenology and lived experience of voices? This is important for a number of reasons. First, we can only develop good theories of the causes of (and, by extension, therapeutic interventions for) voices if we know what voices are actually like (Jones, 2010a). Second, this can help non-voice-hearers who are providing therapeutic interventions to voice-hearers to better understand the problems voice-hearers are having. Finally, it may allow us to work out *why* voices can cause problems, lead to psychiatric diagnoses, and help us to reconsider whether voices necessarily really are a symptom of mental disorder.

Hearing voices in psychotic disorders: prevalence and phenomenology

In contemporary psychiatric classifications, AVHs are listed as characteristic symptoms of a range of psychotic and mood disorders including schizophrenia,[1] schizophreniform disorder, schizoaffective disorder, brief psychotic disorder, bipolar disorder (in both manic and depressive episodes) and major depressive disorder. This section will focus on schizophrenia and bipolar disorder. Throughout the following discussion of prevalence figures, it is worth noting that psychotic symptoms such as AVHs are likely to be under-reported by patients (Fennig *et al.*, 1994).

---

[1] As we saw in Chapter 3, the reliability and validity of the diagnosis of schizophrenia has been questioned. I do not intend to re-visit this debate here (see Bentall, 1992a, 2003; Boyle, 2002 for extensive discussion of this issue). The term will continue to be used here, where it is helpful for the purposes of communication to do so.

Schizophrenia (AVH prevalence c.70%)

Given that AVHs are defined as a 'characteristic symptom' (APA, 2000, p. 312) in the diagnostic criteria for schizophrenia, it is hence unsurprising that those with a diagnosis of schizophrenia have a high prevalence of AVHs. Yet the statement is often made that AVHs 'are common in schizophrenia' or that 'people suffering from schizophrenia also frequently experience various kinds of hallucinations ... such as hearing voices' (Andreasen, 1985, p. 60) *as if this tells us something*. Whilst these statements are obviously correct, their danger is that they could be taken to imply that there is an ontologically independent, eternally existing condition 'out there' called 'schizophrenia', in which AVHs just happen to be very common. This is much like saying that alcohol is frequently found in pubs, or that footballers frequently kick balls. Voices are not characteristic of schizophrenia because they commonly occur in such patients, they are common because they are *defined* as a characteristic symptom. Similarly, Fisher, Labelle & Knott (2008) state that 'One characteristic symptom of schizophrenia is auditory verbal hallucinations (AH), *as* they have a reported prevalence of 50–80%' (p. 3, emphasis added). Yet voices are not a characteristic symptom of schizophrenia *because* they are common in patients with this diagnosis; they are common as the DSM *defines* hearing voices (and particularly certain types) as a characteristic symptom of schizophrenia.

This notwithstanding, the frequency of AVHs in schizophrenia appears to have crept up over the last 100 years. This would appear to reflect changes in the extent to which AVHs are seen as a core symptom of schizophrenia, rather than any absolute increase in levels of AVHs in society per se. In 1908 Kraepelin found that 36 per cent of his first admission dementia praecox patients had auditory hallucinations (Jablensky, 1997). By the late 1960s a cross-cultural World Health Organisation (WHO) study of 811 patients diagnosed with schizophrenia in eight countries found that 47 per cent heard voices (WHO, 1973). More recent studies show that 60–83 per cent of individuals diagnosed with schizophrenia hear voices (Baethge *et al.*, 2005; Bentall & Slade, 1988; Thomas *et al.*, 2007; Wing, Cooper & Sartorius, 1974). The literature on AVH prevalence in schizophrenia has now become too voluminous to review (i.e. in order to create a weighted average prevalence), and in any case, it is somewhat unclear what such a review would achieve. We may therefore take a fair estimate of the prevalence of AVHs in schizophrenia as being around 70 per cent today.

Bipolar disorder (AVH prevalence c.7%)

Bipolar I disorder is characterised by one or more manic or mixed (manic and depressive) episodes. In the DSM-IV-TR (APA, 2000), manic and depressive episodes are recognised as potentially including psychotic features. The DSM notes that with such episodes, hallucinations are likely to be auditory and to have mood-congruent features. For example, in a manic episode, 'God's voice may be heard explaining that the person has a specific mission' (p. 414). In a depressive episode,[2] voices may berate the person for shortcomings or sins, although these are 'usually transient and not elaborate' (p. 412). Yet, the DSM-IV-TR also notes that voices in this condition may also have mood-incongruent content. AVHs are less commonly found in patients diagnosed with bipolar disorder than patients diagnosed with schizophrenia (Baethge *et al.*, 2005). Estimates for the prevalence of AVHs in bipolar disorder range widely. In a review of the prevalence of auditory hallucinations (i.e. not limited to voices) in manic states in 26 studies pre-1990, Goodwin & Jamison (1990) found a prevalence of 18 per cent. However, as Baethge *et al.* (2005) note, most of the studies in Goodwin & Jamison's review lacked the use modern diagnostic criteria, standardised assessments, or included phenomena such as illusions. A study by Keck *et al.* (2003; N = 352) found 37 per cent of bipolar patients reported auditory hallucinations. However, they do not state whether these were specifically voices or not, and there appear to have been an abnormally high number of bipolar patients with a history of such experiences in this sample. In the most recent large-scale study, Baethge *et al.* (2005) found that of 549 hospitalised patients with bipolar diagnoses, 37 (7%) heard voices either at the time of testing, or very recently. Hallucinations per se were more common in patients presenting with mixed (manic and depressive) episodes, than either manic or depressive episodes alone (data on voices was not reported for this comparison). In two recent smaller studies Hammersley *et al.* (2010) found 8 of 40 bipolar patients (20%) heard voices (of these, 7 did so when they were depressed), and Hammersley *et al.* (2003) found 30 of 96 bipolar patients (31%) had auditory hallucinations, of which 11 of these were voices commenting. The higher values found by Hammersley and colleagues appear to be due to these being lifetime prevalence of such experiences. Hence, the best estimate of point prevalence of AVHs in bipolar disorder appears to be that of Baethge *et al.* (2005).

---

[2] In addition to AVHs occurring in depressive episodes within bipolar disorder, they also occur within the context of major depressive disorder (MDD), although little work has been done estimating the prevalence of voices in this condition.

Phenomenology of AVHs in psychotic disorders

In order to establish a picture of what the phenomenology of AVHs is like in people diagnosed with psychotic disorders, we will examine two sources of information. The first is the great descriptive accounts given by Kraepelin and by Bleuler around the turn of the nineteenth/ twentieth century. The second is recent quantitative studies of the phenomenology of AVHs. This approach could be criticised for not using accounts written by voice-hearers themselves. Indeed, many are available (e.g. Romme *et al.*, 2009). However, first-person accounts from qualitative studies will be used to examine the lived experience of voices in psychosis in Chapter 5, and voice-hearers' own voices will also be heard in Chapter 12 when we examine the contested meaning of hearing voices today.

Kraepelin's and Bleuler's accounts of hearing voices in psychosis

Today, the research literature does not contain the rich descriptions of voices that it used to. Studies today are typically quantitative which, whilst very valuable in quantifying how frequent types and properties of voices are, fails to give us a full flavour of the voices. For this we may turn to the great descriptive accounts of the phenomenology of voice-hearing in dementia praecox/schizophrenia provided around the start of the twentieth century by Emile Kraepelin (1919) and Eugene Bleuler (1950).

Kraepelin found that before the onset of voices there were 'usually simple noises, rustling, buzzing, ringing in the ears, tolling of bells . . . knocking, moving of tables, cracking of whips, trumpets, yodel, singing, weeping of children, whistling, blowing, chirping, "shooting and death-rattle"; the bed echoes with shots; the "Wild Hunt" makes an uproar; Satan roars under the bed' (p. 7). Following such experiences, Kraepelin observed that 'then there develops gradually or suddenly the symptom peculiarly characteristic of dementia praecox, namely, the hearing of voices' (ibid.). In terms of the frequency of such experiences, Kraepelin observed that 'Often the voices torment the patient the whole day long, and at night also he hears "telephone gossip", or perhaps he only hears them now and then, not infrequently in the form of single detached remarks' (p. 8). These voices may be one or many: 'Sometimes they shout as in a chorus or all confusedly . . . [one] heard, "729,000 girls"' (ibid.). In addition to sounding like people, voice-hearers could also hear metallic sounds, 'resonant voices' or 'organ voices'(ibid.).

Kraepelin observed that voices were often connected to real external noises. For example, 'The clock speaks as if it were enchanted; the rushing of water is changed into words; each step under the patient speaks; a patient "heard the thoughts of others out of the soles of his boots". Here and there the voices have a rhythmical cadence, probably in connection with the carotid pulse' (ibid.).

In terms of the location of the voice, Kraepelin noted that 'for the most part the origin of the voices is sought for in the external world … The question is about the "address", about "the communicated voices of human beings", about "murmurings and natural spirit-voices", about underground voices from the air, from the ground, voices from Further India and Siberia, whispering voices from the whole of mankind, "voices of spirits which are quite near", of God, the saints and the blessed, of the guardian angel, but especially of all conceivable persons in the neighbourhood' (ibid.). Yet, internally located voices could also occur, either located in the head, 'the brain talks', or the body. 'Many patients hear the voices in the whole body; the spirits scream in the belly, in the feet, and possibly also wander about; a patient heard them speaking in his purse' (ibid.). Different voices could be heard in the patient's different ears. Kraepelin described one patient who had a voice in his right ear saying 'Never', a voice in his left ear saying 'Stupid Jesus God', a voice in the stomach saying 'Blackguard. Point. Good', a voice in his nose saying 'Munich; Ohoboy', a voice in this heart saying 'Boy' and a voice in the right side of his abdomen saying 'Yokel' (ibid.).

In terms of the perceptual nature of the experience, in addition to hearing clear voices, Kraepelin also noted that 'At other times they do not appear to the patients as sense perceptions at all; they are "voices of conscience", "voices which do not speak with words", voices of dead people, "false voices", "abortive voices". There is an "inner feeling in the soul", an "inward voice in the thoughts"; "it is thought inwardly in me"; it "sounded as if thought"; "it was between hearing and foreboding"' (ibid.). Hence, he was clear how heterogeneous the experience is.

What did the majority of voices say? Kraepelin found that 'What the voices say is, as a rule, unpleasant and disturbing … The patient is everywhere made a fool of and teased, mocked, grossly abused, and threatened … Some one calls out: "Rascal, vagrant, miserable scoundrel", "incendiary, parricide", "good-for-nothing", "blackguard", "anarchist, rogue, thieving murderer", "filthy fellow, filthy blockhead, filthy beast"… "town whore", "convict", "criminal". The patient is said to have assaulted a child, seduced a girl with 80,000 marks, had sexual intercourse with his children, eaten human flesh. He is threatened with having his ears cut off, his feet chopped off, with being sawn asunder, with being beheaded ... He must come along; he must be arrested; he has seduced the girl ... Most frequently they are indecent and filthy things that are called out in which impurity and self-abuse play a large part' (p. 9). Bleuler (1950) also noted this, writing that 'Threats and curses form the main and common content of these "voices". Day and night they come from everywhere – from the walls, from above and below, from the cellar and the roof, from heaven and hell, from near and far' (p. 97). Yet, in addition to these negative voices, Kraepelin found that there were also frequently ' "good voices", "good wishes"... God makes known to the patient that he will proclaim him, send him into the world as his son. "Here he is", cries a voice from heaven. He hears that he is a king's son, an officer's son, that he is very musical' (p. 10). Yet voices, Bleuler noted, are very often contradictory, and the roles of pro and con may be taken over by different people. Thus, for example, 'The voice of his daughter tells a patient: "He is going to be burned alive"; while his mother's voice says, "He will not be burned"' (p. 98). Similarly, 'At other times the same voice will amuse itself by driving the patient to utter despair in that they approve of his intentions, or order him to make a certain purchase and then berate him for doing so. The voices command him to go bathing and then jeer at him for obeying' (ibid.).

Kraepelin describes how the voices were often involved with the patient's ongoing life, 'many of the voices make remarks about the thoughts and the doings of the patient' (p. 10). In addition to comprehensible content, Kraepelin also found that 'Often ... in the beginning of the disease or in the more advanced stages what the voices say is indifferent or quite nonsensical and incomprehensible. The patient hears ... "Banker, rich farmer, crash, salt roll"; "Stallion"... "Lavender and crossroads are the strongest explosive", and similar expressions' (p. 10). Another patient of Kraepelin's who was 'quite reasonable' reports that his voices said ' "He veni I came Cham Saul Absalom lyric dropping roast lust Turks"' (p. 11). In addition to these voices, Kraepelin found 'many patients hear perpetually, in endless repetition or with slight changes, the same meaningless sentences' (ibid.).

Kraepelin also found that voices would give commands which would 'forbid the patient to eat and to speak, to work, to go to church; he must run barefoot. "Go on, strike him, beat him", it is said, "go on, go on!", "Hands up!", "Slope arms!", "Put the chair here, stand up!", "Jump in!"' (p. 12). Bleuler (1950) adds to this by noting that 'the voice may forbid the patient to do what he was just thinking of doing' (p. 98). Bleuler also reported a number of further facets. He noted AVHs of the form of a confusing crowd of voices in which 'Often several voices talk at once so that the patient cannot follow them' (p. 99). In terms of person-like characteristics of the voice, Bleuler observed that 'The voices may also reveal information about themselves. They tell who they are, what they look like, where they are, etc, but this is an infrequent occurrence' (1950, p. 99). In terms of the length of the voice's utterances, Bleuler found that, as a rule, patients heard short sentences or individual words, and not long monologues or 'entire sermon[s]' (p. 96). Instead, he found that what he called 'thought-dialogues' were more common, with people dialoguing with their voice, be it God, a persecutor or a protector. Like Kraepelin, he noted that the voices could come from the body, but describes this more vividly: 'Many times ... the whole body will be intoning ... "you whore"' (p. 99). Some voices would come from under the skin, shouting 'Don't let me out' or 'Don't cut it open' (p. 100). Bleuler also noted that there are ' "such vivid thoughts" which are called "voices" by the patients. At other times they are "audible thoughts" or "soundless voices"' (p. 110). To illustrate this, Bleuler notes one patient who described that feeling: 'It was as if someone pointed his finger at me and said "Go and drown yourself". It is as if we were speaking to each other. I don't hear it in my ears, I have the feeling in my breast' (p. 111).

Quantitative accounts of voices in psychosis

Although the above descriptions paint an excellent picture of the experience of voice-hearing in those distressed by the experience, it is not a formal, large-scale, quantitative analysis, and does not allow us to quantify which specific instances of the phenomenon are common or rare. To address this, a number of studies have been performed that allow us to form a quantitative picture of the phenomenology of AVHs in patients diagnosed with psychosis, and particularly in patients diagnosed with schizophrenia. The summary below of the phenomenology of AVHs in psychosis draws on the study of Nayani & David (1996; 100 patients, the majority of whom had a diagnosis of schizophrenia), Garrett & Silva (2003; 28 patients diagnosed with schizophrenia), Leudar et al. (1997; 14 patients diagnosed with schizophrenia), Moritz & Larøi (2008; 45 patients diagnosed with schizophrenia) and Hoffman et al. (2008b; 50 patients diagnosed with schizophrenia or schizoaffective disorder).

Acoustic properties

The first property of voices of interest is the extent to which they live up to their name, i.e. that they are voices just like hearing another person talking to oneself. In fact, the answer one gets to this depends on the study one examines. Garrett & Silva (2003) and Leudar *et al.* (1997) both found that the majority of voices reported by patients were much like hearing other people speak. Leudar *et al.* report that 'All of our informants reported that hearing voices was very much like hearing other people speak' (p. 889) and Garrett & Silva (2003) state that 100 per cent of patients diagnosed with schizophrenia reported hearing 'the voices clearly just as you are hearing the sound of my voice now' (p. 448). However, a number of other studies have found this not to be the case. Moritz & Larøi (2008) found that 31 per cent of patients diagnosed with schizophrenia reported that their voices were indistinguishable from real voices, 31 per cent that they were almost real, and 38 per cent that their voices were not very real. Similarly, Nayani & David (1996) found that 44 per cent of patients reported that their AVHs were more like ideas than external sensations. Indeed, a small number of voice-hearers have what Bleuler (1950) termed 'soundless voices' (p. 110). In such AVHs a message or meaning is communicated to the voice-hearer, but it is not actually heard. As we noted, a patient of Bleuler's who threw himself into the Rhine reported afterwards that 'It was as if someone pointed his finger at me and said "Go and drown yourself"' (p. 111). Pierre Janet also noted this phenomenon, giving the example of a patient who reported that 'it is not a voice, I do not hear anything, I sense that I am spoken to' (Leudar & Thomas, 2000). In a recent study, Moritz & Larøi found that 5 per cent of patients diagnosed with schizophrenia had AVHs that were absolutely silent and could not be heard.

Although voices may sound like external people, this does not mean that they are mistaken for them. Indeed, Leudar *et al.* (1997) found that none of their sample confused their AVHs for other people actually speaking, i.e. they knew when they were hallucinating. Likewise, Mullen (1997) gives an example of a telephonist who, whilst being troubled by constant auditory hallucinations, was nevertheless able to continue to work efficiently and to distinguish between her AVHs and the disembodied voices of callers. Consistent with this, in terms of the reality of voices, Junginger & Frame (1985) found that patients' tendency to rate their voices as real was independent from how similar or dissimilar they said their voices were to auditory experiences. In terms of the relationship between AVHs and the patient's own thoughts, Hoffman *et al.* (2008b) found that the majority of patients (80%) were able to differentiate their AVHs from their normal verbal thoughts most of the time.

In terms of the clarity and volume of voices, Garrett & Silva (2003) and Leudar *et al.* (1997) both report that voices tend to speak clearly, although voices mumbling have also been reported (Nayani & David, 1996). The majority of voices speak at a normal conversational volume, yet whispering or shouting voices occur in around 10–20 per cent of voice-hearers (Moritz & Larøi, 2008; Nayani & David, 1996). The type of voice also affects its volume, with Nayani & David finding 84 per cent of voice-hearers saying that angry voices were typically louder.

Voices may be heard speaking to the voice-hearer through their ears, or the location of the voice may be identified as being in the voice-hearer's head. Nayani & David (1996) found that 49 per cent of the sample heard voices through their ears that originated outside of their head, whereas 38 per cent heard them inside their head, with 12 per cent having voices that varied between these states. Of those who heard externally located voices, 65 per cent said that they experienced their voices as coming from the same direction each time they heard them. Nayani & David report that internally located voices were usually found to be complex, both in their prosody (i.e. their emotional intonation), as well as the number of words they involved. In a sample of 197 voice-hearers (the majority, 81%, with a diagnosis of schizophrenia), Copolov, Trauer & Mackinnon (2004) found that 35 per cent had voices located only inside their head, 28 per cent only outside, and 38 per cent had both types. A key finding was that internal voices were felt to be just as real as external voices. They also found there was no difference between internally and externally located voices in their perceived clarity, volume, tone, content, gender, age (child/adult) and whether the voice spoke in the first, second, or third person. Although command AVHs were not more commonly associated with internal or external voices, patients were more able to resist voices located outside the head (91% could resist) than voices inside the head (76% could resist).

Number, identity and frequency of voices

In terms of the number of voices heard, Nayani & David (1996) found that 66 per cent of participants heard more than one voice. Voice-hearers on average seem to hear around three different voices, with the majority of voices having an identifiable gender, male voices being more common than female ones (Garrett & Silva, 2003; Leudar et al., 1997; Moritz & Larøi, 2008; Nayani & David, 1996). Indeed, Nayani & David found that 71 per cent of both men and women reported their most prominent voice was male. The age of voices is also generally discernible. Nayani & David found that more than 75 per cent of patients stated the voices sounded middle-aged, but patients who were less than 30 were more likely to report that their voices sounded young. Overall, the single most prominent hallucinated voice in their 100 participants was a middle-aged man (34%), a young adult man (24%) or a young female (10%). They also found 71 per cent of patients said that the voice's accent differed from their own (consistent with this, Hoffman *et al.* (2008b) found that 79 per cent said the voice they heard did not sound like their own speaking voice). Thirty per cent described an upper-class voice (a 'BBC voice'). Voices with a Jamaican/Afro-Caribbean accent were most commonly reported by British-born Afro-Caribbean participants.

The majority of voice-hearers claim to know the identity of their voices (Garrett & Silva, 2003; Leudar *et al.*, 1997; Nayani & David, 1996). In some cases the voice may tell the voice-hearer its name, as a normal person would do when introducing him/herself to another (Garrett & Silva, 2003). Who says manners are dead? Nayani & David found that 61 per cent of people stated they knew the identity of one or more of their voices. Fifteen per cent described what the authors term 'delusional' explanations (God, the Devil, robots, etc.), whereas 46 per cent described people (relative, neighbour, etc.). Garrett & Silva give examples of one voice-hearer who heard the voice of her dead daughter, who cried when the patient refused to join her in the grave. In terms of explanations for voices, in Nayani & David's 1996 study, 51 per cent of voice-hearers used accounts involving a clash of forces of Good and Evil, 16 per cent a plot (e.g. CIA bugging the house) and 5 per cent ghosts, spirits or aliens. It is notable how little the typical clash between good and evil voices has been worked into theories of AVHs (see Chapter 9).

The frequency at which voice-hearers hear voices ranges widely. Nayani & David found that 12 per cent of voice-hearers experienced them once or twice a day, 36 per cent several times a day, 37 per cent most of the time and 15 per cent all of the time. Voices lasted seconds or minutes in about 33 per cent of patients, less than an hour in 25 per cent and more than an hour in 42 per cent. The more frequent people's voices were, the more likely they were to speak for longer when they did speak.

What the voices say

What the voices say is quite consistent. The majority of voices in individuals with diagnoses of psychotic disorders attempt to regulate their activity by issuing commands or telling them to perform specific actions, and/or judge them, being typically critical or abusive (Leudar *et al.*, 1997; Nayani & David, 1996; Suhail & Cochrane, 2002). For example, Nayani & David asked patients to give ten examples of their voices, and the most frequently found (in 84% of patients) was a voice that gave commands (e.g. 'get the milk', 'go to the hospital'). Such command

AVHs are particularly distressing when they command people to kill themselves (e.g. 'stab yourself', 'slash your wrists'), harm themselves ('burn yourself', 'go into the road'), kill others ('cut her throat', 'kill your husband and daughter') or harm others ('rape your neighbour', 'hit them') (Byrne *et al.*, 2006). Such voices that command or advise on actions can be seen to be consistent with the historical accounts of voice-hearing in Part I, in which such voices appear in people ranging from Socrates and the Old Testament prophets, to George Trosse and Thomas Schucker, and appear in the clinical observations of physicians from Esquirol onwards.

Consistent with these findings, Lee *et al.* (2004), in a study of 100 patients diagnosed with schizophrenia in Asia, found that 53 per cent reported command AVHs. Interestingly, women were more likely than men to have such AVHs. Of the 33 patients who complied with their command AVHs, 33 per cent committed a violent act in response to the voices, 18 per cent of which were self-injurious acts, and 15 per cent of which were violent acts towards others. Of the 20 participants who were able to ignore the command AVHs, the most commonly adopted strategy was praying (used by 25% of participants).

Leudar *et al.* (1997) observed that if voice-hearers did not comply with these commands, the voice would typically repeat it frequently until it was obeyed or the situation changed, with participants stating that their voices would nag them, bully them, and 'go on'. They also noted that when voices were trying to get the voice-hearer to do something, they were not simply repetitive, like a record stuck in a groove, but would rephrase the directives, or start swearing when not obeyed. However, there may be exceptions, such as voices repeatedly telling the voice-hearer to kill themselves. In terms of other properties of voices, Nayani & David found 77 per cent were critical (e.g. 'you are stupid'), 70 per cent were abusive ('ugly bitch'), 66 per cent were frightening (e.g. 'we're going to kill you'), 66 per cent were third person or neutral ('He's in bed'), 53 per cent were arguing either with the patient or between themselves, and 48 per cent were pleasant (e.g. 'she's alright').[3]

The most common voice utterances Nayani & David (1996) found in patients were vulgar expletives, yet they noted that it was not the case that voices reflected simple expletives like words uttered almost

---

[3] Intriguingly, sometimes very rarely, commands are also experienced via other modalities. For example, ffytche, Lappin & Philpot (2004) report a case of a patient *seeing* grammatically correct, meaningful written sentences or phrases, often in the second person and with a threatening and command-like nature (e.g. 'Don't take your tablets', 'They're after your money, we have got some of them but we are trying to find the others' (p. 81)). This also makes one think of Belshazzar's Feast.

automatically at times of stress (damn, shit, etc.). Instead, they were found to have the morphology of personal insults (an -er ending), specificity tailored to the subject, and often conveying contempt and anger. Similarly, Close & Garety (1998) in a study of AVHs in 30 patients diagnosed with schizophrenia found 53 per cent had negative voices, saying things such as 'Hang yourself, you're evil and damned', 'You're fat, ugly, and useless', 'You're a bloke who whistles a lot', 'You deserve to have a breakdown the way you use people', 'Sell your soul to the devil', 'Kill yourself, chop up your girlfriend', 'F*ck off' (pp. 177–9). As a result, the voice-hearers in this study often interpreted their voice-hearing as being a punishment. This could be from God (e.g. because they had had an abortion), for other wrongdoings, for being a male prostitute.[4] Other explanations were understandably along similar themes, e.g. the voices are from hell and they want their soul, they are evil spirits intent on driving them mad, as well as more benign illness themes.

Positive voices

Positive or benevolent voices are also heard in patients diagnosed with a psychotic disorder, with their prevalence ranging from 8 per cent to 83 per cent (Cheung et al., 1997; Honig et al., 1998; Jenner et al., 2008; Johns et al., 2002; Nayani & David, 1996; Sanjuan et al., 2004; Suhail & Cochrane, 2002). The low end of this estimate (the 8% figure) comes from a study based solely on medical records (Suhail & Cochrane, 2002) and hence appears likely to be an underestimate. Nayani & David's (1996) interview-based study found that 48 per cent of voice-hearers heard pleasant voices, and Honig et al.'s (1998) study, which reported a prevalence of 83 per cent, was also found after face-to-face interviews. In a detailed study of the positive voices in psychiatric out-patients who had been diagnosed with a psychotic disorder, Jenner et al. (2008) found that although only 8 per cent had voices that were predominantly positive, 52 per cent had had some positive voices. Positive voices were found to help with handling the negative voices in 47 per cent of patients who had had positive voices. In terms of the functions of the positive voices in those who had experienced them, 46 per cent said the positive voices wanted to protect them, between 30 per cent and 39 per cent of people said that the positive voices made them confident, calm, kept them company, helped them solve

[4] This raises the issue of shame and guilt which is elaborated upon in Parts III and IV.

problems, develop their talents, helped with daily activities; 25 per cent said the positive voices helped keep them mentally healthy; and 20 per cent that they made them important. The majority of positive voices (68%) wanted to give the voice-hearer advice, and around 40 per cent to help with their decisions, daily activities, or to keep appointments. Positive voices were hence very beneficial to such voice-hearers, and it would have been interesting to find out how patients felt about the thought of medication potentially taking away both the negative voices *and* the positive voices, as 32 per cent wanted to keep their positive voices.

Conversing with voices, and other properties

The majority of voice-hearers appear able to talk interactively with their voices. For example, Garrett & Silva (2003) found that 88 per cent of patients diagnosed with schizophrenia with AVHs could engage in back and forth conversation with their voices. Similarly, Leudar *et al.* (1997) found that 82 per cent of voice-hearers could ask their voices questions and sometimes get answers. Notably, Nayani & David (1996) found that voice-hearers who could *not* talk to their voices were more distressed than those who could.

The content of voices is often novel, with Leudar *et al.* (1997) finding 43 per cent of voice-hearers diagnosed with psychosis heard voices telling them something they did not know. Nevertheless, a large number of voices have repetitive content as well. Hoffman *et al.* (2008b) found that around half of their sample said their voices were either 'often', 'most of the time' or 'always' repetitive. Similarly, Nayani & David (1996) found that 66 per cent of voice-hearers could give examples of repetitive content of their voices, which were usually simple, vulgar insults. Likewise, Chaturvedi & Sinha (1990) found that 39 per cent had recurring content of their voices between different episodes of psychosis. Although repetitive, it is often hard to link voices back to specific memories. For example, Johns *et al.* (2002) found that only 14 per cent of voice-hearers said the hallucinations were 'replays' of memories of voices they had heard before.

In terms of other properties of voices, around a quarter appear to make predictions about the future. Garrett & Silva (2003) found that 25 per cent of voice-hearers had voices which predicted the future, and Leudar *et al.* (1997) found that 18 per cent of voice-hearers had voices which made predictions regarding the consequences of the voice-hearer's actions. Regarding the control voice-hearers have over their voices, Nayani & David (1996) report that 51 per cent were able to exercise some control over the voices, 38 per cent could induce their voices by concentrating on it or asking it questions, whereas 21 per cent said they could sometimes stop them.[5] Finally, Garrett & Silva (2003) found that 31 per cent of patients had voices that occurred in their dreams, too.

In addition to typically having a distinct gender, possessing other distinct auditory properties which differ from the patient's voice, and their ability to hold dialogues with the voice-hearer, voices have a number of other properties that lead the voice-hearer to feel that they are 'real' entities, with a will and existence separate from them. Garrett & Silva (2003) give a number of these. First, voices can show a self-preservative reaction. They found that 15 per cent of patients had voices which knowingly responded to efforts to eliminate them or diminish their power. For example, voices may perceive antipsychotic medications as a threat to them, and urge the patient to refuse it. Voices may also make predictions about the future which, when they come true, add to the voice-hearer's perception of their reality. One patient heard a voice telling him that his doctor would be unable to draw his blood, a prediction that proved correct. Voices also often have a 'not me' content. For example, one patient whose voice called her 'Mommy' stated that 'Maybe it's me. But I wouldn't call myself "Mommy"'. Another person stated they first thought the voices might be her imagination, but came to believe they were not part of her because they were capable of a viciousness she had never seen in herself. Nayani & David (1996) also observe that voice-hearers conveyed a sense of personal intimacy with their voices, both in their knowledge concerning the voice, but mainly by the voice's knowledge of them.[6] For example, in Garrett & Silva's (2003) study, one patient reported a voice which knew details of her rape, even though she had never told anyone else these details. Nayani & David (1996) observe that the price the voice-hearer pays for this is a loss of privacy, which one patient expressed as 'an open mental wound' (p. 186).[7]

---

[5] Whilst I do not know how Nayani & David's sample did this, a common technique used within the Hearing Voices Movement is for the voice-hearer to ask their voices to go away temporarily and come back at say, 5:30 pm, when they will talk to them. It is unknown how many voice-hearers find this effective, though.

[6] In this sense, it can be seen that an unequal power balance exists between the voice-hearer and their voice, see Chapter 12.

[7] The playwright Harold Pinter, in another context, uses the phrase 'the wound is peopled' (Pinter, 2005), and I will suggest in Parts III and IV that a 'peopled wound' may be a good way to conceptualise many instances of voice-hearing.

Change over time

There has not been a great deal of work on how AVHs change over time.[8] Nayani & David (1996) report that patients who had had voices for more than a year were more likely to report complex voices (i.e. a greater number of voices, which uttered more words, and were more likely to have a dialogue with the voice-hearer) than those who had had them for less than a year, suggesting that voices developed in complexity over time. They also noted a trend for voices to change from being externallly to internally located over time. In some cases AVHs may evolve out of much more basic forms of auditory hallucinations. For example, Almeida *et al.* (1993) report the case of a 77-year-old who heard voices.[9] Before hearing voices the patient had lost her husband, and over a period of five years had become increasingly deaf in her right ear, contributing to her becoming more socially isolated. One year before her hospital admission she started to notice 'white noise' in her right ear. This then changed into sounds such as knocking and tapping, then a few weeks later, hearing music. Soon afterwards she began to hear the neighbours' voices commenting on her snoring. As the voices grew more frequent she sought hospital treatment.

AVHs may also evolve out of hypnagogic hallucinations. For example, Bleuler (1950) noted that some AVHs 'first appear as the ordinary dream; then they appear in the hypnagogic state; then finally in the full waking state' (p. 116). Here Emanuel Swedenborg's experiences, as discussed in Chapter 3, are instructive. Swedenborg's voice-hearing experiences were developmentally preceded by hypnagogic hallucinations (Jones & Fernyhough, 2009a). In an earlier paper of mine (Jones, 2010a) I give the example of a voice-hearer diagnosed with schizophrenia, who initially developed an AVH, the content of which was a voice saying (verbatim) phrases which had actually been said to them during a traumatic event. However, over time their AVH changed to become the voice of the same individual (from the traumatic event) but now saying novel things. Hence, it is worth considering the possibility that the mechanisms that may form the original basis for an AVH (e.g. a verbal intrusion of a specific memory of trauma) may later change, resulting in a different type of voice, potentially underpinned by different mechanisms (such as inner speech). Little is known, though, about how this may occur or the neural networks involved in this voice evolution.

---

[8] How voices change in response to antipsychotic medication is discussed in Chapter 8.
[9] Although this individual did not receive a psychiatric diagnosis, the progression of the experience is nonetheless interesting.

A small number of studies have also examined how the voice-hearer's relation to their voice changes over time. For example, Thomas, McLeod & Brewin (2009) found the longer a person has had their voice, the more likely they are to be submissive to it. Much more work remains to be done in this area, though. In Chapter 12 we will examine how some therapeutic interventions can change the voice-hearer's voice over time, and in Chapter 8 how antipsychotic drugs can change the voice over time.

AVHs in other psychiatric and medical conditions: prevalence and phenomenology

Post-traumatic stress disorder (AVH prevalence c.50%)

Post-traumatic stress disorder (PTSD) is defined in the DSM-IV-TR (APA, 2000) as the exposure of a person to a traumatic event which leads to the development of characteristic symptoms such as re-experiencing the event, avoidance of stimuli associated with the trauma and increased arousal (sleep difficulties, hypervigilance, difficulty in concentrating). In some 'severe and chronic cases' the DSM notes that auditory hallucinations may be present, although the diagnostic criteria for PTSD suggest that these are likely to relate to flashbacks to the traumatic event itself. However, as we will see here, such voices are remarkably phenomenologically similar to those in patients diagnosed with psychotic disorders.

According to the research literature, rates of PTSD are high. However, these results should be considered in the context of many experienced clinicians reporting that they actually find AVHs in such patients to be quite rare. This inconsistency remains to be resolved. In a study of 45 participants with PTSD, Anketell et al. (2010) found that 50 per cent heard voices. Of these, half reported their voices as being of people directly involved in their trauma (e.g. the perpetrator). There were both unpleasant voices goading people to kill themselves, as well as supportive voices (e.g. an 'inner guide'). Most voices were located inside individuals' heads, issued commands, and were as loud and clear as a real voice. Only 40 per cent of voice-hearers linked their voices to their earlier traumas. Importantly, the content of the voices was often *symbolically* related to the trauma, and was not like a literal flashback to it. In a small but phenomenologically detailed study of thirty PTSD patients, where the trauma had arisen from a trauma in adulthood (although 50% also reported childhood trauma), Brewin & Patel (2010) found that 67 per cent of patients reported hearing voices. All patients regarded these as being a manifestation of their own thoughts. About half of the sample only heard one voice, with the rest hearing between two and ten voices. Most of the voices were male, and most were recognised, either as being the self, a friend, parent, or other. Most referred to the patient as 'you', and patients typically heard voices many times a day. Twenty-two per cent of patients described the effect of the voice as positive, but 75 per cent said its effect was negative. The majority of patients heard the voice for the first time after the trauma in adulthood. For both positive and negative voices, half of the PTSD voice-hearers were able to disagree with their voices. The positive voices were viewed by the majority of patients as encouraging, rational, supportive and strong. In contrast, the negative voices were viewed by the majority of patients as being critical, angry, intimidating and strong. Brewin (2003) also notes that such voices are likely to comment, not necessarily favourably, on both the PTSD therapist and the process of therapy itself.

In Chapter 11 I will go on to examine the relationship between specifically childhood trauma and AVHs in more detail, but here I will focus on the most studied sub-group of PTSD sufferers with AVHs, namely combat veterans, where it is common to find, to adapt Wilfred Owen, voices parading before helpless hearing. A range of studies have found the occurrence of voices in such individuals (e.g. Brewin & Patel, 2010, N = 93, prevalence = 58%; David et al., 1999, N = 53, prevalence = 38%; Hamner et al., 1999, N = 45, prevalence = 47%; Mueser & Butler, 1987, N = 36, prevalence = 14%; Wilcox, Briones & Suess, 1991, N = 59, prevalence 29%). A weighted average of this limited range of studies suggests that 41 per cent of combat veterans with PTSD hear voices. In the most recent study, which was of 158 ex-servicemen and women from the United Kingdom's armed forces with current, past and no PTSD, Brewin & Patel (2010) asked about voice-hearing experiences, using item 27 of the Dissociative Experiences Scale: 'Some people sometimes find that they hear voices inside their head that tell them to do things or comment on things they are doing. Circle a number to show what percentage of the time this happens to you.' Sixty five per cent of the past PTSD group endorsed this item, 58 per cent of the current PTSD group and 21 per cent of the no PTSD group, thus highlighting that the presence of PTSD is associated with an increased prevalence of AVHs compared to control veterans without PTSD. Culture also appears to play a role in the likelihood of hearing voices in combat veterans, with studies in the United States showing that Hispanic veterans with PTSD are more likely to hear voices than other cultural groups (Mueser & Butler, 1997; Wilcox et al., 1991).

Reports on the phenomenology of voices in combat veterans paint a remarkably consistent picture. The majority have voices which are related to the earlier combat situation, with non-combat-related voices (e.g. voices whispering with unidentifiable content) commonly co-occurring with these combat-related voices (Hamner *et al.*, 1999). Indeed, David *et al.* (1999) found that all voices heard by veterans (mostly of the Vietnam War) in their study 'reflected combat themes and guilt', including hearing voices of dead comrades calling 'help' or 'medic' or 'people screaming in the back of my head' (p. 30). Yet case studies show that the voices that are heard are not typically simple flashback-like experiences to verbalisations at the time of the combat. Although cries and groans from the actual time of combat are sometimes heard (David *et al.*, 1999; Mueser & Butler, 1987), veterans mostly seem to hear voices they could never actually have heard before. For example, Bleich & Moskowits (2000) report the case of a 39-year-old man whose tank was hit by a shell during battle. He was injured and a number of his comrades were killed. Several weeks later he started to hear the voices of his dead comrades accusing him of having betrayed them by leaving them and remaining alive. The voices also commanded him to join them by committing suicide.

Indeed, a very common theme can be seen to run through the voices of veterans: kill yourself. In a study of thirty-six veterans with PTSD, Mueser & Butler (1987) found five heard voices. The first, a Korean War veteran, heard voices inside his head of people he believed he had killed in Korea and of some recently deceased relatives. These voices cried to him, criticised him and encouraged him to kill himself. The second, another Korean War veteran, a week after shooting a Korean soldier who was wounded, started to hear the voice of this soldier urging him to kill himself. The third, a Vietnam War veteran, heard the voice of a friend who had been killed in combat, which sometimes just spoke to him, but at other times told him to kill himself. The fourth, another Korean War veteran, hospitalised with guilt and depression over soldiers he had killed, heard voices of fellow soldiers telling him to kill himself and that it was time for him to join those he had killed. The final voice-hearer, a Vietnam War veteran, was the only one not hearing voices to kill himself – instead he heard the voices of those he had killed, laughter, mortar and gunfire. Notably, these soldiers did not have any other symptoms commonly associated with psychosis, such as delusions. Mueser & Butler's study was also noteworthy for its examination of differences between PTSD patients with and without voices. The only difference to emerge (once one applies a Bonferroni correction to their findings) was that patients with AVHs were more likely than PTSD patients without AVHs to have no leisure activities.

In summary, a large number of studies over the past decades show that the experience of hearing critical or abusive voices is relatively common in soldiers who have been in combat situations such as Vietnam or Korea. The next question we thus have to ask is, has this always been the case? Have soldiers in battles such as in World War Two (WWII), World War I (WWI), the Boer War, the American Civil War, Waterloo, the Wars of the Roses, all commonly experienced such voices following combat? One reason to ask this question is the argument that has been put forward that the form that PTSD symptoms take is culture-bound. Thus, shell-shock after WWI typically took the form of bodily symptoms (tics, body movements), and after the American Civil War took the form of an aching in the left side of the chest and a feeling of a weak heartbeat (Watters, 2010). Although detailed records only go back so far, voices can be seen in the aftermath of both WWII and WWI. For example, in WWII, Gottschalk (2004) relates how James Todd and his friend Fred Buckley were on a naval destroyer ship when it was attacked by a submarine. Fred was killed in front of James, who survived. After the event James started to hear voices saying that he was unworthy of surviving. Voices can also been found in soldiers as part of the shell-shock syndrome following WWI. Indeed, the books and medical journals of the time are full of references to hearing voices in the context of shell-shock (e.g. Eager, 1918; Marr, 1919). We already saw one example in Chapter 3, Box 3.3. To give another example, Eager (1918) gives an example of a 'Private D' who 'was subjected to very heavy bombardment in the trenches, and said that he absolutely could not stand it and had to put his fingers in his ears – it so frightened him'. After being sent back to England following complaining of pains in the head and noises in the ears, he reported that he heard 'the voice of God' reprimanding him for his past misdeeds. Thus, going back a century at least, voices seem to be a fairly consistent and common reaction to combat stress, and from the above, as we will return to in Chapter 11, guilt and shame seem likely to play an important role in these.

Dissociative identity disorder (AVH prevalence: 70–90%)

The essential feature of dissociative disorders, according to the DSM-IV-TR (APA, 2000) is a 'disruption in the usually integrated functions of consciousness, memory, identity, or perception' (p. 519). The most prominent of the dissociative disorders is Dissociative identity disorder (DID; formerly known as multiple personality disorder). DID is characterised by the presence of two or more distinct identities or personalities (which have their own idiosyncratic ways of thinking and viewing the world, self and others), which recurrently take charge of the person's behaviour (DSM-IV-TR). The DSM specifically mentions voices in the context of DID, observing that 'An identity that is not in control may nonetheless gain access to consciousness by producing auditory or visual hallucinations (e.g. a voice giving instructions)' (pp. 526–7). This echoes Morton Prince's model of voice-hearing from Chapter 3. Patients with this diagnosis have often experienced childhood physical and/or sexual abuse, much like many individuals with a diagnosis of psychosis (see Chapter 11).

In terms of prevalence of voice-hearing in DID, a study by Ross, Miller et al. (1990) of 348 patients with multiple personality disorder, found that 71 per cent reported hearing voices commenting, and 74 per cent heard voices arguing. In a sub-set of this sample, 94 per cent said that these voices came from inside their head. Other authors have concluded that up to 90 per cent of DID patients hear voices (Şar & Öztürk, 2008). Hearing voices in DID can take three forms: hearing the voices of alter personalities; voices heard in the context of flashbacks; and hearing voices experiences like those documented in psychotic disorders (Dell, 2006). It is unclear what the various ratios of these types of voices are, but many appear to be those of alter personalities (e.g. Lewis et al., 1997).

Can we distinguish phenomenologically between AVHs in those with a diagnosis of DID and those classified as having a psychotic disorder? Steinberg & Siegal (2008) argue that we can, with 'the voices associated with a person with schizophrenia typically including bizarre and delusional content' and in contrast, the voices of DID patients having 'appropriate content without delusions or bizarreness' (p. 179). Yet it is unclear what they mean by bizarre content, what constitutes 'appropriate content', and they give no detailed phenomenological comparisons. However, a study by Honig et al. (1998) did directly compare the phenomenology of voices heard by patients diagnosed with schizophrenia (N = 18) and patients with DID (N = 15). They found[10] that AVHs in the two groups (SZ vs DID) did not differ greatly on the extent to which the voices talked *to* the patients (94% vs 93%), talked *about* the patients (61% vs 53%), commented on their behaviour (72% vs 80%), commented about others (61% vs 60%), were supportive/encouraging (83% vs 67%), critical/abusive (100% vs 93%), located outside the head (78% vs 67%). The larger differences that did emerge

---

[10] Although Honig et al. (1998) do not report the statistical significance of these comparisons, this can simply enough be worked out from their data. However, none of the differences were statistically significant (using a chi-squared test with a Bonferroni corrected alpha of 0.003). This is likely due to the small sample size not giving the study enough power to detect differences. Hence, here I can only indicate suggestive 'larger' and 'smaller' differences.

showed that DID patients were more likely to have voices inside the head (73% vs 50%) and were less likely to dialogue with the voices (33% vs 67%). In another study comparing AVHs in DID with AVHs in patients diagnosed with schizophrenia, Dorahy *et al.* (2009) found that the DID sample were more likely both to hear voices before the age of 18, to hear more than 2 voices and to hear both child and adult voices. Interestingly, command AVHs were more common in the DID group (72%) compared to patients diagnosed with schizophrenia who had not suffered childhood maltreatment (44%), but comparable to patients diagnosed with schizophrenia who had suffered childhood maltreatment (81%). The voices of DID patients were also more likely to be replays of things that had previously been said to them than in the patients diagnosed with schizophrenia. Going beyond DID specifically, AVHs appear to be associated with dissociative experiences generally. Moskowitz & Corstens (2007) note that, to date, four studies have 'demonstrated robust links between AH and dissociative experiences' (p. 51). Hence, it appears that voices in DID have a significant phenomenological overlap with those in patients who have been given diagnoses of psychotic disorders.

Borderline personality disorder (AVH prevalence c.32%)

A significant number of patients with borderline personality disorder (BPD) experience AVHs. In a study of 171 patients with BPD by Yee *et al.* (2005), 29.2 per cent were found to report voices. In a smaller study of 30 patients with BPD, Kingdon *et al.* (2010) found 50 per cent experienced AVHs. A weighted average of these two studies suggests that a tentative estimate of the prevalence of AVHs in BPD is 32 per cent, although more studies are clearly needed.

Yee *et al.* (2005) examined in detail the voices of 10 individuals with BPD. These voices were found not to be brief and fragmentary, but 'pervasive'. Somewhat paradoxically, 90 per cent of these patients described their voices as having the quality of true perceptions, yet 80 per cent also described the experience as similar to thoughts. All patients had negative voices, including ones which tormented them, instructed them to hurt themselves, and some which were 'multiple, critical, and terrifying [voices, that] ... often came in the form of a scream' (p. 150). However, 40 per cent had protective voices. All 10 patients had experienced having a conversation with their voices, and six had written conversations with them. This phenomenology of voices was similar to that found in an earlier, smaller study by Suzuki *et al.* (1998). In this study of five patients with BPD and hallucinations/delusions, voices were found which tormented and criticised, but these were all reported to be voices of people that patients knew well. One patient, after a fellow patient committed suicide by jumping from the roof of the hospital, began to experience a voice which commanded her to jump from the roof. From these studies it appears that the voices in BPD do not differ significantly in their phenomenology from the voices found in psychosis. This conclusion is supported by a direct comparison of voices in BPD and schizophrenia by Kingdon et al. (2010), who found that there were no significant differences (if a Bonferroni correction is applied for the number of analysis of variance tests they performed) in the frequency, location, duration, loudness, amount of negative content, distress, disruption or controllability between these two groups.

Post-partum voices

Voices may also occur shortly after a woman gives birth.[11] These appear to be relatively rare, occurring after only 0.1 per cent of births (Kaplan & Sadock, 1981, as cited in Aleman & Larøi, 2008).

Epilepsy

AVHs in epilepsy may occur in the context of either simple partial seizures (in which seizure activity is limited to specific regions of the brain and consciousness is not impaired), complex partial seizures (where consciousness is impaired), as well as in the period immediately surrounding generalised tonic-clonic seizures (in which activity spreads over the whole brain leading to 'grand mal' seizures with muscle convulsions and impaired consciousness).

AVHs are most commonly found as part of the seizure pattern in medial and lateral temporal lobe epilepsy (TLE). Although exact prevalence figures for AVHs during seizures are not available, in a study of 8,000 patients with epilepsy which identified 119 patients with seizures with auditory features (which accounts for around 1% of cases of epilepsy), AVHs were found to occur in up to 40 per cent of a sub-set of these patients during simple, complex or generalised seizures (Bisulli et al., 2004). In a study of 666 patients with TLE, Currie et al. (1971) found that auditory hallucinations occurred in 16 per cent of seizures, with elaborate auditory hallucinations being five times rarer than more basic ones.[12] The phenomenology of seizure-related AVHs has been described in a number of case reports. For example, Karagulla & Robertson (1955)

[11] We may note Margery Kempe in Chapter 1.
[12] It is unclear how many, if any, of these were actually speech.

describe the case of an 18-year-old bilingual individual with TLE who, as part of his seizure pattern, heard a voice in his head which spoke in short sentences giving him commands or threatening him, and a 7-year-old boy with TLE who heard a man's voice in his stomach during a seizure, which also gave commands. Other examples of AVHs immediately surrounding seizures are given by Penfield & Perot (1963). Of one patient they noted that 'In the beginning of an attack he would hear a male voice saying, "Someone call a doctor, someone call a doctor". He also stated that at the end of his attacks he heard the same male voice saying, "It's all over, forget the doctor"' (p. 658). Another patient, just before an attack, 'frequently heard a voice saying strange words which he could not understand' (ibid.).

AVHs in epilepsy are also quite common as a result of the schizophrenia-like psychosis that may also co-occur in such patients (see Sachdev, 2004 for a review). Estimates of the prevalence of psychosis in epilepsy vary. For example, a large Danish study by Bredkjaer, Mortensen & Parnas (1998; N = 67,116, Denmark) found a prevalence of 0.4 per cent, whereas Gaitatzis *et al.* (2004; N = 5,834, UK) found a rate of 9 per cent. Following seizures, AVHs may occur in post-ictal states (typically defined as being within a week after a seizure or cluster of seizures, and the associated AVHs lasting less than a few months). Both post-ictal hallucinosis (hallucinations present, but no other psychotic experiences) and post-ictal psychosis may occur. However, it is possible that some post-ictal psychoses may be due to ongoing seizure activity and should therefore be categorised as non-convulsive status epilepticus (Elliott, Joyce & Shorvon, 2009). AVHs may also occur in inter-ictal psychosis (defined as psychotic symptoms in clear consciousness lasting for more than 6 months, and not being related to seizure activity). For example, Takeda *et al.* (2001) reported a 25-year-old woman with TLE who, two days after a cluster of 18 seizures, started hearing the voices of her parents. In one of the largest studies of specifically AVHs in epilepsy (N = 808) Kanemoto, Kawasaki & Kawai (1996) found that a total of 2.2 per cent of epileptic patients with TLE experienced AVHs in the form of voices commenting (data was not reported on other specific types of voices), in periods clearly demarcated from seizures themselves. Of these, 1.1 per cent had inter-ictal psychosis, 0.1 per cent post-ictal psychosis and 1.0 per cent chronic psychosis.

Voices in patients with epilepsy with psychosis have the features of voices associated with psychosis as described above. In a recent study of voices in patients with epilepsy without psychosis (which appear to be inter-ictal AVHs), Korsnes *et al.* (2010), in a small sample (N = 6), found that two-thirds of the patients heard more than one voice, with one-third always hearing the same voice. For all the patients the voices were unpleasant, awful or scary, and lasted for either seconds or minutes. However, phenomenological properties of voices common in patients diagnosed with psychosis were relatively rarer in those patients with epilepsy. For example, only one of the patients (i.e. 17%) had voices which gave commands, and even then it was only 'sometimes'; only 2 patients (i.e. 33%) had voices which talked about events in the world, and only one patient (17%) heard the voices more than once daily. Due to a paucity of large-scale studies, it remains somewhat unclear how much phenomenological similarity is shared between AVHs resulting from epilepsy, and those in individuals with psychiatric diagnoses such as those reviewed above.

Alcohol and hearing voices

Alcohol is known to be able to cause AVHs, although what percentage of people who abuse alcohol go on to experience AVHs is unknown. Alcoholic hallucinosis is characterized by an acute onset of predominantly auditory verbal hallucinations that occur either during or after a period of heavy alcohol consumption (Perme, Chandrasekharan & Vijaysagar, 2003). This term was coined by Bleuler, who believed that alcohol unmasked 'schizophrenic symptoms' (Alpert & Silvers, 1970). The voices may continue even after the patient has stopped drinking. For example, Medlicott (1958) gives the case of a middle-aged man who, after a heavy bout of drinking, began to hear voices. These voices persisted and were of several men and one woman, who swore at him and told him to do things. This did not appear to cause major problems however, as 'after the "voices" started he gave up the roving life he had led, built up a prosperous business, and married ... there has been nothing unusual apparent about him' (p. 670). Medlicott noted that when the individual drank excessively again, the voices would become more insistent.

Hearing voices is also found during alcohol withdrawal (delirium tremens), although visual hallucinations are more common in this condition (Platz, Oberlaender & Seidl, 1995). In a sample of 64 patients with delirium tremens, they found that 76 per cent had auditory hallucinations, and of these, 65 per cent were voices. These voices included ones telling the voice-hearer to kill themselves. The mean length for which the voice-hearing lasted was 57 hours (range 1–720 hours). A number of interesting cases of AVHs in delirium tremens were reported by Bevan Lewis (1885). A 34-year-old man had two attacks of delirium tremens, and heard instructive remarks on God and the Virgin Mary in his right ear, but vulgar and obscene language in his left ear (this echoes a phenomenon noted in some individuals diagnosed with psychotic disorders by Kraepelin and Bleuler, above). Another patient heard a voice in his left ear which used insulting terms, whilst in his right ear he heard a voice using consolatory expressions.[13]

Bleuler observed that AVHs in alcoholic hallucinosis have 'peculiar character: that is they discuss him in the third person; much more rarely they speak to him. These voices threaten him also ... some of them side with the patient' (Bleuler, 1916, as cited in Glass, 1989, p. 31). Indeed, such AVHs are typically threatening and have obscene content (Glass, 1989). Are alcohol-related voices really different to those in psychosis, though? In a comparison between the AVHs of alcoholic patients and the AVHs of psychiatric patients (mainly diagnosed with schizophrenia), Deiker & Chambers (1978) found that AVHs were very similar in these two groups. The groups did not differ in the extent to which the voice was likely to be human speech (although the alcoholics were more likely to hear animal noises), whether the voices spoke exclusively in the second ('you') or third person ('he/she'), or in the voice's gender or identity. However, an earlier study by Alpert & Silvers (1970), who compared the AVHs of 18 patients with alcohol hallucinosis to 45 patients diagnosed with schizophrenia, did find some subtle differences. The patients with alcohol hallucinosis were found to be more likely than the patients with schizophrenia to have voices occurring many times each day (94% vs 66%), to have the source of the voices located externally (100% vs 68%) with a specific location (67% vs 27%). However, the patients diagnosed with schizophrenia were more likely than the alcoholic patients to have their voices become more frequent when they were emotionally aroused (49% vs 17%) and when they were socially isolated (60% vs 6%). Their study did not bear out Bleuler's claim that it was rare for those with alcoholic hallucinosis to be talked to by their voices (as opposed to talked about).

Other drugs and hearing voices

Cannabis use is also thought to be able to cause AVHs, and appears particularly likely to be able to do this in individuals with specific genotypes (Caspi et al., 2005). However, it is unknown what percentage of cannabis users experience AVHs. One qualitative study (Costain, 2008) found some voice-hearers used cannabis because it made their voices 'louder and clearer' which helped them to cope with them, as the

---

[13] It would be interesting to see if this pattern holds more generally, as this would have implications for neural lateralisation of different kinds of voices.

voices became easier to understand and control. Other drugs which may lead to AVHs include ketamine, which has been reported in one case to lead to hearing 'a demon's voice' (Lim, 2003), cocaine (Siegal, 1978), phencyclidine (PCP, or 'angel dust') (Petersen & Stillman, 1978) and some psychedelics. Although the hallucinations resulting from psychedelics such as LSD, psilocybin and dimethyltryptamine (DMT) appear to be predominantly visual or felt-presence experiences (Kleinman, Gillin & Wyatt, 1977), voices are also experienced. In a series of studies in which DMT was administered intravenously, Strassman (2001) found that 'it was quite rare for volunteers to hear formed voices ... rather there were simply sounds ... "whining and whirring" ... "crinkling and crunching"' (p. 148). However, there were some reports of hearing voices; 'an inner voice spoke to me' (p. 8), 'I heard two to three voices talking. I heard one of them say, "He's arrived"' (p. 193). The Copernicus of consciousness, Terence McKenna (1946–2000), also reported hearing voices, in conjunction with visual hallucinations, while under the influence of psilocybin (McKenna, 1993). Similarly, William Burroughs describes hearing voices after taking amphetamines: 'I started hearing whispers from people in the bedspread, and in the window glass, and though I was a little embarrassed at first, I answered them, thinking, why deny anything' (Burroughs, 1971, as cited in Kleinman et al., 1977, p. 569).

Voices very rarely may also occur as the result of side-effects of medications. For example, Paraskevaides (1988) reports that a 50-year-old man with no history of mental illness was given a single tablet of the narcotic analgesic buprenorphine (200mg) after a haemorrhoidectomy and then reported hearing voices which were instructing him to perform various chores on the ward. When interviewed by the duty psychiatrist, the patient stood up and threw himself out of the (4th floor) window. He survived, and later questioning revealed that he had been ordered to jump by the voices. He did not experience any voices subsequently. Another case study reported a woman who began to hear voices after taking the antidepressant drug mirtazapine (Padala et al., 2010). Lantz & Giambanco (2000) report AVHs in a 78-year-old woman following treatment with Celecoxib, a non-steroidal anti-inflammatory agent. Interestingly, for our understanding of how voices may develop, she started by hearing thumping sounds which progressively increased to the experience of hearing voices calling her name and repeating words from the television and radio. After discontinuing the drug, the voices ceased. In the twentieth century, bromides were used in certain sleeping drugs or for 'calming the nerves'. Such bromides have been found to cause the experience of hearing voices (Levin, 1960), most famously being thought to play a role in the voices heard by Evelyn Waugh, which were disclosed in a fictionalised account of his own experiences reported in his novel, *The Ordeal of Gilbert Pinfold* (Lynch, 1986). There is also some evidence that high caffeine intake, particularly under conditions of stress, may make AVHs more likely (Crowe *et al.*, 2011; Jones & Fernyhough, 2009b). Finally, chemicals ingested as toxic fumes may also cause AVHs, with Randolph (1970) noting the case of an individual who developed voices as a consequence of their job disassembling fuel-pump carburettors of aeroplanes (this poor young man's voices did not subside after being removed from the situation, and he remained tragically hospitalised in a mental institution).

Parkinson's disease (AVH prevalence c.8%)

AVHs are found in Parkinson's disease and appear to have a prevalence in the range of 2–10 per cent (e.g. Fenelon *et al.*, 2000; Graham, Grunewald & Sagar, 1997; Holroyd, Currie & Wooten, 2001; Inzelberg, Kipervasser & Korczyn, 1998; Matsui *et al.*, 2007). However, visions are more common than voices in this condition (Henderson & Mellers, 2000; Holroyd, Currie & Wooten, 2001). Studies reporting prevalence have varying estimates (Fenelon *et al.*, 2000, N = 219, 21AVHs; Graham, Grunewald & Sagar, 1997, N = 129, 2AVHs; Holroyd, Currie & Wooten, 2001, N = 98, 2AVHs; Inzelberg, Kipervasser & Korczyn, 1998,[14] N = 121, 10AVHs). A weighted average of these studies gives a prevalence of AVHs of 8 per cent. Inzelberg and colleagues found that all patients who heard voices also experienced visual hallucinations (although not at the same time, i.e. none of the visions talked). These voices were externally located, spoke in the first or second person, and only one voice-hearer had a voice that was imperative (i.e. gave instructions/commands). Only one of Inzelberg *et al.*'s sample volunteered that they heard voices, the rest only reported this when directly challenged, saying that they felt embarrassed about it (and had not told their clinicians either).

Alzheimer's disease (AVH point prevalence c.12%)

Voices also occur in Alzheimer's disease. In a review paper, Bassiony & Lyketsos (2003) found a wide range of prevalence of auditory

---

[14] Inzelberg, Kipervasser & Korczyn's study contains at least one AVH which may be bereavement-related. Indeed, some or many Parkinson's or Alzheimer's patients may have AVHs relating to bereavement rather than their medical conditions.

hallucinations, ranging from 1 per cent to 29 per cent, with a mean value of 12 per cent. They do not, though, state whether these are specifically voices. The prevalence reported by studies varied widely partly because of the methodology used. For example, a study which found a prevalence of 28 per cent (Craig *et al.*, 2005) assessed this by using the criteria 'patient describes hearing voices or acting as if he/she hears voices' (p. 463). Care-givers' accounts also report a higher prevalence than patient accounts (Burns, Jacoby & Levy, 1990). In their large study of 178 patients with Alzheimer's disease, 9.6 per cent were found to hear voices. Furthermore, patients with voices had higher rates of cognitive deterioration than patients without voices. In a later smaller study (N = 56) Forstl *et al.* (1994) found a comparable rate of 12.5 per cent. Little is known about the phenomenology of such voices.

Brain traumas

Moderate to severe head injuries may cause AVHs. Although as many as 50 per cent of individuals with such injuries may experience auditory hallucinations, it is unknown what percentage of these are specifically AVHs (Fujii & Ahmed, 2002). Brain lesions resulting from incidents such as traumatic brain injury, haemorrhage, cerebrovascular disease and tumours, can also result in AVHs. For example, Tanabe *et al.* (1986) found that a lesion (hemorrhagic infarction) in an individual's left superior temporal gyrus caused them to hear a voice in their right ear. In a systematic review of auditory hallucinations following brain lesions, Braun *et al.* (2003) found that in the 19 cases where auditory hallucinations occurred, 74 per cent took the form of hearing voices experiences. These voices could be telling the patient where to go, 'haunting voices', that of a radio announcer, the patient's own voice, children crying, or a murmuring crowd. However, Braun and colleagues note that the phenomenology of AVHs following lesions are different to those experienced in psychosis. Specifically, 'the content of the hallucinated speech does not correspond to any apparent emotional or moral obsession of the patient (as seems to occur in psychosis), the speech is often a conversation among several people known to the patient or singing by a person heard previously by the patient, and the speech is often of a person of the opposite sex' (p. 433). Braun *et al.*'s systematic review of AVHs following brain lesions found that post-lesion AVHs were associated with lesions at a range of points along the auditory pathway (pons, inferior colliculus, medial geniculate body and temporal lobe). They conclude that 'the cases presented here are best explained by a neurotransmitter-independent, modality-specific neuronal loss, resulting in connection-based release of inhibition in the sensory cortex'. However, they note: 'We remain somewhat perplexed, however, by the paucity of published cases of auditory hallucinosis after a thalamic lesion' (p. 444). They also note that whereas the hallucinations of psychotic patients are more frequently auditory, post-lesion hallucinations are more frequently visual. They also advise that 'an isolated report of hallucination should be taken as a potential symptom of a brain lesion and should be diagnostically explored as such' (p. 446). They also note that treatment for such AVHs using therapies with classic neuroleptics, antidepressants or benzodiazepines have generally been found to be unpromising. Hence, it appears that the AVHs resulting from explicit brain injuries, and those of individuals who have received a psychiatric diagnosis, have different causes, phenomenologies and require different types of intervention.

AVHs in deaf individuals

Hearing loss in the elderly can lead to AVHs. For example, Cole *et al.* (2002) found that of 125 people aged over 65 years of age who were referred to a university audiology department for hearing impairments, 2.5 per cent reported hearing voices. However, beyond this, AVHs occur in deaf people who cannot hear normal speech and use lip-reading or sign language as their primary means of communication (for a review, see Atkinson, 2006). There have been two recent detailed empirical studies of this phenomenon. In the earlier of these, 17 deaf individuals diagnosed with schizophrenia were interviewed by du Feu & McKenna (1999) who found that 59 per cent had ongoing AVHs. Patients heard voices which they communicated to the researchers using the sign for talking. Five patients had been deaf since birth, and the majority of the rest were diagnosed as deaf before the age of 18 months. The authors also indicate that it is noteworthy that some also 'reported aspects of speech of which they could have no conception ... [such as] voices belonging to people they knew' (p. 457). Thus, one participant, deaf from birth, identified her voice as being that of a colleague at work – even though she could never actually have heard his voice. Another (also deaf from birth) heard God talking to him through his left ear, and was clear to distinguish between the normal experience of seeing people signing and this experience where he *heard* God. When patients were asked how they were able to hear voices, given that they were deaf, most participants either shrugged or said they didn't know, or indicated they didn't understand the question. The voices were much like those found in patients diagnosed with schizophrenia. They spoke in the second and third person, could be located in or outside the head, or both, and could be nasty or nice.

A later, larger and more detailed study of voice-hearing in deaf people was performed by Atkinson *et al.* (2007), who examined voice-hearing in 27 deaf individuals diagnosed with schizophrenia. They found a range of different types of voice-hearing experiences which were related to the nature of the deafness of the individual (profoundly deaf since birth, deafness onset after a hearing period, etc.). In individuals who had been profoundly deaf since birth, AVHs were reported to be non-auditory (i.e. there was no sound), clear and easy to understand. The deaf voice-hearers were certain that they did not hear any sound when voices were present, and did not consider questions about pitch, volume and loudness relevant to their experiences. This echoed the finding of an earlier study where the researcher asked a deaf participant about the acoustic properties of such hallucinated voices (e.g. pitch, volume or accent) and got the pithy response, 'How do I know? I'm deaf!' (Thacker, 1994, as cited in Atkinson, 2006, p. 702). Atkinson and colleagues found that in voice-hearers who had been profoundly deaf since birth, the identity and gender of the voice was known, but this was not deduced from the way it sounded. Instead, participants reported seeing an image of the voice communicating with them in their mind's eye when voice hallucinations were present. Although all participants had experienced seeing an image of the voice signing or lips moving in their mind, these images were faint, unclear, transparent and never solid. One participant stated (in a translation from British Sign Language) that 'All my voices sign to me, deaf school kids and the pope, even though he is hearing. I am not sure how I can communicate but voice is projected into my brain, it moves in my thoughts … hands and lips move and glow in my mind' (p. 352). Participants' voices were more widely believed to originate inside the head than outside. The voices were never perceived through the ears and there was a sense that participants 'just knew' what the voices were saying and that they might be understood via a sense of telepathy. Atkinson and colleagues note that this conveys that the heard voices are not physically sensual.

In Atkinson *et al.*'s (2007) study, reports of the voices heard by individuals who had some experience of hearing speech and used hearing aids were somewhat contradictory and confused. Voice-hearers were uncertain about whether their voice hallucinations were auditory in nature. The voices appeared to use speech/lip movements to convey their message, as well as fingerspelling and gesture occasionally, and were perceived as sometimes being silently articulated and sometimes having sound. One participant described how 'I hear him shouting through my stomach. I see black shadowy lips in my mind, but I don't lip read them really. It feels like it is in my mind but I use my sense of hearing. I'm not sure if I hear it or not. It's like I just know' (p. 353). In contrast, in individuals who were born moderately or moderately severely deaf and used hearing aids, voices were auditory and they could report that they could always hear sounds when the voices were present, with some participants able to make judgements about auditory proper-ties, including pitch and volume. One participant stated that 'I would hear Peggy Mitchell [from *Eastenders*] talking to me. I don't know how, I was just mad. I didn't lipread her. It was quite clear. I could hear her voice like on the TV. I heard my sister talking to me at night when I was in bed. I definitely heard something, so I put my hearing aids in to check but there was nothing there' (p. 354). Another individual indicated a co-occurring visual component, 'Most of the time the devil speaks and I hear him but sometimes he signs to me and I see him looking at me and signing in my mind' (ibid.).

In addition to the du Feu & McKenna (1999) and Atkinson *et al.* (2007) studies, other facets of voice-hearing which are notable in patients diagnosed with schizophrenia are also found in deaf patients diagnosed with schizophrenia. Thus, some deaf individuals diagnosed with schizophrenia can hear voices inside their body, with Critchley *et al.* (1981) describing a deaf voice-hearer diagnosed with schizophrenia who experienced men and women talking in her chest. One of the voices wanted to marry her. As both the du Feu & McKenna and Atkinson *et al.* studies examined deaf patients diagnosed with schizophrenia, it is not known what the prevalence of voices is in the general deaf population. In contrast, there have been an extensive number of studies of voice-hear-ing in the general population (see Chapter 7).

AVHs in non-verbal quadriplegics

Hamilton (1985) studied 220 individuals who were physically handi-capped to the extent that they required total care, not being able to walk, talk, bathe, toilet or dress themselves. Communication methods were developed and participants were able to signal 'yes' or 'no', via methods such as tongue, lip or hand movements, in response to questions put to them. Seven individuals were found who were able to understand what was said to them, learn and retain information in a normal manner. Asking about hearing voices would not immediately strike one as an obvious question, but nevertheless Hamilton inquired about this. Of the seven, five responded to the question as to whether they heard voices with 'startled expressions followed by excited "yes" signals' (p. 383).

One of the cases was that of Tim, a 27-year-old with a diagnosis of athetoid-spastic quadriplegia due to perinatal hypoxia. Tim felt that it was grossly unfair that he was able to live in this world only as a spectator, and as such was lonely, depressed and angry. The following statement was confirmed by Tim as being true:

You actually hear a voice like there is someone in the room. It's a real voice; you hear him with your ears. It's a man's voice; it is God talking to you. He started after you came here; he never came before [Tim was institutionalised at the age of 14]. You don't know how he comes but you are glad of it. This is unusual; others don't have it. You keep it private. You ask questions, but he does not answer. It is not a two-way conversation; he talks to you. He passes judgment, says what is good or bad. If you have bad thoughts about your parents, he criticizes you. He praises your good actions . . . When you want peace and quiet, which you do often, you can't make him go away . . . When your parents first left you here, you were frightened; then he talked to you and calmed you' (p. 385).

Others in the study reported similar voices. Ron, aged 30, had athetoid-spastic quadriplegia due to a brain injury at birth, and his voice had been with him since childhood. He heard a man's voice, like his uncle, which came from his left side, directed him to do things and was a pleasant voice that kept him company. When Ron disagreed with the voice, it could give him a hard time. Ann, aged 29, first heard her voice when she was moved to a new area of her institution. Both her and Mary, aged 38, heard a voice which told them what is good and bad, and what they should and shouldn't do. Mary's voice told her to forgive her parents (her mother didn't realise Mary could understand everything and didn't work out a yes–no signal with her). The voice sometimes made her feel imposed upon and personally devalued and she was happiest when the voice was absent. The only person with a purely negative voice was Beth, aged 30. What Beth wanted most was what was least available to her: a few close friends who have time to take a special and enduring interest in her. Her voice was like her mother's, and told Beth what to do, and never to talk back. The voice said that her grandmother would die, and it always came at night when everyone was in bed. This voice did not come to help, but wanted to hurt, and Beth was frightened by her. Helen, aged 37, heard her grand-mother's voice, which started soon after she died. None of the voice-hearers interviewed could talk back to their voices, although Larry, 21, notes that although he can't talk back to it, the voice listens to his thoughts. The voice-hearers were also aware of the negative valuation that society puts on voice-hearing.

In summary, the voices that the participants in this study hear are much like those found in patients with psychosis. They occur on a daily basis, have a specific location in external space, involve commands, suggestions relating to ongoing events and often have an evaluative tone. However, unlike in psychosis, these patients could not talk back to their voices. As we will see in Chapter 11, the likely causes of many of these voices (stress, bereavement, loneliness, isolation) may be the same for other individuals who hear voices, irrespective of their diagnosis.

Chapter 4: summary of key points

- AVHs in psychosis have a typical form which involves issuing commands, guidance and evaluative comments directed at the voice-hearer and the ongoing events in their life.
- Such voice-hearers will typically hear a mix of positive and negative voices, although the negative voices predominate.
- The majority of such voice-hearers can hold a conversation with their voices.
- Voices showing self-preservative reactions increase the feeling they are real, and not self-produced.
- There is extensive phenomenological variation within this group with some, for example, stating their voices are like clearly heard external speech, whilst others report voices which are more like ideas than speech.
- The perceived reality of voices in this group is not dependent on whether they are perceived to be external or internal to the head.
- Other types of voices may also be heard, such as repetitive voices, or simply random words. How and why these AVHs may evolve into the more typical, interactive voices is not well understood.
- The phenomenology of AVHs when compared between individuals with different psychiatric diagnoses such as PTSD, dissociative identity disorder, schizophrenia, bipolar disorder and borderline personality disorder shows many more similarities than differences.
- Voice-hearing in certain groups, such as the general deaf population and non-verbal quadriplegics, remains under-researched.
- Voice-hearing across many psychiatric diagnoses and medical conditions may be underpinned by similar causal mechanisms and require similar interventions.

5 The lived experience of hearing voices in individuals diagnosed with a psychotic disorder: or, the journey from patient to non-patient

In Chapter 4 we established what voices are like in people who have received psychiatric diagnoses. This tells us nothing about what it is like for these individuals to live with voices, though, and we may rightly ask what their lived experience of hearing voices is actually like. In the first half of this chapter we will draw on the peer-reviewed qualitative literature in this area. This will show that loss and recovery of basic human needs are fundamental themes reported by voice-hearers who have entered and then emerged from patienthood. The second part of the chapter will then focus on the more radical emancipatory approach to voice-hearing, as developed in the work of Marius Romme and the Hearing Voices Movement (see Chapter 3) and will compare and contrast the conclusions of this approach with the existing qualitative literature.

The lived experience of voice-hearing in individuals diagnosed with psychotic disorders

A decade ago, the Division of Clinical Psychology of the British Psychological Society issued a report addressing recent advances in the understanding of psychosis (BPS, 2000). The report noted that psychological services should 'ask about what the [psychotic] experiences mean to the person and how he or she understands them' (p. 60). In recognition of the importance of gaining knowledge of individuals' own understanding of their experiences of psychosis, the decade since this recommendation has seen the emergence of a significant body of research into this area. This has taken the form of qualitative studies where participants are asked open-ended questions about their experiences, and their replies transcribed verbatim and analysed. This starts to allow some voice-hearers' voices to be heard,[1] although it is noteworthy that it is still a

---

[1] We will examine the debate around hearing voice-hearers' own accounts of their experiences, and the debate over the medical model in Chapter 12.

researcher defining the broad questions, and in many of these studies respondent validation (i.e. asking the participant if they agree with the findings of the study) is not employed. Whilst most studies have studied the general experience of psychosis or schizophrenia, rather than voice-hearing in itself, a picture can still be created from this literature of what the lived experience of voices in people in the psychiatric system is like. Of course, a study of the effects of psychosis on one's life is not necessarily the same as a study of voices on one's life. However, given that the vast majority of people who are given the diagnosis of a psychotic disorder will hear voices, such studies give us a good indication of the struggles and problems that voice-hearers in the psychiatric system are likely to face. Such caveats aside, what does this literature show?

Relationships with voices

Having a voice often means developing a new relationship in one's social world, a relationship of sorts with one's voice. It has been found that patient voice-hearers often develop close relationships with their voices, and react to their verbalisations just as someone would with another person (Benjamin, 1989). Around half of voice-hearers assign names to their voices, again, just as one would with people in the real social world (Chin, Hayward & Drinnan, 2009). Voice-hearers will often be involved in a battle for control and power with their voices. Voices can try and achieve power over the voice-hearer by issuing commands and instructions, and also by having a disturbing 'knowledge' of the voice-hearer's weaknesses, attacking them at this point (ibid.). In response, voice-hearers will employ tactics such as fighting back, or complying with the voices. Many voice-hearers have a sense of closeness with their voices, with one stating that 'I haven't got many friends ... so the only thing I can stay very close to are the voices and I do stay very close to them' (p. 9). However, others reject this sense of closeness, which disturbs them, with one voice-hearer stating that their voices would keep on saying 'that we're all in this together and we're gonna be married with each other for the rest of our lives' (p. 11). Reasons for rejecting this sense of closeness include trying to maintain a sense of self. Going beyond the relationship one has with one's voices, two core themes may be found in the lived experience of voice-hearing, those of loss and regaining.

Loss

Voice-hearing in those who enter the psychiatric system is associated with a loss of many basic human needs, including the loss of safety, security, hope, social relationships, respect, esteem and a purpose in life. This is not to say that they are necessary losses, but rather that individuals who are distressed by their voices, cannot cope with them, and end up in an illness state, typically suffer such losses.

Loss of consensual reality

Qualitative studies show voice-hearers can report that when their voices start they feel like they have lost the sense of living in the same world as everyone else. When they start, voices' onset may be sharp and noticeable, or more gradual (ibid.).[2] This onset of voices is not necessarily perceived as abnormal, with some people noting voices starting, but regarding them as normal: 'I thought that was just the way I was' (Judge et al., 2008, p. 97). Yet numerous voice-hearers start to feel like they are living in a different reality (Dilks, Tasker & Wren, 2010; Mauritz & van Meijel, 2009), and question this new reality, asking what is real and who the voices are (Jarosinski, 2008). The onset of this new reality is often accompanied by feelings of confusion and fear (Boyd & Gumley, 2007). Fear often remains, or is even amplified, by hospital admission (Laithwaite & Gumley, 2007).

Loss of hope

For those hospitalized as a result of their voices, a loss of hope and motivation is common. The loss of a perceived future is a key reason for the loss of hope. One participant in a study bluntly stated 'I don't have a future' (Knight, Wykes & Hayward, 2003, p. 216). Rice (2008) found that 'a positive future was not something they could easily grasp or shape, and to hope for a "recovery" did not seem possible' (p. 971). Jarosinski (2008) found participants' beliefs that they were 'unable to make it on his or her own', was reinforced by their voices. When voice-hearers receive a diagnosis (often of schizophrenia) this can also destroy hope, being experienced as a 'prognosis of doom' (p. 421), with the way it is communicated to them by mental health professionals often not helping (Pitt et al., 2009). Schulze & Angermeyer (2003) noted that participants in their study, including voice-hearers, criticised diagnoses being given with prognoses such as 'You've got schizophrenia, you will be ill for the rest of your life' (p. 304). The biological model used by professionals can also be associated with determinism and hopelessness

---

[2] Hoffman et al. (2008b) found 71% of patients could recall the first time they heard a voice, 48% remembered it vividly and 62% were at least moderately upset by this.

(Thornhill, Clare & May, 2004), with some individuals diagnosed with psychotic disorders reporting having had their hopes crushed by clinicians: 'I had a doctor about ten years ago who said I would never work again' (Chernomas, Clarke & Chisholm, 2000, p. 1518), 'one psychiatrist told me I'd only ever do menial work' (Marwaha & Johnson, 2004, p. 309). Indeed, Tooth *et al.* (2003) found nearly two-thirds of individuals in their study (patients diagnosed with schizophrenia) reported health professionals had had a negative impact on their recovery. One reason was the use of 'you can't' messages, which stripped them of any hope of recovery.[3] When voice-hearers receive a diagnosis, this can also be associated with a loss or change in identity. Dilks, Tasker & Wren (2010) found a participant who described 'beginning to undergo that radically dehumanizing and devaluing transformation from being a person to being an illness ... to being "a schizophrenic" ' (p. 98). Other reasons for loss of hope include loss of employment (Perry, Taylor & Shaw, 2007) and, in the case of mothers with psychosis, having their children taken away from them (Diaz-Caneja & Johnson, 2004). This loss of hope may often lead to a depressed, demotivated state, with McCann & Clark (2004) recording the view of one individual (diagnosed with schizophrenia) who, when asked what they saw themselves doing in the next five years, simply replied 'nothing' (p. 789).

Loss of homeostasis

A number of studies have identified a loss of normal sleeping and eating patterns, and the loss of a normal pain-free state in individuals diagnosed with psychotic disorders (e.g. Koivisto, Janhonen & Vaisanen, 2002), many of whom will be voice-hearers. Medication side-effects are implicated in such changes, with McCann & Clark (2004) quoting one individual remembering that 'I was asleep nearly 18 hours a day' (p. 792). Rofail, Heelis & Gournay (2009) noted that medication could cause patients to be 'hungry all the time' (p. 1491). Physical pain was also a side-effect, with Usher (2001) finding a participant reporting 'What I've been through is like hell ... like a screw being tightened in your brain ... like a pressure point being turned on in your brain ... you feel lethargic and tired but at the same time they give you motor restlessness, it is a weird sensation, you don't feel like getting up to do anything

---

[3] A lack of information or knowledge about how to combat voices may also lead to a loss of hope. Virginia Woolf herself wrote, not long before her suicide, 'I am always hearing voices, and I know I shan't get over it now. I shan't recover this time' (Woolf, as cited in Szasz, 2006, p. 85).

and yet you can't keep still' (p. 148). Roe *et al.* (2009) noted one participant reporting the effect as being 'as if someone pulled the hand brakes in my brain' (p. 41).

Loss of security

Feeling scared and insecure due to the voices themselves is common. Abba, Chadwick & Stevenson (2008) noted that voice-hearers were 'overwhelmed, overtaken, subsumed and defined by a powerful other' (p. 81). One participant stated of their voice, 'it just won't let you lie there and rest ... they're at you 24 hours of the bloody day' (ibid.). Voice-hearers may feel especially vulnerable whilst in hospital (Koivisto, Janhonen & Vaisanen, 2004). For example, Thornhill, Clare & May (2004) noted participants diagnosed with a psychotic disorder used 'imagery about imprisonment and torture to describe the experience of treatment within the mental health system' (p. 188), with one patient describing hospital as like a prison where there was continual danger of attack. Financial security may also be lost due to voice-hearers losing their jobs: 'I couldn't hold down a job due to the way I was feeling' (Gee, Pearce & Jackson, 2003, p. 6). Such financial problems also cause problems with one's living arrangements (Laliberte-Rudman *et al.*, 2000), such as having to downsize or move to a worse neighbourhood, making people feel even more insecure.

Loss of relationships

Hearing voices can also cause severe problems with keeping up one's social relationships. This can lead to chronic loneliness at a time when love and belonging is particularly needed (Mauritz & van Meijel, 2009). Gee, Pearce & Jackson (2003) found individuals diagnosed with schizophrenia, including voice-hearers, 'being quiet and not sociable. Not wanting to go anywhere' (p. 8). One reason for this was problems communicating due to the voices. As one participant stated, 'There's sort of voices and all sorts of mayhem going on inside and there's not enough of your brain left to concentrate on what people are saying' (p. 7). As a result, some studies (e.g. Judge *et al.*, 2008) noted withdrawal being used as a coping mechanism. Chernomas, Clarke & Chisholm (2000) found women diagnosed with schizophrenia talking about the loss of relationships with friends and family who 'didn't understand their illness and with the difficulty they now have ... connecting to the world' (p. 306). Similarly, MacDonald *et al.* (2005) found that some individuals diagnosed with psychosis felt misunderstood by their friends and preferred not to spend time with them. Medication side-effects and diagnosis also impaired relationships, as well as help-seeking. In Usher's (2001) study of individuals diagnosed with schizophrenia, one participant stated that 'I stay at home now and don't go out much because people are sort of put off by the side-effects ... people avoid me or they can't understand me because I slur my words' (p. 149). This also makes voice-hearers feel less able to enter into romantic relationships (Redmond, Larkin & Harrop, 2010). Volman & Landeen (2007) found individuals diagnosed with schizophrenia felt their illness also profoundly impacted on their sexuality, with one problem being medication-related weight gain. They found that social stigma also limited participants' sexual experiences, and that voices could impair relationships. One individual reported that her partner 'tells me that he loves me ... but the voices tell me different' (p. 414). In terms of sex for the purpose of reproduction, Gonzalez-Torres *et al.* (2007) found that this was discouraged in individuals diagnosed with schizophrenia, with one participant saying 'You mention to the psychiatrist that you want to have a child and he says "no, that's not possible, don't even think of it" ' (p. 19). Chernomas, Clarke & Chisholm (2000) found that some women diagnosed with psychosis who had chosen not to have children 'because of their illness' were angry, sad, or resigned about this.

Stigma

Stigma is a major problem,[4] particularly as many voice-hearers receive a diagnosis of schizophrenia. Chernomas, Clarke & Chisholm (ibid.) reported that many women chose not to disclose their diagnosis of schizophrenia to others as 'they don't understand ... especially with schizophrenia, they think they're going to be murdered by you' (p. 1518). Judge *et al.* (2008) found participants diagnosed with psychotic disorders would avoid or delay coming to services because people 'would think you was crazy' and 'I pictured myself being locked up in a cell if I told the truth' (p. 98). Rice (2006) found how one participant's diagnosis of schizophrenia was used against them when testifying against an abuser in court, with a participant stating that 'The police just didn't think I was ... a good enough woman to pursue any charges ... Kind of like a lower class citizen ... a degenerate person'. MacDonald *et al.* (2005) also found that individuals diagnosed with schizophrenia felt

---

[4] For a good discussion of stigma resulting from the way in which the media portrays hearing voices, see Leudar & Thomas (2000). Also see Chapter 12 on the relation between biological models of voices and stigma.

they were viewed as diminished, with one stating that 'it's like first when Aids came out, "Don't touch those people"' (p. 137). Gonzales-Torres *et al.* reported that individuals diagnosed with schizophrenia felt they were treated like 'oddballs' (p. 18) and similarly Chernomas, Clarke & Chisholm (2000) found that they were labelled as 'an oddball', 'a freak' and 'a weirdo' (p. 1519). In Laliberte-Rudman *et al.*'s (2000) study, one even stated that 'I feel ... like a different species'. Rice (2008) found an individual diagnosed with schizophrenia who felt forced to maintain secrecy surrounding her sexual abuse, stating 'there was nobody I could tell it to, because if you told somebody, even today, they think there's something wrong with you, especially if you're schizophrenic ... you have a disease ... you're trash'.

Loss of autonomy and respect

It was noted in Chapter 3 how the asylum system under Tuke encouraged patients to be viewed as children. This appears still to be the case with individuals diagnosed with psychotic disorders today, who can experience a loss of autonomy leading to their not feeling respected (e.g. Wagner & King, 2005; Warren & Bell, 2000). We find statements such as 'I wasn't told what the medication did ... you were just told to take it' (Powell & Clarke, 2006, p. 362) and 'I feel like a guinea pig' (Rofail, Heelis & Gournay, 2009, p. 1492). Humberstone (2002) reported an individual diagnosed with schizophrenia stating how services 'can treat me like a little child, they can treat me like a spastic, they can treat me like a nothing' (p. 370). Voice-hearers often feel that they are not treated as a whole person: 'they [the nurses] really only come around to give needles as though that's all's needed' (Warren & Bell, 2000, p. 199), 'you are now a schizophrenic and we treat you with medication' (Thornhill, Clare & May, 2004, p. 188). Roe *et al.* (2009) quote one participant arguing 'who are you to decide for me that it is better to be fat and happy to be on the safe side? I want to be skinny with episodes ... give me the right to decide for myself' (p. 41). Voice-hearers' physical complaints may also be dismissed: 'Until they discovered what I have (kidney stones), they didn't listen to me, it was all due to nerves' (Gonzales-Torres *et al.*, 2007, p. 18).

Parenthood

Both mothers and fathers (Evenson *et al.*, 2008) who hear voices and receive a psychotic diagnosis face a number of problems. Diaz-Caneja & Johnson (2004) found mothers were concerned at having to cope with both with their children and their voices, especially when medication impaired their ability to look after their children, by slowing them down and reducing their concentration. Both Diaz-Caneja & Johnson and Chernomas, Clarke & Chisholm (2000) found mothers worrying that, due to genetic or environmental factors, their children may also become mentally ill, and their great fear of their children being taken away ('they're gone, and you don't think you have a reason to live', p. 1519). Chernomas, Clarke & Chisholm also emphasised the issues for women diagnosed with a psychotic disorder who became pregnant. Those who got pregnant whilst on antipsychotic drugs were faced with a conundrum; one explained, 'I had to continue taking my medication because without my medication I'm helpless ... What harm is my medication going to do to my child? I don't know. But I knew I couldn't stop taking it' (ibid.).[5]

Regaining

The qualitative literature also shows the important aspects in recovery from voices, which in part circulate around regaining the ability to re-meet the human needs that voices had led to people not being able to meet. Importantly, whilst for some this may involve getting rid of their voices, for others it may involve coming to be able to cope with their voices and to meet their needs whilst still hearing voices.

Regaining reality and self

Many qualitative studies find medication helps control some people's voices, increase feelings of reality and help clear thinking (Rofail, Heelis & Gournay, 2009; see also Appendix A). However, regaining a sense of reality and control does not necessarily involve getting rid of voices; for some it is a case of dealing with them better.[6] As noted earlier, Costain (2008) found some voice-hearers used cannabis precisely because it made the voices 'louder and clearer', which helped them to cope with them, as the voices became easier to understand and control. Another important part of coping with voices is making sense of them (see also

---

[5] Notably, Pawlby *et al.* (2010) have found evidence that challenges previous conclusions that mothers with a diagnosis of schizophrenia have deficits in their interactions with their babies.

[6] An important step in recovery may not be the regaining of the same reality as the majority of the population, but rather the recognition by others of the new reality a voice-hearer is living in. Other people recognising that one's voices are a real experience may also be very helpful to the voice-hearer (Coleman, 2000).

Romme *et al.*, 2009). Sharing the voice-hearing experience with others who do not doubt or question them is important (Dilks, Tasker & Wren, 2010) and voice-hearers commonly seek the company of peers with shared experience (MacDonald *et al.*, 2005). Sense-making is sometimes helped by diagnosis, which can be seen as legitimating participants' experiences (Pitt *et al.*, 2009). Achieving distance from voices, accepting them without being too 'impressed' by them (Roe, Chopra & Rudnick, 2004, p. 125) and mindfulness/detachment have been found to help: 'I just decided to observe basically within myself, just to be aware, and to allow the voices to say whatever they wanted to say' (Nixon, Hagen & Peters, 2010b). Thornhill, Clare & May (2004) described how regaining the self involved escaping the role of a psychiatric patient, which could happen suddenly, with one participant explaining their decision to just 'let go ... of being that mad' (p. 189).

Regaining hope

The importance of regaining hope is clear, evidenced by voice-hearers' statements, such as 'when ... you're hearing voices ... sometimes hope is the only thing you've got' (El-Mallakh, 2006, p. 61). Hope can come back suddenly; 'there was a flash in my mind. I was so sick of being mistreated by everyone that I thought to myself, "Enough is enough" ' (Noiseux & Ricard, 2008, p. 1153) or gradually (Gould, DeSouza & Rebeiro-Gruhl, 2005). The support of friends and family can be crucial to hope returning (Wagner & King, 2004). Medication can also give hope (Usher, 2001), as can religion or spirituality (Humberstone, 2002). As one individual put it, 'If I had no faith, I don't know how I'd get through it. No faith, no hope, no light at the end of the tunnel. I would end it' (Drinnan & Lavender, 2006, p. 323). Powell & Clarke (2006) found that having an understanding that other people are going through the same thing instilled hope. One participant in their study stated that 'reading experiences where people had recovered, it was such a boost, because you thought well, if they can do it, you know, I will be damned if I can't' (p. 363). Schon, Denhov & Topor (2009) revealed that meeting others in the same situation as themselves could give participants 'living proof' of hope. Here we see the importance and inspirational value of recovered voice-hearers (who do or do not still hear voices) who act as positive role models.

Regaining employment

A common theme in studies of individuals diagnosed with psychotic disorders, and hence voice-hearers, is the desire to get back to work

(Marwaha & Johnson, 2005). As one participant in the study of Dilks, Tasker & Wren (2010) put it, 'I want to get back into work, I want to get back into a normal, stable life' (p. 95). Work is often associated with a feeling of being normal, and can be seen as a way of coping (Roe, Chopra & Rudnick, 2004). Several studies have identified barriers to returning to work, with stigma playing a key role. Often voice-hearers will not mention their illness to employers, because 'You wouldn't get taken on in the first place if you told them you had a big mental history' (Marwaha & Johnson, 2005, p. 309). Chernomas, Clarke & Chisholm (2000) identified the barrier of the perceived risk of losing welfare benefits, with one participant diagnosed with schizophrenia stating, 'I want to try to find a job, but I'm scared ... that I'm going to get sick and I'm going to lose my job, and I'm going to have no money and how am I going to get back on welfare?' What voices say can also be a barrier in getting back to work: 'My first priority is to get rid of the voices and then work' (Gioia, 2006, p. 170). Rofail, Heelis & Gournay (2009) also found that medication side-effects impaired some participants' ability to work: 'They make me feel too tired to work my skilled job' (p. 1491).

Regaining relationships, and recovering through them

Friends, family, and the need for constancy, for someone who voice-hearers know would 'be there' (Lencucha et al., 2008, p. 345) are all important. Many voice-hearers may create new and enduring friend-ships with people who share similar voice-hearing experiences (Nixon, Hagen & Peters, 2010a). Indeed, Lencucha, Kinsella & Sumsion (2008) found that participants diagnosed with schizophrenia identified their most important relationships as being ones with people who had know-ledge of living with psychosis. Knight, Wykes & Hayward (2003) also found that solidarity with others was important. One participant diag-nosed with schizophrenia referred to their peer-support group for people who heard voices as giving 'solidarity in people' (p. 217). Although Tooth et al. (2003) found that nearly two-thirds of participants reported that health professionals had a negative impact on their recovery: 'it was the psychiatrist versus us lot [the patients]' (Knight, Wykes & Hayward, 2003, p. 214), Nixon, Hagen & Peters (2010a) found that the majority of participants diagnosed with psychosis in their study stated that mental health professionals were instrumental in their recovery, highlighting the friendship aspect to their relationship with helpful professionals. One participant described how her psychologist did not act as a condescend-ing expert, but 'talked like a friend to me'. Similarly, O'Toole et al. (2004) found that being 'treated like a human being' (p. 321) by mental health professionals was a key to recovery. Being listened to was also important for recovery (McGowan, Lavender & Garety, 2005).[7]

Beyond regaining: the gifts of voices

A number of studies found that voice-hearers with diagnoses of psychotic disorders talked of the gifts that came from their experiences (Woodside, Schell & Allison-Hedges, 2006). Nixon, Hagen & Peters (2010a) found some participants could now connect with their sense of creativity (e.g. through writing about their experiences) and that this was associated with their path to recovery. Some participants also noted the help of spirituality to their recovery, and as a result viewed their psychosis retrospectively as a spiritual gift. Nixon, Hagen & Peters (2010b) also described how some participants 're-aligned their career path to reflect their newfound spiritual awareness'. One participant stated that, 'I don't think I was creative until that [my psychosis] happened'. Voice-hearers may also try to help others with mental health concerns, or become advocates for other service-users, reflecting their increased compassion (Nixon, Hagen & Peters, 2010a). We will examine these aspects more in Chapter 12.

Conclusion

In conclusion, we can see that for voice-hearers who are unable to cope with their voices and who enter the psychiatric system, this can have a pervasive effect on their lives, leading to an illness state. In fact, the experience can be seen to impact upon all of Maslow's (1943) basic human needs. First, basic physiological needs can be affected (such as sleep impairment, physical pain, etc.). Second, one's security needs are not met. This can include losing one's job and hence one's financial security, having to move into worse housing and neighbourhoods, and physical changes to the body and one's health often due to medication side-effects. Third, the need for love and belonging is frustrated due to the impact of the voices on one's ability to function, and the stigma which is associated with the experience. Fourth, one's need for esteem is blocked by stigma affecting how other people view you, what you might come to think of yourself, and what the voices tell you. The need for self-actualisation, i.e. to create, live and be all you can be, is also often blocked. Recovery is hence a long journey to get all this back, and not

---

[7] See Chapter 12 for problems voice-hearers have being listened to.

an easy one. As Milton (1821) put it, 'Long is the way/And hard, that out of hell leads up to light' (p. 47). Once these needs are met again, the voices may have given the person gifts, which they can use to enhance their life and, in Maslow's terminology, get closer to self-actualisation than they were before.

How, then, is recovery to be achieved? Aside from the regaining of basic human needs, this depends in part on what recovery means for the individual voice-hearer in terms of their relationship with their voices. This may range from the desired elimination of the voices,[8] to simply being able to cope with (and not eliminate) the voices, to the successful addressing of emotional issues that potentially underlie the voices.[9] One tool, as highlighted in some of the qualitative accounts above, is anti-psychotic medication. Rigorous quantitative studies of the effectiveness of antipsychotic medication will be examined in Appendix A, and the subjective impact of such medication on voices and the possible biological mechanisms underpinning this action will be discussed in Chapter 8, when we move on to look at the biological causes of AVHs. There is also some evidence that cognitive behavioural therapy (CBT) is also able to reduce the frequency of voices in some cases, and can help people cope better with their voices although, as we will see in Chapter 12, quantitative randomised controlled trials of CBT for AVHs show disappointing results. Before we come on to these quantitative studies later in the book, it is worth noting here that in cognitive models of voice-hearing it is the appraisal of voices rather than the voices per se that is seen as the cause of problems and distress (e.g. Byrne et al., 2006). This conclusion is reinforced by the findings in the next chapter, that many people can function well whilst hearing voices. Thus, voices in themselves may not be pathological, but the inability to cope with them or dysfunctional coping may result in a state that can be labelled illness. In this way recovery may not be a matter of changing oneself from a voice-hearer into a non-voice-hearer, but changing from being a patient voice-hearer into a healthy voice-hearer. That this could validly be considered recovery is what Romme and colleagues have referred to as the emancipation of voice-hearers (Chapter 3; Romme et al., 2009). Given that Romme and colleagues' work on recovery is based on their personal and clinical experience, as well as individual case-studies

---

[8] Although some voice-hearers report feeling lonely when this desired outcome has actually happened (e.g. see Byrne et al., 2006, p. 83).

[9] Furthermore, as well as the voice-hearer's recovery, it has been argued that society also needs to recover from its stigmatisation of voice-hearing to allow the voice-hearer the freedom to walk the street talking to their voices (see Coleman in James, 2001).

(and their work can be seen as more qualitative than quantitative, hence showing a resemblance to the studies reviewed above), their conclusions will be examined here. An important question is how their conclusions as to how recovery can be achieved differ from that found in the review of qualitative accounts discussed above.

Changing the lived experience of voices: Romme's emancipatory approach

Writers within the Hearing Voices Movement, as described in Chapter 3, have argued that 'getting rid of voices is neither necessary, nor that important' (Romme et al., 2009, p. 7). Such writers argue instead that one must change one's relationships with one's voices. This forms part of the Maastricht approach, which we will discuss further in Chapter 12. An important publication relating to recovery within the ethos of the Hearing Voices Movement is *Living with voices: 50 stories of recovery* (Romme et al., 2009), which should be required reading for anyone involved in this area. Based on their review of 50 voice-hearers' own stories of recovery, Romme and colleagues identify nine issues which they argue are important in helping an individual to recover from the distress associated with voices. Many of these are consistent with the conclusions from the review of qualitative studies above. First, Romme *et al.* conclude that *Meeting someone who takes an interest in the voice-hearer* is important. This is consistent with the findings of the first half of this chapter, which showed that being treated as a whole person, rather than simply a drug pin-cushion, was reported as being important to recovery. Second, Romme *et al.* note that *Giving hope, by showing a way out and normalising the experience* is needed. Again, this accords with the crucial importance of hope noted in the first half of this chapter. *Meeting people who accept the voices as real; being accepted as a voice-hearer by others, but also by oneself* is Romme *et al.*'s third criterion. This is consistent with the need to overcome stigma, and the benefits of talking and meeting with others who have the same experience, noted in the first half of this chapter. Romme *et al.* also highlight that *Making choices* is important to recovery. By this they mean that choosing to stay alive, choosing which friends one wants, choosing to develop one's self, choosing to get a job, etc., are important. This adds to the qualitative findings reviewed above by highlighting that the ability to recover human needs has an important step between hoping for recovery of these needs and achieving these needs, namely the need actively to choose to undertake this journey (see also Coleman & Smith, 1997).

Importantly, the qualitative literature reviewed in the first half of this chapter fails to note five (i.e. over half) of the issues that Romme *et al.* (2009) propose are important in recovery, all of which involve the voice-hearer actively engaging with their voices and emotions. These are *Becoming actively interested in the hearing voices experience, Recognising the voices as personal and becoming the owner of your voices, Changing the power structure between you and your voices, Changing the relationship with your voices, Recognising your own emotions and accepting them.* The reason for the qualitative literature not identifying this appears to stem from the different philosophies employed by the majority of the authors of qualitative research and Romme *et al.* Central to their approach (Chapter 3, Chapter 12) is that voices are meaningful experiences, related to the emotions and events in the voice-hearer's life. They argue that recovery can only be achieved by working with the voices, understanding them and their relation to one's own emotions and past, and changing one's relationship with them. This can be achieved both by talking directly to the voices (e.g. using the technique of voice dialogue – see Chapter 12), as well as using clues given by the voices (i.e. their content, age, etc.) as to their relation to events in the voice-hearer's past, which then need to be resolved. Such an approach is generally in contrast to the majority of the qualitative literature, which tends to focus on the negative consequences of the voices, implicitly or explicitly assuming that the way to recover these is hence to eliminate the voices. Here we see radically different routes to recovery. Although the early informal results of Romme's approach appear positive, moving forward there is the need to clearly test its effectiveness in a large-scale randomised controlled trial.

Chapter 5: summary of key points

- Voice-hearing in individuals who are distressed and unable to cope with them (and have hence become psychiatric patients) leads to the loss of basic human needs.
- These include a loss of control over one's mind and body, a loss of security and safety, a loss of social and romantic relationships, a loss of hope and a loss of respect.
- These basic human needs are lost not only due to the direct effects of the voices, but due to factors such as stigma, misunderstanding and negative experiences in the mental health system.
- The process of recovery is likely to be the process of regaining the ability to achieve these needs.
- Hope and positive social relationships are key to the recovery process.

- The voice-hearer who has recovered may or may not still hear voices, and can achieve growth and personal development from the experience they have been through.
- Existing peer-reviewed qualitative studies differ from Romme and colleagues' emancipatory approach to voice-hearing by failing to consider the need to engage with and change one's relationships with voices.
- It may be that the important transition is not from voice-hearer to non-voice-hearer, but from patient voice-hearer to healthy voice-hearer.
- Large-scale randomised controlled trials of Romme *et al.*'s recovery model of voice-hearing are required.

6 Beyond disorder: religious and cross-cultural perspectives

The *Diagnostic and Statistical Manual of Mental Disorders* (DSM) (APA, 2000) is clear to stress that clinicians must take account of cultural factors when making a diagnosis. The authors of the DSM note that, 'In some cultures ... auditory hallucinations with a religious content may be a normal part of religious experience' (p. 306) and give the example of hearing God's voice. Thus, although Szasz (1996) famously quipped that 'If you talk to God you are praying; if God talks to you, you have schizophrenia' (p. 13), the DSM allows that one may hear God's voice and that if this is culturally acceptable, then this is not a sign of mental disorder. But how many people hear what they believe to be God's voice? How do religions today treat the experience of hearing voices (Christianity and Islam will be focused on here), how prevalent is voice hearing in other cultures and how is the experience understood and coped with in these cultures? These are the questions this chapter will set out to examine.

Contemporary religion and hearing voices: Christianity

Evangelical Christianity and hearing the voice of God

The allowance by the DSM that hearing the voice of God may be a normal part of experience in a culture opens the door to a serious study of what leads contemporary individuals to report hearing the 'voice of God', and what this experience is like. In a study of 29 members of an evangelical Christian church, who reported having no previous treatment for mental illness, Davies, Griffin & Vice (2001) found that 59 per cent reported hearing voices. This compared to a rate of 27 per cent in a non-religious control group. The experience of hearing voices was significantly more positive in evangelical Christians than in both non-religious controls and patients diagnosed with psychosis. Interestingly, both the evangelical Christian group and the patients diagnosed with

149

psychosis reported that their most recent hearing voices experience was more positive than their first hearing voices experience.

A later, more detailed study by Dein & Littlewood (2007) tried to gain a better understanding of what hearing the voice of God was actually like. They interviewed 25 individuals, predominantly white Europeans from an English Pentecostal church, who indicated that they had heard the voice of God in response to prayer. Fifteen of the 25 heard God's voice as coming from outside them. The voices were heard at various frequencies, ranging from daily to once every couple of months. The participants felt they had no control over when the voice started or stopped. One way in which God's voice was identified as being His, was the positive emotion and feelings that were associated with the voice: 'an emotion of forgiveness' (p. 219). Other ways it was 'known' that it was God's voice was via 'a sense of knowing on the inside', because it was consistent with biblical teachings or how God should be, and by getting the voice to confess that Jesus Christ is God. God's voice was generally male, although 10 of the 25 reported He had no gender. His voice was typically like a human voice, and was reported as being 'gentle ... not demanding or controlling' (ibid.). One individual described how, at the end of an emotional experience in a church, they heard the voice of God saying 'you need to serve, just be a servant' (p. 220). Another was driving in her car when 'all of a sudden I heard an audible voice ... it said "you will have a son and you will name him Isaac" ' (ibid.). Participants commonly reported being able to have a conversation with God, in which they could question or clarify what the voice said.

Dein & Littlewood (2007) noted that 'God's voice often focuses on immediate issues. He seldom offers metaphysical insights. This seems like a way of regulating and evaluating daily activities and providing guidance to those whom He communicates with' (p. 221). For example, one participant stated that 'I was looking in the mirror one day and God said to me "I don't want you to be afraid of growing your hair" ' (ibid.). When suggesting actions, participants felt that God was not command-ing them, but offering them a choice. In many instances He spoke to participants at the time of a major life crisis: 'I cried out to God saying "If you are real you need to let me know because if you don' I am going to kill myself". ... In that moment I did hear this voice. It wasn't audible but in my mind. It wasn't me, I knew it wasn't and the voice said "Tracey get up, get dressed and walk' " (ibid.). One individual, David, had been diagnosed as having a psychotic breakdown, with AVHs, a number of years earlier. He attributed these voices, which were 'nasty and aggressive ... forceful and pushy' (p. 224) to his illness. However, after recovering from his psychosis, he heard a voice which he attributed to

God. This voice was 'very calm and peaceful and doesn't force you' (ibid.). In terms of the criteria that the pastor of the church used to establish whether someone was hearing the voice of God, he stated that voices should only be understood as being of divine origin when followed by changes in behaviour which are morally significant. In cases where this was not the case, the pastor would judge them to be mistaken, and that instead their experiences had a purely physiological or satanic basis. This echoes the historical Christian discernment criteria as laid out in Chapter 2.

Overall, it is notable how the phenomenological properties of God's voice, such as its tendency to directly address the voice-hearer, to regulate activities with commands and suggestions and to focus on mundane events, are similar to the voices heard by distressed voice-hearers who go on to receive a diagnosis of psychosis (Chapter 4), as well as the voices heard by healthy voice-hearers (which we will examine in the next chapter). Furthermore, like these groups, the voice of God also tended to occur at times of stress (see Chapter 11). This could lead to the interpretation that the evangelical Christians in this study are actually experiencing the same neurophysiological events (as well as emotional conflicts) as individuals with psychosis and healthy voice-hearers, but interpreting the resultant voice-hearing experience in a different way. Yet there do appear to be some important differences in the phenomenology of the 'voice of God', such as the emotions associated with hearing it (e.g. a powerful sense of forgiveness) and this, as well as the cultural context, is likely to influence the attribution of such voices to God.

The contemporary Catholic Church

The Catholic Church's contemporary classification of locutions (heard voices) still follows that of St Augustine and incorporates the three types of voices identified by St John of the Cross (see Chapter 2). For example, Father Jordan Aumann O.P. (1916–2007), the former Director of the Institute of Spirituality at the Pontifical University of St Thomas Aquinas in Rome, divided locutions into three classes (Aumann, 2006). The first are auricular locutions, which 'are words perceived by the bodily sense of hearing by reason of acoustical vibrations. In themselves they may be produced by God, by angels, or by demons. They may also be produced by natural causes, whether physical or psychic. They sometimes seem to proceed from a bodily vision, the Blessed Sacrament, a religious image such as a crucifix, or some other article that is used as an instrument.' The second are imaginative locutions, which 'are words perceived in the imagination and may occur either during sleep or in waking hours. They may proceed from God, the devil, or natural causes. The best rule of discernment is the effects produced in the soul. If they are from God, they cause humility, fervor, desire for self-immolation, *obedience*, desire to perform perfectly one's duties of state. If they proceed from the devil, they cause dryness, inquietude, *insubordination*, etc. The ones that proceed from the individual do not usually produce any noteworthy effects' (emphasis added). The third are intellectual locutions which are 'words perceived directly by the intellect, and the activity is similar to that by which angels would communicate ideas to each other. Two elements concur in this type of locution: the preexisting or infused intelligible species and the supernatural light that illumines and clarifies them. It is beyond the power of the devil to produce a truly intellectual locution, for he cannot operate on the human intellect directly'. This interpretation is still very much in line with the traditional Church discernment criteria we saw in Part I. Such criteria have inherent in them that divine voices only occur in people who will not challenge the Church's authority.

Surprisingly, though, to a secular person at least, perhaps, Catholic theologians are also very willing to embrace an illness meaning of voice-hearing, even in regard to some of their own saints. This may owe something to the influence of Bultmann's (1952) process of demythologisation. Take, for example, St Thomas Aquinas, whom we met in Chapter 1. I have previously examined (McCarthy-Jones, 2011a) how St Thomas is reported to have heard a voice and how contemporary theologians understand this. The meaning that is given to St Thomas's experience by contemporary theologians is a medical one. This has a number of interesting implications, which we will touch on again in Chapter 12.

Exorcism

'I know someone will ask me', wrote C. S. Lewis (2002, p. 46) ' "Do you really mean at this time of day, to re-introduce our old friend the devil – hoofs and horns and all?" Well, what the time of day has to do with it I do not know. And I am not particular about the hoofs and horns. But in other respects my answer is "Yes I do" '. In contrast to C.S. Lewis's willingness to discuss the devil, Porter (2002) claims that: 'These days ... the Roman Catholic or Anglican who claims to be assailed by the Devil has become an embarrassment. His priest may try to persuade him that such doctrines are merely metaphysical; and, if he persists, he may be urged to see a psychotherapist' (p. 33). Porter actually overstates the case here, as the practice of exorcism and deliverance in response to 'possession' and 'demonic voices' continues to be per-formed and taken very seriously particularly by the Catholic Church, but also the Anglican Church.

I have conducted a number of interviews with exorcists in the Catholic Church to examine the nature of voices heard by individuals whom the Church has determined are genuinely under the sway of demonic forces. Whilst I will respect the confidentiality in which I spoke to the fathers, and will not go into details here, I will comment that the phenomenology of many of the voices reported by those experiencing 'demonic possession' closely parallels the phenomenology of negative voices found in distressed voice-hearers with psychiatric diagnoses. Whilst this could lead to a conclusion that to some theolo-gians would suggest that the devil has achieved his greatest trick, I should state here that successful naturalistic attempts to explain some of the content of the 'demonic' voices reported by the fathers still elude me. The atheist should hope this is due to my intellectual failings.[1]

Other contemporary Christian influences

Many individuals who hear voices which do not distress them come to understand them as being that of an angel. Indeed, there is a remarkably large contemporary literature on peoples' experiences with such beings, including accounts of people interpreting voices as coming from angels (e.g. Eckersley, 1996; Heathcote-James, 2001) as well as guides for recognising such angelic voices (e.g. Virtue, 2007) which in turn act to guide others to interpret their experiences in the same light. The Christian Church's traditional discernment criteria in which, for example, clear external voices are spiritually suspect, are not widely employed by the lay public, however. The impact of culture and the absence of traditional discernment criteria are both seen in a report of a voice given by Heathcote-James (2001): 'It was a male voice, very clear and very distinct. It wasn' a voice I recognised, but somehow I knew it was a good voice. My mother said something I hadn't thought of. She said "Maybe it was your guardian angel" ' (p. 113). In such reports there are frequent examples of voices which parallel the religious voices heard in the sixteenth century. Recall from Chapter 2 that St Teresa talked of the sense of peace and/or inner consolation that divine voices could bring. In a contemporary example of this, Heathcote-James describes a

---

[1] These issues will be taken up again in Chapter 12.

woman who had been feeling somewhat depressed, walking through a forest with her dog: 'suddenly I felt a presence by my side (I did not see anything) and I heard a voice speaking to me internally. It said "But you have trust in God"... I felt great [consolation] and joy. I just cannot describe the sense that I felt, it was so beautiful it was indescribable' (p. 123).

Voices also have the potential to lead to conversion experiences today, just as it reputedly did for St Paul around 2,000 years ago. A twentieth-century example is given in Bede Griffiths' autobiography, *The Golden String* (1954), in which the author has a voice-hearing experience which leads him to become a Benedictine monk (Hirsh, 1989). Griffiths recalls that at an important moment in his life he heard a voice saying 'You must go to a retreat' (Griffiths, as cited in Hirsh, 1989, p. 81). Griffiths elaborates on this voice which, in Augustine's classification appears to be an intellectual locution: 'When I say that I heard a voice, I do not mean that I heard any sound. It was simply that this signified to me interiorly, but in such a way that it did not appear to come from myself' (ibid.).

Following George Fox (see Chapter 2), Quakers today still look to 'the "still small voice" that dwells within each of us – the voice of God that speaks to us' (Hamm, 2003, p. 70), be this literally or figuratively. Yet, in contemporary American spirituality, the relation between this still small voice of God and one's own thoughts starts to blur. For example, the presence of God's voice has been considered as part of the contemporary American spirituality observed by Luhrmann (2005). Luhrmann, an anthropologist, noted that this spirituality 'encourages people to attend to the stream of their own consciousness like eager fishermen ... to identify moments of discontinuity that are natural to the flow of our everyday awareness, and actually to interpret them as discontinuous. It encourages them to seek for evidence that they might be hearing a voice spoken by another awareness, be that God, the Holy Spirit, or a shamanic guide' (p. 141). By isolating thoughts which are slightly different in some way, such individuals attribute these to God. For example, in an analysis of Virkler & Virkler's book, *Dialogue with God* (1986), Luhrmann shows how the author describes originally living in a 'rationalist box', yearning to hear the voice of God, but not hearing it. The author then realised that God's voice often sounds like his own, like a flow of spontaneous thoughts, rather than an audible voice, and set out a system in which one has to distinguish God's thoughts and your own. Were St John of the Cross alive today, he would be likely to apply his naturalistic self-talk model to such individuals (see Chapter 2).

Christian cognitive behavioural therapy

People who hear distressing voices in a religious context may receive therapeutic interventions also within this context. Garzon (2009) reports employing Christian cognitive behavioural therapy, based on Anderson's Christ-centred therapy (Anderson, Zuehlke & Zuehlke, 2000) and the Steps to Freedom in Christ programme (Anderson, 2001) with a 32-year-old Brazilian woman, Lucia, who was experiencing (in psychiatric terminology) mood-congruent AVHs in the context of depression. A case history revealed that her problems started surrounding arguments and problems she and her husband were having. She suspected a curse might be the cause of this and had gone to a Macumba practitioner (a form of Brazilian witch doctor) six months before. In a ceremony performed at midnight, the Macumba practitioner had spread faecal material over Lucia's body, placed her in a partially dug grave and poured a herbal solution on her. The curse would only be lifted fully, though, he told her, if she returned the following week for a follow-up session, which would cost $500.[2] It was after this experience that the condemnatory AVHs began.

Garzon (2009) attempted to understand her symptoms from a cognitive biopsychosocial perspective. Key to this was Lucia's unsuccessful attempt to cope with her situation by utilising her Christian faith. The Macumba practitioner exposed her to spiritual deception and created guilt and anxiety, leaving her vulnerable to condemnatory AVHs. This meant that as a therapist he had to deal with her disconnection from her husband and the spiritual crisis she was now facing (e.g. has God rejected me for seeking a black magic resolution to my problems? Am I going to live under a curse the remainder of my life? Can my Christianity help my situation?). Garzon noted that the context of Lucia approaching him was that she expected ministry, not medication. Thus, treatment took the form of one intensive seven-hour session, involving the Steps to Freedom programme. For example, Step 1 involved renunciation of occult involvement. Lucia drew up a list and asked God's forgiveness for these activities and renounced each one individually. She appeared to experience a great sense of relief from her guilt following the activity. Step 3 was forgiveness. Here Lucia had to reconcile with God and to forgive herself. The next week, when Garzon monitored the situation, her AVHs were not recurring. Garzon suggests that she may have been experiencing demonic oppression, but notes that many liberal theologians hearing this account may become squeamish,

---

[2] I do not know if this practice is representative of all Macumba practictioners.

having relegated demons to a past that they now believe has been 'demythologized' (cf. Bultmann, 1952). It is unknown what are the relative merits of psychotherapy compared to medication in such a case, but the form of CBT utilised appeared to address the problems the client bought to therapy and to achieve the goals she set.

Contemporary religion and hearing voices: Islam

Background

The Koran teaches that Allah populated the universe with four types of beings: humans, angels, Iblis (Satan) and djinn (or jinn, in their English rendering) (Stein, 2000). Of these, only humans are visible, but the others are not merely imaginary or symbolic: they coexist with humans, guiding and interfering with their efforts to follow the way of Islam (ibid.). In Islam, heard voices are commonly attributed to jinn, a name derived from the Arabic *ijtinan*, which means 'to be concealed from sight' (Sheikh, 2005). According to Islamic beliefs, jinn are creatures created out of smokeless fire, which live in a parallel world to us where they can see us, interact with us, but cannot be seen by us, except rarely (Khalifa & Hardie, 2005; Sheikh, 2005). They share with humans the characteristics of intelligence and the ability to make moral choices (ibid.), yet they differ from humans by being ruder, more selfish and in not concealing their emotions (Watters, 2010). The cause of having jinn speak to you can include having committed a sin, having someone cast a spell against one, or simply having been in the wrong place at the wrong time (Blom, 2010). Additionally, people who are angry, frightened, about to change social status (e.g. pregnant women, couples about to be married and the dying) are particularly liable to attack by jinn (Crapanzano, 1973).[3] Jinn can both issue threats, insults and command behaviours, or be comforting through offering advice or companionship (Blom, 2010). Jinn are reported to say that they will intensify their attacks on the voice-hearer if the individual speaks of them in front of others (ibid.).[4] Yet jinn are not exorcised like demons in the Christian tradition; instead they are said to be placated with food, drink and dance

---

[3] This echoes the findings which will be discussed in Chapter 11, that hearing voices is likely to occur following stressful or traumatic events. It is notable that many religions have a better idea of the sort of events that may precede voice-hearing experiences than many working in the mind sciences. This suggests, as we will return to later in the book, that the mind sciences need to overcome their hubris surrounding the idea that they have everything to teach, but nothing to learn from religion.

[4] Many secular voice-hearers have told me that their voices have also threatened them not to tell other people about their presence.

in order to make them settle down and act better (Watters, 2010). Given this clear framework, it is unsurprising that Al-Issa & Al-Issa (1970), reporting on hearing voices in Iraq, note that the experience is sometimes 'not regarded as abnormal by the patient or his family'. Clear reasons are available for voice-hearing experiences, such as 'the local belief that members of the Prophet Mohammed's family may appear to give the person advice about his affairs. The spirit of a deceased relative visiting the household is also an accepted phenomenon' (p. 18).

Hearing voices in the context of Islam

Watters (2010) gives a fascinating practical example of voice-hearing in an Islamic woman, Kimwana, who lived in Zanzibar. Kimwana reported that her voices were usually male and spoke to her as if they could 'see to my very soul' (p. 146). Much of the distress caused by the voices was due to their conflicting with Islamic rules of female modesty, reports Watters. While the male voices were occurring, Kimwana felt that she must behave as if there was a man present. The reaction of her family to her experiences was notable, in that there was a calm emotional tone in dealing with her periods of disturbed behaviour. During times of trouble she was allowed to withdraw, without excessive signs of alarm being shown by the family, and during well periods her health was not overtly celebrated. There was hence little pressure for Kimwana to identify herself as someone with a permanent mental illness, such as schizophrenia. It also made her less stressed, as she did not feel she was constantly being monitored or judged. The relation of her experiences to her religion was also noteworthy. The family would often repeat the belief that Allah would never put more burden on a person than they could bear. Indeed, by the family, managing hardships such as Kimwana's behaviour, was seen to be a way to pay off the debts of sinfulness – a continual act of penance. Not only did God's grace await those who suffered, but there was a feeling of gratitude for being able to prove their ability to endure it. Watters noted that the belief in jinn was also beneficial, as everyone on Zanzibar believed, as one family member put it, that we all have 'creatures in our heads' (p. 157). This made unusual behaviour goaded on by voices, e.g. hitting out at someone at the voice's prompting, more understandable and hence less stigmatising, and also led to less shame being attached both to the family and to Kimwana. All of these factors led to Kimwana remaining in her social group rather than being hospitalised and taking on a chronic patient role. Notably, when psychiatry came to Zanzibar, antipsychotics, electro-convulsive therapy and locked wards came too. Jinn were evicted to make way for broken mind narratives, and it is highly debatable how much this actually helped, as patients not getting better were now seen as defying the will of the psychiatrists and family members who were working together to get them well.

Comparing voice-hearing between Saudi Arabia and the United Kingdom

In a series of studies, Wahass & Kent compared voice-hearing and its meaning in Saudi Arabia and the United Kingdom (UK). First, they compared the phenomenology of voices in patients diagnosed with schizophrenia between Saudi Arabia (n=40) and the UK (n=35) (Kent & Wahass, 1996). It was found that the frequency of voices (typically more than once a day), loudness of voices (equally split between loud, average and quiet), amount of distress caused by voices (mostly distressing), difficulty in ignoring voices (mostly difficult to ignore), validity of the voices (mostly difficult not to believe), source of the voices (typically inside the head) and the perceived reality of the voices (typically felt to be real), did not differ between the two groups of patients. Additionally, 100 per cent of both groups of patients heard second-person voices ('you'), which tended to be negative (threatening, criticising, accusing or reviling them), and around two-thirds of each group of patients heard third-person voices ('he/she') of which approximately a third were negative, 10 per cent instructional and 5 per cent friendly in each group. Some differences were found, though. Voices in the UK patients were more likely to be clear (86% vs 58%), to have second-person voices with instructional themes (i.e. telling them what to do or not to do, such as hurting themselves or others; 86% vs 43%) and third-person voices which gave a running commentary (46% vs 10%), whereas the Saudi voices were more likely to have religious themes and 'superstitious' content (i.e. mentions of demons, magic and spirits).

Wahass & Kent (1997a) then compared attitudes in the general population to voices in Saudi Arabia to the UK. Patients attending a general doctor's surgery were asked about the meanings of voices. UK participants were more likely than Saudi participants to think that AVHs were symptoms of schizophrenia (61% vs 19%), and that they were caused by either brain damage (38% vs 9%), 'bad childhood experiences' (35% vs 14%) or stress (74% vs 31%). Saudi Arabian participants were more likely to say that AVHs were due to curses or magic (17% vs 2%), Satan's/Demons' voices (33% vs 5%) and that the person was pretending to hear voices (17% vs 7%). In terms of treatment, only a few of each set of participants felt no treatment was needed (UK: 6%, SA: 5%).

UK respondents were more likely to say that medication (22% vs 5%), psychological therapy (55% vs 33%) or a combination of medical and psychological therapy (63% vs 23%) were needed, as opposed to Saudi respondents, who were more likely to think that religious assistance was needed (66% vs 11%). The UK participants were more likely to disagree with statements that they would socially distance themselves from voice-hearers by discouraging marriage into the family, trusting them to look after their children, or avoid dealing with them.

Finally, Wahass & Kent (1997b) compared psychologists and psychiatrists in the two countries. They found that psychologists and psychiatrists in Saudi Arabia were more likely to take a medical view of hearing voices than their UK counterparts. Although psychiatrists in the UK were more likely to agree that voices were caused by brain damage (62% vs 40%), bad childhood experiences (22% vs 6%), environmental factors (28% vs 8%) and stressful life-events (34% vs 10%), the Saudi Arabian psychiatrists were more likely to think that drug therapy alone would be an effective treatment. Yet Saudi Arabian psychiatrists were also more optimistic that psychological therapy alone would work, and had a greater confidence than UK psychiatrists that a combination of drug and psychological therapy could be effective. We will return to issues surrounding medical and spiritual approaches in Chapter 12.

Cross-cultural prevalence of hearing voices

By looking at religious discourses on voices, we have started to move towards an understanding of how hearing voices is understood outside the dominant Christian culture of the West. We may now consider how voice-hearing is experienced around the world. It appears that voice-hearing is found in all countries on the planet. For example, Murphy *et al.* (1963) wrote to psychiatrists across the world and asked them to state whether they encountered hearing voices in their patients. In all of the countries studied (Australia, Barbados, Brazil, Bulgaria, Canada, Chile, Colombia, Czechoslovakia, Ecuador, Formosa, Germany, India, Japan, Java, Kenya, Kuwait, Hong Kong, Martinique, New Zealand, Nigeria, Norway, Peru, South Africa, South Korea, Thailand, Turkey, Uganda and the USA) hearing voices was never an infrequently found experience in patients. Even in remote communities, such as the Palau people who live on a small Western pacific island, who have subsequently been exposed to Western practices and concepts of schizophrenia, AVHs in distressed individuals have usually been found to involve them commenting on or criticising the voice-hearer

Table 6.1. *Cross-cultural prevalence of AVHs in patients diagnosed with schizophrenia*

City (number in study)	Aarhus (53)	Agra (101)	Cali (101)	Ibadan (120)	London (100)	Moscow (77)	Taipei (86)	Prague (76)
Heard voices	42%	34%	54%	45%	53%	23%	53%	36%
Voices speak to patient	40%	32%	55%*	44%	47%	18%	48%	33%

*It is not clear why more people heard voices speak to them than actual heard voices in this category.
**Data from Washington, USA, not given in report.
Source: WHO. (1973). Report of the international pilot study of Schizophrenia. Geneva: World Health Organization.

(Hammond, Kauders & Macmurray, 1983). Is voice-hearing more common in some of these countries than others, though?

Voice-hearing prevalence in different societies

All existing studies comparing the prevalence of AVH between different locations in the world suffer from the limitation that they examine this prevalence in patients with psychotic disorders, typically schizophrenia. This means that any differences found are likely to tell us more about local differences in how indicative psychiatrists view hearing voices as being a symptom of schizophrenia, and less about whether hearing voices is actually more common in certain places in the world. Nevertheless, what is clear is that hearing voices appears to occur in most cultures and societies across the world (e.g. Ndetei & Vadher, 1984; WHO, 1973). For example, in a 1973 World Health Organisation study, the prevalence of AVHs in patients diagnosed with schizophrenia across a number of countries was examined (Table 6.1). Hearing voices was found in all patients, with prevalence of AVHs in patients with schizophrenia ranging from 23 per cent (Moscow) to 54 per cent (Cali). A more recent study by Thomas *et al.* (2007) found 64 per cent of patients diagnosed with schizophrenia spectrum disorders in India experienced AVHs, whereas 83 per cent of patients diagnosed with schizophrenia in the USA did. However, this is likely to tell us more about how strongly the experience of hearing voices is associated with schizophrenia in the mind of American psychiatrists than Indian ones.

In terms of variations in the phenomenology of voices between cultures, there appears to be a good deal of stability in the types of voices heard. The voices in patients diagnosed with schizophrenia in one country are much like those of patients diagnosed with schizophrenia in another, country, supporting the claim that there is at least one universal class of voice-hearing experience. In the section above on Islam, we have already seen similarities in the voices experienced in Islamic societies compared to the predominantly Christian UK. In another between-cultures study, Suhail & Cochrane (2002) compared Pakistani patients diagnosed with psychosis living in Lahore, Pakistan (N = 98), to white British patients diagnosed with psychosis living in Britain (N = 50). It was found that the Pakistani patients had a higher prevalence of hearing voices (88% vs 52%). Further analyses showed that the white British patients were more likely to experience voices commenting on their behaviour, personality and actions (18% vs 3%), voices calling them bad names (32% vs 8%) and telling them to kill themselves or others (24% vs 6%). Additionally, voices were more likely to talk directly to the white British voice-hearer than the Pakistani voice-hearer in Pakistan (48% vs 21%), and the identity of the voice was more likely to be unknown in the white British sample than the Pakistani sample (56% vs 24%). Suhail & Cochrane also compared the Pakistani patients living in Pakistan to Pakistani patients living in Britain and found that those living in Britain were more likely to have voices commenting (15% vs 3%), voices telling them to kill themselves or others (17% vs 6%). However, as this study was based on patients' case notes, it is possible that the differences between Pakistan and Britain may have been influenced by systematic cross-cultural variations in the importance psychiatrists put on voices, and their tendency to write this down. Yet Suhail & Cochrane note that psychiatrists in both countries will share common training methods and textbooks.

Interestingly, there is also some evidence that hearing voices may evolve into visual hallucinations more often in non-Western cultures. For example, Collomb (1965, as cited in Al-Issa, 1978) in a study of Senegalese patients, found that hearing voices, particularly hearing the Devil's voice, was likely to evolve into visual hallucination of animals that wanted to kill them. However, more research is needed into the inter-relations between AVHs and visual hallucinations.

Within cultures

Differences have been found in the prevalence of voice-hearing between sub-cultures within a country. Chu & Klein (1985) found that hearing voices in the United States was more common in black patients diagnosed with schizophrenia than white patients diagnosed with schizophrenia. This finding could, of course, simply be due to diagnostic biases, with black people being more likely to be diagnosed with schizophrenia if they report AVHs. While this may be the case, there do appear to be genuine differences in voice-hearing prevalence within sub-cultures of a country. For example, in a study of the general population, based on data collected for the *Fourth National Survey of Ethnic Minorities* in the UK, Johns *et al.* (2002) found 1.2 per cent of the white population, 2.8 per cent of Caribbean participants and 0.6 per cent of South Asian had experienced hearing voices in the last year, saying quite a few words or sentences when there was no-one around that might account for it. Only a small percentage of those who reported such experiences had received a diagnosis of, or treatment for, psychosis. This pattern of findings of prevalence of AVHs in the UK being Asian < White < Caribbean has also been found recently in 9–12-year-old children by Laurens *et al.* (2008, 2011, personal communication). Their study of 1,579 children found that the percentages who reported having had a voice-hearing experience were: black Caribbean = 39%, white British = 30% and Asian = 22%. Of course, it may be that within certain cultures voice-hearing is a less stigmatised experience, and so people are more likely to admit hearing them.

The form and content of voices within sub-cultures in a single country may also differ. In a comparison of Pakistani patients with psychosis living in Britain and white Britons with psychosis living in Britain, Suhail & Cochrane (2002) found that although overall levels of hearing voices did not differ significantly (88% vs 72%), the white British voice-hearers were more likely to have voices calling them bad names (32% vs 15%) and to have voices speaking directly to them (48% vs 28%).

Changes in the prevalence of hearing voices may also occur within a society over time. For example Lenz (1964, as cited in Al-Issa, 1995) found that over the past hundred years in Vienna, the prevalence of auditory hallucinations in patients had increased. A study by Diethelm (1956, as cited in Al-Issa, 1978) found a similar pattern in the United States. However, again this may tell us more about changing cultural attitudes or psychiatric classification criteria than indicate any absolute increase in levels of voice-hearing.

Conceptualisation of voices in different societies

In addition to examining whether rates of voice-hearing differ between or within cultures, we may also ask how voices are understood in countries that have not been exposed to Western psychiatric discourses. Indeed, thus far in this book we have mostly focused on hearing voices in WEIRD (Western, Educated, Industrialised, Rich and Democratic) cultures (Henrich, Heine & Norenzayan 2010). We may ask what we can learn from these other societies about hearing voices, rather than just what we can teach them. Schmidt (1968) reports on hearing voices in the Murut of Sarawak, a tribe living in the mountains of Borneo. In the Murut, it is believed that the foremost cause of mental illness is haunted wells. Such an illness is called *ruden rupan*. If a person passes within two feet of one, or more importantly comes into contact with the water, he will hear voices and have visions of people who want to catch him, he therefore runs away. He usually reports that the people who want to kill him are not people who live in his village. He may resort to jumping into the river to drown himself, or hang himself from a tree, from the terror of his hallucinations. Whilst anyone can be affected by this, it is commonest in the young. It is treated by a healing ceremony performed by a native healer, which involves an appeal to the spirits of the well not to disturb the person any more. Thus, even in cultures which do not have our contemporary Western psychiatric criteria, we can see that they still experience similar types of aggressive voices that we do.

Similarly, in a rural Malay community in West Malaysia, Chen (1970) found that hearing voices was commonly associated with a condition called *Gila kena hantu*.[5] This is a form of insanity/severely disorganised mental state, which poses a threat to the community as a whole, as well as the individual sufferer (*gila*). In addition to hearing voices, this condition is characterised by fits of violence and superhuman abilities to cause physical destruction. The cause of the heard voices is thought to be *hantu* (evil spirits) who can enter an individual and whisper in his head, causing AVHs. These *hantu* are indigenous Malay spirits, and distinct from jinn, who may be either malevolent or benevolent. Chen does not indicate if voices per se are seen as pathological, but it appears that it is specifically the violence in this condition that is seen as threatening, rather than the voices per se. If this violence or threat is absent, the individual is not labelled *gila* (insane), but is said to have an illness (*penyakit*), which can either be due to *hantu* or witchcraft. In terms of what brings on the *hantu*, this was seen as potentially being due to mental stress, loss of one's vital force (*semangat*) due to a traumatic event, or incorrect behaviour. In terms of treatment, such individuals would be attended to by the *bomoh*, an individual who knew the folklore of the causes of diseases and their treatment and prevention. Treatment might consist of holding a feast (*kenduri*) to appease the offending spirit.

---

[5] Chen also found that the Malay recognised that AVHs could occur in *Gila merian* (post-partum insanity), with childbirth being thought to attract *hantu*.

If the *bomoh* failed, mental hospitals in urban centres would be consulted, however this was rare, as it was not felt that modern psychiatry was able to treat *hantu*, as it did not believe in them.

Murphy (1976) studied mental illness in both an Eskimo population as well as the Yoruba people of Nigeria. The Eskimos were found to have a concept of *nuthkavihak* ('being crazy'), signs of which included hearing voices, believing oneself to be an animal, refusing to talk, refusing to eat, drinking urine and threatening people. The Yoruba had a concept of *were* ('insanity'), signs of which included hearing voices, tearing off one's clothes, defecating in public, believing that one smells bad, laughing when there is nothing to laugh at and thinking one's food is poisoned. In the Yoruba, *were* people could be seen wandering the streets, sometimes naked, but more often dressed in odd, tattered clothes. They 'almost always [had] long, dirt-laden hair, talking to themselves, picking up objects to save. They usually stayed in one locale, where people fed them generously, allowed them to sleep in the market stalls, teased them mildly or laughed at them for minor deviations, and took action to control them only if the psychotics became violent' (p. 1025).

Crucially, though, Murphy stresses that: 'Of paramount significance is the fact that *were* and *nuthkavihak* were never used for a single phenomenon such as hearing voices, but rather were applied to a pattern in which three or four of the phenomena described above existed together' (p. 1022). Hearing voices on their own was actually a valued experience in these cultures. The ability to hear voices, along with the ability to see things others cannot and to prophesy, is called 'thinness' by Eskimos, and is a characteristic of the shaman. Murphy found that 4 per cent of the Eskimos had performed the shaman role in their lives (compare this figure to the prevalence of voice-hearing in the general population in Chapter 7). Moreover, people who are 'thin' outnumber the insane at least 8 to 1, and 'thin' people are never labelled as a *nuthkavihak*. One Eskimo explained this distinction, saying that 'When the shaman is healing he is out of his mind, but he is not crazy' (p. 1022). Murphy concludes that voices are only sometimes linked to insanity and that this depends on 'the degree to which they are controlled and utilized for a specific social function. The inability to control these processes is what is meant by a mind out of order; when a mind is out of order it will not only fail to control sensory perception but will also fail to control behaviour'. Although Murphy goes on to suggest that 'hearing voices, for example, can be voluntary or involuntary, and that it is mainly the involuntary forms that are associated with *were* and *nuthkavihak*' (ibid.), this is not explicitly stated by participants. The spontaneous form of hearing voices may be more likely to be associated with madness, but this is not a necessary association. What Murphy fails to note is that a number of the experiences which had to co-occur with hearing voices for a label of *were* or *nuthkavihak* to be applied could be seen to be consequences of failing to be able to cope with the voices, following their commands and not being able to manage them.

The terminology used to frame experiences of hearing voices is also important. In Mexican-American families of southern California, there exists a term, *nervios*, which is used to describe the illness of a person with schizophrenia (Jenkins, 1988, as cited in Watters, 2010). This term is used for a range of problems from headaches to grumpy behaviour, a catch-all term to describe mental distress. Hence, this is a hopeful term, as it downplays the gravity of the illness and signifies that it is only a transitory state (ibid.). It also helps not to isolate the experiences of the person with voices, as most people will have experienced some form of *nervios*, making the person with schizophrenia 'just like us only more so' (p. 161).

The change from a rural tribal culture to a more Western society can also affect how people experience voices. For example, Scott (1967) studied one hundred black female psychiatric patients admitted to a mental hospital in South Africa. These appear to be African women who had begun to move away from their tribes into the city. Of these, 85 per cent experienced AVHs; 42 per cent of these voice-hearers heard voices telling them to do certain tasks (e.g. pray, attend church, convert others). One clear difference that was found between the voices of these women and those found in the white population was that whereas the white patients typically did not know who the voices they heard were, the black women were more often able to identify them as known people (e.g. 58% said they were ancestors). Scott also noted that patients admitted to a hospital in a city were more likely to report their voices as being from God (as opposed to ancestors, as found in the tribes). Furthermore, unlike typical voices associated with psychosis, the black women only had accusatory voices in 8 per cent of cases, and the voices hardly ever commented on their actions. Why was this less than the white patients? Scott also noted the conclusion of Blignaut (1958, as cited in Scott, 1967, p. 854) that a greater degree of 'acculturization' (e.g. reading newspapers and watching television – which represents, in Scott's view 'sophistication' and a move away from 'primitive' ancestor cults) might cause accusatory content to increase. It appears that the women may have been much better able to cope with their voices using traditional tribal methods than the services they were offered. In particular, tribal methods would likely have found a way to work with the ancestor voices and to offer understanding, rather than trying to medicalise them away. Indeed, Scott observed that, 'even highly educated and training urban Africans consult the Sangoma [a tribal healer] for what they consider to be outside the White man's medicine' (p. 854). This is likely because tribal healers may have been more effective.[6]

In conclusion, it appears that many cultures accept that hearing voices in and of itself is not a pathological experience. Furthermore, an ability to 'treat' the distressed voice-hearer in the context of their local culture and to value the experience, and take an approach which does not stigmatise or make the voice-hearer feel less valued than other members of the community, and which provides hope, appears to be beneficial for voice-hearers in such cultures.

Cultural differences and hearing voices

Voices in the context of psychosis in the West have a large degree of similarity in both form and content to those in the East. However, differences are apparent, such as voices in the West being more likely to give the voice-hearers instructions, particularly to hurt themselves or others, and being less likely to have religious content. It may be that such differences can best be addressed through an analysis of how guilt and responsibility are understood across cultures. At a more basic level, though, it is known that cultural sponging (i.e. voices soaking up the dominant culture of the voice-hearer) will influence the content of voices. Skirrow et al. (2002) argue that as hallucinations 'are, by definition, self-generated experiences, it seems reasonable to expect that that content of these experiences will reflect the experiences, memories and beliefs of the individual concerned' (p. 87). They demonstrated this by examining the impact of a prominent news event (the 1999 involvement of NATO in the Kosovo conflict and the bombing of Serbia) on the voices of patients in an intensive care unit. They found that during the conflict two individuals had auditory hallucinations involving themes of war, both of whom were aged over 70. Before and after the conflict no voice-hearers had voices involving war. As these older individuals would have had memories of WWII, conflict was likely to have been of more concern to them.

Given that many of the studies reviewed here have employed patients diagnosed with schizophrenia, it remains unknown how voices per se differ between cultures, because due to the diagnostic criteria for schizophrenia, this will naturally produce two fairly homogeneous

[6] Here we may note the improved outcomes of schizophrenia in developing, as opposed to developed countries (Jablensky & Sartorius, 2008; WHO, 1973).

groups of voice-hearers who have distressing voices. Yet, given suggestive evidence for variation in prevalence rates between cultures, how might we explain this? Al-Issa (1995) has proposed that culture affects the prevalence of hallucinations such as AVHs due to: (1) cultural attitudes affecting a person's 'familiarity with their own fantasy and imagination' (p. 368), leading to a confusion between reality and fantasy, and (2) cultural beliefs affecting people's levels of expectancy and suggestibility. In 'less rational cultures' (p. 370), Al-Issa argues, people are encouraged to be more introspective, which leads to their becoming more aware of private mental events and reporting more hallucinations. On the other hand, he argues that in 'Western rational scientific society' (p. 369) voices are considered negative due to their potential to interfere with daily activities, hence people become less aware of the workings of their own minds, and this increases the threshold of noticing such imaginings and people hallucinate less. Whilst I would not agree with the implied association with irrationality and hearing voices, some parts of this argument do seem valid. For example, the great inward-looking contemplative mystics (e.g. St John of the Cross (Chapter 2) and the Desert Fathers (Chapter 1)) who cultivated silence and introspection, did appear more likely to have voice-hearing experiences than the general population.

Conclusions

By adding the findings of this chapter to the findings of Part I, we may now conclude that there is a common basic form of voice-hearing experience involving commands, comments and evaluations of the voice-hearer's thoughts and actions, which is found across both time (i.e. throughout much of documented history) and space (i.e. across all countries of the world today). In the West a common perception is that hearing voices is a sign of madness, with Goffman (1962) noting that the significance of hearing voices with madness is a culturally derived and socially engrained stereotype. As Al-Issa (1978) notes, this is internalised by the voice-hearer, the psychiatrist and the members of society. This leads to hearing voices being reacted to with alarm and anxiety by the voice-hearer, their friends, family and psychiatrist, which is unlikely to be of help to the voice-hearer. We may recall from Part I that the development of a particular concept of self in the West (i.e. self-disciplined, self-contained, self-determining and rational) encourages the view that intrusive thought/perceptual experiences are threatening. In contrast, in many non-Western societies and sub-cultures in the West, voices may be viewed as less threatening, and hence be reacted to more calmly. Al-Issa argues that because Western models portray voices as random, spontaneous, unpredictable and largely uncontrollable, this also makes the patient more anxious, as he has limited means to control them. In contrast, as we have seen, in cultures where spirits are understood to cause AVHs, there are prescribed theological and social ways to control voices, to give the experience meaning and to offer the voice-hearer some control and hope. If the voice-hearer is then able to take up a specific role in the society, such as a shaman or medium, this enables meaning and coping by reintegrating the voice-hearer into society, rather than abandoning them at its borders. Ritual may also help, by limiting AVHs to socially prescribed times and places.

In the West, the dominance of scientific naturalism and materialism lead to a view that there is an objective, measurable world out there that is reality. In contrast, both within sub-cultures of the West, and in other societies, hearing voices either occurring spontaneously or being induced by drugs, ritual or trance is understood to open a doorway to a hidden reality which is more real than the 'normal' world. In this view, voices can be seen as more real than the real world (Karlsson, 2008).

Culture and religious factors are hence not primitive ways of understanding voices, but complex systems designed to allow individuals to cope with their experiences. This may be the reason why outcomes for patients' diagnosed schizophrenia are better in the developing, as opposed to developed world (Jablensky & Sartorius, 2008; WHO, 1973). It appears that the hegemonic Western mind sciences would do well to look to theologians and individuals from other cultures to see what they can teach them about voices, and not just vice-versa.

Chapter 6: summary of key points

- Hearing voices appears to be experienced in all cultures across the globe today, only being associated with madness in some societies.
- Western models of self may encourage perceptions of voice-hearing as threatening, making the experience more distressing than necessary.
- Voices in the Western world appear more likely to tell the voice-hearer to hurt themselves or others than voices in non-Western societies.
- Religious frameworks can provide meaningful ways for people to understand voices they hear, reduce the anxiety associated with the experience and aid coping.
- The 'voice of God' shows many phenomenological similarities with the voices heard by distressed voice-hearers who are given psychiatric diagnoses, but also some notable differences, such as the positive emotions associated with the experience.

- Therapy can work within this religious framework, potentially using religious concepts of love, forgiveness and tolerance, which appear suited to working with the distressing experience of hearing voices, particularly given the issues of guilt and shame we will later see are often associated with them (Chapter 11).
- Contemporary Western mind sciences should look to learn from how voices are understood and managed by religions and other cultures, rather than simply imposing its own understanding onto them.

7 The phenomenology of hearing voices in people without psychiatric diagnoses

In the previous chapter we examined people exempt from the DSM on the grounds that their beliefs were consistent with their culture or society. What, then, about another group of people exempt from the DSM, namely those in the general population who hear voices but cope with them well?[1]

Hearing voices in the general population

Hypnagogic and hypnopompic voice-hearing experiences

Hallucinations on the border of sleep are referred to as hypnagogic if occurring in the transition between waking and sleep, or hypnopompic if occurring in the transition between sleep and waking (Mavromatis, 1988). Hypnagogic and hypnopompic (H&H) hallucinations appear to be broadly similar and can be treated as a single class of experience. H&H voice-hearing experiences appear to be the most common form of voice-hearing experience in the general population (Ohayon, 2000). They can include hearing one's name being called, neologisms, irrelevant statements, nonsense, quotations, references to spoken conversation and remarks directed to oneself (Mavromatis, 1988). Voices may also take the form of meaningful responses to one's current thoughts, but such statements are typically not directed at anybody (ibid.).

A number of systematic studies of H&H voice-hearing experiences have been performed. Ohayon (2000), in a study of 13,057 people in the general population, found that 2.4 per cent reported some form of auditory hallucination in the H&H states (with most of these in the hypnagogic, as opposed to hypnopompic). However, student populations report much higher levels of H&H AVHs. Jones, Fernyhough & Meads (2009)

---

[1] i.e. in the terminology of the DSM, those who do not suffer social or occupational impairment.

found that 49 per cent of students had heard someone calling their name in the H&H state, and 5 per cent experienced this frequently or very frequently. Forty four per cent had heard a voice that was familiar to them, and 31 per cent had heard the voice of a person they could not identify. In a more detailed later study, Jones, Fernyhough & Larøi (2010) examined H&H voice-hearing experiences in 325 students. One hundred and eight (i.e. 33% of the sample) indicated that they heard voices in the H&H state, and were happy to answer follow-up questions. In terms of clarity, only 22 per cent said they heard clear words, with most (43%), hearing only the odd clear word. Forty-six per cent reported one-off voices, 12 per cent reported the voice of the same person all the time and 42 per cent reported a mix of one-off and recurrent voices. Eighty-one per cent of participants who had heard a voice in the H&H state had had the experience of hearing a voice of a person they recognised, whereas 70 per cent had had the experience of hearing a voice of a person unknown to them. Of the 108 students who had experienced H&H AVHs, 42 per cent reported that the voices talked directly to them. Both nice (17%), nasty (9%) and mundane (35%) things were said by the voice. Over half of the participants (53%) had spoken back silently to the voices and around a third (32%) had spoken back aloud to them: 8 per cent had managed to engage the voice in a form of conversation. Notably, unlike the voices found in clear consciousness in those diagnosed with psychosis, only 4 per cent of participants reported, in the H&H state, experiencing voices commanding them or advising them to do things. Hence, phenomeno-logical analyses suggested that there may be two different types of AVHs occurring in the H&H state, which may not share common mechanisms. However, in a recent functional magnetic resonance imaging (fMRI) study of the neural responses to sound in those prone to H&H hallucin-ations, Lewis-Hanna et al. (in press) found that similar areas were hyper-active in this group, compared to patients diagnosed with schizophrenia who hear voices. More work is hence needed into the continuity of AVH phenomenology and cause between AVHs experienced in the waking and H&H state.

Voices in clear consciousness

Starting with the study of Sidgwick et al. (1894), as mentioned in Chapter 3, there have been a large number of studies, particularly in the past couple of decades, of the prevalence of voice-hearing in the general population. These studies have typically focused on what St Augustine termed corporeal voices (i.e. hearing an external spoken voice), with more subtle voice-hearing experiences such as intellectual

Table 7.1. *Hearing voices in the general population (selected large-scale studies)*

Study	N	Details	Sample	%	Prevalence
Auditory hallucinations (voices, noises and other sounds)					
Shevlin et al. (2007)	5,983	Auditory hallucinations May have included sleep-related experiences	Population	8.3	Lifetime
Olfson et al. (2002)	1,005	Auditory hallucinations May have included sleep-related experiences	Population	12.7	Lifetime
Caspi et al. (2005)	802	Hearing things or voices that other people cannot hear Excluded sleep-related voices	Population	3.4	Lifetime
Ohayon (2000)	13,057	Hearing sounds, music or voices which other people cannot hear Excluded sleep-related voices	Population	0.6	Lifetime
Hearing voices (potentially including those on the border of sleep)					
Ross, Joshi & Currie (1990)	1,055	Number who said that the statement 'Some people sometimes find that they hear voices inside their head which tell them to do things or comment on things they are doing' had been true of them at some time	Population	26.0	Lifetime
Verdoux et al. (1998)	462	Hearing voices (in people with no psychiatric history)	GP patients (non-psychosis)	16.0	Lifetime
		(voices conversing)		(4.8)	
		(voices commanding)		(4.8)	
Hearing voices (excluding those on the borders of sleep, and related to drugs/alcohol)					
Sidgwick et al. (1894)	17,000	Hearing voices	Population	2.9	Lifetime
Tien (1991)	18,572	Auditory hallucinations of all forms	Population	2.2	Lifetime
Caspi et al. (2005)	802	Hear voices commenting on what you were doing or thinking	Population	1.0	Unstated
		Hear voices telling you what to do		0.6	
		Hear two or more voices talking to each other that other people could not hear		0.6	
		Carry on conversations with the voices that other people could not hear			
Johns et al. (2002)	7,849	Number who have heard voices saying quite a few words or sentences*	Population	1.1	Annual
Johns et al. (2004)	8,520	Number who have heard voices saying quite a few words or sentences Excluded those with probable psychosis (n = 60)	Population	1.1 0.7	Annual

*Weighted average of 2,867 white, 1,205 Caribbean and 3,777 South Asian participants.
Source: Compiled by the author.

locutions not being studied. In this section our focus will be on the prevalence and phenomenology of voice-hearing experiences in the general population. Data on the prevalence of AVHs from a number of large studies is presented in Table 7.1.

The Sidgwick *et al.* study found 2.9 per cent of people (493/17,000) reported having experienced hearing voices (auditory vocal hallucinations in their terminology) in the absence of any visual or tactile component. Of these people, 43 per cent said they had heard the voice of a living person, 14 per cent dead people, 41 per cent unrecognised voices and 1 per cent the voice of an angel or religious phantasm. Of those who gave the age that they were at the time they heard the voice, the most common age ranges were 20–29 years (42%), 10–19 years (20%) and 30–39 years (18%). Of the first-hand accounts of voice-hearing Sidgwick *et al.* collected,[2] the majority of voice-hearing experiences (47%) were simply hearing one's own name called, with 35 per cent hearing words other than their name and 17 per cent hearing no definite words.

The closest to a modern replication of the Sidgwick *et al.* study is the study of Tien (1991, see Table 7.1). Tien does not explicitly state in his paper that hearing voices is being looked at (referring instead to 'auditory hallucinations'), however, the text implicitly suggests that it is hearing voices that is being asked about. Tien also does not actually numerically report the prevalence figures for hearing voices, instead presenting a graph of prevalence by age. The graph shows that approximately 2.2 per cent of people reported hearing voices (high of 3.2% at 18–19 years, low of 1.5% at age 30–39). Tien also examined whether or not the voices were associated with impaired functioning. It appears (again, reading from Tien's graphs) that around 0.7 per cent of people had consulted a professional or taken medication for their voices more than once and had voices which interfered with their life or activities a lot, whereas 1.5 per cent heard voices with no impairment of function or distress (a ratio of non-impairment to impairment of just over 2:1). Further graphs show that 1.8 per cent of men and 2.8 per cent of women heard voices. In women the highest prevalence was 5 per cent at the age of 18–19, whereas for men the mean prevalence remained fairly consistent at all ages.

Although the studies of Sidgwick *et al.* (1894) and Tien (1991) suggest that hearing voices (excluding those experienced on the borders of

[2] This specific set of data was not for voices heard on their own, and in about 50% of cases other modalities of hallucination were concurrently experienced (see Sidgwick *et al.*, 1894, p. 131).

sleep and due to drugs/medical conditions) occurs in 2–3 per cent of people in the general population, the studies of Johns and colleagues and Caspi *et al.* (2005) suggest that hearing voices saying more than the odd word (i.e. saying quite a few words or sentences) only occurs in around 1 per cent of people (Table 7.1). Johns *et al.* (2002) also examined whether participants who reported hearing voices saying quite a few words or sentences met the criteria for psychosis using the Present State Examination (Wing, Cooper & Sartorius, 1974). It was found that of the sub-set of the 1.2 per cent who did report this experience and who were interviewed, 25 per cent met criteria for a psychotic disorder, 56 per cent criteria for an affective disorder and 19 per cent did not meet any diagnostic criteria.

Tien's and Sidgwick's work suggests that the prevalence of voices is greater in the young (although we should note that AVHs due to deafness in old age, and losing one's spouse, are also potential triggers for hearing voices). Consistent with this, a more recent and detailed twenty-year longitudinal study (starting with 591 participants and with 62 per cent of participants continuing to participate over the 20-year period) by Rossler *et al.* (2007) found that the proportion of people who said that the statement that they had been distressed by 'hearing voices that other people don't hear' in the past month applied to them 'a little bit' at age 20–21 was 3.2 per cent, at age 22–23 was 2.2 per cent, at age 28–30 was 1.0 per cent, at age 30–31 was 1.1 per cent, at age 35–36 was 1.0 per cent and at age 40–41 was 0.1 per cent.[3] The rates of those who said that this statement applied to them 'moderately' was much lower, peaking at 0.7 per cent at age 28–30. This also showed a trend to decrease over time, from 0.4 per cent at age 20–21 to 0 per cent at age 40–41. This supports a greater prevalence of distressing AVHs among the young.

In our discussion of AVHs in the H&H state, it was noted that the prevalence is much higher in student populations than in the general population. This pattern is also found for AVHs in clear consciousness. In contrast to the general population surveys discussed above, where the prevalence of voice-hearing is in the low single digits, studies in student/college populations have found that the *majority* of such individuals report having had some form of voice-hearing experience at some time in their life. For example, Posey & Losch (1983) examined hearing voices experiences in a college student population, focusing on the experience of hearing a voice fully aloud 'as if someone had spoken' (p. 101). Of the sample, 71 per cent reported having heard a voice in

[3] This would not, of course, pick up people who had the experience but were not distressed by it.

some form (and it appears this was not in the H&H state). The most common single experience, reported by 39 per cent of the sample, was hearing one's name being called when no-one was there. In addition, 11 per cent reported that they had literally heard God's voice, and 11 per cent had also heard voices which offered comfort or advice in situations similar to that of hearing a voice coming from the back seat of the car when driving: 5 per cent had experiences like talking to a dead relative and hearing their voice respond. Specific examples of participants' experiences included: 'I was sitting on a hillside letting my mind fully wander when I actually heard someone or something say "It's beautiful isn't it." It scared the hell out of me' (p. 102); 'When I'm alone driving I started to hear me talk to me. It is as if I'm beside myself engaging in a conversation with myself' (p. 105); 'The voices seem not to want to harm me, but to calm me down or to warn me' (p. 106). One of the participants who heard the voice of God reported that it came from the middle of his chest, and sounded something like his own voice. Very similar rates were found in college students (N = 586) by Barrett & Etheridge (1992). In this study, 64 per cent had heard their own name being called in a shop, 13 per cent had heard voices from the back of the car whilst driving and 6 per cent had had a conversation with a dead relative.

Why should the prevalence of hearing voices in students be so much higher than in the general population? One possibility is that such experiences are much more common in the young, but as we saw in the Rossler et al. (2007) study discussed above, although the prevalence of voices (associated with distress) in young adults is higher, it was still in the low single-figure digits. Another more likely possibility is that the questions asked of students, being much more specific (rather than the generic 'have you heard voices' questions of general population surveys, which are also often asked in the context of pathology), led to a greater possibility of recall of the experience. Evidence that this might be the case comes from a study of AVHs in mental health nurses (Millham & Easton, 1998), which asked the same questions as had been asked by Posey & Losch (1983). This study found that a near majority of mental health nurses had had an AVH, with 42 per cent having heard their name called whilst out and 13 per cent had heard a voice from the back of the car whilst driving.

AVHs in the general population appear to be more likely to occur when there is external noise that may be misinterpreted, or an absence of noise. Taking the latter first, it has been found that AVHs may occur spontaneously in the general population during sensory deprivation, with 15 per cent of people, on average, hearing either music or voices (Zuckerman, 1969). In addition to sensory isolation, social isolation also appears to be a trigger for hearing voices, particularly when undergone in conjunction with ambiguous unpatterned noise, a combination of factors which often occurs in lone explorers. One good example is that of Charles Lindbergh. Lindbergh successfully completed the first solo transatlantic flight (from New York to Paris) in his single-engine, single-seater plane, the *Spirit of St Louis*, in 1927. Although alone during his flight, Lindbergh was surrounded by engine noise, which he had to continually listen to in order to monitor for problems. Lindbergh stated that: 'First one then another presses forward to my shoulder to speak above the engine's voice . . . [or they] come out of the air itself, clear yet far away . . . conversing and advising me on my flight, discussing problems of my navigation, reassuring me, giving me messages of importance unattainable in ordinary life' (Lindbergh, as cited in Maitland, 2008, p. 61). Solo sailors also commonly report AVHs, coming from the noises around them, with the sailor Bill Howell reporting in his sailing log that 'Usual voices in the rigging calling "Bill, Bill" rather high pitched' (Howell, as cited in ibid., p. 62).

AVHs in the general population also appear to occur under conditions of extreme stress or at problematic periods in life, in which they often have a highly beneficial function. Elsewhere I have termed these 'voices that save' (Jones, 2010b). For example, the mountaineer Joe Simpson (Simpson, 1988), after a horrific climbing accident, was forced to descend from the mountain Siula Grande with a broken leg by crawling for four days back to base camp. During the latter stages of his infernal journey, he began to hear a voice which was 'clean and sharp and commanding' (p. 141) and which told him to 'Go on, keep going' (p. 147).[4] During a period of his life he was significantly negatively affected by alcohol, Sir Anthony Hopkins is also reported as hearing a voice. He is said to have described how 'It was as if a voice said, "Ready! Go!" It was that clear, the voice of God. The best part of myself, my subconscious, came to rescue me. I don't know how. I had no religious connection or a connection to what I thought was God' (Hopkins, 2009).[5] Similarly, Heathcote-James (2001)

---

[4] We may contrast this with an account of Oliver Sachs from an incident when he, too, was dragging himself back along a mountain path after a fall. Sachs reports stopping due to exhaustion and thinking in his normal inner speech, 'why not a little rest – a nap maybe'. He then countered this by replying to himself in his inner speech, 'Don't listen to it ever. You've got to go on' (Sachs, as cited in Stephens & Graham, 2000, p. 147). Thus, a thought for which Sachs experienced mental agency, Simpson did not.

[5] I have attempted to contact Sir Anthony to get his corroboration of this media report (which should hence be treated with caution), but with no joy to date. However, in an unauthorised biography of Hopkins (Falk, 2004), he is quoted as saying: 'There was this extraordinarily powerful voice inside my head and it said "It's all over. Now you can start living, but remember it all because it has been for a purpose." And instantly I knew what it was. It was God' (p. 88).

reports numerous examples of people hearing voices, such as ones warning them that 'the boiler's overheating' (p. 116), or, like Joe Simpson, encouraging them to 'keep going' (p. 122) in times of despair.[6] This fascinating class of voices remains under-researched. From an evolutionary point of view, it makes sense that we should have the capacity to generate these 'voices that save', however, why they should need to be experienced as non-self-produced is unclear. It may be that the force of such auditions, and their tendency to take the form of a command which compels one to perform the action, make them more effective cognitions than simply our normal thoughts in such circumstances.

AVHs in children and adolescents (prevalence 5–32%)

Most large-scale studies show that around 5 to 10 per cent of children and adolescents will hear voices (Table 7.2). In Horwood et al.'s (2008) study, 18.8 per cent of voice-hearing children had auditory hallucinations occurring weekly or more frequently. In Scott et al.'s (2009) study, whereas 4 per cent reported hearing voices sometimes, a further 2 per cent reported hearing them often. However, in a more recent study of children aged 9–12 at primary schools in London, Laurens et al. (2008, 2011, personal communication) found that 32.1 per cent responded affirmatively to the question 'Have you ever heard voices that other people could not hear?'. The reasons for the greater prevalence in this study are unclear.

Bartels-Velthuis, Jenner & van de Willige (2010) report that in their study 15 per cent of children experienced substantial suffering and problem behaviour as a result of voices. Suffering and anxiety associated with the voice was greater in girls than in boys. Interestingly, Dhossche et al. (2002) reported that social phobia was more strongly associated with auditory than visual hallucinations, and that adolescents with voices were more likely to go on to develop depression or substance misuse disorders at eight-year follow-up.

A more detailed study of the negative effects that voice-hearing can have on children was performed by Escher et al. (2004). They found that 70 per cent of children had problems at home and 82 per cent at school, due to the voices. These problems included difficulty paying attention at school, problems at home due to performing actions to placate the voices (e.g. stealing, running up and down the staircase, touching tiles) which

---

[6] These voices have clear parallels to the motivation purposes of inner speech, see Chapter 9.

Table 7.2. *Hearing voices in children and adolescents in the general population*

Study	N	Age	Prevalence	Prevalence period
Studies asking about auditory hallucinations				
Dhossche *et al.* (2002)	909	11–18 years	5%*	Lifetime
Horwood *et al.* (2008)	6,455	12 years	7.3%*	Six months
Scott *et al.* (2009)	1,261	13–17 years	6%*	Lifetime
Studies asking about specifically auditory verbal hallucinations				
Bartels-Velthuis *et al.* (2010)	3,870	7–8 years	9%	Annual
Laurens *et al.* (2008, 2011, personal communication)	1,579	9–12 years	32.1%	Lifetime

*Figure for auditory hallucinations, so may have included non-verbal auditory hallucinations (e.g. music).
Source: Compiled by the author.

irritated family members. Problems were also caused by the child talking out loud in public, smashing things, or being provoked into quarrels. As a result, 41 per cent of voice-hearing children said they had been punished because of things they did that were connected to the voices. Talking to their parents about their voices was beneficial. For example, one child was able to explain to her father: 'That's why I couldn't play chess with you yesterday, the voices told me not to' (p. 216). Escher and colleagues also found that 16 per cent of children became so afraid as a result of the voices that they couldn't move, talk or think. In the first year of their study, Escher and colleagues found that 52 per cent of children said that they could not refuse to do what the voices commanded them to do, 39 per cent were being blackmailed by them, and 47 per cent of them had voices which interfered with their making their own choices. Some children became unable to decide what to eat, drink, wear, or even what kind of shampoo to use. Interestingly, it was noted that many of the voice-hearing children's ability to cope with emotions was very weak. Rather than a child expressing an emotion, the voice may express it instead, with one girl reporting that: 'I can never get angry, the voices get angry instead' (p. 217).

Escher *et al.* (2002) have also examined the persistence of AVHs in children. Eighty children (with a mean age of 13 years) with AVHs were followed up at one-year, two-year and three-year intervals. After 3 years there had been a 60 per cent cumulative discontinuation of voices. If children could identify triggers of time and place (e.g. only hearing voices at school or when alone in one's bedroom at night), then the voices were more likely to discontinue. Twenty per cent of children's voices stopped without any engagement with mental health services. For an excellent examination of hearing voices in children, see Escher & Romme (2010).

Healthy voice-hearers

Prevalence

The voices we have examined so far in the general population are typically fairly infrequent, brief and only rarely complex. However, from Part I of this book we already know that throughout history there have been people who had frequent and complex AVHs and coped with them quite well. How can we estimate the prevalence of such healthy voice-hearers today? The first question that arises is, how many people in the general population today have frequent AVHs and yet have not been in contact with mental health services? From Table 7.1, it would appear that an upper limit for this figure is around 1 per cent of the general population.[7] However, the question then arises as to what proportion of people are coping well with these experiences and what percentage are potentially suffering in silence and could really use some help. Unfortunately we do not have conclusive data to answer this question, and what follows will have to be a very basic approximation.

The best data we have comes from Johns *et al.* First, we have Johns *et al.*'s (2002) finding that 1.2 per cent of the general population[8] hear such voices. The first problem here is that Johns and colleagues do not clearly state what proportion of this 1.2 per cent have either contacted psychiatric services or taken antipsychotic medication. The intimation in Table 2 of their paper is that it could be as high as almost half of this 1.2 per cent (they note that 0.5% of the total white population reported treatment or diagnosis for a psychotic disorder). Of the sub-sample of this 1.2 per cent they interviewed, approximately 25 per cent met criteria for a psychotic disorder, 57 per cent met criteria for affective disorders (and presumably a key part of meeting such criteria was distress and impairment), and only 19 per cent did not meet the diagnostic criteria for any psychiatric disorder. The figure for healthy voice-hearers could

---

[7] i.e. using the figures from Johns and colleagues' and Caspi *et al.*'s studies of the experience of complex and extensive voices experienced in the last year. This assumes, of course, that all people who had voices felt able to admit to them, which is potentially unlikely.
[8] I use here the 1.2% figure reported by Johns *et al.* (2002) for white participants, who form the majority of the UK population.

hence be as low as 0.2 per cent of the population (1.2% × 0.19). Yet this 0.2 per cent figure may be too low, as Johns *et al.*'s (2004) general population study found that after excluding individuals with probable psychosis, 0.7 per cent of participants reported this experience of hearing quite a few words or sentences. Another problem with these studies of Johns and colleagues is that we only know that such individuals had heard quite a few words or sentences, and not how often they heard such voices. Another source of data we have, which is less methodologically rigorous but still suggestive, is the report of Romme & Escher (1989), who asked voice-hearers in the general population to contact them to tell them about their experiences (see Chapter 3). They found that of the 450 voice-hearing respondents, 300 could not cope with their voices, whereas 150 could cope. This does not help us accurately establish the prevalence of healthy voice-hearing, but could be taken to suggest that for every two people who contact psychiatric services about voices they cannot cope with, another one may hear voices they can cope with and not need to contact psychiatric services (i.e. are a healthy voice-hearer). By this logic, and using a back-of-an-envelope calculation, if around 2 per cent of the population are diagnosed with either schizophrenia or bipolar disorder, and around half of these individuals hear voices (i.e. 1% of the population), then we could estimate that half of this number of people (i.e. 0.5%) in the general population hear voices they can cope with. Finally, Sommer *et al.* (2010) found that of 4,135 members of the general population who completed an on-line questionnaire on hallucinations, 103 (i.e. 2.5%) who did not meet criteria for a diagnosis of schizophrenia, bipolar disorder, or result from drug/alcohol abuse were identified as having AVHs. Of these, 91 per cent had no disturbance of their lives by the voices (i.e. social or occupational impairment). Of course, this 2.5 per cent is unlikely to be generalisable to the general population, as the sample was self-selecting (i.e. people with voice-hearing experiences may have been more keen to participate in a hallucinations questionnaire study than non-voice-hearing people, hence inflating the prevalence figure).[9] Thus, if we are making a conservative estimate, it appears the best figure we currently have, after averaging the figures for individuals in the general population with significant voice-hearing experiences in the absence of disorder of 0.2 per cent from Johns *et al.* (2002) and 0.7 per cent from Johns *et al.* (2004), is that 0.45 per cent of the population can be viewed as healthy voice-hearers. However,

---

[9] Indeed, quite sensibly, Sommer and colleagues make no attempt to estimate the prevalence of healthy voice-hearers from the data in their study.

we should note that more detailed studies are urgently required in this area, and that this figure is only a tentative estimate.

Voice-hearing experiences in healthy voice-hearers are given a range of meanings, which will be discussed in Chapter 12. Here, though, we focus on the phenomenology of such voices (which, of course, cannot be entirely separated from their meaning). What, then, are the voices heard by healthy voice-hearers like? This can be answered by an examination of the research literature, as well as an examination of accounts of healthy voice-hearers in their own words. To give a brief illustration, Honig *et al.* (1998) give an example of a healthy voice-hearer, a 42-year-old mother of two who has a private practice as a psychic healer. She hears a number of voices, her earliest voice, which started in childhood, speaking to her in the second person and with which she communicates for the benefit of herself and her clients. Her voices are protective and give her care, comfort and advice. The voices also talk among themselves, but she is not afraid of them, and they do not restrict her life. She was repeatedly physically and sexually abused as a child,[10] and her voices have helped her pull through difficult times. She was punished as a 5-year-old child for repeating in class at school what her voices said to her, and as a result she did not discuss them with others again until she was 34 years old.

In a large systematic study, Sommer *et al.* (2010) studied 103 healthy voice-hearers. These individuals were members of the general population who had completed a hearing voices questionnaire, then been interviewed by a trained psychologist over the telephone. They had voices distinct from their thoughts, and which had a 'hearing' quality. They had never been diagnosed with or treated for a psychiatric disorder, and had not abused drugs or alcohol in the last three months. The individuals were found to have experienced voices for a mean duration of 29 years, with mean age at onset of 14 years. Over the last week, on average they had experienced 3.6 hearing voice experiences. Eighteen per cent had commenting voices, and 11 per cent had voices which spoke to each other. The majority (71%) never had voices with negative content, 25 per cent heard both positive and negative voices, with 4 per cent experiencing only negative voices. Nearly all participants (91%) did not report any disturbance of daily life by their voices. In terms of explanations, 58 per cent believed they had a real, external source, mainly benevolent spirits. Fifty-five per cent reported that they could stop their voices if they wanted to, for example, at inconvenient

---

[10] A common story in voice-hearers, see Chapter 11.

moments. It was found that 'the subjects with AVH did not have clinic-ally relevant delusions, disorganization, or negative symptoms, nor did they meet criteria for schizotypal, schizoid, or paranoid personality disorder'. Notably (again, see Chapter 11), compared to non-voice-hearing controls, there were higher levels of childhood trauma in the healthy voice-hearers.

Phenomenological comparison

How do the voices of healthy voice-hearers differ from voice-hearers with psychiatric diagnoses? Based on diagnostic criteria for psychotic dis-orders, it should be expected that such individuals may hear voices very much like those in psychiatric patients, but in the absence of social or occupational impairment (which is necessary for a psychiatric diagno-sis). Factors that cause these voices not to be life-impairing are likely to be that they have less distressing content and are more controllable. This is indeed what we find.

In the largest study of its kind, Daalman et al. (2010) compared the phenomenology of AVHs in 118 patients diagnosed with psychosis, with 111 'otherwise healthy individuals'. The patient group experi-enced less control over their voices, more frequently heard voices speaking in the third person, were older when they first heard a voice (by 9 years), and had voices which were more frequent, distressing and emotional, as well as being longer in duration. No differences were found in the perceived location (inside/outside head), loudness, and number of voices. In attempting to distinguish between the two groups the authors note that: 'Having control over the AVH for most of the time, hearing voices less than once a day, age of onset before 16 years of age, and hearing voices with a predominantly positive content are good predictors that a person does not have a psychotic illness' (p. 188). Of course, it may be argued that such variables do not actually tell us whether someone has an illness or not, but rather whether or not they are likely to be distressed by their voices. This issue will be returned to in Chapter 12.

In a comparison of 14 patients diagnosed with schizophrenia who heard voices and 14 healthy individuals (students) who heard voices, Leudar et al. (1997) found the voices of the two groups to differ in only a very limited number of ways. The voices of the patients were more likely to be those of a public figure, to advise specific actions, to have violent content and to give new information and less likely to be the voice of a family member, to inhibit actions, have mundane content, to evaluate others, or to ask questions. In a study by Honig et al. (1998)

comparing 18 patients diagnosed with schizophrenia to 15 healthy voice-hearers, patients were found to be significantly more afraid of their voices, more likely to have voices that disturbed daily life, to get into problems due to the voices, not to be in control of the voices, and for the voice to be more in control (using a conservative Bonferroni adjusted alpha of $p < 0.001$). In fact, in this study all the patient group had negative voices, as compared to only 53 per cent of the healthy voice-hearers, with both groups having a high prevalence of positive voices (83% vs 93%, respectively). Both Honig *et al.* and Leudar *et al.* note their surprise at the remarkable similarities of the voices of patients diagnosed with schizophrenia and healthy voice-hearers. The logical conclusion is that it is not hearing voices per se that is associated with problems, but rather that voices that are harder to cope with (e.g. which are all negative) are associated with problems and entry into the psychiatric/mental health system.

In another examination of healthy voice-hearers, in a national campaign in New Zealand, Beavan & Read (2010) appealed for members of the general public over the age of 18, 'who have heard voices that no one else can hear' (p. 201) to contact them. Of the 154 participants who responded and completed a questionnaire on voice-hearing, 46 per cent had voices who said mostly friendly and/or helpful things, 24 per cent had voices which said mostly negative and/or unhelpful things and 14 per cent had voices that said mostly neutral things. A subset of 50 of these voice-hearers were then interviewed. It was found that no participants heard positive voice content only, 3 participants heard negative content only and 6 heard neutral content only. Most commonly (in 22 of the 50 cases), participants reported hearing all three types of voice content. Fifty eight per cent had some positive voices, and of these, 38 per cent offered advice or guidance, 24 per cent provided information, 20 per cent said nice things to the person, 16 per cent offered encouragement and 28 per cent gave comforting words. For example, 'Mr O' would often hear a male voice saying 'You can do anything. You're unbelievable.' Moving beyond positive voices, 76 per cent of those interviewed had negative voices: 30 per cent offered negative advice or guidance, 50 per cent criticised the person, 32 per cent told them to harm themselves or others, 16 per cent criticised others. Mrs A reported hearing her mother's voice regularly putting her down: 'When I make a little mistake over something, like I've misread the bus timetable and I find I've missed the bus or something, something quite trivial, and I will hear this voice saying, "You're rubbish, you're no good, you're incompetent, you've got no common sense, I always knew you couldn't manage without me"' (p. 203). Those with negative voice content were more likely to have had contact with mental health services. People who were disturbed or upset by their voices were more likely to have voices that talked or argued with each other, voices that commented on them, to hear voices that talked for longer, disturbed their contact with others, took over their thoughts and over which they had less control. Conversely, people who had a positive emotional reaction to their voices were more likely to have voices with positive content, which acted as a helpful guide, have shorter duration, disturb their contact with others less and over which they had more control.

It is possible that healthy voice-hearers who quite happily experience benevolent voices may later come to experience malevolent voices which cause them significant distress and lead to an illness state. It appears that negative life events can sometimes be the triggers for such changes. For example, Escher & Romme (2010) give the example of 'Laura', who heard positive voices from the age of six, until they turned negative at age twelve. Looking back at Laura's history, it was established that she had been sexually abused by her boyfriend's friends at age twelve. However, out of the entire population of healthy voice-hearers, it remains unclear what percentage may later develop problems relating to their voices, or problematic experiences that often occur with voices such as delusions or thought disorder. Due to this association between voices and psychopathology, it is often argued that hearing voices of any kind is an indication that one is in the prodromal stage of schizophrenia (e.g. Yung *et al.*, 2003). Studies which have looked at this have focused on individuals classified as having an 'at risk mental state' (ARMS), which includes those with 'attenuated psychotic symptoms' (e.g. auditory distortions less intense than AVHs), 'brief limited intermittent psychotic symptoms' (e.g. hearing voices twice a month for six months, or every second day for six days before resolving spontaneously), or 'trait and state risk factors' (such as low mood or anxiety in conjunction with a family history of psychosis) (Yung *et al.*, 2003). Mason *et al.* (2004) found, in a sample of 74 individuals who met the criteria for ARMS, that having auditory hallucinations in the ARMS state was a significant predictor to having a diagnosis of a psychotic disorder at one-year follow-up. However, little is known about the exact probability of anyone who hears voices later experiencing mental distress. We saw in Chapter 5 the sorts of reasons that led voices to come to result in social and occupational impairment, but more work is needed on the developmental progression of voices and how they may come to result in problems such as thought disorder and delusions.

Conclusions

Asking members of the general population if they have ever heard voices yields a positive response from around 2–3 per cent of people. If people are asked about specific voice-hearing experiences (and it has mainly been students who have been asked such questions), then this rate jumps enormously. Hence, there is the need to ask such specific questions to the general population to try more accurately to establish how many people have heard such voices. Such experiences of voice-hearing are typically brief and infrequent, but as there have been throughout history, there are a number of healthy voice-hearers in the general population who hear more frequent and extensive voices. The exact number of such individuals is still very poorly known, although here it has been estimated that 0.45 per cent of the population are healthy voice-hearers. The voices heard by such individuals are very similar phenomenologically to those who are distressed by their voices and have become psychiatric patients. The reason healthy voice-hearers are not distressed by their voices appears to be that they have more positive content, and that they have more control over them. This suggests that hearing voices in itself is not an illness or pathological, but rather that hearing predominantly negative voices one cannot cope with leads to an illness state.

We may integrate the findings of this chapter with Chapter 4's findings of the prevalence of voices in those with psychiatric diagnoses. Table 7.3 attempts to approximate broadly how many adults in Western society regularly hear complex voices, and of all Western voice-hearers, what diagnostic categories (or lack of them) they are likely to be given. This table has a large number of methodological limitations, and is for indicative purposes only, yet it acts as a potentially useful ballpark estimate of these figures.[11] It appears that around 2.1 per cent of adults in the general population hear extensive, complex voices. These figures suggest that around 37 per cent of voice-hearers receive a diagnosis of a psychotic disorder (schizophrenia or bipolar disorder), 31 per cent of voice-hearers receive a diagnosis of borderline personality disorder, and that

[11] Obvious limitations include (a) the inexact voice prevalence rates used for each category, which would ideally be based on a weighted average of all methodologically sound studies of voice-hearing prevalence for a given diagnosis, (b) the very limited work done on the actual prevalence of healthy voice-hearers, and (c) this work being drawn mainly from studies done on white individuals in the USA and UK. Furthermore, this table notably excludes voices due to substance abuse (due to a lack of reliable estimates of this) as well as voice-hearing in the general population that is associated with undiagnosed psychotic disorders. It also uses a lifetime prevalence figure for healthy voice-hearing, rather than a point prevalence.

Table 7.3. *Estimated prevalence of voices by diagnosis*

Diagnosis[a]	Point prevalence of disorder (A)[b]	Point prevalence of AVHs in this group (B)	% of people in society and have this label who hear voices (A × B)	% of all voice-hearers who have this label [(A × B)/2.09 × 100%]
Schizophrenia	1%	70%	0.7	33.5
Bipolar I disorder	1%	7%	0.07	3.3
PTSD	0.4%[c]	50%	0.2	9.6
BPD	2%	32%	0.64	30.6
Healthy voice-hearers	0.45%[d]	100%	0.45	21.5
Alzheimer's disease	0.15%[e]	12%	0.018	1.0
Parkinson's disease	0.15%[f]	8%	0.012	0.5
Total			**2.09**	**100**

[a] Dissociative identity disorder is not included due to lack of clear estimates of point prevalence of this disorder.

[b] As per DSM-IV-TR (APA, 2000) unless not given in DSM, in which case another appropriate estimate was located.

[c] Murthy *et al.* (2001).

[d] I have taken the conservative estimate of this figure from the discussion earlier in the chapter.

[e] No clear data available, estimate same as that for Parkinson's disease.

[f] UK Government, Department of Work and Pensions figure.

Source: Compiled by the author.

people with a diagnosis of PTSD make up around 10 per cent of all voice-hearers. In addition, it appears that around 21 per cent of all voice-hearers are healthy voice-hearers. That this is so low says, in part, something about the lack of effectiveness, or knowledge of, management techniques for voice-hearing.

Phenomenological sub-types

Having now examined the phenomenology of heard voices, can we distinguish any clear patterns emerging? From this review of the phenomenology of voices in this section of the book, and those encountered in our historical review in Part I, I would suggest that we can conceive of two phenomenological sub-types of hearing voices experiences.

Type 1 (Dynamic) AVHs: These are voices which have content relating to the ongoing thoughts and behaviours of the voice-hearer.

These typically involve commands, advice or suggestions, as well as evaluative comments. I term these 'Dynamic AVHs' to contrast them with the Type 2 AVHs below. These appear to be the most common type of AVH, being found in a range of people, from those diagnosed with psychotic disorders to healthy voice-hearers.

Type 2 (Static) AVHs: These AVHs are those either identified by the voice-hearer as memory-like, in the sense that they can be seen to be verbatim memories of actual events, or they are isolated fragments of voices which are unrelated to the voice-hearer's ongoing actions and life. These appear to be more common in epilepsy and dissociative personality disorder than in individuals diagnosed with psychosis, or healthy voice-hearers.

Type 1 AVHs appear to consist of two sub-types.

Type 1a: Hypervigilance

These voices are heard during exposure to unpatterned sound and are located externally. Such a type of AVH has been noted from Aristotle to Burton to Kraepelin to solo adventurers today. The term hypervigilance hallucination was coined by Dodgson & Gordon (2009) and we will examine this further in Chapter 10.

Sub-type 1b: Ex nihilo   In contrast to hypervigilance AVHs, these are not dependent on the presence of external sound to trigger them (i.e. they come from nothing in the external world, being solely dependent on internal stimuli) and may be located in or outside the head.

We are now left with the question as to whether this distinction is phenomenologically valid, and if so, why it is important in any case. Although I believe this typology is clearly discernible in phenomenological descriptions of voices, it of course remains to be empirically validated in large-scale quantitative studies using appropriate statistical techniques. If this distinction is validated, then we are left with a number of further questions as to the implications of this for research and clinical intervention strategies. In terms of research, it is quite possible that these types of voices are underpinned by separate causal mechanisms, albeit with some commonalities. For example, I will suggest later that Type 1 AVHs may have their roots in inner speech and Type 2 AVHs their roots in memory. If this is the case, then this is likely to require experimental designs that account for and address this issue. For example, how do the neural correlates of these two types of voices differ? In terms of clinical intervention strategies, it may be that different techniques are required to help aid voice-hearers cope with these different types of voices (or to treat these voices). Hence, it may be that a 'one size fits all' approach to coping with/treating voices is not appropriate. For example, as we will discuss in Chapter 12, the technique of voice dialogue is likely to be effective for Type 1b AVHs, but perhaps not Type 1a or Type 2 AVHs. At present I have written as if these two types of voices are mutually exclusive, but it is quite likely that the same individual may experience both, or that one type may evolve from the other. For example, it has been suggested to me that what I have termed Type 1b AVHs (*ex nihilo*) may evolve from Type 1a (hypervigilance) AVHs (Dodgson, personal communication). All of these issues remain questions for future work to address.

Chapter 7: summary of key points

- Large-scale population studies show AVHs are found in clear consciousness in around 2–3% of the general population, yet these seem to be simple and brief.
- When studies ask participants (typically students) specific questions about their voice-hearing experiences, this uncovers much higher levels of voice-hearing, with a majority of respondents typically reporting having heard voices at least once.
- More complex and extended AVHs appear to occur in around 1% of the general population, with a conservative estimate being that 0.45% of the population hear such voices in the absence of social/occupational impairment ('healthy voice-hearers').
- The phenomenology of voices heard by healthy voice-hearers is very similar to that of individuals who have distressing voices and go on to receive psychiatric diagnoses, with the main differences being that healthy voice-hearers' voices have more positive content, and that they have more control over their voices.
- Hearing voices does not seem indicative of pathology in and of itself.
- Hearing voices occurs in between 5 and 32% of children.
- Approximately 34% of voice-hearers have a diagnosis of schizophrenia, 31% a diagnosis of borderline personality disorder, 21% no psychiatric diagnosis (healthy voice-hearers) and 10% a diagnosis of PTSD.
- An examination of the phenomenology of AVHs suggests two subtypes: Type 1 (Dynamic) and Type 2 (Static), which may have different causes and require different interventions.

Part III

The causes of hearing voices

Introduction to Part III

Having established in the previous chapters what the phenomenology of AVHs is like, we are now in a position to try and attempt to explain what causes these experiences. For any who question the need to understand the causes of voices, we may refer to the words given to the Merovingian by the Wachowski brothers in the film *The Matrix Reloaded*. '*Why* is the only source of real power, without it you are powerless' (Wachowski & Wachowski, 2003).

Chapter 8 will examine the neural underpinnings and biology of AVHs.

Chapters 9 and 10 will then examine the cognitive psychology of AVHs, being guided by both the phenomenology of AVHs as well as the findings from Chapter 8. Chapter 9 will focus specifically on inner speech models, with Chapter 10 looking predominantly at memory and hypervigilance models.

Chapter 11 will go beyond the confines of an individual's head to examine environmental factors that may cause someone to hear voices, and how these work through an individual's biology.

8 Neuroscience and hearing voices: it's the brain, stupid?

Before we begin this chapter, a word on terminology. First, I am going to use the terms 'voice-hearing brain', SZ:AVH+ (an individual diagnosed with schizophrenia and who hears voices) and SZ:AVH− (an individual diagnosed with schizophrenia but who does not hear voices). Such phrases have the potential to objectify, and similar phrases, such as Bartels-Velthuis, Jenner & van de Willige's (2010) term 'AVH-positive children' (p. 43) suggest the voice-hearer has tested positive for a disease. In regard to the term 'voice-hearing brain', it will quite rightly be pointed out that brains do not hear voices, people do. Also, given that in Chapter 7 we saw AVHs occur in a number of people in the general population, all brains could be seen as potentially voice-hearing brains under the right (or wrong) conditions. However, the terminology I employ here is simply meant to be a convenient shorthand way of referring to participants in the studies, and to make the text less cumbersome. It should also be noted that use of this terminology is not to endorse the concept of schizophrenia, whose reliability and validity has been questioned (Bentall, 2003; Boyle, 2002), although the distress and suffering of individuals with such a diagnosis is very real.

Getting our bearings

Before we start on this journey, it may help to get our bearings in the brain. Figure 8.1 shows a side-on diagram of the cortical regions of the brain (the front on the left, the back on the right), and, importantly for the purposes of models of AVHs, indicates Broca's area (typically associated with overt speech and inner speech production), Wernicke's area (typically associated with speech perception) and the arcuate fasciculus white matter pathway that links them together. Although there is also another indirect pathway that links Broca's and Wernicke's area, which runs through the inferior parietal cortex (Catani, Jones & ffytche, 2005), this pathway has been much less studied in relation to AVHs, and so will not be focused upon here. In Figure 8.1 the four lobes of the

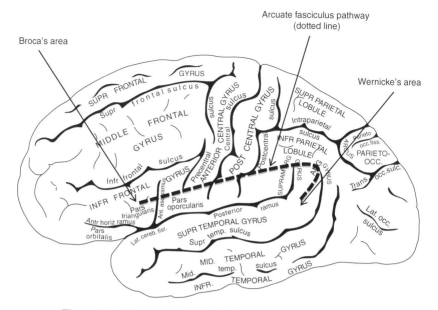

Figure 8.1. The cortex of the brain
Source: Taken from Wikipedia Commons at http://commons.wikimedia.
org/wiki/File:Mediaal_(gray).PNG

brain can also be broadly determined, being the frontal lobe (broadly corresponding to the areas labelled superior, middle and inferior frontal gyri), the temporal lobe (broadly corresponding to the areas labelled superior, middle and inferior temporal gyri), the parietal lobe (the superior and inferior parietal lobules) and the occipital lobe (broadly located around the area marked 'lat occ. sulcus').

Early neuro-stimulation studies

A relatively simple way to find out what brain areas might be involved in AVHs is to electrically simulate the brain directly and see whether it causes AVHs. This is precisely what Penfield & Perot (1963) did. During neurosurgery on 520 patients with epilepsy, which involved removing portions of the scalp in order to be able directly to access the brain, they were able to use an electrode to electrically stimulate the brain directly. As the patients had only received local anaesthetics to their scalps and the brain itself does not feel pain, the patients were wide awake and able to report on what they saw, felt or heard during this process.

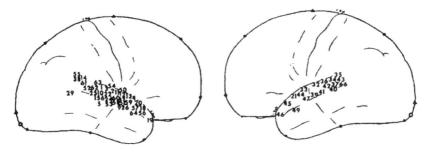

Figure 8.2. Areas of direct brain stimulation resulting in auditory hallucinations
Source: Reproduced from Penfield, W. & Perot, P. (1963). The brain's record of auditory and visual experience. *Brain*, 86, 595–696, by permission of Oxford University Press.

Before their study, in a review of the case histories of 1,132 of their patients suffering from focal epilepsy, Penfield & Perot had identified no patients with auditory hallucinations who had their focus of epileptic discharge outside of the temporal lobe. This suggested to them that stimulating the temporal lobe would be likely to produce auditory hallucinations. Consistent with their prediction, they found that only stimulation of a specific temporal lobe structure, the superior temporal gyrus (STG), resulted in auditory hallucinations. Overall, Penfield & Perot elicited from the STG either a voice, voices, music or a meaningful sound from 66 different stimulation points in 24 patients. Of these auditory experiences, they note: 'a voice or voices was the most common response' which resulted from stimulation of 46 cortical points. Of these 46 points, 31 resulted in voices that were recognised/known to the patient. There was a trend for voices to result more often from STG stimulation of the non-dominant hemisphere (i.e. in right-handed people, the right hemisphere). Figure 8.2 shows the specific areas in the right and left hemisphere that, when stimulated, gave rise to auditory hallucinations.

Within the STG, if the primary auditory cortex (and Heschl's gyrus) was stimulated, patients reported hearing non-linguistic simple sounds, such as buzzing or whistling. However, they report in some cases that when the electrode was then moved towards Wernicke's area, actual voices were heard. For example, they report that 'In Case 29 ... an electrode was inserted into the anterior transverse temporal gyrus and the patient reported, "a buzzing". As the electrode was withdrawn, so that it came into the cortex of the first temporal gyrus, he exclaimed, "Someone is calling"' (p. 666). Stimulation of the STG led to a range of AVHs, which included patients reporting 'I heard voices' (p. 651), 'my mother and father talking' (p. 645), and 'something like a crowd' (p. 640). In addition to AVHs, musical hallucinations and forms of non-verbal auditory hallucinations (e.g. bangs) were also caused. Notably, only a small number of the total number of stimulations of the temporal lobe (7.7%) actually led to any form of hallucination.

Mahl *et al.* (1964) also investigated the effects of direct stimulation of the left temporal lobe, although they only used a single patient with epilepsy. On one occasion the patient reported hearing a conversation between two people. At another time she reported hearing some kind of offensive word. Although I have used the word 'hear', interestingly the authors report that when questioned in detail, 'the patient cannot decide whether she actually heard people saying words to her or whether she thought about the words' (p. 347). Furthermore, the authors note that what she heard were 'not merely words which she associates with past events; the words, sentences, and conversations occur at the time she reports them' (ibid.). Yet, the authors conclude that 'we cannot tell whether the hallucinatory experiences were the equivalent of dreams or psychotic hallucinations or the equivalent of an exact playback' (p. 357). Ferguson *et al.* (1969) also reported upon the effects of direct electrical stimulation of the brain, but in this case specifically the left amygdala region and anterior hippocampus. This did not result in any AVHs, although visual hallucinations did occur. Consistent with the above pattern of findings, the use of the more recent and advanced mag-netoencephalography (MEG: which examines the magnetic field change associated with changes in electrical activity in the brain) technique has found that AVHs occurring in epilepsy are associated with spikes of activity in the STG (Mohamed *et al.*, 2006). Finally, it is also worth noting an unexpected case of AVHs caused by stimulation of an area long thought to have an involvement in AVHs, but not reported on by Penfield & Perot (1963) as causing AVHs when directly stimulated. Lesser *et al.* (1984) report that direct electrical stimulation of Broca's area caused a patient to report AVHs, which spoke in the patient's voice and said single words, phrases or sentences. Nevertheless, the authors were careful to note that stimulation of this area may have led to activation in temporal lobe regions, which in turn could have been the cause of the patient's AVH.

What can we conclude from such studies as to the causes of AVHs? Is it likely that spontaneous epileptic electrical activation in the superior temporal gyrus is a model for all AVHs? First we may note that David (1994), after reviewing the phenomenology of the AVHs Penfield & Perot (1963) elicited, notes that 'it is striking how *unlike* the reports [of AVHs during electrical stimulation] are of auditory hallucinations described by psychotic patients' (p. 271, emphasis added). Specifically, David argues that only 5 of the 40 cases reported by Penfield & Perot show 'verbatim accounts of clear [AVHs]' (ibid.). However, this does not necessarily invalidate the model, as not all AVHs in patients diagnosed with psychosis are clear (Chapter 4), and we may note two other cases in addition to the ones David reports: case 15, 'voices yelling at me' (p. 630), and case 29, 'a man's voice, I could not understand what he said' (p. 640). As another argument against the phenomenological similarity between these induced AVHs and those found in patients diagnosed with psychosis, David also observes that two-thirds of patients in the Penfield & Perot study were able to identify their AVHs as voices from their past (indeed, Penfield & Perot themselves note that 'the patient usually recognizes it [the induced AVHs] spontaneously as coming from his past'). We may further add that we do not see many phenomenological parallels in the AVHs created in these studies to common properties of the voices of individuals diagnosed with psychosis (or healthy voice-hearers), such as commands. However, some common properties can be seen (e.g. being shouted at, and voices directly addressing the patient). Yet overall, it appears that spontaneous focal epileptic activity in the STG is likely not to be a good model of all AVHs. However, this may be a good model for the Type 2 (Static) AVHs highlighted in Chapter 7.

Before proceeding, it is worth considering if we can even model epileptic AVHs as resulting simply from focal epileptic activity in the STG. We saw in Chapter 4 that AVHs in non-psychotic patients with epilepsy have a phenomenology different from that of individuals diagnosed with psychosis in many ways (e.g. commands are rare) (Korsnes et al., 2010). But even though such AVHs appear to be phenomenologically distinct from those found in psychosis, on a dichotic listening task non-psychotic epilepsy patients with inter-ictal AVHs have been found to have patterns of neural activation similar to that of SZ:AVH+ (ibid.). This suggests that AVHs in epilepsy may involve more than simply activations in just the STG. More research thus remains to be done on commonalities and differences in both the phenomenology of AVHs and the neural activation during AVHs, between patients with epilepsy (without psychosis) and those found to be typical of a cluster of psychiatric diagnoses (and in people without psychiatric diagnoses) in Chapter 4.

The neuroscience of hearing voices

Although we saw in Chapter 4 that the phenomenology of AVHs in patients diagnosed with psychosis was much like that of individuals with

AVHs who had been given other psychiatric disorders, or indeed the AVHs of healthy voice-hearers, the rest of this chapter, after a few brief comments, will focus solely on studies employing patients diagnosed with schizophrenia with AVHs (SZ:AVH+). I do this in order to allow comparability across studies, as inclusion of studies of AVHs in individuals diagnosed with other psychiatric disorders, due to the different medication regimes of such patients, may cause confounds and confuse the emerging picture of neural activation/structural changes uniquely associated with AVHs. However, it is likely that the neural processes involved in SZ:AVH+ are the same as those in individuals with phenomenologically similar AVHs but with different (or no) psychiatric diagnoses. For example, a study published just as I was making the final changes to this book (and hence not included in the analyses in the rest of this chapter) found that the neural regions activated during AVHs in SZ:AVH+ were not different to that during AVHs in healthy voice-hearers (Diederen et al., in press). Similarly, a study by Knöchel et al. (in press), discussed in more detail later, found that changes to the corpus callosum were associated with hallucination severity (although AVHs specifically were not reported on) in patients diagnosed with schizophrenia, and that a trend towards a similar pattern was also found in relation to hallucination-proneness in healthy individuals. Furthermore, (a) AVHs in patients with epilepsy diagnosed with psychosis have been found to be associated with a wide range of neural changes (for example, fronto-temporal white matter abnormalities, Flugel et al., 2006), (b) AVHs in Parkinson's disease have been found to be associated with hypoperfusion in the bilateral prefrontal cortex and right STG (Matsui et al., 2006), and (c) AVHs in patients with Alzheimer's disease has been found to be associated with smaller parahippocampal gyrus volumes (Forstl et al., 1994), all areas that will be highlighted as important in the review below of AVHs in SZ:AVH+. Although more work does remain to be done both on phenomenological and neural differences in AVHs between these psychiatric diagnoses (and to link specific aspects of phenomenology of AVHs to neural activations), it appears that such findings at least support a symptom-based approach to AVHs.

Structural neuroimaging studies of AVHs

Structural imaging studies of the brain using magnetic resonance imaging can shed light on how the brain of voice-hearers is different to that of non-voice-hearers. Whilst older studies focused on grey matter structures in the brain (which contain the nerve cell bodies themselves), more recent studies have been able to examine white matter tracts in the

Table 8.1. *Structural studies comparing SZ:AVH+ to healthy controls*

Study	N (SZ/HC)	Method	Superior temporal gyrus	Insula
Hubl *et al.* (2010)	13:13	MRI (DTI)	↑ (right)	–
Cachia *et al.* (2008)	30–28	MRI (VBM)	↓ (bilateral)*	–
García-Martí *et al.* (2008)	18–11	MRI (VBM)	↓ (bilaterally)	↓ (bilaterally)
Hugdahl *et al.* (2008)	6–12	MRI (VBM)	↓ (left)	X
O'Daly *et al.* (2007)	28–32	MRI (VBM)	↓ (right)	↓ (bilaterally)
Shapleske *et al.* (2002)	41–32	MRI (VBM)	X	↓ (bilaterally)
Shapleske *et al.* (2001)	74–32	MRI (ROI)	X	–
Havermans *et al.* (1999)	15:17	MRI (ROI)	X	–

* Sulcation in this region was lower.
– = area not examined, SZ = patients diagnosed with schizophrenia,
HC = healthy controls, X = no differences found.
Source: Compiled by the author.

brain (responsible for the transmission of signals between grey matter areas, and which may both cause activity in grey matter structures to be either excited or inhibited).

Structural imaging studies of grey matter in SZ:AVH+

To date there have been 15 structural imaging studies which have examined grey matter (GM) volumes in relation to AVHs in patients diagnosed with schizophrenia. These are grouped below based on the nature of the analyses they performed.

SZ:AVH+ compared to healthy controls (HCs)

Eight studies have employed this design (Table 8.1). The only replicated findings are that SZ:AVH+ have reduced STG GM volumes (found in 4 of 8 studies) and reduced insula volumes (3 of 4 studies) compared to HCs. Yet the most recent study (Hubl *et al.*, 2010) found *increased* STG volumes in SZ:AVH+ compared to HCs. An obvious limitation of comparing SZ:AVH+ to HCs is that structural changes identified may not be specific to the presence of AVHs but to factors associated with a diagnosis of schizophrenia, or may result from the documented effects of antipsychotic medication on both cortical and sub-cortical GM volumes (Dazzan *et al.*, 2005; Gur *et al.*, 1998). For example, Vernon *et al.* (2010) found, in rats, that antipsychotic administration (both haloperidol and

Table 8.2. *Grey matter volumes in participants with SZ:AVH+ compared to SZ:AVH−*

Study	N (SZ:HC)	Method	Superior temporal gyrus
Hubl *et al.* (2010)	13:13	MRI (DTI)	↑ (right)
Shin *et al.* (2005)	17:8	MRI (VBM)	−
Onitsuka *et al.* (2004)	13:6	MRI (ROI)	↓ (left)
Shapleske *et al.* (2002)	41:31	MRI (VBM)	X
Shapleske *et al.* (2001)	44:30	MRI (ROI)	X
Havermans *et al.* (1999)	15:15	MRI (ROI)	X
DeLisi *et al.* (1994)	Not reported	MRI (ROI)	X

olanzapine) caused a 6–8 per cent decrease in whole brain volume, driven mainly by a reduction in frontal cerebral cortex volume. We thus need to turn to studies which compare patients diagnosed with schizophrenia with and without AVHs, which will be more useful, as both will be on antipsychotic medication, eliminating this as a potential confound.

SZ:AVH+ vs SZ:AVH−

Seven studies have been done of this design (Table 8.2) which attempt to identify structural changes specific to AVHs, rather than schizophrenia per se. The only area identified by more than one study has been the STG. However, whereas Onitsuka and colleagues (2004) found smaller STG volumes specific to SZ:AVH+, this was not replicated by the six other studies, five of which found no differences, and one which found an increased volume specifically in Heschl's gyrus. Inconsistencies in these studies may result from the small number, the relatively small sample sizes often employed, the potentially confounding presence of varying levels of hallucinations in other modalities/other positive symptoms and inconsistencies in the definitions of SZ:AVH+ and SZ:AVH− used. For example, whereas one study (Shapleske *et al.*, 2001) defined SZ:AVH− as those with a score less than 2 on the Scale for Assessment of Positive Symptoms (SAPS) (Andreasen, 1984) Auditory Hallucination item, another (Onitsuka *et al.*, 2004) defined SZ:AVH− as those with a zero score on this measure.

AVH severity correlated with GM volumes

Eight studies of this design have been performed (Table 8.3). Studies have used a range of measures of AVH severity, including the

Table 8.3. *Correlations of severity of AVHs with grey matter volumes*

Study	N	Method	Superior temporal gyrus	Inferior frontal gyrus	Postcentral gyrus
Nenadic *et al.* (2010)	99	MRI (VBM)	↓ (bilaterally)	X	↓ (left)
Modinos *et al.* (2009)	26	MRI (VBM)	X	↑ (left)	X
García-Martí *et al.* (2008)	18	MRI (VBM)	X	↓ (left)	↓ (right)
Gaser *et al.* (2004)	85	MRI (DBM)	↓	↓ (right)	
Shapleske *et al.* (2001)	74	MRI (VBM)	X	–	–
Levitan *et al.* (1999)	30	MRI (ROI)	↓ (left)	–	–
Cullberg *et al.* (1992)	33	CT	–	–	–
Barta *et al.* (1990)	15	MRI (ROI)	↓ (left)	–	–

PSYRATS-AH (Haddock *et al.*, 1999), the SAPS Auditory Hallucination item and the sum of the SAPS Auditory Hallucination, Voices Commenting and Voices Conversing items. The most consistent finding was that four of the seven studies examining the STG found smaller STG volumes to be associated with more severe AVHs. Of the four studies examining the inferior frontal region, two found reduced volumes to be associated with more severe AVHs, one found an increased volume to be associated with more severe AVHs, and one found no relation. The only other replicated finding was that two studies (out of three) found reductions in the post-central gyrus GM volume to be associated with increased levels of AVHs. One further study (Cachia *et al.*, 2008) examined the correlation between AVH severity and measures of gyrification and sulcation in the temporal lobe, but failed to find any significant correlations.

Structural imaging studies of white matter and connectivity in AVHs

One initial source of evidence that white matter (WM) problems are related to AVH comes from studies of the condition metachromatic leukodystrophy, a demyelinating genetic disorder which occurs in about 1/40,000 people (Black, Taber & Hurley, 2003). The loss of WM is most prominent in the frontal and parietal lobes, and this is associated with hearing voices and a range of other experiences (ibid.).

The WM tract most likely to be of relevance to AVHs (and hence the most studied) is the arcuate fasciculus (AF). The AF is the main part of the larger superior longitudinal fasciculus (SLF) which connects the front and back of the brain (Bernal & Ardila, 2009). The lateral part of the AF contains shorter U-shaped fibres that connect a range of areas, including Broca's area to Wernicke's area (Hubl *et al.*, 2004) via a possible relay station in the premotor or motor cortex (Bernal & Ardila, 2009).

Four studies have simply examined WM volume (rather than tract integrity) in those with AVHs. Compared to HCs, O'Daly *et al.* (2007) found that SZ:AVH+ had reduced WM volume in the left but not the right STG, as well as in the right inferior longitudinal fasciculus. Although Shapleske *et al.* (2002) when comparing SZ:AVH+ to HCs also found reduced WM in the right frontal lobe near the SLF, and increased WM in the left temporal-parietal connecting tracts, when they compared SZ:AVH+ to SZ:AVH− they found no differences. Similarly, Rossell *et al.* (2001) found no difference in the size of the CC between SZ:AVH+ and SZ:AVH−. However, Seok *et al.* (2007) did find a WM volume difference specific to SZ:AVH+, with WM density in the left SLF being significantly increased in SZ:AVH+, but not different in SZ:AVH− compared to HCs.

Going beyond simple volumetric measurements of WM, diffusion tensor imaging (DTI) allows the assessment of the integrity of WM tracts in the brain. When water is within WM tracts, its direction of diffusion is primarily limited to being parallel to it (Basser, Mattiello & Lebihan, 1994). The degree of restriction on the direction of flow of water molecules is termed fractional anisotropy (FA). DTI works by assessing the FA of water in WM tracts. Lower relative FA indicates damaged WM (Le Bihan *et al.*, 2001), including loss of structural organisation and the expansion of extracellular space (Dong *et al.*, 2004). Increased relative FA, however, can be taken to mean increased anatomical connectivity (Hubl *et al.*, 2004).[1]

Five DTI studies have focused specifically on AVHs. As shown in Table 8.4, Hubl and colleagues (2004) and Rotarska-Jagiela and colleagues (2009) both found increased FA values in the arcuate fasciculus in SZ-AVH+ compared to HCs. Yet de Weijer *et al.* (2011), Seok *et al.* (2007) and Shergill *et al.* (2007) found lower FA values in SZ:AVH+ compared to HCs (note, the Shergill study is not cited in the SZ:AVH+ vs HCs section of Table 8.4, as only two-thirds of patients, not all, had AVHs). The only studies (Hubl *et al.*, 2004; Seok *et al.*, 2007) to have compared SZ:AVH+ with SZ:AVH− found increased FA in the SLF in

---

[1] Basically, imagine water flowing in a straight pipe. If you make holes in the side of the pipe and damage it, the water will start spurting out in all directions (low relative FA), whereas if the pipe has no holes in the side and is nice and smooth inside, the water will all flow in the same direction along the pipe (high relative FA).

Table 8.4. *Diffusion tensor imaging studies of AVHs*

Study	N	Arcuate fasciculus	Cingulum	Corpus callosum
FA in SZ:AVH+ compared to HCs				
de Weijer *et al.* (2011)	44SZ-AVH+ 42HC	↓ (bilaterally)	X	–
Rotarska-Jagiela *et al.* (2009)	12SZ-AVH+ 12HC	↑ (bilaterally)	X	↓
Seok *et al.* (2007)	15SZ-AVH+ 22HC	↓ (left)	↓	X
Hubl *et al.* (2004)	13SZ-AVH+ 13HC	↑ (temporoparietal region, bilaterally) ↓ (all other parts)	X	– ↓
FA in SZ:AVH+ vs SZ:AVH−				
Seok *et al.* (2007)	15SZ-AVH+ 15SZ-AVH−	↑ (left frontal portion)	↑ (left caudal)	X
Huble *et al.* (2004)	13SZ-AVH+ 13SZ-AVH−	↑ (all parts bilaterally)	↑	↑
Correlation between AVH severity and FA values				
Rotarska-Jagiela *et al.* (2009)	12SZ-AVH+	+ve (bilateral)	−ve (left)	X
Seok *et al.* (2007)	15SZ-AVH+	+ve (left frontal)	+ve (anterior)	X
Shergill *et al.* (2007)	33SZ	+ve (bilateral)	+ve (anterior)	X

Source: Compiled by the author.

SZ:AVH+. In addition to the DTI studies presented in Table 8.4, a further study examined functional connectivity between neural areas, comparing SZ:AVH+ and HCs, and assessing concurrent activation in these areas. This study by Vercammen *et al.* (2010a) found significantly decreased connectivity between the left temporoparietal junction (TPJ) and the right homotope of Broca's area in SZ:AVH+ compared with HCs.

A number of studies have examined the relation between WM connectivity and AVH severity. All studies employing DTI and examining the AF found that AVH severity was associated with increased FA (Table 8.4). The majority of studies also found a positive correlation between AVH severity and FA in the cingulum. Although all studies found that AVH severity in SZ:AVH+ correlated with increased FA values in the AF, when compared to HCs, the studies were divided as to whether SZ:AVH+ had higher or lower absolute levels of FA in this region. It is somewhat paradoxical that, for example, Seok and colleagues (2007) found that SZ:AVH+ had lower FA values in the AF than HCs, but within the SZ:AVH+ group higher FA values (i.e. those nearer the scores of HCs) had more severe AVHs. On balance, the following picture emerges. It appears that, compared to healthy controls, SZ:AVH+ have lower FA in the AF (here I give weight to the largest study in this area, coming from the excellent Dutch research group of Iris Sommer and colleagues), but that this is associated with a diagnosis of schizophrenia per se. Within the group of patients diagnosed with schizophrenia, higher FA in the AF is associated with more severe voices. Thus patients diagnosed with schizophrenia have an absolute hypo-connection in the AF, but hearing voices within this group is associated with relative hyper-connection in the AF. Confused? Me too.

Although the studies reported in Table 8.4 did not reliably find FA in the CC to be specifically related to AVHs, a recent study by Knöchel *et al.* (in press) has found that lower CC volumes and fibre integrity in patients diagnosed with schizophrenia are associated with more severe hallucinations (the scale they used was a measure of hallucinations per se, rather than specifically AVHs, and hence this study is not included in Table 8.4). Finally, it is notable that connectivity problems may be related to specific types of voices. For example, Lee *et al.* (2009) found FA values in the left STG correlated positively with levels of voices commenting (but not conversing). This again points us to the potential existence of sub-types of voices with different underlying neural mechanisms as proposed in Chapter 7. Voices commenting may fit into my class of Type 1b voices, underpinned by neural connectivity problems with inner speech (Chapter 9), and voices conversing may fit into my class of Type 2 voices (specifically Type 2b voices – see Chapter 11), underpinned by spontaneous, epileptic-like activity in the STG. This, of course, remains speculative.

In addition to these DTI studies, a number of studies have examined functional connectivity between neural areas in voice-hearers. Vercammen *et al.* (2010a) studied the functional connectivity between neural areas in SZ:AVH+ while at rest. It was found that AVH severity correlated negatively with functional connectivity between the left TPJ and the bilateral anterior cingulate, as well as with functional connectivity between the left TPJ and the bilateral amygdala. Gavrilescu *et al.* (2010) found that, when at rest, inter-hemispheric connectivity between both left and right primary auditory cortex, and left and right secondary auditory cortex, was worse in SZ:AVH+ than both HCs and SZ:AVH−. In addition, Hashimoto *et al.* (2010) found that the severity of AVHs was correlated with the functional connectivity between the left sylvian-parietal-temporal area and the anterior insula, a pathway which the authors note is critical for speech production (Hickok & Poeppel, 2007). Moving away from studies while voice-hearers are 'at rest', Raij et al. (2009) failed to find any regions of the brain that coupled (i.e. covaried) with Broca's area differently during AVHs and during non-AVH periods in the scanner. However, they did find that during AVHs, coupling between left Broca's area and the bilateral supratemporal cortex, right posterior temporal lobe and middle right anterior cingulate cortex, all correlated with the subjective reality of patients' voices. Furthermore, during AVHs the coupling between Broca's area and the right posterior STG, as well as Heschl's gyrus in the left auditory cortex, also correlated with the perceived reality of voices. The reality of AVHs correlated negatively with the coupling between Broca's area and the posterior cingulate cortex. As we will see later, such findings are consistent with models in which (inner) speech production areas fail to communicate with other regions of the brain (such as speech perception areas), resulting in AVHs.

Functional neuroimaging studies of AVHs

Activity during AVHs

Sixteen studies (4 PET, 12 fMRI) have examined the neural activity in SZ:AVH+ associated with the presence of AVHs, compared to non-AVH periods (Table 8.5). Overall, 69 per cent of studies found activation in the STG, 63 per cent in cingulate regions, 56 per cent in the middle temporal gyrus, 50 per cent in the inferior frontal gyrus (IFG), and 25 per cent in the parahippocampal gyrus, insula, middle frontal gyrus and cerebellum. Activation in these regions was not consistently found to be specific to a given hemisphere, or to occur bilaterally, though. A limitation of all but two of the studies was their sample size. Today it is generally accepted that a sample size of more than twenty participants is required for a functional magnetic resonance imaging (fMRI) study to produce reliably replicable findings (Thirion et al., 2007). However, only two studies had a sample size in excess of this (Diederen et al., 2010; Sommer et al., 2008). Areas identified by both of these studies were bilateral activation in the IFG (primarily in the right hemisphere), the STG, insula, supramarginal gyrus and cerebellum.

Activity preceding AVHs

As studies of neural activation during AVHs cannot distinguish between activity resulting in their production and activity resulting from their

Table 8.5. *Functional imaging studies of AVHs in SZ:AVH+*

Study, imaging method (N)	AH assessment	IFG	MFG	Insula	STG	MTG	Cingulate	Parahippo-campal cortex	Other regions
Diederen et al. 2010, fMRI (24)	Balloon squeeze	Bilateral	Right	Bilateral	Bilateral	Bilateral			Post- and pre-central gyrus, inferior parietal lobule, cerebellum, bilateral supermarginal and superior frontal gyrus
Raij et al. 2009, fMRI (11)	Button press	Bilateral					Right	Right	Right posterior and left anterior temporal lobe
Sommer et al. 2008, fMRI (24)	Balloon squeeze	Bilateral		Bilateral	Bilateral		Left		Medial frontal and supramarginal gyrus, right cerebellum
Copolov et al. 2003, fMRI (8)	Button press	Right			Left	Right	Left	Left	Right medial frontal
Shergill et al. 2001, fMRI(1)	Post-scan report			Right	Right	Right	Left posterior	Right	
Shergill et al. 2000, fMRI (6)	Post-scan report	Left	Bilateral	Bilateral		Bilateral	Anterior bilateral	Left	Right central gyrus, thalamus, parietal lobule, left hippocampus
Van der Ven et al. 2005, fMRI (6)	Button press				Bilateral HG*				
Lennox et al. 2000, fMRI (4)	Button press		Left		Bilateral	Bilateral			

Study	Activation state							Other areas
					Left, incl HG	Left		
Dierks et al. 1999, fMRI (3)	Button press	Bilateral			Left, incl HG			Left amygdala, hippocampus
Lennox et al. 1999, fMRI (3)	Button press	Right	Right	Bilateral	Right	Right	Right anterior	Right cuneus
Bentaleb et al. 2002, fMRI (1)	AVH prevented by noise			Left PAC	Right			
Woodruff et al. 1995, fMRI (1)	Finger raise			Right	Right	Right	Right anterior	Thalamus. Right prefrontal, premotor and parietal cortex
McGuire et al. 1993, PET (12)	Symptomatic v remitted	Left					Left anterior (trend level)	
Parellada et al. 2008, PET (9)	Symptomatic v remitted						Anterior	SMA, medial superior frontal area, cerebellum
Silbersweig et al. 1995, PET (6)	Button press				Right		Right anterior	Bilateral — Bilateral thalamus, right putamen and caudate, left cerebellum
Suzuki et al. 1993, PET (5)	Symptomatic v remitted			Left			Anterior	

* In 50% of patients.

HG = Heschl's gyrus, PAC = primary auditory cortex

consequences (Hoffman *et al.*, 2008a), studies have also examined the activity in the seconds immediately preceding onset of AVHs. In the largest of the four studies done in this area, Diederen *et al.* (2010: $N = 15$) examined neural activation in the six-seconds preceding AVHs, the onset of which SZ-AVH+ indicated by squeezing a balloon, compared to the six second periods preceding random balloon squeezes (not followed by AVHs). AVHs were most prominently preceded by deactivation in the left parahippocampal gyrus, and also by deactivation in the left STG, right inferior frontal (Broca's area) and left middle frontal gyri, right insula and left cerebellum. The finding of deactivation in the parahippocampal gyrus was also found in an earlier, smaller study by Hoffman *et al.* (2008a: $N = 6$) in the period 4.5–1.5s before AVHs. However, Hoffman and colleagues also found deactivation in the anterior cingulate, and activation, not deactivation, of the insula. Although Hoffman and colleagues suggested that insula activation may be due to preparation for motor movement to signal AVH-onset, Diederen and colleagues' study, which also found insula involvement whilst controlling for motor movements, suggests this is not the case. Diederen and colleagues' finding of a role for the inferior frontal gyrus was not replicated by Hoffman and colleagues, however Shergill and colleagues (2004: $N = 2$) did report activation of the inferior frontal gyrus (although the left, and not the right) preceding AVHs.

A consistent finding of earlier smaller studies (Hoffman *et al.*, 2008a; Lennox *et al.*, 1999; Shergill *et al.*, 2004), not found by Diederen and colleagues (2010), was activation around the middle temporal region preceding onset of AVHs specifically the right middle temporal region preceding onset of AVHs. Hoffman *et al.* (2008a) account for this by arguing that the middle temporal gyrus activation represents initial verbal content and/or prosody, which is then subsequently sent to the STG which creates the acoustic element of the AVH. Consistent with this, Shergill and colleagues (2004) found that it was only as individuals became aware of the AVH that activation spread to the bilateral STG and MTG. This led them to propose that 'activation in the temporal cortex [was] mainly occurring when the participant subsequently perceived auditory speech' (p. 517). Hoffman *et al.* (2008a) similarly concluded that 'more robust bilateral activation in the superior temporal gyrus arose somewhat later perhaps at hallucination onset – than the middle temporal gyrus activation' (p. 425). Overall, we are still in need of more large-scale studies (i.e. $N > 20$) of the activation preceding AVHs to form a reliable picture of the neural regions involved. However, we may tentatively suggest that involvement of inferior frontal and parahippocampal regions preceding AVHs suggests that inner speech and memory-based processes, respectively, are involved in generating the raw material of AVHs, with activation of the STG then reflecting the perception of the AVH.

Summary of functional and structural neuroimaging studies

The most consistent findings that emerge from the above are: (1) an association between AVHs and structural abnormalities in the STG and IFG; (2) an association between AVH severity and hyperconnectivity in the AF; (3) functional activation during AVHs being most consistently seen in the IFG, STG, insula, cingulate, cerebellum and supramarginal gyrus; and (4) forms of activation/deactivation immediately preceding AVHs in the parahippocampal cortex, insula and IFG.

Lateralisation studies

The two largest fMRI studies of neural activation during AVHs discussed earlier in this chapter both found particularly the right IFG (including Broca's area) to be activated during AVHs (Diederen et al., 2010; Sommer et al., 2008). This suggests that laterality may be an important factor. Yet although Diederen, Sommer & Tendolkar (2011) in a pilot study found that language production was more lateralised to the right hemisphere in SZ:AVH+ compared to HCs, there was no difference in lateralisation between healthy voice-hearers and HCs. The authors thus suggest that lateralisation to the right in SZ:AVH+ is associated with psychosis per se, not AVHs. However, the frequency of AVHs in the SZ:AVH+ were significantly greater than the healthy voice-hearers. Hence, more work remains to be done to resolve this question.

If we turn away from changes in lateralisation in Broca's area to changes in lateralisation in temporal regions, the evidence for a link between unusual lateralisation and AVHs is stronger. Here we may first consider evidence from dichotic listening (DL) tasks. DL tasks are a non-invasive way to test hemispheric asymmetry and are also a test of the functional integrity of left temporal lobe language areas (Hugdahl, 1988). In this task, single auditory stimuli (such as consonant-vowel syllables, e.g. /ba/, /ta/, /ga/) are presented to both ears simultaneously, and the participant has to attempt to correctly identify the stimuli they heard, or if they heard two, which they heard best. It is typical for healthy individuals more often to report the stimuli reported to the right ear, as this information has direct access to the left temporal lobe, which is superior to the right temporal lobe in language-processing ability (ibid.).

In contrast, the stimuli presented to the left ear is initially sent to the right temporal lobe before having to be transferred across the corpus callosum to the left temporal lobe, which delays and attenuates the signal (ibid.). Using a DL procedure, several studies have shown that those with AVHs do not show the typical right ear advantage (e.g. Levitan, Ward & Catts, 1999). Recently, Løberg, Jørgensen & Hugdahl (2004) found that SZ:AVH+ showed the opposite pattern of ear advantage to HCs, showing a left ear, not a right ear advantage. Patients with a diagnosis of schizophrenia with a history of AVHs, but no current AVHs, did not show this left ear advantage. In addition to this finding, McKay, Headlam & Copolov (2000), as part of a comprehensive assessment of auditory processing between SZ:AVH+ and SZ:AVH−, found very few group differences, but did find that the former group were impaired compared to the latter on performance on a left monaural speech perception test, suggesting impaired right auditory cortex dysfunction or a problem in signalling between the auditory areas of the two hemispheres. This finding is supported by a recent study which (although using a global measure of hallucinations, rather than AVHs per se) found that in patients diagnosed with schizophrenia there was an association between hallucination severity and the extent to which the normal brain asymmetry in the temporal lobe (left greater than right), in terms of both volume and functional activation, was reduced (Oertel et al., 2010).

Transcranial magnetic stimulation

Another methodology that allows us to investigate the neural activity associated with AVHs is transcranial magnetic stimulation (TMS). Whereas with electroconvulsive therapy,[2] best known to the public from the film One Flew Over the Cuckoo's Nest, a gross electric shock is simply applied to the patient's head, the induction of electrical current in the brain by TMS is precise, painless and done while one is wide awake. TMS works by holding a stimulator coil over the desired area of the scalp. A rapidly changing magnetic field in the coil induces an electrical current in the cortex directly below the coil, and can be aimed with an accuracy of around 1 cm. fMRI can be used to identity where a specific neural structure is in the individual participant, to ensure that the desired area is being stimulated. The electrical field induced in the cortex then causes the neurons in this area to fire. In slow TMS (done

[2] A systematic review by Tharyan & Adams (2005) suggested that ECT, when combined with antipsychotic medication, may prove beneficial for patients diagnosed with schizophrenia.

at a frequency of around 1Hz) this reduces the excitability of the region targeted. Given that some theories posit that AVHs are due to hyper-activation of speech perception areas, TMS can be used to try to reduce AVHs. At present, though, this technique is used as a last resort with medication-resistant patients (Aleman & Larøi, 2008).

Aleman, Sommer & Kahn (2007) in a meta-analysis of TMS for AVHs, found that TMS over the left TPJ region reduced the severity of AVHs (but not other positive symptoms) for some (but not all) patients. This suggests a key role for the left TPJ in the generation of AVHs in some patients. Since this meta-analysis, further studies have replicated the finding that TMS over the left TPJ region improves AVHs (Vercammen et al., 2009). Some such studies have also used fMRI-guided TMS, in which fMRI is used to identify the location of brain activity during AVHs, then TMS is applied to this specific region. For example, Jardri et al. (2007) found that fMRI-guided TMS over the left TPJ cortex resulted in a 47 per cent improvement in an 11-year-old child's AVHs. This was a clinically significant improvement, and the child was able to return to school. We may ask what specific properties of AVHs, TMS actually improves. Horacek et al. (2007) found that the loudness, salience of the voices, as well as the amount of distress the voice-hearer experienced, were all imporved by TMS over the left TPJ. However, other facets, such as the frequency of voices, their reality, the number of voices, and the length of their utterances were not found to be significantly reduced by TMS.

Given that inferior frontal regions have been suggested to be involved in AVHs in the above review, what happens when TMS is conducted Broca's area? Although TMS over Broca's area has not been found to be beneficial for AVHs (Hoffman et al., 2007; Schonfeldt-Lecuona et al., 2004), it has been found that, for SZ: AVH+ with continuous AVHs, the greater the coupling between right Broca's area and Wernicke's area is, the less effective TMS over TPJ regions is, and, for SZ: AVH+ with intermittent AVHs, that the greater the amount of activation in Broca's area during AVHs, the less effective TMS over the TPJ is (Hoffman et al., 2007). Again this starts to push us towards the need to posit the existence of sub-types of voices, which have different underpinning neural mechanisms, and may require different forms of treatment. This could be taken to suggest that whilst some AVHs are due to hyperactivity of the TPJ, others have their roots in connectivity problems between speech production and speech perception regions.

Aside from reducing cortical excitability, how does TMS have its effect? First, TMS may increase functional activity between areas of the brain that are 'disconnected' in patients with AVHs. For example,

TMS over the left TPJ results in an increase in connectivity between the left TPJ and the right insula in patients with AVHs (Vercammen *et al.*, 2010b). Second, at a cognitive level, which we will discuss further in the next chapter, improvements in source monitoring resulting have been found to result from TMS over the left TPJ (Brunelin *et al.*, 2006b). The meaning of this will be examined in the next chapter. It has also been found by Horacek *et al.* (2007) that TMS exerts its effects by both transcallosal as well as intrahemispheric connections, reducing brain metabolism in the left STG and its interconnected regions (e.g. hippocampus, insula), but increasing metabolism in the contralateral cortex and in the frontal lobes (e.g. the middle frontal gyrus). The potentially interhemispheric effects of TMS on language areas have also been noted by Andoh & Martinot (2008). They argue that TMS can cause functional reorganisation in homologous areas to where the 'virtual lesion' occurs, in order to compensate for the stimulated and disturbed area. Given the electrophysiological evidence for an involvement of the right TPJ (Line *et al.*, 1998; see electrophysiological section below) and right Broca's area (Sommer *et al.*, 2008) in AVHs, this may explain how left TPJ TMS can cause improvement in AVHs. Finally, it has also been proposed that TMS may exert its effect at a neurochemical level by inhibiting subcortical dopamine release (Aleman, Sommer & Kahn, 2007). It is such neurochemistry to which we now turn.

Neurotransmitters, antipsychotic drugs and AVHs

Insights into the proximal biological causes of AVHs can also be gained from studies of voice-hearers who have been treated with antipsychotic medication. Before we start building any model of AVHs based on the proposed mechanisms underpinning antipsychotic drug treatment, it is worth considering how effective these drugs are. Whilst estimates of their short- and long-term effectiveness vary, they do at least appear to be helpful for some voice-hearers (see Appendix A for further discussion).

Exactly what happens to people's AVHs when they take antipsychotic medication which has a useful effect? In an early study, Elkes & Elkes (1954) found that of the two patients in their sample who heard voices, chlorpromazine did not make the voices disappear, but only made the patients less bothered by them (i.e. the patients didn't shout and scream at their voices as much). For example, one patient stated that his voices 'did not worry him so much' (p. 563), and another who had been hearing a voice called 'Mr Knock', who put 'filthy thoughts into her mind', reported after chlorpromazine treatment that 'she did not bother any more with Mr. Knock' as he 'did not annoy her so much' (ibid.). Fifty years later, Mizrahi *et al.* (2005), in a study of the effects of antipsychotic medication, found that before treatment patients thought that the medication would both eradicate the voices and help them be more detached from them. However, after six weeks the patients found that the drugs helped them be more detached from their symptoms – 'help deal, help stop thinking, and make the symptoms not bother' (p. 862) – but were less effective in taking away the voices altogether. Thus, while some patients find medication is able to eliminate their voices, for others the voices remain but are relegated to the backs of their mind, rather than vanishing (Kapur *et al.*, 2006).

A recent study by Schneider *et al.* (in press) examined how specific properties of voices changed over time in twenty-eight patients with a diagnosis of schizophrenia who were being treated with antipsychotic medication. This sample was a mix of first-episode admission and repeat admissions, and hostile and severely suspicious patients were excluded from the analyses. The outcome measure was the PSYRATS-AH, which assesses properties of voices including their frequency, duration, location, loudness, beliefs re-origin (i.e. caused by external events in the world versus being internal, self-related events), amount of negative content, degree of negative content, amount of distress, intensity of distress, disruption and voice-hearer control. Overall, 40 per cent of the patients stated that antipsychotic medication reduced their hallucinations. Four sub-scales of the PSYRATS-AH (using univariate tests) showed significant improvements, namely frequency (38% reduction in mean score), loudness (20% reduction), beliefs re-origin (42% reduction) and disruption (33% reduction). Reductions in loudness and disruption were found after 4 weeks, yet reductions in frequency and changes in the beliefs regarding the origin of the voice were found only after 10 weeks. Thus, there appears to be a two-stage effect of antipsychotics on voices: first a reduction in frequency and loudness, followed later by a reduction in the amount of disruption the voices caused and the patients' beliefs about the origin of the voices. Of course, given that there was no control group, we cannot necessarily attribute the causes of the change in the voices to drugs, as opposed to other factors associated with being treated.[3]

Biological mechanism of antipsychotic medication

Of the more than 100 antipsychotic medications available, all have the effect of decreasing dopamine levels (Kapur, 2003). In particular,

[3] See also Miller (1996) on changes in hallucinations following treatment.

D2 dopamine receptors are blockaded (Stahl, 2008). Hyperactivity of the mesolimbic dopamine pathway, which projects from the ventral tegmental area (VTA) in the brain stem to the nucleus accumbens in the ventral stratium (Stahl, 2008) has been proposed to be responsible for hallucinations (Weinberger, 1987), and particularly auditory hallucinations (Stahl, 2008).

Thus, if a pure D2 dopamine antagonist (i.e. a 'typical' antipsychotic such as chlorpromazine or haloperidol) is applied, this reduces the activation of the hyperactive D2 dopamine receptors in the mesolimbic dopamine pathway (Stahl, 2008). However, this action also reduces activity in other 'innocent' regions of the brain where there are D2 receptors. For example, D2 receptors working away in the nigrostriatal pathway also have their activity reduced and this causes as side-effects so-called extrapyramidal symptoms, which can include tremors and shaking and tardive dyskinesia (facial and tongue movements and grimacing) (ibid.).

Why should such over-activity of mesolimbic D2 receptors cause AVHs? At least two reasons exist. The first, as Stahl (ibid.) describes, is that there is a cortico-striatal-thalamic-cortical loop which creates a thalamic sensory filter controlling the amount of information that is sent to the cortex. In brief, the corticoacumbens glutamate pathway runs from the prefrontal cortex (PFC) to an area of the ventral striatum known as the nucleus accumbens. This in turn has inhibitory gamma-aminobutyric acid (GABA) connections to the thalamus. There is then a separate, direct route from the thalamus back to the prefrontal cortex, the thalamocortical pathway. This creates a circular loop between the thalamus and PFC which enables the amount of information that the thalamus sends to the PFC to be controlled in a form of 'sensory filter', which stops too much of the sensory traffic coming into the thalamus from escaping to the cortex, where it may overwhelm or confuse cortical information processing. In this loop, dopamine inhibits the GABA neurons which project to the thalamus. Thus, if dopamine levels increase here, the GABA neurons cannot inhibit the activity of the thalamus as effectively, leading to more information getting through the sensory filter of the thalamus. It has thus been proposed that if there is N-methyl-d-aspartate (NMDA) hypofunction in the VTA, this results in (1) mesolimbic dopamine hyperactivity, which reduces the ability of the GABA neurons running from the nucleus accumbens to the thalamus to inhibit the thalamus's activity, and (2) corticoacumbens glutamate pathway hypoactivity, which further reduces the firing of the GABA neurons in the nucleus accumbens, leading to further reduced inhibition of the thalamus. This, in theory, leads to the sensory filter function of the thalamus breaking down, allowing more information to pass from the thalamus to the PFC, which may lead to AVHs (all taken from Stahl, 2008).

A second theory is the motivational salience hypothesis put forward by Kapur (2003). According to this hypothesis, excess dopamine makes internal representations of precepts, language and memories more salient. In particular, the mesolimbic dopamine system has been argued to be a critical component in the 'attribution of salience', a process in which 'events and thoughts come to grab attention, drive action, and influence goal-directed behavior because of their association with reward or punishment' (ibid., p. 14). Dopamine also adds flavour to the experience, making such experiences either desirable or aversive (Kapur, 2003). This theory is attractive, as it offers an explanation for the finding, described above, that patients' AVHs do not always vanish, but just bother them less.

But why should there be over-activity of D2 receptors in the first place?[4] As Stahl (2008) describes, going back a step to examine what normally influences the level of dopamine in the mesolimbic dopamine pathway, it has been found that the glutamate projection from the brain stem effects the mesolimbic dopamine pathway. The cortical brain stem glutamate connection normally acts as a brake on the mesolimbic dopamine pathway by an inhibitory GABA interneuron in the VTA. Hence, it is proposed that hypoactivity of NMDA receptors in this pathway means that the mesolimbic dopamine neurons are not inhibited and thus become hyperactive. This is all well and good but, as will be discussed in detail in Chapter 11, we need to go back further in the aetiological chain to the events happening in people's lives that cause dopamine levels potentially to change.

In contrast to the typical antipsychotics, atypical antipsychotics act both to block D2 receptors and serotonin 5HT2A receptors (Stahl, 2008). However, as atypical antipsychotics have been found to be no more effective than typical antipsychotics (Lewis & Lieberman, 2008), the additional serotonin action of these drugs may not tell us much about the mechanisms underlying AVHs.

Electrophysiological studies

Electrophysiological techniques are able to examine the electrical activity in the brain with a higher temporal resolution than fMRI, and can hence give us further insights into the neuroscience of AVHs. One

---

[4] In Chapter 11 we will go outside the head to look at events in the world that might cause such changes.

well-studied area is mismatch negativity. Normally when we hear a series of similar sounds and then a new sound appears, the brain reacts by generating an electrophysiological response called a mismatch negativity (MMN). This MMN involves automatic, pre-attentive detection of auditory changes (Näätänen, 1990). It has been proposed that the MMN arises by the novel stimulus being compared to our memory of the usual stimulus. If there is a discernible difference between the incoming auditory stimulus and the existing memory trace, the MMN is generated (ibid.). In a study of the MMN in SZ:AVH+ and SZ:AVH−, Fisher et al. (2008) report that reductions in frontal MMN amplitude are associated with clearer AVHs, and suggest that there is a relationship between AVHs and preconscious auditory stimulus detection. They also note two previous reports showing an association between pre-attentive processing and AHs, with MMNs in left frontal/temporal sites being negatively correlated with AH ratings (e.g. Hirayasu et al., 1998). However, no MMN differences were found by van Lutterveld et al. (2010) in healthy voice-hearers. They did, though, find an increased P300 response in healthy voice-hearers. The P300 event-related potential is a positive electroencephalograph (EEG) deflection which occurs approximately 300ms after the presentation of an anomalous stimuli, and is thought to represent conscious processing of stimuli (Näätänen, 1990) and to be related to the degree of attentional resources that are deployed. Others have found reduced P300 activity over the left temporal lobe to be specific to SZ:AVH+ (Havermans et al., 1999). Indeed, Papageorgiou et al. (2004) found that P300 amplitudes over the left temporoparietal region and at the left prefrontal area were lower in SZ: AVH+ before antipsychotic medication, as compared to after treatment.

What appears particularly promising are studies that have examined EEG coherence in SZ:AVH+ while they were hallucinating and while they were not. EEG coherence is basically a measure of how strongly two regions of the brain are talking to each other. High coherence indicates a high functional connectivity between these two areas, which may be either exciting or inhibiting each other (Sritharan et al., 2005). They found that although coherence in the EEG alpha-band between Broca's and Wernicke's areas did not differ between voice-hearing and non-voice-hearing states, there was an increase in coherence between the right and left STG during AVHs. The authors suggest this may implicate the interhemispheric pathway between the auditory association areas in the two hemispheres in AVHs.[5]

---

[5] Much like Julian Jaynes (2000) proposed (Chapter 1).

Another very interesting finding is that in a study of eight SZ: AVH+, Line *et al.* (1998) found EEG activity one second before AVH onset occurring over the right temporoparietal region one second prior to the patient's report of AVH onset. The authors note that the right temporoparietal cortex is involved in the process of self-recognition, and since their study many have found this region is involved in such judgements (see Decety & Sommerville, 2003). For example, Keenan *et al.* (2001) found that during a Wada test (where one hemisphere is anaesthetised, the right hemisphere in this case) an individual was not able to recognise his own face, and thalamic-temporoparietal lesions have been found to impair the recognition of one's movements as one's own (Daprati *et al.*, 2000). Yet outside of AVH episodes, using probe tones Ford *et al.* (2009) found that SZ: AVH+ had a lower electrophysiological response in their *left* (but not right) primary auditory cortex than SZ:AVH−. They took this to indicate that a non-speech area of auditory cortex (Heschl's gyrus) was 'turned on' and 'tuned in' in voice-hearers in order to process internal acoustic information, and that this came at the cost of being able to process sounds in general (p. 65). The electrophysiological work of Ford and colleagues is discussed in more detail in relation to inner speech models in Chapter 9. For a good review of electrophysiological studies of hallucinations, the interested reader should consult van Lutterveld, Sommer & Ford (2011).

A particularly novel development arising from EEG studies in relation to AVHs comes from the study of microstates. These are transiently stable (*c.*100–200ms) distributed neural networks, which have been referred to as the 'atoms of thought', as they are thought to reflect specific conscious experiences (Lehmann & Koenig, 1997). Kindler *et al.* (2010) investigated such microstates in relation to specifically AVHs, looking at microstates in SZ:AVH+ when they were at rest. It was found that AVHs were associated with a shortening of a specific type of sub-second EEG microstate (class D, which has a fronto-central distribution). The authors suggest this microstate provides a protective cognitive function, and they speculatively propose that its shortened duration may impair the correction of errors involving misattributing self-generated inner speech to external sources. We will return to inner speech models in Chapter 9.

Genetics

What role might genetics play in AVHs? Given the areas found above to be involved in AVHs, we should expect that genetic research into AVHs would target genes involved in these regions. Indeed, Hugdahl *et al.* (2008), in a review of the current state of knowledge of genetics and AVHs, suggest that genes involved in speech and language are likely to be implicated. The FOXP2 gene they note is a potential candidate, as patients with abnormal FOXP2 function show disturbed activation of language-related brain regions, such as underactivation of Broca's area (Liégeois *et al.*, 2003). They also observe that polymorphisms in FOXP2 have recently been associated with auditory hallucinations in patients diagnosed with schizophrenia (Sanjuan *et al.*, 2006). Another gene that Hugdahl and colleagues highlight is the cholecystokinin type A receptor (CCK-AR) gene, which impacts upon dopamine levels, and has been found to be related to persistent AVHs by Sanjuan *et al.* (2004). They also note Sun *et al.*'s (2005) finding of a gene (LMO4) being expressed differentially in left and right peri-Sylvian regions of the embryonic human brains, and speculate that given the laterality issues highlighted here in AVHs, this may play a role.

Thomas *et al.* (2007) found a correlation between the presence of AVHs in patients diagnosed with schizophrenia spectrum disorders and the presence of AVHs in a sibling of theirs who also had a schizophrenia spectrum disorder (77 pairs of twins in the USA). However, this was not found in a larger sample in India (136 pairs), which may have resulted from the overall higher prevalence of hearing voices in the American sample (83.4%) as compared to the Indian sample (64.3%). The authors take this to suggest a significant impact of non-shared environmental factors in the aetiology of hearing voices, but note that three other studies have failed to find correlations between AVHs in siblings who both have schizophrenia spectrum disorders (DeLisi *et al.*, 1987; Kendler *et al.*, 1997; Hwu *et al.*, 1997, as cited in Thomas *et al.*, 2007).

AVHs in other contexts have also started to be studied in terms of their genetics. In epilepsy research, Winawer *et al.* (2000) have linked the syndrome of autosomal dominant partial epilepsy with auditory features (ADPEAF) in families to an area of chromosome 10q. AVHs in Alzheimer's has been found to be associated with a specific genetic polymorphism of the 5-HT2A receptor polymorphism 102-T/C, with those with some form of the C102 allele being more likely to have AVHs (Holmes *et al.*, 1998).

Yet all voice-hearing genetic research is still in its infancy, and it appears most likely that epigenetic processes, interactions between genes, environment and psychological factors (see Chapter 11) will play a role in the genesis of AVHs.

Table 8.6. *Summary of neurophysiological findings*

Methodology	Finding
Neuroimaging studies	• Grey matter abnormalities in the STG and IFG • Hyperconnectivity in the arcuate fasciculus • Functional activation during AVHs in the IFG, STG, insula, cingulate, cerebellum and supramarginal gyrus • Activity immediately preceding AVHs in the parahippocampal cortex, insula and IFG
Lateralisation	• Signalling abnormalities between left and right temporal lobes, or right hemisphere dysfunction
Transcranial magnetic stimulation (TMS)	• Overactivity in temporoparietal junction • Role for connectivity between Broca's and Wernice's areas
Psychopharmacology	• Increased mesolimbic D2 dopamine activity
Electrophysiological	• Increase in coherence between right and left STG during AVHs • Increase in EEG activity one second before AVH onset over right temporoparietal region • Impaired communication (corollary discharge signal) between speech production and speech perception areas (see Chapter 9)

Building a neurobiological model of AVHs

How can we draw the findings of this chapter together? Table 8.6 summarises the key findings from this review. These may be integrated into a neuroanatomical model of AVHs, but before doing this it is worth noting the heterogeneity of the findings. How can we explain, for example, that some neuroimaging studies find Broca's area activation during AVHs, whilst others do not? We already noted sample size issues as a potential cause of this, but given that we identified two types of AVHs in Chapter 7, Type 1 (Dynamic), with its two sub-types, and Type 2 (Static), we must allow that these different types of AVHs (or indeed, other more fine-grained phenomenological distinctions) may have different neural underpinnings. This may explain some of the variability in the findings. Contrastingly, it may be that the same AVH can be caused by different neural pathways. These issues remain to be clarified.

One recent neuroanatomical model of AVHs is that of Allen *et al.* (2008). They propose that bottom-up dysfunction[6] occurs through

---

[6] I apologise for using the language of dysfunction as is common in this area. This is not meant to imply that voice-hearing is pathological. I am using the term in the sense of 'different to how non-voice-hearers' neural systems work' and it is not meant to imply judgement.

spontaneous hyperactivity in the STG which primes these areas, leading to 'over-perceptualization' (p. 187). This may result in increased bottom-up modulation from the auditory cortex to other cortical regions which let the person experience and perceive their own internal auditory activity in a more vivid sense. Such perceptions are likely to be felt as non-self-produced, they argue, due to a weakening of top-down control from ventral anterior cingulate, prefrontal, premotor and cerebellar cortices leading to poor self-monitoring and impaired experiences of agency. Areas involved in the regulation of emotion (e.g. parahippocampal and cingulated regions) then contribute to the affective valence of AVHs.

Allen *et al.* note that their model allows for 'a disconnection model, in which frontal regions fail to prime perceptual centres regarding the internal origin of self-generated speech' (p. 188) as well as for the possibility of reduced control by monitoring centres. Disconnection models of AVHs (e.g. Friston & Frith, 1995) propose that such experiences arise due to a failure of the connections between the frontal cortex and the temporal lobe.[7] Such models draw on studies like that of Muller-Preuss & Jurgens (1976, as cited in Friston & Frith, 1995), who found that specific cells in the auditory cortex of squirrel monkeys responded to externally produced sounds, but not to self-generated sounds from the monkey itself. Ploog (1979, as cited in Friston & Frith, 1995) concluded that the inhibition of these cells during self-produced vocalisation was caused by corollary discharge associated with vocalisation, possibly from the anterior cingulate cortex, which projects not only to Broca's area, but also to auditory areas. As applied to AVHs, this means such experiences could be understood as self-formed words and utterances that are experienced as externally produced. Yet Allen *et al.* (2008) also claim that 'we also hypothesise an increased activation or hypercoupling of speech production centres in the inferior frontal cortex and speech perception areas in left temporoparietal cortex' (p. 188). It is hard to see how one can simultaneously advocate a disconnection and hyperconnection model between frontal and temporal regions.

The neuroimaging findings reviewed here support Allen *et al.*'s proposal of involvement of the STG in AVHs. Both structural GM changes in the STG, its activation during AVHs, and its abnormal connectivity with language production areas suggest a key role for it in AVHs. However, Allen *et al.*'s model is unclear about what is the cause of the over-activity in the STG. At least two possibilities exist. First, AVHs

---

[7] We will see more evidence for such models in the next chapter.

could be conceived of as resulting from focal activity of an epileptic nature, originating solely in the STG. Indeed, as we saw at the start of this chapter, direct electrical cortical stimulation of the STG is sufficient for AVHs to occur (Penfield & Perot, 1963). Yet this seems unlikely to be the primary cause of AVHs, due to the variety of neural regions found to be associated with AVHs in this chapter. Indeed, the above findings support David's (1999) proposal that AVHs 'cannot be regarded as random "discharges" from a diseased brain, but rather as the distorted output of a complex cognitive system' (p. 95).

A more nuanced model, as suggested by Hunter *et al.* (2006) is that activity in the anterior cingulate cortex (ACC) (involved in attentional processes) drives spontaneous fluctuations of activity levels in the STG which result in AVHs. In support of this proposal, Hunter and colleagues found, using fMRI, that when non-voice-hearing individuals sat in silence, there were clear 'intermittent episodes of strikingly increased activity within speech-sensitive regions'. These regions included the left STG and the medial transverse temporal gyrus (the site of primary auditory cortex). These fluctuations were also accompanied by increases in activation in the anterior cingulate cortex, as well as in the right insula. Hunter and colleagues note that although such experiences did not result in AVHs in healthy individuals, a greater magnitude of such fluctuations could be the basis for AVHs.[8] The proposal for an involvement of the ACC in a similar way is supported by Fletcher *et al.* (1999), who observe that in addition to the STG in non-voice-hearing individuals being affected by activity in the PFC and the ACC individually, it is also sensitive to a combination of activity in the ACC and PFC above and beyond its sensitivity to activity of either region in isolation. They suggest that this reflects a modulatory effect of the ACC on prefrontal interactions with the superior temporal cortex. Indeed, the ACC has strong reciprocal connections with both the prefrontal and superior temporal cortices, which allow it to modulate the prefrontal inhibition of temporal regions (Fletcher *et al.*, 1999). In people at risk for development of schizophrenia, increased activation of the ACC and increased effective connectivity between this region and temporal and frontal areas has been found (Allen *et al.*, 2010). Allen and colleagues suggest that this is because it is attempting to compensate for a fronto-temporal system which was faulty, but had not yet failed (a failure which would result in the onset of AVHs). However, Hunter and colleagues' 'spontaneous fluctuation' model still needs to be able to account for the specific

---

[8] This will be discussed further in Chapter 10 as part of the default network.

phenomenology of AVHs as laid out in Chapter 4. For example, why should such spontaneous fluctuations so often result in commands or meaningful comments directed to the voice-hearer about ongoing events in their life?

In addition to the ACC, and in line with the evidence from this review, STG activation appears to result from temporally prior inputs from other neural areas such as the inferior frontal gyrus (via the AF) and/or the parahippocampal gyrus. Structural abnormalities in the IFG, in conjunction with its hyperconnectivity to the STG, may create abnormal activation in the STG, further kindled by structural abnormalities in the STG itself. Similarly, disinhibiton of the parahippocampal gyrus preceding AVHs may cause abnormal activation in the STG. The trend for studies to find STG/MTG activation increasing in the temporal lead-up to AVHs, with peak activation during the AVH itself, also suggests that activity in this area is caused by prior activation in other neural areas. The anterior cingulate may still play a role in modulating this network (see Chapter 10).

Whereas Allen *et al.* (2008) focus on a front-to-back disconnection, the evidence from EEG studies reviewed here suggests that side-to-side disconnection, specifically between the left and right STG, may play a role. This, when taken in conjunction with the lateralisation studies, and Vercammen *et al.*'s (2010a) work showing disconnectivity between regions such as the left TPJ and the right insula, suggests that a complex network of bilateral frontal and bilateral temporal regions may underpin AVHs. It is notable how both recent EEG and fMRI studies are finding more evidence of right hemisphere involvement.

Allen *et al.*'s (2008) model does not address (and was not intended to) the inter-relations between dopamine and neuroanatomical findings. Here we may consider Gray's (1998) theory. In this, structural abnormalities in the hippocampus, amygdala and temporal/frontal cortex cause hyperactivity in the mesolimbic dopamine pathway, which in turn causes a disruption to the integration of past experiences with current stimuli, which results in AVHs. In this model the limbic forebrain (e.g. prefrontal cortex, ACC), creates predictions of the upcoming state of the world from the person's current motor programmes, which it transmits to the nucleus accumbens via the subiculum (the inferior part of the hippocampus), which compares the expected state to the actual state. In voice-hearers it is proposed that the input from the hippocampus to the nucleus accumbens is disrupted leading, chemically, to hyperactivity in the mesolimbic dopamine pathway and, experientially, to novel, unexpected events, which are experienced as AVHs. Items which are unexpected are reactivated by feedback from the comparator system to those areas of the sensory neocortex (visual, auditory, somatosensory, etc.) in which they have just been non-consciously analysed. It is this reactivation by feedback from the comparator that selects these items for entry into consciousness. In this chapter we saw evidence of a role for the parahippocampal gyrus preceding AVHs. Gray (1995) argues that activity around this hippocampal region relates to its role as a 'novelty detector' that automatically draws attention when the organism is confronted with an unpredicted situation. Gray notes that the involvement of this area means that items that should be treated as 'expected/familiar' are in fact treated as 'unexpected/novel'. Others have focused specifically on the interaction between dopamine and cingulate regions, with Dolan *et al.* (1995) proposing that AVHs result from 'dysregulation in the dopaminergic modulation of cingulate neuronal activity with a resulting impairment in the functional integration of more remote, but anatomically connected, cortical regions' (p. 182).

The next chapters will attempt to translate these neuroanatomical findings into an explanation at the neurocognitive level. However, this will not be straightforward, given the multiple cognitive and affective functions of many grey matter structures in the brain. Such findings are open to multiple interpretations, and the meaning of the activation of these areas at the neurocognitive level is underdetermined. As Hein & Knight (2008) observe, 'the same brain region can support different cognitive operations depending on task-dependent network connections' (p. 2125). For example, although Allen *et al.* (2008) propose that the involvement of the parahippocampal gyrus relates to its role in emotional memory, it is also possible that its involvement could relate to attentional or self-monitoring processes. In order to assess what neurocognitive explanation is most suited to the current pattern of findings, it is necessary to assess whether leading neurocognitive models of AVHs are able to account for the findings of this review, and if not, then to consider how to potentially extend or revise these accounts based on these findings.

Chapter 8: summary of key points

- Spontaneous epileptic discharges in the STG are unlikely to be a good model for all AVHs (possibly accounting for Type 2, but not Type 1 AVHs).
- Neuroimaging studies typically show AVHs to be associated with grey matter abnormalities in the STG and the IFG, and hyperconnectivity in the AF.

- Functional activation during AVHs typically occurs in the IFG, STG, insula, cingulate, cerebellum and supramarginal gyrus, whilst activity immediately preceding AVHs is typically seen in the parahippocampal cortex, insula and IFG.
- TMS studies suggest that overactivity in the temporoparietal junction, as well as connectivity between Broca's and Wernice's areas, may be involved in AVHs.
- Increased dopamine activity may make certain cognitions more salient and play a key role in the generation of AVHs.
- Electophysiological studies show an increase in coherence between right and left auditory association areas during AVHs, as well as an increase in EEG activity one second before AVH onset over right temporoparietal region.
- A neuroanatomical model of AVHs can be built around impaired connectivity between frontal speech production areas and temporal/parietal regions involved in speech perception (with a potential modulatory role for the anterior cingulate), and impaired interhemispheric connectivity between auditory association areas.
- More research is needed into such neural underpinnings, however, using large samples and a variety of techniques, linking the specific phenomenological properties of AVHs to neural mechanisms.
- There is a need to build neurocognitive models to help us better understand AVHs, a task which we turn to next.

Attempting to deduce what causes AVHs simply from neurological findings is problematic, not least because of the multiple functions of each region of the brain. There is hence the need for an account at the neuropsychological level because, as Churchland (1986) has argued, 'neuroscience needs psychology because it needs to know what the system does' (p. 373). Similarly, Coltheart & Langdon (1998) argue that 'it can be very hard to understand what a system is actually doing if one's only information about it is a description at the physical-instantiation level. A description at the abstract-theory level will be far more enlightening' (p. 150). Thus, co-activation of, for example, Wernicke's and Broca's areas of the brain in AVHs is relatively uninformative unless we know what cognitive functions these areas are involved in. Furthermore, as most areas of the brain are involved in many possible tasks (i.e. the meaning of their activation is underdetermined), it makes sense to be guided by an explanation of AVHs which proposes what normal cognitive processes have gone awry to produce them.[1] Yet this can be a two-way process, as functional neuroimaging can be used to inform and challenge a model of AVHs which was initially conceived in pure cognitive psychological terms (Buchsbaum & D'Esposito, 2008). For example, if cognitive models of AVHs had no mention of memory processes, and neuroimaging studies showed neural areas associated with memory to light up during AVHs, then cognitive models would need to be updated to take into account the likely involvement of memory processes.

Frogs and salt

If one rules out the theory that AVH comes from an external, ontologically independent, supernatural being, then we are left with AVHs having

---

[1] Or, less negatively, potentially to understand what functional purpose AVHs might be providing.

their root in internally generated cognitions.[2] This actually only leaves a relatively limited number of ways to explain voice-hearing and as such (as we have seen in Part I) similar theories of voice-hearing have re-occurred in each new generation, most of them orbiting around the central idea that voices are our own thoughts/memories/waking dreams. Indeed, Bentall (1990) has noted that 'there is one fundamental assumption that all the theories [of AVHs] have in common: that hallucinators mistake their own internal, mental, or private events for external, publicly observable events' (p. 88). Thus, conceptually we have not really advanced much from Aristotle's salty frogs (Chapter 1), and hence what follows in essence is an exploration of the nature of the frog and the mechanics of salt.

A useful starting point for our examination of voices is Behrendt's (1998) observation that AVHs tend to converge on the idea that 'hallucinations are regarded as self-generated events such as memories, inner speech, thoughts, or verbal images that are experienced as alien to the self' (p. 236). There is a lot in this sentence, and in essence the next two chapters will be spent unpacking it and then examining the evidence for it. Behrendt's observation can be split into two parts.

First, there is the proposal that what I will call the 'raw material' of voices (i.e. the processes that produce the content of the AVHs) is some form of memory, inner speech, thought or verbal imagery. That some combination of these processes is involved in AVHs appears hard to argue with. Yet, this immediately raises the question as to what each of these processes are, how they differ, how they are related and which is/are involved in voices. For example, how is inner speech different to thought? Is memory involved in thought? Which of these play a role in voices?[3]

Second, there is Behrendt's proposal that these events are self-generated, yet are experienced as alien to the self. Perhaps this would be better phrased as internally generated cognitions which are experienced as alien to the self (ask yourself here, does the 'self' produce cognitions, or does the self merely experience cognitions?). In either case, once we have determined what the raw material of voices is, we will need to explain why such internally generated cognitions are not felt to be 'mine'. What causes this, to use Graham & Stephens' (1994) term, 'introspective alienation' (p. 95)?

---

[2] Of course, these two accounts are not necessarily mutually exclusive, with those such as St Thomas Aquinas (see Chapter 1) arguing that angels moved the humours inside us to result in divine voice-hearing. See Chapter 12.
[3] This is clearly fertile ground for philosophers.

In addition to answering these two questions, a neurocognitive theory of AVHs will also need to account for all other potential aspects of the phenomenology of the voice a person hears. For example, as we saw in Parts I and II, voices can exist on a continuum running from a clear, external voice with another person's accent to a voice that is either more thought-like, or soundless. It also needs to be accounted for why AVHs have characteristic pragmatics, such as their tendency to appear as second-person assertive utterances (e.g. commands). To date, no theory has been entirely successful in accounting for all of these aspects of the phenomenon (Jones & Fernyhough, 2007b). Three key contemporary psychological theories of AVHs will be primarily examined here: inner speech models (the focus of this chapter), and then memory-based and hyper-vigilance models in Chapter 10. These theories are not mutually exclusive, and as will be made clear later, there is more work to be done to try to integrate these theories into a more comprehensive model(s), as I will attempt to do in Chapter 10 and the Conclusion of this book.

Inner speech theories of AVHs

Inner speech theories of AVHs, which in essence propose that AVHs are inner speech that is not recognised as such, have a long historical pedigree and are probably the theory of AVHs most widely subscribed to by psychologists. As we have seen, around half a millennium ago St John of the Cross (Chapter 2) thought many AVHs could be explained in this way. Around a century and a quarter ago, the French psychologist Eggers (1881, as cited in Pintner, 1913, p. 129) likewise argued that some of the voices we encountered in Part I, such as the daemon of Socrates and the voices of Joan of Arc, were simply inner speech asserting itself with greater insistence than is usual in ordinary individuals. Indeed, the ubiquity of inner speech led Buss (1966) to argue that 'the normal individual thus operates so as to make auditory hallucinations likely were he to become psychotic'. To jump ahead slightly, it will be argued here that in terms of our distinction made in Chapter 7, it appears that if inner speech is involved in AVHs, then it is likely to be able to account for Type 1 (Dynamic), but not Type 2 AVHs.

What is inner speech?

What do we mean by 'inner speech'? As Carruthers (2002) notes, most cognitive scientists hold a communicative conception of language, which views it as an input–output system for central cognition, with thinking itself undertaken in some other form of representation (which Fodor, 1975, terms 'mentalese'). At the other end of the spectrum exists views, such as those held by early behaviourists, which equate thought with inner speech, claiming thought to be merely speech without sound (e.g. Watson, 1920). Treading a middle path between Fodor and Watson, a Vygotskian account of inner speech fits with cognitive conceptions of language which see it as having a constitutive role in cognition that goes beyond the straightforward communication of information (Jones & Fernyhough, 2007a).

Vygotsky (1934/1987) proposed that thought and speech could be visualised as two intersecting circles. The overlapping region of thought and speech represents what may be termed verbal thought or inner speech. Such a conception allows that, whilst thought may occur in the medium of inner speech, there remains 'a large range of thinking that has no direct relationship to verbal thinking' (p. 115). This position is consistent with evidence of the need for verbal thought in some forms of thinking, as well as the possibility of thought without language (see Jones & Fernyhough, 2007a).

In Vygotsky's theory, inner speech represents the endpoint of a developmental process in which external discourse gradually becomes internalized to form verbal thought. His ideas about inner speech form part of a broader theory of the social origins of higher mental processes. This theory is encapsulated in his well-known claim that every mental function appears twice in development: first on the interpsychological plane, as a function distributed between individuals, and second on the intrapsychological plane, as an internalised version of that previously external function. Understanding the development of inner speech is hence likely to be crucial to understanding inner speech. Fernyhough (2004) argues that the development of inner speech from external speech happens in four stages. At Level 1 (external dialogue), children engage in overt, out-loud 'social speech' directed at conversing with others (Berk, 1992). For example, a child and caregiver might engage in social speech whilst undertaking the collaborative solving of a jigsaw puzzle ('where do you think that piece goes?' 'I don't know, but it must go with the rest of the blue pieces', 'well according to the picture they're all up on the left', etc.). At Level 2 (private speech), children conduct these dialogues in overt, out-loud 'egocentric' or self-directed speech, which is also termed private speech. This private speech is not aimed at communicating with others, but is 'speech for oneself intimately and usefully connected with ... thinking' (Vygotsky, 1934/1986, p. 228). Vygotsky argued that overt private speech, which can be seen eventually to die out in children, does not stop, but 'goes underground'

(p. 33) to form inner speech. In this view, private speech acts as a waystation on the developmental path leading from external to inner speech (Fernyhough, 2004).

Yet Vygotsky (1934/1986) argued against an interpretation of this new inner speech as simply 'speech minus sound' (p. 235), instead proposing it to be an entirely new species. Speech, Vygotsky proposed, undergoes a number of important structural changes as it is internalised. Foremost among these changes are condensation and abbreviation. Using an example from external speech, Vygotsky notes that if a bus is seen to be arriving, the speaker will not say 'the bus for which we are waiting is coming', but rather simply 'coming'. This is possible because, as Berk (1992) puts it, 'the self is a highly sympathetic and understanding listener' (p. 21). Furthermore, Vygotsky proposed that inner speech also shows a 'preponderance of the sense of its word over its meaning' (p. 244), with the personal sense of a word taking precedence over its traditional meaning. Additionally, he proposed that there was an 'influx of sense' (p. 246) into words in inner speech, leading to them having more associations for the individual than for a traditional dictionary definition. Such qualities of inner speech lead to it being experienced not as 'a series of fully formed utterances, but rather as a fragmentary, condensed series of verbal images' (Fernyhough, 2004, p. 54). This allows us to understand inner speech as itself having two forms which Fernyhough's (2004) model distinguishes between. The first is what Fernyhough terms expanded inner speech (Level 3), which can be seen to be much like speech without sound – thinking to ourselves in our heads in full sentences, much like when we speak aloud. This form of inner speech over time undergoes a syntactic and semantic abbreviation process, described above, which results in what Fernyhough terms condensed inner speech (Level 4), which Vygotsky refers to as 'thinking in pure meanings'. This distinction between expanded and condensed inner speech is supported by findings from the study of children's private speech (Fernyhough, 2009), evidence from introspection (Martínez-Manrique & Vicente, 2010), as well as self-talk in athletes (Hardy, Hall & Hardy, 2005).

The fact that inner speech develops from external speech means it is likely to have specific properties. Central to the Vygotskian conception of inner speech is the assumption that, like its developmental precursor private speech, it will retain certain characteristics of the external discourse from which it is derived. In particular, several authors (e.g. Wertsch, 1980) have noted that one implication of Vygotsky's theory is that inner speech will have a dialogic structure. Here we may recall Socrates' answer to Theaetetus when asked to define thought: 'the talk which the soul has with itself ... [the soul] when it thinks, is merely conversing with itself, asking itself questions and answering' (Plato, 1987, 189e). Somewhat more recently this dialogic structure of thought can be seen nicely in an account given by the always entertaining Richard Feynman, who reports that when thinking aloud (which we can see as a publicly observable, vocalised manifestation of expanded inner speech), 'I argue with myself. I have two voices that work back and forth', giving the example of saying ' "The integral will be larger than this sum of the terms, so that would make the pressure higher, you see?" "No, you're crazy." "No, I'm not! No, I'm not!" I say' (Feynman, as cited in Szasz, 1996, p. 6). Expanded inner speech is proposed to retain the give-and-take quality of external dialogue and, like in the Feynman example, to be a dialogue with one's self (where the other half of the dialogue may actually be another person). Importantly, this dialogic pattern may also be found in condensed inner speech, where the linguistic accoutrements of dialogue become jettisoned and inner speech becomes a process of 'thinking in pure meanings' (Vygotsky, 1934/1987; Fernyhough, 1996). To put it another way, the conversation that we have with ourselves does not cease when it ceases to be conducted in explicit, syntactically expanded questions and answers (Jones & Fernyhough, 2007a). A further implication of inner speech developing from external dialogue is that, as Fernyhough (2004) has argued, it should literally be shot through with other voices. Thus, we should literally use/experience other people's voices in the inner dialogues we have. Indeed, Bakhtin (2003) has argued that 'two voices is the minimum for life, the minimum for existence' (p, 252). Yet this has received little study, and the phenomenology of inner speech is still relatively unexplored (although see Hurlburt & Heavey, 2006). However, in a recent study with a student population, myself and Charles Fernyhough found that 26 per cent of students reported experiencing the voices of other people in their inner speech (McCarthy-Jones & Fernyhough, in press). A good example of this dialogic thought involving the voices of others is seen in Bakhtin's (2003) analysis of the thought of Raskolnikov in Dostoevsky's *Crime and Punishment*. Bakhtin observes that 'he does not think about phenomena, he speaks with them... he addresses himself (often in the second person singular, as if to another person)... he tries to persuade himself, he taunts, exposes, ridicules himself... his inner speech is filled with other people's words... he inundates his inner speech with these words of others' (pp. 237–8). Other psychological theories also propose a role for other voices in our inner speech. For example, Dialogical Self Theory proposes that inner speech can involve multiple sets of characters, with autonomous thought centres, that interact in verbal and non-verbal dialogical forms in an imaginal space (e.g. Hermans & Dimaggio, 2004).

But *why* do we internalise speech? Vygotsky argued that the internalisation of previously external verbal activity was an essential component in children's developing self-regulation of behaviour and cognition. Although we cannot directly observe the inner speech of others, the private speech of children is observable, and studies of children's private speech have shown that it often contains utterances that have a self-directive function (Luria, 1961). The dialogic nature of private speech (and, by extension, inner speech) guarantees that children become able to take the role of the questioner, adviser and director in the regulation of their activity. As Vygotsky (1978) put it, the use of verbal mediation means that humans are able to 'control their behavior from the outside' (p. 40). This linkage to control of behaviour immediately makes one think of the high prevalence of commands in AVHs.

Is inner speech happening during AVHs?

Electroencephalograph and subvocalisation studies

One way in which it has been investigated whether inner speech is the raw material of AVH is through studies of small movements of the speech musculature during AVHs. As Slade & Bentall (1988) note, inner speech during activities such as silent reading (Faaborg-Anderson & Edfelt, 1958),[4] imagining people speaking (Jacobson, 1932) and silently formulating counterarguments to statements one disagrees with (Cacioppo & Petty, 1981) has been found to be associated with electromyography (EMG) activity in the speech musculature (e.g. in the throat and lips). This leads to the hypothesis that if the raw material of AVHs is inner speech, then we should be able to detect subvocalisations going on during AVHs. The first large-scale test of this hypothesis was performed by Louis Gould in 1948. Gould attached electroencephalograph (EEG) sensors to the lower lip and chin (as well as to eye, jaw, larynx and bicep regions) of 100 non-voice-hearing controls, and 100 psychiatric patients who heard voices. Participants were asked to close their eyes, the lights were turned off and EMG recordings were made for between 6 and 18 seconds.[5] Twenty-eight per cent of the control group showed EMG activity in their vocal musculature during the experiment, as compared to 83 per cent of the patients Gould adjudged to be currently hearing voices, and

---

[4] Ironically, their paper was published in a journal with a title very hard to read at one's first attempt: *Acta Ortolaryngologia* (now try saying it quickly a few times).
[5] Problematically, Gould did not actually ask the patients if they heard voices during this period, but simply adjudged from case notes how many were likely to be hearing voices during the experiment (he estimated it was 77% of patients).

10 per cent of the patients he adjudged not to be currently hearing voices. Although suggestive, due to a range of methodological problems, the study could not establish that subvocal speech caused voices.[6] Similarly equivocal evidence for EMG activity in speech musculature at the same time as, or preceding AVHs, was found by McGuigan (1966), Inouye & Shimizu (1970) and Junginger & Rauscher (1987), as all these studies had mixed findings and suffered from methodological problems (see Green & Kinsbourne, 1990). Furthermore, both Roberts, Greenblatt & Solomon (1951) and Green & Kinsbourne failed to find consistent evidence for EMG activity being associated with AVHs.

Rather than relying on EMG readings, a small number of studies have examined the content of the amplified subvocal speech that some patients make surrounding their AVHs. Gould (1949) amplified the subvocalisations of a patient (L.M.) whose voices had begun not long after her husband's death. These subvocalisations were not audible to the unaided ear, and could only be heard when the patient held a microphone to her mouth and lips and the signal was amplified. It was found that her subvocal speech was much more rapid than her ordinary voice (speaking about twice as quickly) and had 'a different quality which could be identified as a "male voice" ' (p. 421). The voice varied in its intensity and force. It was found that the content of her subvocalisations closely matched the content of her voices. For example, when the amplified subvocal speech was heard to say 'I don't think this is fair, do you?... On the level . . . something else', the patient reported her voice as saying 'I don't think this is fair. Isn't she on the level with you or something else?' (ibid.). When the investigator found it hard to hear the amplified subvocal speech, the patient reported the same about her voices. Interestingly, in terms of the dialogic nature of inner speech noted above, it was found that the subvocal speech sometimes had a dialogue, with the two sides of the conversation occurring on expiration and inspiration of breath. Gould (p. 422) gives the example below, and during this time the patient reported hearing two separate voices, an upper and lower:

ON EXPIRATION: 'Oh, she is certainly the wisest one in the world'
ON INSPIRATION: 'No she is not'
ON EXPIRATION: 'I don't know if she is on the level'
ON INSPIRATION: 'What is she going to do?'
ON EXPIRATION: 'I don't know what she is going to do'

---

[6] For example, the voice-hearing patients could simply have been responding in their inner speech to what the voices were saying to them. Furthermore, Gould did not report whether increased muscle activity in patients was specific to the speech musculature, or whether it was also found in other muscles.

During distraction tasks, subvocal speech production stopped, although it is not stated if the voices did, too.

In a more recent study of this design, Green & Preston (1981) examined a 51-year-old male patient diagnosed with schizophrenia who heard a female voice ('Miss Jones'), whilst simultaneously and unbeknownst to him, making quiet, unintelligible whisperings. A throat microphone was attached to his larynx and the output amplified so that the patient could hear his own vocalisations as they happened. When the patient was left on his own, his whispering could be heard to be saying 'You shouldn't speak to him', 'It's me. We're on tape'. Later, the patient's amplified whisper said 'I love him and I want him and you won't let him out of the hospital'. This segment of the tape was then played back to him, and the patient commented: 'It's funny that she should speak to me and then it's my voice speaking. What happened?'. The interviewer then asked the patient's voice the direct question as to where Miss Jones' boyfriend was. The patient said aloud in his normal voice, addressing Miss Jones, 'Where's your other boyfriend?'. The amplified whisper then said, 'He's here with you', and the patient reported in his normal voice that his voice had just said 'He's here with me'. Thus, in this case, the patient's voice appeared to be his own subvocal whispering. As the authors note, his whispers referred to him as 'he', commented on his actions, gave him instructions, used vulgar phrases the patient did not and interrupted him whilst he was saying something else. This is much like the Type 1 (Dynamic) AVHs noted in Chapter 7. Why the patient should have been producing such speech in the second person at first seems puzzling, but a dialogic theory of inner speech (described above) offers an explanation for this. It is worth noting, before moving on, that studies of subvocalisation associated with AVHs, or studies which attempt to amplify subvocalisations of voice-hearers, have not been performed for the past few decades. The reasons for this are unclear.

One of Gould's (1950) early studies also supplemented his EMG studies with phenomenological data, reporting on the phenomenology of AVHs in 84 patients with AVHs and examining their similarity to their thoughts. Gould found a number of examples where patients became aware that their voices were actually their own thoughts. Patient H.B. 'had auditory hallucinations one week after admission. He later stated that he thought he heard his own voice' (p. 111). Patient A.P. started hearing voices in his head: 'At first he realised it was his own self talking, but then he gradually laughed at the idea and thought it really came from the outside'. When the voices stopped, A.P. stated: 'I am quite positive that it [hearing voices] is caused by lack of conversation-opportunities to speak to people. If a person doesn't have the opportunity to speak to someone he will speak to himself'. Patient M.L. noted: 'I thought they were really voices but it was really *myself thinking to myself*. At first *I thought it was someone talking to me*' (p. 111). Such a conclusion is also reached by many patients during the process of cognitive behavioural therapy (see Chapter 11), again supporting the claim that misattributed inner speech forms the raw material of AVHs.

Another way to address whether inner speech is occurring during AVHs is to ask the voice-hearer to perform a task that decreases their ability to perform inner speech and to see if this reduces their AVHs. Bick & Kinsbourne (1987) tested this by asking SZ:AVH+ to open their mouths wide open for a minute, a task thought to disrupt (note, disrupt, not stop) the ability to perform inner speech (try it for yourself to see if it does). After the study, participants were asked if they had experienced AVHs, and it was found that there had indeed been a decrease in AVH− frequency in 14 out of 18 patients. Such a decrease was not found for control tasks, in which participants had to close their eyes or make a fist. Interestingly, they also found that 18 out of 21 healthy individuals who were able to hallucinate when under hypnosis, also had this ability impaired when they opened their mouths wide. However, this finding was not replicated in a later study by Green & Kinsbourne (1990), who examined the effects on AVHs when patients did three tasks thought to reduce inner speech (opening mouth, biting tip of tongue, humming a single note quietly) and two control tasks (squeezing fists, raising eyebrows). Of these five tasks, the only one which reduced the frequency of AVHs whilst the patient was doing it was humming, which reduced AVHs in 17 of 20 participants, reducing overall levels of AVHs by 59 per cent. Notably, when Green & Kinsbourne examined how much EMG activity each of these five tasks generated in the speech muscula-ture, the only task to approach significance was humming, suggesting that it was its ability to interfere with inner speech that accounted for its clinical effectiveness in reducing AVHs. Of relevance to the previous chapter which highlighted the potential for the STG and IFG to be involved in AVHs, humming notes has been found to be associated with bilateral activation of the STG and IFG (Özdemir, Norton & Schlaug, 2006). Evenson (1987) also reports success in reducing AVHs using humming.

Other studies have also looked to engage the vocal production system, to examine the effects of this on AVHs. It has been found that reading aloud reduces AVHs during the duration of the activity (Margo, Hemsley & Slade, 1981). Yet, not only reading, but also listening to sounds, and particularly meaningful speech, has been found to reduce AVHs.[7] For example, Margo, Hemsley & Slade found that when participants with AVHs listened to more meaningful sounds (interesting passages of text) their AVHs became less frequent compared to when they listened to less meaningful sounds (boring text, passages in a foreign language). Subvocal counting has also been found to be an effective long-term intervention in 18 per cent of voice-hearers (Nelson, Thrasher & Barnes, 1991), and listening to music via headphones has also been found to be effective in some voice-hearers (Na & Yang, 2009; Nelson, Thrasher & Barnes, 1991).[8] It remains to be established if listening to people speaking via headphones (e.g. audiobooks) whenever voices start, is more effective than listening to music upon onset.[9] It is also interesting in this context to recall the Islamic woman, Kimwana, whose story we heard in Chapter 6. Kimwama found that reading and listening to the Koran was beneficial for the voices she heard (Watters, 2010).

Evidence of an involvement of inner speech from neuroimaging studies

Neuroimaging studies can also help us establish if there is a role for inner speech in AVHs. At least two strands of evidence are available here. First, do the structural and functional imaging studies of AVHs reviewed in the previous chapter support an involvement of inner speech areas during AVHs? Second, when voice-hearers perform inner speech, is there abnormal neural activation? In order to answer the first question, we need to know what neural regions are involved in inner speech production.

Inner speech (as silent articulation)

A number of neuroimaging studies have been performed to investigate the neural correlates of silent articulation in healthy participants (see Jones, 2009, for a review). These studies typically show that regions associated with this form of inner speech are the left IFG (Broca's area), the left insula, the supplementary motor area (SMA) and left

---

[7] Recall that Gould found that subvocal speech stopped during distraction techniques in his single-person case study described above.

[8] As a personal aside, my own tinnitus stops when external noise is present, but re-emerges when quiet resumes.

[9] As we will discuss in Chapter 12, whether this is likely to be a fruitful long-term strategy is doubtful.

STG, left inferior parietal region and the right posterior cerebellar cortex. Evidence for an involvement of Broca's area in inner speech also comes from a transcranial magnetic stimulation (TMS) study of Aziz-Zadeh *et al.* (2005), who showed that TMS over Broca's area interfered with the ability to perform inner speech.

A range of these inner speech-related areas were highlighted in the previous chapter as being associated with AVHs. Specifically, the structural grey matter changes in the IFG, the altered connectivity of white matter pathways between the IFG and the STG, and the trend for the IFG to be activated immediately before AVHs are also consistent with a proposed role for inner speech in AVHs. Interestingly, the two largest fMRI studies of neural activation during AVHs in this review both found particularly the right IFG (including Broca's area) to be activated during AVHs (Diederen *et al.*, 2010; Sommer *et al.*, 2008). Inner speech models which previously built on an early study showing left Broca's area involvement in AVHs (McGuire, Murray & Shah, 1993) have hence been adapted (Sommer *et al.*, 2008) to propose that inner speech produced in the right hemisphere homologue of Broca's area may be the raw material of AVHs. Although it is too early to conclude on right Broca's area's involvement in AVHs (due to the lack of the replication of this finding yet by other research groups), the present evidence tentatively supports theories which propose a key role for right hemisphere speech production areas in AVHs (Jaynes, 2000; Mitchell & Crow, 2005).

Studies which have examined whether the neural correlates of inner speech (again, somewhat problematically operationalised simply as silent articulation) in SZ:AVH+ differs to that of non-voice-hearing controls, have failed to find any differences (McGuire *et al.*, 1995; Shergill *et al.*, 2000b). However, both these studies employed voice-hearers in remission, and not individuals who were currently hearing voices. These studies also compared an inner speech condition with a baseline condition where participants were resting. Inner speech may hence have been occurring in the baseline condition, reducing the power of the study to identify unique activation associated with inner speech (Jones & Fernyhough, 2007a). Furthermore, the most informative comparison is likely not to be between a 'self-produced inner speech' and a 'no self-produced inner speech' condition. Instead, as voice hearing appears to involve a confusion between inner speech and heard speech, we are likely to learn more from a relative comparison of inner speech and hearing external speech in voice-hearers compared to controls. In a recent study which did just this, Simons *et al.* (2010) compared the neural activity in healthy controls and patients diagnosed with schizophrenia with a history of AVHs[10] when performing inner speech and when listening to external speech. It was found that the controls and SZ:AVH+ did not differ in patterns of neural activation in key language areas when listening to external speech. However, when performing inner speech, differences were found between the two groups in terms of the degree of change occurring from their pattern of activation in the listening condition. One key area of difference was the left STG. This area was activated in both controls and SZ:AVH+ during listening to external speech. Compared to this level of activation, controls showed much less activity in the STG when performing inner speech; however the reduction in STG activation was not as great in SZ:AVH+. A second difference was that control subjects showed increased activation of the anterior cingulate in the inner speech condition as compared to the listening to external speech condition, whereas patients did not show this increase. We will return to what this may mean later (a potential impairment of corollary discharge signal from inner speech production areas to the STG), and for the time being note only that inner speech in patients with AVHs is not accompanied by the normal differentiating neural features that distinguish it from heard speech in non-voice-hearers.

Auditory verbal imagery

Although evidence for differences in the neural correlates of silent articulation between voice-hearers and non-voice-hearers is somewhat mixed, this is of course only one form of inner speech. To use Fernyhough's (2004) terms, the silent articulation employed in such studies is monologic (i.e. does not have the give and flow of a dialogue) expanded inner speech and does not involve other voices, with which, as noted above, ecologically valid inner speech has been argued to be literally shot through. A more fertile ground for neural differences in inner speech between voice-hearers and non-voice-hearers may therefore be an examination of differential activation when imagining the voices of other people in one's head. The production of imagined speech in our head is termed auditory verbal imagery (AVI). That this may be a profitable area of investigation comes from Shergill et al.'s (2000a) observation that when they were fMRI scanning patients with schizophrenia during AVHs, 'The pattern of activation we observed during auditory hallucinations is remarkably similar to that seen when healthy volunteers imagine another person talking to them (auditory verbal imagery)' (p. 1036). Specifically, they observed common activation of

---

[10] Although it is not clear if they were experiencing voices at the time of the study.

the bilateral frontal and temporal gyri, along with right-sided precentral and inferior parietal gyri. Of course, given the phenomenological similarities between these two experiences, a large degree of neural concordance is to be expected.

Two studies (McGuire *et al.*, 1995; Shergill *et al.*, 2001a) have addressed the question as to whether voice-hearers show neural differences to non-voice-hearers when performing AVI. These employed a paradigm where participants had to complete sentences silently in their head, such as 'I like . . .', or 'I like being . . .'. In addition to doing this in their own voice, participants were also asked to imagine either the sentence being spoken in their own voice (first-person AVI), or, after having heard another person's voice being played to them on tape, to imagine that person's voice saying the sentence to them in the form 'You like . . .' (second-person AVI), or 'He likes x' (third-person AVI). Non-voice-hearing individuals, when performing AVI, are known to activate the normal areas involved in inner speech (e.g. left Broca's area, left parietal cortex), but with the addition of activation in the left precentral gyrus and STG, and the right homologues of all of these areas. Activation in the right homologue of Broca's area during such tasks is notable given the findings, discussed above, pointing to activation of right Broca's area in AVHs. When patients diagnosed with schizophrenia and with a history of AVHs are compared to non-voice-hearers when doing AVI tasks, a number of differences emerge. McGuire *et al.* (1995) found that SZ:AVH+ in remission, compared to SZ:AVH−, showed reduced activation in the left middle temporal gyri, the rostral SMA, and a posterior region spanning primary and secondary visual areas and the adjacent cerebellar cortex. Using fMRI, Shergill *et al.* (2001a) found that when voice-hearers in remission imagined others speaking to them, there was less activation in the posterior cerebellum, hippocampal complex and lenticular nuclei bilaterally, and also the right thalamus, MTG and STG, and left nucleus accumbens. Thus, the only region identified by both these studies as differentiating voice-hearers from non-voice-hearers was reduced activation in the voice-hearers in the temporal lobe regions of the STG and MTG during AVI. Again, we will come to what this means later in the chapter (i.e. potential impairment of corollary discharge signal from inner speech production areas to the STG).

An argument from phenomenology

Another way to evaluate the inner speech account of voices is to examine whether the phenomenology of AVHs is, in fact, similar to that of inner speech. A *prima facie* case for the involvement of inner speech in AVHs concerns a basic commonality between the two kinds of experience, namely that both involve some form of internal verbal mentation, or 'voice in the head'.

First, in terms of the content of inner speech, if one's own inner speech is the raw material of AVHs, then we should also not be surprised that the existing thoughts and ideas of voice-hearers may come to be reflected in part or much of the content of the AVHs (Skirrow et al., 2002) which indeed they do (Leudar & Thomas, 2000). For example, Sonnemans in his account of his voice-hearing experience notes that he takes it for 'granted that, in some way, I create those voices myself. It relates to how I look at myself' (Romme et al., 2009, p. 249). Similarly, derogatory voice content is linked with depression (Soppitt & Birchwood, 1997), suggesting the voice may reflect the voice-hearer's own thoughts about themselves. There is also an established relationship between the content of earlier traumatic events (e.g. combat trauma, abuse, etc.) and voice content (Chapter 4; Chapter 11). Thus, as David (1994) has argued, AVHs are clearly not 'merely outpourings from an abnormal brain' (p. 271), but instead are often meaningfully related to the voice-hearer's own thoughts. We may also note here that in cognitive behavioural therapy (CBT) some voice-hearers come to recognise their voices as actually being their own thoughts (e.g. Byrne et al., 2006); however, the phenomenological transformation that occurs during this transition remains to be studied in depth (see Chapter 12 for more on CBT for AVHs).

Second, given the role of inner speech in controlling behaviour, we would expect that if AVHs are grounded in inner speech they also would often be linked to behaviour control. The high frequency of command AVHs, such as 'get the milk' or 'go to the hospital', reported by 84 per cent of voice-hearers in Nayani & David's (1996) phenomenological survey, is therefore consistent with inner speech's developmental linkage with the control of action. Indeed, Nayani & David's phenomenological study of voices noted that AVHs 'bear a strong resemblance to patterns of thought that are part of the normal experience of making decisions' (p. 184). Leudar et al. (1997), based on their findings that AVHs are typically 'focused on the regulation of everyday activities' (p. 896) have also noted that this is consistent with an inner speech account.

Third, inner speech, as we have noted, has been proposed to take the form of a dialogue. When performing inner speech under normal circumstances, as Stanghellini & Cutting (2003) have put it, 'we experience at the same time a sense of unity and a sense of duality . . . we experience a sense of unity but not of singularity' (p. 123). Inner speech models based on a conception of inner speech as being dialogical, are hence consistent with the form of many AVHs which question/command the voice-hearer and respond to the questions of the voice-hearer. Essentially, the dialogic form of inner speech, which may involve us asking ourselves questions and then answering them ourselves (Fernyhough, 2004), is consistent with the basic form of such AVHs. Consistent with this, Leudar et al. (1997) have also noted that AVHs 'are characterized by the same dialogical structures one finds in ordinary speech' (p. 896). Similarly, Beck & Rector (2003) have argued that when patients engage in an internal debate or dialogue, especially internal debates, the more salient side may be transformed into an AVH (although they do not suggest why only this other side becomes transformed). In one kind of internal dialogue, they note the 'voice of authority', such as commands, criticisms, or evaluations, frequently prevails and may become audible. Here they give the example of a patient approaching a vending machine who had the thought, 'Should I get a coke or a cup of water?' and then heard the command, 'You should get the water.' Beck & Rector also claim that at other times, the 'self-indulgent response' may be vocalised, with the more permissive cognition being dominant. Here they cite the example of the same patient, sitting in the group room, who thought, 'I shouldn't eat another snack', and then heard the indulgent voice state 'You can eat the snack.' Such reports are consistent with inner speech models, such as that of Stanghellini & Cutting (2003) which argues 'AVHs are disorders of self-consciousness that are best understood as the becoming conscious of inner dialogue' (p. 126).

In a related proposal, Fowler et al. (2006) have proposed a basis for AVHs in inner speech, but inner speech conceived of as rumination and inner dialogue. Specifically, due to the association between trauma and AVHs (see Chapter 11), Fowler et al. propose rumination or inner dialogue about interactions with an abuser, for example, may be the raw material for many AVHs. This would predict the content of AVHs to be likely to 'reflect patterns of rumination or internal dialogue about self in relationship to what a shaming and insulting abuser might say about one's current actions' (p. 113). Jones & Fernyhough (2008b) have also proposed a similar model. These accounts are consistent with the phenomenology of many AVHs which, as noted in Chapter 4, are not the same as what was said during/surrounding earlier trauma, yet related to it. For example, in veterans it is what a dead man they killed would be likely to say (but not what he did say) that forms the content of the AVH (Chapter 4).

That voices are related to one's inner speech is also suggested by studies of AVHs in bilingual individuals. Although Hemphill (1971, as cited in Wang, Morales & Hsu, 1998) found that patients diagnosed with schizophrenia in South Africa who could speak, understand and think in both English and Afrikaans typically heard voices speaking in their first language only, Wang, Morales & Hsu (ibid.) failed to replicate this. For example, Wang and colleagues give the example of one voice-hearer who stated that 'When I thought in English they [the voices] spoke in English; when I thought in Chinese, they spoke in Chinese' (p. 502). Another voice-hearer who used to speak in Spanish, and heard Spanish voices, now noted that 'Now I think in both English and Spanish, so they speak in both English and Spanish' (ibid.). Wang, Morales & Hsu concluded that voices 'mostly reflect the subject's thinking process' (p. 503).

Interestingly, inner speech models can actually predict the phenomenology of one of the more unusual forms of AVHs (Jones, 2010). As noted above, Vygotsky (1987) proposed that inner speech typically becomes syntactically and semantically condensed and abbreviated, losing most of its structural and acoustic qualities, becoming a process of 'thinking in pure meanings'. If inner speech forms the raw material for AVHs then, in addition to fully formed words or sentences being experienced as AVHs, it can be predicted that some would also have this quality of 'pure meaning'. In our discussion of the phenomenology of AVHs (Part II) just such voices were identified: the 'soundless voices' that both Bleuler (1950, p. 110) and Janet noted, as well as the intellectual locutions described by St Augustine and experienced by many (Part I). The 'influx of sense' inherent to inner speech noted by Vygotsky earlier, is also consistent with the finding that voices, as St Teresa put it (see Chapter 2), can 'contain a world of meaning such as the understanding alone could never put rapidly into human language'.

One area of inner speech that has not been explored in detail in relation to AVHs is Hurlburt & Schwitzgebel's (2007) differentiation between inner speech and inner hearing. These authors note that whilst inner speech is experienced as 'going away', 'produced by' and 'under the control of' the individual, and is 'just like speaking aloud except no sound', in contrast, inner hearing is the experience of a sound which is 'coming toward', 'experienced by' and 'listened to' by the individual (p. 257). In these terms, many AVHs are more phenomenologically consistent with inner hearing than inner speech. These two different experiences remain to be worked into theories of AVHs, and their neural underpinnings established.

However, these accounts with their focus on the voice-hearer's own thoughts as being the basis for AVHs, need to reconcile themselves with Hoffman et al.'s (2008b) finding that in a patient sample of voice-hearers, 'respondents reported that verbal content of voices was distinct from verbal thought either most of the time or all of the time' (p. 1170).

Furthermore, in an investigation of thoughts preceding AVHs, Stinson *et al.* (2010) found that only 30 per cent of AVHs involved links between the content of antecedent thoughts and AVHs. Of this 30 per cent, one-third involved direct mirroring (e.g. thought: 'my friend hasn't rung me', AVH: 'your best friend hates you and that's why he didn't ring you'), and two-thirds involved having some related content (e.g. thought: 'someone might be out to get me', AVH: 'we will kill you'). Cleverly, Stinson *et al.* then tested if these preceding cognitions were likely to be causative. In a virtual reality environment (in which a social situation was simulated), they asked one group of patients to think these potentially triggering thoughts, but not the other group. It was found that there was no difference in the frequency of occurrence of AVHs in these two groups. Many voices may hence not be related to ongoing conscious thought/inner speech. Hence, this questions how often AVHs are related to one's own ongoing (conscious) thoughts. Here we may start to wonder if, in addition to the conscious stream of thought we are aware of, there are similar streams of thought going on unconsciously, which take the form of language and are produced by another semi-autonomous cognitive centre(s). This could include a dissociated inner speech cognitive centre, or at least a competing set of periodically stabilising neural networks involving speech production, operating semi-autonomously from normal inner speech. Here, though, we are venturing into spectacularly speculative avenues. However, there is some precedence for this argument (e.g. Morton Prince's theories from Chapter 3) and tangential empirical support, and we will return to this in the concluding chapter of this book).

Is it me? Why don't people know it's their own inner speech?

From the above it appears at least plausible that Type 1 (Dynamic) AVHs may have their raw material in inner speech. The next key question is why such internally generated inner speech comes not to be experienced as generated/authored by the self. Two main accounts have been put forward for this, which can be related to each other. The first is a top-down account based around the concept of source monitoring. The second is a bottom-up account which employs a corollary discharge/forward prediction model.

Source monitoring accounts

The fundamental tenet of many psychological theories of AVHs is that voice-hearers have a problem with the mechanism that allows the internally generated cognitions the brain produces to be experienced as self-produced. This results in internal productions being misattributed to an external source, although when we say 'misattribution', this is not to imply this is a conscious strategy; instead, such decisions are likely made pre-consciously (Ditman & Kuperberg, 2005). This mechanism has been investigated through experimental designs that attempt to answer the question as to whether those with AVHs are more likely than those without AVHs to mistake their own current or past actions/speech/thought/memories for someone else's actions/speech/thought/memories. In the psychological literature, the ability to identify the source of an event (e.g. did I say that word vs did I just think that word?; did I say that word or did someone else say that word?) comes under the broad category of source monitoring. This term covers both the ability to distinguish between externally perceived events and imagined events (reality monitoring), self- and non-self-produced events (self-monitoring) and specifically self- and non-self-produced speech (verbal self-monitoring, or VSM).

Bentall (2003) has argued that the ability to tell whether a given cognitive event is an internally, self-generated thought/imaginary creation, or an externally generated, real voice is a skill which we have. Bentall argues that perceptual states do not come with labels on them, such as 'real' or 'imaginary', and that instead we have to work this out based on a range of cues. This account draws on the source monitoring paradigm developed by Johnson, Hashtroudi & Lindsay (1993) which examines the factors that influence our decision as to whether a given event is a memory of something we perceived, or a memory of something we thought ourselves. To illustrate this, Bentall gives the example of Paul McCartney, who awoke with the tune to his song 'Yesterday' in his head, and then had to spend a couple of days trying to work out whether this was a memory of something he had heard before, or whether it was something new. Johnson, Hashtroudi & Lindsay's work indicates that the cues we use to distinguish between self- and other generated events include sensory qualities (the more vivid the event is, the more likely we are to think it was a real event), plausibility (the less plausible it is, the more likely we are to think it was not a real event) and cognitive effort (if the thought involved a lot of effort to create it in the first place, e.g. thinking of a vegetable beginning with the letter 'o', then this is more likely to be later recalled as being self-produced. Contrastingly, things that come to mind easily may feel more like memories of real events). Expectations are also argued to play a role, with those who allow for the existence of spirits, for example, being more likely to attribute a self-generated event to the agency of another. A bias towards detecting stimuli in the environment (a response bias) may also play a role, with a lowered criterion for the detection of external events, so when there is either no stimulation (e.g. during sensory deprivation) or confusing stimulation (e.g. white noise) those prone to AVHs are more likely to mistake thoughts for perceptions of external events (this will be discussed in detail in Chapter 10 in relation to hypervigilance AVHs). Stress may also play a role in making people make hasty and inaccurate decisions as to whether a thought is internally or externally generated.

One facet of source monitoring that has been particularly well studied in relation to AVHs is the amount of cognitive effort involved in producing cognitions. Certain thoughts (termed intrusive thoughts) occur with little accompanying sense of cognitive effort. More specifically, intrusive thoughts are generally defined as thoughts that are unwanted or unintended, perceived as uncontrollable, ego-dystonic and capable of interrupting ongoing activity, and are typically associated with negative affect and attempts to suppress them (Varese & Bentall, 2011). The occurrence of such thoughts may hence seed AVHs due to their proclivity to be associated with source monitoring errors. There are a number of studies showing a positive association between levels of intrusive thoughts and levels of AVHs (e.g. Morrison & Baker, 2000). Furthermore, Brébion et al. (2009) found that incorrect intrusions from memory were associated specifically with AVHs, rather than other unusual experiences. In their study, patients diagnosed with schizophrenia were shown a number of words then later asked to write down as many of these words as they could remember. It was found that the number of words that patients wrote down that were not on the original list (extra-list intrusions) were positively associated with their levels of AVHs (but not with visual hallucinations or delusions). Although the authors noted that this correlation was weak (but still significant) in those with AVHs, it was found that in the subset of patients who had at least one extra-list intrusion, this correlation between AVHs and number of extra-list intrusions was much stronger ($r = 0.60$, $p < 0.005$). The authors concluded that these intrusions, which reflect misattribution of internally produced words to the experimental list, seem to be selectively associated with AVHs.

To this discussion of cognitive effort I would add a consideration based on the work of J. J. Gibson (1977) and his concept of affordances. In essence, Gibson noted that when we perceive things in the environment we perceive their affordances, that is, the actions that they permit. It could hence be argued that when we perceive something (e.g. a telephone or a knife), it metaphorically calls out potential actions to us (e.g. pick up the phone or cut yourself, etc.). In this sense, some

AVHs could result in spontaneous language activation resulting from the perceived affordance of a specific object, which could be experienced as alien due to the low cognitive effort involved in the generation of such cognitions (i.e. low effort as they are inherent in the object itself to some degree).

Going beyond intrusive thoughts per se, it has been argued that an individual's beliefs about their thoughts (their meta-cognitive beliefs) are also likely to impact upon the decision to attribute their thoughts to another source. Morrison, Haddock & Tarrier (1995) have argued that intrusive thoughts come to be labelled as non-self-produced (and hence experienced as AVHs) due to an attempt to reduce negative affect associated with cognitive dissonance (Festinger, 1957) resulting from a conflict between what happens in one's mind and what one thinks should happen in one's mind. In this model, intrusive thoughts, and particularly those with content incongruent with what the person thinks one should think, occurring in individuals who have meta-cognitive beliefs such as 'I should always be in control of what I think', and 'I am responsible for what I think', may lead them to (unconsciously) attribute such thoughts to an external (non-self) person, leading to AVHs. However, a recent meta-analysis by Varese & Bentall (2011) found that although there was a robust relation between hallucination-proneness and meta-cognitive beliefs in non-clinical samples (mainly university students), in clinical samples, after controlling for comorbid symptoms, the relationship between hallucination-proneness and meta-cognitive beliefs was weak. In addition to their work on motivational factors, Morrison and colleagues have also found that voice-hearers experience self-produced words and thoughts as feeling less self-produced as do controls (Baker & Morrison, 1998) and that this is particularly the case when voice-hearers have their attention focused on their thoughts (as opposed to the external environment) (Ensum & Morrison, 2003). This suggests there may be some fundamental losing of agency of the thoughts of those with AVHs when one is focused in on oneself. However, as we will see in Chapter 10, Dodgson & Gordon (2009) present a model in which attention specifically focused outwards, not inward, is related to a certain form of AVHs.

It could be argued that because intrusive thoughts may take the form of intrusive images as well as intrusive verbal thoughts, then we would expect to see an equal prevalence of visual and verbal hallucinations in schizophrenia, for example, which in fact we do not, as voices are more common (e.g. Thomas et al., 2007). However, as Hagenaars et al. (2010) have noted, intrusive verbal thoughts and intrusive verbal images are sub-served by two separate cognitive systems, hence not requiring us to predict equal prevalence of visual and verbal hallucinations.

Next we will examine a number of studies which have experimentally examined whether individuals with AVHs show a pattern of source monitoring errors as compared to non-voice-hearers. These may be divided into memory-based and instantaneous on-line studies, and will be examined in turn.

Source monitoring: judgements on events in the past

A proxy measure that has been developed to assess whether voice-hearers tend to attribute their own thoughts to other people is to examine whether they tend to make retrospective judgements that words they earlier read, or thought up in response to the experimenter's instructions, were actually read or produced by the experimenter. A recent review of this area by Ditman & Kuperberg (2005) concluded that there was inconclusive evidence that making such misattributions is specific to those with AVHs. They suggested the evidence was inconclusive likely because the studies had a significant memory component, which may not be involved in the immediate attributions made about ongoing inner speech. We may also consider an alternative explanation, though. Given the neuroimaging findings that those with AVHs differ to non-voice-hearers not on silent articulation tasks (which is much like the reading tasks used in source monitoring studies), but on imagined speech, this suggests no consistent differences were found by Ditman & Kuperberg (2005) because the studies they reviewed involved thoughts generated in one's own voice, which are not the raw material of AVHs. Indeed, a more recent study by Brunelin et al. (2006a) did include an imagination condition in their source monitoring study when comparing SZ:AVH+ to SZ:AVH−. In one condition (say-imagine) participants had to distinguish words they themselves had earlier said from those they had earlier imagined themselves saying. In the second condition (hear-imagine) they had to distinguish between words they had heard the experimenter say, and words they had imagined the experimenter saying. SZ:AVH+ did not differ to SZ:AVH− on the say-imagine task. However, SZ:AVH+ were more likely than SZ:AVH− to think words they had imagined the experimenter saying had actually been said by the experimenter. The authors also noted that the two groups did not differ on a measure of positive symptomatology (after AVHs scores had been excluded), suggesting that this difference was specific to voices.

Yet the most convincing evidence for a causal role of source monitoring in AVHs comes from a study by Brunelin et al. (2006b).

In this study, a source monitoring task was administered to patients with AVHs before and after transcranial magnetic stimulation treatment (which reduced their AVHs). Although the source monitoring task employed was the slightly cruder reading task rather than the apparently more sensitive speak-imagine condition of Brunelin *et al.* (2006a) it was nevertheless found that improvements in AVHs correlated with improvements in source monitoring. This suggests (although it cannot prove causation) that if source monitoring improves, then this may enable the person to recognise their own cognitions as their own, and is the reason that their AVHs reduce.

Source monitoring: judgements on current events

Whereas the above studies have examined participants' retrospective judgements (which may be a poor proxy for the process of recognising inner speech in real time) the verbal self-monitoring (VSM) paradigm has examined, in real time, the ability to recognise whether an event was self- or other-produced. The design of VSM studies involves the participant first speaking a word into a microphone. One of four voices is then immediately played back to them via headphones saying the word they have just said: (1) their own voice, (2) their own voice distorted by a number of semi-tones, (3) another person's voice[11] and (4) another person's voice distorted by a number of semi-tones. The person then has to judge whether the voice they hear over the headphones is their own or another person's. Johns *et al.* (2001) employing this design found that the number of errors (being unsure, or incorrectly identifying the voice) participants made when their own distorted voice was played back to them did not differ between SZ:AVH+ and SZ:AVH−. However, SZ:AVH+ were more likely to make misidentification errors, i.e. getting the identity (self vs other) of the voice wrong, and not just saying 'unsure'. SZ:AVH+, but not SZ:AVH− or healthy controls, were also more likely to make errors when the words used were derogatory. However, SZ:AVH+ made misidentification errors for derogatory words by both thinking their voice was that of another, and that the voice of another was their own. If this error was at the root of voice-hearing, we would have expected it to be that SZ:AVH+ would mistake their own voice for another's, but not vice versa. Other studies have identified another problem, namely that levels of delusions, and not the presence

---

[11] In case you are wondering how this is done, the words are pre-specified so that the experimenter can pre-record another person's voice saying the same word, and then play it back to the participant after they have said that word.

of AVHs, relate to performance on this task (Allen *et al.*, 2006; Cahill, Silbersweig & Frith, 1996). A further problem for this paradigm is that the pattern of errors made by individuals with affective psychosis with AVHs is not the same as that in SZ:AVH+ (Johns *et al.*, 2006), with the former tending to make more 'unsure' rather than misattributions. Finally, the findings of such studies have been shown to be explainable by a general externalising bias employed under conditions of uncertainty (Allen *et al.*, 2004).

These results notwithstanding, we may still learn about the mechanisms underlying AVHs by examining the neural correlates of participants' misattributions. Allen *et al.* (2007), using fMRI, examined the neural correlates of making such errors. It was found that whereas both healthy controls and SZ:AVH− showed increased activity in the STG when listening to the speech of another compared to one's own speech, SZ:AVH+ showed no difference in STG activation between these two categories. When a distorted voice was heard by healthy controls and SZ:AVH−, as compared to a non-distorted voice, the anterior cingulate gyrus showed increased activation. However, in SZ:AVH+ such activation did not increase. These findings are hence consistent with the neuroimaging evidence noted in Chapter 8, and an account in which AVHs result due to a failure of the ACC to modulate the activity in the left STG.

One of the most recent VSM studies (Kumari *et al.*, 2010) found that whereas hearing distorted speech (compared to non-distorted speech) caused healthy controls to have increased levels of activation in the right temporal lobe, right IFG and right parietal regions, the opposite pattern of activity was found in patients diagnosed with schizophrenia, who showed decreased levels. This tendency to have decreased (as opposed to increased) activation in these regions when moving from undistorted to distorted feedback conditions was associated with poor performance at correctly identifying the voice. Furthermore, this correlated with levels of hallucinations,[12] i.e. patients with more hallucinations showed lower levels of activity in the right temporal lobe (e.g. the STG), IFG and parietal regions during distorted (as compared to undistorted) speech. However, problematically, no indication is given if this relation would still be significant if levels of delusions were controlled for.

In conclusion, the evidence from VSM studies is at best inconclusive at present. Notwithstanding this conclusion, we may use the concept of

---

[12] Although this was a global measure of hallucinations, hence including visual hallucinations as well as AVHs.

VSM to explain why, at a neural level, inner speech in the form of silent articulation does not differ between voice-hearers (in remission) and non-voice-hearers, but auditory verbal imagery (imagining speech) does differ between the same voice-hearers and non-voice-hearers (see Jones & Fernyhough, 2007a, for a full discussion). Silent articulation is thought to involve low levels of activation of the VSM system (McGuire *et al.*, 1996). Although generating verbal mentation in one's own voice will be a relatively automatic process, mentally imitating another voice presumably requires internal inspection of this imagined speech (necessary to assess whether the voice has the prosody, tone, pitch and rhythms of the voice it is intended to be (ibid.)), placing high demands on the VSM system. The greater demands of mentally imitating another voice are consistent with healthy participants rating such a task as subjectively more difficult than silent articulation (Shergill *et al.*, 2001). The proposal that high VSM tasks are problematic for voice-hearers has been experimentally tested by Shergill *et al.* (2003), who hypothesized that if the VSM load involved in silent articulation could be increased, then differences would be found between AVH-hearers and healthy controls. Accordingly, Shergill *et al.* (ibid.) asked participants covertly to articulate the word 'rest' either once every four seconds (low VSM condition) or once every second (high VSM condition). It was found that lateral temporal cortex activation (where VSM appears to have its neural correlates, with greater levels of activation signifying greater engagement of VSM systems) increased with the faster rate of covert generation in healthy participants. In contrast, in patients diagnosed with schizophrenia with a history of AVHs (but, at the time of study, in clinical remission) less activation was shown in the right (but not left) superior temporal gyrus, the right parahippocampal gyrus and the right cerebellar cortex when compared to controls performing the faster rate of covert generation. This result is in agreement with the finding above of Kumari *et al.* (2010) which also found decreases (as opposed to the expected increase) in VSM areas during tasks requiring high levels of VSM in voice-hearers. It may therefore be, as I have argued elsewhere based on a review of the neuropsychological evidence (Jones & Fernyhough, 2007a) that, as Hoffman *et al.* (2008b) have more recently put it, 'source monitoring mislabeling may selectively attach to verbal imagery of non-self speakers rather than ordinary inner speech' (p. 1172). This proposal could be tested by seeing whether differences between voice-hearers and non-voice-hearers on an overt speech equivalent of AVI (e.g. doing impersonations of other people's voices) are found in the Johns *et al.* VSM paradigm.

Meta-analysis of source monitoring/self-recognition studies

In an attempt to determine a clear picture from the large numbers of source monitoring studies, Waters *et al.* (in press) performed a meta-analysis of studies of self-recognition in patients diagnosed with schizophrenia compared to healthy controls. This included studies such as Johns and colleagues' VSM studies discussed above, as well as a range of source monitoring studies which asked participants to make judgements as to the origin of earlier self/other produced words or actions. It was found that SZ:AVH+ were significantly worse than SZ:AVH−, on self-recognition tasks. Specifically, SZ:AVH+ were found to be significantly worse in studies requiring a judgement on action-identity (that's me vs that's not me) and on action-recognition tasks (that's mine vs that's not mine). Notably, this study also found that recognition of new items (when participants had to identify whether items on a list were self-produced, other produced, or brand new items not seen before) did not differ between SZ:AVH+ and SZ:AVH−. This, the authors noted, points to a specific difficulty with self-recognition, rather than recognition per se. The authors concluded that the 'remarkable consistency across studies indicates that self-recognition deficits occur across all action modalities, timing delays, and regardless of the design measuring self-recognition'. They also note that as self-recognition deficits were seen on immediate conditions and after a delay, it seems likely that processing abnormalities in patients with auditory hallucinations occurs in the early stages of presentation (which in memory tasks might be referred to as encoding), rather than in memory-based processes. Yet perhaps the findings of this meta-analysis need to be treated with some caution, given that the 'top-line' findings of studies such as Johns and colleagues obscure issues such as the potentially confounding relationship between VSM and delusions, as well as patients showing VSM errors making them in both directions (i.e. self to other, as well as other to self, with the latter not being predicted by a VSM account of voices).

Bottom-up models: the forward model and corollary discharge

As noted above, Bentall (1990) has argued that cognitions do not come stamped with a label telling us whether they are self-produced or not. A weak version of bottom-up neurological accounts would agree with this, arguing that neurological events produce cognitions with specific properties (unexpectedness, vividness, etc.) which are then evaluated (pre-consciously) by source monitoring skills. However, a strong bottom-up model of AVHs would argue that inner speech can come stamped with an 'it's me' tag.

We encountered the idea of a disconnection model in the previous chapter. The idea that AVHs could result from a failure in the brain's self-monitoring (feed forward or corollary discharge) systems was first put forward by Feinberg (1978) and was subsequently developed by Frith and colleagues (e.g. Frith, 1992; Frith, Blakemore & Wolpert, 2000). Frith and colleagues most clearly worked out their model in relation to actions, developing the idea that the brain has what they term a neurocognitive action self-monitoring system (NASS) (Frith, Blakemore & Wolpert, 2000). This idea was based on Miall & Wolpert's (1995) forward model, which was developed to model systems in which, due to temporal constraints, it makes sense to base decisions on the predicted consequences of actions. The NASS model may be summarised as follows (adapted from Blakemore, 2003; Frith, Blakemore & Wolpert, 2000). First, a representation is created of what motor command is needed to achieve a particular goal, based on the estimated current state of the system and the desired end-state. The motor command needed to achieve this goal is then issued. In parallel to this, an efference copy of the motor command is also issued. The efference copy is used by the brain, in conjunction with knowledge of the current state of the system, to create a prediction of what will happen if this motor plan is executed. It is proposed that if the actual sensory feedback matches the predicted state, then awareness of initiation of movement will remain based on the predicted state. In this scenario, awareness of performing a motor action is hence based on the predicted state, which is available before the movement is actually performed. This results in individuals being aware of the occurrence of their motor action around 50 to 100 ms before they have actually moved (which has been experimentally demonstrated, e.g. Haggard, Newman & Magno, 1999; Libet et al., 1983). If the action is self-produced, then predicted sensory feedback should be cancelled out by reafference from the actual sensory feedback. If this occurs, then there is perceptual sensory attenuation of the motor act, meaning that one does not feel or pay as much attention to the movement. If the actual movement does not match the predicted movement, due for example to a defective predicted state mechanism, then the predicted sensory feedback and actual sensory feedback signals will not cancel each other out. Frith, Blakemore & Wolpert (2000) use this postulated mechanism to explain why an action may be actively experienced as performed by the self or passively experienced as performed by an alien 'other'. Blakemore (2003) has detailed the specific mechanism through which we may come to experience an action as authored by another. She claims that it is the predicted sensory feedback not matching and consequently not cancelling out the actual feedback, leading to greater activity in the parietal cortex, which makes the movement feel 'externally controlled' (p. 651). Support for this proposal comes from the work of Spence *et al.* (1997), who also suggest that over-activity of the parietal cortex may contribute to the feeling that willed actions are externally controlled in patients suffering from delusions of control.

The mechanism through which we come to experience an action as authored by ourselves has been detailed by Frith (2002). Frith claims that we get our awareness of authoring movements before the comparison has been made between the predicted and actual feedback. To argue for this, Frith draws on Wegner & Wheatley's (1999) work showing that the temporal contiguity of a thought of what is about to happen (e.g. hearing the word 'swan') followed by it actually happening (e.g. finding that your hand has just moved a pointer to a swan) causes the emotion of self-authorship.[13] Wegner (2002) calls this 'apparent mental causation' (p. 64). Frith applies this to the forward model by suggesting that, what Wegner (p. 325) calls the 'emotion' of self-authorship, is created when awareness of an action about to occur, based on the predicted state (available 50–100 ms before we move, as discussed above), is promptly followed by the actual action. The forward model can be applied to deviations from the normal processes of action authorship in the following way. If the predicted state mechanism is malfunctioning, either through efference copy information not reaching it or through some other impairment, then first, Wegner's mechanism of apparent mental causation cannot work, meaning that the actor does not feel the authorship emotion, even though the action is self-initiated. Second, the high level of parietal cortex activation (due to non-cancellation of predicted and actual feedback) is the same as if the movement were passive (i.e. caused by someone else). This gives the event the same 'feel' as a passive or externally caused action, and the actor hence feels as though someone else caused the action.

This detailed exposition of the NASS may be applied to AVHs (see Jones & Fernyhough, 2007b). This has been done in two ways. First,

---

[13] For example, earlier today I walked into my study and without paying any attention to what I was doing, flicked on the light switch. At exactly the same time I stubbed my toe on a hairdryer lying on the floor, and had the unnerving sensation that it was me kicking the hairdryer that had caused the light to come on. Two lessons: one, temporal contiguity can lead to false experiences of causation, and two, keep hairdryers in cupboards.

Seal, Aleman & McGuire (2004) propose that due to a failure in the NASS, the predicted sensory consequences of inner speech initiation become distorted or absent, resulting in inner speech being produced with an associated experience of unintendedness. The origins of this inner speech (i.e. whether it is self- or other-produced) is thus experienced in 'various states of ambiguity ... rather than two distinct states of awareness (self/other)' (p. 65). The proposal is then made that top-down factors, such as attributional biases, lead to the unintended inner speech being experienced as other-generated. An alternative application of Frith and colleagues' forward model to AVHs has been observed by Jones & Fernyhough (2007b). This notes that the forward model outlined by Frith *et al.* does not state that the absence (or distortion) of the predicted state causes the experience of unintendedness, which is then resolved into a feeling of self- or other-authorship by preconscious attributions. Instead, as discussed above, the forward model has a two-part mechanism, in which the emotions of self-authorship or other-authorship of an action are determined by the Frith–Wegner and Blakemore mechanisms, respectively. This model proposes that, as in Seal *et al.*'s model, the brain either produces a degraded predicted state or fails to produce a predicted state at all. The reasons for this are still poorly understood, but it seems likely that it will involve a particular neurological deficit, potentially modulated by stress. The consequences of failing to generate a coherent predicted state from the initial inner speech motor command are likely to be that awareness of performing inner speech cannot occur, as Libet *et al.*'s (1983) work suggests it would, 50–100 ms before inner speech actually occurs. Consequently, Wegner's (2002) mechanism of apparent mental causation (responsible for generating the emotion of self-authorship) is unable to operate. Instead, Blakemore's (2003) mechanism of non-cancellation of predicted and actual feedback, leading to increased parietal cortex activation and hence the feeling of external control, would be operative, leading the event to be attributed to an external cause.

Electrophysiological studies have given us an insight into how this efference copy mechanism may work. Such studies are based around the proposal that the self-monitoring system works through a corollary discharge system in which discharges from the motor speech-producing areas in the frontal lobes 'warn' the auditory cortex that self-produced speech is about to be produced (Creutzfeldt, Ojeman & Lettich, 1989). This is postulated to work through the motor speech-producing areas' corollary discharge deactivating the auditory cortex when self-produced speech is about to occur (Ford & Mathalon, 2005). Thus, speech production areas 'tell' the speech perception areas that incoming speech is self-produced by reducing the activity in the speech perception areas, leading to the resulting speech being recognised as our own. Evidence for the existence of this mechanism originally came from a study by Creutzfeldt, Ojeman & Lettich (1989). In this study, recordings were taken from the surfaces of the right and left temporal cortices (which were exposed to allow surgery) while patients talked and listened to others talking. When the patients were talking, suppression of activity in a third of MTG neurons was found. Such signalling between these areas is thought to occur via the arcuate fasciculus linking Broca's and Wernicke's areas.

Ford and colleagues used the electrophysiological technique of event-related potentials (ERPs) to study the activation of such areas during inner speech in patients diagnosed with schizophrenia (Ford et al., 2001). In this experiment, N1 ERPs were used as a measure of engagement of the auditory cortex during inner speech. N1 is generated by the STG of the auditory cortex in response to auditory stimuli of all kinds (ibid.). Participants were asked to repeat typical hallucinatory statements (e.g. 'That was really stupid') silently to themselves for 30 seconds, whilst brief auditory stimuli were presented via headphones. It was found that, in healthy participants, the N1 response to brief auditory sounds during 'inner speech' (construed here as repeating silently the hallucinatory-type statements) decreased significantly as compared to baseline. In contrast, patients diagnosed with schizophrenia showed no significant difference in N1 response between these two conditions. Ford et al. interpreted this to show that, whereas healthy individuals dampen their auditory cortex response during self-produced speech, as if to warn the auditory cortex that the sound is internally produced, patients diagnosed with schizophrenia do not, and this may lead to them experiencing their own self-produced speech as having an external source. Yet, Ford et al. failed to find a significant correlation between levels of hallucinations and the N1 effect, suggesting that other factors must be causally involved in AVHs beyond damping of the auditory cortex response during the silent recitation of sentences. A later study by Ford & Mathalon (2005) also failed to link corollary discharge abnormalities (assessed through frontal–temporal gamma synchrony) to AVHs.

However, when Heinks-Maldonado et al. (2007) utilised the VSM task of Johns et al. (2001) described above, they found that the normal pattern of increased suppression of the N1 response when hearing back one's normal speech (as compared to one's distorted speech) was not found in those with AVHs. Specifically, severity of AVHs was associated with smaller differences in N1 response between the distorted and non-distorted own speech condition. Furthermore, Ford *et al.* (2007) tested the proposal that the transmission of an efference copy from speech production to speech perception area was an emergent property of a self-organising system, which was accomplished by the synchronisation of oscillatory activity among distributed neuronal assemblies. A specific frequency of synchronous oscillations may identify spatially separated neural populations as belonging to the same functional network (ibid.). Thus, if the forward model mechanism involves speech production and perception areas communicating with each other, then an enhancement of neural synchrony between these areas should be evident before execution of motor acts, such as talking. Consistent with this proposal, Ford and colleagues found that both healthy comparison subjects and patients diagnosed with schizophrenia showed an increase in phase synchrony during the 150 ms preceding speaking in the 15.62 Hz frequency range, which they suggest is a pre-movement burst of synchronous neural activity which reflects the forward model preparing the brain for the sensory consequences of its own actions. In line with their previous work, this pre-speech signal was smaller in patients, and was not associated with suppression of cortical responsiveness to speech sounds in 125–100ms before speech onset. However, crucially in this study they found that hallucination severity was related to pre-speech synchrony. However, they noted that at present they could not determine whether it was the case that there was a faulty corollary discharge *to* the auditory cortex or whether there was faulty processing of the information *in* the auditory cortex. Nevertheless, it appears fair to conclude that the electrophysiological data is suggestive of a relationship between AVHs and an impaired corollary discharge mechanism.

Is the neuroimaging evidence consistent with a failure in self-monitoring?

The neuroimaging studies discussed in the previous chapter may be examined to see if they support the proposal that a form of self-monitoring deficit is involved in AVHs. The (anterior) cingulate, STG and MTG are all areas which have been shown to be involved in self-monitoring (Carter *et al.*, 2001; McGuire, Silbersweig & Frith, 1996) and it has been suggested that the right anterior cingulate may 'tag' an auditory event as originating from the external world (Szechtman *et al.*, 1998). The parahippocampal gyrus has also been found to be involved in meta-cognitive 'self or other' decision making (Schmitz, Kawahara-Baccus & Johnson, 2004), and the insula and cerebellum have been found to be involved in producing the experience of agency

(Farrer & Frith, 2002; Yomogida *et al.*, 2010). All of these areas were identified in Chapter 8 as either functionally involved immediately preceding AVHs (parahippocampal gyrus, insula), during AVHs (STG, insula, cingulate, cerebellum), or structurally different in patients with AVHs (STG). We may also note that the cerebellum has been found to be involved in making successful decisions as to whether a given event was actually perceived or whether it was imagined (Simons *et al.*, 2006).

Furthermore, the abnormalities in white matter in the arcuate fasciculus documented in voice-hearers in Chapter 8 are also consistent with a corollary discharge abnormality occurring between the two ends (Broca's and Wernicke's areas) of this signalling pathway, resulting in a failure to 'label' inner speech as self-produced. The deactivation of the parahippocampal gyrus preceding AVHs has been argued to be consistent with inner speech theories by Hoffman (2010), who speculates that this could form part of a cognitive state preceding AVHs which takes the form of a 'listening attitude' that predisposes people to AVHs. It is hence quite possible to interpret the neuroimaging studies of neural activity associated with AVHs as reflecting failures in a self-monitoring network.

Other variants on source monitoring accounts for why inner speech is felt as alien

A number of other accounts have also been proposed as to why inner speech is experienced as alien. First, we may note motivational accounts in which voices are disowned and attributed to another as they express content which is disavowed by the individual. An obvious problem with this account is that it cannot explain voices which are not inconsistent with the voice hearer's own beliefs. Indeed, Stephens & Graham (2000) note this account somewhat 'smacks of outdated Freudianism or self-help paperbacks' (p. 52). Second, Fernyhough's (2004) re-expansion model proposes that when condensed inner speech becomes re-expanded under conditions of stress or cognitive challenge (becoming Level 3 expanded inner speech), this may result in AVHs. Third, Diederen *et al.* (2010) have proposed that inner speech originating in right Broca's area is at the root of AVHs (see Chapter 8) and that this inner speech is experienced as alien, due to self-monitoring being harder when language activity is 'derived from cortical areas in two hemispheres' (p. 2). This focus on the right hemisphere homologue of Broca's area is a notable new trend of recent fMRI studies of AVHs. One problem this theory solves is the selectivity problem (Gallagher, 2004, see below), namely why some, but not all, inner speech utterances are experienced as AVHs (i.e. in this model, only inner speech produced by the right, and not the left Broca's area is the raw material of AVHs). Cutting (1990) also argues for the involvement of the right hemisphere in an inner speech-based model. His theory is based on his claim that thoughts are stamped as uniquely ours by the prosody system, which is located in the right hemisphere. If this stamping is impaired, Cutting argues, then the tone of inner speech would not sound right and might sound like someone else's, resulting in an AVH. Cutting also speculatively argues that this could explain the grammatical transformations that occur in AVHs. For example, he states that 'The peculiar grammatical transformation from "I" to "You", "He" or "She" may be partly due to the attenuation of the right hemisphere's deep-level grammatical representation of the self, and partly due to the preserved ability of the left hemisphere to provide superficial grammatical transformations' (p. 264). Further empirical studies are needed of all these proposals, and we will return to this in Chapter 10. However, it is worth noting that Cutting's account conflicts with the findings of Gould (1949) noted earlier in the chapter, which showed a voice-hearer to *already* be producing subvocal speech in another person's voice, and in the second person. This finding of Gould (as well as dialogic theories of inner speech) suggests that no explanation may be needed for mysterious grammatical transformations from 'I' to 'you', as inner/subvocal speech is already being produced in the 'you' modality.

A further theory of why inner speech is not recognised as one's own (Sass, 1992; Sass & Parnas, 2003) proposes that schizophrenia generally, as well as AVHs specifically, result from hyper-reflexivity. That is, such individuals more closely monitor their inner experiences and mental life than normal, and this leads to their alienation from their inner experiences resulting in AVHs. This theory has been further developed by Stanghellini & Cutting (2003). Empirically, such theories receive some support from Ensum & Morrison's (2003) finding noted above, that voice-hearers experience self-produced words and thoughts as feeling less self-produced than do controls, particularly when they have their attention focused on their thoughts (as opposed to the external environment). However, if this theory was correct, then meta-cognitive beliefs such as cognitive self-consciousness should be expected to be more prevalent in such individuals. However, Varese & Bentall's (2011) meta-analysis of meta-cognition in voice-hearers found no strong evidence for this. Furthermore, this theory would appear to predict that all inner speech would be experienced as AVHs, whereas individuals with AVHs appear to have normal inner speech (Langdon *et al.*, 2009). Although such evidence arguing against a hyper-reflexivity theory of

AVHs comes from research done with patient populations, it may be that other types of AVHs, such as those experienced by mystics, both historical (e.g., St John of the Cross) and contemporary, may indeed have a root in such intensive introspection. Again, this opens the door to the idea that different types of AVHs may have different causes. The hyper-reflexivity theory also shows how a close consideration of the phenomenology of AVHs can lead to new theories of their causation.

Other forms of support for inner speech theories

AVHs in the deaf

Support for AVHs being rooted in inner speech/verbal thought, also comes from studies of voice-hearing in deaf individuals (Atkinson *et al.*, 2007). Internally generated sign language in deaf individuals without AVHs (which could be referred to as 'inner signing' as opposed to 'inner speech') has been found to result in activation of the same key neural areas as are activated during inner speech in hearing individuals, such as left Broca's area (McGuire *et al.*, 1996). However, sign language differs from speech, in that perception involves the direct analysis of the movements made by the language articulator, namely the hands and/or lips (Atkinson *et al.*, 2007). Atkinson and colleagues argue that if AVHs really are misidentified internal thoughts' they should appear in ways that are unique to the individual, and given the different route to the formation of thought that deaf people have, and their reliance on the visual channel for both speech and sign language perception, we should expect the occurrence of more diverse voice phenomena than seen in hearing people. The Atkinson *et al.* study (described in Chapter 4), was the first to provide convincing evidence that many voice-hearing deaf individuals who reported visual phenomena were experiencing a sub-visual precept of the voice rather than a true primary visual hallucination. This imagery was 'frequently described as being like a black/grey shadowy figure or face, with hands and/or lips that moved as it communicated and only appeared when the voice was present' (p. 357). Such voices, Atkinson *et al.* suggest, may be similar to the subvocal imagery generated by a signer asked to imagine a story told in British Sign Language by someone they know. Atkinson *et al.* propose that deaf people's thought processes, like those of hearing people, are based primarily on an articulatory code which remains largely preconscious and closed to introspection. In their model, thoughts encoded in terms of premotor articulations enter explicit awareness during AVHs, leading to the perception of articulatory percepts, which are interpreted as non-self produced. Atkinson et al. propose that these 'voices' usually take an auditory-verbal form in hearing individuals' because the brain associates speech articulations with audible speech. Thus, they argue that when hearing people describe 'hearing a voice', they may actually be perceiving an auditory trace 'ancillary to motor subvocalisations' (p. 358). This is an interesting model, and can be integrated with efference copy models of AVHs, making it a promising candidate for future research.

Inner speech, source monitoring, imaginary companions and AVHs

Fernyhough *et al.* (2007) have proposed that during the development of inner speech, children who are in the process of internalising speech may be particularly likely to confuse actual incidences of their inner speech for external verbal speech. They propose that this may be due to their generally weak understanding of the thinking process, combined with their immature source monitoring capacities, which can result in the imaginary companions that young children have been found to have. A number of studies have found that children with imaginary companions are more likely to have AVHs when listening to ambiguous stimuli. For example, Pearson *et al.* (2001) found that 9–11-year-olds who currently had imaginary companions were more likely to 'hallucinate' words when listening to mashed-up human speech in white noise than those who did not have imaginary companions. However, this study was done by playing a tape to the children in a large group in a class-room setting, which introduced a range of methodological problems (e.g. social pressures to write down words). Furthermore, imaginary companions are thought to fall off significantly after the age of 10 (Taylor, 1999). Fernyhough *et al.* (2007) addressed this limitation by utilising a much younger sample of children tested on a one-on-one basis, finding that 4–8-year-olds listening to prerecorded jumbled-up speech were more likely to report hearing real words in this tape if they had a (parentally corroborated) imaginary companion. This study also controlled for age, gender, verbal ability and understanding of the concept of stream of consciousness. As a result, Fernyhough and colleagues suggest that the same source monitoring problems that may cause imaginary companions in children may also underpin AVHs in adults.

How does inner speech come to be perceived as speech?

If we accept that inner speech is the raw material of (some) AVHs, and that a combination of source monitoring and efference copy/forward models can explain why it is not felt to be self-produced, this still leaves inner speech models needing to explain why inner speech comes to have specific acoustic properties, e.g. being a heard voice. It appears likely that the corollary discharge model, in addition to explaining the loss of agency over inner speech, is also likely to account for why some voices are experienced as heard. Failure to inhibit the temporal cortex during inner speech production could lead not only to inner speech not being experienced as self-produced, but also as a speech perception.

Another approach to this problem has been to suggest that inner speech has more acoustical properties in voice-hearers than non-voice-hearers. For example, a recent study found that approximately 40 per cent of patients diagnosed with schizophrenia who had AVHs rated their own thoughts as having some acoustical properties, as opposed to being absolutely silent (Moritz & Larøi, 2008). This compared to a rate of only 20 per cent in non-voice-hearing controls. This led the authors to argue that AVHs may be associated with abnormalities with sensory inner perception 'which apparently arise already at the stage of thoughts' (p. 105).

An alternative approach is to question the degree to which an experience being labelled as a voice is to do with its acoustical properties. Stephens & Graham (2000) have argued that 'something can count as a voice without being experienced as audition-like or mistaken for sensory perception of another's speech' (p. 114). For example, they note what they term a fast confabulation account of voices, drawing on a discussion by Dennett (1991). In this account, someone finds themselves possessing certain information and then tells themselves a post-hoc story about how they acquired it, convincing themselves that they had a 'vivid, richly detailed conscious experience of a voice' (Dennett, 1991, as cited in Stephens & Graham, 2000, p. 28). Here it is useful to note Hoffman's (1986) introduction to the realm of AVHs of an idea from Daniel Dennett. Dennett differentiates between the occurrence of an imagery event, which he calls α, and the immediate cognitive consequences of α, which he terms the β-manifold of α. In essence, this proposal states that it there is no a priori way to tell whether a given property of an AVH (being a heard voice, for example) is present at the α stage, or whether it is part of a relatively automatic inference that someone makes about the voice (i.e. it is part of the β-manifold). Whilst we have seen in Gould's (1949) study that the subvocal voice already had the properties of another person's voice (i.e. it was present at the α stage, and not just a β-manifold), it is possible that for other people the vocal characteristics are part of the β-manifold, and not present at the α stage. Unfortunately, we just do not know enough about this yet. It is also worth noting, as we saw in Chapter 4, that not all voices have the phenomenology of a heard voice just like hearing a 'real' person speak. Although some voices have this nature, voices exist on an acoustic continuum running from clearly heard voices to more thought-like voices, to soundless voices.

Problems with inner speech theories of AVHs

Although the above review has highlighted a number of areas of evidence suggestive that at least some AVHs have a basis in inner speech, such theories also have a number of problems. First, inner speech theories can only account for a subset of the voice-hearing experience. AVHs which have a basis in actual memories (Type 2) do not seem readily explainable by this account, and these are likely to be better accounted for by memory-based models (see Chapter 10). Furthermore, as Waters, Badcork & Maybery (2006) have argued, inner speech models cannot explain other types of AVH, such as the voices of crowds, or other non-verbal auditory hallucinations, such as environmental noise and music. Indeed, Nayani & David (1996) found the latter to be quite frequent, with 36 per cent of patients diagnosed with schizophrenia who had AVHs also reporting musical hallucinations, and 16 per cent reporting elemental sounds such as clicks and bangs (recall here the results of Penfield & Perot's (1963) direct stimulation of the STG). However, given that voice-hearers with diagnoses such as PTSD have both flashback/memory-like AVHs (Type 2) in addition to voices which they could not have heard before which make negative comments about their thoughts, behaviours and being (Type 1), it may be that these two types of AVHs share some common mechanisms. For example, it may be that the final common pathway of AVHs is the STG, with input into this region from both speech systems and memory systems, as well as spontaneous fluctuations in this region, able to cause AVHs. We will return to this issue in the conclusion of the book.

A second problem is that some of the predictions that stem from certain inner speech theories of AVHs have been falsified. For example, one interpretation of inner speech theories of AVHs, given they predict that some inner speech utterances transform into AVHs, is that the frequency of subjective inner speech in those with AVHs should be less than those without AVHs. Second, given that AVHs have a characteristic form (e.g. speaking in the second or third person), then presumably inner speech theories would predict that voice-hearers would be more likely to speak to themselves in the second or third person (in order to create the raw material for AVHs). A study by Hurlburt (1990) began to give some answers to these questions by asking four individuals diagnosed with schizophrenia to reflect upon and describe their inner world at random intervals, when signalled to do so by a beeper. As part of this task, patients reported on their inner speech. Of the four patients surveyed, only two experienced AVHs. One reported AVHs that were 'occasionally dimly present' (p. 157), whereas another 'frequently heard voices ... which she understood to be the voices of beings she called gods'. The former patient frequently reported inner verbal experiences 'entirely similar to those given by non-schizophrenic [*sic.*] subjects' (p. 191), whereas the latter, who frequently heard second- and third-person AVHs, reported inner speech as being in her own voice with the same vocal characteristics as if she were speaking aloud. This suggests the inner speech of such voice-hearers actually bears no resemblance to their voices and is much like non-voice-hearing individuals. However, this study was limited by the small sample and not being designed to answer these specific questions.

A recent study I was involved with (Langdon *et al.*, 2009) was able more directly to answer these questions. In this study we carried out interviews with 29 SZ:AVH+ and 42 non-voice-hearing members of the general population, asking about the inner speech of each group, as well as the voices of the SZ:AVH+ group. We found the inner speech of the two groups were very similar. No significant differences existed between the two groups in terms of the intelligibility, speed and the pragmatics of inner speech. There was, however, a non-significant trend towards fewer SZ:AVH+ than controls reporting dialogic inner speech (i.e. inner speech as a back-and-forth conversation). No relations were found between the inner speech and voices of the SZ:AVH+ group. Individuals with many voices had the same amount of inner speech as patients with few voices. The speed, volume and intelligibility of patients' inner speech was not related to the speed, volume and intelligibility of their voices. There was no relationship between the tendency for SZ:AVH+ to experience their AVHs as talking to them directly and their own tendency to talk directly to themselves in their own inner speech. Similarly, there was no relationship between the tendency for SZ:AVH+ to hear voices conversing and their tendency to have inner speech in the form of having a conversation with oneself. There were also no concordances between the usage of personal names, second-person or third-person pronouns in inner speech and the frequency with which similar terms of address were used by voices.

What are the implications of these findings for inner speech theories of AVHs? It could be argued that inner speech in the second and third person was automatically experienced as AVHs in patients, and this is the reason why patients with second- and third-person AVHs did not report any such inner speech (this would fit with Gould's (1949) findings discussed above). If this second- and third-person inner speech took the form of the other side of a dialogue the patient was having with an imaginary interlocutor, this would explain why there was a trend for patients to have less dialogic inner speech. Yet what appears to come out of these findings clearly is that silent articulation in one's own voice is unlikely to be the source of AVHs. However, our study did not ask about the extent to which the voices of other people existed in the voice-hearer's normal inner speech.

Given that voice-hearers have normal inner speech, this raises the problem which Gallagher (2004) has termed the selectivity problem. This asks the question as to why, if inner speech is the raw material of AVHs, is not all the inner speech of voice-hearers experienced as alien? Explanations of this tend to be centred around the proposal that it is only under conditions of stress and cognitive challenge that inner speech comes to be experienced as an AVH. For example, the same factors may be involved that Bentall (1990) has described as affecting our judgement about whether an event is public or private: namely, factors such as stress-induced arousal, our ability to use cues, perceptual attenuation, or effects of suggestion. However, this explanation has something of a post hoc flavour to it. It also cannot account for why voice-hearers may be interrupted by their voices, or have their voices speak over them. However, the theory that AVHs result from activity in Broca's area in the non-dominant hemisphere, provides a way around this problem.

Another problem is that activation of Broca's area during AVHs is taken to imply a causal role for inner speech in AVHs. However, Broca's area activation may be a result of AVHs, not a cause. Motor theories of speech perception propose that the perception of speech involves activation of the speech production system (Liberman & Mattingly, 1985). Indeed, Broca's area has been shown to be activated by speech perception (e.g. Watkins & Paus, 2004). Although immediately after birth, speech does not activate Broca's area (instead only activating the STG) by the age of six months, speech perception activates both Broca's area and the STG, providing evidence of a developmental linkage between these two areas (Imada et al., 2006). Imada and colleagues note that this fits with the onset of imitation and canonical babbling, which begin around 5–6 months of age, both of which rely on the development of the connection between auditory cortical areas and speech motor areas. Although it could be argued that the activation in the IFG seen immediately preceding AVHs (Chapter 8) suggests it does play a causal role, STG activation also seen preceding AVHs in some studies still allows that such IFG activation could be an effect of this STG activation.

Hence, more large-scale studies of the activation preceding AVHs are needed to help resolve this question.

In addition to the issues raised above surrounding the involvement of Broca's area, we may also question whether other evidence cited in support of inner speech theories actually does support them. For example, as noted above, it is commonly argued that studies showing reading aloud reduces AVHs during the duration of the activity (Margo, Hemsley & Slode, 1981) support a role for inner speech in AVHs. However, it has been found that speech serves to constrain spontaneous activation in left-sided speech-sensitive temporal regions (Hunter *et al.*, 2006). Thus, it may be that such tasks are effective not because they reduce inner speech, but rather, because they stop the temporal lobe activating spontaneously and producing speech perceptions.

Another problem is that top-down source monitoring accounts assume that properties of the voices (such as their vividness, lack of cognitive effort, confusion caused by stress, etc.) result in inner speech being ascribed to another, causing an AVH. However, when voice-hearers are actually asked what makes them think their voices are non-self entities (i.e. the voice is that of a being which is an entity independent from themselves), Garrett & Silva (2003) found voices 'Predicting the future', 'Showing self-preservative reactions' and 'Having a "not me" content' were key reasons which led participants to feel this way. Whilst this could be integrated into a source monitoring account (these being reasons why an individual might unconsciously attribute the voice to another), it starts to push us towards an alternative reason why voices may be perceived to be non-self-produced, namely that *they are non-self-produced*. They may be produced by the brain, but not the self. But what, then, is the relation between the brain and the self? Do we think, or do thoughts just occur? Frankfurt (2007) notes that 'to some of the thoughts that occur in our minds ... we are mere passive bystanders'. Such thoughts, he argues, 'do not occur by our own active doing. It is tempting, indeed, to suggest that they are not thoughts that we think at all, but rather thoughts which we find occurring in us ... It is not incoherent ... to say that a thought that occurs in my mind may or may not be something I think' (p. 59). Thus, some thoughts may be things that happen to us, rather than things we create. We may often be witnesses to thoughts, not originators. Here a Buddhist perspective may prove useful, introducing the concept of 'thoughts without a thinker' (e.g. Epstein, 1999). It may be that cultural factors, as noted in Part I may wrongly encourage us to think that we generate, and are responsible for, all our thoughts. We will return to this issue in the Conclusion of the book.

Conclusions

In conclusion, evidence from a number of sources, including studies of amplified whisperings, neuroimaging studies of AVHs which provide structural and functional evidence suggestive of a role for Broca's area in AVHs and of abnormal connectivity between inner speech production areas and speech perception areas, phenomenological concordances between inner speech and some types of AVH, parallels between the developmental purposes of inner speech and the high frequency of command AVHs, parallels between the neural activation associated with imagined others speaking to us and that associated with AVHs, and electrophysiological studies linking corollary discharge abnormalities to AVHs, all suggest a role for inner speech in AVHs. In particular, inner speech accounts seem suited to explaining Type 1 AVHs. However, a number of problems for inner speech theories remain to be resolved. These include their inability to account for non-verbal auditory hallucinations, the lack of concordance bweteen the voice-hearer's normal inner speech and their voices, and the fact that not all inner speech utterances in voice-hearers result in voices. Here we may be forced to move away from a model where our own self-voiced inner speech is the raw material of voices, to a model involving inner speech emanating from right Broca's area, auditory verbal imagery produced in the voice of another, or more speculatively, dissociated inner speech cognitive centres.

Nevertheless, at present it appears that the production of both inner speech and auditory verbal imagery (AVI) by individuals who hear voices is associated with a failure to activate temporal lobe structures such as the STG and MTG, as well as the anterior cingulate. Given that the anterior cingulate has connections to the prefrontal regions as well as the auditory association cortex (see Paus *et al.*, 1993), it is possible that the anterior cingulate plays a role in transmitting the efferent outputs from the speech production regions. This may occur by its modulating activity in the STG (Simons *et al.*, 2010). Abnormal activity in the anterior cingulate may lead to a failure to dampen speech perception areas when inner speech is being performed, leading to it being tagged as non-self-produced. Top-down factors are also likely to play a role, in addition to abnormal activity in the direct efference pathway (arcuate fasciculus) between speech production and speech perception areas. AVI may be associated with sub-vocal speech production, and also with a failure in regions involved in both agency and memory processes such as the hippocampus, insula and cerebellum. Yet the number of problems identified with this account suggest the need for some form of profound revision of this theory. We will turn next to alternative, although related accounts, to see what they can explain, before returning to how existing inner speech theories may be amended in the Conclusion of this book.

Chapter 9: summary of key points

- A number of small studies, in need of modern and larger-scale replication, have found the content of voice-hearers' subvocal speech to match the content of their AVHs.
- A Vygotskian model of inner speech is important for our understanding both of what ecologically valid inner speech is like, as well as for the development of inner speech models of AVHs.
- Inner speech models of AVHs have a number of strengths' including some key phenomenological similarities between inner speech and AVHs, and suggestive evidence from neuroimaging studies of the neural regions activated during AVHs, and from corollary discharge studies of inner speech in voice-hearers.
- They are also supported by voice-hearers who either spontaneously, or as a result of psychotherapy (e.g., CBT) come to view their voices as actually being their own thoughts.
- However, such models are limited to explaining Type 1 AVHs, and not Type 2 AVHs or non-verbal auditory hallucinations.
- Inner speech models also have a number of significant problems, such as the lack of concordance between a voice-hearer's normal inner speech and their voices, and the episodic nature of voices (i.e. not all inner speech is experienced as alien).
- This suggests that inner speech accounts need to be reconceptualised by focusing on areas such as auditory verbal imagery (the production of other people's voices in inner speech), the output of right Broca's area, or dissociated inner speech cognitive centres. Furthermore, inner speech models need integrating with other cognitive models in order to be able to better explain AVHs.

10   Neuropsychological models II: memory and hypervigilance

The previous chapter focused on the most studied model of AVHs, the inner speech model, as a potential explanation for Type 1 AVHs. Here we turn our attention to two other models which address some aspects of AVHs not accounted for by inner speech models, and briefly examine the theories of two prominent AVH researchers, Christopher Frith and Ralph Hoffman.

Intrusions from memory

The idea that AVHs are reactivated memories has been around since Aristotle, being mentioned by St Augustine, as well as proto-psychiatrists such as Esquirol and Baillarger, and physicians such as Samuel Hibbert (Part I). Both in the twentieth century, and today, variants of such models remain popular.

West's memory-based model

West's (1962) perceptual release theory proposed that AVHs were 'previously recorded information: percepts, engrams, templates, neural traces, etc' (p. 281). West proposed this theory could account for both dreams and waking hallucinations, and was based on two assumptions. The first, echoing Aristotle, was that 'life experiences affect the brain in such a way to leave permanent neural traces, templates or engrams' (p. 278) which then form the basis of memory, thought and imagination West's second assumption was that psychobiological forces, inside and outside the individual, exert an integrating and organising influence on memory traces and affects the way they are woven into images, dreams, fantasies and hallucinations. Most sensory impulses, West notes, are normally excluded from consciousness by a scanning and screening mechanism. When sensory input decreases, she proposed, there is then less input to inhibit the emergence of perceptual traces which may then be released in 're-experienced in familiar or new combinations' (p. 279) through the firing of 'perception-bearing circuits' (p. 280) which may come to be experienced as hallucinations. Thus, she predicts that hallucinations will be found in conditions of reduced sensory input (e.g. sensory deprivation), but also, given that consciousness operates at an optimal level of arousal, in conditions of over-arousal (e.g. due to extreme anxiety).

Whilst this theory has many useful ideas (e.g. that ongoing events affect how memory is weaved into ongoing thought, and that memory hence does play some role in shaping the contents of AVHs), this theory also has a number of problems. As Slade & Bentall (1988) note, this theory places too much emphasis on sensory deprivation as conditions under which AVHs occur. In practice AVHs during sensory deprivation are a relatively rare occurrence, with no real phenomenological resemblance to the more common AVHs seen in those diagnosed with psychosis, for instance (Chapter 4). Slade & Bentall hence conclude this theory on its own is unlikely to be able to be a sufficient explanation of AVHs. To this I would add a number of other criticisms. First, this theory makes no effort to engage with the phenomenology of AVHs, and does not offer an account of why they have the typical phenomenology that they do. Second, it cannot explain a number of findings we have previously examined, e.g. the involvement of Broca's area, or why white noise should encourage AVHs. As such, a more advanced memory-related model is required.

Waters and colleagues' AVHs-as-memories model

Most recently, Waters et al. (2006) have proposed a model in which AVHs result from the unintentional activation of memories. This model has the significant advantage over any previous memory-based model of being supported by evidence garnered from well-designed empirical studies. Waters et al. argue that auditory hallucinations (AHs), including AVHs, are a result of the 'unintentional activation of memories' (p. 65) or, as they put it elsewhere, that they result from 'the failure to inhibit memories of prior events' (Badcock et al., 2005, p. 132). In their memory-based model they propose there are two fundamental factors that lead to AVHs.

First, there is a failure in what they term 'intentional inhibition'. This means that the normal ability to keep information out of consciousness fails. However, such a deficit on its own is not enough to explain AVHs. If this deficit alone occurred one would simply experience thoughts coming into one's head, which one would recognise as one's own but could not stop. This would then lead to experiences found in obsessive compulsive disorder (OCD), rather than AVH-like experiences. There-fore, the authors propose a second-stage deficit is also necessary for an individual to have AVHs, and this to be a context memory deficit. Context memory allows us to bind different contextual evidence together in order to help us locate a memory in a context, and hence to be able to identify it as a memory. Thus, if I have a memory of my grandfather shouting at me, it may be easier to experience this as a hallucinated voice if I can't tie this memory to a specific instance, e.g. my grandfather shouting at me in a park because I had just kicked a football in through the open window of an ice-cream van (and no, dear reader, I didn't do this).

Waters and colleagues' introduction of the idea that there are common characteristics in OCD and AVHs (e.g. Badcock *et al.*, 2007), which may be due to a shared failure in the mechanism underlying the first step of their model (intentional inhibition) is intriguing. In fact, if we go beyond what the authors themselves have written on this topic, we can see very strong phenomenological similarities between the thoughts in OCD and the voices in AVHs.[1] First, the thoughts in OCD have a compelling nature. You do not *have* to go home to check as to whether you have left the gas on or not, but you feel a strong urge to. The thought is hard to resist. A parallel can be seen here with command AVHs; you do not have to respond to the voice telling you to hurt yourself, for example, but it can be very hard not to, and sometimes voice hearers report temporary relief by complying with the voice (e.g. Byrne *et al.*, 2006, p. 73).[2] Second, the obsessional thoughts in OCD (Rachman, 1997) are by definition repetitive, and often centred on a common theme, as can be AVHs (e.g. Hoffman *et al.*, 2008b). Take, for instance, this example of thoughts in OCD given by Rachman of an 'affectionate and attentive grandmother [who] had recurrent images of throwing her beloved grandson over the balcony' (p. 794), or of another patient who was deeply religious but had recurrent and violent obscene images about the Church and the Virgin Mary. These experiences only need a soft phenomenological push (e.g. to have an auditory flavour, and to come from another) for us to recognise them as being just like typical AVHs (as described in Chapter 4). Indeed, the key differences appear to be that whereas those with OCD experience their thoughts as their own, those

---

[1] Indeed, Criterion A of the DSM-IV-TR definition of OCD bears a remarkable similarity to a description of what AVHs are like (albeit AVHs are not recognised as the product of one's own mind).

[2] Although, as noted earlier, some voice-hearers can be mocked by their voices for carrying out an action the voice had just told them to do.

with AVHs 'attribute their intrusive cognitions to a nonself origin' (Badcock *et al.*, 2007, p. 79), and experience a perceptual flavour to the thought. This theory that there may be shared processes underpinning both obsessional thoughts in OCD, and AVHs with repetitive content, leads to empirically testable predictions. For example, if an individual is suffering from a voice which has a repetitive, OCD-like nature, and we hypothesise that this voice is formed by the same processes that create the thoughts found in OCD, then treating such an AVH with an anti-obsessional medication designed for use with OCD patients, should be effective. Although there have been no large scales tests of this theory, consistent with this proposal Stephane, Polis & Barton (2001) report two cases of AVH with being improved by anti-obessional medications. The first of these individuals had an AVH which always had the same repetitive content: 'Do it, hang yourself in the bathroom'. This voice was 'decreased' (although it is not stated by the authors what 'decreased' actually means in terms of how the voice, or the voice-hearer's reaction to the voice, changed) by fluvoxamine, an anti-obsessional medication. Stephane and colleagues argue that such voices form a clear sub-set of the hearing voices experience. This appears a promising avenue for future work. One key question to be addressed here is whether such repetitive voices can evolve into more complex and novel AVHs.

Experimental evidence for the AVHs-as-memories model

Waters and colleagues' theory is supported by some well-designed studies carried out by the authors. First, Waters *et al.* (2003) investigated intentional inhibition in SZ:AVH+. This study employed two tasks to assess this construct. The first was the Hayling Sentence Completion Test. In this participants have to complete the last word of a sentence, but not with the obvious word. Thus, the participant may be given the sentence, 'The cat sat on the . . .'. If they said the word 'mat' this would count as a failure of intentional inhibition. In the second task, the Inhibition of Currently Irrelevant Memories (ICIM) task was used to examine how participants' memories of previously seen stimuli affect their memory on a recognition task. It was found that the severity of the patients' AVHs correlated with the extent of their failure of intentional inhibition. This effect was specific to AVHs, and not to any other positive or negative symptoms associated with schizophrenia. A later study by this group (Badcock *et al.*, 2005) compared three groups: SZ:AVH+, SZ:AVH− and healthy controls. Using the ICIM task, they found that SZ:AVH+ fared worse than SZ:AVH−, who in turn did worse than healthy controls. From this study the authors highlighted the problems those with AVHs had in suppressing memories that are not relevant to current reality.

Having established a deficit in intentional inhibition, this group then examined context memory deficits. Waters *et al.* (2006) analysed data on context memory, as assessed by a task in which participants had to assess *who* did something, and *when* it happened. In session one participants either watched the experimenter put two cards with pictures of household objects into a pair, or they themselves made a pair of two objects together. In session two, done thirty minutes later, this was repeated with different objects. Five minutes after the second session, the participants were asked to look at a number of pairs of items, and decide first whether this was one of the pairs that had been done in the experiment. If they thought it was, then they had to say (a) whether this pair had been made in the first or second session (*when*), and (b) whether it was them or the experimenter who had made the pair (*who*). They had previously found (Waters *et al.*, 2004) that patients diagnosed with schizophrenia did worse than healthy controls in being able to recognise the 'who' and 'when'. Waters *et al.* (2006) found that SZ:AVH+ did not perform any worse than SZ:AVH− on the 'when' part of the task. However, performance on the 'who' part of the task, which can be seen to assess self-monitoring, was worse in SZ: AVH+ than SZ:AVH−, and correlated negatively with severity of AVHs.

Finally, this group then examined data on the co-occurrence of intention inhibition and context memory deficits. Waters *et al.* (2006) found that 89.5 per cent of SZ:AVH+ had deficits (defined as 1 standard deviation less than controls) in both of these abilities, as compared to only 33.3 per cent of SZ:AVH−. Overall, although weakened by the fact that some hallucinating patients do not show both deficits, and some non-hallucinating patients do show both deficits, intentional inhibition and context memory do appear to be associated with AVHs (Aleman & Larøi, 2008).

Argument from phenomenology

A key way to evaluate any model of AVHs, as we have seen in the previous chapter on inner speech, is to examine whether the model predicts, or is at least consistent with the phenomenology of AVHs. Are the properties of AVHs, then, consistent with a model which views them as the 'unintentional activation of memories' or 'the failure to inhibit memories of prior events'? Waters *et al.* (2006) have argued that 'the proposal of auditory hallucinations as memories' is indeed consistent with the phenomenology of AVHs and can explain why 'entire dialogues from a conversation may be recalled' and 'why voices often refer to the patient's personal details' (p. 76). However, these examples of voices are not typical of the phenomenology of AVHs (see Chapter 4). Indeed, it is not entirely clear if the authors are claiming that this account can explain all AVHs, or just a subset (such as Type 2 AVHs). A more detailed consideration of this model based on the extent to which it accords with the phenomenology of AVHs is hence required.

The phenomenology of a number of AVHs do indeed appear to be consistent with the AVHs-as-memories account, particularly those where their content can be directly linked to memories of previous traumatic/ abuse experiences. This makes intuitive sense, as intrusive trauma memories are known to contain sensory fragments of the traumatic experience (Ehlers, Hackmann & Michael, 2004), which would give such memories a heard quality – a voice. In such cases AVHs do seem to be decontextualised intrusions of material from memory. As will be discussed in more detail in Chapter 11, there is substantial evidence demonstrating that AVHs are associated with earlier experiences of physical and sexual abuse (e.g. Hammersley et al., 2003). However, there has been significantly less research into the concordance between the actual content of the AVH and the auditory experiences undergone during and surrounding such abuse. If verbatim memories associated with the trauma (e.g. what an abuser said) are the basis of some AVHs, then concordance between the content of AVHs and trauma memories would be expected. Direct evidence for this comes from findings showing that the content of AVHs can be linked to traumatic experiences. Read & Argyle (1999) found that in three of seven instances in which content of the AVHs of patients diagnosed with schizophrenia was recorded, the content could be linked to physical or sexual abuse. For example, command hallucinations to self-harm were found to be experienced as being that of their abuser. Similarly, Fowler (1997) reported a history of trauma in fourteen of twenty four patients with psychosis who experienced hallucinations, and in four of these fourteen patients the voice heard was appraised as being that of the abuser. In addition, some content of the voices matched utterances heard at the time of the abuse. We may also propose that voice-hearers who have suffered childhood abuse, and today hear voices with content such as 'If you tell anyone, I'll kill you', may be re-experiencing what was said during the abuse. Such parallels have led Read et al. (2005) to claim that 'some psychotic hallucinations appear to be nothing more or less than memories of traumatic events' (p. 341).[3]

---

[3] See Chapter 11.

Despite the suggestive evidence above, further consideration shows the AVHs-as-memories account to be in phenomenological accordance with only a (relatively small) subset of AVHs. First, in the study of Fowler (1997) cited above, only in four of the total of twenty-four voice-hearers studied could the content of voices be seen as 'sometimes' being suggestive that these were memories. In the remainder of the sample who had a history of trauma, meaningful connections could be made between the trauma and the voices, but these connections were thematic (e.g. both the voices and trauma involved humiliation) rather than involving a direct relation between the content of the voices and what was said during and surrounding the trauma. Similarly, Hardy *et al.* (2005) found only 7 per cent of individuals with AVHs were rated as demonstrating clear concordance between the theme and content of the trauma and the themes and content of the voices. Hardy and colleagues also found that 42 per cent of people with hallucinations, who reported having current problems with past trauma, had no association between the content of their hallucinations and the past trauma. Instead, when we consider the phenomenology of AVHs as discussed in Part II of this book, we see that what are common are critical comments, or comments about the person's day-to-day experiences, with AVHs being 'focused on the regulation of everyday activities' (Leudar *et al.*, 1997, p. 896). Similarly, recall from Chapter 4 that Nayani & David (1996) found AVHs to typically be 'minutely engaged in the apprehension of objective reality' (p. 185). It is hard to understand how simple intrusions from memory of past verbalisations could function in such a role. It is also worth noting that Nayani & David observe that AVHs tend to evolve over time with the voices 'fashioning increasingly detailed dialogues with or about the patient' (p. 187). Again, it is hard to see how verbal intrusions from memory could create such an interactive dialogue with the voice-hearer. That some AVHs are not simply an intrusive memory of verbalisations experienced in and surrounding trauma/abuse, or more generally, but are instead more of a dynamic creation, is suggested by the technique of voice dialogue (see Chapter 12). Whilst Hoffman *et al.* (2008b) found voices to be more repetitive, in terms of their content, than the voice-hearer's normal verbal thought, suggesting that intrusive memories may play a role, we may note from our review in Chapter 4 that Leudar *et al.* found 43 per cent of psychotic voice-hearers heard voices telling them something they did not know, and Johns *et al.* (2002) found that only 14 per cent of voice-hearers said the hallucinations were 'replays' of memories of voices they had heard before. Such findings pose problems for a simple intrusion from memory account.

Other types of AVHs are also hard for the AVHs-as-memories account to explain. For example, AVHs may take the form of crowds of mumbling voices (Nayani & David, 1996). This seems an unusual form for an intrusive memory to take. While it is well documented that trauma leads to intrusive recollections of the experience and surrounding events (Ehlers, Hackmann & Michael, 2004), it is unclear why anyone should experience an intrusive memory of mumbling voices.[4] The same argument applies to non-verbal AHs. As Bleuler (1950) noted, in addition to AVHs, 'blowing, rustling, humming, rattling, shooting, thundering, music, crying and laughing' (p. 96) may also be heard. Although Waters and colleagues argue that their model can explain such types of AVHs, it would appear that these experiences, with seemingly[5] random content, are instead more parsimoniously accounted for by a bottom-up model, which views such experiences as caused by random, epileptic-like neural activity in the STG. We will return to this issue later.

In conclusion, it appears from the above that such AVHs-as-memories models can only account for the phenomenology of a minority of types of AVH. For example, this may be applicable to the minority of individuals (c.10%–20%) whose voices include content that can be linked directly back to memories of trauma. These are what I termed in Chapter 7, Type 2 AVHs. However, what I have termed Type 1 AVHs, which form the majority of AVHs, and which are related to the ongoing patterns of activity in the voice-hearer's life, seem to be inconsistent with a memory-based account.

Evidence from neuroimaging of AVHs

The evidence from neuroimaging studies of AVHs in Chapter 8 may also be considered in the context of memory-based models. Given the key role of the parahippocampal gyrus in memory (Diederen et al., 2010), the involvement of this area preceding the onset of AVHs could be seen to be consistent with the memory-based model. Diederen et al. have noted that the parahippocampus plays a central role in memory recollection, receiving perceptual information from association cortices, such as the language areas, exchanging this with the hippocampus, and redistributing it to the association cortices. As such, they propose that

---

[4] Although one could understand these as having occurred at the same time as trauma, potentially.

[5] Again, here we assume that these sounds have no meaning to the voice-hearer. Yet it may be worth asking voice-hearers if these sounds are associated with anything in their eyes. For example, these may have been sounds heard during abuse. Of course, they may not be, but the dangers of simply assuming they are random noises are great.

disinhibition of the parahippocampal gyrus preceding AVHs, may trigger the bilateral language-related areas originally involved in the perception of speech. Activation in inferior frontal gyrus and insula could be then explained as a result of the information redistributed to them by the parahippocampus, preparing them for activation in the course of hallucinations (ibid.). Similarly, cerebellum activity associated with AVHs, interpreted in inner speech models as being involved due to its role in agency-related processes, could also be accounted for in a memory-based model due to its role in memory-based processes (Okano *et al.*, 2000).

Conclusions

The AVHs-as-memories model appears only to be able to account for a small sub-set of AVHs (Type 2 AVHs). However, an examination of Waters and colleagues' memory-based model appears to suggest that they are actually describing two different types of model. Explicitly, as we have seen, they refer to a model based in 'the failure to inhibit memories of prior events' (Badcock *et al.*, 2005, p. 132), and arguing AVHs are a result of the 'unintentional activation of memories' (Waters *et al.*, 2006, p. 65). This is the model that appears to be able to account for Type 2 AVHs. However, by drawing the intriguing parallel with OCD, this suggests that Waters and colleagues are implicitly arguing for a thought-based model. I described earlier how the phenomenology of thought in OCD has a number of very marked similarities to AVHs, hence suggesting it is thoughts we should be focusing on, rather than just intrusions from memory. More evidence for a relation between AVHs and OCD comes from Guillem *et al.* (2009), who found that levels of AVHs correlated positively with levels of compulsions (when controlling for levels of delusions), and went on to suggest that 'hallucinations and compulsions may both reflect a decrease capacity to inhibit behaviors or thoughts' (p. 361). Here again we see thought, rather than memory, being referred to.[6]

The thought-based model that Waters and colleagues implicitly refer to, which draws on these parallels to OCD, appears to have the potential to account for many of the phenomenological properties of Type 1 AVHs, and appears particularly suited to repetitive AVHs. However, some involvement of memory is strongly suggested by the current neuro imaging evidence. If memory-based models of AVHs can be integrated

---

[6] Of course, thought and memory are not opposites, and are inherently linked (as will be discussed in the Conclusion to this book).

with verbal thought models more generally (such as the inner speech models discussed in the last chapter), then we may be able to develop an account with greater explanatory power. We will return to what such an account might look like in the Conclusion of this book.

Hypervigilance model of AVHs

That people may hear words in unpatterned sounds such as the roar of the sea (e.g. Evagarius, Chapter 1), the rush of the wind, or the hum of engine noise (Chapter 7), has long been known (e.g. Aristotle, Burton, Part I). More recently, Dodgson & Gordon (2009) have proposed a theory of AVHs which, in line with the phenomenological heterogeneity of AVHs we have seen earlier, only attempts to explain a specific subset of AVHs. In this model they focus on what they term 'hypervigilance hallucinations' (p. 326) which they argue are always located externally as they are based on (or at least derived from) real sensory experiences. This can be seen to form a subset of Type 1 (Dynamic) AVHs (termed Type 1a in Chapter 7).

Dodgson & Gordon's model is based on the idea that cognitive biases exist in voice-hearers for detecting certain personally salient words in the environment, resulting in them hearing these words in ambiguous noise, causing an AVH. In their model of hypervigilance AVHs, a precipitating event (such as a stressful life-event, drug misuse, etc.) triggers a distressing emotional state. This leads the individual to generate thoughts regarding a potential threat to themselves and then to become hypervigilant for this threat stimulus. Due to the resulting cognitive bias, they are then particularly likely to detect this threat stimulius in ambiguous patterns of noise, resulting in an AVH. Dodgson & Gordon argue that these hypervigilance hallucinations should be viewed as evolutionary by-products of a cognitive system designed to detect threat and avoid false negatives. This model will be explained in more detail below.

Perceptual biases

Dodgson & Gordon begin by noting that the cocktail party effect (Cherry, 1953) illustrates that there is a natural tendency to suddenly hear personally salient information in the external environment. In the cocktail party effect, a person who is unaware of the content of a neighbouring conversation will suddenly become aware of hearing their name, should it be mentioned. We have all likely had this experience. There is hence a cognitive bias towards recognising certain salient stimuli (such as our names) which is to be found in all of us, and it is this which may be exaggerated in some voice-hearers. In particular, a bias towards detecting stimuli in ambiguous conditions has been experimentally demonstrated in individuals with AVHs using signal detection studies. Signal detection theory (SDT) (Green & Surets, 1966) is a mathematical model of how we detect whether a stimulus was present. Experimentally, this is assessed by presenting an individual with a background of unstructured sound (e.g. white noise, random conversational background) and asking them whether they hear a specific word or sound in this (the 'signal'). On any given trial an individual is required to determine whether there is noise, or noise with a signal in it. Four outcomes are possible: there is a signal and the person thinks there is one (a hit); there is a signal but the person thinks there isn't a signal (miss); there is no signal but the person thinks there is (false alarm); or there is no signal and the person thinks there is no signal (correct rejection). A person's performance on the task can be divided into two components: their perceptual sensitivity and their response bias. Perceptual sensitivity is a measure of the general effectiveness of the perceptual system to detect a signal (i.e. the sensitivity of your hearing), whereas response bias represents the individual's criterion for deciding whether a perceived event is an actual stimulus. If one has a greater response bias, then this is manifested through the person having less misses in SDT tasks, but more false alarms (which can be conceived of as hallucinations).

The earliest SDT study of voice-hearing by Bentall & Slade (1985) examined the SDT performance of hallucinating and non-hallucinating patients diagnosed with schizophrenia. Participants were required to listen to white noise and state whether or not they heard the word 'who' during it. In half of the trials this word was actually there, in half it was not. Patients with AVHs were found not to have more perceptual sensitivity than controls (i.e. their hearing was no worse or better than controls), but they did have a greater perceptual bias to detect a signal (more recent studies will be discussed below). Based on the premise that patients with AVHs are more likely to detect signals when they are not there, Dodgson & Gordon (2009) employ error management theory (Haselton & Nettle, 2006) to explain why this might occur. This theory proposes that many human judgements are made in conditions of uncertainty, where there are differential costs for false positives and false negatives. In this model, it is proposed that evolution is likely to lead to a bias which is functional and adaptive. Thus, if an individual is trying to recognise noises in a wood, it may be potentially fatal to fail to recognise the sound of an approaching bear (false negative). However, incorrectly thinking a bear is approaching when it is not (false positive) does not have severe consequences for an individual's fitness.

Case example

To illustrate their model, Dodgson & Gordon (2009) present a case study. Michael presented with AVHs in which he heard people calling him a 'nonce' [slang for paedophile]. During his assessment, Michael disclosed that around the age of fifteen he had masturbated to a variety of sexual fantasies, one of which was about his younger sister, who at the time was about eight years old. On returning to his parental home, Michael became concerned that his previous sexual fantasies were highly inappropriate and suggested he was a paedophile, leading to intense shame. Later in life he became preoccupied by what he used to do, began to become anxious about what would happen if other people knew about these thoughts, and feared exposure. He became convinced that other people might think he was a paedophile and started to actively scan background noise from the street to see if anybody was calling him a 'nonce'. This increased his sleep deprivation and levels of arousal, which led to a vicious circle or open system where the psychotic systems exacerbated his distress, until he was eventually admitted to hospital.

One of the most important aspects of Dodgson & Gordon's model is the focus on a specific type of effect which is proposed to play a role in the genesis of AVHs: shame. Dodgson (personal communication) has argued, on the basis of clinical experience, that shame is the key emotion in AVHs. Shame can lead to people trying to cope with thoughts by trying not to think about the shame-inducing event. Yet attempting to suppress thoughts about an event can trigger intrusive thoughts (Gilbert, 1992), which source monitoring errors may lead to be experienced as an internal voice (see Jones & Fernyhough, 2006, for more on thought suppression and AVHs).

Linking the hypervigilance model to inner speech and other models of AVHs

Dodgson & Gordon's (2009) model appears to be both a pleasing model of AVHs, as well one which is clinically useful (Dodgson, personal communication). We may add that such voice-hearers might have other cognitive biases that lead them to hear words in ambiguous stimuli. For example, they may rush to judge what the word they hear is, and exhibit a form of jumping to conclusions bias. An early study by Heilbrun & Blum (1984) which required participants to guess the meaning of mono-syllabic words spoken against decreasing levels of white noise, found results consistent with this; hallucinators responded rapidly on this task, but made more errors than controls.[7] Overconfident decision making has been found with those with AVHs in a number of studies. Mintz & Alpert (1972) found a poor relation between hallucinating individuals' accuracy when listening to voices against white noise and their confidence in their judgements. Alpert (1985) also found that individuals with hallucinations were inappropriately confident when guessing the contents of brief phrases played through a low-pass filter. This suggests that individuals with hypervigilance AVHs (but not necessarily all forms of AVH) may show a form of jumping to conclusions bias.

A number of other findings, not mentioned by the authors, are relevant to the hypervigilance model. Dolgov & McBeath (2005) have previously suggested that attentional processes may shift the decision criteria in patients with AVHs in order to create a decrease in misses (the stimulus not being detected when it is actually there) as well as a corresponding increase in false alarms (hallucinations). One implication of this is that this increased attention should actually lead to improved performance by patients with AVHs on certain tasks. Schneider & Wilson (1983) investigated this, examining the performance of SZ:AVH+, SZ:AVH− and healthy controls on a task where they had to respond to frequent and infrequent tones with different button presses. It was found that although the SZ:AVH+ were slower than controls, they were faster than SZ:AVH−. Although Schneider & Wilson used non-verbal stimuli, a later study by Vercammen et al. (2008) used an SDT task involving speech. In addition to the well-documented response bias in SZ:AVH+, they again found that although SZ:AVH+ were worse than healthy controls on perceptual sensitivity, they were better than SZ:AVH−.

Vercammen et al. attempt to explain this finding in two ways. First, they note that those with AVHs may scan their environment for auditory input more than patients without AVHs. However, they do not suggest why this may be the case. Here Dodgson & Gordon's (2009) proposal that patients are used to scanning the environment for threats, due to previous negative life events,[8] may provide the answer, if we can see this increased threat scanning as translating into better scanning abilities per se. A second explanation that Vercammen and colleagues offer is that the increased performance of SZ:AVH+ is due to the increased imagery–perception interaction in this population. The term 'imagery–perception' interaction refers to the increased likelihood that a perception

---

[7] It is not known what the phenomenology of these AVHs were.
[8] Hence, we can also link this into the voice-hearers' possible history of trauma – see Chapter 11.

will take place after it has just been imagined. This concept proposes that stimuli which are presented at the edge of a person's ability to detect them are likely to be detected more often when a person has just imagined that stimulus. In a previous study Aleman *et al.* (2003) had investigated this in an SDT task in SZ:AVH+. In this study a tone was presented to participants (either 440Hz or 1000Hz) for one second, and they were then asked to imagine the tone for the next 2 seconds. A burst of white noise was then presented, which on 50 per cent of the trials contained a target stimulus (25% of trials the 440Hz tone, and 25% the 1000Hz tone) at the auditory threshold of the subject. On each trial, participants indicated verbally whether or not they perceived a target stimulus. The difference between the number of stimuli detected when the image was identical to the target stimulus, and when it was not, is a measure of the interaction between imagery and perception. It was found that severity of AVHs in patients correlated with this measure of imagery–perception interaction. Specifically, patients with more severe AVHs were more likely to perceive a stimulus after they had been imagining it. Aleman and colleagues explain this result by considering how, in the SDT task, participants must match their memory image of the word they are attending for with the actual stimulus. If the degree of overlap between these is sufficient, they will answer that they detected a signal. These findings have led Vercammen *et al.* to suggest that it is the combination of imagery–perception interactions and a response bias that lead to AVHs. However, they puzzle over why voice-hearers do not continually hallucinate, with instead only certain words as their AVHs (cf. Gallagher's, 2004, selectivity problem). Here, Dodgson & Gordon's (2009) account can offer an explanation. It is only personally salient words specific to the individual that form the basis of AVHs.

Imagery and AVHs

We may digress here, briefly, into the relation between mental imagery and AVHs. Vercammen and colleagues' theory that top-down process (expectations, auditory verbal imagery [AVI], etc.) can influence perception, resulting in AVHs, can explain the paradoxical findings that both a lack of auditory input (i.e. silence) and degraded stimuli (e.g. white noise) increase levels of AVHs – as both of these make AVI more likely to be experienced as perceptions – whereas clear auditory stimuli (speech, music etc.) makes AVHs less frequent (e.g. Margo, Hemsley & Slade, 1981) by interfering with AVI. Vercammen *et al.*'s (2008) findings can also help us understand the mental imagery and AVHs literature better. As noted in Chapter 9, the source monitoring framework proposes more vivid imaginings will be less distinguishable from actual perceptions, leading to a greater frequency of reality monitoring errors. Indeed, a long-standing theory of voices has been that they occur in people who have abnormally vivid mental imagery (e.g. Galton, 1907). In a slightly different vein, Horowitz (1975) implied that voices resulted from a tendency for voice-hearers to typically have less vivid mental imagery, with voices resulting from any vivid imagery they did then have being attributed to an external source.[9] However, there is no good evidence that voice-hearers have unusually vivid (or un-vivid) mental imagery (Aleman et al., 2003; Bentall, 1990). Yet Aleman et al.'s concept of imagery–perception interaction, which is based around the idea that you are more likely to think you hear something if you are currently imagining it, helps explain why imagery plays a role in AVHs, i.e. even though it is not more vivid, it influences perception more in those with AVHs.

A classic study which can be interpreted in this light is the White Christmas study of Mintz & Alpert (1972). In this study, participants were asked to close their eyes and imagine the song *White Christmas* was being played. When this was done with SZ:AVH+ and SZ:AVH− it was found that 95 per cent of SZ:AVH+ reported hearing at least 'a vague impression' of the record playing as compared with 50 per cent of the SZ:AVH− group. Furthermore, 10 per cent of the SZ:AVH+ (and none of the SZ:AVH−) believed the record had actually been played.[10] This finding was later replicated by Young et al. (1987). Whilst Bentall (1990) has interpreted such findings as showing an increased willingness in patients with AVHs to describe imagined events as real, it may instead be that it is actually a demonstration of Aleman et al.'s (2003) imagery–perception interaction. What, then, might underlie this imagery–perception interaction? One possibility is that it is anterior cingulate activation, as discussed in Chapter 8. We may also again note that the cerebellum, found to be implicated in Chapter 8 in AVHs, is involved in making successful distinctions between imagined and perceived events (Simons et al., 2006).

---

[9] Hoffman (1986) also notes an account which argues that there is less inner speech in those with AVHs, so instances of it are more likely to be experienced as alien. However, there is no evidence that there is less inner speech in those with AVHs (Langdon et al., 2009).

[10] It could be argued that being a psychiatric patient makes one more likely to be compliant (cf. the relation between psychiatry and authority, as argued for by Pinel, etc., Chapter 3), however, this would not explain the difference between SZ:AVH+ and SZ:AVH−.

Frith's models of AVHs

We have already met some of the work of Christopher Frith in the previous chapter. There we saw his theory that a failure in a self-monitoring mechanism which normally lets us be aware of our actions before we perform them (or in the case of AVHs, allowing us to be aware that we have produced inner speech before it actually happens) helps explain why inner speech may be experienced as alien. However, it is also worth noting some of Frith's earlier theories.

In 1979, Frith proposed that AVHs were the result of the voice-hearer becoming aware of what are usually unconscious verbal processes (Frith, 1979). Specifically, he proposed that when sound is heard the brain considers the possibility that this sound may be speech, and creates a guess or hypothesis as to what word(s) it may be. If an individual becomes aware of these early guesses, argued Frith, this could result in AVHs. This theory lacks any explanation for the characteristic phenomenology of AVHs, though, with it being unclear, for example, why people would consistently guess that they were being told to do things (i.e. hearing commands). However, we could tie this account into the hypervigilance model of AVHs suggested above. Later, Frith (1992) proposed that what entered awareness was the detached content of failed metarepresentations. Central to this theory is the concept of metarepresentation. A simple representation of the physical world might involve, for example, the thought 'it is raining'. When we consider the mental states of others (or even ourselves), though, we have to create representations of their representations (hence, a metarepresentation). Thus, I represent this representation in the mind of my friend and hence have the metarepresentation that 'she believes "it is raining"'. Frith highlights three areas where metarepresentations play a key role: awareness of goals, awareness of our own intentions, and awareness of the intentions of others. He then proposes that if metarepresentation fails, an individual is just left with the content of the proposition. Thus, if I had metarepresentation regarding my friend Ed's views on me that 'Ed believes "you should listen to more Bob Dylan"', then a failure of metarepresentation would lead to the free-floating notion of 'you should listen to more Bob Dylan' being experienced and resulting in an AVH. Frith has since repudiated this theory (Frith & Gallagher, 2002), although my friend Ed still thinks I should listen to more Bob Dylan. Frith has since moved to the position, as noted above, that it is not a problem of awareness of ours and others' intentions, but in the awareness of the initiation of such thoughts, that results in AVHs. However, in the Conclusion we will return to this original theory, which still seems to have some valuable components.

Hoffman's models of AVHs

Over the years Ralph Hoffman has developed a number of influential models of AVHs. In 1986, he proposed a model in which verbal imagery/ inner speech which is not consistent with consciously accessible goals and discourse plans (high-level goals for what we intend to achieve with our speech) comes to be experienced as unintended and hence results in AVHs. A number of problems exist with this account.[11] First, and this is for me the primary problem, is a lack of phenomenological evidence that voices are actually inconsistent with voice-hearers' current goals. Hoffman notes as evidence for breakdowns in discourse plans the disordered overt speech in some patients diagnosed with schizophrenia. However, reliance on this fails to explain why voices occur in people without diagnoses of schizophrenia and who do not have disordered speech. Second, a number of philosophers (e.g. Akins & Dennett, 1986) have also offered philosophical critiques of the problems in which classifying thoughts as intentional resulted. For example, the notion of intentional thought is open to the criticism that it leads to an infinite regress, with the intention to think a thought itself being a thought, which must then be preceded by an intention to think that thought, which is also a thought, etc. Finally, given that the majority of the population are likely to have thoughts not consistent with their current goals, thoughts which come 'out of the blue', this model would appear to predict that hearing voices would be much more common than it actually is. Furthermore, individuals with obsessive compulsive disorder have instances of verbal imagery not consistent with consciously accessible goals, which are experienced as unintended and yet are not experienced as an AVH. Although Hoffman (1986) argues that such mentation is still 'intentional', other factors, such as context memory problems as found by Waters and colleagues above, are hence likely to be necessary.

Hoffman (ibid.) also proposed in this model the idea that a 'parasitic memory' (p. 513) existing in long-term memory could also be a factor in causing AVHs. He proposed that such parasitic memories could enter into working memory, disrupt the normal language planning process, be experienced as inconsistent with current goals, feel unintended, and hence result in an AVH. He argues that this would result in AVHs having the form of 'a small number of rigidly repeated expressions' (p. 514), which he argued was phenomenologically consistent with his impression 'that schizophrenic [sic.] voices are not very creative or expressive and

---

[11] For a good critique see Stephens & Graham (2000).

frequently consist of a small number of rigidly repeated expressions' (ibid.). This appears a good model of such voices, and in the next chapter when we look at trauma, we will see good candidates for what events may form this parasitic memory. However, the big problem for this model is that, as we saw in Part II, not all voices are a 'small number of rigidly repeated expressions'. We are hence left with the question as to whether this model can be adapted to account for a wider range of AVHs, or whether different accounts are needed for different types of voices, or whether such AVHs seed the later development of more complex voices.

Around a decade later, Hoffman & McGlashan (1997) argued that AVHs were the result of synaptic elimination (such as that experienced in adolescence), and showed using a connectionist model that removing a high level of working memory connections produced spontaneous speech percepts that simulated hallucinated speech or 'voices'. This account had the novel benefit of offering an evolutionarily based account, in which a certain level of synaptic elimination led to improved perceptual abilities, but too much led to voices. Again, though, this model offers no clear explanation of why voices should have the phenomenology that they do, and it is unclear whether this model claims to account for all AVHs, or just a subset.

Most recently, Hoffman (2007) has proposed that due to the social nature of humans, the brain, in the absence of verbal social stimuli, may produce its own spurious cognitions which come to be experienced as voices. Here Hoffman draws on parallels with Charles Bonnett syndrome, in which loss of visual input leads to bizarre visual hallucinations. In addition to the evidence Hoffman provides, this model is consistent with the finding that voices can fulfil social functions for voice-hearers who lack normal social contact (e.g. Beavan, 2011).[12] We may also note that the relationship between loneliness and AVHs has previously been documented. Nayani & David (1996) in their study of one hundred voice-hearing patients found that 80 per cent said being alone worsened their AVHs, and Escher & Romme (2010) found being alone was a trigger for voices in 32 per cent of children. We may also consider here the accounts of voice-hearing in non-verbal quadriplegics discussed in Chapter 4, where loneliness did appear to play a role in the aetiology of the voices, possibly along with the stress of being moved into an institution. Yet trying to extend Hoffman's model, we may ask what

[12] We may also reach back across history here to note that Margery Kempe most often heard a voice in the silence of a church, should this be a valid report rather than one aimed to stress the religious nature of her experiences.

emotions are felt when one is alone. Nayani & David found that a mood of sadness was most commonly cited as preceding AVHs (being much more common than fear) with such sadness being 'not infrequently in association with being alone or lonely and seemed to form an important context for the emergence of the [AVH]' (p. 184). Similarly, Escher & Romme (2010) also report that, in their study of children who heard voices, 49 per cent said the voices would appear when they were sad. It may be that being alone is not necessarily the trigger for voices, but the type of emotions that one feels when one is alone.

Although this model offers an insightful account of situations when voices may occur, and importantly takes into account our social nature, it only explains a small corner of the hearing-voices experience. For example, it does not engage with the role of previous events in the voice-hearer's life, and does not predict much about the specific phenomenology that AVHs should have (e.g. it cannot explain why commands are such a frequent occurrence). This raises the question as to whether social isolation is a cause of AVHs, or simply a trigger for them once other events have led to their genesis. This model hence appears likely to be an important facet of a more comprehensive model. It also suggests that more detailed studies of the relation between loneliness, social isolation and hearing voices are likely to prove very worthwhile. This focus on social factors brings us nicely onto our next chapter.

Chapter 10: summary of key points

- The AVHs-as-memories model when limited to intrusive memories can only account for a subset of AVHs (Type 2).
- The development of this account along the lines of a thought-based model, which draws on phenomenological similarities between obsessive compulsive disorder and AVHs, has a much greater explanatory power.
- The syntheses of such a model with inner speech-based models need to be considered to see if they can be synthesised to form a more satisfying model of AVHs which can account for Type 1 and Type 2 AVHs.
- Dodgson & Gordon's hypervigilance model offers a valuable contribution to our understanding of AVHs, and specifically Type 1a.
- Social isolation and loneliness may play a role in triggering AVHs.

11 The wound is peopled: from world to brain and back again

Years of insanity have made this guy crazy   Woody Allen

So far we have predominantly focused on a pinky-grey-coloured object weighing 1.4kg with a volume of $0.015m^3$. This has been at the expense of another somewhat larger object, bluey-green in colour, weighing around 6,000,000,000,000,000,000,000,000kg, with a volume of around $1,000,000,000,000,000,000,000m^3$ and which, rather importantly for our current purposes, is roamed by around 7,000,000,000 strange ape-like creatures who are often not very nice to each other. This may have proved something of an oversight. Neglect of context, argued John Dewey, is the greatest single disaster which thinking can incur.

What, then, of the world? In biopsychosocial models of phenomena, the social world and the individual's psychological and biological reaction to it are emphasised. However, in 2005, a year when sales of antipsychotic drugs topped $6bn, the President of the American Psychiatric Association wrote that 'Financial incentives and managed care have contributed to the notion of a "quick fix" by taking a pill and reducing the emphasis on psychotherapy and psychosocial treatments ... as a profession, we have allowed the biopsychosocial model to become the bio-bio-bio model' (Sharfstein, 2005, p. 3). This 'bio-bio-bio' model also tends to reflect a view of voices as being what William Battie in Chapter 2 termed 'Original Madness' (an endogenously arising brain disorder) rather than what he termed 'Consequential Madness' (an experience linked to events which occurred in the external world). Whilst there is obviously an important place for a biological understanding of hearing voices, the choice to focus one's attention solely on biological mechanisms and to provide accounts only in these terms is not a scientific choice. It is a political one. The effects of focusing solely on causes inside the brain are multiple, and the social and political impacts of locating causes of distress inside the head, rather than in societal causes, have been spelt out elsewhere (e.g. Smail, 2005).

Here it is useful to introduce the concept of distal and proximal causes of events. Whereas a proximal cause is the link in a causal chain which immediately precedes an event, links in the causal chain that are prior to the final link are termed distal causes (Jackson & Coltheart, 2001). For example, while the immediate, proximal cause of a stomach pain may be an acidic meal, the more removed, distal cause may be stress over a period of years causing a proneness to stomach ulcers, possibly with a genetic predisposition to develop such ulcers. In Chapter 8 we examined the most immediate and proximate causes of voices – the brain – pressing our noses up close against the causal window. However, by focusing solely on proximal cause of voices in the brain, trying to deduce their causes by a cross-sectional approach (both temporally and literally), we neglect more distal causes, events occurring 'out there' in the world that have caused the brain to be the way it is. A consideration of all these causes is needed for a scientific account of the causes of voices, and to help us to understand how and where to target interventions. As we will come to see later in this chapter, an epigenetic biopsychosocial approach is needed which looks at the interaction between events in the world and the individual's genetic make-up, in the societal context they occur in.

Looking out into the world can help suggest testable hypotheses for the causes of hearing voices, and their specific properties, which could not be found by looking at brains alone. For example, by looking in at the brain, Badcock (2010) has argued that it is abnormal functioning in the anterior auditory pathway which underpins the predominance of male voices in AVHs. Basing an account of AVHs in the fundamental structure of the auditory system is a laudable idea, and may lead to progress in our understanding of AVHs. However, it should supplement, not replace, a consideration of other causes based in life-events or societal structures. For example, as we will see later in this chapter, a significant percentage of voice-hearers have been victims of childhood abuse. When we note that 95 per cent of the perpetrators of CSA are male (e.g. Dubé & Hébert, 1988), this suggests another factor which may contribute to why the voices individuals hear are identified as being predominantly male. Furthermore, in a patriarchal society, the voice of the male is the voice of authority, and given that commands are common in AVHs, this may help us understand this predominance of male voices.

In this chapter we will be concerned with remedying the problem of focusing only on proximal causes, by examining the potential distal causes of hearing voices. Many of the historical vignettes in Part I pointed to possible causes (Boxes 2.3, 3.1, 3.4). Chapters 9 and 10, which examined how AVHs may relate to cognitive processes such as inner speech, memory and hypervigilance, further hinted at potentially causative events, with the real world emerging through discussions of the potential role of emotions such as shame, and events such as trauma. A particularly useful concept that emerges from Chapter 9 is the Vygotskian idea that inner speech is an internalisation of a process that originally took place externally, overt dialogue. The alchemists had the axiom 'as above, so below', and rejigging this in a Vygotskian manner we may say 'as outside, so inside'. The point of this is to suggest that what is going on inside our heads is likely to be related to what has been going on in the world (hardly a revolutionary suggestion, but one which is often overlooked). The social relations we engage in are transported into and acted out within our own heads. To understand what is within, we must therefore look without. Given that AVHs are often destructive, abusive and threatening, we should not expect what we find outside to be pretty.

Traumatic life events and hearing voices

In earlier chapters we have already seen stressful or traumatic life events preceding transitory examples of voice-hearing in the general popula-tion, be this the voice heard by Joe Simpson whilst descending in agony from Siula Grande, or the voices occurring to Charles Lindbergh during the stress of constantly listening to the whine of the 236 kg of whirring metal keeping him aloft. When we turn to those who regularly hear complex voices, there is not ample space here to do justice to the research into trauma and AVHs, and even less to be able to amply communicate the sheer horror of the experiences many people with AVHs have been through before they enter psychiatric services. Here I will endeavour to argue two points. First, that there is a strong and likely causative relation between traumatic events and AVHs, and second that this relation is non-diagnosis specific, i.e. that irrespective of what psychiatric diagnosis you have (PTSD, schizophrenia, bipolar), your AVHs may be the result of traumatic events.

The origin of the word trauma is in the Greek word for wound (Becker *et al.*, 2003). The American Psychiatric Association (APA, 2000) gives examples of traumatic events, which include directly experiencing military combat, personal assault (physical, sexual, robbery, mugging), torture, severe automobile accidents, as well as witnessing, or simply hearing of, unexpected deaths of close others. Although such events are likely to be traumatic to most, more generally what is experienced as traumatic by one individual may not be by another. Given the subjectivity inherent to what is traumatic, it has hence been noted that trauma therefore has its effects through the prism of meaning (Becker *et al.*, 2003). For example, in the hearing voices literature

Romme & Escher (1989), who equate traumatic events with emotional events, and allow that experiences such as being in love or moving house, which many may not commonly associate with the word 'trauma', may be traumatic. I will hence use the term trauma broadly to refer to an event which results in an intense emotional experience in an individual, and which typically overwhelms their normal coping abilities.

By definition the voices experienced by individuals with a diagnosis of PTSD are preceded by a traumatic event. Individuals with dissociative identity disorder (DID) in whom AVHs are also frequent (Chapter 4) have also been found to have high rates of childhood trauma such as sexual and/or physical abuse (Ross, Norton & Wozney, 1989). We found in Chapter 4 that although flashback-like AVHs (Type 2) were found in these groups, a very common form of AVH that either co-occurred with such AVHs or dominated the clinical presentation were Type 1 AVHs (i.e. those which gave commands, commented, were interactively involved with the voice-hearer's current life, and were hence not flashback-like). Given the presence of these Type 1 AVHs in individuals diagnosed with psychosis (as well as in healthy voice-hearers) in addition to those with PTSD and DID, taking a complaint-orientated approach to AVHs (Chapter 3) may suggest that these phenomenologically similar AVHs may share a common cause, and hence that one such cause may be trauma.

The written accounts of voice-hearers' life stories (Dillon, 2010; Romme et al., 2009), and testimony presented by voice-hearers at conferences (e.g. Dillon, 2009) clearly suggests a causative role for trauma and stressful life-events in the genesis of at least some AVHs. Formal quantitative research now offers some support to the intuitions from such accounts. Indeed, probably the most important body of research relating to AVHs over the last two decades has been that which has shown a link between traumatic experiences and AVHs. There is now substantial evidence demonstrating that hallucinations in general (Read et al., 2003), AVHs specifically (Morrison & Peterson, 2003; Offen, Waller & Thomas, 2003), and particularly AVHs that take the form of commands to hurt the self or others (Hammersley et al., 2003) are associated with earlier experiences of trauma, such as physical and sexual abuse.

The types of trauma preceding AVHs can vary greatly. In a review of the stories of recovery of 50 voice-hearers, Romme et al. (2009) noted 24 people had suffered sexual abuse, 14 had suffered emotional abuse, 6 had experienced adolescent problems, 5 had suffered physical abuse, 4 had had high levels of stress and 2 were bullied. In another study, Romme & Escher (1989) found that 70 per cent of voice-hearers from the general population stated that their voices began after a traumatic or emotional event. These events included an accident (4%), divorce or death (14%), a psychotherapy session (12%), spiritism (4%), and other events (36%) such as being in love, moving or pregnancy. Similarly, Escher *et al.* (2004) found that in 75 per cent of children, traumatic events or circumstances beyond their control had occurred at the onset of hearing voices. In 23 per cent of the children a period of grief (e.g. a death in the family) accompanied the onset of voices, and here Escher *et al.* suggest that the child not being allowed to express their grief could be a particular trigger. Furthermore, 24 per cent had problems at home during the onset of the voices (divorce, moving house, etc.) and 19 per cent had problems at school (e.g. being bullied, problems with teachers, learning ability problems, etc.). As a result of this, Escher *et al.* propose that 'it might be more adequate to interpret hearing voices as a reaction to serious life problems with which a child has difficulties coping; or, formulated differently, as a signal of serious life problems, instead of a symptom of a psychiatric illness in itself' (p. 218).

As it is not possible to review all traumatic events that have been linked with hearing voices here, in this chapter we will focus on two traumatic events, bereavement and childhood abuse, and in particular the best studied form of such abuse: childhood sexual abuse (CSA).

Hearing voices and bereavement

Two centuries ago, grief was officially regarded as a cause of death (Parkes, 1964). The potent mix of grief, depression, sleep disturbances and loneliness following bereavement is well documented (Clayton, Desmarais & Winokur, 1968; Osterweiss, Solomon & Green, 1984). Although some widows/widowers ask 'What's the good of being left behind?' (Grimby, 1993, p. 75), some are not entirely left behind; the voice of the departed can remain. The experience of hearing a voice following bereavement is found cross-culturally, from the East to the West, with these experiences being viewed as more normal in countries such as Japan than in the UK (Rees, 1971; Yamamoto *et al.*, 1969). In an early study, Rees (1971; N = 293) found that 13 per cent of bereaved people, most of them aged over 60, had heard the voice of their deceased spouse. Women (14%) were slightly more likely to experience such voices than men (11%). These voices occurred at various points throughout the day (i.e. there is no reason to believe these were solely hypnagogic/hypnopompic phenomena). The longer the marriage had been, the more probable hallucinations of all forms were. The majority of individuals (67%) found this experience was helpful, with the majority of the remainder finding them neither helpful nor unpleasant. Indeed, unpleasant voices were rare. Only 28 per cent had told anyone about their experiences, and only 15 per cent had told more than one person. None had told doctors and only one had told a clergyman. Although most people could give no reason for why they had not told anyone, those who did give a reason most commonly cited fear of ridicule.

In a later study of fifty people in their early 70s whose spouses had died within the previous year, Grimby (1993) found that one month after bereavement, 30 per cent were hearing the voice of their partner. Three months after bereavement 19 per cent were now hearing their voice, and by one year after bereavement, 6 per cent were still hearing their dead partner's voice. Most would only admit to these experiences after the interviewer had informed them about the commonness and normality of post-bereavement hallucinations. As with Rees's (1971) study, the majority of people found these experiences to be pleasant. Once the experience had proved pleasant and occurred once, people typically wanted it to happen again. Interestingly, hearing the voice of the dead partner was found by Grimby to be more frequent among men with low self-esteem (although no details are given on the content of the AVHs of this subgroup) and more frequent in the very lonely and severely crying participants (cf. Hoffman's (2007) model of AVHs).

Why should AVHs occur following bereavement? It would appear that social interaction decreasing and loneliness increasing following bereavement (Grimby, 1993), alongside increases in negative affect, the role of expectation (one gets used to hearing one's partner) and the firm establishment of the voice of the other in one's own inner speech and memory, are likely to be the key aetiological drivers. Why are they slightly more common in women? Grimby has suggested that it is because widows may be more likely to have been impacted by socio-economic and cultural factors following their husband's deaths, such as loss of financial security and self-identity.

Hearing voices and childhood abuse

There were nearly 800,000 verified cases of child maltreatment in 2007 in the United States alone, in addition to reported cases that were not verified and incidents that were simply not reported. Sixty percent of those children suffered from neglect, 10% were physically abused, and almost 2000 children died, most of them younger than 4 years of age ... These statistics represent the experiences of individual children who have suffered nonaccidental physical and emotional injuries, primarily from caregivers, including broken bones, black eyes, ruptured eardrums, tearing around the genital area, inadequate nutrition, clothing, and medical care, and constant derogation and ostracism (Twardosz & Lutzker 2010, p. 59).

Being the victim of childhood abuse has been found to have a dose-response relationship with psychosis, with experiencing mild, moderate and severe abuse being associated with 2, 11 and 48 times, respectively the likelihood of having 'pathology level' psychosis, compared to individuals with no childhood trauma (Janssen *et al.*, 2004). A similar pattern has also been found specifically in relation to AVHs, with multiple traumas being associated with a higher probability of having AVHs. For example, Read *et al.* (2003) found that whereas 15 per cent of individuals with CSA experienced command AVHs, telling them to kill or harm themselves, and 18 per cent of those with CPA (childhood physical abuse) had such voices, those who had experienced both CSA and CPA had a 29 per cent prevalence of such AVHs. The same pattern was found in adults: 20 per cent of adults with adult sexual abuse (ASA) and 13 per cent of adults with adult physical abuse (APA) heard voices telling them to kill or harm themselves, but individuals with both APA and ASA had a 29 per cent prevalence of such voices. Similarly, Shevlin *et al.* (2007) found that the more traumatic events an individual had suffered as a child (out of the four they examined: neglect, physical abuse, sexual abuse, or sexual molestation) the more likely they were to have experienced AVHs.

Childhood sexual abuse

The specific type of childhood abuse that has received the most attention in relation to AVHs is CSA. Another reason for focusing our attention specifically on CSA in this brief review, as opposed to CPA, for example, is that CSA has been found to be associated with mental health problems to a greater extent than CPA (Fergusson, Boden & Horwood, 2008). In early studies of the effects of CSA, Ellenson (1985, 1986) found that many female incest survivors experienced hallucinations in a range of modalities including the visual (e.g. shadowy figures, movements in peripheral vision), the auditory (e.g. intruder sounds) and specifically the auditory verbal (e.g. voices giving commands, voices persecuting the voice-hearer, or voices helping the voice-hearer). More recent research (e.g. Read *et al.*, 2003) has led to the suggestion that there is a specific relationship between CSA and AVHs, with Hammersley & Fox (2006) arguing that in studies of psychosis and childhood trauma the link between CSA and AVHs 'is consistently the most reliable finding' (p. 152).

Table 11.1. *AVHs and childhood sexual abuse in psychiatric patients*

Study	Psychiatric diagnoses of population	If had AVHs, what % had CSA?	If had CSA, what % had AVHs?
Honig *et al.* (1998), N = 33	Majority schizophrenia	33 (11/33)	n/a
Read *et al.* (1999), N = 22	Majority depression	n/a	53 (9/17)
Hammersley *et al.* (2003), N = 96	Bipolar	37 (11/30)	73 (11/15)
Offen *et al.* (2003), N = 26	Majority schizophrenia	38 (10/26)	n/a
Read *et al.* (2003), N = 200	Majority depression	39 (21/54)	53 (21/40)
Andrew *et al.* (2008), N = 22	No diagnoses reported	50 (11/22)	n/a
Anketell *et al.* (2010), N = 20	PTSD	15 (3/20)	43 (3/7)
Weighted average		**36 (67/185)**	**56 (44/79)**

Table 11.2. *AVHs and childhood sexual abuse in non-psychiatric populations*

Study	Population	If had AVHs, what % had CSA?	If had CSA, what % experienced AVHs?
Honig *et al.* (1998), N = 15	Individuals with no psychiatric history, but with AHs	33 (5/15)	n/a
Andrew *et al.* (2008), N = 21	Individuals with no psychiatric history, but with AVHs	14 (3/21)	n/a
Weighted average for individuals with AVHs but no psychiatric history		**22 (8/36)**	**n/a**
Shevlin *et al.* (2007), N = 5,877	General population	7 (36/489)[a] 16 (80/487)[b]	21 (36/174)[a] 16 (80/485)[b]

[a] = CSA – rape, [b] = CSA – molestation

A recent review of mine of the relation between AVHs and CSA examined the existing literature in this area (McCarthy-Jones, 2011b). In this paper, I noted that only a relatively small number of small sample studies have specifically examined the relation between CSA and AVHs, Tables 11.1 and 11.2 show the rates of AVHs in those with CSA, and the rates of CSA in those with AVHs, found by these existing studies.

As can be seen from Table 11.1, 36 per cent of psychiatric patients with AVHs report CSA, and 56 per cent of psychiatric patients who have experienced CSA report AVHs. Table 11.2 shows that, albeit in a very small sample, 22 per cent of 'healthy voice-hearers' have experienced CSA. In comparison, a minimum of 21 per cent of members of the general population who have experienced CSA report AVHs, and of those in the general population who report having had an AVH at least 16 per cent report having experienced CSA. Other results from these studies are also noteworthy. Read *et al.* (2003) examined the impact of the type of CSA (incest and non-incest related) on AVHs. It was found that those who had experienced CSA involving incest had significantly higher rates of AVHs (32% had voices commenting) than those with CSA that did not involve incest (0% had voices commenting).

Going beyond associations, results from quantitative studies have been used to argue that 'child abuse is a *causal* factor for ... voices commenting and command hallucinations' (Read *et al.*, 2005, p. 330, emphasis added), yet the causal role of CSA specifically has not been addressed. However, clinical experience, first-person testimonies from individuals who hear voices (see Romme *et al.*, 2009) and a range of case studies (e.g. Heins, Gray & Tennant, 1990; Kaufman *et al.*, 1997; Lysaker, Buck & Larocco, 2007) are all suggestive of a causal role for CSA in the development of AVHs. If CSA does cause AVHs, then we would expect levels of AVHs to be higher in those who have experienced CSA than those who have not. Table 11.3 shows that, in line with this prediction, there are typically higher rates of AVHs in those who have experienced CSA, as opposed to those who have not.

However, the studies in Table 11.3 suffer from significant design limitations. First, only one of these studies (Shevlin *et al.*, 2007), which is discussed further below, controlled for any potentially confounding variables which were likely to be present in individuals with CSA and which have been found by other studies to be associated with AVHs. A key such variable is emotional abuse. Üçok & Bikmaz (2007), although not finding individuals with and without CSA to differ in their levels of AVHs, did find that both AVHs, and specifically commenting voices, were more common in those who had experienced childhood emotional abuse, than those who had not experienced such abuse. Sommer *et al.* (2010) also found childhood emotional abuse levels to be greater in (non-psychiatric) voice-hearers than healthy controls.

A second potentially confounding variable is depression. Mundy *et al.* (1990), in a study of homeless adolescents (N = 96), found a positive correlation between AVHs and extra-familial CSA (but not familial CSA). However, they also found depression to positively correlate with

Table 11.3. *AVHs in those with and without childhood sexual abuse*

Study	Comparison		Finding
Hammersley *et al.* (2003)	Bipolar patients with CSA (n = 15)	Bipolar patients with no CSA (n = 81)	(1) Auditory hallucinations were over 3 times more common in those with CSA (73%) than those without CSA (23%) (2) Voices commenting were over 6 times more common in those with CSA (40%) than those without CSA (6%)
Read *et al.* (2003)	Psychiatric patients with CSA (n = 40)	Psychiatric patients without CSA (n = 108)	(1) Auditory hallucinations were nearly 3 times more common in those with CSA (53%) than those without CSA (18%) (2) Voices commenting were nearly 6 times more common in those with CSA (28%) than those without CSA (5%) (3) Voices commanding were over 7 times more common in those with CSA (15%) than those without CSA (2%)
Shevlin *et al.* (2007)	Individuals with CSA-rape (n = 174)	Individuals without CSA-rape (n = 5732)	Auditory hallucinations (AHs) were over 2 times more common in those with CSA-rape (21%) than those without CSA-rape (8%)
	Individuals with CSA-molestation (n = 485)	Individuals with no CSA-molestation (n = 5415)	AHs were over 2 times more common in those with CSA-molestation (16%) than those without CSA-molestation (8%)
Üçok *et al.* (2007)	1st episode schizophrenia patients (n = 17) with CSA	1st episode schizophrenia patients (n = 40) without CSA	No difference in levels of AVHs between the two groups or in levels of voices commenting

levels of AVHs, and their results section (although not entirely clear) appears to state that the correlation between extra-familial CSA and AVHs was not significant when depression levels were controlled for. Other factors which were not controlled for by the studies in Table 11.3, but which have been found to be associated with AVHs include childhood physical abuse (Read *et al.*, 2003), and bullying (Campbell & Morrison, 2007). Other potentially confounding variables include schizotypy and delusion-proneness. Indeed, Sommer *et al.* (2010) have argued that trauma results in AVHs through its effects on schizotypy and delusion-proneness. In a correlational study, Sommer *et al.* (2010) found that the presence of AVHs was predicted by schizotypy (which correlated strongly with delusion-proneness) and a family history of AVHs (at trend level), but not by trauma levels (assessed by a composite measure of sexual, physical and emotional abuse, as well as physical and emotional neglect levels). Sommer *et al.* interpreted their findings as suggesting that the relation between trauma and AVHs is due to child-hood trauma leading to an 'altered (more paranoid) perception of the world', reflected in increased levels of schizotypy and delusion-proneness, 'which in turn may confer risk to AVH' (p. 7).

The one study in Table 11.3 which did control for some confounding variables was Shevlin *et al.* (2007). This study controlled for age, sex, depression, urbanicity, income and drug/alcohol dependence. After con-trolling for these variables, it still found a significant relation between CSA and auditory hallucinations. It also offers some suggestive evidence that even when controlling for levels of physical abuse and neglect, CSA may still be uniquely associated with a higher risk of AVHs. After controlling for the variables noted previously, Shevlin *et al.* found that having one of four potential types of childhood trauma (neglect, physical abuse, rape, molestation) was associated with a 1.62-times increased probability of having AVHs. This probability increased to 2.36 times if someone had two of these traumas, and 4.15 times if someone had three of these traumas. It hence appears likely that the additive effects of either of the CSA traumas would lead to a significant increase in the probability of having AVHs over and above the effects of neglect or physical abuse.

At present we are forced to conclude that whilst the quantitative evidence is highly suggestive of a causal relation between specifically CSA and AVHs, due to the problems with internal and external validity of existing studies this evidence is not conclusive (McCarthy-Jones, 2011b). We may therefore turn to other avenues that may shine light on the relation between childhood abuse more generally, and AVHs.

Phenomenological evidence for a link between childhood trauma and AVHs

The past may not repeat itself, but it certainly rhymes

Mark Twain

Hardy *et al.* (2005) have noted four relations are possible between trauma and AVHs. First, there may be a direct link in which the content of AVHs is directly related to a memory of the traumatic event (i.e. what I have termed a Type 2 AVH). Second, there may be an indirect link, in which the AVH is not like a flashback of verbatim memory, but where there is a thematic link or some clear commonality, e.g. the voice of the abuser is heard, but s/he is saying new things which s/he had not said before (which I have termed a Type 1 AVH). Third, trauma may act as a stressor that triggers AVHs, but does not inform or relate to their content. Finally, there may be no relation between trauma and AVHs.

In order to help address this question, the phenomenology of AVHs needs to be examined in relation to the trauma that people report. However, there have been very few studies of this type, reflecting the prevailing late twentieth-century scepticism that the content of AVHs was in any way meaningful.

We have already noted in Chapter 10 that the content of some voices is directly related to childhood abuse. For example, Read & Argyle (1999) found, in three of seven instances in which content of the AVHs of patients diagnosed with schizophrenia was recorded, that the content could be linked to physical or sexual abuse. For example, one patient heard command hallucinations to commit suicide, and identified the voice as that of the alleged perpetrator of the abuse. Another patient heard the voice of his abuser (his father) saying, 'You have died' or 'You were shot'. In a later study, Read et al. (2003) reported one participant, whose records stated that they were 'abused over many years through anal penetration with the use of violence' (ibid.), who had an AVH in which the perpetrator's voice told the participant to touch children. Similarly, Reiff et al. (in press) found some direct links between child abuse and AVHs (e.g. being raped as a child, and then in later life experiencing AVHs which threatened rape). Another participant who was sexually abused at age 8 had AVHs which took 'the form of the "voice of the abuser" ' (ibid.).

Despite this suggestive evidence for a direct relation, further consideration shows that direct links only appear to occur in a relatively small sub-set of AVHs. Again, as noted earlier in Chapter 10, Fowler (1997) found only in 4 of the total 24 voice-hearers studied (17%) could the content of voices be seen as 'sometimes' being suggestive that these were memories. In the remainder of the sample who had a history of trauma, meaningful connections could be made between the trauma and the voices. However, such connections were thematic (e.g. both the voices and trauma involved humiliation) rather than involving a direct relation between the content of the voices and what was said during and surrounding the trauma. Similarly, the study by Reiff et al. (in press) found that the majority of AVHs showed thematic links to abuse (e.g. threats/deprecation in the original abuse and threatening/deprecative AVHs) rather than being direct memories of the abuse itself.

This direct/indirect relation issue was more clearly addressed in a study by Hardy *et al.* (2005), who investigated the links between hallucinations and trauma in a sample of 75 patients with diagnoses of non-affective psychotic disorders (i.e. schizophrenia, schizoaffective disorder) who all had hallucinations. Although Hardy and colleagues do not state whether the hallucinations were predominantly AVHs or not, due to the very limited number of studies of this type we will assume that the results of this study may be applicable specifically to AVHs. Hardy and colleagues found that forty of the 75 patients reported having experienced trauma, and that 32 of these patients had experienced the trauma before the onset of mental health problems. The most common traumas were bullying (30%), adult sexual abuse (20%), childhood sexual abuse (17.5%) and being attacked with a weapon (12.5%). Blind raters then analysed whether the trauma events were related to patient's hallucinations (patients themselves were not asked if they saw a connection). It was found that five of these 40 participants (i.e. 12.5%) had a direct link between their trauma and their hallucination (e.g. if threatened with a gun they had a hallucination involving a gun). Twenty-three participants (58%) had an indirect thematic link between their trauma and their hallucination (with themes of either guilt, threat, humiliation or intrusiveness occurring both in their trauma and in their hallucination). A further 17 participants (42.5%) had hallucinations with no relation to their trauma. Thus in the overall sample of patients with AVHs, only five out of the total of seventy five patients (7%) were rated as demonstrating clear direct concordance between the content of their voices and the content of a traumatic event, yet twenty-three (31%) of the overall sample could link their AVHs thematically back to a traumatic event. Limitations to this study include that trauma may have been under-reported, and patients themselves were not asked if they could see a link between their voices and previous events in their lives. Further investigation of the presence of trauma, or asking recovered voice-hearers about links between their voices and their traumas, may show that the figures of Hardy *et al.* are underestimates.

In terms of other studies of linkages between trauma and voices, Andrew, Gray & Snowdon (2008) found greater scores on the Impact of Events Scale (Horowitz, Wilner & Alvarez, 1979), a measure of 'the extent to which a traumatic event is reverberating in the mind' (Andrew, Gray & Snowdon, 2008, p. 1412) to be associated with more malevolent, omnipotent and less benevolent voices. Another factor related to the malevolence of AVHs has been found to be age at the time of CSA.

Offen, Waller & Thomas (2003) found that CSA occurring at an earlier age was associated with a greater belief that the voices were malevolent.

In conclusion, in a sizeable minority of cases at least, the content of AVHs can be linked to earlier traumatic events. This connection appears more commonly to be a thematic link to earlier traumas, than a direct link to what was said at the time of the trauma. It appears that the extent of the impact of the trauma on the individual, as well as factors such as the age at abuse, may also be important in determining the content of the voice. This offers support for (at least) an indirect causal role of such experiences in AVHs. However, as always, more research is needed into the relation between trauma and AVH content, and factors that may mediate this relation. Furthermore, as Romme *et al.* (2009) have suggested that such voices may be a defence mechanism for dealing with the emotions raised by these events, phenomenological studies of AVH content and its relation to trauma may be a good way to empirically test this claim.

Neuroscienific frameworks for understanding how childhood trauma may cause AVHs

Pérez-Álvarez *et al.* (2008) have argued that 'hallucinations occur more for interpersonal reasons than merely due to neurocognitive causes' (p. 77). This resonates well with the findings reviewed in this chapter. However, there is the need to integrate the interpersonal with the neurocognitive, tracing how the former impacts upon the latter. The field of developmental traumatology attempts to trace the neurobiological impact of trauma on the developing child (Crozier *et al.*, 2011). It considers how specific facets of traumatic experiences (such as the type, age of onset and duration of child maltreatment) and other biopsychosocial factors (e.g. the child's temperament, social support for the child and family) relate to specific neurobiological changes in the brain. In animal studies, early experiences of trauma have been found to be associated with long-term alterations in coping, emotional and behavioural dysregulation, altered responsiveness of the neuroendocrine system to stressful experience, as well as affecting brain structure, neurochemistry and gene expression (see Cicchetti & Walker, 2001). In human studies, people who have experienced childhood trauma have been found to have a range of structural changes to their brains as compared to non-abused individuals. Smaller anterior cingulate cortex volumes have been found in individuals with abuse-related PTSD (Kitayama, Quinn & Bremner, 2006), as well as individuals with multiple adverse childhood events (Cohen *et al.*, 2006), compared to healthy controls. Changes in STG volumes have been found to relate to traumatic events such as neglect, physical abuse, sexual abuse and emotional maltreatment (De Bellis *et al.*, 2002a), anxiety (De Bellis *et al.*, 2002b) and depression (Caetano *et al.*, 2004). Altered STG volumes have been found to be associated with parental verbal abuse (Tomoda *et al.*, 2011), and such verbal abuse has also been found to be associated with a reduction in fractional anisotropy in the arcuate fasciculus (Choi *et al.*, 2009). Childhood emotional maltreatment has been found (after effects of sexual and/or physical abuse were controlled for) to be associated with 'profound' reductions of medial prefrontal cortex (i.e. medial prefrontal gyrus and anterior cingulate gyrus) volumes (van Harmelen *et al.*, 2010). We hence see that key neural areas involved producing voice-hearing experiences, such as the anterior cingulate, the STG and the arcuate fasciculus (Chapter 8) are impacted by traumatic events.

An additional factor that appears to determine the neurological consequences of child abuse is the age of the child when the abuse occurs. For example, Andersen *et al.* (2008) found that hippocampal volumes were reduced in those who experienced CSA at ages 3–5 years and 11–13 years, corpus callosum volumes were reduced in those with CSA occurring at ages 9–10 years, and that the frontal cortex was attenuated in subjects with CSA at ages 14–16 years. In addition to structural changes, Read *et al.* (2001) have also noted similarities between abused individuals and patients diagnosed with schizophrenia on measures such as hyper-responsivity of the stress system (i.e. the hypothalamic-pituitary-adrenal axis), and activation of dopamine systems. Such findings appear to offer support for the 'traumagenic neurodevelopment model' of schizophrenia (and hence, by extension, AVHs) of Read and colleagues.

Although this research is still in its relative infancy, it appears plausible that childhood traumatic events may be the cause of the structural and functional neuroimaging findings in some voice-hearers, as well as some of the neurotransmitter changes. Furthermore, such findings may be worked into other accounts of voice-hearing. For example, the neural changes resulting from trauma could be integrated with Hoffman & McGlashan's (1997) synaptic elimination model of AVHs discussed in the last chapter. Similarly, traumatic events would seem good candidates for the parasitic memories proposed to be important in AVHs by Hoffman (1986), or seeds for ruminative inner dialogue as discussed in Chapter 9. In the Conclusion of this book we will return to this issue.

Psychological frameworks for understanding how childhood trauma, and trauma more generally, may cause AVHs

There are a number of theoretical reasons for expecting the relation between trauma and AVHs to be a causal one. Hammersley *et al.* (2003) have noted that traumatic events such as CSA are likely to produce intrusive memories, occurring automatically and with low cognitive effort, two factors which Bentall (2003) notes are likely to lead to source monitoring errors (see Chapter 9) and which will encourage the misattribution of such experiences to a non-self source, leading to AVHs. Kilcommons *et al.* (2008) propose that traumatic events lead to a change in the individual's beliefs (negative cognitions about the self and world) and a shattering of the individual's basic assumptions about the self (self-worth, vulnerability), the world and others (in relation to fairness, dangerousness, trustworthiness, equality) which may confer a vulnerability to the development of AVHs. There may also be a causal link between CSA and AVHs through the mechanism of dissociation. For example, Allen, Coyne & Console (1997) have argued that trauma-induced dissociation may hamper reality testing, leaving individuals 'vulnerable to the nightmarish inner world' (p. 332). There is hence likely to be a complex interaction between attachment style, coping strategies, stress-reactivity and CSA, which still needs to be examined in more detail in prospective studies.

Nijenhuis & Van der Hart (1999) argue that AVHs may result from dissociation in which one dissociative part of the personality becomes trauma-fixed and aurally impinges upon the normal, everyday functioning part of the personality. The theory is that traumatic events are stored in an unintegrated manner in the brain and are not integrated into autobiographical memory. This work has been developed by Steel, Fowler & Holmes (2005) who argue that, in the case of trauma and PTSD, memories of traumatic hotspots (Ehlers & Clark, 2000) are not processed in the normal manner by the hippocampus. Instead, during highly traumatic events, information by-passes the hippocampus and is processed via the amygdala, in order to enable a faster release of stress hormones. Although this allows faster processing, it does not allow the hippocampus to perform its normal role of integrating information within a spatial and temporal context. This leads to the information becoming separated from other material in the form of what Brewin, Dalgleish & Joseph (1996) have termed a 'situationally-accessible memory'. Such a memory is vulnerable to being triggered and entering intrusively into consciousness when stimuli associated with the original trauma occur. This situation can then in theory be modified by mentally revisiting the situation, talking about it, allowing the hippocampus to code it correctly, making the event into a normal 'verbally accessible memory'. Again, if such memories and events are present, psychotherapy supported by appropriate medication, rather than salience-reducing medications alone, would seem to be appropriate.

Given that not all individuals who experience trauma go on to develop voices, a crucial question is what factors determine who develops voices and who doesn't? The answers to such questions are likely to be crucial in allowing interventions to help people cope effectively with traumas they have been through. Aside from ways of preventing trauma and abuse happening in the first place (which should obviously be done even if this was not connected to AVHs), this is perhaps the next most important area for contemporary research. At present we can only speculate on what factors may be important in causing the transition from trauma to AVHs, based on clinical experience and parallel studies from other areas.

Clinical experience suggests that one very important factor in whether voices develop or not following trauma is the shame associated with the experience. As noted in Chapter 10, it has been argued that shame is one of the key emotions associated with AVHs (Dodgson & Gordon, 2009). Research from other psychiatric diagnoses suggests this is a plausible claim. For example, Andrews et al. (2000) examined what factors led victims of violent crime (defined as actual or attempted physical or sexual assault, or bag snatch) to develop PTSD symptoms (although voices were not looked at specifically). One month after the crime, it was found that shame (such as feeling they should have done more to stop it, looking bad to others during it, or having bodily signs of the crime) and anger with others were both significant predictors of levels of PTSD symptoms. However, it was found that shame surrounding their experience of crime was the only predictor, six months after the incident, of PTSD symptoms. In a meta-analysis of risk factors for PTSD, Brewin, Andrews & Valentine (2000) found some evidence that events following a trauma, such as lack of social support, or further experiences of stress, were also influential in predicting whether PTSD would develop. Furthermore, Canton-Cortes et al. (2011) found that in 163 female students who had experienced CSA, those who blamed themselves had more avoidant coping strategies, which in turn led to more severe PTSD symptomatology. As a result, they suggest that it would be beneficial to intervene to modify children's attributions of self-blame relating to their abuse. Consistent with this, other studies have found the attributions made by survivors of CSA have been found to affect outcome with, for example, self-blame being associated with increased PTSD symptoms and depression (Feiring, Taska & Chen, 2002; Kolko, Brown & Berliner, 2002). It is plausible that emotions such as guilt, shame, self-blame and anger, as well as a lack of social support, lead to traumas reverberating in the mind to a greater degree, and play a role in the development of malevolent voices (see Andrew, Gray & Snowden, 2008, as discussed above). It has also been found that attachment security mediates the relation between CSA and the emergence of trauma symptoms generally (Aspelmeier, Elliott & Smith, 2007).

In regard to the debate about whether certain forms of abuse are more likely than others to result in voices, a useful concept here is unifinality (Cicchetti & Rogosch, 1996). Unifinality refers to a single end point (in this case, AVHs) being reached by different developmental pathways. It may be that the particular form of childhood abuse (e.g. sexual, physical, emotional) is less influential in the potential future development of AVHs than the meaning of the experience to the individual (attributions of self-blame, feelings of shame) and the level of social support available after the trauma (McCarthy-Jones, 2011b). For example, the ability of an abuser to make the victim feel that they were responsible for what happened, or the victim's body's potential to react with arousal even in abuse situations can lead to feelings of guilt and shame, and have been highlighted to me by some voice-hearers as being, in their view, critical to the reason their abuse led to voice-hearing. In line with this proposal, we may add that CSA, for example, has been found to be more likely to result in psychiatric disorders generally if the perpetrator was related to the victim, if force or threats were used, or if someone the victim told did not believe them, did not support them, or punished them for the abuse (Bulik, Prescott & Kendler, 2001), all factors which affect the meaning of the abuse, and the available coping strategies.

Conclusion: trauma, emotions and voices

In conclusion, there is clear evidence of an association between CSA, as well as trauma more generally, and AVHs. Mental health professionals should hence routinely ask voice-hearers about such trauma, and CSA specifically, particularly with individuals who have received a diagnosis of schizophrenia, whom previous research shows are less likely to be asked previous experiences of being abused (Read & Fraser, 1998). Guidelines as to when and how to ask about CSA have already been laid out (Read, Hammersley & Rudegeair, 2007) and should be employed. In terms of a causal relation between CSA and AVHs, whilst there are good theoretical reasons, indicative quantitative empirical research, as well as case-study and first-person accounts, for a role of CSA in the aetiology of AVHs, this remains to be firmly established. Nevertheless, the evidence is suggestive that there is likely to be a causal relation. It appears Freud was probably wrong to recant on the role of childhood abuse in hearing voices (Chapter 3). Further research into the potentially causative relation between AVHs and CSA, as well as trauma more generally, is needed, and is the best way for researchers to honour the stories many voice-hearers themselves relate (McCarthy-Jones, 2011b).

Such research should likely consider that a key factor that determines whether trauma leads to voice-hearing may be the attendant emotions involved. In particular, shame and guilt appear likely to mediate the relation between trauma and voice-hearing. First, the findings reported in this chapter are suggestive of this. Second, when we consider many of the examples of voice-hearing reported in the three historical chapters of this book (Part I), we see many examples of shame and guilt as precursors to voice-hearing (e.g. Boxes 2.3, 3.1, 3.4 and 12.1). Third, when in Chapter 4 we considered what the voices say in psychosis, we saw examples of patients reporting that they think their voices may be a punishment for having had an abortion, or result from other wrongdoings such as being a male prostitute in one case. Again, guilt and shame emerge as key emotions here. Similarly in Chapter 4 it appears likely that such emotions are likely to play a role in the development of voice-hearing of combat veterans. Finally, the work done on the Hypervigilance model of Dodgson & Gordon (2009) also points towards a role for shame (Chapter 10). It is worth stating that this is not to say that shame and guilt play a role in all voice-hearing experiences, but rather that they may be important in many, and it is worth examining this.

This focus on the relation between emotions and voice-hearing acts as a much needed counterbalance to the previous chapters, which have focused much more on the role of cognition (thought) rather than affect (feeling) in voice-hearing. Given Nietzsche's (2001) argument that 'thoughts are the shadows of our feelings – always marker, emptier and simpler' (p. 137), we should expect that highly emotional events, such as the ones reviewed above, will be the source of the cognitions at the root of voice-hearing. However, we may also ask how voice-hearers deal with their emotions, and if voice-hearers may come to react to emotions differently to non-voice hearers. One way we can deal with our emotions is to attempt to suppress them. The concept of emotional suppression refers to inhibiting one's behavioural responses (e.g. facial or vocal expressions) to emotional stimuli, and has been found to actually have a number of negative consequences (see Badcock, Paulik & Maybery, 2011). In a recent study, they found that those SZ:AVH+ who used emotional suppression more, heard more frequent, longer and louder voices. If we assume the techniques we learn to use to cope with emotions are developed in childhood, then again, we can reach back to a link between early childhood experiences, emotions, coping and voices.

Could problems with processing emotion also be related to AVHs? As we noted briefly in Chapter 9, Cutting (1990) has argued that thoughts are stamped as uniquely ours by the prosody system, which is located in the right hemisphere. If this stamping is impaired, Cutting argues, then the tone of inner speech would not sound right and might sound like someone else's, resulting in an AVH. Consistent with this proposal, Rossell & Boundy (2005) found that SZ:AVH+ although not performing differently to SZ:AVH− on test of facial emotion recognition, did perform worse on a test of auditory emotion recognition. Shea et al. (2007) also found SZ:AVH+ to be worse than SZ:AVH− at an emotional prosody task. These behavioural differences are reflected at the neural level. In an fMRI study of responses to emotional auditory stimuli, Sanjuan et al. (2007) found greater levels of activation in a range of neural regions (orbitofrontal cortex, temporal cortex, insula, cingulate and the amygdala) in SZ:AVH+ as compared to healthy controls. Although Shea et al. (2007) argue that such findings are consistent with Cutting's model, this model still fails to account for why some, and not all, inner speech is experienced as AVHs. Furthermore, it may be that these auditory emotional processing difficulties are a result of other factors specific to AVHs (e.g. trauma) than being a cause of AVHs. For example, it is known that early life stress can result in deficits in affective processing (Pechtel & Pizzagalli, 2011).

In terms of future work, it should be noted that little research has been done on the potential lag between experiencing childhood trauma and the development of AVHs. For some the onset may be instant, whilst for others the onset may be longer. As Herman (2001) notes, survivors of abuse may successfully manage adult life until defensive structures break down due to precipitating events such as the failure of a marriage, the birth of a child, the illness or death of a parent. This has been described as the 'sleeper effect' of trauma (Briere, 1992). Thus trauma may have the ability to cause AVHs on its first occurrence, or childhood trauma may act as a risk factor for a later trauma to cause AVHs to emerge. We see this in numerous accounts of voice-hearers (see Romme et al., 2009).

Finally, we may also pause here to reconsider our Type 2 AVHs. In Chapter 7, Type 2 AVHs were defined as those either identified by the voice-hearer as memory-like, in the sense that they can be seen to be verbatim memories of actual events, or they are isolated fragments of voices which are unrelated to the voice-hearer's ongoing actions and life. Inherent to the definition is that there may be two sub-types here. Having considered the role of trauma here, and seen the effects of direct electrical stimulation of the STG in Chapter 8, we may now pull Type 2 AVHs into two sub-types. Type 2a, which I will term Traumatic Memory AVHs, can be seen to be those resulting from memories of trauma which have not been processed in a normal manner. Here Brewin's (1996) concept of a 'situationally-accessible memory' appears useful for explaining the origins of such voices. In contrast, Type 2b Random AVHs are those not relating from the unusual processing of traumatic memories, but from spontaneous electrical fluctuations in the STG, as elicited by Penfield & Perot (1963) or those explained by Hunter *et al.*'s (2006) model of AVHs. Such voices are phenomenologically distinct from Type 1 AVHs in that they do not relate to the ongoing thought processes of the individual, and may be random and un-understandable.

Social rank, the social world and AVHs

Going beyond traumatic events, there are a number of other types of events in our social world that may be linked to the hearing voices experience. Behrendt (1998) has proposed a model of AVHs which is based around the observation that the evaluation of our social rank is an important human need. If an individual feels an increased pressure to infer the value of the self from social situations, pays increased attention to the social environment, and focuses on how/what others think and say about them, then this, he argues, may produce AVHs. Permanent social stress is one factor he suggests may increase attention towards events that communicate a social message. Behrendt argues that out of the entire range of hallucinations that SZ:AVH+ could have, the fact that they predominantly experience AVHs would be consistent with attention being focused on others' comments on their social status. In terms of social defeat, we may also note that Edwards *et al.* (1966) in a study of 51 alcoholics who had been sleeping rough, found that the majority had experienced hearing voices.

We may extend this account based on observations of what social defeat does to the neurology of an individual. In rats, both social threat (Tidey & Miczek, 1996) and social defeat leads to increases in dopamine levels in the mesolimbic dopamine pathways (Anstrom, Miczek & Budygin, 2009), precisely the same areas as identified in

Chapter 8 as being where excesses in dopamine are thought to be targeted by antipsychotic medication. Why does this happen? Tidey & Miczek propose that this results from increased attention to the threat, or due to attempts by the rat to cope. Indeed, they state that the observation that 'dopamine release in nucleus accumbens and prefrontal cortex is heightened while an animal is exposed to an aversive environmental stimulus is significant given growing clinical evidence that stressful experiences may precipitate the onset of schizophrenia' (p. 148). Thus, we may legitimately potentially attribute the cause of any 'imbalance' in mesolimbic dopamine activity in voice-hearers to environmental events. We may further note that of all classes of stressful event, specifically social-evaluative stressors have been found to cause particularly large responses from the stress system in terms of cortisol release (see Jones & Fernyhough, 2007c).

In addition to considering social rank and social defeat in the aetiology of AVHs, social rank theory has also been used to help understand the relationship between the voice-hearer and their voice. Birchwood *et al.* (2000) found that the power differential between a voice-hearer and their voice was predicted by the perceived power differential between themselves and significant other real people in their social world. However, this study was not able to determine whether people's relations with others in their social world determined how they related to their voices, or whether hearing voices led to reduced social rank and status compared to others, potentially through the mediating variable of depression. A later study by Birchwood *et al.* (2004) attempted to determine which of these models was correct. In a study of 125 patients diagnosed with schizophrenia who had AVHs, it was found that the best fitting model was one where it was the voice-hearer's social rank/status that determined their relationship to their voices. Thus it appears that a low social rank/status causes people to relate to their voices in this way.

Social rank has also been found to affect how one responds to specific commands of voices. Fox, Gray & Lewis (2004), in a study of command AVHs, examined two groups of voice-hearers who complied with the commands their voices gave, one group who complied with their voices' commands to hurt themselves, and another group who complied with their voices' commands to hurt others. It was found that the self-harm group reported significantly higher ratings of inferiority in social relationships, whereas the other-harm group reported significantly higher ratings of superiority within social relationships. Thus, a voice-hearer's social relationships and social rank can have a major impact on how they experience and relate to their voices.

From psychology towards sociology

Ingleby (1981) has argued that psychiatry 'protects the efficient functioning of social institutions by converting the conflict and suffering that arises within them into "symptoms" of essentially individual (or at best familial) "malfunctioning"; it thus attempts to provide short-term technological solutions to what are at root political problems' (p. 44). When we note that only 0.3 per cent of all schizophrenia research has investigated the roles child abuse and neglect may play in its development, and only 0.9 per cent has studied the role of poverty (Read et al., 2009), we see that Ingleby may have a point here. There is hence the urgent need for research into the social and societal causes of AVHs. If traumatic events, such as child abuse, are playing a role in AVHs, we must then ask what causes people to commit child abuse in the first place. One set of factors are macroscopic socio-economic ones. For example, abuse and maltreatment of children has been found to relate to levels of unemployment in society (Ben-Arieh, 2010; Kassim & Kasim, 1995; Krugman et al., 1986; Zuravin, 1989). Given that sexual abuse and rape are often more about power than sex, we should not be surprised that societal factors which act to make individuals powerless, such as unemployment, are associated with such crimes. Based on similar reasoning, I would not be surprised if future research found income inequality (Wilkinson, 2005) to be linked to levels of hearing voices. The point being made here is that to understand AVHs we must go beyond the proximal causes to the very distal causes which are hidden over the horizon. By doing so we may be able to rectify the current situation in which, as Smail (2005) has argued, psychology 'has done more to mystify the human condition than just about any other even remotely intellectual enterprise' (p. i).

Factors such as urban environments, migrant status and discrimination have all been linked to psychosis (see Bentall & Fernyhough, 2008). However, less work has been done specifically on the relation between these factors and hearing voices. A number of interesting studies have been done, though. For example, Bartels-Velthuis, Jenner & van de Willige (2010) in a study of voice-hearing in 7–8-year-old children found that only 3 per cent of children in urban schools experienced AVHs, as compared to 10 per cent of children in rural schools. Although this finding is in the opposite direction to what would be predicted from the psychosis literature, the authors also found that AVHs had more impact upon children in urban environments. This may be because urban areas provide toxic social circumstances such as victimisation and powerlessness (Bentall & Fernyhough, 2008), which make the voices more negative. More work is needed in this area, though.

Epigenetics

We have cast our eyes over the typically short-sighted causal horizon to more distal factors in the previous section, but we must also consider other causes closer to the individual. For example, part of the cause of voices may be due to events occurring while the individual is still in the womb. Bartels-Velthuis, Jenner & van de Willige (2010) found that children aged 7–8 who heard voices were more likely to have a mother who had had an infection during pregnancy. They also found evidence that children with AVHs showed some developmental delay in 'fine motor activity, adaptive, personal/social behaviour in the first 12 months' (p. 43), compared to non-voice-hearing children. Research has also found that children at a greater genetic risk for later receiving a diagnosis of schizophrenia[1] have reduced superior temporal lobe volumes (Rajarethinam *et al.*, 2004), suggesting this may act as a trait risk factor for AVHs. However, it is unclear whether the IFG and arcuate fasciculus which connects it to the STG, are also similarly associated with genetic factors. Nevertheless, the finding discussed in Chapter 9 that immediately after birth, speech does not activate Broca's area (instead only activating the STG) and that by the age of six months, speech perception activates both Broca's area and the STG, providing evidence of a developmental linkage between these two areas (Imada *et al.*, 2006), suggests environmental insults, or genetic factors controlling this process, could play a role in the development of heard voices. Such studies caution us that, in order to fully understand the causes of voices, the biological must meet the social to create an integrated account of the causes of hearing voices, with potentially separate accounts required for both different types of AVHs, and different voice-hearers' own pathways to voices.

This leads us to the concept of epigenetics. This concept notes that the socio-environmental events which happen to an individual influence the process of gene transcription (Read *et al.*, 2009), basically switching the activity of certain genes on or off. An epigenetic approach to voices proposes that they will best be explained by an interaction between the genetic make-up of an individual and the events in their environment. Such an approach moves beyond a simple dichotomy where the environmental or one's genetic make-up are seen to be *the* cause of AVHs. Read *et al.* give an informative example from the work of Meaney and colleagues who found in rodents that maternal care (licking and grooming)

---

[1] Although the genetics of 'schizophrenia' remain a contentious area (see Read *et al.*, 2009).

impacted the development of pups. Pups who did not receive such care had greater reactivity of their stress system, leading to increased anxiety and startle responses. The epigenetic mechanism behind this was that maternal care influenced the transcription of genes that supported the forebrain regulation of the stress system. Thus, in effect the environment signals to an individual's genes what sort of world they are coming into, activating/deactivating certain genes to tailor the person to be able to best survive in this world (i.e. if the world is hostile, it makes sense to be anxious and careful in it). Hence, an epigenetic approach to voices would examine how environmental events (e.g. negative life events) interact with an individual's genes (possibly having a greater effect in individuals with certain genotypes) to lead to the experience of hearing voices.

Changing causes, changing treatments?

Once we accept that voices may have meaningful content, and are likely to be related to past/current emotional issues in people's lives, then this potentially shifts the focus of treatment for AVHs from an emphasis solely on medication, to addressing the emotional issues in the lives of voice-hearers. If, as Romme *et al.* (2009) have argued, voices are fundamentally linked to emotional events in people's lives, and that voices are potentially useful messengers or representations of these emotions, then working with these emotions may be the best way to help people either cope with voices, or resolve them through recognising them as aspects of their own thought. Whilst the meaning of voices will be examined in more detail in the next chapter, some observations may be made here regarding the implication of this meaning of voices for treatment.

We discussed in Chapter 8 how antipsychotics often have their effects not by making voices vanish, but by making them less salient. This immediately becomes problematic if we come to understand voices as communicating real problems in the voice-hearer's life. To illustrate the effect of antipsychotics in animals, Kapur (2003) describes the research of Courvoisier (1956, as cited in Kapur, 2003). In the classic behaviourist paradigm, Courvoisier trained rats to associate a ringing bell with an electric shock, resulting in the rats trying to avoid the mere sound of the bell on its own. However, when the rats were given an antipsychotic they stopped avoiding the bell, even though they were perfectly capable of running away from it, but still responded to the electric shocks themselves. It was as if the bell was less salient to them. In fact, Kapur notes that Delay *et al.* (1952, as cited in Kapur, 2003) observed that the 'état d'indifférence' resulting from chlorpromazine resembled the effects of lobotomy, which was prevalent in those times (Chapter 3). This raises some questions about how antipsychotics should be used. If the voice is indeed communicating or representing some emotional problem in one's life, would not a better long-term strategy be to address the problem rather than to continually numb oneself to it? An example of this can be seen in Escher & Romme's (2010) work, such as in the case of 'Daisy', whose voices had started when her grandmother died. Daisy was not allowed to express her grief and it was only after she had been able to talk about it openly, particularly with her mother, that the voices disappeared. In this view, antipsychotics may have a role to play in controlling the voices whilst the emotional/psychological causes of the problems in the individual's life are dealt with, and then the medication slowly tapered off. Indeed, as Kapur (2003) has noted: 'At present, for most patients we provide modifiers of the biological process (antipsychotic drugs) but provide no specific help for the cognitive-psychological resolution' (p. 17). However, psychological help for voice-hearers has made advances in the last decade. After a further examination of the meanings of hearing voices in the next chapter, we will return to treatments for voices. Finally, as many distressing voices appear to have interpersonal roots, an examination of the distal socio-economic factors which affect how we relate to each other and what we do to each other leads us towards politics. If we really listen, voices may be heard to tell us more about broken societies than broken brains. This should make us question exactly where interventions should be targeted.

Conclusions: the wound is peopled

Here I would like to start reconsidering what the above findings might imply for the meaning we give to hearing voices and how we understand their causation, although meaning will be more thoroughly explored in Chapter 12. In this chapter we have seen that traumatic and adverse life events appear to play a role in the development of hearing voices. We can add this to the finding noted in Chapter 4 of the high prevalence of hearing voices in individuals with PTSD who have experienced traumas ranging from car accidents to combat trauma. Given the root of the word 'trauma' in the Greek term for 'wound', this suggests we can see some (although likely not all) experiences of voice-hearing as being a form of wound. We may also note from our examination of the phenomenology of hearing voices (Part II) that people in the voice-hearer's social world, and often those involved in traumatic events happening to the voice-hearer, inform the identity of the voice. In this sense, then, we may be able to understand some experiences of hearing voices as a peopled wound. As well as potentially making more sense of the experience than the nihilistic proposal that hearing voices is an endogenous brain disease, this may have benefits for the public's view and relationships with people who frequently hear voices, as we will see in the next chapter.

One limitation of viewing voices as a peopled wound is that it can encourage a passive view of voices, suggesting they simply express the wound. Instead, we may go back to Bleuler (Chapter 3), who argued that experiences such as voices could be seen as the 'expression of a more or less unsuccessful attempt to find a way out of an intolerable situation' (1950, p. 460). In this account, voices may actually be quasi-adaptive attempts to solve a problem, rather than simply an expression of it. Research into this area is still in its infancy, however Marius Romme (personal communication) has found that often, if voices are directly asked what they want, they claim to have come to protect the voice-hearer (see also Chapter 12). Much more work into this area is needed and this functional nature of voices still needs to be rigorously empirically tested.

Given the role of environmental events in the aetiology of voice hearing, this suggests, as Read, Bentall & Fosse (2009) have argued, that there is the urgent need for more research into the social and psychological causes of AVHs, within an epigenetic framework, rather than context-less brain research. In this sense, given that the 1990s were labelled the Decade of the Brain, it would be nice to think that this current decade could be the Decade of the Person in the World. Of course, given the powerful forces with interests in maintaining a focus on the brain, rather than the world people are living in, I suspect this is unlikely to happen. Although a model of voices solely focused on the brain is bad science, it is good politics. Ideally, an epigenetic model which considers the more distal causes of these events (the socio-economic factors that seed such experiences) should lead us to consider 'treating' our society, as well as the distressed individual. Rather than continually fishing drowning people out of rivers, we may wish to go upstream and see who or what is pushing them into the river in the first place. And stop them.

Chapter 11: summary of key points

- There is a greater need to look out into the world to examine what life events may play a causal role in AVHs (irrespective of diagnosis).
- Both PTSD and DID are known to have their roots in trauma, and there is highly suggestive evidence that AVHs in many voice-hearers

(irrespective of diagnosis, or lack of it) are caused by traumas, such as childhood sexual abuse.

- Attempts are underway to examine how the effects of trauma on the brain may lead to the neural changes we know to be associated with AVHs.
- Shame and guilt appear to be important in mediating the relation between trauma and AVHs.
- Clinicians need to ask about potential trauma in voice-hearers, and relate this to their AVHs.
- Relating trauma to the content of people's voices shows them to be meaningful and can affect the way we wish to therapeutically intervene.
- A model of voices which concentrates solely on the brain functioning of voice-hearers is bad science, but good politics.
- An epigenetic model, which considers the interaction between events in the individual's environment, and their biological/genetic make-up, appears the best way forward for models of voices.
- Voices may be viewed as a peopled wound.
- More attention is needed to the potential distal causes of AVHs, such as socio-economic factors which lead to conditions of powerlessness, the impact of a ruthless hierarchical society which can lead many to feel inferior and worthless, both of which can ferment abuse, a lack of self-compassion, and ultimately may lead to negative and destructive AVHs.

Part IV

The meanings of hearing voices

Introduction to Part IV

In Part I we examined a history of hearing voices in which we saw the to-and-fro of discourses surrounding what the experience of hearing voices was deemed to mean. Part II showed us what voices are like today, as well as how they are interpreted and experienced in psychiatric, secular and religious contexts, as well as some examination of their cross-cultural occurrences. In Part III the cognitive neuroscience perspective on voices were examined, as well as the role of events in the life of the voice-hearer in the aetiology of voices. We can now bring these together as part of an examination of the meanings of voice-hearing today.

12 The struggle for meanings

What does it mean to hear voices today? In popular culture, the mere experience is typically associated with pathology. For example, in *Harry Potter and the Chamber of Secrets*, J. K. Rowling writes that 'Hearing voices no one else can hear isn't a good sign, even in the wizarding world'. Within the research community, a continuum of views exist. At one end exist positions such as that of Stephane, Barton & Boutros (2001), who stress the findings discussed in Chapter 8, to argue that 'AVH is a symptom of brain disease just like blindness or hemiplegia'[1] (p. 186). Such a position, echoing George Trosse's 'crack'd Brain' (Chapter 2), can lead to people with experiences such as voices being understood to have a 'broken brain' (Andreasen, 1985, p. 1). Seen through this lens hearing voices is a biological illness, a necessarily pathological experience. At the other end of the spectrum exists views such as those of Marius Romme, who argues that hearing voices is a natural human variation which typically results from a personal emotional crisis, and that voice-hearers need to be emancipated, not cured (Romme, personal communication). In this view, voices are associated with illness only when the individual is unable to cope with them. This latter approach has led to a greater attention to the meaning of the experience to the person hearing voices. As Hornstein (2009) notes, for people who hear voices the experience 'isn't about "scrambled electrical signals" or "new breakthroughs in the exciting world of brain research". They write of captivity, insight and resilience' (p. xvii). From this viewpoint, 'Madness is more code than chemistry. If we want to understand it, we need translators – native speakers, not just brain scans' (p. xix). We hence need to turn to voice-hearers' own expert accounts of their own experience to get a fuller view of what meanings are being given to voice-hearing today.

---

[1] Paralysis of one side of the body.

Reclaiming experience: who speaks?

In Chapter 2 we saw Martin Luther observing that religious voice-hearers were 'taught by doctors ... [to] say that one's complexion or melancholy is to blame, or the heavenly planets, or they invent some other natural cause' (ibid.). Today distressed voice-hearers are still told what the 'real' cause of their experiences is, namely that it is a symptom of a brain disease. Many voice-hearers find this of little value, feeling it ignores the reality of their voices and invalidates their experiences (Cockshutt, 2004). Furthermore, patients are taught how to speak about their voices, being given a vocabulary (auditory verbal hallucinations[2]) and are given a clear indication of which aspects of their experience are important (e.g. whether the voice is heard as coming from inside or outside the body is important for some reason). The voice-hearer is thus taught 'psy-speak', and given an alien mould to force their own experiences into. If they insist on an unauthorised explanation, they are said to show a lack of 'insight'. As we saw in Part I, throughout history voice-hearers have followed a similar historical trajectory to women, children, the disabled and people of a non-white skin colour – their voices and opinions have been dismissed as unreliable, and those in a position of power have spoken for them and over them.

Frank (1995) argues that 'whereas modern medicine began when clinicians asserted their authority as scientists by imposing specialised language on their patients' experiences ... The postmodern experience of illness begins when ill people recognise that more is involved in their experiences than the medical story can tell' (p. 6). Frank links this change explicitly into post-colonialism, which he defines as 'the demand to speak rather than being spoken for and to represent oneself rather than being represented' (p. 13), in which 'the story teller seeks to reclaim her own experience of suffering' (p. 18). In terms of hearing voices, this suggests voice-hearers might think differently from imposed stories, and learn about their own meaning of their experiences, by hearing themselves tell their stories, absorbing others' reactions and experiencing their stories being shared in places such as Hearing Voices Groups (e.g. Romme & Escher, 1993). Indeed, Escher, Hackmann & Michael (2004) note that 'By individualising voice-hearers and forbidding them to talk about their experiences, we alienate them from their own experiences and separate them from sources of help, the support of others, and

---

[2] In Karlsson's (2008) qualitative study of 23 individuals who heard voices, the term 'hallucination' was never used by voice-hearers to describe their experiences, preferring their own terms instead.

we make it more difficult for them to understand how the voices influ-ence their daily life' (p. 218). Following the rise of the Hearing Voices Movement (Chapter 3), voice-hearers have fought to achieve a space where their voices can be heard. The first step has been to reclaim their experience as their own.

This approach can be seen in an important paper by Dillon & May (2002), which begins by noting how 'clinical language has colonised experiences of distress and alienation' (p. 25). This colonisation means, argue Dillon & May, that 'recovery seems to be about a decolonizing process, a reclaiming of experience'. They define reclaiming experience as 'our right to define ourselves. The right to find our own voice to describe our experiences and our lives' (ibid.). Ron Coleman (2000), a voice-hearer, trainer and activist, has advanced similar arguments, placing 'great store in the idea of who has ownership within the experi-ence of mental distress' (p. 56). He goes on to argue that the psych-iatrists' ownership of a supposed expert knowledge gives them great power over their clients, and that 'the real expert of the client's experi-ence is the client' (ibid.). In this new discourse, Dillon & May argue that voices should be seen as both meaningful and valid, allowing 'the right to be different' and the reclaiming of voices. Dillon & May ask what stories and systems enable voice-hearers to reclaim their experiences. They argue that 'supportive places to tell your story and make sense of taboo experiences are essential to any liberation process' and cite Hearing Voices Groups as such places. Many others have also advanced argu-ments that can be employed to argue that voice-hearers need to be able to reclaim their experience (e.g. Geekie, 2004; Shotter, 1981).

This involves viewing voices as more than just a symptom, which the 'psy' disciplines often convert it into. As Longden (Romme *et al.*, 2009) notes in relation to her voices, 'What started off as an experience became a symptom' (p. 143). This transformation of voices from experiences to symptoms can also be seen in a recent paper by Sommer *et al.* (2010) entitled 'Healthy Individuals With Auditory Verbal Hallucinations; Who Are They? Psychiatric Assessments of a Selected Sample of 103 Sub-jects'. In this paper, Sommer and colleagues attempt to distinguish whether 'AVH in healthy subjects may exist as an isolated symptom' or whether it forms part of a more general 'vulnerability to other aspects of schizophrenia'. This statement immediately raises the question as to why, if the individuals are healthy, should hearing voices be a 'symptom' of anything? Elsewhere the same research group refer to healthy voice-hearers as 'otherwise healthy individuals' (Daalman *et al.*, 2010), again implicitly assuming that the voice-hearing is unhealthy. This again shows the tendency to view AVHs as a symptom of a disease.

Similarly, in Chapter 3 we noted the rise of the approach of 'médecine retrospective' in the nineteenth century. Today this approach continues to be popular, with people arguing that historical figures who heard voices and who explained their voice-hearing experiences in religious terms were actually mentally ill. For example, as we noted in Chapter 1, the prophet Ezekiel claimed to hear the voice of God. In contrast, Stein (2010) in a paper in the *British Journal of Psychiatry*, argues that these were command hallucinations, and basically diagnoses Ezekiel with schizophrenia. Similarly, Johnson (1994) argues that Swedenborg, whom we met in Chapter 2 and who explained his voices in a religious context, also had schizophrenia. Given that the main purpose of diagnosis is to establish the appropriate treatment for an individual (Moncrieff, 2010) we may ask, what exactly are the authors of such retrospective diagnoses trying to achieve in relation to people whose atoms we now regularly breathe in? In fact, this is actually two separate questions: one, what do the authors think they are trying to do, and two, what are they actually doing? In terms of the second question, such work functions to give legitimacy to current psychiatric diagnostic classifications (e.g. schizophrenia) in that if they have existed throughout history, then they must be 'real'. Furthermore, they argue for the uni-meaning of an experience, i.e. the person might think they are having a religious experience, but they are 'really' suffering from a brain disease, and colonise the explanation of the historical figure. Such work which pathologises religious individuals can create a 'religiousity gap' (Dein *et al.*, 2010) between psychiatry and those with religious beliefs. As a result, Dein *et al.* have argued that 'individuals with religious beliefs may be extremely reluctant to engage with psychiatric services that they perceive to be atheistic, scientific and disparaging of religion' (p. 63), and give the example of the ultra-Orthodox Hasidic Jewish community in London, who 'treat psychiatry and psychology with great suspicion and are generally reluctant to attend psychiatric consultations for fear of misdiagnosis' (ibid.).

In response to papers which have pathologised religious figures, other historical analyses have examined whether such an approach is appropriate (Leudar & Thomas, 2000) or have argued that psychiatric diagnoses are not appropriate, as the individuals in question were examples of hallucinations in the sane. For example, in the case of Swedenborg (Jones & Fernyhough, 2007), I argued that his experiences were best understood as 'Hallucinations without mental disorder'. However, this paper still colonised Swedenborg's own explanations and vocabulary, with our own contemporary terminology. In a later paper on St Thomas Aquinas (McCarthy-Jones, 2011a), I tried to avoid this problem by using the term 'hallucinations' to refer to Aquinas's experiences, using the strike-through to indicate that using the term 'hallucination' was problematic. In this paper I tried to reach an understanding of St Thomas's experiences based on a biopsychosocial approach, rather than the prevailing biological models. However, it could still be argued that all historical analyses function as a battleground for the validity of contemporary approaches to voice-hearing. As a result, they likely tell us more about prevailing attitudes and approaches to voice-hearing than about the historical figure themselves. This is, of course, not a profound insight and will be obvious to many, anyway.

It could be argued that rather than undertaking such historical analyses, time may be more profitably spent on contemporary critiques of diagnostic classifications (e.g. Bentall, 2003) and on examining how psychiatry can meet the needs of religious individuals with distressing mental experiences. Yet I believe real benefits are possible from examination of religious figures' accounts of voice-hearing if such accounts are approached with humility. For example, in an analysis of St John of the Cross's writings on voice-hearing, I argued against the traditional view that it is solely the case that the contemporary mind sciences can help us understand a figure such as St John better, instead proposing that St John can educate the mind sciences in relation to the hearing voices experience (Jones, 2010b). Specifically, as St John was conceptualising voices through a different set of eyes to psychiatry (i.e. through the phenomenological lens of religion rather than medicine) his account of the phenomenology of voices could help us better understand voices by identifying features of them that the contemporary mind sciences have overlooked. For example, St John notes a category of voices which could be termed 'voices that save', as well as stressing that more meaning is often communicated by voices than is given in the words themselves (density of meaning). These are important aspects of voice-hearing which the contemporary mind sciences have overlooked, and need to be used to feed into our accounts of what causes voices. If we do not know what we are trying to explain, how can we explain it properly? This opens the door to an approach to voices where religion and the mind sciences may learn from each other (a bi-directional relationship) rather than the mind sciences simply overwriting religious discourse with medical terminology (a uni-directional relationship).

Rather than simply overwriting a voice-hearer's own narrative with a medical one, what may be a more fruitful approach? Frank's (1995) work can be used to suggest that hearing voices requires telling two stories. The first story is that needed to repair the damage that voice-hearing has done to the voice-hearer's sense of where they are in life, and where they may be going. These stories must then be told to self and other. Yet this is not easy, as voice-hearing can turn people into what Ronald Dworkin has called a 'narrative wreck' (p. 54). The way for voice-hearers to recover, in Frank's model, is through telling stories; not stories that reflect the self, but stories that actively create it. Frank can also help us think about what a recovered voice-hearer might call themselves. He argues that the term survivor 'does not include any particular responsibility other than continuing to survive' (p. 137). However, if one calls oneself a witness, then this means one assumes a responsibility for telling what happened. The witness offers testimony to a truth that is generally unrecognised. Today we see this in action, with voice-hearers who have suffered early traumatic experience which they have linked to their voices, speaking out in witness to the link between these events and rejecting a simplistic, decontextualised biomedical, pathology model of voice-hearing.

Voice-hearers' explanations for their experiences

Geekie (2004) argues that there are two broad ways voice-hearers can deal with their experiences. 'Sealing over' involves dismissing the experience as being of little personal relevance, whereas 'integration' involves having a curiosity about the experience and trying to establish its personal significance. This leads to different models being used by different individuals. Whilst medical explanations are suited to the 'sealing over' type of approach and will be favoured by some, other voice-hearers will want 'integration'-based accounts, and draw on explanations not just limited to a medical explanation, instead creating their own explanations for their experiences drawing on a range of available discourses (e.g. spirituality) or the sense their voices make in the context of their lives (Cockshutt, 2004; Jones, Guy & Ormrod, 2003).[3] Karlsson (2008) found that the explanations people themselves had for the causes of their voices included natural reactions to stress, loneliness, sorrow, a life crisis, telepathy, ghosts, demons or spiritual guides. In this study, many voice-hearers felt that their voices were meaningful in some way. One participant, Anna, stated that she had to go through voice-hearing in order to get through the traumatic experiences of her childhood: 'the psyche knows best what it needs, and if it needs voices then you get voices. I needed voices' (p. 369). Another participant, Yolanda, felt her

[3] Similarly, Read & Harré (2001) found that the general public tended to reject biological and genetic explanations of mental health problems in favour of psychosocial explanations which focused on negative life events (see below).

voices, which came on after a split from her boyfriend, started because she needed to 'observe that [her] body was so tired' (ibid.). Such meanings facilitate coping with AVHs, and make sense of the experience in the context of the voice-hearer's own life.

Other qualitative studies have identified a range of themes relating to voice-hearers' search for the cause of their experiences. Voice-hearers consider causes such as abuse and other traumatic experiences in child-hood (Holzinger *et al.*, 2003; Nixon, Hagen & Peters, 2010b). Life events such as changes or losses in their social network, low self-esteem, or having done 'bad things' (e.g. stealing) are cited as potential causes (Barker, Lavender & Morant, 2001). Genetic factors may also be blamed as well as illness, neurotransmitter imbalances, society/ environment, loneliness, drugs/alcohol, magical and spiritual influences, self-blame and personality (Holzinger *et al.*, 2003). In this latter study, some voice-hearers highlighted emotional sensitivity as being a cause of voices, with one stating that 'if you're both a sensitive child and a sensitive adult, then you're more likely to get such an illness' (p. 159). Drinnan & Lavender (2006) found that self-identified triggers included difficulties at work or with study, financial problems, problems with accommodation, religious concerns, adolescence, drug and alcohol use, and stopping medication. Many voice-hearers hence have great expertise in creating meaningful explanations for the causes and triggers of their own voices, which in turn facilitates their coping.

What do mental health professionals think cause voices?

How do voice-hearers' varied explanatory frameworks referred to above compare to that of mental health professionals? The medical model remains the dominant paradigm in which mental health professionals understand AVHs. Wahass & Kent (1997c) found that the majority of UK psychiatrists were most likely to agree that the cause of hearing voices was either biochemical disturbances or brain damage. In contrast, only around a third or less said stressful life events, environmental factors or bad childhood experiences were causes. Although the majority of UK psychologists also agreed that biological disturbances and brain damage could cause voices, a majority also said stressful life events caused voices (although still only around a third said bad childhood experiences or environmental factors could cause them).

Given this medical model, and the perceived root of AVHs in de-contextualised brain disturbances, this is likely to lead to mental health professionals viewing the content of AVHs as being of little or no interest or relevance. In contrast, as noted above, voice-hearers take their voices to be meaningful phenomena and wish to discuss them. This is bound to lead to conflict. On paper, though, this is not the case. One study has looked at how mental health professionals deal with the actual content of AVHs. Aschebrock *et al.* (2003) asked 58 mental health practitioners and researchers (47% mental health nurses, 22% psychiatrists, 19% clinical psychologists, with the rest belonging to other disciplines, e.g. occupational therapists) about (1) their perceived costs and benefits of attending to the content of patients' hallucinations, (2) the extent to which they did this and (3) their training regarding examining content. Sixty per cent of participants had 10+ years' experience working with patients with psychosis. Most (71%) rated it as important to attend to the content of hallucinations, citing benefits such as that it helped to understand and formulate patients' problems. Furthermore, 48 per cent of the sample said that the content of hallucinations were 'understandable' in the context of patients' lives (of course, this means 52% did not state this position). One stated that 'I often find a lot of sense and "meaning" behind people's psychotic experiences and the content begins to make a lot of sense when you begin to explore the psychotic's [*sic.*] life experience enough' (p. 308). In terms of drawbacks, 28 per cent said that they were worried that attending to content may lead to 'reinforcing of psychotic experiences' (ibid.). Rather oddly, one stated that 'You might "understand" the psychosis so well that you miss the fact that the patient is psychotic' (ibid.). In terms of training, 38 per cent of participants said they had had little or no training in how to deal with the content of hallucinations (in fact, the majority of clinical psychologists said this, but only 15% of the psychiatrists).

Is engagement with the content of voices what is found in practice, though? To test this, McCabe *et al.* (2002) studied how psychiatrists interacted with their patients. They videotaped 32 sessions of psychiatrists consulting with patients diagnosed with schizophrenia or schizoaffective disorders. Seven different psychiatrists participated in the study, and consultations lasted around 15 minutes. A typical average consultation involved the psychiatrist reviewing the patient's mental state, medication regime and any side effects, their social and occupational activities, living arrangements, finances and contact with other mental health professionals. It was found that patients actively tried to talk about the content and meaning of their hallucinations and delusions, but that the psychiatrists were reluctant and uncomfortable talking about them, and 'hesitated and avoided answering the patients' questions, indicating reluctance to engage with these concerns' (p. 1150). Furthermore, they 'responded with a question rather than with an answer, and smiled or laughed (when informal carers were present), indicating that they were reluctant to engage with patients' (p. 1148). This conflict between the patient wanting to talk about their symptoms and the psychiatrist not wanting to,[4] led to notable 'interactional tension' (p. 1149). The authors also note that 'the growing number of organisations started by patients and carers (for example, the Hearing Voices Network) to provide an opportunity to talk about psychotic symptoms reflects a wish for this aspect of the illness to be addressed' (p. 1150).

In response to this study, a psychiatrist (Rajesh, 2003) wrote to the *British Medical Journal* (BMJ) to defend the situation, noting, among other points, that (1) conversations with psychotic patients were unlikely to be normal due to thought disorder, negative symptoms (poverty of thought), and other abnormalities of affect [implication: patients can't talk meaningfully about their voices], (2) because the session is only 15 minutes long, the things that are of maximum benefit to the client need to be focused on [implication: talking about the experiences of voices is not of maximal benefit], and (3) psychiatrists should avoid duplication of work done by other services [i.e. other services are already talking to people about the meaning of their voices]. In their reply to this, McCabe *et al.* (2003) wondered 'when the right occasion is and to whom patients should talk about their psychotic symptoms if not their psychiatrist?' (p. 550). A medical director of a psychiatric hospital in the Netherlands also wrote in to the BMJ, stating that: 'As a psychiatrist I was trained to listen. But also not to listen. There is little or no place for psychotic content in textbooks'. He goes on: 'My own experience is that taking some time to discuss seriously the . . . messages that voices bring is highly appreciated by patients and, believe it or not, often time saving. It taught me a lot about these psychotic experiences that is found nowhere in psychiatry textbooks' (van Meer, 2003, p. 549). Indeed, as McCabe & Priebe (2008) note, part of the problem seems to be that there is little 'systematic, theoretically informed training on how clinicians should respond' (p. 405).

Given this clash of explanatory frameworks, it is unsurprising that voice-hearers often have negative experiences of treatment (Chapter 5). Plenty of first-person accounts written by voice-hearers support this claim. One voice-hearer who had been sexually abused as a child reported that 'My therapist didn't tell me anything more than "swallow your medication and keep your mouth shut. Keep the lid on the cesspool"' (Romme *et al.*, 2009, p. 248).

---

[4] We seem to have reached the other end of the pendulum from psychoanalysis, where the old joke goes, 'After twelve years of therapy, my psychoanalyst said something that brought tears to my eyes. He said "No hablo ingles"'.

The basis for voices being an illness

Is the mere experience of hearing voices a sign of illness? Kapur (2003) argues that as long as the voices people hear 'remain private affairs, they are not an illness by society's standards. It is only when the patient chooses to share these mental experiences with others, or when these thoughts and percepts become so salient that they start affecting the behavior of the individual, that they cross over into the domain of clinical psychosis' (p. 16). Kapur's first criterion for hearing voices being an illness, 'sharing one's experience with others', is a strange one. There are not any cancers that become malignant simply by people telling others about them, and it is unlikely that the next breakthrough in cancer research will be the finding that just not telling anyone about one's cancer turns out to be the long searched for cure. The second criterion for illness, the impact on behaviour, is also problematic. For those whose voices help them on a spiritual journey, aid their work or life, an illness model does not seem appropriate. Instead it appears likely that only when individuals cannot cope with their voices and this leads to negative effects on their life, is an illness model appropriate. But then it is not the voices that are a necessary sign of illness, but rather the failure to cope with them.

That a given voice is not necessarily pathological is reflected (on paper, at least) in the present psychiatric classification system, with the DSM-IV-TR (APA, 2000) defining voice-hearing as a mental disorder only if it causes social and occupational impairment. Two people could hear exactly the same voice, with exactly the same underlying biological cause; one could be impaired by it, not cope and fail to function in society, and therefore be defined as having a mental disorder, and the other could cope with it well, perhaps interpreting it in a spiritual light, and not have a mental disorder. This has led Johnstone (2000) ironically to note that there are hence two ways one can officially recover from voices. The first is not to be distressed by them anymore, and to recover one's social and occupational roles. The second is to become part of a culture that values or accepts voice-hearing. If it is a cultural norm, then you are not mentally ill (i.e. you can't be beaten by the 'delusion stick'). This may mean moving elsewhere, or more radically it may mean lobbying for change in society's views of hearing voices. The obvious parallel here is homosexuality, often noted by members of the Hearing Voices Movement, which was officially a mental disorder until it was removed from the DSM-III in 1973, and hence millions of people recovered overnight (ibid.). Szasz (1996) also draws a parallel with homosexuality, but also with masturbation. Just as self-stimulation was long regarded as an abnormal and dangerous practice, he argues that hearing voices has suffered the same fate.[5] What other arguments could be used to argue that hearing voices per se is an illness? It may be thought that AVHs (and particularly command AVHs) are a sign of pathology, as they make people more likely to be dangerous and violent. A review by Bjorkly (2002) found, though, that 'there is no evidence that auditory command hallucinations are dangerous per se. There is some, but so far inadequate, evidence that voices ordering acts of violence towards others may increase compliance and thereby be conducive to violent behaviour' (p. 612). Braham, Trower & Birchwood (2004) also were forced to conclude with uncertainty on this issue. Although there are many instances of people citing commanding AVHs as the cause of violent acts they went on to perform, this subset of voice-hearing experiences does not indicate hearing voices per se is pathological. Sara Maitland gives an example of such lumping together: 'I said to a psychiatrist that there must be something wrong, when people are unable to distinguish between Peter Sutcliffe [the Yorkshire Ripper] and William Blake [who as a boy saw angels sitting in a tree on Peckham Rye, "bright wings bespangling every bough like stars"] and he said, "There's no difference." I said, "Excuse me, there's a massive difference between writing a lot of beautiful but rather strange poetry and going out and murdering a lot of women"' (Walsh, 2007). Moving beyond questions of illness, the relevant issue then becomes what factors mediate the relation between having command AVHs and actually acting on these. It has been found that having co-existing delusions, knowing the identity of the voice, believing the voices to be real, and having less frequent voices, makes following the voices' commands more likely, with beliefs about the command being more important than the phenomenology of the voice (Shawyer et al., 2008).

The most obvious answer as to why hearing voices per se is seen as illness is that those who present to mental health services with voices typically do so as they are distressed by them. This creates a fundamental association in mental health professionals' minds between voice-hearing and distress. This then comes to be reflected in psychiatric textbooks and filters through to society (along with the media's predominant focus on the negative effects of hearing voices), as the sole representation of hearing voices (see Leudar & Thomas (2000) for a good examination of the relation between the media and AVHs). In the absence of evidence

[5] Szasz views hearing voices as self-conversation (here I agree), but specifically self-conversation which the individual is unwilling to take responsibility for, and hence seems to view hearing voices as a *moral* failure (here I do not agree).

of people living with, coping with and valuing their voices, this picture is unlikely to change. However, due to the training being done for mental health services by representatives from the Hearing Voices Movement, and public awareness-raising work by this Movement, the necessary association between voices and illness is beginning to change.

For the subset of voices that lead to distress and impairment, and could validly be labelled an illness experience, what causes this distress and impairment – i.e. what is it about the voices, the person hearing them, or the interaction between the two that leads to an illness state? From our examination of the phenomenology of voices in Part II, it is intuitively clear why many voices are experienced as distressing by voice-hearers themselves: their negative content. This is supported by Beavan & Read's (2010) finding that voice content was the only predictor of voice-hearers' levels of distress (see also Close & Garety, 1998). Yet some people have voices with negative content, but can still function well with them and do not wish to be rid of them (e.g. Romme et al., 2009).[6] Indeed, these negative voices may be seen as useful messengers, offering useful advice, albeit in the form of metaphors (ibid.; Romme & Escher, 2000). It has also been argued that it is the misinterpretation of the message voices bring that leads to distress, and that if voices are asked directly what they want, they often claim to have come to protect the voice-hearer (Romme, personal communication). In this view, it is a dysfunctional relation between the person and their voice that leads to problems.[7] For example, Romme (personal communication) gives the example of a voice-hearer who had a voice saying 'you may as well be dead'. Discussions with the voice-hearer led to the finding that this voice reflected the fact that in self-preservative situations she did not do anything to protect herself, and that if she did not change her behaviour, she may as well be dead. The voice-hearer was thus able to move from a position where she thought the voice wanted her to be dead to a position where she saw it as trying to help her defend herself more. In such a view, voices are not an illness per se, but only result in this

---

[6] It may be objected to that people with voices who are unable to rid themselves of them may find rationales to value the experience (Miller, O'Connor & DiPasquale, 1993), and hence that the experience is not 'really' valued. It is possible this may be the case in some voice-hearers, but appears to be unlikely to be the case in all voice-hearers who value their voices.

[7] This is, of course, central to CBT approaches, already discussed. The work on social rank discussed in Chapter 11 is also relevant here, individuals with low social rank tend to relate to their voices in a similar way. Aiding the person to be more assertive and socially valued may hence improve their relations with their voices (Byrne et al., 2006). However, the Romme example given here goes beyond these approaches, by assuming voices are meaningful metaphors.

when their meaningful and potentially adaptive response to events in the voice-hearer's life (which are intimately tied up with their own emotional and cognitive reactions to these events) are not recognised and are coped with poorly. However, I suspect many might be wondering whether voices are 'really' metaphors, or whether this is something that is just being read into them. Here the proof is likely to be in the pudding. If a meaningful account of the voices (a 'construct' – see Box 12.3 and below) is created, and working with this leads to the voices improving, then this suggests such an approach is valid. Yet it remains unclear whether some voices are simply meaningless, and not connected with life events, and what the ratio of meaningless versus meaningful voices may be. A lot more systematic research into this area is needed here.

In addition to distress, impairment, and hence illness, resulting from some specific properties of the voice and the voice-hearer's interaction with their voices, some of the distress and impairment associated with voice-hearing may come from other sources, such as how society views voices and hence how it treats voice-hearers. McGruder (2002) offers an insightful analysis of why experiences such as hearing voices are seen as problematic in our contemporary society, and this analysis accords well with the findings from Part I of this book. McGruder argues that voices are threatening because they suggest a 'different relationship to the commonly accepted version of reality' (p. 65). Specifically, they represent a 'reversal of what Western humans, in the last few hundred years, have come to value as the essence of human nature. Because our culture so highly values a certain unitariness of consciousness and an illusion of self-control and control of circumstance, we become abject when contemplating mentation that seems more changeable, less restrained and less controllable, more open to outside influence, than we imagine our own to be' (ibid.). Thus, as was argued in Part I, as society has become more committed to a model of self in which one is self-disciplined and self-controlled, which we noted was linked to the rise of capitalism, intrusions such as voices, particularly when they influence people's behaviour, are viewed as highly suspect. This suggests that a change in how we view the nature of our consciousness, and a change in the amount of responsibility we feel for thoughts that occur in us may change how we view voices and the amount of distress they cause. As McGruder puts it, 'When humans do not assume that they have rather complete control of their experiences, they do not so deeply fear those who appear to have lost it'. Furthermore, we should note the society that a biomedical disease model emerges from. It is a society which likes to focus on explanations of behaviour at the level of the individual, rather than at macro-level social explanations, and which is built on a capitalist base which has a powerful financial and political interest in medicalising distress (McGruder, 2002; Smail, 2005).

Much is made about the neural changes associated with hearing voices, as we saw in Chapter 8, as if this somehow clinches the argument that it is necessarily an illness and a pathological experience. In a recent editorial in the BMJ, Lieberman & First (2007) argued that 'evidence shows' that hearing voices and the other symptoms of schizophrenia 'are manifestations of brain pathology. Schizophrenia is not caused by disturbed psychological development or bad parenting. Compared with normal controls, people with schizophrenia have abnormalities in brain structure and function seen on neuroimaging and electrophysiological tests. In addition, the evidence that vulnerability to schizophrenia is at least partly genetic is indisputable' (p. 108). I will pass over the absurd intimation in this sentence that life events have no impact upon the brain, and simply note that it is the findings of neural signatures associated with voice-hearing (as we saw in Chapter 8) that leads researchers to state with confidence, therefore, that voices are 'a symptom of brain disease' (Stephane, Barton & Boutros, 2001, p. 186). But just because something is associated with neurological changes does not make it a disease. Bentall (1992b) has made this point satirically by proposing happiness be classified as a mental disorder, due to its tendency to be associated with reckless behaviour and the presence of demonstrable neural changes. We[8] are hence left to decide whether hearing voices is a desirable experience or not, and what factors effect this.

In a 2001 debate in the pages of the *Psychologist* magazine, a debate relevant to our current discussion took place. Ivan Leudar, a psychologist, and Anthony David, a psychiatrist, addressed the question whether voice-hearing was associated with mental illness (David & Leudar, 2001). Both authors had their own grounds on which they found voices to be pathological. David first argued that 'A voice-hearer who is not in any distress, who lives a fruitful and productive life according to commonsense criteria, would never even enter the arena in which the possibility of mental illness was up for discussion'. However, David later started to slip back from this position into an illness discourse, stating that voice-hearing 'on its own seems only marginally pathological'. He then added that 'the fact that it [i.e. voice-hearing] frequently (in about 70 per cent of cases[9]) occurs alongside other more bizarre

---

[8] You may well wonder who 'we' includes.

[9] I am not aware where this figure comes from, nor what sort of differences are being referred to regarding the difference between a normal and a 'bizarre' hallucinatory experience.

hallucinatory experiences, does suggest that bracketing them under the heading of illness is not unreasonable'.

In response, Leudar, like William James before him, argued that voices should be judged 'according to whether they are reasonable, and in terms of their consequences for life: in other words, pragmatically'. For Leudar, voices indicate problems when, for example, they are out of touch with mundane reason and when they are a source of unreasoned and impulsive action. David disagreed with this, asking Leudar 'to justify whose reason is his gold standard, and what are the criteria for "out of touch"?' Leudar also observes that voices can be distressing 'because of the meaning of the experience in our culture', and that the media portrayal of them as symptoms of illness and signs of unreason means that if people hear voices they may think themselves going insane, and question whether, for example, they can trust themselves with their families. He therefore argues that whether or not voices are pathological is socially and culturally contingent. David disagrees with this, stating 'the less we resort to the shifting sands of cultural values and the more we seek to apply universal standards (e.g. third person commenting voices are usually pathological), the less open to abuse and innocent mistakes psychiatry will become'. Leudar also argued that 'The madness of some hallucinations is in their involuntariness, delirious content, falsity, childish terror of the hallucinator: in other words, nothing specific to hallucinating'. Again, David challenges this, arguing voices are inherently frightening, stating that their delirious content, their falsity and their terror are 'highly specific to hallucinations, they are part and parcel and not mere add-ons'.

In terms of the interpretations of the experience, David argues that 'if they are memories, fantasies, fears, why not call them that?'. He then proposes that if we 'collude with the compartmentalisation of experiences' this can lead to multiple personality disorder, and concludes that 'While there are dangers in seeming to denigrate a person's experience with a pathological label, there are equivalent dangers in reifying them'. Leudar then adds, 'Would I say that voices are a secret and forgotten source of wisdom? Clearly not today'. This is based on his observation that the content of voices today, in his view, tends to be mundane, and that even religious voices in the past were mundane, although what religious voice-hearers inferred from their voices was not.

What can we take from these exchanges? It is notable that no voice-hearers, such as a representative from the Hearing Voices Movement, were invited to take part in the debate. Obviously the meaning of hearing voices can be decided without actually asking any voice-hearers! Most of the issues I come to next could already have been resolved had a voice-hearing representative from the Hearing Voices Movement been present in the debate, as they could have answered these points succinctly and from a position of personal experience. First, we may consider the validity of David's claim that 'A voice-hearer who is not in any distress, who lives a fruitful and productive life according to commonsense criteria, would never even enter the arena in which the possibility of mental illness was up for discussion' (p. 256). I suspect many voice-hearers may have had different experiences. Such a statement also suggests that the decision to label a voice-hearer with a tag of mental illness is always an objective process, rather than sometimes being a tool used by non-voice-hearers against voice-hearers to achieve goals of power (think back to Georgina Weldon). Second, David puts forward a version of the 'can of worms' argument, namely that working with the voice-hearer's voices can have a negative effect. Indeed, as Romme & Escher (2000) note, many psychiatrists believe that listening to the content of voices 'increases the hearer's undesirable fixation on this "unreal" world' (p. 14). If there is good empirical evidence out there for the claim that such engagement has a negative effect, I am not aware of it. Indeed, stories of voice-hearers' recoveries (e.g. Romme et al., 2009) and the claims of Moskowitz & Corstens (2007) actually suggest that engaging with the voices can have a positive effect on the voice-hearers' life. Again, a randomised controlled trial of these two contrasting approaches could be used to resolve this question empirically.

Another issue raised by this debate is that of absolutism regarding the causes and meanings of voices. I would agree with David's implied proposition that there is a 'correct' causal story to be told in the case of any given voice-hearer. Indeed, I am committed to the proposal that there is a scientifically determinable distil and proximal causal mechanism which underpins voices (although different voices may have different causes). However, the meaning of the experience, or more specifically whether it is viewed as being intrinsically pathological, is a political/ cultural one rather than a scientific question. Bracken & Thomas (2005) describe how the different meanings people give to hearing voices can cause conflict today. For example, given that a number of people in the community hear voices, cope well with them, employing a range of medical, spiritual, or paranormal explanations, they ask whether such individuals should be viewed as undiagnosed patients in a 'pre-schizophrenic' state who are 'to be considered at risk of developing schizophrenia and thus in need of early intervention?' (p. 43). They argue that such a position is problematic. However, to my eyes this would appear to be an empirical question. If one hundred people at a given point in time unproblematically hear voices, then at a later point in time a certain percentage will have problems resulting from these voices. That people should be advised on this potential, told what life events may cause their voices to become problematic, and given some form of coping strategies to consider seems commonsensical.

More pertinently, Bracken & Thomas note that 'the question is this; what right do we have to impose on others explanations for their experiences that may conflict with their understanding?' (p. 43). In order to address this question, it is worth considering the circumstances under which someone would want to impose their opinion of the meaning of voice-hearing onto the voice-hearer. In terms of healthy voice-hearers, in theory at least, it would appear unlikely that anyone should want to change the voice-hearers' own personal understanding of their voices, unless the explanation is threatening to another. Thus, the Enthusiasts in the seventeenth century used their voices to assert claims of authority and status, and the Church imposed its own views onto them. Today, if a healthy voice-hearer were to claim they heard the voice of God and used this to try and influence people, the validity of their account would also be questioned. In terms of voice-hearers who are distressed by their voices and consult mental health services, such services will likely try and impose their own understanding on the voice-hearer as part of their well-intentioned attempt to help, potentially seeing the voice-hearer's own explanation as part of what is causing them distress. Perhaps lessons here can be learnt from the Hearing Voices Movement, in which leading writers (e.g. Romme *et al.*, 2009) typically argue that trauma (or more accurately, problems dealing with the emotions resulting from trauma) plays a causal role in creating an individual's voices, yet, much like in CBT, there is still the acceptance that a person's own explanation may be worked with collaboratively. For example, if a voice-hearer has a telepathic explanation for their experiences, Coleman & Smith (1997) suggest that one can work with this belief, considering 'psychic self-defence', for example. Therapists undoubtedly have a challenging job in this area, but it is likely that more training of therapists by recovered voice-hearers, or voice-hearers who have been distressed by their voices and then recovered, training as therapists, will help provide sensitive, respectful and effective reduction of distress.

Problems with a purely biomedical model of hearing voices

In Chapter 11 we examined the distal causes of hearing voices, which pointed towards the necessity of a biopsychosocial account of voices. In addition to this scientific argument for a move away from a 'bio-bio-bio' model, we may also consider the negative effects of viewing hearing voices as a biological malfunction. First, McGruder (2002) argues that people with 'deviant mental content' are 'not well served by the current positivistic tunnel vision of our biomedical culture that sees [them] ... as biochemical products of an abnormal nervous system' (p. 62). Indeed, Jung (1977) argued that 'The dogma, or intellectual superstition, that only physical causes are valid still bars the psychiatrist's way to the psyche of his patient and impels him to take the most reckless and incalculable liberties with this most delicate of all organs' (p. 349). In addition to these problems and the incompatibility of purely biomedical models of AVHs with voice-hearers' own explanations, there lies another problem. We are told that social stigma, cruelty and prejudice result from 'a failure to realise that mental illness is a physical illness, and illness caused by biological forces' (Andreasen, 1985, p. 2). Given the impact of the Decade of the Brain (the 1990s) on society, the continued stigma undergone by voice-hearers in the lived experience of psychosis (Chapter 5) suggests this account is false. Indeed, it has been suggested that a problem with the biological model of mental illness is that it might actually *increase* stigma. Corrigan & Watson (2003) observe that 'Biological explanations may also imply that people with mental illness are fundamentally different or less human' (p. 478) and a number of studies show this to be the case.

A revealing study by Mehta & Farina (1997) involved setting up a task where participants had to teach a 'patient with mental illness' to learn a certain pattern of button presses. They had to administer 'somewhat painful' electric shocks to the other person to give them feedback when they went wrong. Unbeknownst to the participant, the 'patient with mental illness' was actually only an actor, a confederate of the experimenter. In one condition the 'patient' said their mental illness was due to 'some things that happened to me as a kid' (psychosocial explanation). In a second condition the patient said their mental illness was 'just like any other [illness] which affected my biochemistry' (biomedical explanation). I suspect you know what is coming next. Yes – participants increased the severity of shocks more quickly to the 'patient' who gave a biomedical explanation, as compared to the psychosocial explanation. The authors concluded: 'The disease model engenders a less favourable estimation of the mentally disordered than the psychosocial view ... Viewing those with mental disorders as diseased sets them apart and may lead to our perceiving them as ... almost a different species'. This is consistent with the lived experience of voice-hearers in the context of psychosis, as we saw in Chapter 5. Here the idea I introduced in the previous chapter of voice-hearing being a 'peopled wound' may prove useful in reducing stigma, as well as being an accurate description of some, although perhaps not all, voice-hearing experiences.

Similarly, in a study of 469 people, Read & Harré (2001) found that in the general public, biological and genetic causal beliefs are related to negative attitudes, including perceptions that 'mental patients' are dangerous, anti-social and unpredictable, and a reluctance to become romantically involved with them. In contrast, the amount of reported personal contact with people who had received psychiatric treatment was correlated with positive attitudes. Read & Harré hence recommend that destigmatisation programmes consider abandoning efforts to promulgate illness-based explanations and focus instead on increasing contact with and exposure to users of mental health services.

Pathological and non-pathological voices

One clear alternative to medical and pathology discourses are spiritual/religious interpretations of voices, as noted in Chapter 6. To give a contemporary example, Rohnitz reports that after a suicide attempt birds started to talk to her, and later a tree. This, she notes, 'was a spiritual experience, which stimulated me. The birds told me that I was their friend, that I was part of the universe. This experience was positive' (Romme et al., 2009, p. 105). This has led to a focus on the spiritual aspects of psychosis in general (Clarke, 2001; Cook, Powell & Sims, 2009). Much effort has been spent on trying to decide how to distinguish between pathological and non-pathological voices. In particular there has been great interest in how 'spiritual' and 'pathological' voices differ.

A real-life example of the conflict between the medical and spiritual paradigms is to be found in the work of Luske (1990). Luske reports on the competing models of meaning used by patients and staff on a ward. One patient, Vern, 'has insisted all along that his experiences are of a religious nature and in no way indicative of mental illness' despite openly acknowledging that 'psychic pain attends his spiritual quest' (p. 97). In one conversation with a staff member (Cathy), Vern (who claims he talks to God, and hence presumably hears voices) is told, 'Vern, you can't keep avoiding what's going on with you. It's not some [with irony] "religious breakthrough", it's a psychotic episode. That's what it's called: psychosis, schizophrenia. You may not want or like it ... But that's what it is. *That's the reality*' (pp. 96–7, emphasis added). When Vern reacts to such statements by replying 'Why are you trying to cut me down and going on like that?' Cathy again replies 'I am the voice of reality, that's all I am' (p. 89). The power to define what reality is, is an awesome responsibility, and is hardly ever recognised as such. As the doctor on Vern's ward notes, it is the staff's job to use all available means to get Vern to replace his version of his experiences with their psychiatric construction 'psychotic illness'. Vern's priority, says Cathy, 'should be getting a source of income, then housing, food' (p. 102). These may not be Vern's priorities, but of course this is irrelevant to mental health services, whose mandate is to get an individual functioning in a capitalist society again. This, of course, is not the fault of staff within the mental health system, many of whom may be frustrated in their attempts to help a person with their personal and spiritual growth by the fact that this is not recognised as an outcome measure.

All sorts of problems are thrown up by such interactions, many of which we do not have good answers for. As noted earlier in this chapter, we can see the voice-hearer's own explanation being colonised by the psychiatric explanation. Not only is the imposition of someone else's interpretation onto the voice-hearer's experiences problematic in and of itself (Bracken & Thomas, 2005), but it is also self-defeating for the ostensibly therapeutic aims of mental health services. How Vern is meant to engage with people who simply tell him he is wrong and are not prepared to accept the reality of his experiences is somewhat beyond me. The argument could quite plausibly be made, as many have done before in similar cases, that what Vern is being treated for is not aberrant biology, but aberrant values. Going beyond this debate, it would in any case appear to make more sense to consider the content of the conversation between Vern and 'God', work out what issues these potentially reflect in Vern's life and work on these, rather than simply tell Vern he lacks insight into his illness. Vern is certainly in pain and needs help, but the best way to provide this help remains a contentious issue.

The question as to how we can differentiate spiritual and pathological voices has received extensive attention (e.g. Clarke, 2001; Jackson & Fulford, 1997). This may seem like an academic debate, but the label that is attached to a voice-hearer's experiences has a real-world impact on how the voice-hearer is treated (by friends, family and mental health services) and whether they are medicalised, for example. As we saw in Chapter 3, Underhill (1911), following William James, proposed spiritual voices were distinguished from pathological voices by 'their life-enhancing quality' (p. 323). In a seminal contemporary study, Jackson & Fulford (1997) argued that pathological and spiritual experiences could not be distinguished on the basis of factors such as their form or content alone, or by their relationship with other psychopathological experiences. Instead they argue that the distinction depends on the way the experience is embedded in the values and beliefs of the person concerned. A contrasting approach comes from Lukoff (1985), who has argued for a diagnostic category which he terms Mystical Experience with Psychotic Features. In this view an experience may be described as psychotic (i.e. involving hallucinations and delusions) but yet still be spiritually meaningful, hence moving away from an either/or style debate.

My own view is that if we accept that the labels 'spiritual' or 'pathological' do not refer to ontologically independent objects, and that the usage of one or other of these terms is dependent on a complex mesh of factors involving properties of the voice, individual and societal factors (which should be the topic of investigation themselves), the situation starts to become clearer. Too often investigations in this area assume that there is a right answer, and that at the end of the quest we can open the AVH box, look inside and see whether there is a label saying 'spiritual experience' or 'pathological experience'. A better approach may be to return to Wittgenstein's proposal to work out the meaning of these terms by examining how they are used. Or we may examine the factors that push people towards explaining their voices in a 'spiritual' or 'pathological' framework. Here it is informative to consider people who have experienced voices and attributed some to an illness and others to God. Such an individual is reported by Dein & Littlewood (2007). 'David had been diagnosed with a mental illness and was hearing voices in the context of this.[10] He describes how "When I was going through my breakdown I would get quite nasty and aggressive thoughts and voices in my head, which I didn't know how to handle. These were very forceful and pushy' (p. 13). David understood these voices as 'psychotic voices'. However, after recovering from his episode of diagnosed mental illness he began to hear a voice again, but this time he identified it not as a psychotic voice, but as the voice of God. When asked how he distinguished between the two voices, he stated that 'God says something and doesn't force you, so you do what you like with it. It is much easier to respond than with a negative voice'. This was in contrast to the 'psychotic voices' which 'you can't refuse to do something when you hear them. They are very pushy' (p. 13). God, said David, 'tells you what you should do but basically it is up to you'. If he asks God a direct question, ' "Should I go for this job, for instance, or should I do such-and-such?", the only time you will get a no, is when it is for your benefit and it is not good for you' (ibid.).

---

[10] Consistent with the role of negative life events we found in the previous chapter, David had experienced a difficult and unhappy childhood, including bullying at school, and the voices started after a marital breakdown resulted in a period of depression.

Related to this is that one rarely discussed factor in the decision as to whether one is labelled as having a meaningful spiritual experience or a psychotic experience is the level of power and prestige the voice-hearer themself holds. For example, it was widely reported that George W. Bush claimed to have heard God's voice telling him to invade Iraq: 'God would tell me, "George, go and fight these terrorists in Afghanistan". And I did. And then God would tell me "George, go and end the tyranny in Iraq". And I did' (Bush, 2005). Bush was not labelled with an illness and removed from office on the basis of such reports. Likewise, Emanuel Swedenborg, whom we met in Chapter 3, had a high social standing and this undoubtedly played a role in the acceptance of his experiences by others. This is not to say that pathology is never attributed to voice-hearers of high social standing, only that claims that such experiences are spiritual ones are, on balance, more likely to hold more sway if one has such a standing.

It would be remiss to move on without confronting the question as to whether it really is possible to hear voices from supernatural entities. Most people try to avoid answering this question, and it is probably not in the top ten routes to tenure. For example, in their work on voices, Moskowitz & Corstens (2007) state that they 'do not take a position ... as to whether AH [i.e. AVHs] may, under some circumstances, represent a "genuine" spiritual experience'. It is hard to stand still on a moving train, though. One could quite simply say that it is a question of faith as to whether one accepts the possibility of such experiences. However, is it possible to take an evidence-based position on this question? Wiebe (2004) argues that one can. Based on his detailed phenomenological study of visions, voices and exorcisms, he argues that 'the conjecture that evil spirits exist has some plausibility' (p. 58), and that 'claims that God and other spirits are real are rationally defensible' (p. 152). Wiebe (2000) is led to this conclusion in particular through his investigation of contemporary visions of Christ, which he argues 'elude adequate naturalistic explanation at present' (p. 139). However, history shows that what was once unknown and attributed to God is quickly taken away from Him when the naturalistic mechanisms behind such events come to be understood. It would hence not appear wise to base one's faith too firmly on ostensibly divine revelations today. However, for a given voice, how could one prove that it was not divine/demonic in origin? Moskowitz & Corstens (2007) argue that even if it is allowed that there may be genuine spiritual experiences, adequate means to distinguish such experiences from those better explained by neuro-psychological mechanisms remain to be established and that the two cannot be adequately distinguished at present. However, in practice it is hard to conceive of a way such experiences could ever be empirically distinguished between. Studies which show quasi-hallucinatory spiritual experiences can be induced through electromagnetic stimulation of the brain (Persinger, 1993), or hypothetical studies involving functional magnetic imaging of the brains of people whilst they were hearing 'the voice of God' do not logically compel us to deny the possibility of supernatural communication. It would be interesting to discover what neurologically minded theologians would see as convincing evidence of divine locutions today. However, I suspect evidence for a divine source would likely be seen as coming from the content of the voice (e.g. being told things one could not possibly know), rather than its neural correlates. The question of God is unlikely ever to be settled in an fMRI scanner, and I suspect this is probably the way He would want it.

Voices and creativity

The range of meanings of hearing voices is expanded when we note the number of great thinkers, artists and musicians that have experienced voices. As we saw in Chapter 3, the existence of such individuals greatly influenced the 1850s debate of the French proto-psychiatrists as to the meaning of hearing voices. In addition to such voice-hearers explicitly mentioned in Part I, we may add the creative genius that was William Blake. Blake writes in a letter that he heard the voice of his brother, with whom 'I converse daily & hourly ... I hear his advice and even now write from his Dictate' (Blake, as cited in Gardner, 1998, p. 97). Why did Blake hear his brother's voice? We may note that his brother had died thirteen years earlier and that Blake had 'sat up for a whole fortnight with his brother Robert during his last illness' (ibid.). As one writer understatedly puts it, Blake's 'peace of mind was much broken' (ibid.). The writer Virginia Woolf also heard voices[11] (Zwerdling, 1986), although appears not to have coped well with them, as did the musician Robert Schumann, who also struggled to cope (Box 12.1). Today the Beach Boys musician Brian Wilson (Box 12.2) hears voices, although appears to have found ways to cope with them.

   Although it is unclear if creative, artistic individuals are more likely to hear voices than the general population, we may ask if there is any reason to suspect that they might. Posey & Losch (1983), following Jaynes' (2000) suggestion that voices originate in the right hemisphere, have suggested

---

[11] One voice which Woolf heard was that of her mother, which she appears to have actually exorcised by writing *To The Lighthouse*, which can be seen as a reply to her mother, argues Zwerdling (1986).

Box 12.1: The voices of Robert Schumann

Robert Schumann (1810–56), the great German romantic composer, was himself a voice-hearer. His hallucinations began one night, when Schumann heard a single tone which would stop and start. During the next day this ceased, but a day later he was hearing sounds again, which according to his wife Clara was 'music that is so glorious, and with instruments sounding more wonderful than one ever hears on earth' (Ostwald, 1987, p. 4). This music-hearing continued to the extent that Clara writes that 'he heard entire pieces from beginning to end, as if played by a full orchestra' (p. 5). At best this experience would force him to stop reading the paper, but the overwhelming nature of the experience started to impair his own ability to think creatively. Schumann himself referred to this as 'Exquisite suffering' in his diary (p. 5). This music was then expanded to be accompanied by angels singing.

However, then they changed. His wife, Clara, recorded 'a frightful change! The angel's voices transformed themselves into the voices of demons, with horrible music. They told him he was a sinner, and that they wanted to throw him to hell ... Half an hour later he said the voices had become friendly again and were trying to give him courage' (p. 6).

Schumann found the uncontrollability of the voices very distressing. Clara wrote that 'he asked to go to the insane asylum because he could no longer control his mind and did not know what he would do at night' (p. 7). The next day Schumann threw himself off a bridge into the Rhine, but was rescued. He was then willingly hospitalised in an asylum, and did not see Clara again until two-and-a-half years later. On 27 July 1856 Clara was able to see Schumann in hospital, where she noted that 'he was always talking a lot with his spirits' (p. 292). He died in the asylum two days later.

that voices will be more common in people who 'skilfully engage in behaviours thought to be more dependent on the right rather than left hemisphere such as those pertaining to music, art, poetry and spatial maths skills'. In the sample of college students they examined, students who did three or more of specific artistic activities (painting, sculpture, playing musical instruments, writing poetry, drawing or enjoying mathematics) had higher rates of hearing voices. Consistent with this, today we find a range of prominent mathematicians, writers and musicians who hear voices, and are actually helped by their voice(s), and who provide them with novel and useful information (e.g. Malone, 2006).

Box 12.2: Bad vibrations: the Beach Boys' Brian Wilson

In an interview in *ABILITY* magazine, the creative genius behind the Beach Boys, Brian Wilson (2011), described how he has been hearing voices since he was 25 years old: 'for the past 40 years I've had auditory hallucinations in my head, all day every day, and I can't get them out. Every few minutes the voices say something derogatory to me, which discourages me a little bit, but I have to be strong enough to say to them, "Hey, would you quit stalking me? F*** off! Don't talk to me – leave me alone!" I have to say these types of things all day long. It's like a fight.' He describes how 'I dread the derogatory voices I hear during the afternoon. They say things like, "You are going to die soon", and I have to deal with those negative thoughts. But it's not as bad as it used to be'.

In terms of his explanation for the voices, he notes that 'I'd taken some psychedelic drugs, and then about a week after that I started hearing voices, and they've never stopped. For a long time I thought to myself, "Oh, I can't deal with this." But I learned to deal with it anyway'.

Although the voices at times have become so overwhelming that he didn't want to be alive anymore, Wilson describes that he got through this because 'my friends constantly assure me I'm going to be okay ... and they will help me through it'. In terms of other coping strategies, he notes that 'When I'm on stage, I try to combat the voices by singing really loud. When I'm not on stage, I play my instruments all day, making music for people. Also, I kiss my wife and kiss my kids. I try to use love as much as possible.'

He also reports how 'I've been seeing a psychiatrist once a week for 12 years now, and he's become a really close friend of mine. We talk and he helps me out. He tells me, "Well when you hear the voices, why don't you make a joke and say to them, 'How are you doing, Voices? How are you doing today?' You know, talk humorously to them." I tried that out and it works a little bit.' Wilson also takes medication for his voices and notes that it 'dulls you a little bit at first, but once you get used to it, it doesn't bother your creative process'. In another interview, his wife Melinda stresses: 'The inner strength that it takes for him to get up every day to deal with the voices in his head ... he's not this meek, weak person people think he is ... Brian is strong. He chose to live' (Powell, 2008).

Although Wilson (2011) identifies psychedelic drugs as a cause of his voices, we may note that in his autobiography Wilson (1996) gives more details on who the voice he hears is: 'Permutations of my dead father's voice filled my head' (p. 15). Given what we discussed in Chapter 11, you can probably guess what is coming

Box 12.2: (cont.)

next. Wilson (ibid.) describes that during his childhood his father
was 'volatile, unpredictable, violent' (p. 27). He recalls how his
father forced him to defecate on the floor in front of him, and made
his mother watch, too, which made Brian feel 'beaten, abused,
soiled' (p. 28). He notes that 'I've never forgotten this incident . . .
the anger has never gone away' (ibid.). He also notes that, aged
eight, 'My dad yelled at or beat me so often that all he had to do
was look at me and I'd flinch' (p. 31). Given this, perhaps the
Maastricht approach to voices (see below), might help this musical
genius deal with his voices and the potential emotional issues
attached to them, in addition to short-term strategies of
distraction.

Voices may thus help us find parts of 'ourselves' which we cannot
consciously access, and further study of this may help shed light on the
creative process. An intriguing example here is a contemporary case,
reported in the BMJ, in which an otherwise healthy woman started to
hear voices telling her to get a brain scan for a tumour. Eventually she
persuaded her doctor to give her a brain scan, which actually did find a
tumour that was subsequently removed. After this, the voices stopped
(Azuonye, 1997). The issues surrounding voices and creativity, with
voice-hearers in some cases even being dictated books by their voices,
starts to raise profound questions about the relation between thought,
consciousness, self and hearing voices. A greater and more detailed
philosophical consideration of this area is much needed.

**What should we be doing? Changing meanings,
changing treatments**

Meaning is as important as medicine in recovery. As Thomas, Bracken &
Leudar (2004) note, 'A concern with meaning makes it possible for us to
wonder at how the person integrates puzzling and distressing experience
within his or her life. We may then understand how some people cope
with their experiences [voices], and others do not. From this point on
recovery becomes a possibility' (p. 22). The twin pillars of the meaning
the Hearing Voices Movement has given to voices may be seen to be that
(1) voices are not a sign of pathology in themselves, instead it is the
failure to cope with them that leads to illness, and (2) that they reflect
meaningful emotional issues in the voice-hearer's life. Such pillars can be
seen to greater or lesser degrees in a range of talking therapies for voices.

Cognitive behavioural therapy for AVHs

The most widely employed psychological therapy for AVH is cognitive behavioural therapy (CBT). Indeed, in the United Kingdom the National Institute for Health and Clinical Excellence (2009) now recommends that CBT is offered to all patients diagnosed with schizophrenia. CBT interventions are built on cognitive models of voice-hearing in which it is the appraisal of voices rather than the voices per se that is seen as the primary cause of distress (e.g. Byrne et al., 2006; Chadwick & Trower, 2006). Therefore it is the distress associated with hearing voices that is the primary target of treatment, rather than attempting to eliminate the voices. As such, CBT for AVHs is typically built around creating links between a client's cognitive appraisals of their voices and their emotional and behavioural responses. In such CBT, normalisation of voice-hearing can help the client with anxiety associated with the experience of hearing voices. Going beyond this, CBT aims to facilitate the voice-hearer to test out their dysfunctional beliefs about the voice's level of power and control, and to undertake behavioural experiments to establish that not doing what the voice commands does not result in physical harm or punishment (Byrne et al., 2006). Coping strategies such as distraction may also be employed, as well as many of the techniques that voice-hearers themselves have developed to cope with their voices (see Farhall, Greenwood & Jackson, 2007, for a review of such coping techniques and their effectiveness).

Based on individual case-reports it appears that CBT for voice-hearing is effective in the short term at least. For example, Byrne et al. (2006) give the example of 'Janice', a 28-year-old woman, married with two children. Her voices appear to have developed at the age of 12 as a form of friendship, due to her being a lonely, isolated child. At this time they were helpful and comforting companions. At the age of 15 she was raped violently by her then boyfriend, but would not go to the police for fear of what her parents would say. She became pregnant and was encouraged by her family to have an abortion. It was shortly after the termination that her voices turned nasty and have continued to be this way to the time she presented for CBT. Here she reported that the voices commanded her to hurt herself and others (e.g. 'put your head in the oven', 'cut yourself'). They also threatened her daughter ('I will get her'). In addition, the voices commented critically and abusively on Janice ('you're not doing that properly', 'you're a stupid cow'). Her therapist worked on a range of techniques with Janice, including distraction techniques (e.g. keeping busy), problem solving (if the voices commanded her to burn herself in the kitchen, then leave the room and go into the garden), self-care (sleeping well and taking medication). Janice saw her voices as being more powerful than her (comparing herself to a mouse and her voice to a monster). Therapy involved the therapist asking Janice to run round the room, then when she did not, asking her in a sterner voice to do it. This helped Janice see she could choose not to act on the voices commands. Janice's beliefs that the voices could harm her were then challenged, for example by the therapist directly challenging Janice's voice to cut off the therapist's finger (Janice reported the voices went silent). Janice was also taught to ask the voices for evidence of their claims, and to see that the voices' threats did not actually materialise in the world. The relation between the voices and Janice's trauma was also explored, and the hypothesis examined that the content of the voices might reflect Janice's own feelings about herself. Janice confirmed this, saying that it was sometimes hard to work out what was herself and what was the voices. As she said, 'It's really eerie trying to work out which part is me and which part is the voices' (p. 82). It was proposed that a lack of nurture as a child led to the benevolent voices, with the trauma being responsible for them turning nasty. After 27 sessions of CBT, Janice reported feeling stronger, more confident and more knowledgeable about the voices (and superior to them), although at 12-month follow-up this had changed for the worse, being much like when she had entered therapy. This case was also complicated by the fact that Janice was also simultaneously having ECT for depression, which made it harder for her to concentrate and remember. It was also notable that Janice also found that during therapy her voices stopped when she took a new antipsychotic medication. When this happened Janice missed her voices, even the negative ones, stating: 'I've got no-one to talk to now' and 'nobody wants to know me now the voices have gone' (p. 83). However, after a stressful visit to see her children, the voices returned.

Although case-studies like the above, as well as non-controlled trials, have found CBT for AVHs to be effective (e.g. Morrison, 2001), when we turn to evidence garnered from studies with the gold standard of design, randomised controlled trials (RCTs), the evidence for CBT's effectiveness becomes much weaker. In the past decade, as far as I can see, there have been seven RCTs which have reported on the effectiveness of CBT for AVHs. Three of these found no evidence that CBT was more effective than control groups (e.g. psychoeducation, supportive counselling, treatment as usual) for the treatment of AVHs (Cather et al., 2005; Durham et al., 2003; Lewis et al., 2002). However, all of these used total scores on the PSYRATS-AH as their outcome measure, hence potentially missing specific facets of voices that were improved by CBT. Furthermore, these three studies all used CBT for psychosis, rather than CBT specifically tailored for voices. Two other studies, both of which were RCTs for CBT for psychosis, have examined changes in scores on the three subscales of the PSYRATS-AH (physical, emotional, and cognitive). Valmaggia *et al.* (2005) found that although CBT led to greater reductions in participants' scores on the physical and cognitive subscales of the PSYRATS-AH, neither of these gains was maintained at six-month follow-up. Although Morrison *et al.* (2004b) found that their CBT group had lower scores than their control group on all three subscales of the PSYRATS-AH, only lower scores on the cognitive subscale were maintained at 12-month follow-up. Morrison and colleagues also found that whereas in the control group there was no change in the percentage of patients who were hallucination-free pre- and post-treatment (50%), in the CBT group the percentage of hallucination-free patients increased from 39 per cent to 63 per cent, suggesting that CBT might actually be able to eliminate voices. Though, at 12-month follow-up, only 46 per cent were still hallucination-free. However, the Morrison *et al.* study did not use a non-CBT therapy control group (instead just using a waiting list control), limiting our ability to attribute the therapeutic effects to CBT specifically.

In another RCT for CBT for psychosis, which used a different outcome measure (the Beliefs About Voices Questionnaire; (BAVQ) (Chadwick, Lees & Birchwood, 2000)), Peters *et al.* (2010) found that neither the malevolence nor omnipotence of voices was reduced, compared to controls, in the CBT group. Although resistance to voices was reduced, this was not maintained at three-month follow-up. Thus, CBT for psychosis has little unambiguous empirical evidence for its benefit for those with AVHs compared to control conditions. One reason for this may be that the percentage of time in CBT for psychosis sessions that actually focus on voices can be in the mid-to-low single digits (Farhall *et al.*, 2009), with voice-hearers bringing different goals to therapy, such as social functioning. However, one RCT has examined the effects of CBT specifically designed for those with voices on their AVHs. Trower *et al.* (2004) gave cognitive therapy for command hallucinations (CTCH) to fifteen voice-hearers and compared the effects of this to a group of seventeen patients who received treatment as usual. At the end of the six months of CBT (sixteen sessions per patient) the omnipotence of voices had decreased (as assessed by the BAVQ), as had the distress associated with the voices (PSYRATS-AH: Distress), and frequency of the voices (PSYRATS-AH: Frequency). Voice hearers also rated themselves as having more control over their voices

(PSYRATS-AH: Control). However, at six-month follow-up, only the omnipotence, control over voices and VPD power remained significantly reduced.

It hence appears that CBT tailored specifically for certain types of disturbing voices may be more effective than CBT for psychosis per se. However, certain facets of voices, such as their malevolence, seem stubbornly resistant to CBT. Given the role of trauma we have seen in this chapter, it may be that the voices may be a secondary problem to other emotional issues in the voice-hearer's life, and that CBT should focus on addressing issues surrounding any potential underlying trauma (trauma-focused CBT) or emotional problems, rather than initially target the voices themselves. Of course, this depends on what the client own goals are for therapy.

In addition to the reasons already outlined, why may CBT be failing to impact upon the voices of voice-hearers, according to these RCTs? Why may formal RCTs of CBT be appearing to show disappointing results? One potential reason is that the small sample sizes employed by many of these studies have resulted in their being under-powered, only allowing the detection of large-effect sizes. This would allow that CBT is effective for AVHs, but that existing studies have not been large enough to detect this. Another potential reason that voices may be resistant to CBT is because CBT is resistant to voices. CBT, in contrast to the Maastricht Approach (see below) may still be viewing voices as 'the enemy'. Indeed, the terminology used is often reminiscent of a battle about to commence, with Birchwood & Trower (2006) referring to the 'armamentarium of CBT' (p. 107). Furthermore, we may be erring by assessing the success of such CBT for voice-hearers by focusing on the changes in voices themselves. As Pérez-Álvarez et al. (2008) have noted, the effectiveness of CBT has typically been assessed according to criteria more akin to that of medication, which is the reduction or elimination of voices, rather than a genuine acceptance that full recovery can be achieved whilst still hearing voices. Although more recent CBT work appears to be moving away from this approach, it remains to be seen how this can lead to improved assistance for distressed voice-hearers.

Other psychotherapeutic techniques

In contrast to standard CBT, another psychotherapeutic technique for voices appears particularly promising, as it builds on the findings discussed in Chapter 11 which suggest that guilt and shame play an important role in AVHs. Hence, this appears to get closer to the core issues associated with many voices. Compassionate Mind Training

(CMT) (Gilbert & Irons, 2005) builds on the idea that people with high levels of shame find it hard to be self-supporting or self-reassuring, in part because they have never learned to be this way, due to their history of being shamed and criticised. By helping such people to develop self-compassion and self-soothing, perceived threats can be reduced. In one application of this technique to voice-hearers, Mayhew & Gilbert (2008) found that CMT 'had a major effect on voice-hearers' hostile voices, changing them into more reassuring, less persecutory and less malevolent voices' (p. 133). The first participant in their study was notable, given the discussion above relating to shame, in that he 'had a sexual secret that he was ashamed of, that led him to worry about others discovering this secret and then punishing and rejecting him' (p. 121). The third participant heard a voice telling him he was a paedophile. Both these voice-hearers' back stories echo the case study of Dodgson & Gordon (2009) discussed in Chapter 10, again suggesting that guilt and shame may be central to voice-hearing. By practising compassionate thoughts, and bringing to mind compassionate images that helped them create these compassionate thoughts, the clients in this study found their voices became less negative.

Although a very small scale study (N = 3), both the promising results of this study, combined with the congruence of its theory with the findings discussed in Chapter 11, suggest large-scale trials of this intervention are justified. It also has the advantage of being consistent with the reports of some voice-hearers themselves, who state that a key part of their recovery was when they were able to find themselves 'not-guilty' in relation to the abuse they had suffered. As Coleman (2000) puts it in regard to a fellow voice-hearer, Jenny, he was working with, 'she had to find herself innocent of any fault within the abuse . . . It did not matter that I like many others told Jenny that she was the victim in this situation what mattered is what Jenny thought . . . [she] had to put herself on trial and in order to do this had to go through the experience again and again from every conceivable angle until she could say with real conviction I am innocent' (p. 76).

Other related cognitive therapies and techniques have also been developed and tested for voice-hearing, although these have not been empirically tested to the extent that formal CBT has. These include Acceptance and Commitment Therapy (Bach & Hayes, 2002) and mindfulness training (Chadwick, Taylor & Abba, 2005). Acceptance and Commitment Therapy (ACT) is particularly notable for differing from CBT by not attempting to change voice-hearers' beliefs about their voices. Instead ACT first aims to get voice-hearers to accept their voices, i.e. not to suppress or avoid them, or to struggle or fight with them, but to 'just notice' them. This approach hence takes seriously the Archbishop of Canterbury, Rowan Williams' (2003) observation that 'the real hell is never to be able to rest from the labours of self-defence' (p. 48). Second, ACT aims to allow voice-hearers to commit to taking action based on their own life goals, rather than on the commands of the voices (Bach & Hayes, 2002). The interested reader should consult these papers for more details, or consult the excellent paper of Pérez-Álvarez *et al.* (2008) for a lively and stimulating review. Going beyond such cognitive therapies, more radical techniques advocate active engagement with the voice hearer's voices. This arises from the Maastricht approach to hearing voices, to which we turn next.

The Maastricht approach

The 'Maastricht approach' developed by some of the leading figures in the Hearing Voices Movement has the meaning of the experience of hearing voices at its heart (see Box 12.3). In this approach, tools such as the *Maastricht Hearing Voices Interview* (Romme & Escher, 2000) or Coleman & Smith's (1997) workbook, *Working with Voices: From Victim to Victor*, can be used to create links between each of the voice-hearers' voices and events in their life. This involves actively listening to the content of voice-hearer's voices, and trying to understand their meaning in the context of the voice-hearers' life. To take an example here, one voice-hearer reports how their voices had uncovered a number of uncomfortable things he had been trying to avoid thinking or feeling, such as that he had problems with relating to other people, self-confidence, sexuality and anxiety, and that 'the voices had in fact been right' (Romme *et al.*, 2009, p. 109). He thus used the voices to spur changing his life for the better, after having forgiven the voices and asking them for forgiveness in turn (note here a use of an approach similar to Compassionate Mind Training). This individual also notes that by his psychiatrist giving him the minimum amount of medication he is able to function and enjoy life, rather than being given the high doses which make him unable to function at all.

Within this approach the appropriate form of treatment depends on the stage at which the voice-hearer is. Romme & Escher (2000) argue that there are three phases of voice-hearing. The first is the startling phase, which is when the voice-hearer is still overwhelmed by the voices, leading to confusion. At this stage the voice-hearer is unlikely to be able to talk about their voices and their content, as the voices may forbid it, or will punish them for talking about them by becoming louder. At this stage the 'construct' of the Maastricht approach cannot yet be

Box 12.3: The Maastricht approach to hearing voices

The Maastricht approach to hearing voices is built on three tenets: (1) The phenomenon of hearing voices is more prevalent in the general population than was previously believed, (2) voice-hearing is a personal reaction to life stresses, whose meaning and purpose can be deciphered, with the voice often taking the form of a metaphor, and (3) voices are best considered a dissociative experience, and not a psychotic symptom. Given this, a medication only approach which rejects the proposed meaningfulness of voices is seen not only to reject the voices, but also the person. The approach stresses how voice-hearers who come to psychiatric services have become stuck in destructive communication patterns with their voices. The Maastricht approach looks for a way for people to change their relations with their voices, make sense of them, and hence cope better.

A key tool in this approach is the Maastricht Hearing Voices Interview (Romme & Escher, 2000), which aims to structure information relating to the voice-hearer and their voices. It is completed in conjunction with the voice-hearer and helps them to explore their own experiences, achieve distance from the voices and plan treatment. The interview includes sections on the characteristics of the voices, personal history of voice-hearing (e.g. 'What were the personal and social circumstances when the voices appeared for the first time?'), what the voices say, triggers, the impact of the voices on life, one's balance of relationship with one's voices, coping strategies and experiences in childhood.

The authors report that the interview itself can be a significant step in the process of recovery, and can have a therapeutic effect itself, because voice-hearers became 'aware of the meaning of their voices, the relationship with their emotions and important issues in their lives, and felt stimulated to try other coping strategies'. From the interview two questions are then to be answered, 'who do the voices represent?' and 'what problems do the voices represent?' This 'breaks the code' of the voices and results in what is termed the 'construct'. This is achieved by an active collaboration between the voice-hearer and professional. This then forms the basis for treatment, which has three goals: (1) to identify the most hindering aspects of the voices, choose a strategy and practise this method, (2) to improve the voice-hearer's relationship with difficult emotions and adopt alternative coping mechanisms for dealing with those emotions, and (3) to deal with the historical events that have been difficult to accept, and work through the associated anxiety and guilt.

(Taken from Corstens, Escher & Romme, 2008)

introduced, although the interview may be done. Key treatments here are anxiety management, providing information, trying medication and social support (ibid.).

The second of Romme & Escher's phases of voice-hearing is the organisation phase, where the voice-hearer has grown more used to their voices and is looking for ways to deal with them. Here the 'construct' can be discussed and developed with the voice-hearer. Recommended treatment here can involve a range of CBT techniques (although we have seen problems with the effectiveness of such techniques in this chapter), rebalancing the voice-hearer's power relation with their voices, and gaining insight into their personal meaning. The third phase is the stabilisation phase. This is where the relation between the person and their voices is more balanced. Here the voices are felt to belong to the voice-hearer, because 'what they say clearly applies to them' (p. 60). At this stage, treatment works by solving problems in daily life linked to the voices, recognising social disempowerment, rebuilding social networks and achieving independence (ibid.). In my view, this is likely to be particularly important if trauma is related to the voices because, as Herman (2001) notes, the central experiences of psychological trauma are disempowerment and disconnection from others.

One specific technique that has evolved out of the Hearing Voices Movement is that of voice dialogue (Hayward & May, 2007; Moskowitz & Corstens, 2007; Romme & Escher, 1993).[12] In this technique, the therapist asks permission from the voice-hearer to speak directly to his or her voices, and then proceeds to respectfully 'interview' the voice as one might a new acquaintance (Moskowitz & Corstens, 2007). The timing and reasons for the voice coming into being, its relation to the person, and what it 'wants' are all explored. This is repeated for all voices (that allow contact), with the person usually taking a seat in a different chair in the room for each voice they speak to. The results of this intervention can include a decrease in the perceived 'destructiveness' of the voices, including a transformation from 'negative' to 'positive' voices with increased understanding from the person, along with an increased capacity (and willingness) to dialogue with the voices. Corstens (in Moskowitz & Corstens, 2007) notes that from his work with this technique, no person has so far become more psychotic, and quality of life is sometimes substantially improved (see Box 12.4 for an example). This technique can only be done if the person can have a dialogue with their voices, which as we saw in Chapter 4,

---

[12] Reports of similar techniques can also be found in earlier literature (e.g. Van Dusen, 1972).

Box 12.4: An example of the Voice Dialogue technique

'Karen', although hearing voices since her childhood, had a steady job and coped well until, when aged 20, she joined a religious sect. The sect told her that her voices were 'instruments of the devil' and that she should get rid of them. The four male voices she heard then became more negative and disturbing, commenting on her behaviour and her thinking, and telling her to kill herself. After having received a range of diagnoses including schizophrenia and borderline personality disorder, spending four years living in a psychiatric hospital, where antipsychotic medication helped her anxiety but not her voices, she presented for treatment.

The first session started with the therapist asking Karen for her permission to talk to her voices. She agreed, and the therapist interviewed each voice in turn. Each voice reported that they entered into Karen's life when she was aged four, a time when she was feeling quite lonely and had been sexually abused. The voices said their job was to help Karen feel less lonely and overcome difficult moments. Before the sect had made her reject the voices, Karen had accepted the voices and they felt acknowledged. But when Karen began to reject her voices, so they too rejected her – becoming very negative and telling her to kill herself. The voices told the therapist that they wanted Karen to accept them again, as she used to do. Karen, who was able to 'overhear' the therapist talking to the voices, agreed and began setting aside time in the evening to engage with the voices.

By the next session, two of the voices had disappeared, and those that remained were easy to ignore. The voices became more positive, no longer criticising Karen or telling her to kill herself. Therapy ended a few sessions later. When Karen contacted the therapist four years later, she reported that she was happy and living with her two young children in a new city. She had not been psychiatrically hospitalised, but still took a very low dose of antipsychotic medication. She only heard one voice, but it was positive and supportive and she liked talking to it.

(from Moskowitz & Corstens, 2007)

many can. However, as Trower *et al.* (2004) have noted, some voice-hearers may be afraid of communicating information about their voices, fearing that the voices will harm them for doing this. Similarly, other voice-hearers' voices may specifically tell them not to disclose their presence to others, and not to tell others about what they say. This echoes the historical example of Joan of Arc (Chapter 1), whose voices appear to have told her not to communicate certain things to the court. Although talking directly to one's voices is anathema to the traditional psychiatric approach, in addition to these case-reports, and Romme and colleagues' published stories of recovery (e.g. Romme *et al.*, 2009), there are a number of peer-reviewed studies that provide evidence suggesting that this may be a useful approach. For example, Nayani & David (1996) found that voice-hearers who *could not* talk to their voices were more distressed than those who could. Additionally, Romme *et al.*'s approach suggests that if, in addition to a dominant negative voice, the voice-hearer also hears a positive voice in the background, they could be encouraged to use this as an ally against the negative voice. Again, although traditionally this would be seen as feeding into the patient's problems, recall here the study of Jenner *et al.* (2008) discussed in Chapter 4, which found patients with positive voices could use them as an ally against their negative voices. In conclusion, although this technique appears promising, engaging as it does with the emotions and voices of the voice-hearer, there have been no published randomised controlled trials of the effectiveness of this approach yet, and its effectiveness hence remains to be established in this manner.

Another technique which is employed by the Maastricht approach is that of re-authoring lives. This draws on the work of Michael White (see Stewart, 1998). In this approach, one asks questions so that the voice-hearer starts to see the voices as personalities. This helps them see the voices as the expression of a specific background, with it being 'their history that gives the voices identity' (Romme & Escher, 2000, p. 87). White observed that voices spoke as experts to the voice-hearer, acting as if they did not need to justify their views, or disclose the source of their authority. In order to remedy this, White advised that voice-hearers 'expose' (ibid.) the voice, asking it about its purpose and motive to aid de-authorising it. This helps change the voice-hearer's relation with their voices (ibid.). Moving beyond the voices themselves, core to Escher & Romme's (2010) work with children who hear voices is working with the voice hearer's emotions. If children have not been allowed to express their anger or sadness, for example, by working with them on these emotions the voices may disappear or change their relationship with the child to a more positive footing.

In summary, an approach which assumes the content of voices to be meaningful, engages directly with the voices, works with the underlying emotions of the voice-hearer, recognises voice-hearers as experts on their experience, encourages hearing voices groups and offers training to professionalise voice-hearers, appears promising. Such an approach appears likely to be more effective than an impoverished approach involving antipsychotic medication alone, accompanied by techniques that many psychiatric nurses have told me they were trained to employ;

namely, if a patient reports hearing a voice, then distract them by playing Scrabble. Again, though, as I have stressed earlier, wider recognition of the effectiveness of the Maastricht approach is likely to require random-ised controlled trials of its effectiveness. However, evidence of effective-ness alone may be insufficient for the widespread implementation of an approach, and here we may briefly turn to the informative example of the Soteria study.

Soteria

In Chapter 1 we encountered the fourth-century desert monk, Evagrius Ponticus, the originator of the concept of deadly sins. The Soteria study, according to its designer, Loren Mosher (1933–2004), commit-ted the four deadly sins of psychiatry: 'demedicalizing madness, de-hospitalizing people, de-psychopharmacologizing, and de-professional-izing' (Mosher, 1997, as cited in Johnstone, 2000, p. 212). Soteria (from the Greek for deliverance/salvation) was a community-based, experimental residential treatment run in the San Francisco Bay area in the 1970s and 1980s. It drew on the power of human relationships, was not run by doctors and nurses, tried to use antipsychotic medica-tion as infrequently as possible, ideally not at all, and offered an alternative for patients to hospitalisation (not a follow-up to it). The non-professional staff did not wear uniforms, aimed to provide a simple home-like atmosphere, were taught, and believed, that human involve-ment and understanding were critical to healing interactions. They were not there to observe in experimental fashion, but were there to 'be-with' the patients (like an LSD trip guide might be), working 36–48-hour shifts to facilitate this. There were no locks on the doors, restraints or seclusion rooms. The contextual restraints were that every-one should be treated with dignity and respect, have sanctuary, quiet, safety, support and protection, and that the atmosphere be imbued with hope. The rules that there were forbade violence, and did not allow 'tourists' or illegal drugs into the house (for a full description, see Mosher & Hendrix, 2004).

This all sounds very nice and 'right-on', and many would be sceptical about such an approach. What differentiated this study from many other earlier attempts to treat individuals diagnosed with schizophrenia in this manner was that it was a rigorous scientific study. The study recruited first-episode patients diagnosed (using DSM guidelines) with schizo-phrenia. Patients in a first cohort (n = 79) were first assigned to either Soteria or standard medical treatment on a consecutive space available basis. Patients in a second cohort (n = 100) were randomly allocated to one of these conditions. This resulted in 82 patients being treated at Soteria and 97 with standard medical treatment. After six weeks both groups showed significant improvement, and to a comparable degree (Mosher & Menn, 1978; Mosher, Vallone & Menn, 1995). Notably, whereas nearly all of those in the standard medical treatment condition were given continuous doses of antipsychotic medication, only 24 per cent received some at Soteria, and only 16 per cent received a substantial dose (>7 days treatment). At two-year follow-up (68 Soteria patients, 61 controls) it was found that patients in the Soteria group had a significantly better global outcome, with a 20 per cent greater chance of being in the lowest psychopathology category, and being less likely to have been re-admitted.

However, this study was criticised on a number of grounds. Carpenter & Buchanan (2002) argued that the Soteria study was 'based on an anti-medication model and anti-disease model ideology. These are not valid models ... and invalid models should not be the basis for the diagnosis and treatment of this most severe of human illnesses' (p. 577). However, criticism of the philosophy of the project is not a criticism of its results. Second, Carpenter & Buchanan argue that a study by Carpenter *et al.* (1990, as cited by Carpenter & Buchanan, 2002) had shown that continuous mainten-ance antipsychotic treatment was more effective than targeted drug treatment for relapse prevention. However, a study of Lehtinen *et al.* (2000) has provided evidence that points in the other direction. The Lehtinen study devised an experimental group in which a 'minimal neuroleptics use' regime was used. In the first three weeks after admission neuroleptic drug treatment, whenever possible, was not started. If the patient's condition had clearly improved during this initial phase, drug use was postponed even further or avoided totally. This condition was then compared to another condition where neu-roleptics were used as per usual practice, which in most cases meant immediate use. Both groups also received treatment by the psycho-therapeutic and family-centred principles of the Finnish treatment model. At two-year follow-up, the two groups were comparable on all outcome measures except that the experimental group actually had significantly less hospital re-admission, had a significantly higher level of global functioning and showed a trend towards showing less psych-otic symptoms. Carpenter & Buchanan's third argument was that 'no evidence for recovery is presented. The study criteria for recovery was staying off drugs'. However, Mosher and colleagues did present data on levels of psychopathology and outcome measures which did not include whether the patient stayed on drugs or not.

Conclusion

The lessons of Soteria are multiple, and amongst them is that sometimes evidence just isn't enough. The Soteria study makes it clear that alternative forms of meanings and treatments will face resistance from traditional approaches. Given that many in the Hearing Voices Movement understand it as being a civil rights movement, this underlines an awareness that issues of power are central to the essentially political movement it represents. However, this is not to dismiss the new scientific understanding of voices that this movement can lead to and is leading towards, through a consideration of the role of trauma in voices, and new interventions based on engagement with the voice hearer's voices and emotions. How the relation will evolve between the existing organs of meaning, treatment and research, and the Hearing Voices Movement and voice-hearers more generally, is unclear. In particular, the argument that voice-hearers need emancipating is likely to prove contentious, especially when applied to voice-hearers who have been given a diagnosis of schizophrenia, present with a range of other complaints (delusions, thought disorder etc.) and are in significant distress. Furthermore, the diversity of views of voice-hearers and those within the Hearing Voices Movement as to the meaning of voices means it will face the typical internal problems of any political organisation, which may impact upon its interactions with establishment organisations.

We have seen a range of explanation thus far, but what meanings might we still be missing? To my eyes there is still a lack of focus on the distal social causes that engender AVHs. Yes, abuse seems to play a role in the aetiology of voices, but what societal factors encourage abuse to occur? Here the nature of hierarchical Western capitalist societies need to come under scrutiny, with powerlessness, unemployment, income inequality (Wilkinson & Pickett, 2009) and their affective and behavioural consequences, clearly being relevant to an understanding of the causes of voices. The attitude that a given society breeds in us towards ourselves, others, as well as to the very planet we live on (Jensen, 2000), shows us that a consideration of the meaning and causes of voices must lead far, far beyond the brain.

Chapter 12: summary of key points

- The meaning of voice-hearing remains contested, as it has throughout history.
- Voice-hearers are now re-claiming their voices and experiences in a movement which has clear parallels to both the women's liberation movement and decolonisation struggles.

- Hearing voices is not an illness per se, but the inability to cope with the experience can lead to illness.
- Voice-hearers need to be recognised by mental health professionals as potential experts on their own experiences.
- New voice-hearers who are distressed by their experiences need recovered voice-hearers to continue to act as witnesses to their experiences, and as evidence of recovery.
- Mental health professionals and voice-hearers need further dialogue to help understand each other's positions better.
- Biomedical models actually increase stigma surrounding voices.
- Medication has a useful role to play in recovery.
- Randomised controlled trials of CBT show disappointing results, suggesting modifications are needed, or larger trials.
- Compassionate Mind Treatment appears a promising new technique for helping voice-hearers.
- The Maastricht approach offers a radical new approach to coping with, making sense of, and recovering from voices.
- The new technique of voice-dialogue offers a novel way to work with voices.
- These new approaches are in need of large-scale randomised controlled trials to demonstrate their effectiveness to the scientific community and policy makers.
- The meaning of voices cannot be limited to the brain, but points towards distal social factors which must also be confronted, and hence to politics.

Conclusion Moving towards new models
of hearing voices

In Norse mythology the god Odin had two ravens, Hugin ('thought') and Munin ('memory'), who flew across the world to bring him information (Orchard, 1997).[1] If voices have their roots in thought and memory, how might we use this fable to help understand the core aspects of hearing voices? First, thought and memory inhabit the world and bring their information to Odin from it. Voices, too, appear to fly to the ears of the hearer from (traumatic/emotional) events that have happened in the outside world. Second, following Baillarger,[2] it may be that the ravens bring things back the individual did not ask for or expect. Third, the birds are independent of Odin and bring things to him, yet they are also in some way part of him. Fourth, we may consider the relation between these two birds. In the previous chapters we have seen a separation between memory-based and inner speech-based models of voice-hearing. But might these creatures be the same bird? Finally, although the birds' tongues may seem foreign to those who are not Odin, if we listen carefully we may find meaning in their message.

What voices are we trying to explain?

Parsimony suggests that there should be one model to explain all types of AVHs; one explanation to rule them all, to echo Tolkien. Historically, voices have been viewed in this way, as if they are a homogeneous category of experiences which can all be explained by one model. Each new theory of hearing voices has hence been criticised by researchers for not accounting for all types of voices. But what parsimony pulls together, phenomenology can pull apart. In this book I have argued that there are phenomenologically discernible sub-types of voices, each of which may

---

[1] The idea that thought and memory can be represented as birds visiting and then returning from distant places is common in early Germanic and Celtic verse (Orchard, 1997).
[2] See Chapter 3.

Table C.1. *Type 1 and Type 2 AVHs*

Type	Characteristics	Potential intervention
Type 1a: Hypervigilance	• Reflect hyper-salient words/ phrases • Simple in form • Heard in external noise • Heard outside head	• Work on thoughts and emotions of voice-hearer • Potential for neuroleptic medication and TMS as short-term aid
Type 1b: *Ex nihilo*	• Reflect ongoing inner dialogue • Complex in form • Not dependent on external noise • May be inside or outside head	• Work on thoughts and emotions of voice-hearer • Potential for neuroleptic medication and TMS as short-term aid
Type 2a: Reactivated memories	• Not inner dialogue-related • Reflect earlier traumatic memories	• Trauma-focused CBT • EMDR
Type 2b: Random	• Not inner dialogue-related • Unrelated to current events	• Transcranial magnetic stimulation

Source: Compiled by the author.

have a different cause and hence require its own model, and its own clinical intervention where necessary. This is not to say that there is no overlap in terms of common pathways and mechanisms shared between these different types of voices, but rather that they are distinct enough to require consideration on their own.

In Chapter 7 I introduced the distinction between what I termed Type 1 (Dynamic) AVHs and Type 2 (Static) AVHs. These two types of AVHs, and their subtypes, are shown in Table C.1. To recap, Type 1 AVHs are those characterised by having content relating to the ongoing thoughts and behaviours of the voice-hearer, and typically involve commands, advice or suggestions, as well as evaluative comments. Type 1 AVHs have two sub-types: *Type 1a: Hypervigilance*, being those identified by Dodgson & Gordon (2009), which are characterised by being heard during exposure to un-patterned sound, with a perceived source/ location which is outside of the head, and *Type 1b: Ex nihilo*, which are not dependent on the presence of external sound to trigger them. It may further be possible to subdivide these Type 1b voices into those with repetitive content (a sub-type highlighted by Stephane, Polis & Barton (2001b), and those with more extended, novel content. Type 2 AVHs were defined in contradistinction to Type 1 AVHs. These voices are those identified by voice-hearers as either being memory-like in the sense that they can be seen to be verbatim memories of actual events, or being isolated fragments of voices that are unrelated to the voice-hearer's ongoing actions and life. In Chapter 11, Type 2 AVHs were more clearly divided into two types: *Type 2a: Reactivated memories*, voices that directly reflect memories of earlier traumatic events, and *Type 2b: Random*, which are voices with random content.

Type 1 AVHs appear to have their roots in the voice hearer's own thoughts/inner dialogue, and are phenomenologically consistent with the form and developmental purpose of dialogic inner speech. Type 1a AVHs are well modelled by Dodgson & Gordon's (2009) hypervigilance model, and Type 1b AVHs by forms of inner speech models. Type 2a AVHs are consistent with models derived from traumatic memory research (e.g. Brewin, 1996) and Type 2b AVHs fit into Hunter *et al.*'s (2006) model of AVHs, or epilepsy-based models.

In terms of treatment for those seeking help for distressing voices, Type 1 AVHs, given their likely root in the voice-hearer's own thoughts and emotions, appear best treated through a form of talking therapy that addresses these issues (e.g. the Maastricht approach, and psychotherapies such as Compassionate Mind Training), supported by neuroleptic medication where required. Of course, the evidence for such talking therapies still needs to be rigorously established by randomised controlled trials. Furthermore, those voices with a repetitive content, which may have their roots in many of the same cognitive processes underlying the thoughts in OCD, may successfully be helped by anti-obsessional medications, although again the evidence for this at the present time is limited. Type 2a AVHs appear best treated through techniques tailored specifically for PTSD, such as trauma-focused CBT or eye movement desensitisation and reprocessing (EMDR). Type 2b appear the most 'neurological' of the four and hence treatments such as transcranial magnetic stimulation (TMS) may be particularly suited here.

This proposal is, of course, speculative, and remains in need of empirical testing. However, it is in good company, as this book has shown that the causes of AVHs are still poorly understood, and that both many existing and developing therapies lack firm empirical support from the gold standard of evidence, randomised controlled trials. To be clear, I am not arguing that of these four types of voices (1a, 1b, 2a, 2b) only one occurs in any given individual. Indeed, these types of voices often co-occur in an individual, possibly due to the shared mechanisms involved. For example, PTSD is probably the best example of Type 1b and Type 2a AVHs co-occurring. This means a range of treatments may be needed for any given individual. If these voices are related, then we may ask why they co-occur. At present something of an iron curtain exists been between inner dialogue-based and memory-based AVHs, with these models seen as competing and mutually exclusive. It should be considered how these two models may be seen to work together.

When Hugin met Munin

We have seen evidence that traumatic/emotional events are likely at the root of a significant number of voices. Employing a memory-based model we may therefore wish to say that these are simply intrusive memories. Yet, as we noted in Chapter 10, the phenomenology of AVHs in those with trauma histories is not always that of verbatim memories, instead often being only thematically related to them. This pushes us back towards an inner speech-based account. However, can we start to link inner speech- and memory-based models together (i.e. link Type 1 and Type 2a AVHs)? One way to this may be through a consideration of what thought is like, and the role of memory in thought.

Spontaneous thought and AVHs: a role for the default network?

In Chapter 9 it was shown how neuroimaging studies of inner speech involved assessing the activation associated with a person generating a sentence or word in inner speech while in the scanner. To work out the neural activity associated with such inner speech, these studies calculate the neural activation associated with this task, then subtract the activity in the brain when the subject is simply 'at rest' in the scanner. However, it has been noted that some verbal thought is naturally also going to be occurring during this 'rest' condition (Jones & Fernyhough, 2007a). The spontaneous thought occurring in this 'rest' condition is today studied through the concept of the default network.

As Raichle (2006) has noted, less than 10 per cent of our synapses carry incoming information from the external world. It should hence be unsurprising that we spend a lot of time in our own worlds. Indeed, other methodologies have confirmed that people spend a large amount of time engaged in internally-directed spontaneous thought (Hurlburt, 1990; Singer, 1966). Such spontaneous thought is primarily about typical life events (Singer & Antrobus 1963) and can involve words, images, or meaningful thought without words or images (Hurlburt, 1990). The default network in the brain is said to underpin this form of thinking (Raichle et al., 2001). This network increases its activity when we relax our attention on the world and start to have spontaneous cognitive processes (thoughts/images) which often involve remembering the past and imagining the future (Andrews-Hanna et al., 2010b), and is then suppressed when we turn our attention to specific tasks in the world. Its activation is associated with neural activation in the middle temporal gyrus, medial prefrontal cortex, inferior parietal regions, posterior cingulate/retrosplenial cortex and hippocampal regions (Buckner, Andrews-Hanna & Schacter, 2008). Of course, a number of events could be occurring in the default network beyond thought. Hence, is it informative to examine activation specifically associated with the occurrence of spontaneous thoughts (termed 'stimulus-independent thought' or 'mind wandering'). It has been found using fMRI in healthy individuals that such thoughts are associated with activation in the bilateral STG, MTG, insula, cingulate and frontal and pre-frontal regions (Mason et al., 2007), all regions linked to AVHs (Chapter 8).

What is this default network for? Buckner & Carroll (2007) argue that it is likely to be functional and adaptive, even if it is not directed toward immediate behaviour, as evolutionarily it makes sense we must be doing something useful, as the amount of energy the brain uses in the default network is not much less than when it is doing specific tasks (Raichle & Mintun, 2006). It has been observed by Andrews-Hanna et al. (2010a) that the default network may be involved in two opposing functions: (1) internal mentation and/or (2) monitoring the external environment (the 'Sentinel Hypothesis'). Andrews-Hanna et al. (ibid.) found evidence for the former, with activity increasing in the default network when participants had spontaneous cognitions, as compared to when they attended to the external environment. It was also found that participants' spontaneous thoughts mainly involved their past and future, especially the recent past and immediate future. These results are consistent with the notion that individuals spontaneously draw on details from their past and flexibly recombine these details into novel future events. As Buckner & Vincent (2007) have observed: 'the default network engaged during passive task states is suspiciously similar to the core brain network engaged when people imagine themselves in alternative perspectives to the present, such as when remembering the past or envisioning the future' (p. 1093). Indeed, Andrews-Hanna et al. (2010a) found that spontaneous thoughts about the past and the future were associated with increased functional coupling between the medial temporal lobe (MTL) and specific cortical regions within the default network (bilateral ventromedial PFC, posterior inferior parietal lobule and the retrosplenial cortex), all corresponding to an MTL subsystem within the default network that may support memory retrieval and thoughts about the future (Andrews-Hanna et al., 2010). Consistent with this, a range of studies have found the MTL to be involved in both memory for past events (Squire, Stark & Clark, 2004), as well as the imaginative creation of new thoughts and scenarios (Hassabis *et al.*, 2007; Schacter & Addis, 2009). In terms of the function of this process, Andrews-Hanna *et al.* (2010a) note that pondering over our recent past may allow us to consolidate significant events, whereas envisioning our personal future enables us to entertain plausible future scenarios, experiencing them before they happen.

Does the default network function differently between voice-hearers and non-voice-hearers? Whilst AVHs specifically have not yet been looked at in relation to the default network (and it would be of benefit to do this), Garrity *et al.* (2007) have found differences in the default network between patients diagnosed with schizophrenia and healthy controls. First, patients showed greater deactivation in areas of the frontal gyrus involved in the default mode. Second, patients showed decreased activation in the anterior cingulate relative to comparison subjects. Third, a larger region of the parahippocampal gyrus was included in the default mode of patients versus comparison subjects. In another study comparing patients diagnosed with schizophrenia and healthy controls, Whitfield-Gabrieli *et al.* (2009) found that activity in default network regions was not suppressed as much during tasks in patients. Specifically, the medial prefrontal cortex remained more active in patients, and showed greater connectivity to other regions in the default network (e.g. the posterior cingulate). There is hence suggestive evidence that spontaneous thought, at least at a neural level, may be different in voice-hearers compared to non-voice-hearers.

Could the default network be involved in AVHs? On the one hand, given that the default network is involved in task independent thought, we would not expect it to be involved in Type 1 AVHs, which are typically related to the ongoing activities of voice-hearers. However, given Hoffman's (1986) argument that voices are often experienced as inconsistent with existing goals and discourse plans, activity in the default network could be a candidate for the production of the thoughts that form the basis for such voices. Furthermore, two of the areas noted by Garrity *et al.* (2007) as being differentially activated in the default network in patients diagnosed with schizophrenia, the parahippocampal region and the anterior cingulate, were noted in Chapter 8 as key regions involved in AVHs. We may also add that Whitfield-Gabrieli *et al.* (2009) note that the medial prefrontal cortex, which they found hyperactivated in patients diagnosed with schizophrenia, is normally activated during self-referential tasks (i.e. events in which others' actions refer to one's self). This could be seen to explain why voices are experienced as talking to the voice-hearer and being directed at them, rather than just being passively overheard.

If spontaneous thoughts generated by default network activity were to be the raw material of some AVHs, then factors that increase default network activity should be linked to increased levels of AVHs. Thus, given that loneliness and isolation appear to be likely to increase spontaneous inner mentation, we would predict these would be associated with AVHs, which indeed they are. In terms of existing theories, the concept of the default network could clearly be profitably employed in conjunction with both Hoffman's social de-afferentation model (Chapter 10; Hoffman, 2007) and his unintentional thought model (Hoffman, 1986). Yet we are still talking about thought; how might memory play a role here?

Memory and verbal thought

Research into memory has highlighted that it is typically a creative, (re-)constructive process, rather than simply a matter of retrieving exact records of previous events (Conway & Pleydell-Pearce, 2000; Schacter & Addis, 2007; Schacter, Norman & Koutstaal, 1998). Thus, when we remember, this is not like taking a DVD out of its case, popping it into the DVD player and getting a verbatim playback of what happened. Instead we actively construct events, and we construct the future much like we construct the past, using what Hassabis and colleagues have termed 'scene construction' (e.g. Hassabis et al., 2007). Indeed, Buckner & Carroll (2007) have noted the extensive overlap in the brain network activated during fMRI studies of remembering the past, thinking about the future, the 'default network' and stimulus independent thought. There is hence likely to be a complex relation between memory and ongoing verbal inner speech processes, which are not yet fully understood. With this caveat in mind, we may now try to sketch out why many AVHs can have their origin in memories (e.g. of a traumatic event), but are not typically verbatim playbacks of such events.

If memories of trauma exist, then these may be particularly influential building blocks for ongoing spontaneous cognitions about the world. Such memories could be seen to be the parasitic memories referred to by Hoffman (1986), and the 'situationally accessible memories', which have been processed outside normal mechanisms, of Brewin, Dalgleish & Joseph (1996). These memories may become key building blocks for ongoing verbal thought process involving taking the view of another (see below) on our experiences, which would then have the form of inner speech (e.g. commands, evaluative comments etc.), but are informed or flavoured by these memories. Thus a spontaneous thought relating to oneself, made from the perspective of another, may be specifically coloured, through the influence of these memories, by what an abuser, for example, would have said. There may be a form of memory–inner speech continuum which underpins different AVHs. AVHs resulting from material at the memory extreme of the continuum come to have the form of reactivated trauma memories; AVHs resulting from material at the inner speech extreme have the form of commands, comments and evaluations much like the person's own voice; and the middle ground characterised by highly activated trauma memories informing ongoing inner dialogue may result in voices with the form of inner speech, but felt to be that of an abuser, for example. If such an account could lead to an explanation of the content of many AVHs, we could then explain why such experiences are felt to be alien and have acoustic properties through the bottom-up corollary-discharge and top-down source monitoring models we discussed in Part III. Although this is a broad brush sketch, it at least suggests that a rapprochement between inner speech and memory models is possible, even if not in the exact way I have high-lighted, and that such an account may have greater explanatory power than either alone. However, much more thinking around these issues is required.

More thoughts on thought

What is most problematic for the development of any inner speech account of AVHs is that we still know next to nothing about thought itself. Until we have some idea of the nature of thought and how the brain produces it, it remains very hard to assess how unusual manifest-ations of it result in AVHs. How can we know how thoughts relate to voices until we know what thinking itself is like? We have already seen how a traditional corollary discharge account views AVHs as resulting from efference copy signals from inner speech productions in left Broca's area not being communicated correctly to the left speech perception regions of the brain, but what other accounts may we consider?

A good starting place for a brief consideration of some of the issues here is the theory of Morton Prince, mentioned in Chapter 3. Prince proposed the idea that AVHs resulted from our main personality hearing the thought of a sub-personality. This account has a nagging sense of phenomenological resonance with Type 1 AVHs. For instance, recall from the Introduction that Aldous Huxley talked of strange psycho-logical creatures leading an autonomous existence, and the individual within the context of Islam in Chapter 6 who talked of the 'creatures in our heads'. By locating the source of the voice in a separate cognitive centre, this would explain how voices can be autonomous from our normal stream of consciousness. However, such an account has many limitations. An obvious problem is that it assumes that there is a core self, which many philosophers of mind would disagree with, instead arguing that there is simply a narrative centre of gravity (Dennett, 1991) which solders thoughts into a coherent but illusory sense of self. In such a model, thoughts are not produced by the self in the first place. Here we may return to argument from Chapter 9 that voices may be experienced as non-self produced because they (and indeed all thoughts) *are* non-self produced. Stephens & Graham (2000), drawing on Frankfurt's (2007) observation as noted earlier (Chapter 9), that some thoughts are not thought by us, but only found to be incurring in us, to conclude that we are just passive bystanders to some of our thoughts and that there are thoughts which are not ones '*we think* at all, but rather thought which we *find* occurring in us' (p. 59, emphasis in original). They conclude that the sense of mental agency for our thoughts comes from whether or not a person is convinced that such thoughts represent his intentional state (i.e. his own beliefs and desires). If we are alienated from thoughts, then AVHs result. What this account implies is that thoughts start off not being ours, and that we create mental agency for this by working them into ourselves at a later time. This can be tied into a Buddhist approach in which there are 'thoughts without a thinker' (Epstein, 1999). Indeed, a greater appreciation of Buddhist philosophy of mind may help voice-hearers cope better with their voices/thoughts, and indeed this forms the backbone of third-generation cognitive behavioural therapy in which mindfulness plays a central role (e.g. Chadwick, Taylor & Abba, 2005).

Consistent with this account, work with split-brain patients (in whom the corpus callosum which joins the two hemispheres of the brain together has been cut for medical reasons) has led to the proposal that we have an 'interpreter' module in our left hemisphere which is responsible for weaving together a coherent narrative and sense of self from the diverse events that happen to us (Gazzaniga & LeDoux, 1978). However, split-brain studies have also found that the two hemispheres of the brain are able to have different 'personalities', so to speak. For example, Gazzaniga & LeDoux (1978) report how the patient P.S. when asked what he would like to be, responded (via his left hemisphere which can generate speech) that he would like to be a draughtsman. However, although P.S.'s right hemisphere could not speak, it was able to give responses by spelling out answers using Scrabble tiles. When his right hemisphere was asked what it wanted to be, the answer given was 'automobile race', presumably meaning 'it' wanted to be a racing driver. Here we start to move away from a position where all thoughts start off equal to a model where thoughts generated in specific regions of the brain may be less consistent with our centre of narrative gravity than others.

Locating the origin of voices in the speech productions of the homo-logue of Broca's area in the 'silent' right hemisphere (i.e. on the opposite side of the brain to our normal speech production area) is one way to operationalise Prince's theory. Such a model feels right, given that we want to acknowledge that voices come from within, and yet are still not part of 'us'.[3] Sommer & Diederen (2009), building on their research group's most recent large scale neuroimaging studies (reviewed in Chapter 8), which show right Broca's area activation during AVHs, have proposed voices to originate in the right hemisphere homologue of Broca's area. They also note some phenomenological accords between AVHs and the speech that can be created by the right hemisphere in patients with severe aphasia, which are often repetitive, simple, 'automatic speech' utterances, with little variation, which often consist of terms of abuse or swear words. However, whilst some AVHs have this phenomenology, not all do, and we may need to postulate that these right hemisphere auto-matic speech productions are able to become more complex over time (Nayani & David, 1996). However, the automatic speech idea is consist-ent with the form of many AVHs which are typically, as Bleuler noted (Chapter 3), short utterances (and not sermons by the voice) or take the form of a dialogue with the voice-hearer. Given that answers are often inherent in questions, it is fairly simple to understand how voices could be easily created in response to questions from the voice-hearer. Hence, this appears a promising account of AVHs. We could also tie this account into J. J. Gibson's (1977) concept of affordances noted in Chapter 9. Here the affordances of objects could potentially generate automatic speech in the right hemisphere (e.g. pick up the cup) which is experienced as an AVH. This proposal could be empirically tested by seeing if objects with obvious affordances (e.g. cutlery) trigger AVHs in those with frequent AVHs more than objects which less clearly afford actions (e.g. a scrap of paper). How-ever, even when we have offered an account of the non-self nature of AVHs, it still remains to be explained why the voice is experienced as that of another person with specific acoustic properties.

Becoming the other

As we saw in Chapter 9, Hoffman (1986) has argued that it is problem-atic to tell whether certain properties of AVHs are inherent to them

---

[3] As we noted in Chapter 1, Julian Jaynes (2000) proposed such a theory (albeit locating the source of the voices in right Wernicke's, not right Broca's area).

(α properties) or are added on later by relatively automatic inference processes (β-manifold). One such property is the identity of the speaker of the voice. As we have seen, a number of theories have proposed that the raw material of AVHs is inner speech conceptualised as speaking silently in our own voice, which then somehow is misinterpreted as another's voice (i.e. is part of the β-manifold), and gets grammatically transformed (i.e. from one's first-person voice into 'he/she'). In line with such theories, we might suggest that if the raw material of at least some AVHs are coarse, vulgar, automatic speech productions from the right hemisphere, then these are likely to be interpreted as being those of people who have said similar things in the past, e.g. an abuser. In this sense, the specific person a voice is interpreted as representing is part of the β-manifold.

Arguing against this, though, Gould's (1949) study suggests that at least some voice hearers' subvocal speech is already in the form of another person's voice speaking, and it may be that the vocal character-istics of another person are (at least sometimes) an α property of the voice.[4] Dialogic theories of inner speech also suggest that the 'otherness' of the voice may be an α property of the it voice, as they argue our inner dialogue is literally shot through with other voices. This raises the question as to whether the voices that are heard by voice-hearers actually exist in all individuals, potentially occurring outside of their normal awareness. Kapur's (2003) finding that antipsychotics reduce the sali-ence of voices, also raises the question as to whether voice-hearers are having unusual thoughts which become more salient and are experi-enced as voices, or whether all individuals have such thoughts, but they are not normally salient to them. In addition to dialogic inner speech theories, we may also consider another reason why we may all (possibly unconsciously) generate the voices of others' in our head. Let us postu-late that, like the voices of voice-hearers, all individuals generate other people's voices commenting on them and evaluating them, albeit with this normally taking place outside conscious awareness. If this were to be the case, why would evolution have created this situation? The obvious answer is that as a social species it is highly advantageous to know what others are thinking of us, and hence to view ourselves as others do – making us objects to ourselves. If the other has been made more salient (e.g. one has been attacked/abused by others in the past, is a migrant in a new and strange land, or is living in a dangerous environment) then such verbalisations may also become more likely. Given the high demands

---

[4] It is obviously perilous to base too much on this single study, and more studies of associated sub-vocal speech are needed.

such cognitions would place on the verbal self-monitoring system, such thoughts could be likely to be experienced as alien. This has echoes of Frith's (1992) metarepresentational theory (Chapter 10), in that it places the content of AVHs in the process of taking others' perspectives on ourselves.[5] How might we test this theory? One way would be to examine if implicit awareness of others is heightened in voice-hearers, which could be done both in an fMRI scanner as well as at a behavioural level. Such an account would also open up a way to explain why delusions are commonly found in association with voices. For example, by paying more attention to the (potentially malevolent) actions of others, one makes oneself more vulnerable to delusions of reference and of persecution. Such proposals are, of course, in need of empirical testing.

Bringing it all back home

As I have argued above, it is unlikely that a single model will cover all voice-hearing experiences. However, I will put forward the following as what I believe is a useful framework for understanding many of the voices that we have seen in this book.

In the beginning was the world. In any given society in this world, socio-economic structures encourage individuals to relate and behave towards each other in a particular way. A child is born into a specific society, possibly with a predisposition to react to certain events by hearing voices (e.g. through genes coding for the development of the superior temporal gyrus). Events in this society happen to this child and the epigenetic interaction between these events and their genetic make-up result in the development of specific ways of reacting to, and coping with the world. The child then experiences a traumatic/emotional event(s), the probability of which is influenced by the socio-economic conditions of the society. In addition to some events which are likely to be experienced as traumatic/emotional by nearly everyone, both the culture the child lives in, and their own developmental history, will play a role in influencing what events are experienced this way. Traumatic events may include sexual abuse, bullying, deaths of friends and family and parental divorce. Such factors can be seen as the distal causes of voice-hearing.

Some individuals may immediately react to such emotional experiences by hearing voices, which may either be benevolent or malevolent. In this sense, the evoked emotions speak through the person in the form

---

[5] This also echoes a proposal of Christopher Frith that voices may result from our mental models of others which have gained a semi-autonomous existence (Malone, 2006).

of voices. Whether these voices simply express the evoked emotions, or are a form of coping mechanism, remains to be clearly established. The question as to why some individuals develop voices in response to such events and others do not remains one of the biggest unknowns in voice-hearing research.[6] Aside from factors specific to the child's earlier development, one possible candidate is the meaning such events have for the individual, and the coping mechanisms available. If the child is made to feel emotions such as shame or guilt, is isolated from social support, and/or deals with their emotions by suppressing them, then voice-hearing appears more likely to develop.[7] For others who do not start hearing voices at this time, such events may form a vulnerability to voice hearing, which may only come to be triggered (or indeed occur in the absence of such earlier traumatic events) by further stressful life events in later life. These later triggers may include events such as re-victimisation, giving birth, the death of a family member, physiological stress resulting from illicit drug use, or the general stresses of adolescence. Again, guilt and shame are likely to play a key role in many such trigger events. Traumatic events may also change benevolent voices in those already with them into malevolent voices.

In terms of the proximal causes of hearing voices, Type 2a AVHs (traumatic memories) may result from intrusions of verbal imagery from the traumatic experience which were not processed in the normal way at the time (Brewin, 1996). Trauma may also lead to the individual becoming hypervigilant for certain words or phrases, leading to Type 1a AVHs. These AVHs may then evolve into Type 1b AVHs, now no longer requiring the presence of ambiguous external sound to trigger them. Similarly, as Kraepelin (1919) noted, random and nonsensical voices (Type 2b AVHs) may also come to evolve into more complex voices, like the Type 1b AVHs described here. Likewise, as was the case with Schumann's voices (Box 12.1), AVHs may develop from initial auditory hallucinations involving noises or music. Why this happens is unclear but it may potentially be due to some form of stabilisation and elaboration of a neural network, which initially only permitted fleeting thoughts or sounds to be experienced as alien (with Hunter et al.'s (2006) model based in spontaneous fluctuations in the STG model being a possible starting point here, as well as Dodgson &

---

[6] It may be that whilst some develop voices in response to such events, others will self-harm or develop eating disorders, for example.

[7] Although many writers from the Hearing Voices Movement have argued for a role of emotion in the genesis of voices, the proposed causal sequence from emotion to voice remains to be established in any detail.

Gordon's (2009) model), resulting in more complex AVHs which enter into an attractor state which has a form and structure like inner speech. Although it is still somewhat unclear, Type 1b AVHs are likely to have their raw material in either dialogic inner speech/spontaneous thoughts flavoured by memories of voices of other people from traumatic events and which involve taking the perspective of another on oneself, or to be right hemisphere speech productions. It appears possible, drawing the parallel with obsessive compulsive disorder, that these thoughts would usually be inhibited, but that inhibition mechanisms break down somehow.[8] A better understanding both of the nature of thought, as well as the neural correlates of AVHs, should help us better answer this specific part of the puzzle of voices. Such raw material is then experienced as non-self produced due to a failure in either bottom-up and/or top-down mechanisms. First, corollary discharge mechanisms appear to play a key role in failing to tag these cognitions as self-produced. The exact regions affected by this failure are still somewhat unclear, however it appears likely that a key region here is the left temporoparietal junction, with signals from both frontal speech production regions and right hemisphere auditory association areas failing to correctly alert this area of their activities. It also seems likely that the anterior cingulate is also involved in causing disruption of such efferent signals, and that input from the parahippocampal gyrus plays an important, but still unclear, role in this process. In addition to bottom-up factors, top-down factors such as imagery–perception interactions and source-monitoring and verbal self-monitoring factors are also likely to play a role in the assessment that the cognition is an alien voice.

The content of the voice, the reactions of close others as well as society in general, and the help/coping mechanisms available to the voice-hearer all play a role in whether hearing the voice(s) leads to distress and dysfunction, and hence an illness state, or whether the voice is unproblematic, or even helpful, resulting in the individual remaining healthy. The voice may be interpreted as a pathological and/or spiritual experience, depending on the way the experience is embedded in the values and beliefs of the voice-hearer.

---

[8] We are still left with the question as to whether the thoughts that are the raw material of AVHs are a special form of thought which are more compelling than your average thought (again, drawing a parallel with OCD here). Why these thoughts should be this way is unclear; it may be due to the associated emotions, rather than an inherent property of the thought.

Interventions and liberations

As how we understand the causes of voices influences the meaning we give to them, how would the account laid out above impact upon the meaning we give to voices? First, this model stresses that the content of voices is meaningful in many cases, being related to the voice-hearer's own thoughts and emotions, and hence needs to be attended to (although that does not mean they should literally be obeyed, obviously). Furthermore, given that it roots many voices in previous life events of the voice-hearer, this recognises that the voice-hearer is the person with the expertise needed to make the links between their voices and their life.

What, then, of the dilemma, noted earlier, of the clash between mental health professionals' explanatory models, and those of voice-hearers?[9] Therapists undoubtedly have a hard job negotiating this divide. However, this is not just a dilemma for those working within the system. Many within the Hearing Voices Movement, although on paper accepting that all explanatory models are welcome, still prioritise trauma-based models (i.e. some models are more equal than others). Although it could be argued that this potential tension within the movement still remains to be resolved, as the movement does not impose trauma-based models, but encourages voice-hearers to make their own links between their past and their voices, this problem is minimised. If an individual comes to a mental health professional for help with their voices, it is likely that they are still developing explanations for their experiences. Whilst their beliefs may be dysfunctional in many ways, they may also be acting as coping mechanisms and should not be dismissed. Furthermore, as Geekie (2004) notes, clinicians who insist on telling clients what their experience means, risk alienating them and missing out on the chance to learn from the voice-hearer. It is likely to be beneficial if the therapist is able to give the voice-hearer hope, employ a biopsychosocial model (rather than a stigmatising biomedical model), and to treat the voice-hearer as a person and not just a chemical imbalance to be corrected. Furthermore, as Dein *et al.* (2010) have recommended, the initial psychiatric assessment for voice-hearers in distress should be 'far more than a symptom inventory; it needs to be, wherever possible, *an enquiry into meaning*' (p. 64, emphasis added).

A greater knowledge of the history of hearing voices can aid the therapist's engagement with the distressed voice-hearer, helping them see the range of different explanations that have been given to

---

[9] Although, again, it should be stressed the two groups are not mutually exclusive.

the voice-hearing experience, linking their experience with a long line of previous hearers (and hence not alienating them from humanity), and allowing them to decide for themselves on the meaning of their own personal experiences. Hearing voices groups may also help to reduce the isolation associated with hearing voices. Depending on the voice-hearer's own preferred approach to their voices, there may be a need to take a spiritual history of the person, and work with their beliefs surrounding their voices in this manner (Pargament, 2007). Furthermore, for those with voices and Christian religious beliefs, for example, a form of Christian CBT (Chapter 6) may prove beneficial. Not only this, but just as psychiatry at its birth imported many concepts from Christian treatments (Chapter 3), today the greater use of concepts from Christianity, such as forgiveness and love, may also prove beneficial. Indeed, such concepts are now appearing in Compassionate Mind Training. A greater dialogue between theology and psychiatry surrounding AVHs would undoubtedly be of benefit to both parties (McCarthy-Jones, 2011a). Of course, there are significant issues at the interaction of these two disciplines which remain to be resolved. For example, if an individual with religious beliefs hears voices, should their psychiatrist pray with them (Dein et al., 2010)? Furthermore, it appears that both disciplines' attempts to own the experience have distorted their view of what voices are typically like. They generally appear to be less mystical and wise than many theologians have argued, but less pathological and random than many mind scientists have argued. This is not to say, though, that at the extremes they may not take these forms.

The acceptance of voice-hearing as not pathological per se is also important. In this way the emancipation of voice-hearers is an important goal, though of course no-one can achieve this but voice-hearers themselves. As I have stressed throughout this book, there is likely to be no one-size-fits-all model, and some voices may be better understood as endogenously occurring, spontaneous brain events, and trying to decode their meaning vis-à-vis the voice-hearer's life may, at best, be a fruitless task. However, whilst there are dangers in starting from the assumption that the content of all voices has meaning, it is probably more dangerous to assume from the outset that they are meaningless.

There is still the need to create greater public understanding of voice-hearing, in terms of what it is like and what it means (and doesn't mean). Written publications and artistic representations are likely to play a useful role here.[10] However, ultimately, people who have come through

---

[10] For an example in the visual arts, see the work of the artist Susan Adams, www.susan-j-adams.co.uk/voices.html.

the turmoil of what life has thrown at them, have found a way to manage their ensuing voice-hearing experiences, still hear voices, and now act as witnesses and living embodiments of hope to those who are just starting their journeys of healing, are among the most inspirational people in our society. Such individuals are those who truly have the power to change public perceptions. There is also the need to firmly establish experts-by-experience in positions of power within the mental health system, in order that they can meaningfully influence policy decisions. Also, there is the need to offer training to allow research to be performed by experts-by-experience, and to facilitate voice-hearers to help educate professionals as to what may be missing or wrong with existing models of research. Given that 'hearing voices' is often used as a rhetorical club to knock others down with, as a way to discount someone's views, it behoves us all to be more considerate in how we use this term. Perhaps there are no better words than those of William James, who counselled 'A certain tolerance, a certain sympathy, a certain respect, and above all a certain lack of fear, seem to be the best attitude we can carry in our dealing with these regions of human nature' (James, as cited in Rubin, 2000, p. 199).

Does this book suggest how techniques to aid individuals distressed by their voices should change? What appears important is establishing why the voices are problematic, and the development of interventions which are informed by about what we know about the causes of voices. First, in terms of targeting the voices themselves, a comprehensive range of interventions should be made available, in addition to established approaches such as medication, once a sufficient evidence base has been developed. Such interventions can work on four facets of voices; their salience, the beliefs the voice-hearer holds about their voices, the way the voice-hearer engages with their voices, and the potential linkage between the voices and earlier traumatic life events (and, hence, the relation between the voice-hearer and their own emotions). Anti-psychotic medication and transcranial magnetic stimulation (TMS) may prove beneficial in reducing the salience of the voices for some individuals, giving the voice-hearer some temporary relief if required. Along similar lines, acceptance and commitment therapy (ACT) may aid the voice-hearer's detachment from their voices, making their voices less salient and less influential on their life and behaviour. Cognitive behavioural therapy may be useful in helping the voice-hearer change their beliefs about their voices (e.g. their power, their uncontrollability and their meaning), and hence reducing their distress. In terms of the way the voice-hearer engages with their voices, whilst medication, TMS and ACT can all help the voice-hearer de-engage from their voices (which may be temporarily beneficial), there is also likely to be a longer term need for engagement with voices and the life events and emotions underpinning them.[11] Indeed, a significant danger is that voices with their causal roots in emotional events are treated solely by biological interventions (e.g. neuroleptic medication, transcranial magnetic stimulation) which simply suppress them and do not allow these emotional issues to be resolved.[12] As Milton wrote, 'Who overcomes by force hath overcome but half his foe' (Milton, 1821, p. 24). A parallel here could be drawn with nineteenth-century vivisectionists who routinely severed the vocal cords of animals before operating on them, which stopped them screaming (or as the literature put it, emitting 'high pitched vocalizations') during the experiment (Jensen, 2000). If a voice is a reflection of emotion, suppression can only be a short-term aid, not a long-term strategy. This highlights the urgent need for more research into the potential causal mechanisms linking voices and earlier traumatic/emotional experiences, and randomised controlled trials of potential benefits of working with the thoughts and emotions of the voice-hearer. It is also clear that it is important for therapeutic interventions to focus on more than just the distressing voices themselves. Given that many of the problems caused by voices are social, financial, and self-esteem related (i.e. the problems are rooted in the loss of basic human needs) there is the need to provide increased help and support at these levels too. This may involve services holding hope for the voice-hearer when they cannot, aiding re-employment, re-entry into the social world, establishing Hearing Voices Groups, taking a personal interest in the voice-hearer and actively fighting for their recovery. In this sense, as Coleman (2009) has put it, 'recovery is living'. Or, more broadly, as Marlow says in Conrad's *Lord Jim*, 'strictly speaking, the question is not how to get cured, but how to live' (p. 198). This book has also pointed to the need to look beyond interventions based at the level of the individual, and towards examining

---

[11] Here the innovative techniques of the Maastricht Approach (e.g., voice dialogue), as well as Compassionate Mind Training, may be of use to voice-hearers. However, as noted earlier, the potential effectiveness of these techniques remains in need of rigorous scientific testing. More generally, there is the need for voice-hearers to be given a range of interventions to choose from, in order to achieve their own specific goals. For example, some voice-hearers may have the goal of simply eliminating their voices. Given that antipsychotic medication can achieve this goal in some (but not all) voice-hearers, this may hence be an appropriate choice for some. However, voice-hearers with other goals, such as retaining their voices but having a greater sense of control over them, and with the voices behaving better, will likely need to choose other forms of intervention.

[12] Although, of course, some people may desire such treatment and find it is sufficient for them.

how a societal structure that encourages us to behave in a destructive manner towards each other may also be targeted for change.

In terms of future work into voices, it is likely to be fruitful to examine in more detail the links between emotions, how emotions are dealt with, previous events in the voice hearer's life and their voices. Furthermore, a return to the phenomenology of voices themselves is likely to be beneficial. The phenomenology of voices gives us many clues to their origins, and we likely need to start by listening better. The form of voices may also be informative, with aspects of voices such as their tendency to take the form of negative voices offset by positive voices needing to be more clearly worked into models of voices, as well as models of thought itself. Overall, a biopsychosocial, epigenetic approach is needed which links the events that happen to voice-hearers, the meaning of such events to the voice-hearer, how they attempt to cope with them, and the biological reactions and down-stream neural consequences of such events. More work is hence needed across the spectrum, from proximate biological causes to distal socio-economic causes. This may be done in conjunction with an emancipatory approach to voice-hearing, and with the full recognition that our answer to the voice-hearing conundrum is as much a political one as it is a scientific one. Furthermore such future research should be truly multidisciplinary in nature. As I have only started to demonstrate in this book, it is by drawing on insights from multiple disciplines, including theology, the medical humanities, sociology, literary and English studies and philosophy, that we can approach a better understanding of the experience of hearing voices, its meanings and causes, and look towards the development of better therapeutic interventions, and more meaningful scientific research.

Are voices distressing? Quite often, yes. Can they be worked with and resolved? Yes. Are voices a sign of illness in themselves? No. Can they result in a state which could be classified as illness? Yes. What are voices signs of? Underlying emotional issues, a societal structure that creates catastrophic human interactions, a brain disease, supernatural communication, a mental illness, the inherent power of human thought? I have laid out in this book the meanings that I favour, but what they are more widely understood to be is a question that will be determined not by this book, but by those with power, as has always been the case. We seem to be at a juncture in history when the power balance is again shifting, but this time due to the increasing influence of a movement of voice-hearers themselves and their allies. How the meaning changes and what voices become is hence the next chapter in the history of hearing voices. Franz Fanon wrote that 'For the black man there is only one destiny. And it is white'. For most of history, voice-hearers have only had one destiny, and that is silence. The silence of the voices they hear has been the definition of health, and their own opinions on the meaning of their voices when in conflict with the prevailing paradigm, be this medical or religious, have been silenced. Silence is meant to be broken, though, and voices are meant to be heard. The future looks positive.

Appendix A: AVHs and antipsychotic medication

It would seem a straightforward question to ask how many out of 100 patients diagnosed with schizophrenia who hear voices, when treated with antipsychotic medication, will experience a beneficial effect on their voices as a result of the medication itself. Indeed, asking the question is simple, it is getting a straight answer which is surprisingly hard. The question also has a number of parts. First, are antipsychotics an effective treatment for people who hear voices, in both the short and/or long term? If they are, then three further questions are pertinent: how big is this effect, how do the voices and/or the person's relation to the voices actually change, and what causes this at a biological level?

Anti-psychotic medications broadly fall into two types, the older 'typical' antipsychotics (e.g. chlorpromazine/Thorzine or haloperidol/Haldol) and the newer 'atypical' antipsychotics (e.g. risperidone, olanzapine, clozapine). In the large-scale randomised controlled clinical trials of these drugs, changes in levels of AVHs are not typically reported on specifically. Instead, a general measure of positive symptoms (e.g. hallucinations, delusions) is employed, typically being assessed by the Positive and Negative Symptom Scale (PANSS) or the Brief Psychiatric Rating Scale (BPRS). If we assume that positive symptom levels can be taken as a proxy measure of levels of AVHs (and it is not clear that this is a valid assumption), then evidence of changes in positive symptoms would suggest that voices are indeed being helped.

There is a large research literature showing that antipsychotic medications are beneficial for positive symptoms for a number of patients (see Kane & Marder, 1993). Some note that some patients diagnosed with schizophrenia are 'exquisitely responsive' (Brown & Herz, 1989, p. 123). Clinicians typically state, from their experience, that around two-thirds of patients diagnosed with schizophrenia respond to antipsychotic medications. Similarly, a respected psychiatric textbook also states that when patients diagnosed with acute schizophrenia are given antipsychotic medication, 'approximately 60 percent will improve to the extent that they will achieve a complete remission or experience only mild

375

symptoms; the remaining 40 percent of patients will improve but still demonstrate variable levels of positive symptoms that are resistant to the medications' (Sadock, Kaplan & Sadock, 2007, p. 489). No references are provided for this claim, however. In the introduction sections of psychiatric research papers a broad consensus can be seen in the effectiveness researchers believe antipsychotic drugs have. Hoffman *et al.* (2008b) state that AVHs 'remain poorly or incompletely responsive to currently available treatments in approximately 25% of cases' (p. 1167), and Vercammen *et al.* (2009) state that 'AVH persist in about 25% of cases' (p. 172). Both of these studies, and many more, cite as evidence for this claim the paper of Shergill, Murray & McGuire (1998). The Shergill, Murray & McGuire paper itself states that 'in 25–30% they [AVHs] are refractory to traditional antipsychotic drugs' and cites as its evidence Meltzer (1992) and Kane *et al.* (1988). But what do these two papers say?

The Meltzer (1992) study cites a study by Brenner *et al.* (1990) as its evidence that there is a 'consensus that 5 to 25 percent of schizophrenic patients may be considered unresponsive to antipsychotic drug therapy to a clinically significant extent' (p. 516), and the Kane *et al.* (1988) study cites Davis (1980). What do the Brenner *et al.* (1990) and Davis (1980) papers actually say?

The Brenner *et al.* study cites three peer-reviewed papers (Davis, 1976; Losonczy *et al.*, 1986; and Vaughn *et al.*, 1984) to support its claim that the 'consensus is that from 5 to 25 percent of schizophrenic patients are partially or totally unresponsive to antipsychotic drug therapy' (p. 551). The Davis study cites Cole, Goldberg & Davis (1966), Cole, Goldberg & Klerman (1964) and Goldberg, Klerman & Cole (1965). We then must track down these papers to see what they say.

The Davis (1976) study also cites Cole, Goldberg & Klerman (1964) and Goldberg, Klerman & Cole (1965) as its source of data. The Vaughan *et al.* (1984) study is not a study of the effectiveness of antipsychotic medication, and the Losonczy *et al.* (1986) study found that of 19 patients with schizophrenia (who had been kept medication free for two weeks before the study) only 7 showed improvement (using, as they state a 'generous criteria' for improvement, p. 979) after four weeks. The Cole, Goldberg & Davis (1966) study is not a peer-reviewed paper.

When we get to the Cole, Goldberg & Klerman (1964) and Goldberg, Klerman & Cole (1965) studies, we finally actually get to some empirical data. I took you through the long and winding journey above to show how many links we have to go through actually to get back from claims to original data. The Cole, Goldberg & Klerman (1964) study was a six-week randomised controlled trial (double-blind) of the effectiveness of chlorpromazine, fluphenazine, thioridazine and placebo on the symptoms of newly admitted patients diagnosed with schizophrenia. This study reported a significant decrease in auditory hallucinations in the overall drug group compared to placebo; however, we are not told the significance level of this difference, and hence, given the number of total comparisons they made (13), it is unclear if this would still have remained significant after a Bonferroni correction was applied. Furthermore, the measure used to assess levels of auditory hallucinations was a scale resulting from a new factor analysis done by these authors of items on the Inpatient Multidimensional Psychiatric Scale (Lorr & Klett, 1966). It is unclear exactly which items the authors included on this auditory hallucinations factor, and whether this was a psychometrically valid measure. However, the authors report that at the end of the trial, 46 per cent of patients in the drug group had no symptoms or only borderline illness, suggesting that there was a marked improvement in auditory hallucinations.

The Goldberg study was a six-week, randomised controlled trial (double-blind) of the effectiveness of chlorpromazine, fluphenazine, thioridazine and placebo on the symptoms of newly admitted patients diagnosed with schizophrenia. This did specifically report on AVHs, with their measure consisting of two questions: (1) To what extent does he appear preoccupied or distressed by hallucinatory voices (e.g. voices that accuse, blame or threaten)?, (2) ... hears voices that ordered him to carry out or perform certain tasks? Patients on placebo saw their mean AVH scores go from 12.9 to 8.0, a significant improvement ($p < 0.01$).[1] Patients on drug treatments saw their mean AVH scores go from 12.9 to 5.2, also a significant improvement ($p < 0.01$). The decrease in symptoms was reported as being significantly greater in the drug group than the placebo group, but only at $0.05 > p > 0.01$. However, if a Bonferroni correction had been applied to the significance level to take into account the increased chance of a Type 1 error due to the number of statistical comparisons made, then the antipsychotics would not have been more effective than placebo. Furthermore, whereas there were 45 per cent of patients with AVHs in the drug group, there were only 34 per cent of patients with AVHs in the placebo group. This could mean that there was less scope for improvement in scores in the placebo group.

Thus, we see an interesting contrast between the start of our journey here, where we were told that only 25 per cent of patients are medication

---

[1] No Bonferroni corrections were applied.

resistant, to the sources of the evidence cited to support this claim, one of which actually shows that antipsychotic drugs are no better than placebo for treating AVHs, and the other which does show improvement due to the drugs, but does not report all the data one would want to be happy that these conclusions were reliable and/or valid.

These individual trials aside, what does the larger picture of evidence say about the effectiveness of antipsychotics? One of the earliest of the typical antipsychotics, as noted in Chapter 3, was chlorpromazine. So does chlorpromazine improve positive symptoms? The first question is what source to take our evidence from. Given that Perlis *et al.* (2005, as cited in Bentall, 2009) found that psychiatric drug trials sponsored by a pharmaceutical company or in which at least one of the authors has a declared financial conflict of interest, were 4.9 times more likely to report a positive result than an independently funded trial, we need to be selective in our sources of evidence. One good source is likely to be the independent Cochrane Library. In a Cochrane Library systematic review of randomised controlled trials reporting on the efficacy of chlorpromazine compared to placebo, Adams *et al.* (2007) first observed that 'Even though chlorpromazine has been used as an antipsychotic drug for decades, there are still a surprisingly small number of well-conducted randomised, placebo-controlled trials measuring its efficacy and potential to cause adverse effects' (p. 13). The results of their review of these well-conducted studies concluded that 'In spite of 45 years of research on this benchmark anti-psychotic treatment, very little can be said from trials regarding its direct effect on mental state in general or specific symptoms of schizophrenia' (p. 11). Indeed, they 'found no short term difference in mental state using a cut-off point of at least a 50% decline in score to indicate "improvement"' (p. 9). It is 'humbling' to think, wrote the authors, that 'perhaps, for every six people treated with this compound, five may have been given the drug with no important clinical responses beyond a placebo effect'. So why is chlorpromazine so widely used? The authors suggest that 'The use of chlorpromazine for millions of people is based on clinical experience rather than the poorly reported trials that involve, in total, only a few thousand participants' (p. 13).

One reason the authors may have failed to find an improvement is as they defined improvement as a 50 per cent decline in today scores. However, typical trials for interventions in schizophrenia, be they drug trials or CBT trials, define clinical improvement as a 20 per cent reduction in symptom measure scores (e.g. Breier *et al.*, 2000; Tarrier *et al.*, 2000). But what does this actually represent, in the real world, in terms of improvement? Leucht *et al.* (2005) argue that a 25–30 per cent

BPRS score reduction means that the patient is showing minimal improvement, and that a 55 per cent change represents 'much improvement'. In terms of hallucinations, what would a 25 per cent improvement represent? The hallucinations item on the BPRS is a six-point scale running from 2 (Very mild: While resting or going to sleep, sees visions, smells odours or hears voices, sounds, or whispers in the absence of external stimulation, but no impairment in functioning) to 7 (Extremely Severe: Persistent verbal or visual hallucinations throughout the day OR most areas of functioning are disrupted by these hallucinations). If someone had a score of 7, and their score reduced by 20 per cent to a score of 5 on the scale, then the drugs are seen to be working. Thus a change from 'Extremely Severe' (score of 7) voices to 'Moderately Severe' voices (score of 5: Experiences daily hallucinations OR some areas of functioning are disrupted by hallucinations) would be seen as the drugs working. As such, drugs can be classified as working even if you still are experiencing daily hallucinations. This is not to minimise the potential impact of this, though, as it may potentially make a big difference to someone's life. It is also worth noting that we do not know whether specific sub-types of AVHs (e.g. commands, running commentaries, voices making short, repetitive statements) tend to respond more than others to medication.

Because the typical antipsychotics have a number of specific side-effects, newer 'atypical' antipsychotics were developed. Individual drug company-sponsored trials show positive results. For example, in a randomised controlled trial (RCT), McEvoy et al. (2007) found that 64 per cent of patients treated with olanzapine, 58 per cent of patients treated with quetiapine and 65 per cent of patients treated with risperidone had their hallucinations improved to the point where they scored 3 or less on the PANSS hallucinations item 'at some point during the study' (p. 1057). A score of 3 on the PANSS represents 'One or two clearly formed but infrequent hallucinations, or else a number of vague abnormal perceptions which do not result in distortions of thinking or behaviour'. However, it is notable that not only did 70 per cent (yes, 70%) of patients discontinue their medications during the 52-week trial, but that the PANSS hallucination score used as the outcome measure was not the patient's score at the end of the trial, but apparently the lowest value it reached at any point of the trial. Other individual studies such as Robinson et al. (2006) have also found a significant improvement in hallucinations (classed as a rating of mild or better) in around 50 per cent of patients treated with either risperidone (54% response) or olanzapine (44% response). As in both of these studies one or more of the authors had either served as a speaker or a consultant, or received research support from pharmaceutical companies, these should be treated with some caution, given the findings of Perlis *et al.* noted above.

Turning to Cochrane Library reviews, we may ask, what is the evidence base for the effectiveness of atypical antipsychotics? In a systematic review of RCTs of the effectiveness of risperidone versus placebo, Rattehalli, Jayaram & Smith (2010) initially note a clear effect of risperidone on psychiatric symptoms. However, of the seven RCTs examined there was one outlier, an equivocal trial which was sponsored by a research charity. As the authors note, the other studies 'were sponsored by an interested pharmaceutical industry ... We found very few data reported on mental state for the comparison of risperidone versus placebo and what we do have is difficult to trust. Further confusing matters is that such a fall [the 20% fall] in PANSS ... may not be clinically meaningful. PANSS negative and positive symptom sub scores as well as measures of depression, cognitive function and verbal memory are unconvincing of any meaningful difference between the drug and placebo' (p. 15). Rattehalli and colleagues further note that 'There is a likelihood of a significant bias favouring risperidone, given the fact that the majority of trials were funded by the manufacturer of the drug itself. The magnitude of author-industry affiliation seems to be high in the included papers which has to make the reader more sceptical about any positive findings. There is a significant relationship between funding source and study outcome, with industry-funded studies favouring the innovative (sponsored) treatments over others to a greater degree than non industry-funded studies' (p. 16). Rattehalli and colleagues conclude that 'Risperidone may well help people with schizophrenia, but the data in this review are unconvincing. People with schizophrenia or their advocates may want to lobby regulatory authorities to insist on better studies being available before wide release of a compound with the subsequent beguiling advertising' (p. 18).

If a patient is classed as treatment-resistant to antipsychotic medication (i.e. has failed to respond to at least two antipsychotic medications, having been on each for at least 6–8 weeks) then clozapine may be prescribed. However, clozapine's potential for agranulocytosis and consequent need for frequent blood count monitoring have limited its use to otherwise treatment-refractory patients diagnosed with schizophrenia. In examining the effectiveness of clozapine, it should hence be borne in mind that response will likely be lower than the first-line atypicals. In a review of 31 studies involving 2,589 patients, Wahlbeck *et al.* (2000) found that 'for every 100 people with schizophrenia given clozapine for a few weeks 18 will have a discernible clinical improvement ... For every 100 people treated for at least 26 weeks with clozapine, 17 will improve clinically' (p. 11). Thus overall, 'Treating five people with schizophrenia [with clozapine] will result in one of them showing a clinical improvement' (p. 10).

The drug trials above have typically examined the short-term effects of antipsychotic medication. In the long term, though, is antipsychotic medication better than no antipsychotic medication? It appears it may not be. In a meta-analysis of long-term outcomes (> 1 yr) of schizophrenia in first- and second-episode patients who were given antipsychotic medication and similar patients who were unmedicated, Bola (2006) found no significant differences.

Other problematic issues surrounding antipsychotic drugs

One of the most surprising findings in the field of schizophrenia research is the five-year follow-up study of the International Pilot Study of Schizophrenia (WHO, 1979), which examined outcomes of schizophrenia in patients with this diagnosis in a series of countries across the world. As this study was performed in the 1970s, the 'obvious' expectation was that patients in the West, who had benefited from the advanced psychopharmacological antipsychotic drugs, such as chlorpromazine, would have better outcomes than patients in other less developed parts of the world. However, it was found that the developing nations (India, Colombia and Nigeria) had better outcomes (with more having no symptoms at follow-up, and less having chronic psychosis) than patients in the developed countries (Denmark, England, Russia, Czechoslovakia and the USA). This result was replicated later in the Determinants of Outcome of Severe Mental Disorders study (Jablensky et al., 1992). Yet it is important to note that this study did not find the outcome of patients in the developing countries to be uniformly better, as compared to the outcome in developed countries (Jablensky & Sartorius, 2008). Thus, for example, although complete clinical remission was more common in developing country areas than in developed countries (37% vs 16%), the proportions of continuous unremitting illness did not differ between these two types of country (11% vs 17%). Importantly, though, patients in developing countries experienced significantly longer periods of unimpaired functioning in the community, although only 16 per cent of them were on continuous antipsychotic medication (compared with 61% in the developed countries). Taking all patients together, the best predictors of outcome were type of onset (insidious vs acute) and type of setting (developed vs developing country), followed by less strong predictors of marital status, gender, social isolation and drug abuse (ibid.).

Another problem that can be levelled at antipsychotic medications is, as Johnstone (2000) proposes, that drugs act to suppress symptoms rather than allow people to understand them. Johnstone also observes how psychiatrists switch between medical (e.g. biochemistry) and psychological (e.g. concepts such as projection), not being sure which is correct and how the two are related. As Johnstone notes, 'the switch from psychotherapeutic to medical language has very little to do with the patient and his/her problems. It tends to occur when mental health professionals, and psychiatrists in particular, reach the limits of their own ability to see someone's distress in psychological terms and to bear the feeling this stirs up' (p. 34). Johnstone argues that as psychiatrists are not given detailed training in counselling, these limits are reached rapidly. As one patient she notes puts it, 'I feel that, essentially, when a doctor prescribes a pill for me, it's to put *him* out of *my* misery' (p. 34, emphasis in original).

Clinicians on the ground

Although not the result of controlled scientific studies, it is worth considering what clinicians and physicians report seeing 'on the ground', in terms of the clinical effects of antipsychotics on voices. This is especially important given, as Adams *et al.* (2007) argued above, that it is such clinical experience that forms the basis of prescribing antipsychotics. A study by Lecrubier *et al.* (2007) examined reports from 872 physicians on 6,523 patients regarding the symptom changes of patients diagnosed with schizophrenia whom they were prescribing antipsychotics. Of the 3,845 patients with hallucinations (of all forms, not just AVHs), physicians reported that 51 per cent of hallucinations were generally well controlled by antipsychotic drugs. However, antipsychotics were rated as providing little or no control of hallucination in 11 per cent of patients, and only some control in 38 per cent of patients. But what 'control' means is unclear, and the studies we have previously reviewed above suggest that a significant amount of such effectiveness may be due to placebo effects.

Time of response

In theory, because dopamine blockade happens within hours of starting medications (Tauscher *et al.*, 2002), the effects of the atypical antipsychotics on symptoms such as voices should be on this time frame. Although for a long time it was thought that antipsychotics took a number of weeks to work, this has been found not to be the case in more recent studies. In a meta-analysis of 7,450 patients in 42 studies, Agid *et al.* (2003) found a reduction in symptoms of psychosis in the first week. Furthermore, Kapur *et al.* (2005) found psychotic symptoms were reduced after 24 hours (and after only 2 hours in the case of intramuscular olanzapine). However, Gunduz-Bruce *et al.* (2005) found that the median length of time that hallucinations took to respond to medication (defined as an absence of hallucinations for 6 weeks) was 27 days (mean = 59 days). Hallucinations which were more severe responded more slowly, and patients with a higher parental social class had a slower response to medication (the meaning of this last finding is unclear).

References

Abba, N., Chadwick, P. & Stevenson, C. (2008). Responding mindfully to distressing psychosis: A grounded theory analysis. *Psychotherapy Research*, 18, 77–87.

Adams, C. E., Awad, G., Rathbone, J. & Thornley, B. (2007). Chlorpromazine versus placebo for schizophrenia. *Cochrane Database of Systematic Reviews*, 2, CD000284.

Agid, O., Kapur, S., Arenovich, T. & Zipursky, R. B. (2003). Delayed onset hypothesis of antipsychotic action – a hypothesis tested and rejected. *Archives of General Psychiatry*, 60, 1228–35.

Akins, K. A. & Dennett, D. C. (1986). Who may I say is calling? *Behavioral and Brain Sciences*, 9, 517–18.

Aleman, A. (2001). Hallucinations and the cerebral hemispheres. *Journal of Psychiatry & Neuroscience*, 26, 64.

Aleman, A., Böcker, K. B. E., Hijman, R., de Haan, E. H. F. & Kahn, R. S. (2003). Cognitive basis of hallucinations in schizophrenia: Role of top-down information processing. *Schizophrenia Research*, 46, 175–85.

Aleman, A. & Larøi, F. (2008). *Hallucinations: The science of idiosyncratic perception*. Washington DC: American Psychological Association.

Aleman, A., Sommer, I. E. & Kahn, R. S. (2007). Efficacy of slow repetitive transcranial magnetic stimulation in the treatment of resistant auditory hallucinations in schizophrenia: A meta-analysis. *Journal of Clinical Psychiatry*, 68, 416–21.

Al-Issa, I. (1978). Social and cultural aspects of hallucinations. *Psychological Bulletin*, 84, 570–87.

(1995). The illusion of reality or the reality of illusion: Hallucinations and culture. *British Journal of Psychiatry*, 166, 368–73.

& Al-Issa, B. (1970). Psychiatric problems in a developing country: Iraq. *International Journal of Social Psychiatry*, 16, 15–22.

Allen, J. G., Coyne, L. & Console, D. A. (1997). Dissociative detachment relates to psychotic symptoms and personality decompensation. *Comprehensive Psychiatry*, 38, 327–34.

Allen, P., Amaro, E., Fu, C. H. Y., Williams, S. C. R., Brammer, M. J., Johns, L. C. *et al.* (2007). Neural correlates of the misattribution of speech in schizophrenia. *British Journal of Psychiatry*, 190, 162–9.

Allen, P., Freeman, D., Johns, L. & McGuire, P. (2006). Misattribution of self-generated speech in relation to hallucinatory proneness and delusional ideation in healthy volunteers. *Schizophrenia Research*, 84, 281–8.

Allen, P., Johns, L. C., Fu, C. H., Broome, M. R., Vythelingum, G. N. & McGuire, P. K. (2004). Misattribution of external speech in patients with hallucinations and delusions. *Schizophrenia Research*, 69, 277–87.

Allen, P., Larøi, F., McGuire, P. K. & Aleman, A. (2008). The hallucinating brain: A review of structural and functional neuroimaging studies of hallucinations. *Neuroscience and Biobehavioral Reviews*, 32, 175–91.

Allen, P., Stephan, K. E., Mechelli, A., Day, F., Ward, N., Dalton, J. *et al.* (2010). Cingulate activity and fronto-temporal connectivity in people with prodromal signs of psychosis. *Neuroimage*, 49, 947–55.

Almeida, O. P., Forstl, H., Howard, R. & David, A. S. (1993). Unilateral auditory hallucinations. *British Journal of Psychiatry*, 162, 262–4.

Alpert, M. (1985). The signs and symptoms of schizophrenia. *Comprehensive Psychiatry*, 26, 103–12.

& Silvers, K. N. (1970). Perceptual characteristics distinguishing auditory hallucinations in schizophrenia and acute alcoholic psychoses. *American Journal of Psychiatry*, 127, 298–302.

Andersen, S. L., Tomoda, A., Vincow, E. S., Valente, E., Polcari, A. & Teicher, M. H. (2008). Preliminary evidence for sensitive periods in the effect of childhood sexual abuse on regional brain development. *Journal of Neuropsychiatry and Clinical Neurosciences*, 20, 292–301.

Anderson, N. T. (2001). *Steps to freedom in Christ: The step-by-step guide to freedom in Christ*. Ventura, CA: Gospel Light.

Anderson, N. T., Zuehlke, T. E. & Zuehlke, J. S. (2000). *Christ centered therapy*. Grand Rapids, MI: Zondervan.

Andoh, J. & Martinot, J.-L. (2008). Interhemispheric compensation: A hypothesis of TMS-induced effects on language-related areas. *European Psychiatry*, 23, 281–8.

Andreasen, N. C. (1984). *The Scale for the Assessment of Positive Symptoms (SAPS)*. The University of Iowa.

Andreasen, N. (1985). *The broken brain: The biological revolution in psychiatry*. New York, NY: Harper and Row.

Andrew, E. M., Gray, N. S. & Snowden, R. J. (2008). The relationship between trauma and beliefs about hearing voices: A study of psychiatric and non-psychiatric voice hearers. *Psychological Medicine*, 38, 1409–17.

Andrews, B., Brewin, C. R., Rose, S. & Kirk, M. (2000). Predicting PTSD symptoms in victims of violent crime. The role of shame, anger, and childhood abuse. *Journal of Abnormal Psychology*, 109, 69–73.

Andrews-Hanna, J. R., Reidler, J. S., Huang, C. & Buckner, R. L. (2010a). Evidence for the default network's role in spontaneous cognition. *Journal of Neurophysiology*, 104, 322–35.

Andrews-Hanna, J. R., Reidler, J. S., Sepulcre, J., Poulin, R. & Buckner, R. L. (2010b) Functional-anatomic fractionation of the brain's default network. *Neuron*, 65, 550–62.

Angst J. & Marneros, A. (2001). Bipolarity from ancient to modern times: Conception, birth and rebirth. *Journal of Affective Disorders*, 67, 3–19.

Anketell, C., Dorahy, M. J., Shannon, M., Elder, R., Hamilton, G., Corry, M. et al. (2010). An exploratory analysis of voice hearing in chronic PTSD: Potential associated mechanisms. *Journal of Trauma and Dissociation*, 11, 93–107.

Anstrom, K. K., Miczek, A. & Budygin, E. A. (2009). Increased phasic dopamine signalling in the mesolimbic pathway during social defeat in rats. *Neuroscience*, 161, 3–12.

APA (1952). *Diagnostic and Statistical Manual of Mental Disorders. First Edition*. Washington DC: American Psychiatric Association.

(1968). *Diagnostic and Statistical Manual of Mental Disorders. Second Edition*. Washington DC: American Psychiatric Association.

(1980). *Diagnostic and Statistical Manual of Mental Disorders. Third Edition*. Washington DC: American Psychiatric Association.

(1994). *Diagnostic and Statistical Manual of Mental Disorders. Fourth Edition*. Washington DC: American Psychiatric Association.

(2000). *Diagnostic and Statistical Manual of Mental Disorders. Fourth Transitional Edition*. Washington DC: American Psychiatric Association.

Aquinas, T. (1927). *Summa theologica* [Summary of theology] (trans. Fathers of the English Dominican Province). London: Burns Oates and Washbourne.

Aristotle (1908/1984). On Dreams (trans. J. I. Beare). *The complete works of Aristotle: The revised Oxford translation*. Princeton University Press.

Aschebrock, Y., Gavey, N., McCreanor, T. & Tippett, L. (2003). Is the content of delusions and hallucinations important? *Australasian Psychiatry*, 11, 306–11.

Aspelmeier, J. E., Elliott, A. N. & Smith, C. H. (2007). Childhood sexual abuse, attachment, and trauma symptoms in college females: The moderating role of attachment. *Child Abuse & Neglect*, 31, 549–66.

Athanasius (1994). *Nicene and post-Nicene Fathers*, Volume IV, Second Series. P. Schaff and H. Wallace (eds). *Athanasius: Select Works and Letters. Life of Antony* (pp. 188–221).

Atkinson, J. R. (2006). The perceptual characteristics of voice-hallucinations in deaf people: A review. *Schizophrenia Bulletin*, 32, 701–8.

Gleeson, K., Cromwell, J. & O'Rourke, S. (2007). Exploring the perceptual characteristics of voice-hallucinations in deaf people. *Cognitive Neuropsychiatry*, 12, 339–61.

Augustine, St (1982). *The literal meaning of Genesis* (Vol. II) (trans. J. H. Taylor). Ramsey, NJ: Paulist Press.

Aumann, J, (2006). *Spiritual Theology*. London, UK: Continuum.

Aziz-Zadeh, L., Cattaneo, L., Rochat, M. & Rizzolatti, G. (2005). Covert speech arrests inducted by rTMS over both motor and nonmotor left hemisphere frontal sites. *Journal of Cognitive Neuroscience*, 17, 928–38.

Azuonye, I. O. (1997). A difficult case: Diagnosis made by hallucinatory voices. *British Medical Journal*, 315, 1685–6.

Bach, P. A. & Hayes, S. C. (2002). The use of acceptance and commitment therapy to prevent the rehospitalisation of psychotic patients: A randomized controlled trial. *Journal of Consulting and Clinical Psychology*, 70, 1129–39.

Bacon, F. (1605/2002). *Francis Bacon: the major works.* (B. Vickers (ed.)). Oxford University Press.

Badcock, J. C. (2010). The cognitive neuropsychology of auditory hallucinations: A parallel auditory pathways framework. *Schizophrenia Bulletin*, 36, 576–84.

Badcock, J. C., Paulik, G. & Maybery, M. T. (2011). The role of emotion regulation in auditory hallucinations. *Psychiatry Research*, 185, 303–8.

Badcock, J. C., Waters, F. A. V. & Maybery, M. (2007). On keeping (intrusive) thoughts to one's self: Testing a cognitive model of auditory hallucinations. *Cognitive Neuropsychiatry*, 12, 78–89.

Badcock, J. C., Waters, F. A. V., Maybery, M. T., & Michie, P. T. (2005). Auditory hallucinations: Failure to inhibit irrelevant memories. *Cognitive Neuropsychiatry*, 10, 125–36.

Baethge, C., Baldessarini, R. J, Freudenthal, K., Streeruwitz, A., Bauer, M. & Bschor, T. (2005). Hallucinations in bipolar disorder: characteristics and comparison to unipolar depression and schizophrenia. *Bipolar Disorders*, 7, 136–45.

Baker, C. & Morrison, A. P. (1998). Metacognition, intrusive thoughts and auditory hallucinations. *Psychological Medicine*, 28, 1199–208.

Baker, P. (1985). *Hearing voices.* Manchester, UK: Hearing Voices Network.

Bakhtin, M. (2003). *Problems of Dostoevsky's poetics.* University of Minnesota Press.

Barker, S., Lavender, T. & Morant N. (2001). Client and family narratives on schizophrenia. *Journal of Mental Health*, 10, 199–212.

Barrett, T. R. & Etheridge, J. B. (1992). Verbal hallucinations in normals 1: People who hear 'voices'. *Applied Cognitive Psychology*, 6, 379–87.

Barta, P. E., Pearlson, G. D., Powers, R. E., Richards, S. S. & Tune, L. E. (1990). Auditory hallucinations and smaller superior temporal gyral volume in schizophrenia. *American Journal of Psychiatry*, 147, 1457–62.

Bartels-Velthuis, A. A., Jenner, J. A. & van de Willige, G. (2010). Prevalence and correlates of auditory vocal hallucinations in middle childhood. *British Journal of Psychiatry*, 196, 41–6.

Basser, P. J., Mattiello, J. & Lebihan, D. (1994). MR diffusion tensor spectroscopy and imaging. *Biophysical Journal*, 66, 259–67.

Bassiony, M. M. & Lyketsos, C. G. (2003). Delusions and hallucinations in Alzheimer's disease: Review of the brain decade. *Psychosomatics*, 44, 388–401.

Battie, W. (1758). *A treatise on madness.* London, UK: Brunner/Mazel.

Baumgarten, A. I., Assmann, J. & Strosmsa, G. G. (eds). (1998). *Self, soul, & body in religious experience.* Leiden, Netherlands: Brill Academic Publishers.

Beavan, V. (2011). Towards a definition of 'hearing voices': A phenomenological approach. *Psychosis*, 3, 63–73.

 & Read, J. (2010). Hearing voices and listening to what they say: The importance of voice content in understanding and working with distressing voices. *Journal of Nervous and Mental Disease*, 198, 201–5.

388   References

Beck, A. T. & Rector, N. A. (2003). A cognitive model of hallucinations. *Cognitive Therapy and Research*, 27, 19–52.

Becker, D. F., Daley, M., Gadpaille, W. J., Green, M. R., Flahery, L. T., Harper, G. *et al.* (2003). Trauma and adolescence 1: The nature and scope of trauma. *Adolescent Psychiatry.* 27, 143–63.

Beers, C. W. (1908). *A mind that found itself.* 4th edn. New York, NY: Longmans, Green and Co.

Behrendt, R. -P. (1998). Underconstrained perception: A theoretical approach to the nature and function of verbal hallucinations. *Comprehensive Psychiatry*, 39, 236–48.

Ben-Arieh, A. (2010). Socioeconomic correlates of rates of child maltreatment in small communities. *American Journal of Orthopsychiatry*, 80, 109–14.

Benjamin, L. S. (1989). Is chronicity a function of the relationship between the person and the auditory hallucination? *Schizophrenia Bulletin*, 15, 291–310.

Bennett, A. E. & Cesarman, F. C. (1953). Transorbital lobotomy: Its use in relapsing psychotic states. *California Medicine*, 78, 453–5.

Bentaleb, L. A., Beauregard, M., Liddle, P. & Stip, E. (2002). Cerebral activity associated with auditory verbal hallucinations: A functional magnetic resonance imaging case study. *Journal of Psychiatry & Neuroscience*, 27, 110–15.

Bentall, R. P. (1990). The illusion of reality: A review and integration of psychological research on hallucinations. *Psychological Bulletin*, 107, 82–95.

(ed.) (1992a). *Reconstructing schizophrenia.* London, UK: Routledge.

(1992b). A proposal to classify happiness as a psychiatric disorder. *Journal of Medical Ethics*, 18, 94–8.

(2003). *Madness explained.* London, UK: Penguin.

(2006). Madness explained: Why we must reject the Kraepelinian paradigm and replace it with a complaint-orientated approach to understanding mental illness. *Medical Hypotheses*, 66, 220–33.

(2009). *Doctoring the mind.* London, UK: Penguin.

Bentall, R. P. & Fernyhough, C. (2008). Social predictors of psychotic experiences: Specificity and psychological mechanisms. *Schizophrenia Bulletin*, 34, 1012–20.

Bentall, R. P. & Slade, P. D. (1985). Reality testing and auditory hallucinations: A signal-detection analysis. *British Journal of Clinical Psychology*, 24, 159–69.

Berk, L. E. (1992). Children's private speech: An overview of theory and the status of research. In R. M. Diaz & L. E. Berk (eds), *Private speech: From social interaction to self-regulation* (pp. 17–53). Hove, UK: Lawrence Erlbaum Associates.

Bernal, B. & Ardila, A. (2009). The role of the arcuate fasciculus in conduction aphasia. *Brain*, 132, 2309–16.

Berrios, G. E. (1990). A theory of hallucinations: Auguste Tamburini. *History of Psychiatry*, 1, 145–50.

(2002). *The history of mental symptoms: Descriptive psychopathology since the nineteenth century.* Cambridge University Press.

& Dening, T. R. (1996). Pseudohallucinations: A conceptual history. *Psychological Medicine*, 26, 753–63.

Bevan Lewis, W. (1883). Cerebral localisation in its relationships to psychological medicine. *British Medical Journal*, 2, 624–8.

(1885). Magnan on certain peculiar features in bilateral hallucinations. *Brain*, 7, 562–4.

Bick, P. A. & Kinsbourne, M. (1987). Auditory hallucinations and subvocal speech in schizophrenic patients. *American Journal of Psychiatry*, 144, 222–5.

Birchwood, M., Gilbert, P., Gilbert, J., Trower, P., Meaden, A., Hay, J. *et al.* (2004). Interpersonal and role-related schema influence the relationship with the 'dominant voice' in schizophrenia: A comparison of three models. *Psychological Medicine*, 34, 1571–80.

Birchwood, M., Meaden, A., Trower, P., Gilbert, P. & Plaistow, J. (2000). The power and omnipotence of voices: Subordination and entrapment by voices and significant others. *Psychological Medicine*, 30, 337–44.

Birchwood, M., & Trower, P. (2006). The future of cognitive-behavioural therapy for psychosis: Not a quasi-neuroleptic. *British Journal of Psychiatry*, 188, 107–8.

Bisulli, F., Tinuper, P., Avoni, P., Striano, P., Striano, S., d'Orsi, G. *et al.* (2004). Idiopathic partial epilepsy with auditory features (IPEAF): A clinical and genetic study of 53 sporadic cases. *Brain*, 127, 1343–52.

Bjorkly, S. (2002). Psychotic symptoms and violence toward others – a literature review of some preliminary findings: Part 2. Hallucinations. *Aggression and Violent Behavior*, 7, 605–15.

Black, D. N., Taber, K. H. & Hurley, R. A. (2003). Metachromic leukodystrophy: A model for the study of psychosis. *Journal of Neuropsychiatry and Clinical Neurosciences*, 15, 289–93.

Black, J. A. & Green, A. (1992). *Gods, demons, and symbols of ancient Mesopotamia: An illustrated dictionary*. University of Texas Press.

Blakemore, S.-J. (2003). Deluding the motor system. *Consciousness and Cognition*, 12, 647–55.

Blakemore, S.-J., Wolpert, D. M. & Frith, C. D. (2002). Abnormalities in the awareness of action. *Trends in Cognitive Sciences*, 6, 237–42.

Bleich, A. & Moskowits, L. (2000). Post traumatic stress disorder with psychotic features. *Croatian Medical Journal*, 41, 442–5.

Bleuler, E. (1950). *Dementia praecox or the group of schizophrenias*. New York, NY: International Universities Press.

Blom, J. D. (2010). *A dictionary of hallucinations*. Berlin, Germany: Springer.

Blumenfeld-Kosinski, R. (2006). *Poets, saints, and visionaries of the Great Schism*. University Park, PA: Pennsylvania State University Press.

Böcker, K. B., Hijman, R., Kahn, R. S. & de Haan, E. H. (2000). Perception, mental imagery and reality discrimination in hallucinating and non-hallucinating schizophrenic patients. *British Journal of Clinical Psychology*, 39, 397–406.

Bola, J. R. (2006). Medication-free research in early episode schizophrenia: Evidence of long-term harm? *Schizophrenia Bulletin*, 32, 288–96.

Borch-Jacobsen, M. (2001). Making psychiatric history: Madness as folie à plusieurs. *History of the Human Sciences*, 14, 19–38.

Bourguignon, E. (1970). Hallucinations and trance: An anthropologist's perspective. In W. Keup (ed.), *Origins and mechanisms of hallucination.* New York, NY: Plenum Press.

Bowman, K. M. & Raymond, A. F. (1931). A statistical study of hallucinations in the manic-depressive psychoses. *American Journal of Psychiatry,* 11, 299–309.

Boyd, T. & Gumley, A. (2007). An experiential perspective on persecutory paranoia: A grounded theory construction. *Psychology and Psychotherapy: Theory, Research and Practice,* 80, 1–22.

Boyle, M. (2002). *Schizophrenia: A scientific delusion?* 2nd edn. London: Routledge.

BPS (2000). *Understanding mental illness and psychotic experiences: A report by the British Psychological Society Division of Clinical Psychology.* Leicester, UK: British Psychological Society.

Bracken, P. & Thomas, P. (2005). *Post-psychiatry: Mental health in a postmodern world.* Oxford University Press.

Braham, L. G., Trower, P. & Birchwood, M. (2004). Acting on command hallucinations and dangerous behavior: A critique of the major findings in the last decade. *Clinical Psychology Review,* 24, 513–28.

Braun, C. M., Dumont, M., Duval, J., Hamel-Hebert, I. & Godbout, L. (2003). Brain modules of hallucination: An analysis of multiple patients with brain lesions. *Journal of Psychiatry & Neuroscience,* 28, 432–49.

Brébion, G., David, A. S., Bressan, R. A., Ohlsen, R. I. & Pilowsky, L. S. (2009). Hallucinations and two types of free-recall intrusion in schizophrenia. *Psychological Medicine,* 39, 917–26.

Bredkjaer, S. R., Mortensen, P. B. & Parnas, J. (1998). Epilepsy and non-organic, non-affective psychosis. National epidemiological study. *British Journal of Psychiatry,* 172, 235–8.

Breier, A., Buchanan, R. W., Irish, D. & Carpenter, W. T. Jr. (2000). Clozapine treatment of outpatients with schizophrenia: Outcome and long-term response patterns. *Psychiatric Services,* 51, 1249–53.

Brenan, G. (1975). *St John of the Cross: His life and poetry.* Cambridge University Press.

Brenner, H. D., Dencker, S. J., Goldstein, M. J., Hubbard, J. W., Keegan, D. L., Krugerm G. *et al.* (1990). Defining treatment refractoriness in schizophrenia. *Schizophrenia Bulletin,* 16, 551–61.

Brewin, C. R. (2003). *Posttraumatic stress disorder: Malady or myth?* New Haven, CT: Yale University Press.

Brewin, C. R., Andrews, B. & Valentine, J. D. (2000). Meta-analysis of risk factors for posttraumatic stress disorder in trauma-exposed adults. *Journal of Consulting and Clinical Psychology,* 68, 748–66.

Brewin, C. R., Dalgleish, T. & Joseph, S. (1996). A dual representation theory of post traumatic stress disorder. *Psychological Review,* 103, 670–86.

Brewin, C. R., & Patel, T. (2010). Auditory pseudohallucinations in United Kingdom war veterans and civilians with posttraumatic stress disorder. *Journal of Clinical Psychiatry,* 71, 419–25.

Briere, J. (1992). Methodological issues in the study of sexual abuse effects. *Journal of Consulting & Clinical Psychology,* 60, 196–203.

Brown, W. A. & Herz, L. R. (1989). Response to neuroleptic drugs as a device for classifying schizophrenia. *Schizophrenia Bulletin*, 15, 123–9.

Brunelin, J., Combris, M., Poulet, E., Kallel, L., D'Amato, T., Dalery, J. *et al.* (2006a). Source monitoring deficits in hallucinating compared to non-hallucinating patients with schizophrenia. *European Psychiatry*, 21, 259–61.

Brunelin, J., Poulet, E., Bediou, B., Kalle, L., Dalery, J., D'Amato, T. *et al.* (2006b). Low frequency repetitive transcranial magnetic stimulation improves source monitoring deficit in hallucinating patients with schizophrenia. *Schizophrenia Research*, 81, 41–5.

Bucher, B. & Fabricatore, J. (1970). Use of patient-administered shock to suppress hallucinations. *Behavior Therapy*, 1, 382–5.

Buchsbaum, B. R. & D'Esposito, M. (2008). The search for the phonological store: From loop to convolution. *Journal of Cognitive Neuroscience*, 20, 762–78.

Buckner, R. L., Andrews-Hanna, J. R. & Schacter, D. L. (2008). The brain's default network: Anatomy, function, and relevance to disease. *Annals of the New York Academy of Sciences*, 1124, 1–38.

Buckner, R. L. & Carroll, D. C. (2007a) Self-projection and the brain. *Trends in Cognitive Sciences*, 11, 49–57.

Buckner, R. L., & Vincent, J. L. (2007b). Unrest at rest: Default activity and spontaneous network correlations. *Neuroimage*, 37, 1091–6.

Bulik, C. M., Prescott, C. A. & Kendler, K. S. (2001). Features of childhood sexual abuse and the development of psychiatric and substance use disorders. *British Journal of Psychiatry*, 179, 444–9.

Bultmann, R. (1952). *Theology of the New Testament* (trans. Kendrick Grobel). London, UK: SCM Press.

Burns, A., Jacoby, R. & Levy, R. (1990). Psychiatric phenomena in Alzheimer's disease. *British Journal of Psychiatry*, 157, 72–94.

Burns, C. E. S., Heiby, E. M. & Tharp, R. G. (1983). A verbal behaviour analysis of auditory hallucinations. *The Behavior Analyst*, 6, 133–43.

Burton, R. (1621/1821). *The anatomy of melancholy*. Vol. I. London: Longman and Co.
(1621/1859). *The anatomy of melancholy*. Vol. III. Boston, MA: William Veazie.

Bush, G. (2005). George Bush: 'God told me to end the tyranny in Iraq'. Retrieved 10 October 2010 from www.guardian.co.uk/world/2005/oct/07/iraq.usa.

Buss, A. H. (1966). *Psychopathology*. New York, NY: John Wiley & Sons.

Byrne, S., Birchwood, M., Trower, P. E. & Meaden, A. (2006). *A casebook of cognitive behaviour therapy for command hallucinations: A social rank theory approach*. London, UK: Routledge.

Cachia, A., Paillere-Martinot, M. L., Galinowski, A., Januel, D., de Beaurepaire, R., Bellivier, F. *et al.* (2008). Cortical folding abnormalities in schizophrenia patients with resistant auditory hallucinations. *Neuroimage*, 39, 927–35.

Cacioppo, J. T. & Petty, R. E. (1981). Electromyograms as measures of affectivity and information processing. *American Psychologist*, 36, 441–56.

Caetano, S. C., Hatch, J. P., Brambilla, P., Sassi, R. B., Nicoletti, M., Mallinger, A. G. et al. (2004). Anatomical MRI study of hippocampus and amygdala in patients with current and remitted major depression. *Psychiatry Research-Neuroimaging*, 132, 141–7.

Cahill, C., Silbersweig, D. & Frith, C. (1996). Psychotic experiences induced in deluded patients using distorted auditory feedback. *Cognitive Neuropsychiatry*, 1, 201–11.

Campbell, M. L. C. & Morrison, A. P. (2007). The relationship between bullying, psychotic-like experiences and appraisals in 14–16-year olds. *Behaviour Research and Therapy*, 45, 1579–91.

Cangas, A. J., Sass, L. A. & Pérez-Álvarez, M. (2008). From the visions of St Teresa of Jesus to the voices of schizophrenia. *Philosophy, Psychiatry and Psychology*, 15, 239–50.

Canton-Cortes, D., Canton, J., Justicia, F. & Cortes, M. R. (2011). A model of the effects of child sexual abuse on post-traumatic stress: The mediating role of attributions of blame and avoidance coping. *Psicothema*, 23, 66–73.

Carpenter, W. T. & Buchanan, R. W. (2002). Commentary on the Soteria project: Misguided therapeutics. *Schizophrenia Bulletin*, 28, 577–81.

Carroll, B. E. (1997). *Spiritualism in antebellum America*. Bloomington, IN: Indiana University Press.

Carruthers, P. (2002). The cognitive functions of language. *Behavioral and Brain Sciences*, 25, 657–74.

Carter, C. S., MacDonald, A. W., Ross, L. L. & Stenger, V. A. (2001). Anterior cingulate cortex activity and impaired self-monitoring of performance in patients with schizophrenia: An event-related fMRI study. *American Journal of Psychiatry*, 158, 1423–8.

Caspi, A., Moffitt, T. E., Cannon, M., McClay, J., Murray, R., Harrington, H. et al. (2005). Moderation of the effect of adolescent-onset cannabis use on adult psychosis by a functional polymorphism in the Catechol-O-Methyltransferase gene: Longitudinal evidence of a Gene X environment interaction. *Biological Psychiatry*, 57, 1117–27.

Catani, M., Jones, D. K. & ffytche, D. (2005). Perisylvian language networks of the human brain. *Annals of Neurology*, 57, 8–16.

Cather, C., Penn, D., Otto, M. W., Yovela, I., Mueser, K. T. & Goff, D. C. (2005). A pilot study of functional Cognitive Behavioral Therapy (fCBT) for schizophrenia. *Schizophrenia Research*, 74, 201–9.

Cavanna, A. E., Trimble, M., Cinti, F. & Monaco, F. (2007). The 'bicameral mind' 30 years on: A critical reappraisal of Julian Jaynes' hypothesis. *Functional Neurology*, 22, 11–15.

Chadwick, P., Lees, S. & Birchwood, M. (2000). The revised Beliefs About Voices Questionnaire (BAVQ-R). *British Journal of Psychiatry*, 177, 229–32.

Chadwick, P., Taylor, K. N. & Abba, N. (2005). Mindfulness groups for people with psychosis. *Behavioural and Cognitive Psychotherapy*, 33, 351–9.

Chaturvedi, S. K. & Sinha, V. K. (1990). Recurrence of hallucinations in consecutive episodes of schizophrenia and affective disorder. *Schizophrenia Research*, 3, 103–6.

Chen, P. C. Y. (1970). Classification and concepts of causation of mental illness in a rural Malay community. *International Journal of Social Psychiatry*, 16, 205–15.

Chernomas, W. M., Clarke, D. E. & Chisholm F. A. (2000). Perspectives of women living with schizophrenia. *Psychiatric Services*, 51, 1517–21.

Cherry, E. C. (1953). Some experiments on the recognition of speech, with one and two ears. *Journal of the Acoustical Society of America*, 25, 975–9.

Cheung, P., Schweitzer, I., Crowley, K. & Tuckwell, V. (1997). Violence in schizophrenia: Role of hallucinations and delusions. *Schizophrenia Research*, 26, 181–90.

Chin, J. T., Hayward, M. & Drinnan, A. (2009). 'Relating' to voices: Exploring the relevance of this concept to people who hear voices. *Psychology and Psychotherapy: Theory, Research and Practice*, 82, 1–17.

Choi, J., Jeong, B., Rohan, M. L., Polcari, A. M. & Teicher, M. H. (2009). Preliminary evidence for white matter tract abnormalities in young adults exposed to parental verbal abuse. *Biological Psychiatry*, 65, 227–34.

Chu, C. & Klein, H. E. (1985). Psychosocial and environmental variables in outcome of black schizophrenics. *Journal of the National Medical Association*, 77, 793–6.

Churchland, P. S. (1986). *Neurophilosophy: Toward a unified science of the mind/ brain*. Cambridge, MA: MIT Press.

Cicchetti, D. & Rogosch, F. A. (1996). Equifinality and multifinality in developmental psychopathology. *Development and Psychopathology*, 8, 597–600.

Cicchetti, D., & Walker, E. (2001). Stress and development: Biological and psychological consequences. *Development and Psychopathology*, 13, 413–18.

Clark, S. (1999). *Thinking with demons: the idea of witchcraft in early modern Europe*. Oxford University Press.

Clarke, I. (2001). *Psychosis and spirituality: Exploring the New Frontier*. London: John Wiley & Sons.

Clayton, P., Desmarais, L. & Winokur, G. (1968). A study of normal bereavement. *American Journal of Psychiatry*, 125, 168–78.

Close, H. & Garety, P. (1998). Cognitive assessment of voices: Further developments in understanding the emotional impact of voices. *British Journal of Clinical Psychology*, 37, 173–88.

Cockshutt, G. (2004). Choices for voices: A voice hearer's perspective on hearing voices. *Cognitive Neuropsychiatry*, 9, 9–11.

Cohen, R. A., Grieve, S., Hoth, K. F., Paul, R. H., Sweet, L., Tate, D. *et al.* (2006). Early life stress and morphometry of the adult anterior cingulate cortex and caudate nuclei. *Biological Psychiatry*, 59, 975–82.

Cole, J. O., Goldberg, S. C. & Davis, J. M. (1966). Drugs in the treatment of psychosis: Controlled studies. In P. Solomon (ed.), *Psychiatric Drugs*. New York, NY: Grune & Stratton.

Cole, J. O., Goldberg, S. C. & Klerman, G. L. (1964). Phenothiazine treatment in acute schizophrenia. *Archives of General Psychiatry*, 10, 246–61.

Cole, M. G., Dowson, L., Dendukuri, N. & Belzile, E. (2002). The prevalence and phenomenology of auditory hallucinations among elderly subjects attending an audiology clinic. *International Journal of Geriatric Psychiatry*, 17, 444–52.

Coleman, R. (2000). *Recovery, an alien concept?* Gloucester, UK: Handsell.
  (2009, September). Talk given at the First International Hearing Voices World Congress, Maastricht, Holland.
  & Smith, M. (1997). *Working with voices: Victim to victor.* Gloucester, UK: Handsell.

Coltheart, M. & Langdon, R. (1998). Autism, modularity and levels of explanation in cognitive science. *Mind & Language*, 13, 138–52.

Conrad, J. (1900). *Lord Jim.* New York, NY: McClure, Phillips & Co.

Conway, M. A. & Pleydell-Pearce, C. W. (2000) The construction of autobiographical memories in the self-memory system. *Psychological Review*, 107, 261–88.

Cook, C., Powell, A. & Sims, A. (2009). *Spirituality and psychiatry.* London: Royal College of Psychiatry.

Copolov, D. L., Seal, M. L., Maruff, P., Ulusoy, R., Wong, M. T. H., Tochon-Danguy, H. J. *et al.* (2003). Cortical activation associated with the experience of auditory hallucinations and perception of human speech in schizophrenia: A PET correlation study. *Psychiatry Research: Neuroimaging*, 122, 139–52.

Copolov, D., Trauer, T. & Mackinnon, A. (2004). On the non-significance of internal versus external auditory hallucinations. *Schizophrenia Research*, 69, 1–6.

Corrigan, P. W. & Watson, A. C. (2003). At issue: Stop the stigma: Call mental disease a brain disease. *Schizophrenia Bulletin*, 30, 477–9.

Corstens, D., Escher, S. & Romme, M. (2008). In A. Moskowitz, I. Schafer and M. J. Dorahy (eds). *Psychosis, trauma, and dissociation: Emerging perspectives on severe psychopathology.* Chichester, Sussex: John Wiley & Sons.

Costain, W. F. (2008). The effects of cannabis abuse on the symptoms of schizophrenia: Patient perspectives. *International Journal of Mental Health Nursing*, 17, 227–35.

Craig, D., Mirakhur, A., Hart, D. J., McIlroy, S. P. & Passmore, A. P. (2005). A cross-sectional study of neuropsychiatric symptoms in 435 patients with Alzheimer's disease. *American Journal of Geriatric Psychiatry*, 13, 460–8.

Crapanzano, V. (1973). *The Hamadsha: A study in Moroccan ethnopsychiatry.* Berkeley, CA: University of California Press.

Creutzfeldt, O., Ojeman, G. & Lettich, E. (1989). Neuronal activity in the human lateral temporal lobe: II. Responses to the subject's own voice. *Experimental Brain Research*, 77, 476–89.

Critchley, E., Denmark, J., Warren, F. & Wilson, K. (1981). Hallucinatory experiences of prelingually profoundly deaf schizophrenics. *British Journal of Psychiatry*, 138, 30–2.

Crowe, S. F., Barot, J., Caldow, S., D'Aspromonte, J., Dell'Orso, J., Di Clemente, A. *et al.* (2011). The effect of caffeine and stress on auditory hallucinations in a non-clinical sample. *Personality and Individual Differences*, 50, 626–30.

Crozier, J. C., Van Voorhees, E. E., Hooper, S. R. & De Bellis, M. D. (2011). Effects of abuse and neglect on brain development. *Child Abuse and Neglect*, 5 16–25.

Cullberg, J. & Nyback, H. (1992). Persistent auditory hallucinations correlate with the size of the 3rd ventricle in schizophrenic-patients. *Acta Psychiatrica Scandinavica*, 86, 469–72.

Currie, S, Heathfield, K. W. G., Henson, R. A. & Scott, D. F. (1971). Clinical course and prognosis of temporal lobe epilepsy: A survey of 666 patients. *Brain*, 94, 173–90.

Cutting, J. (1990). *The right cerebral hemisphere and psychiatric disorders*. Oxford University Press.

Cutting, J. & Shepherd, M. (eds) (1987). *Clinical roots of the schizophrenia concept: Translations of seminal European contributions on schizophrenia*. Cambridge University Press.

Daalman, K., Boks, M. P., Diederen, K. M., de Weijer, A. D., Bloma, J. D., Kahn, R. S. *et al.* (2010). Same or different? Auditory verbal hallucinations in healthy and psychotic individuals. *Schizophrenia Research*, 117, 188–9.

Daprati, E., Sirigu, A., Pradat-Diehl, P., Franck, N. & Jeannerod, M. (2000). Recognition of self-produced movement in a case of severe neglect. *Neurocase: The Neural Basis of Cognition*, 6, 477–86.

David, A. S. (1994). The neuropsychological origin of auditory hallucinations. In A. S. David and J. C. Cutting (eds), *The neuropsychology of schizophrenia*. London, UK: Psychology Press.

(1999). Auditory hallucinations: Phenomenology, neuropsychology and neuroimaging update. *Acta Psychiatrica Scandinavica*, 99, 95–104.

(2004). The cognitive neuropsychology of auditory verbal hallucinations: An overview. *Cognitive Neuropsychiatry*, 9, 107–24.

David, D., Kutcher, G. S., Jackson, E. I. & Mellman, T. A. (1999). Psychotic symptoms in combat-related posttraumatic stress disorder. *Journal of Clinical Psychiatry*, 60, 29–32.

David, T. & Leudar, I. (2001). Head to head: Is hearing voices a sign of mental illness? *The Psychologist*, 14, 5, 256–9.

Davies, M. F., Griffin, M. & Vice, S. (2001). Affective reactions to auditory hallucinations in psychotic, evangelical and control groups. *British Journal of Clinical Psychology*, 40, 361–70.

Davis, J. M. (1976). Recent developments in the drug treatment of schizophrenia. *America Journal of Psychiatry*, 133, 208–14.

Schaffer, C. B., Killian, G. A., Kinard, C. & Chan, C. (1980). Important issues in the drug treatment of schizophrenia. *Schizophrenia Bulletin*, 6, 70–87.

Dawkins, R. (2007). *The god delusion*. London, UK: Transworld.

Dazzan, P., Morgan, K. D., Orr, K., Hutchinson, G., Chitnis, X., Suckling, J. *et al.* (2005). Different effects of typical and atypical antipsychotics on grey matter in first episode psychosis: The AE SOP study. *Neuropsychopharmacology*, 30, 765–74.

De Bellis, M. D., Keshavan, M. S., Frustaci, K., Shifflett, H., Iyengar, S., Beers, S. R. *et al.* (2002a). Superior temporal gyrus volumes in maltreated children and adolescents with PTSD. *Biological Psychiatry*, 51, 544–52.

De Bellis, M. D., Keshavan, M. S., Shifflett, H., Iyengar, S., Dahl, R. E., Axelson, D. A. *et al.* (2002b). Superior temporal gyrus volumes in pediatric generalized anxiety disorder. *Biological Psychiatry*, 51, 553–62.

De Boismont, A. B. (1860) *On Hallucinations* (trans. R. T. Hulme). Columbus, OH: Joseph H. Riley.

de Weijer, A. D., Mandl, R. C. W., Diederen, K. M. J., Neggers, S. F. W., Kohn, R. S., Hulshof, H. E. *et al.* (2011). Microstructural alterations of the arcuate fasciculus in schizophrenia patients with frequent auditory verbal hallucinations. *Schizophrenia Research*, 130, 68–77.

Decety, J. & Sommerville, J. A. (2003). Shared representations between self and other: A social cognitive neuroscience view. *Trends in Cognitive Sciences*, 7, 527–33.

Deiker, T. & Chambers, H. E. (1978). Structure and content of hallucinations in alcohol withdrawal and functional psychosis. *Journal of Studies on Alcohol*, 39, 1831–40.

Dein, S. & Littlewood, R. (2007). The voice of God. *Anthropology and Medicine*, 14, 213–28.

Dein, S., Cook, C. C. H., Powell, A. & Eagger, S. (2010). Religion, spirituality and mental health. *Psychiatrist*, 34, 63–4.

Delisi, L. E., Hoff, A. L., Neale, C. & Kushner, M. (1994). Asymmetries in the superior temporal lobe in male and female first-episode schizophrenic patients: Measures of the planum temporale and superior temporal gyrus by MRI. *Schizophrenia Research*, 12, 19–28.

Dell, P. F. (2006). A new model of dissociative identity disorder. *Psychiatric Clinics of North America*, 29, 1–26.

Dennett, D. (1991). *Consciousness explained.* London, UK: Penguin.

(1995). *Darwin's dangerous idea.* London, UK: Penguin.

Dhossche, D., Ferdinand, R., Van der Ende, J., Hofstra, M. B. & Verhulst, F. (2002). Diagnostic outcome of self-reported hallucinations in a community sample of adolescents. *Psychological Medicine*, 32, 619–27.

Diaz-Caneja, A. & Johnson S. (2004). The views and experiences of severely mentally ill mothers – A qualitative study. *Social Psychiatry and Psychiatric Epidemiology*, 39, 472–82.

Diederen, K. M. J., Daalman, K., de Weijer, A. D., Neggers, S. F. W., van Gastel, W., Blom, J. D. *et al.* (in press). Auditory hallucinations elicit similar brain activation in psychotic and nonpsychotic individuals. *Schizophrenia Bulletin.*

Diederen, K. M. J., Neggers, S. F. W., Daalman, K., Blom, J. D., Goekoop, R., Kahn, R. S. *et al.* (2010). Deactivation of the parahippocampal gyrus preceding auditory hallucinations in schizophrenia. *American Journal of Psychiatry*, 167, 427–35.

Diederen, K., Sommer, I. & Tendolkar, I. (2011). Language lateralization in healthy people with auditory verbal hallucinations: A pilot study. Unpublished manuscript. Retrieved 3 January 2011 from www.ru.nl/ publish/pages/565158/kellydiederen.pdf.

Dierks, T., Linden, D. E. J., Jandl, M., Formisano, E., Goebel, R., Lanfermann, H. *et al.* (1999). Activation of Heschl's gyrus during auditory hallucinations. *Neuron*, 22, 615–21.

Dilks, S., Tasker, F. & Wren, B. (2010). Managing the impact of psychosis: A grounded theory exploration of recovery processes. *British Journal of Clinical Psychology*, 49, 87–107.

Dillon, J. (2009, September). *Survival techniques: An exploration of hearing voices, self-harm, eating 'dis-orders' and dissociation as the consequence of surviving childhood trauma.* Paper presented at the First World Congress on Hearing Voices, Maastricht, Netherlands.

(2010). The tale of an ordinary girl. *Psychosis*, 2, 79–83.

Dillon, J., & May, R. (2002). Reclaiming experience. *Clinical Psychology*, 17, 25–7.

Ditman, T. & Kuperberg, G. R. (2005). A source-monitoring account of auditory verbal hallucinations in patients with schizophrenia. *Harvard Review of Psychiatry*, 13, 280–99.

Dodds, E. R. (1951). *The Greeks and the irrational.* University of California Press.

Dodgson, G. & Gordon, S. (2009). Avoiding false negatives: Are some auditory hallucinations an evolved design flaw? *Behavioural and Cognitive Psychotherapy*, 37, 325–34.

Dolan, R. J., Fletcher, P., Frith, C. D., Friston, K. J., Frackowiak, R. S. J. & Grasby, P. J. (1995). Dopaminergic modulation of an impaired cognitive activation in the anterior cingulate cortex in schizophrenia. *Nature*, 378, 180–2.

Dolgov, I. & McBeath, M. K. (2005). A signal-detection-theory representation of normal and hallucinatory perception. *Behavioral and Brain Sciences* 28, 761–2.

Dong, Q., Welsh, R. C., Chenevert, T. L., Carlos, R. C., Maly-Sundgren, P., Gomez-Hassan, D. M. *et al.* (2004). Clinical applications of diffusion tensor imaging. *Journal of Magnetic Resonance Imaging*, 19, 6–18.

Dorahy, M. J., Shannon, C., Seagar, L., Corr, M., Stewart, K., Hanna, D. *et al.* (2009). Auditory hallucinations in Dissociative Identity Disorder and schizophrenia with and without a childhood trauma history similarities and differences. *Journal of Nervous and Mental Disease*, 197, 892–8.

D'Orsi, G. & Tinuper, P. (2006). 'I heard voices . . .': From semiology, a historical review, and a new hypothesis on the presumed epilepsy of Joan of Arc. *Epilepsy & Behavior*, 9, 152–7.

Drinnan, A. & Lavender, T. (2006). Deconstructing delusions: A qualitative study examining the relationship between religious beliefs and religious delusions. *Mental Health, Religion and Culture*, 9, 317–31.

Du Feu, M. & McKenna, P. (1999). Prelingually profoundly deaf schizophrenic patients who hear voices: A phenomenological analysis. *Acta Psychiatrica Scandinavica*, 99, 453–9.

Dubé, R. & Hébert, M. (1988). Sexual abuse of children under 12 years of age: A review of 511 cases. *Child Abuse & Neglect*, 12, 321–30.

Durham, R. C., Guthrie, M., Morton, V., Reid, D. A., Treliving, L. R., Fowler, D. *et al.* (2003). Tayside-Fife clinical trial of cognitive-behavioural therapy for medication-resistant psychotic symptoms: Results to 3-month follow-up. *British Journal of Psychiatry*, 182, 303–11.

Eager, R. (1918). War psychoses occurring in cases with a definite history of shell shock. *British Medical Journal*, 1(2989), 422–5.

Ebbell, B. (1937). *The Papyrus Ebers: The greatest Egyptian medical document.* Oxford University Press.

Eckersley, G. S. (1996). *An angel at my shoulder: True stories of angelic encounters.* London, UK: Rider.

Edwards, G., Hawker, A., Williamson, V. & Hensman, C. (1966). London's Skid Row. *Lancet*, 1, 249–52.

Ehlers, A. & Clark, D. M. (2000). A cognitive model of posttraumatic stress disorder. *Behaviour Research and Therapy*, 38, 319–45.

Ehlers, A., Hackmann, A. & Michael, T. (2004). Intrusive re-experiencing in post-traumatic stress disorder: Phenomenology, theory, and therapy. *Memory*, 12, 403–15.

Eigen, M. (2005). *Psychotic core.* London, UK: Karnac.

Ellenson G. E. (1985). Detecting a history of incest: A predictive syndrome. *Social Casework: The Journal of Contemporary Social Work*, 66, 525–32.
(1986). Disturbances of perception in adult female incest survivors. *Social Casework: Journal of Contemporary Social Work*, 67, 149–59.

Elias, N. (1970). *What is society?* New York, NY: Columbia University Press.
(1991). *The society of individuals.* Cambridge, UK: Blackwell.

Elkes, J. & Elkes, C. (1954). Effect of chlorpromazine on the behaviour of chronically overactive psychotic patients. *British Medical Journal*, 560–5.

Elliott, B. Joyce, E. & Shorvon, S. (2009). Delusions, illusions and hallucinations in epilepsy: 2. Complex phenomena and psychosis. *Epilepsy Research*, 85, 172–86.

Elliott, D. (2002). Seeing double: Jean Gerson, the discernment of spirits, and Joan of Arc. *American Historical Review.* 107, 26–54.

El-Mallakh, P. (2006). Evolving self-care in individuals with schizophrenia and diabetes mellitus. *Archives of Psychiatric Nursing*, 20, 55–64.

Ensum, I. & Morrison, A. P. (2003). The effects of focus of attention on attributional bias in patients experiencing auditory hallucinations. *Behaviour Research and Therapy*, 41, 895–907.

Epstein, M. (1999). *Thoughts without a thinker: Psychotherapy from a Buddhist perspective.* London, UK: Duckworth.

Escher, S. & Romme, M. (2010). *Children hearing voices: What you need to know and what you can do.* Ross-on-Wye, UK: PCCS Books.

Escher, S. A., Romme, M., Buiks, A., Delespaul, P. & Van Os, J. (2002). Independent course of childhood auditory hallucinations: A sequential 3-year follow-up study. *British Journal of Psychiatry*, 181(suppl. 43), s10–s18.

Escher, S., Morris, M., Buiks, A., Delespaul, Ph., Van Os, J. & Romme, M. (2004). Determinants of outcome in the pathways through care for children hearing voices. *International Journal of Social Welfare*, 13, 208–22.

Esquirol, E. (1845). *Mental maladies: a treatise on insanity* (trans. E. K. Hunt). Philadelphia, PA: Lea and Blanchard.

Evagrius. (n.d., a). *Praktikos.* Retrieved 12 December 2011 from www.ldysinger.com/evagrius/01_Prak/00a_start.htm.
(n.d., b). *Peri Logismo.* Retrieved 12 December 2011 from www.ldysinger.com/evagrius/04_Peri-Log/00a_start.htm.

Evenson, E., Rhodes, J., Feigenbaum, J. & Solly, A. (2008). The experiences of fathers with psychosis. *Journal of Mental Health*, 17, 629–42.

Evenson, R. C. (1987). Auditory hallucinations and subvocal speech. *American Journal of Psychiatry*, 144, 1364–5.

Faaborg-Anderson, K. & Edfelt, A. W. (1958). Electromyograph of intrinsic and extrinsic laryngeal muscles during silent speech: Correlation with reading activity. *Acta Ortolaryngologia*, 49, 478–82.

Falk, Q. (2004). *Anthony Hopkins: The biography*. London, UK: Virgin Books.

Fann, K. T. (1971). *Wittgenstein's conception of philosophy*. Berkeley: University of California Press.

Farhall, J., Greenwood, K. M. & Jackson, H. J. (2007). Coping with hallucinated voices in schizophrenia: A review of self-initiated strategies and therapeutic interventions. *Clinical Psychology Review*, 27, 476–93.

Farhall, J., Freeman, N. C., Shawyer, F. & Trauer, T. (2009). An effectiveness trial of cognitive behaviour therapy in a representative sample of outpatients with psychosis. *British Journal of Clinical Psychology*, 48, 47–62.

Farrer, C. & Frith, C. D. (2002). Experiencing oneself vs another person as being the cause of an action: The neural correlates of the experience of agency. *Neuroimage*, 15, 596–603.

Feinberg, I. (1978). Efference copy and corollary discharge: Implications for thinking and its disorders. *Schizophrenia Bulletin*, 4, 636–40.

Feiring, C., Taska, L. & Chen, K. (2002). Trying to understand why horrible things happen: Attribution, shame, and symptom development following sexual abuse. *Child Maltreatment*, 7, 25–39.

Fenelon, G., Mahieux, F., Huon, R. & Ziegler, M. (2000). Hallucinations in Parkinson's disease: Prevalence, phenomenology and risk factors. *Brain*, 123, 733–45.

Fennig, S. M., Bromet, E., Jandorf, L., Schwartz, J., Lavell, J. & Ram, R. (1994). Eliciting psychotic symptoms using a semi-structured diagnostic interview. *Journal of Nervous and Mental Disease*, 182, 20–6.

Ferguson, S. M., Rayport, M., Gardner, R., Kass, W., Weiner, H. & Reiser, M. F. (1969). Similarities in mental content of psychotic states, spontaneous seizures, dreams, and responses to electrical brain stimulation in patients with temporal lobe epilepsy. *Psychosomatic Medicine*, 31, 479–98.

Fergusson, D. M., Boden, J. M. & Horwood, L. J. (2008). Exposure to childhood sexual and physical abuse and adjustment in early adulthood. *Child Abuse & Neglect*, 32, 607–19.

Fernyhough, C. (1996). The dialogic mind: A dialogic approach to the higher mental functions. *New Ideas in Psychology*, 14, 47–62.

(2004). Alien voices and inner dialogue: Towards a developmental account of auditory verbal hallucinations. *New Ideas in Psychology*, 22, 49–68.

(2009). Dialogic thinking. In A. Winsler, C. Fernyhough & I. Montero (eds), *Private speech, executive functioning, and the development of verbal self-regulation*. Cambridge University Press.

Fernyhough, C., Bland, K., Meins, E. & Coltheart, M. (2007). Imaginary companions and young children's responses to ambiguous auditory stimuli: Implications for typical and atypical development. *Journal of Child Psychology and Psychiatry*, 48, 1094–101.

Feroli, T. (2006). *Political speaking justified: Women prophets and the English Revolution*. Cranbury, NJ: Associated Universities Press.

Festinger, L. (1957). *A theory of cognitive dissonance*. Stanford University Press.

ffytche, D. H., Lappin, J. M. & Philpot, M. (2004). Visual command hallucinations in a patient with pure alexia. *Journal of Neurology Neurosurgery and Psychiatry*, 75, 80–6.

Finnis, J. (1998). *Aquinas*. Oxford University Press.

Fisher, D. J., Labelle, A. & Knott, V. J. (2008). Auditory hallucinations and the mismatch negativity: Processing speech and non-speech sounds in schizophrenia. *International Journal of Psychophysiology*, 70, 3–15.

Fitch, R. H., Miller, S. & Tallal, P. (1997). Neurobiology of speech perception. *Annual Review of Neuroscience*, 20, 331–53.

Flanagan, S. (1998). *Hildegard of Bingen, 1098–1179: A visionary life*. London, UK: Routledge.

Flaum, M., O'Leary, D. S., Swayze, V. W., Miller, D. D., Arndt, S. & Andreasen, N. C. (1995). Symptom dimensions and brain morphology in schizophrenia and related psychotic disorders. *Journal of Psychiatric Research*, 29, 261–76.

Fletcher, P., McKenna, P. J., Friston, K. J., Frith, C. D. & Dolan, R. J. (1999). Abnormal cingulate modulation of fronto-temporal connectivity in schizophrenia. *Neuroimage*, 9, 337–42.

Flugel, D., Cercignani, M., Symms, M. R., O'Toole, A., Thompson, P. J., Koepp, M. J. et al. (2006). Diffusion tensor imaging findings and their correlation with neuropsychological deficits in patients with temporal lobe epilepsy and interictal psychosis. *Epilepsia*, 47, 941–4.

Fodor, J. (1975). *The language of thought*. Cambridge, MA: Harvard University Press.

Fogleman, A. (2009). Finding a middle way: Late medieval naturalism and visionary experience. *Visual Resources*, 25, 7–28.

Forbes Winslow, L. S. (1879). *Private asylums. British Medical Journal*, 1, 128–9.

Ford, J. M., Roach, B. J., Jorgensen, K. W., Turner, J. A., Brown, G. G., Notestine, R. et al. (2009). Tuning in to the voices: A multisite fMRI Study of auditory hallucinations. *Schizophrenia Bulletin*, 35, 58–66.

Ford, J. M. & Mathalon, D. H. (2004). Electrophysiological evidence of corollary discharge dysfunction in schizophrenia during talking and thinking. *Journal of Psychiatric Research*, 38, 37–46.

    (2005). Corollary discharge dysfunction in schizophrenia: Can it explain auditory hallucinations? *International Journal of Psychophysiology*, 58, 179–89.

Ford, J. M., Mathalon, D. H., Kalba, S., Whitfield, S., Faustman, W. O. & Roth, W. T. (2001). Cortical responsiveness during inner speech in schizophrenia: An event-related potential study. *American Journal of Psychiatry*, 158, 1914–16.

Ford, J. M., Roach, B. J., Faustman, W. O. & Mathalon, D. H. (2007). Synch before you speak: Auditory hallucinations in schizophrenia. *American Journal of Psychiatry*, 164, 458–66.

Forstl, H., Burns, A., Levy, R. & Cairns, N. (1994). Neuropathological correlates of psychotic phenomena in confirmed Alzheimer's disease. *British Journal of Psychiatry*, 165, 53–9.

Foucault, M. (2006). *History of madness* (trans. J. Khalfa). Oxford, UK: Routledge.

Fowler, D. (1997). 'Direct and indirect links between the content of psychotic symptoms and past traumatic experience: Evidence from therapists' reports from the London–East Anglia study of cognitive behaviour therapy for psychosis'. Paper presented at the British Association of Behavioural and Cognitive Psychotherapy Annual Conference.

Fowler, D., Freeman, D., Steel, C., Hardy, A., Smith, B., Hackman, C. *et al.* (2006). The catastrophic interaction hypothesis: How do stress, trauma, emotion and information processing abnormalities lead to psychosis? In W. Larkin and A. P. Morrison (eds). *Trauma and psychosis: New directions for theory and therapy*. London, UK: Routledge.

Fox, G. (1808). *Journal. Vol 1*. Philadelphia, PA: Fry and Kammerer.

Fox, J. R. E., Gray, N. S. & Lewis, H. (2004). Factors determining compliance with command hallucinations with violent content: The role of social rank, perceived power of the voice and voice malevolence. *The Journal of Forensic Psychiatry and Psychology*, 15, 511–31.

Franck, N., Rouby, P., Daprati, E., Dalery, J., Mari-Cardine, M. & Georgieff, N. (2000). Confusion between silent and overt reading in schizophrenia. *Schizophrenia Research*, 41, 357–64.

Frank, A. (1995). *The wounded storyteller*. University of Chicago Press.

Frankfurt, H. G. (2007). *The importance of what we care about: Philosophical essays*. Cambridge University Press.

Freud, S. (1901/1958). The psychopathology of everyday life. In J. Strachey (ed. and trans.), *The standard edition of the complete psychological works of Sigmund Freud* (Vol. VI). London, UK: Hogarth Press.

Friston, K. J. & Frith, C. D. (1995). Schizophrenia: A disconnection syndrome. *Clinical Neuroscience*, 3, 89–97.

Frith, C. D. (1979). Consciousness, information processing and schizophrenia. *British Journal of Psychiatry*, 134, 225–35.

   (1992). *The cognitive neuropsychology of schizophrenia*. Hove, UK: Lawrence Erlbaum.

   (2002). Attention to action and awareness of other minds. *Consciousness and Cognition*, 11, 481–7.

Frith, C. D., Blakemore, S. J. & Wolpert, D. M. (2000). Explaining the symptoms of schizophrenia: Abnormalities in the awareness of action. *Brain Research Reviews*, 31, 357–63.

Frith, C. & Gallagher, S. (2002). Models of the pathological mind: An interview with Christopher Frith. *Journal of Consciousness Studies*, 9, 57–80.

Frith, C., Rees, G. & Friston, K. (1998). Psychosis and the experience of self – Brain systems underlying self-monitoring. *Neuroscience of the Mind on the Centennial of Freud's Project for a Scientific Psychology*, 843, 170–8.

Fujii, D. & Ahmed, I. (2002). Psychotic disorder following traumatic brain injury: A conceptual framework. *Cognitive Neuropsychiatry*, 7, 41–62.

Fuller Torrey, E. & Yolken, R. H. (2010). Psychiatric genocide: Nazi attempts to eradicate schizophrenia. *Schizophrenia Bulletin*, 36, 26–32.

Furdell, E. L. (2002). *Publishing and medicine in early modern England*. University of Rochester Press.

Gaitatzis, A., Carroll, K., Majeed, A. & Sander, W. (2004). The epidemiology of the comorbidity of epilepsy in the general population. *Epilepsia*, 45, 1613–22.

Gallagher, S. (2004). Neurocognitive models of schizophrenia: A neurophenomenological critique. *Psychopathology*, 37, 8–19.

Galton, F. (1907/2011). *Inquiries into human faculty and its development*. Retrieved 10 November 2011 from http://galton.org/books/human-faculty/text/galton-1883-human-faculty-v4.pdf.

Garcia-Marti, G., Aguilar, E. J., Lull, J. J., Marti-Bonmati, L., Escarti, M. J., Manjon, J. V. *et al.* (2008). Schizophrenia with auditory hallucinations: A voxel-based morphometry study. *Progress in Neuro-Psychopharmacology & Biological Psychiatry*, 32, 72–80.

Gardner, S. (1998). The tiger, the lamb and the terrible desert. Cranbury, NJ: Fairleigh Dickinson University Press.

Garrett, M. & Silva, R. (2003). Auditory hallucinations, source monitoring, and the belief that 'voices' are real. *Schizophrenia Bulletin*, 29, 445–57.

Garrett, M., Stone, D. & Turkington, D. (2006). Normalizing psychotic symptoms. *Psychology and Psychotherapy – Theory Research*, 79, 595–610.

Garrity, A. G. Pearlson, G. D. McKiernan, K. Lloyd, D., Kiehl, K. A. & Calhoun, V. D. (2007). Aberrant 'default mode' functional connectivity in schizophrenia. *American Journal of Psychiatry*, 164, 450–7.

Garzon, F. (2009). Rethinking integration: A prodding case in Brazil. *Journal of Psychology and Christianity*, 28, 78–83.

Gaser, C., Nenadic, I., Volz, H. P., Buchel, C. & Sauer, H. (2004). Neuroanatomy of 'hearing voices': A frontotemporal brain structural abnormality associated with auditory hallucinations in schizophrenia. *Cerebral Cortex*, 14, 91–6.

Gavrilescu, M., Rossell, S., Stuart, G. W., Shea, T. L., Innes-Brown, H., Henshall, K. *et al.* (2010). Reduced connectivity of the auditory cortex in patients with auditory hallucinations: A resting state functional magnetic resonance imaging study. *Psychological Medicine*, 40, 1149–58.

Gazzaniga, M. S. & LeDoux, J. E. (1978). *The integrated mind*. New York, NY: Plenum Press.

Gee, L., Pearce, E. & Jackson M. (2003). Quality of life in schizophrenia: A grounded theory approach. *Health and Quality of Life Outcomes*, 1, 1–11.

Geekie, J. (2004). Listening to the voices we hear: Clients' understandings of psychotic experiences. In J. Read, L. Mosher & R. Bentall (eds), *Models of madness: Psychological, social and biological approaches to schizophrenia*. London, UK: Routledge.

Gerson, J. (1998). *Jean Gerson: Early works* (trans. B. P. McGuire). New York, NY: Paulist Press.

Gibson, J. J. (1977). The theory of affordances. In R. Shaw & J. Bransford (eds), *Perceiving, acting, and knowing: Toward an ecological psychology*. Hillsdale, NJ: Erlbaum.

Gilbert, P. (1992). *Depression: The evolution of powerlessness*. Hove, UK: Erlbaum.

& Irons, C. (2005). Focused therapies and compassionate mind training for shame and self attacking. In P. Gilbert (ed.), *Compassion: Conceptualisations, research and use in psychotherapy*. Hove, UK: Routledge.

Gioia, D. (2006). Examining work delay in young adults with schizophrenia. *American Journal of Psychiatric Rehabilitation*, 9, 167–90.

Glass, I. B. (1989). Alcoholic hallucinosis: A psychiatric enigma – 1. The development of an idea. *British Journal of Addiction*, 84, 29–41.

Goffman, E. (1962). *Asylums: Essays on the social situation of mental patients and other inmates*. Chicago, IL: Aldine.

Goldberg, S. C., Klerman, G. L. & Cole, J. O. (1965). Changes in schizophrenic psychopathology and ward behaviour as a function of phenothiazine treatment. *British Journal of Psychiatry*, 111, 120–3.

Goldstein, J. E. (2001). *The French psychiatric profession in the nineteenth-century*. University of Chicago Press.

Gonzalez-Torres, M. A., Oraa, R., Aristegui, M., Fernandez-Rivas, A. & Guimon, J. (2007). Stigma and discrimination towards people with schizophrenia and their family members: A qualitative study with focus groups. *Social Psychiatry and Psychiatric Epidemiology*, 42, 14–23.

Goodwin, F. K. & Jamison, K. R. (1990). *Manic-depressive illness*. New York, NY: Oxford University Press.

Gottschalk, L. A. (2004). *World War II: Neuropsychiatric casualties, out of sight, out of mind*. New York, NY: Nova Science Publishers.

Gould, A., DeSouza, S. & Rebeiro-Gruhl, K. L. (2005). And then I lost that life: A shared narrative of four young men with schizophrenia. *British Journal of Occupational Therapy*, 68, 467–73.

Gould, L. N. (1948). Verbal hallucinations and activity of vocal musculature. *American Journal of Psychiatry*, 105, 367–72.

(1949). Auditory hallucinations and subvocal speech. *Journal of Nervous and Mental Disease*, 109, 418–27.

(1950). Verbal hallucinations as automatic speech. *American Journal of Psychiatry*, 107, 110–19.

Graham, G. & Stephens, G. L. (1994). *Philosophical psychopathology*. Boston, MA: MIT Press.

Graham, J M., Grunewald, R. A. & Sagar, H. J. (1997). Hallucinosis in idiopathic Parkinson's disease. *Journal of Neurology, Neurosurgery & Psychiatry*, 63, 434–40.

Gray, J. A. (1995). The contents of consciousness: A neuropsychological conjecture. *Behavioral and Brain Sciences*, 18, 659–722.

(1998). Integrating schizophrenia. *Schizophrenia Bulletin*, 24, 249–66.

Green, D. M. & Surets, J. A. (1966). *Signal detection theory and psychophysics*. New York, NY: Krieger.

Green, M. F. & Kinsbourne, M. (1990). Subvocal activity and auditory hallucinations: Clues for behavioural treatments. *Schizophrenia Bulletin*, 16, 617–25.

Green, P. & Preston, M. (1981). Reinforcement of vocal correlates of auditory hallucinations by auditory feedback: A case study. *British Journal of Psychiatry*, 139, 204–8.

Griffiths, B. (1954). *The golden string: An autobiography*. New York, NY: Templegate.

Grimby, A. (1993). Bereavement among elderly people: Grief reactions, post-bereavement hallucinations and quality of life. *Acta Psychiatrica Scandinavica*, 87, 72–80.

Guillem, F., Satterthwaite, J., Pampoulova, T. & Stip, E. (2009). Relationship between psychotic and obsessive compulsive symptoms in schizophrenia. *Schizophrenia Research*, 115, 358–62.

Gunduz-Bruce, H., McMeniman, M., Robinson, D. G., Woerner, M. G., Kane, J. M., Schooler, N. R. et al. (2005). Duration of untreated psychosis and time to treatment response for delusions and hallucinations. *American Journal of Psychiatry*, 162, 1966–9.

Gur, R. E., Maany, V., Mozley, D., Swanson, C., Bilker, W. & Gur, R. C. (1998). Subcortical MRI volumes in neuroleptic-naive and treated patients with schizophrenia. *American Journal of Psychiatry*, 155, 1711–17.

Haddock, G., McCarron, J., Tarrier, N. & Faragher, E. B. (1999). Scales to measure dimensions of hallucinations and delusions: The psychotic symptom rating scales (PSYRATS). *Psychological Medicine*, 29, 879–89.

Hagenaars, M. A., Brewin, C. R., van Minnen, A., Holmes, E. A. & Hoogduin, K. A. L. (2010). Intrusive images and intrusive thoughts as different phenomena: Two experimental studies. *Memory*, 18, 76–84.

Haggard, P., Newman, C. & Magno, E. (1999). On the perceived time of voluntary actions. *British Journal of Psychology*, 90, 291–303.

Hamilton, J. (1985). Auditory hallucinations in nonverbal quadriplegics. *Psychiatry*, 48, 382–92.

Hamm, T. D. (2003). *The Quakers in America*. New York, NY: Columbia University Press.

Hammersley, P., Dias, A., Todd, G., Bowen-Jones, K., Reilly, B. & Bentall, R. P. (2003). Childhood trauma and hallucinations in bipolar affective disorder: Preliminary investigation. *British Journal of Psychiatry*, 182, 543–7.

Hammersley, P. & Fox, R. (2006). Childhood trauma and psychosis in the major depressive disorders. In W. Larkin & A. P. Morrison (eds), *Trauma and psychosis: New directions for theory and therapy*. London, UK: Routledge.

Hammersley, P., Taylor, K., McGovern, J. & Kinderman, P. (2010). Attributions for hallucinations in bipolar affective disorder. *Behavioural and Cognitive Psychotherapy*, 38, 221–6.

Hammond, K. W., Kauders, F. R. & Macmurray, J. P. (1983). Schizophrenia in Palau: A descriptive study. *International Journal of Social Psychiatry*, 29, 161–70.

Hamner, M. B., Frueh, B. C., Ulmer, H. G. & Arana, G. W. (1999). Psychotic features and illness severity in combat veterans with chronic posttraumatic stress disorder. *Biological Psychiatry*, 45, 846–52.

Hardy, A., Fowler, D., Freeman, D., Smith, B., Steel, C., Evans, J. *et al.* (2005). Trauma and hallucinatory experiences in psychosis. *Journal of Nervous and Mental Disease*, 193, 501–7.

Hardy, J., Hall, C. R. & Hardy, L. (2005). Quantifying athlete self-talk. *Journal of Sports Sciences*, 23, 905–17.

Harley, T. A. (2010). *Talking the talk: Language, psychology and science.* London, UK: Psychology Press.

Haselton, M. G. & Nettle, D. (2006). The paranoid optimist: An integrative evolutionary model of cognitive bias. *Personality and Social Psychology Review*, 10, 47–66.

Hashimoto, R., Lee, K., Preus, A., McCarley, R. W. & Wible, C. G. (2010). An fMRI study of functional abnormalities in the verbal working memory system and the relationship to clinical synptoms in chronic schizophrenia. *Cerebral Cortex*, 20, 46–60.

Hassabis, D., Kumaran, D., Vann, S. D. & Maguire, E. A. (2007). Patients with hippocampal amnesia cannot imagine new experiences. *Proceedings of the National Academy of Sciences USA*, 104, 1726–31.

Havermans, R., Honig, A., Vuurman, E. F. P. M., Krabbendam, L., Wilmink, J., Lamers, T. *et al.* (1999). A controlled study of temporal lobe structure volumes and P300 responses in schizophrenic patients with persistent auditory hallucinations. *Schizophrenia Research*, 38, 151–8.

Hayward, M. & May, R. (2007). Daring to talk back. *Mental Health Practice*, 10, 12–15.

Heathcote-James, E. (2001). *Seeing angels.* London, UK: John Blake.

Heidegger, M. (1962). *Being and time* (trans. J. Macquarrie and E. Robinson). New York, NY: Harper & Row.

Heilbrun, A. B. & Blum, N. A. (1984). Cognitive vulnerability to auditory hallucination: Impaired perception of meaning. *British Journal of Psychiatry*, 144, 508–12.

Hein, G. & Knight, R. T. (2008). Superior temporal sulcus - It's my area: Or is it? *Journal of Cognitive Neuroscience*, 20, 2125–36.

Heinks-Maldonado, T. H., Mathalon, D. H., Houde, J. F., Gray, M., Faustman, W. O. & Ford, J. M. (2007). Relationship of imprecise corollary discharge in schizophrenia to auditory hallucinations. *Archives of General Psychiatry*, 64, 286–96.

Heins, T., Gray, A. & Tennant, M. (1990). Persisting hallucinations following childhood sexual abuse. *Australian and New Zealand Journal of Psychiatry*, 24, 561–5.

Henderson, M. J. & Mellers, J. D. C. (2000). Psychosis in Parkinson's disease: 'Between a rock and a hard place'. *International Review of Psychiatry*, 12, 319–34.

Henrich J., Heine, S. J. & Norenzayan, A. (2010). The weirdest people in the world. *Behavioral and Brain Sciences*, 33, 61–135.

Herman, J. L. (2001). *Trauma and recovery.* London, UK: Pandora.

Hermans, H. J. M. & Dimaggio, G. (eds) (2004). *The dialogical self in psychotherapy.* London, UK: Brunner-Routledge.

Heyd, M. (1995). *Be sober and reasonable: The critique of enthusiasm in the seventeenth and early eighteenth centuries.* New York, NY: Brill.

Hibbert, S. (1824). *Sketches of the philosophy of apparitions.* Edinburgh: Oliver & Boyd.

Hickok, G. & Poeppel, D. (2007). The cortical organization of speech perception. *Nature Reviews Neuroscience,* 8, 393–402.

Hill, C. (1991). *The world turned upside down: Radical ideas during the English Revolution.* London, UK: Penguin.

Hirayasu, Y., Potts, G. F., O'Donnell, B. F., Kwon, J. S., Arakaki, H., Akdaq, S. J. *et al.* (1998). Auditory mismatch negativity in schizophrenia: Topographic evaluation with a high-density recording montage. *American Journal of Psychiatry,* 155, 1281–3.

Hirsh, J. C. (1989). *The revelations of Margery Kempe. Paramystical practices in late medieval England.* Leiden, Netherlands: Brill.

Hobbs, C. J., Hanks, H. G. I. & Wynne, J. M. (2004). *Child abuse and neglect: A clinician's handbook.* London: Churchill Livingstone.

Hoffman, R. E. (1986). Verbal hallucinations and language production processes in schizophrenia. *Behavioral and Brain Sciences,* 9, 503–48.

   (2007). A social deafferentation hypothesis for induction of active schizophrenia. *Schizophrenia Bulletin,* 33, 1066–70.

   (2010). Revisiting Arieti's 'listening attitude' and hallucinated voices. *Schizophrenia Bulletin,* 36, 440–2.

Hoffman, R. E. & McGlashan, T. H. (1997). Synaptic elimination, neurodevelopment, and the mechanism of hallucinated 'voices' in Schizophrenia. *American Journal of Psychiatry,* 154, 1683–9.

Hoffman, R. E., Anderson, A. W., Varanko, M., Gore, J. C. & Hampson, M. (2008a). Time course of regional brain activation associated with onset of auditory/verbal hallucinations. *British Journal of Psychiatry,* 193, 424–5.

Hoffman, R. E., Hampson, M., Wu, K., Anderson, A. W., Gore, J. C., Buchanan, R. J. *et al.* (2007). Probing the pathophysiology of auditory/ verbal hallucinations by combining functional magnetic resonance imaging and transcranial magnetic stimulation. *Cerebral Cortex,* 17, 2733–43.

Hoffman, R. E., Varanko, M., Gilmore, J. & Mishara, A. L. (2008b). Experiential features used by patients with schizophrenia to differentiate 'voices' from ordinary verbal thought. *Psychological Medicine,* 38, 1167–76.

Holmes, C., Arranz, M. J., Powell, J. F., Collier, D. A. & Lovestone, S. (1998). 5-HT2A and 5-HT2C receptor polymorphisms and psychopathology in late onset Alzheimer's disease. *Human Molecular Genetics,* 7, 1507–9.

Holroyd, S., Currie, L. & Wooten, G. F. (2001). Prospective study of hallucinations and delusions in Parkinson's disease. *Journal of Neurology, Neurosurgery and Psychiatry,* 70, 734–8.

Holzinger, A., Kilian, R., Lindenbach, I., Petscheleit, A. & Angermeyer M. C. (2003). Patient's and their relatives' causal explanations of schizophrenia. *Social Psychiatry and Psychiatric Epidemiology,* 38, 155–62.

Honig, A., Romme, M., Ensink, B., Escher, S., Pennings, M. & Devries, M. (1998). Auditory hallucinations: A comparison between patients and non-patients. *Journal of Nervous and Mental Disease,* 186, 646–51.

Hopkins, A. (2009). *Golden voice saved me from alcoholism.* Retrieved 11 June 2009, from http://hearingvoicesmovement.blogspot.com/2008/06/ anthony-hopkins-golden-voice-saved-me.html.

Horacek, J., Brunovsky, M., Novak, T., Skidlantova, L., Klirova, M.,
Bubenikova-Valesova, V. *et al.* (2007). Effect of low-frequency-TMS on
electromagnetic tomography (LORETA) and regional brain metabolism
(PET) in schizophrenia patients with auditory hallucinations.
Neuropsychobiology, 55, 132–42.

Hornstein, G. (2009). *Agnes's jacket: A psychologist's search for the meanings of
madness.* New York, NY: Rodale Books.

Horowitz, M. (1975). Hallucinations: An information processing approach. In
R. K. Siegel & L. J. West (eds), *Hallucinations: Behavior, experience and
theory.* New York, NY: Wiley.

Horowitz, M., Wilner, N. & Alvarez, W. (1979). Impact of Event Scale:
A measure of subjective stress. *Psychosomatic Medicine*, 41, 209–18.

Horwood, J., Salvi, G., Thomas, K., Duffy, L., Gunnell, D., Hollis, C., *et al.*
(2008). IQ and non-clinical psychotic symptoms in 12-year-olds:
results from the ALSPAC birth cohort. *British Journal of Psychiatry*, 193,
185–191.

Hubert, S. J. (2002). *Questions of power: The politics of women's madness narratives.*
London, UK: Associated University Presses.

Hubl, D., Dougoud-Chauvin, V., Zeller, M., Federspiel, A., Boesch, C., Strik,
W. *et al.* (2010). Structural analysis of Heschl's Gyrus in schizophrenia
patients with auditory hallucinations. *Neuropsychobiology*, 61, 1–9.

Hubl, D., Koenig, T., Strik, W., Federspiel, A., Kreis, R., Boesch, C. *et al.*
(2004). Pathways that make voices – White matter changes in auditory
hallucinations. *Archives of General Psychiatry*, 61, 658–68.

Hugdahl, K. (ed.) (1988). *Handbook of dichotic listening: Theory, methods and
research.* Chichester, UK: John Wiley & Sons.

Hugdahl, K., Løberg, E. M., Specht, K., Steen, V. M., van Wageningen, H. &
Jorgensen, H. A. (2008). Auditory hallucinations in schizophrenia:
The role of cognitive, brain structural and genetic disturbances in the left
temporal lobe. *Frontiers in Human Neuroscience*, 1, 6.

Humberstone, V. (2002). The experiences of people with schizophrenia
living in supported accomodation: A qualitative study using grounded
theory methodology. *Australian and New Zealand Journal of Psychiatry*,
36, 367–72.

Hunter, M. D., Eickhoff, S. B., Miller, T. W. R., Farrow, T. F. D., Wilkinson,
I. D. & Woodruff, P. W. R. (2006). Neural activity in speech-sensitive
auditory cortex during silence. *Proceedings of the National Academy of Sciences
of the United States of America*, 103, 189–94.

Hurlburt, R. T. (1990). *Sampling normal and schizophrenic inner experience.*
New York, NY: Plenum Press.

Hurlburt, R. T., & Heavey, C. L. (2006). *Exploring inner experience: The
Descriptive Experience Sampling Method.* Amsterdam/Philadelphia: John
Benjamins.

Hurlburt, R. T., & Schwitzgebel, E. (2007). *Describing inner experience?:
Proponent meets skeptic.* Cambridge, MA: MIT Press.

Huxley, A. (1972). *The doors of perception: And heaven and hell.* London, UK:
Chatto & Windus.

Imada, T., Zhang, Y., Cheour, M., Taulu, S., Ahonen, A. & Kuhl, P. K. (2006). Infant speech perception activates Broca's area: A developmental magnetoencephalography study. *NeuroReport*, 17, 957–62.

Ingleby, D. (1981). Understanding 'mental illness'. In D. Ingleby (ed.), *Critical psychiatry: The politics of mental health*. New York, NY: Penguin.

Ingram, A. (1998) *Patterns of madness in the eighteenth century: A reader*. Liverpool University Press.

Inouye, T. & Shimizu, A. (1970). The electromyographic study of verbal hallucination. *Journal of Nervous and Mental Disease*, 151, 415–22.

Inzelberg, R., Kipervasser, S. & Korczyn, A. D. (1998). Auditory hallucinations in Parkinson's disease. *Journal of Neurology, Neurosurgery and Psychiatry*, 64, 533–5.

Irving, J. (2011). *Interviews: John Irving, the art of fiction No. 93. The Paris Review.* Retrieved 11 March 2011 from www.theparisreview.org/interviews/2757/the-art-of-fiction-no-93-john-irving.

Izumi, Y., Terao, T., Ishino, Y. & Nakamura, J. (2002). Differences in regional cerebral blood flow during musical and verbal hallucinations. *Psychiatry Research: Neuroimaging*, 116, 119–23.

Jablensky, A. (1997). The 100-year epidemiology of schizophrenia. *Schizophrenia Research*, 28, 111–25.

Jablensky, A., & Sartorius, N. (2008). What did the WHO studies really find? *Schizophrenia Bulletin*, 34, 253–5.

Jablensky, A., Sartorius, N., Ernberg, G. Anker, M., Korten, A., Cooper, J. E. *et al.* (1992). Schizophrenia: Manifestations, incidence and course in different cultures. A World Health Organization ten-country study. *Psychological Medicine Monograph Supplement*, 20, 1–97.

Jacobson, E. (1932). Electrophysiology of mental activities. *American Journal of Psychology*, 64, 677–94.

Jackson, M. & Fulford, K. W. M. (1997). Spiritual experience and psychopathology. *Philosophy, Psychiatry, & Psychology*, 4, 41–66.

Jackson, N. E. & Coltheart, M. (2001). *Routes to reading success and failure: Toward an integrated cognitive psychology of atypical reading*. Hove, UK: Lawrence Erlbaum Associates Ltd.

James, A. (2001). *Raising our voices: An account of the Hearing Voices Movement*. Gloucester, UK: Handsell.

James, T. (1995) *Dreams, creativity, and madness in nineteenth-century France*. Oxford: Clarendon Press.

James, W. (1960/1902) *The varieties of religious experience*. London: Collins.

Janssen, I., Krabbendam, L., Bak, M., Hanssen, M., Vollebergh, W., de Graaf, R. *et al.* (2004). Childhood abuse as a risk factor for psychotic experiences. *Acta Psychiatrica Scandinavica*, 109, 38–45.

Jardri, R., Delevoye-Turrell, Y., Lucas, B., Pins, D., Bulot, V. Delmaire, C. *et al.* (2007). Clinical practice of rTMS reveals a functional dissociation between agency and hallucination in schizophrenia. *Neuropsychologica*, 47, 132–8.

Jarosinski, J. M. (2008). Exploring the experience of hallucinations from a perspective of self: Surviving and persevering. *Journal of the American Psychiatric Nurses Association*, 14, 353–62.

Jaspers, K. (1962) *General psychopathology*. Manchester University Press.

Jaynes, J. (1986). Consciousness and voices of the mind. *Canadian Psychology*, 27, 128–48.

(2000). *The origin of consciousness in the breakdown of the bicameral mind*. New York, NY: Mariner Books.

Jenner, J. A., Rutten, S., Beuckens, J., Boonstra, N. & Sytema, S. (2008). Positive and useful auditory vocal hallucinations: Prevalence, characteristics, attributions, and implications for treatment. *Acta Psychiatrica Scandinavica*, 118, 238–45.

Jensen, D. (2000). *A language older than words*. New York, NY: Souvenir Press.

Johns, L. C., Cannon, M., Singleton, N., Murray, R. M., Farrell, M., Brugha, T. et al. (2004). Prevalence and correlates of self-reported psychotic symptoms in the British population. *British Journal of Psychiatry*, 185, 298–305.

Johns, L. C., Gregg, L., Allen, P. & McGuire, P. K. (2006). Impaired verbal self-monitoring in psychosis: Effects of state, trait and diagnosis. *Psychological Medicine*, 36, 465–74.

Johns, L. C., Nazroo, J. Y., Bebbington, P. & Kuipers, E. (2002). Occurrence of hallucinatory experiences in a community sample and ethnic variations. *British Journal of Psychiatry*, 180, 174–8.

Johns, L. C., Rossell, S., Frith, C., Ahmad, F., Hemsley, D., Kuipers, E. & McGuire, P. K. (2001). Verbal self-monitoring and auditory verbal hallucinations in patients with schizophrenia. *Psychological Medicine*, 31, 705–15.

Johnson, F. H. (1978). *The anatomy of hallucinations*. Chicago, IL: Nelson-Hall.

Johnson, J. (1994). Henry Maudsley on Swedenborg's messianic psychosis. *British Journal of Psychiatry*, 165, 690–1.

Johnson, M. K., Hashtroudi, S. & Lindsay, D. S. (1993). Source monitoring. *Psychological Bulletin*, 114, 3–28.

Johnstone, E. C., Frith, C. D., Crow, T. J. & Owens, D. G. C. (1988). The Northwick Park 'functional' psychosis study: Diagnosis and treatment response. *Lancet*, 322, 8603, 119–25.

Johnstone, L. (2000). *Users and abusers of psychiatry*. London, UK: Routledge.

Jones, S., Guy, A. & Ormrod, J. A. (2003). A Q-methodology study of hearing voices: A preliminary exploration of voice-hearers' understanding of their experiences. *Psychology and Psychotherapy: Theory, Research and Practice*, 76, 189–209.

Jones, S. R. (2009). The neuropsychology of covert and overt speech: Implications for the study of private speech in children and adults. In A. Winsler, C. Fernyhough and I. Montero (eds), *Private speech, executive functioning, and the development of verbal self-regulation*. Cambridge University Press.

(2010a). Do we need multiple models of auditory verbal hallucinations? Examining the phenomenological fit of cognitive and neurological models. *Schizophrenia Bulletin*, 36, 566–75.

(2010b). Re-expanding the phenomenology of hallucinations: Lessons from sixteenth century Spain. *Mental Health, Religion, and Culture*, 13, 187–208.

Jones, S. R. & Fernyhough, C. (2006). The roles of thought suppression and metacognitive style in proneness to auditory verbal hallucinations in a non-clinical sample. *Personality and Individual Differences*, 41, 1421–32.

(2007a). Neural correlates of inner speech and auditory verbal hallucinations: A critical review and theoretical integration. *Clinical Psychology Review*, 27, 140–54.

(2007b). Thought as action: Inner speech, self-monitoring, and auditory verbal hallucinations. *Consciousness and Cognition*, 16, 391–9.

(2007c). A new look at the diathesis-stress model of schizophrenia: The primacy of uncontrollable and social-evaluative situations. *Schizophrenia Bulletin*, 33, 1171–7.

(2008a). Speaking back to the spirits: The voices and visions of Emanuel Swedenborg. *History of the Human Sciences*, 21, 1–31.

(2008b). Rumination, reflection, intrusive thoughts, and hallucination-proneness: Towards a new model. *Behaviour Research and Therapy*, 47, 54–9.

(2009a). Did Emanuel Swedenborg have near-death experiences? Envisioning a developmental account of NDEs. *Journal of Near-Death Studies*, 27, 157–87.

(2009b). Caffeine, stress, and proneness to psychosis-like experiences: A preliminary investigation. *Personality and Individual Differences*, 46, 562–4.

Jones, S. R., Fernyhough, C. & Larøi, F. (2010). A phenomenological survey of auditory verbal hallucinations in the hypnagogic and hypnopompic states. *Phenomenology and the Cognitive Sciences*, 9, 213–24.

Jones, S. R., Fernyhough, C. & Meads, D. (2009). In a dark time: Development, validation, and correlates of the Durham Hypnagogic and Hypnopompic Hallucinations Questionnaire. *Personality and Individual Differences*, 46, 30–4.

Judge, A. M., Estroff, S. E., Perkins, D. O. & Penn, D. L. (2008). Recognizing and responding to early psychosis: A qualitative analysis of individual narratives. *Psychiatric Services*, 59, 96–9.

Julian of Norwich (1977). *Julian of Norwich: Showings* (trans. E. Colledge and J. Walsh). Mahweh, NJ: Paulist Press.

Jung, C. G. (1960). *The psychogenesis of mental disease* (trans. R. F. C. Hull). London: Routledge & Kegan Paul.

(1963). *Memories, dreams, reflections* (trans. R. Wilson and C. Wilson). London: Collins and Routledge & Kegan Paul.

(1977). *The collected works*. Vol. XVIII: *The symbolic life*. London: Routledge & Kegan Paul.

Junginger, J. & Frame, F. P. (1985). Self-report of the frequency and phenomenology of verbal hallucinations. *Journal of Nervous and Mental Disease*, 173, 149–55.

Junginger, J. & Rauscher, F. P. (1987). Vocal activity in verbal hallucinations. *Journal of Psychiatric Research*, 21, 101–9.

Kallmann, F. J. (1938). *The genetics of schizophrenia*. New York, NY: Augustin.

Kane, J., Honigfeld, G., Singer, J. & Meltzer, H. (1988). Clozapine for treatment-resistant schizophrenia. A double-blind comparison with chlorpromazine. *Archives of General Psychiatry*, 45, 789–96.

Kane, J. M. & Marder, S. R. (1993). Psychopharmacologic treatment of schizophrenia. *Schizophrenia Bulletin*, 19, 287–302.

Kanemoto, K., Kawasaki, J. & Kawai, I. (1996). Postictal psychosis: A comparison with acute interictal and chronic psychoses. *Epilepsia*, 37, 551–6.

Kant, I. (2002/1766) *Kant on Swedenborg: Dreams of a spirit seer and other writings*, trans. G. R. Johnson and G. A. Magee. Westchester, PA: Swedenborg Foundation.

Kapur, S. (2003). Psychosis as a state of aberrant salience: A framework linking biology, phenomenology, and pharmacology in schizophrenia. *American Journal of Psychiatry*, 160, 13–23.

Kapur, S., Agid, O., Mizrahi, R. & Li, M. (2006). How antipsychotics work – From receptors to reality. *NeuroRX*, 3, 10–21.

Kapur, S., Arenovich, T., Agid, O., Zipursky, R., Lindborg, S. & Jones, B. (2005). Evidence for onset of antipsychotic effects within the first 24 hours of treatment. *American Journal of Psychiatry*, 162, 939–46.

Karagulla, S. & Robertson, E. E. (1955). Psychical phenomena in temporal lobe epilepsy and the psychoses. *British Medical Journal*, 1, 748–52.

Karlsson, L.-B. (2008). 'More real than reality': A study of voice-hearing. *International Journal of Social Welfare*, 17, 365–73.

Kassim, K. & Kasim, M. S. (1995). Child sexual abuse: Psychosocial aspects of 101 cases seen in an urban Malaysian setting. *Child Abuse & Neglect*, 19, 793–9.

Kaufman, J., Birmaher, B., Clayton, S., Retano, A. & Wongchaowart, B. (1997). Case study: Trauma-related hallucinations. *Journal of the American Academy of Child and Adolescent Psychiatry*, 36, 1602–5.

Kavanaugh, K. & Rodriguez, O. (1991). *The collected works of St. John of the Cross*. Washington DC: ICS Publications.

Keck, P. E., McElroy, S. L., Havens, J. R., Altshuler, L. L., Nolen, W. A., Frye, M. A. *et al.* (2003). Psychosis in bipolar disorder: Phenomenology and impact on morbidity and course of illness. *Comprehensive Psychiatry*, 44, 263–9.

Keenan, J. P., Nelson, A., O'Connor, M. & Pascual-Leone, A. (2001). Self-recognition and the right hemisphere. *Nature*, 409(6818), 305.

Kendall, R. E. (2001). The distinction between mental and physical illness. *British Journal of Psychiatry*, 178, 490–3.

Kent, G. & Wahass, S. (1996). The content and characteristics of auditory hallucinations in Saudi Arabia and the UK: A cross-cultural comparison. *Acta Psychiatrica Scandinavica*, 94, 433–7.

Khalifa, N. & Hardie, T. (2005). Possession and jinn. *Journal of the Royal Society of Medicine*, 98, 351–3.

Kilcommons, A. M., Morrison, A. P., Knight, A. & Lobban, F. (2008). Psychotic experiences in people who have been sexually assaulted. *Social Psychiatry and Psychiatric Epidemiology*, 43, 602–11.

Kindler, J., Hube, D., Stirk, W. K., Dierks, T. & Koenig, T. (2010). Resting-state EEG in schizophrenia: auditory verbal hallucinations are related to shortening of specific microstates. *Clinical Neurophysiology*, 122, 1179–82.

King-Lenzmeier, A. H. (2001). *Hildegard of Bingen: An integrated vision.* Minnesota, MN: Liturgical Press.

Kingdon, D. G., Ashcroft, K., Bhandari, B., Gleeson, S., Warikoo, N., Symons, M. *et al.* (2010). Schizophrenia and Borderline Personality Disorder: Similarities and differences in the experience of auditory hallucinations, paranoia, and childhood trauma. *Journal of Nervous and Mental Disease*, 198, 399–403.

Kinnier Wilson, J. V. (1965). *An introduction to Babylonian psychiatry.* In *Studies in honor of Benno Landsberger on his seventy-fifth birthday.* University of Chicago Press (pp. 289–98).

Kitayama, N., Quinn, S. & Bremner, J. D. (2006). Smaller volume of anterior cingulate cortex in abuse-related posttraumatic stress disorder. *Journal of Affective Disorders*, 90, 171–4.

Kleinman, J. E., Gillin, J. C. & Wyatt, R. J. (1977). A comparison of the phenomenology of hallucinogens and schizophrenia from some autobiographical accounts. *Schizophrenia Bulletin*, 3, 560–86.

Knight, M. T. D., Wykes, T. & Hayward P. (2003). 'People don't understand': An investigation of stigma in schizophrenia using interpretative phenomenological analysis (IPA). *Journal of Mental Health*, 12, 209–22.

Knöchel, C., Oertel-Knöchel, V., Schönmeyer, R., Rotarska-Jagiela, A., van de Ven, V., Prvulovic, D. *et al.* (in press). Interhemispheric hypoconnectivity in schizophrenia: Fiber integrity and volume differences of the corpus caltosum in patients and unaffected relatives. *NeuroImage.*

Koivisto, K., Janhonen, S. & Vaisanen L. (2002). Applying a phenomenological method of analysis derived from Giorgi to a psychiatric nursing study. *Journal of Advanced Nursing*, 39, 258–65.

Kolko, D. J., Brown, E. J. & Berliner, L. (2002). Children's perceptions of their abusive experiences: Measurement and preliminary findings. *Child Maltreatment*, 7, 41–53.

Korsnes, M. S., Hugdahl, K., Nygard, M. & Bjørnaes, H. (2010). An fMRI study of auditory hallucinations in patients with epilepsy. *Epilepsia*, 51, 610–17.

Kraepelin, E. (1919). *Dementia praecox and paraphrenia* (trans. R. M. Barclay, G. M. Roberson (ed.)). Chicago Medical Book Co. (Original work published 1896.)

Kramer, H. & Sprenger, J. (1486/2000). *The malleus maleficarum.* Escondido, CA: The Book Tree.

Kramer, S. N. (1971). *The Sumerians: Their history, culture and character.* University of Chicago Press.

Krugman, R. D., Lenherr, M., Betz, L. & Fryer, G. E. (1986). The relationship between unemployment and physical abuse of children. *Child Abuse and Neglect*, 10, 415–18.

Kuipers, E., Garety, P., Fowler, D., Garety, D., Chisholm, D., Freeman, D. *et al.* (1997). The London-East Anglia randomised controlled trial of cognitive-behavioural therapy for psychosis. I. Effects of the treatment phase. *British Journal of Psychiatry*, 171, 319–27.

Kumari, V., Fannon, D., Ffytche, D. H., Raveendran, V., Antonova, E., Premkumar, P. *et al.* (2010). Functional MRI of verbal self-monitoring in schizophrenia: Performance and illness-specific effects. *Schizophrenia Bulletin*, 36, 740–55.

Laing, R. D. & Esterson, A. (1964). *Sanity, madness and the family.* London: Tavistock Publications.

Laithwaite, H. & Gumley, A. (2007). Sense of self, adaptation and recovery in patients with psychosis in a forensic NHS setting. *Clinical Psychology and Psychotherapy*, 14, 302–16.

Laliberte-Rudman, D., Yu, B., Scott, E. & Pajouhandeh, P. (2000). Exploration of the perspectives of persons with schizophrenia regarding quality of life. *American Journal of Occupational Therapy*, 54, 137–47.

Lambert, W. G. (1963). *Babylonian wisdom literature.* Oxford University Press.

Langdon, R., Jones, S. R., Connaughton, E. & Fernyhough, C. (2009). The phenomenology of inner speech: Comparison of schizophrenia patients with auditory verbal hallucinations and healthy controls. *Psychological Medicine*, 39, 655–63.

Lantz, M. S. & Giambanco, V. (2000). Acute onset of auditory hallucinations after initiation of celecoxib therapy. *American Journal of Psychiatry*, 157, 1022–3.

Laurens, K. R., Hodgins, S., Taylor, E. A. & Murray, R. M. (2011). Is earlier intervention for schizophrenia possible? Identifying antecedents of schizophrenia in children aged 9–12 years. In A. S. David, P. McGuffin & S. Kapur (eds), *Schizophrenia: The Final Frontier.* London, UK: Psychology Press.

Laurens, K. R., West, S. A., Murray, R. M. & Hodgins, S. (2008). Psychotic-like experiences and other antecedents of schizophrenia in children aged 9–12 years: A comparison of ethnic and migrant groups in the United Kingdom. *Psychological Medicine*, 38, 1103–11.

Le Bihan, D., Mangin, J. F., Poupon, C., Clark, C. A., Pappata, S., Molko, N. *et al.* (2001). Diffusion tensor imaging: Concepts and applications. *Journal of Magnetic Resonance Imaging*, 13, 534–46.

Lecrubier, Y., Perry, R., Milligan, G., Leeuwenkamp, O. & Morlock, R. (2007). Physician observations and perceptions of positive and negative symptoms of schizophrenia: A multinational, cross-sectional survey. *European Psychiatry*, 22, 371–9.

Lee, K., Yoshida, T., Kubicki, M., Bouix, S., Westin, C. F., Kindlmann, G. *et al.* (2009). Increased diffusivity in superior temporal gyrus in patients with schizophrenia: A Diffusion Tensor Imaging study. *Schizophrenia Research*, 108, 33–40.

Lee, T., Chong, S. A., Chan, Y. H. & Sathyadevan, G. (2004). Command hallucinations among Asian patients with schizophrenia. *Canadian Journal of Psychiatry*, 49, 838–42.

Lehmann, D. & Koenig, T. (1997). Spatio-temporal dynamics of alpha brain electric fields, and cognitive modes. *International Journal of Psychophysiology*, 26, 99–112.

Lehtinen, V., Aaltonen, J., Koffert, T, Rakkolainen, V. & Syvalahti, E. (2000). Two-year outcome in first-episode psychosis treated according to an integrated model: Is immediate neuroleptisation always needed? *European Psychiatry*, 15, 312–20.

Leighton, S. R. (1982). Aristotle and the emotions. *Phronesis*, 27, 144–74.

Lencucha, R., Kinsella, E. A. & Sumsion, T. (2008). The formation and maintenance of social relationships among individuals living with schizophrenia. *American Journal of Psychiatric Rehabilitation*, 11, 330–55.

Lennox, B. R., Bert, S., Park, G., Jones, P. B. & Morris, P. G. (1999). Spatial and temporal mapping of neural activity associated with auditory hallucinations. *Lancet*, 353, 644–30.

Lennox, B. R., Park, S. B. G., Medley, I., Morris, P. G. & Jones, P. B. (2000). The functional anatomy of auditory hallucinations in schizophrenia. *Psychiatry Research: Neuroimaging*, 100, 13–20.

Lesser, R. P., Lueders, H., Dunner, D. S., Hahn, J. & Cohen, L. (1984). The location of speech and writing functions in the frontal language area. *Brain*, 107, 275–91.

Leucht, S., Kane, J. M., Kissling, W., Hamann, J., Etschel, E. & Engel, R. (2005). Clinical implications of Brief Psychiatric Rating Scale scores. *British Journal of Psychiatry*, 187, 366–71.

Leudar, I. & Sharrock, W. (2003). Changing the past? *History of the Human Sciences*, 16, 105–21.

Leudar, I. & Thomas, P. (2000) *Voices of reason, voices of insanity: Studies of verbal hallucinations*. London, UK: Routledge.

Leudar, I., Thomas, P., McNally, D. & Glinski, A. (1997). What voices can do with words: pragmatics of verbal hallucinations. *Psychological Medicine*, 27, 885–98.

Levin, M. (1960) Bromide hallucinosis. *Archives of General Psychiatry*, 2, 429–33.

Levitan, C., Ward, P. B. & Catts, S. V. (1999). Superior temporal gyral volumes and laterality correlates of auditory hallucinations in schizophrenia. *Biological Psychiatry*, 46, 955–62.

Lewis, A. (1978). Psychiatry and the Jewish tradition. *Psychological Medicine*, 8, 9–19.

Lewis, C. S. (2002). *The complete C. S. Lewis*. San Francisco, CA: Harper.

Lewis, D. O., Yeager, C. A., Swica, Y., Pincus, J. H. & Lewis, M. (1997). Objective documentation of child abuse and dissociation in 12 murderers with dissociative identity disorder. *American Journal of Psychiatry*, 154, 1703–10.

Lewis, S. & Lieberman, J. (2008). CATIE and CUtLASS: Can we handle the truth? *British Journal of Psychiatry*, 192, 161–3.

Lewis, S., Tarrier, N., Haddock, G., Bentall, R., Kinderman, P., Kingdon, D. *et al.* (2002). Randomised, controlled trial of cognitive-behavioural therapy in early schizophrenia: Acute-phase outcomes. *British Journal of Psychiatry*, 181 (suppl. 43), s91–s97.

Lewis-Hanna, L. L., Hunter, M. D., Farrow, T. F. D., Wilkinson, I. D. & Woodruff, P. W. R. (in press). Enhanced cortical effects of auditory stimulation and auditory attention in healthy individuals prone to auditory hallucinations during partial wakefulness. *Neuroimage.*

Liberman A. M. & Mattingly, I. G. (1985). The motor theory of speech perception revised. *Cognition*, 21, 1–36.

Libet, B., Gleason, C. A., Wright, E. W. & Pearl, D. K. (1983). Time of conscious intention to act in relation to onset of cerebral activity (readiness potential): The unconscious initiation of a freely voluntary act. *Brain*, 106, 623–42.

Lieberman, J. A. & First, M. B. (2007). Renaming schizophrenia. *British Medical Journal*, 334, 108.

Lieberman, J. A., Stroup, S. & Perkins, D. O. (eds) (2006). *The American Psychiatric Publishing textbook of schizophrenia*. Washington DC: American Psychiatric Publishing.

Liégeois, F., Baldeweg, T., Connelly, A., Gadian, D. G., Mishkin, M. & Vargha-Khadem, F. (2003). Language fMRI abnormalities associated with FOXP2 gene mutation. *Nature Neuroscience*, 6, 1230–7.

Lim, D. (2003). Ketamine associated psychedelic effects and dependence. *Singapore Medical Journal*, 44, 31–44.

Line, P., Silberstein, R. B., Wright, J. J. & Copolov, D. L. (1998). Steady state visually evoked potential correlates of auditory hallucinations in schizophrenia. *Neuroimage*, 8, 370–6.

Littre, E. (1860). Un fragment de médecine rétrospective, *Philosophie Positive*, 5, 103–20.

Løberg, E. M., Jørgensen, H. A. & Hugdahl, K. (2004). DL in schizophrenic patients: Effects of previous vs. ongoing auditory hallucinations. *Psychiatry Research*, 128, 167–74.

Long, A. A. (2009). How did Socrates divine sign communicate with him? In S. Ahbel-Rappe and R. Kamtekar (eds), *A companion to Socrates*. London, UK: Blackwell.

Lorr, M. & Klett, C. J. (1966). *Inpatient multidimiensional Psychiatric Scale: Manual*. Palo Alto, CA: Consulting Psychologists Press.

Losonczy, M. F., Song, I. S., Mohs, R. C., Small, N. A., Davidson, M., Johns, C. A. *et al.* (1986). Correlates of lateral ventricular size in chronic schizophrenia, I: Behavioral and treatment response measures. *American Journal of Psychiatry*, 143, 976–81.

Luhrmann, T. M. (2005). The art of hearing God: Absorption, dissociation and contemporary American spirituality. *Spiritus: A Journal of Christian Spirituality*, 5, 133–57.

Lukoff, D. (1985). The diagnosis of mystical experiences with psychotic features. *Journal of Transpersonal Psychology*, 17, 155–81.

Lukoff, D., Lu, F. & Turner, R. (1992). Towards a more culturally sensitive DSM-IV: Psychoreligious and psychospiritual problems. *Journal of Nervous and Mental Disorders*, 180, 673–82.

Luria, A. R. (1961). *The role of speech in the regulation of behavior*. Harmondsworth, UK: Penguin.

Luske, B. (1990). *Mirrors of madness: Patrolling the psychic border*. New York, NY: Aldine De Gruyter.

Lynch, J. J. (1986). Evelyn Waugh during the 'Pinfold' years. *Modern Fiction Studies*, 32, 543–59.

Lysaker, P. H., Buck, K. D. & Larocco, V. A. (2007). Clinical & psychosocial significance of trauma history in the treatment of schizophrenia. *Journal of Psychosocial Nursing and Mental Health Services*, 45, 44–51.

MacAvoy, L. H. (2003). *The book of Margery Kempe*. Cambridge: D. S. Brewer.

MacDonald, E., Sauer, K., Howie, L. & Albiston, D. (2005). What happens to social relationships in early psychosis? A phenomenological study of young people's experiences. *Journal of Mental Health*, 14, 129–43.

MacDonald, M. (1983). *Mystical bedlam: Madness, anxiety and healing in seventeenth-century England*. Cambridge University Press.

Mahl, G. F., Rothenberg, A., Delgado, J. M. R. & Hamlin, H. (1964). Psychological response in the human to intracerebral electrical stimulation. *Psychosomatic Medicine*, 26, 337–68.

Maitland, S. (2008). *A book of silence*. London, UK: Granta.

Malone, D. (Producer and Director). (2006, June 18). *Voices in My Head* [Television broadcast]. London: Channel 4.

Margo, A., Hemsley, D. R. & Slade, P. D. (1981). The effects of varying auditory input on schizophrenic hallucinations. *British Journal of Psychiatry*, 139, 122–7.

Marneros, A. (2008). Psychiatry's 200th birthday. *British Journal of Psychiatry*, 193, 1–3.

Marr, H. C. (1919). *Psychoses of the war: Including neurasthenia and shell shock*. New York, NY: Oxford University Press.

Marti-Bonmati, L., Lull, J. J., Garcia-Marti, G., Aguilar, E. J., Moratal-Perez, D., Poyatos, C. *et al.* (2007). Chronic auditory hallucinations in schizophrenic patients: MR analysis of the coincidence between functional and morphologic abnormalities. *Radiology*, 244, 549–56.

Martínez-Manrique, F. & Vicente, A. (2010). 'What the . . .?' The role of inner speech in conscious thought. *The Journal of Consciousness Studies*, 17, 141–67.

Marwaha, S. & Johnson, S. (2005). Views and experiences of employment among people with psychosis: A qualitative descriptive study. *International Journal of Social Psychiatry*, 51, 302–16.

Maslow, A. (1943). A theory of human motivation. *Psychological Review*, 50, 370–96.

Mason, M. F., Norton, M. I., Van Horn, J. D., Wegner, D. M., Grafton, S. T. & Macrae, C. N. (2007). Wandering minds: The default network and stimulus-independent thought. *Science*, 315(5810), 393–5.

Mason, O., Startup, M., Halpin, S., Schall, U., Conrad, A. & Carr, V. (2004). Risk factors for transition to first episode psychosis among individuals with 'at-risk mental states'. *Schizophrenia Research*, 71, 227–37.

Masson, J. M. (2003). *The assault on truth: Freud's suppression of the seduction theory*. New York, NY: Ballantine Books.

Matsui, H., Nishinaka, K., Oda, M., Hara, N., Komatsu, K., Kubori, T. *et al.* (2006). Hypoperfusion of the auditory and prefrontal cortices in Parkinsonian patients with verbal hallucinations. *Movement Disorders*, 21, 2165–9.

Maudsley, H. (1869). Emanuel Swedenborg. *Journal of Mental Science*, 15, 417–36.

Mauritz, M. & van Meijel, B. (2009). Loss and grief in patients with schizophrenia: On living in another world. *Archives of Psychiatric Nursing*, 23, 251–60.

Mavromatis, A. (1988). *Hypnagogia: The unique state of consciousness between wakefulness and sleep*. London, UK: Routledge & Kegan Paul.

Mayhew, S. & Gilbert, P. (2008). Compassionate mind training with people who hear malevolent voices: A case series report. *Clinical Psychology and Psychotherapy*, 15, 113–38.

McCabe, R., Heath, C., Burns, T. & Priebe, S. (2002) Engagement of patients with psychosis in the consultation: Conversation analytic study. *British Medical Journal*, 325, 1148–51.

McCabe, R. & Priebe, S. (2003). Author's reply [Letters to editor]. *British Medical Journal*, 326, 550.

(2008). Communication and psychosis: It's good to talk, but how? *British Journal of Psychiatry*, 192, 404–5.

McCann, T. V. & Clark, E. (2004). Embodiment of severe and enduring mental illness: Finding meaning in schizophrenia. *Issues in Mental Health Nursing*, 25, 783–98.

McCarthy-Jones, S. (2011a). Seeing the unseen, hearing the unsaid: Hallucinations, psychology, and St Thomas Aquinas. *Mental Health, Religion and Culture*, 14, 353–69.

(2011b). Voices from the storm. A critical review of quantitative studies of auditory verbal hallucinations and childhood sexual abuse. *Clinical Psychology Review*, 31, 983–92.

McCarthy-Jones, S. & Fernyhough, C. (in press). The varieties of inner speech: Links between quality of inner speech and psychopathological variables in a sample of young adults. *Consciousness & Cognition*.

McDougall, W. (1927). *An outline of abnormal psychology*. London, UK: Meutheun.

McEvoy, J. P., Lieberman, J. A., Perkins, D. O., Hamer, R. M., Gu, H., Lazarus, A. *et al.* (2007). Efficacy and tolerability of olanzapine, quetiapine, and risperidone in the treatment of early psychosis: A randomized, double-blind 52-week comparison. *American Journal of Psychiatry*, 164, 1050–60.

McGowan, J. F., Lavender, T. & Garety P. A. (2005). Factors in outcome of cognitive-behavioural therapy for psychosis: Users' and clinicians' views. *Psychology and Psychotherapy: Theory, Research and Practice*, 78, 513–29.

McGruder, J. (2002). Life experience is not a disease or why medicalizing madness is counterproductive to recovery. *Occupational Therapy in Mental Health*, 17, 59–80.

McGuigan, F. J. (1966). Covert oral behaviour and auditory hallucinations. *Psychophysiology*, 3, 73–80.

McGuire, P. K., Murray, R. M. & Shah, G. M. S. (1993). Increased blood flow in Broca's area during auditory hallucinations in schizophrenia. *Lancet*, 342(8873), 703–6.

McGuire, P. K., Silbersweig, D. A. & Frith, C. D. (1996). Functional neuroanatomy of verbal self-monitoring. *Brain*, 119, 907–17.

McGuire, P. K., Silbersweig, D. A., Murray, R. M., David, A. S., Frackowiak, R. S. J. & Frith, C. D. (1995). Functional anatomy of inner speech and auditory verbal imagery. *Schizophrenia Research*, 15, 91–2.

(1996). Functional anatomy of inner speech and auditory verbal imagery. *Psychological Medicine*, 26, 29–38.

McKay, C. M., Headlam, D. M. & Copolov, D. L. (2000). Central auditory processing in patients with auditory hallucinations. *American Journal of Psychiatry*, 157, 759–66.

McKenna, T. (1993). *True hallucinations: Being an account of the author's extraordinary experiences in the devil's paradise.* San Francisco, CA: Harper.

McPherran, M. L. (1993). *The religion of Socrates.* Pennsylvania State University Press.

Medlicott, R. W. (1958). An inquiry into the significance of hallucinations with special reference to their occurrence in the sane. *International Record of Medicine and General Practice Clinics*, 171, 664–77.

Mehta, S. & Farina, A. (1997). Is being 'sick' really better? Effect of the disease view of mental disorder on stigma. *Journal of Social and Clinical Psychology*, 16, 405–19.

Mellor, C. S. (1970). First rank symptoms of schizophrenia. *British Journal of Psychiatry*, 117, 15–23.

Meltzer, H. Y. (1992). Treatment of the neuroleptic-nonresponsive schizophrenic patient. *Schizophrenia Bulletin*, 18, 515.

Meyer-Lindenberg, J. (1991). The holocaust and German psychiatry. *British Journal of Psychiatry*, 159, 7–12.

Miall, R. C. & Wolpert, D. M. (1995). An internal model for sensorimotor integration. *Science*, 269, 1880–2.

Midelfort, H. C. E. (1999). *A history of madness in sixteenth-century Germany.* Stanford University Press.

Milev, P., Ho, B. -C., Arndt, S., Nopoulos, P. & Andreasen, N. C. (2003). Initial magnetic resonance imaging volumetric brain measurements and outcome in schizophrenia: A prospective longitudinal study with 5-year follow-up. *Biological Psychiatry*, 54, 608–15.

Miller, L. J. (1996). Qualitative changes in hallucinations. *American Journal of Psychiatry*, 153, 265–7.

Miller, L. J., O'Connor, E. & DiPasquale, T. (1993). Patients' attitudes toward hallucinations. *American Journal of Psychiatry*, 150, 584–8.

Millham A. & Easton, S. (1998). Prevalence of auditory hallucinations in nurses in mental health. *Journal of Psychiatric Mental Health Nursing*, 5, 95–9.

Milton, J. (1821). *Paradise lost.* London, UK: John Bumpus.

Mintz, S. & Alpert, M. (1972). Imagery vividness, reality testing, and schizophrenic hallucinations. *Journal of Abnormal Psychology*, 19, 310–16.

Mitchell, R. L. C. & Crow, T. J. (2005). Right hemisphere language functions and schizophrenia: The forgotten hemisphere? *Brain*, 128, 963–78.

Mizrahi, R., Bagby, M., Zipursky, R. B. & Kapur, S. (2005). How antipsychotics work: The patient's perspective. *Progress in Neuro-Psychopharmacology & Biological Psychiatry*, 29, 859–64.

Modinos, G., Vercammen, A., Mechelli, A., Knegtering, H., McGuire, P. K. & Aleman, A. (2009). Structural covariance in the hallucinating brain: A voxel-based morphometry study. *Journal of Psychiatry & Neuroscience*, 34, 465–9.

Mohamed, I. S., Otsubo, H., Pang, E., Chuang, S. H., Rutka, J. T., Dirks, P. *et al.* (2006). Magnetoencephalographic spike sources associated with auditory auras in paediatric localisation-related epilepsy. *Journal of Neurology, Neurosurgery and Psychiatry*, 77, 1256–61.

Moncrieff, J. (2010). Psychiatric diagnosis as a political device. *Social Theory & Health*, 8, 370–82.

Moritz, S. & Larøi, F. (2008). Differences and similarities in the sensory and cognitive signatures of voice-hearing, intrusions and thoughts. *Schizophrenia Research*, 102, 96–107.

Morrison, A. P. (2001). Cognitive therapy for auditory hallucinations as an alternative to antipsychotic medication: A case series. *Clinical Psychology and Psychotherapy*, 8, 136–47.

Morrison, A. P. & Baker, C. A. (2000). Intrusive thoughts and auditory hallucinations: A comparative study of intrusions in psychosis. *Behaviour Research and Therapy*, 38, 1097–1106.

Morrison, A. P., French, P., Walford, L., Lewis, S. W., Kilcommons, A., Green, J. *et al.* (2004a). Cognitive therapy for the prevention of psychosis in people at ultra-high risk: Randomised controlled trial. *British Journal of Psychiatry*, 185, 291–7.

Morrison, A. P., Haddock, G. & Tarrier, N. (1995). Intrusive thoughts and auditory hallucinations: A cognitive approach. *Behavioural and Cognitive Psychotherapy*, 23, 265–80.

Morrison, A. P. & Peterson, T. (2003). Trauma, metacognition and predisposition to hallucinations in non-patients. *Behavioural and Cognitive Psychotherapy*, 31, 235–46.

Morrison, A. P., Renton, J. C., Williams, S., Dunn, H., Knight, A., Kreutz, M. *et al.* (2004b). Delivering cognitive therapy to people with psychosis in a community mental health setting: An effectiveness study. *Acta Psychiatrica Scandinavia*, 110, 36–44.

Mosher, L. R. & Hendrix, V. (2004). *Soteria: Through Madness to Deliverance.* San Francisco, CA: XLibris.

Mosher, L. R. & Menn, A. (1978). Communcity residential treatment for schizophrenia: Two-year follow-up data. *Hospital & Community Psychiatry*, 29, 715–23.

Mosher, L. R , Vallone, R. & Menn, A. Z. (1995). The treatment of acute psychosis without neuroleptics: Six-week psychopathology outcome data from the Soteria project. *International Journal of Social Psychiatry*, 41, 157–73.

Moskowitz, A. & Corstens, D. (2007). Auditory hallucinations: Psychotic symptom or dissociative experience? *The Journal of Psychological Trauma*, 6, 35–63.

Mueser, K. T. & Butler R. W. (1987). Auditory hallucinations in combat-related chronic posttraumatic stress disorder. *American Journal of Psychiatry*, 44, 299–302.

Mullen, P. E. (1997). The mental state and states of mind. In R. Murray, P. Hill & P. McGuffin (eds), *The essentials of postgraduate psychiatry*. Cambridge University Press.

Mundy, P., Robertson, M., Robertson, J. & Greenblatt, M. (1990). The prevalence of psychotic symptoms in homeless adolescents. *Journal of the American Academy of Child and Adolescent Psychiatry*, 29, 724–31.

Murphy, H. B. M., Wittkower, E. D., Fried, J. & Ellenberger, H. (1963). A cross-cultural survey of schizophrenia symptomatology. *International Journal of Social Psychiatry*, 10, 237–49.

Murphy, J. M. (1976). Psychiatric labelling in cross-cultural perspective. *Science*, 191, 1019–28.

Murthy, R. S., Bertolote, J. M., Epping-Jordan, J. A., Funk, M., Prentice, T., Saraceno, B. *et al.* (2001). *The World Health report mental health: New understanding new hope*. Geneva: World Health Organization.

Na, H. J. & Yang, S. (2009). Effects of listening to music on auditory hallucination and psychiatric symptoms in people with schizophrenia. *Journal of Korean Academy of Nursing*, 39, 62–71.

Näätänen, R. (1990). The role of attention in auditory information-processing as revealed by event-related potentials and other brain measures of cognitive function. *Behavioral and Brain Sciences*, 13, 201–32.

National Institute for Health and Clinical Excellence (2009). *CG82 Schizophrenia (update): Quick reference guide*. London, UK: NICE.

Nayani, T. H. & David, A. S. (1996). The auditory hallucination: A phenomenological survey. *Psychological Medicine*, 26, 177–89.

Ndetei, D. M. & Vadher, A. (1984). A comparative cross-cultural study of the frequencies of hallucinations in schizophrenia. *Acta Psychiatrica Scandinavica*, 70, 545–9.

Neckelmann, G., Specht, K., Lund, A., Ersland, L., Smievoll, A. I., Neckelmann, D. *et al.* (2006). MR morphometry analysis of grey matter volume reduction in schizophrenia: Association with hallucinations. *International Journal of Neuroscience*, 116, 9–23.

Nelson, H. E., Thrasher, S. & Barnes, T. R. E. (1991). Practical ways of alleviating auditory hallucinations. *British Medical Journal*, 302, 327.

Nenadic, I., Smesny, S., Schlosser, R. G. M., Sauer, H. & Gaser, C. (2010). Auditory hallucinations and brain structure in schizophrenia: Voxel-based morphometric study. *British Journal of Psychiatry*, 196, 412–13.

Nietzsche, F. (2001). *The gay science* (B. Williams, ed.). Cambridge University Press.

Nijenhuis, E. R. S. & van der Hart, O. (1999). Forgetting and re-experiencing trauma: From anesthesia to pain. In J. Goodwin & R. Attias (eds), *Splintered reflections: Images of the body in trauma*. New York, NY: Basic Books.

Nixon, G., Hagen, B. & Peters, T. (2010a). Recovery from psychosis: A phenomenological inquiry. *International Journal of Mental Health and Addiction*, 8, 620–35.

(2010b). Psychosis and transformation: A phenomenological inquiry. *International Journal of Mental Health and Addiction*, 8, 527–44.

Noble, T. F. X, Strauss, B., Osheim, D., Neuschel, K, Accampo, E., Roberts, D. D. *et al.* (2008). *Western Civilization: Beyond boundaries.* Boston, MA: Houghton Mifflin Company.

Noiseux, S. & Ricard N. (2008). Recovery as perceived by people with schizophrenia, family members and health professionals: A grounded theory. *International Journal of Nursing Studies*, 45, 1148–62.

Noll, R. (2007).*The encyclopedia of schizophrenia and other psychotic disorders.* New York: NY: Infobase Publishing.

O'Brien, M. A. (1924/2003). *Madness in ancient literature.* Whitefish, MT: Kessinger Publishing Co.

O'Daly, O. G., Frangou, S., Chitnis, X. & Shergill, S. S. (2007). Brain structural changes in schizophrenia patients with persistent hallucinations. *Psychiatry Research-Neuroimaging*, 156, 15–21.

O'Toole, M. S., Ohlsen, R. I., Taylor, T. M., Purvis, R., Walters, J. & Pilowsky L. S. (2004). Treating first episode psychosis – The service users' perspective: A focus group evaluation. *Journal of Psychiatric and Mental Health Nursing*, 11, 319–26.

Obermeier, A. & Kennison, R. (1997). The privileging of visio over vox in the mystical experiences of Hildegard of Bingen and Joan of Arc. *Mystics Quarterly*, 23, 137–63.

Oertel, V., Knöchel, C., Rotarska-Jagiela, A., Schönmeyer, R., Lindner, M., van de Wen, V. G. *et al.* (2010). Reduced laterality as a trait marker of schizophrenia—Evidence from structural and functional neuroimaging. *The Journal of Neuroscience*, 30, 2289–99.

Offen, L., Waller, G. & Thomas, G. (2003). Is reported childhood sexual abuse associated with the psychopathological characteristics of patients who experience auditory hallucinations? *Child Abuse & Neglect*, 27, 919–27.

Ohayon, M. M. (2000). Prevalence of hallucinations and their pathological associations in the general population. *Psychiatry Research*, 27, 153–64.

Okano, H., Hirano, T. & Balaban, E. (2000). Learning and memory. *Proceedings of the National Academy of Sciences of the United States of America*, 97, 12403–4.

Okasha, A. & Okasha, T. (2000). Notes on mental disorders in pharaonic Egypt. *History of Psychiatry*, 11, 413–24.

Olfson, M., Lewis-Fernandez, R., Weissman, M. M., Feder, A., Gameroff, M. J., Pilowsky, D. *et al.* (2002). Psychotic symptoms in an urban medical practice. *American Journal of Psychiatry*, 159, 1412–19.

Olin, R. (1999). Auditory hallucinations and the bicameral mind. *Lancet*, 354, 166.

Onitsuka, T., Shenton, M. E., Salisbury, D. F., Dickey, C. C., Kasai, K., Toner, S. K. *et al.* (2004). Middle and inferior temporal gyrus gray matter volume abnormalities in chronic schizophrenia: An MRI study. *American Journal of Psychiatry*, 161, 1603–11.

Orchard, A. (1997). *Cassell's dictionary of Norse myth and legend.* London, UK: Cassell.

Osterweiss, M., Solomon, F., & Green, M. (eds) (1984). *Bereavement: Reactions, consequences, and care.* Washington, DC: Yale University Press.

Ostwald, P. (1987). *Schumann: The inner voices of a musical genius.* Boston, MA: Northeastern University Press.

Owen, A. (1989). *The darkened room: Women, power, and spiritualism in late Victorian England.* University of Chicago Press.

Özdemir, E., Norton, A. & Schlaug, G. (2006). Shared and distinct neural correlates of singing and speaking. *NeuroImage*, 33, 628–35.

Padala, K. P., Padala, P. R., Malloy, T. & Burke, W. J. (2010). New onset multimodel hallucinations associated with mirtazapine: A case report. *International Psychogeriatrics*, 22, 837–9.

Papageorgiou, C., Oulis, P., Vasios, C., Kontopantelis, E., Uzunoglu, N., Rabavilas, A. *et al.* (2004). P300 alterations in schizophrenic patients experiencing auditory hallucinations. *European Neuropsychopharmacology*, 14, 227–36.

Parellada, E., Lomena, F., Font, M., Pareto, D., Gutierrez, F., Simo, M. *et al.* (2008). Fluordeoxyglucose-PET study in first-episode schizophrenic patients during the hallucinatory state, after remission and during linguistic-auditory activation. *Nuclear Medicine Communications*, 29, 894–900.

Paraskevaides, E. C. (1988). Drug points: Near fatal auditory hallucinations after buprenorphine. *British Medical Journal*, 296, 214.

Pargament, K. I. (2007). *Spiritually integrated psychotherapy: Understanding and addressing the sacred.* New York, NY: Guilford Press.

Parkes, C. M. (1964). Recent bereavement as a cause of mental illness. *British Journal of Psychiatry*, 110, 198–204.

Paus, T., Petrides, M., Evans, A. C. & Meyer, E. (1993). Role of the human anterior cingulate cortex in the control of oculomotor, manual, and speech responses: A positron emission topography study. *Journal of Neurophysiology*, 70, 453–69.

Pawlby, S., Fernyhough, C., Meins, E., Pariante, C. M., Senevirante, G. & Bentall, R. P. (2010). Mind-mindedness and maternal responsiveness in infant-mother interactions in mothers with severe mental illness. *Psychological Medicine*, 40, 1861–9.

Pearson, D., Burrow, A., FitzGerald, C., Green, K., Lee, G. & Wise, N. (2001). Auditory hallucinations in normal child populations. *Personality and Individual Differences*, 31, 401–7.

Pechtel, P. & Pizzagalli, D. A. (2011). Effects of early life stress on cognitive and affective function: An integrated review of human literature. *Psychopharmacology*, 214, 55–70.

Peers, E. A. (1943). *Spirit of flame: A study of St John of the Cross.* London, UK: Student Christian Movement Press.

Penfield, W. & Perot, P. (1963). The brain's record of auditory and visual experience. *Brain*, 86, 595–694.

Penn, D. L., Meyer, P. S., Evans, E., Wirth, R. J., Cai, K. & Burchinal, M. (2009). A randomized controlled trial of group cognitive-behavioral therapy vs. enhanced supportive therapy for auditory hallucinations. *Schizophrenia Research*, 109, 52–9.

Pérez-Álvarez, M., García-Montes, J. M., Perona-Garcelán, S. & Vallina-Fernández, O. (2008). Changing relationship with voices: New therapeutic perspectives for treating hallucinations. *Clinical Psychology and Psychotherapy*, 15, 75–85.

Perme, B., Chandrasekharan, R. & Vijaysagar, K. J. (2003). Follow-up study of alcoholic hallucinosis. *Indian Journal of Psychiatry*, 45, 244–6.

Perry, B. M., Taylor, D. & Shaw, S. K. (2007). 'You've got to have a positive state of mind': An interpretative phenomenological analysis of hope and first episode psychosis. *Journal of Mental Health*, 16, 781–93.

Persinger, M. A. (1993). Vectorial cerebral hemisphericity as differential sources for the sensed presence, mystical experiences and religious conversions. *Perceptual and Motor Skills*, 76, 915–30.

Persons, J. B. (1986). The advantages of studying psychological phenomena rather than psychiatric diagnoses. *American Psychologist*, 41, 1252–60.

Peters, E., Landau, S., McCrone, P., Cooke, M., Fisher, P., Steel, C. *et al.* (2010). A randomised controlled trial of cognitive behaviour therapy for psychosis in a routine clinical service. *Acta Psychiatrica Scandinavica*, 122, 302–18.

Peterson, D. E. (1982). *A mad people's history of madness*. University of Pittsburgh.

Petersen, R. C. & Stillman, R. C. (eds) (1978). Phencyclidine: An overview. *National Institute on Drug Abuse Research Monograph Series*, 21.

Philo Judaeus. (2011). *The Decalogue, Book 26*. Retrieved 12 February 2011 from www.ecmarsh.com/crl/philo/book26.htm.

Pinter, H., (2005). *Various voices: Prose, poetry, politics (1948–2005)*. London, UK: Faber & Faber.

Pintner, R. (1913). Inner speech during silent reading. *Psychological Review*, 20, 129–53.

Pitt, L., Kilbride, M., Welford, M., Nothard, S. & Morrison, A. P. (2009). Impact of a diagnosis of psychosis: User-led qualitative study. *Psychiatric Bulletin*, 33, 419–23.

Plato (1987). *Theaetetus* (trans. R. H. Waterford). London, UK: Penguin. (2003). *The last days of Socrates* (trans. H. Tredennick). London, UK: Penguin.

Platz, W. E., Oberlaender, F. A. & Seidl, M. L. (1995). The phenomenology of perceptual hallucinations in alcohol-induced delirium tremens. *Psychopathology*, 28, 247–55.

Plutarch (1878). A discourse concerning Socrates's daemon, in *Plutarch's Morals* (trans. W. W. Goodwin). Boston, MA: Little, Brown and Co.

Porter, R. (1987). *Mind-forg'd manacles: A history of madness in England from the Restoration to the Regency*. Boston, MA: Harvard University Press. (2002). *Madness: A brief history*. Oxford University Press.

Posey, T. B. & Losch, M. E. (1983). Auditory hallucinations of hearing voices in 375 normal subjects. *Imagination, Cognition and Personality*, 2, 99–113.

Powell, A. (2008). *A beach boy's own story*. Retrieved 10 March 2011 from www. telegraph.co.uk/culture/music/3554479/Brian-Wilson-a-Beach-Boys-own-story.html.

Powell, J. & Clarke, A. (2006). Information in mental health: Qualitative study of mental health service users. *Health Expectations*, 9, 359–65.

Prince, M. (1922). An experimental study of the mechanism of hallucinations. *British Journal of Medical Psychology*, 2, 165–208.

Rachman, S. (1997). A cognitive theory of obsessions. *Behavior Research and Therapy*, 35, 793–802.

Raichle, M. E. (2006). The brain's dark energy. *Science*, 314, 1249.

Raichle, M. E. & Mintun, M. A. (2006). Brain work and brain imaging. *Annual Review of Neuroscience*, 29, 449–76.

Raichle, M. E., MacLeod, A. M., Snyder, A. Z., Powers, W. J., Gusnard, D. A. & Shulman, G. L. (2001). A default mode of brain function. *Proceedings of the National Academy of Sciences USA*, 98, 676–82.

Raij, T. T., Valkonen-Korhonen, M., Holi, M., Therman, S., Lehtonen, J. & Hari, R. (2009). Reality of auditory verbal hallucinations. *Brain*, 132, 2994–3001.

Rajarethinam, R., DeQuardo, J. R., Miedler, J., Arndt, S., Kirbat, R., A. Brunberg, J. *et al.* (2001). Hippocampus and amygdala in schizophrenia: Assessment of the relationship of neuroanatomy to psychopathology. *Psychiatry Research: Neuroimaging*, 108, 79–87.

Rajarethinam, R. P., DeQuardo, J. R., Nalepa, R. & Tandon, R. (2000). Superior temporal gyrus in schizophrenia: A volumetric magnetic resonance imaging study. *Schizophrenia Research*, 41, 303–12.

Rajarethinam, R., Sahni, S., Rosenberg, D. R. & Keshavan, M. S. (2004). Reduced superior temporal gyrus volume in young offspring of patients with schizophrenia. *American Journal of Psychiatry*, 161, 1121–4.

Rajesh, G. S. (2003). Design of study has several problems [Letters to the editor]. *British Medical Journal*, 326, 549.

Randolph, T. G. (1970). Domiciliary chemical air pollution in the etiology of ecologic mental illness. *International Journal of Social Psychiatry*, 16, 243–65.

Rankin, P. M. & O'Carroll, P. J. (1995). Reality discrimination, reality monitoring and disposition towards hallucination. *British Journal of Clinical Psychology*, 34, 517–28.

Rattehalli, R. D., Jayaram, M. B. & Smith, M. (2010). Risperidone versus placebo for schizophrenia. *Cochrane Database of Systematic Reviews*, 20, CD006918.

Read, J., Agar, K., Argyle, N. & Aderhold, V. (2003). Sexual and physical abuse during childhood and adulthood as predictors of hallucinations, delusions and thought disorder. *Psychology and Psychotherapy: Theory, Research and Practice*, 76, 1–22.

Read, J. & Argyle, N. (1999). Hallucinations, delusions, and thought disorder among adult psychiatric inpatients with a history of child abuse. *Psychiatric Services*, 50, 1467–72.

Read, J. & Fraser, A. (1998). Abuse histories of psychiatric inpatients: To ask or not to ask? *Psychiatric Services*, 49, 355–9.

Read, J., Hammersley, P. & Rudegeair, T. (2007). Why, when and how to ask about childhood abuse. *Advances in Psychiatric Treatment*, 13, 101–10.

Read, J. & Harré, N. (2001). The role of biological and genetic causal beliefs in the stigmatisation of mental patients. *Journal of Mental Health*, 10, 223–35.

Read, J., Perry, B., Moskowitz, A. & Connolly, J. (2001).The contribution of early traumatic events to schizophrenia in some patients: A traumagenic neurodevelopmental model. *Psychiatry: Interpersonal and Biological Processes*, 64, 319–45.

Read, J., Van Os, J., Morrison, A. P. & Ross, C. A. (2005). Childhood trauma, psychosis and schizophrenia: A literature review with theoretical and clinical implications. *Acta Psychiatrica Scandinavica*, 112, 330–50.

Read, J., Bentall, R. & Fosse, R. (2009). Time to abandon the bio-bio-bio model of psychosis: Exploring the epigenetic and psychological mechanisms by which adverse life events lead to psychotic symptoms. *Epidemiologia e Psichiatria Sociale*, 18, 299–310.

Reddoch, M. J. (2010). *Dream narratives and their philosophical orientation in Philo of Alexandria*. Unpublished doctoral dissertation, University of Cincinnati.

Redmond, C., Larkin, M. & Harrop, C. (2010). The personal meaning of romantic relationships for young people with psychosis. *Clinical Child Psychology and Psychiatry*, 15, 151–70.

Rees, W. D. (1971). The hallucinations of widowhood. *British Medical Journal*, 210, 37–41.

Reeve, J. (1661/2003). *Divine looking glass or the third and last testament of Our Lord Jesus Christ*. Whitefish, MT: Kessinger Publishing Co.

Reiff, M., Castille, D. M., Muenzenmaier, K. & Link, B. (in press). Childhood abuse and the content of adult psychotic symptoms. *Psychological Trauma. Theory, Research, Practice, and Policy*.

Rice, E. (2006). Schizophrenia and violence: The perspective of women. *Issues in Mental Health Nursing*, 27, 961–83.

  (2008). The invisibility of violence against women diagnosed with schizophrenia: A synthesis of perspectives. *Advances in Nursing Science*, 31, 9–21.

Roberts, B. H., Greenblatt, M. & Solomon, H. C. (1951). Movements of the vocal apparatus during auditory hallucinations. *American Journal of Psychiatry*, 108, 912–14.

Robinson, D. G., Woerner, M. G., Napolitano, B., Patel, R. C., Sevy, S. M., Gunduz-Bruce, H. *et al.* (2006). Randomized comparison of olanzapine versus risperidone for the treatment of first-episode schizophrenia: 4-month outcomes. *American Journal of Psychiatry*, 163, 2096–102.

Roe, D., Chopra, M. & Rudnick, A. (2004). Persons with psychosis as active agents interacting with their disorder. *Psychiatric Rehabilitation Journal*, 28, 122–8.

Roe, D., Goldblatt, H., Baloush-Klienman, V., Swarbrick, M. & Davidson, L. (2009). Why and how people decide to stop taking prescribed psychiatric medication: Exploring the subjective process of choice. *Psychiatric Rehabilitation Journal*, 33, 38–46.

Rofail, D., Heelis, R. & Gournay, K. (2009). Results of a thematic analysis to explore the experiences of patients with schizophrenia taking antipsychotic medication. *Clinical Therapeutics*, 31 Suppl. 1, 1488–96.

Rojcewicz, S. J. & Rojcewicz, R. (1997). The 'human' voices in hallucinations. *Journal of Phenomenological Psychology*, 28, 1–41.

Romme, M. & Escher, S. (1989). Hearing voices. *Schizophrenia Bulletin*, 15, 209–16.

——— (1993). *Accepting voices*. London, UK: MIND.

——— (2000). *Making sense of voices: A guide for professionals who work with voice hearers*. London, UK: MIND.

Romme, M., Escher, S., Dillon, J., Corstens, D. & Morris, M. (2009). *Living with voices: 50 stories of recovery*. Ross: PCCS Books.

Rosenhan, D. L. (1973a). On being sane in insane places. *Science*, 179, 250–8.

——— (1973b). Reply to letters to the editor. *Science*, 180, 365–9.

Ross, C. A., Joshi, S. & Currie, R. (1990). Dissociative experiences in the general population. *American Journal of Psychiatry*, 147, 1547–52.

Ross, C. A., Miller, S. D., Reagor, P., Bjornson, L., Fraser, G. A. & Anderson, G. (1990). Schneiderian symptoms in multiple personality disorder and schizophrenia. *Comprehensive Psychiatry*, 31, 111–18.

Ross, C. A., Norton, R. G. & Wozney, K. (1989). Multiple personality disorder: An analysis of 236 cases. *Canadian Journal of Psychiatry*, 34, 413–18.

Rossell, S. L. & Boundy, C. L. (2005). Are auditory-verbal hallucinations associated with auditory affective processing deficits? *Schizophrenia Research*, 78, 95–106.

Rossell, S. L., Shapleske, J., Fukuda, R., Woodruff, P. W. R., Simmons, A. & David, A. S. (2001). Corpus callosum area and functioning in schizophrenic patients with auditory-verbal hallucinations. *Schizophrenia Research*, 50, 9–17.

Rossler, W., Riecher-Rossler, A., Angst, J., Murray, R., Gamma, A., Eich, D. *et al.* (2007). Psychotic experiences in the general population: A twenty-year prospective community study. *Schizophrenia Research*, 92, 1–14.

Rotarska-Jagiela, A., Oertel-Knoechel, V., DeMartino, F., van de Ven, V., Formisano, E., Roebroeck, A. *et al.* (2009). Anatomical brain connectivity and positive symptoms of schizophrenia: A diffusion tensor imaging study. *Psychiatry Research-Neuroimaging*, 174, 9–16.

Rowe, D. (2000). Foreword. In L. Johnstone, *Users and abusers of psychiatry*. London, UK: Routledge.

Rows, R. G. (1916). Mental conditions following strain and nerve shock. *British Medical Journal*, 1, 441–3.

Rubin, J. (2000). William James and the pathologizing of human experience. *Journal of Humanistic Psychology*, 40, 176–226.

Russell, D. A. (2010). Introduction. In D. A. Russell, G. Cawkwell, W. Deuse & J. Dillon. *On the daimonion of Socrates: Human liberation, divine guidance and philosophy*. Tubingen, Germany: Mohr Siebeck.

St John of the Cross. (1943). *The complete works of Saint John of the Cross*. Vol. I. (trans. E. A. Peers). London, UK: Burns Oates.

St Teresa of Avila. (2007). *Interior castle* (trans. E. A. Peers). New York, NY: Dover.

——— (2008). *The life of St Teresa of Avila*. New York, NY: Cosimo.

Sachdev, P. (2004). Schizophrenia-like psychosis and epilepsy: The status of the association. *American Journal of Psychiatry*, 155, 325–36.

Sadock, B. J., Kaplan, H. I. & Sadock, V. A. (2007). *Kaplan & Sadock's synopsis of psychiatry*. 10th edn. Philadelphia, PA: Lippincott Williams & Wilkins.

Sanjuan, J., Lull, J. J., Aguilar, E. J., Marti-Bonmati, L., Moratal, D., Gonzalez, J. C. *et al.* (2007). Emotional words induce enhanced brain activity in schizophrenic patients with auditory hallucinations. *Psychiatry Research: Neuroimaging*, 154, 21–9.

Sanjuan, J., Toirac, I., Gonzalez, J. C., Leal, C., Molto, M. D., Najera, C. *et al.* (2004). A possible association between the CCK-AR gene and persistent auditory hallucinations in schizophrenia. *European Psychiatry*, 19, 349–53.

Sanjuan, J., Tolosa, A., Gonzalez, J. C., Aguilar, E. J., Perez-Tur, J., Najera, C. *et al.* (2006). Association between FOXP2 polymorphisms and schizophrenia with auditory hallucinations. *Psychiatric Genetics*, 16, 67–72.

Sar, V. & Öztürk, E. (2008). Psychotic symptoms in complex dissociative disorders. In A. Moskowitz, I. Schafer & M. J. Dorahy (eds), *Psychosis, trauma, and dissociation: Emerging perspectives on severe psychopathology*. Chichester, Sussex: John Wiley & Sons.

Sarbin, T. R. (1967). The concept of hallucination. *Journal of Personality*, 35, 359–80.

Sarbin, T. R. & Juhasz, J. B. (1967). The historical background of the concept of hallucination. *Journal of the History of the Behavioural Sciences*, 3, 339–58.

Sass, L. (1992). *Madness and modernism: Insanity in the light of modern art, literature and thought*. New York, NY: Basic Books.

Sass, L. & Parnas, P. (2003). Self, consciousness and schizophrenia. *Schizophrenia Bulletin*, 29, 427–44.

Saunders, C. (2005). 'The thoughtful maladie': Madness and vision in medieval writing. In C. Saunders and J. Macnaugton (eds), *Madness and creativity in literature and culture*. London, UK: Palgrave Macmillan.

Schacter, D. L. & Addis, D. R. (2007). The cognitive neuroscience of constructive memory: Remembering the past and imagining the future. *Philosophical Transactions of the Royal Society: B Biological Sciences*, 362 (1481), 773–86.

(2009). On the nature of medial temporal lobe contributions to the constructive simulation of future events. *Philosophical Transactions of the Royal Society: B Biological Sciences*, 364(1521), 1245–53.

Schacter, D. L., Norman, K. A. & Koutstaal, W. (1998). The cognitive neuroscience of constructive memory. *Annual Review of Psychology*, 49, 289–318.

Schmidt, K. E. (1968). Some concepts of mental illness of the Murut of Sarawak. *International Journal of Social Psychiatry*, 14, 24–31.

Schmidt, L. E. (2002) *Hearing things: Religion, illusion, and the American enlightenment*. London: Harvard University Press.

Schmitz, T. W., Kawahara-Baccus, T. N. & Johnson, S. C. (2004). Metacognitive evaluation, self-relevance, and the right prefrontal cortex. *Neuroimage*, 22, 941–7.

Schneider, K. (1959). *Clinical psychopathology.* New York, NY: Grune & Stratton.

Schneider, S. D., Jelinek, L., Lincoln, T. M. & Moritz, S. (in press). What happened to the voices? A fine-grained analysis of how hallucinations and delusions change under psychiatric treatment. *Psychiatry Research.*

Schneider, S. J. & Wilson, C. R. (1983). Perceptual discrimination and reaction time in hallucinatory schizophrenics. *Psychiatry Research,* 9, 243–53.

Schon, U. -K., Denhov, A. & Topor, A. (2009). Social relationships as a decisive factor in recovering from severe mental illness. *International Journal of Social Psychiatry,* 55, 336–47.

Schonfeldt-Lecuona, C., Gron, G., Walter, H., Buchler, N., Wunderlich, A., Spitzer, M. *et al.* (2004). Stereotaxic rTMS for the treatment of auditory hallucinations in schizophrenia. *Neuroreport,* 15, 1669–73.

Schulze, B. & Angermeyer M. C. (2003). Subjective experiences of stigma. A focus group study of schizophrenic patients, their relatives and mental health professionals. *Social Science and Medicine,* 56, 299–312.

Scot, R. (1584). *The discoverie of witchcraft.* Retrieved 15 December 2010 from www.esotericarchives.com/solomon/scot16.htm.

Scott, E. H. M. (1967). A study of the content of delusions and hallucinations in 100 African female psychotics. *South African Medical Journal,* 9, 853–6.

Scott, J., Martin, G., Bor, W., Sawyer, M., Clark, J. & McGrath, J. (2009). The prevalence and correlates of hallucinations in Australian adolescents: Results from a national survey. *Schizophrenia Research,* 107, 179–85.

Scull, A. (1979). *Museums of madness: The social organization of insanity in nineteenth-century England.* New York, NY: St Martin's Press.

(1981). *Madhouses, mad-doctors and madmen.* University of Pennsylvania Press.

(2006). *The insanity of place/the place of insanity: Essays on the history of psychiatry.* London, UK: Routledge.

Schussler, R. (2009). Jean Gerson, moral certainty and the Renaissance of ancient scepticism. *Renaissance Studies,* 23, 445–62.

Scurlock, J. (1995). Death and the afterlife in Ancient Mesopotamian thought. In Jack M. Sasson (ed.), *Civilizations of the ancient near east.* NY: Charles Scribners Sons. Vol. III. pp. 1883–93.

(2006). *Magico-medical means of treating ghost-induced illnesses in Ancient Mesopotamia.* Ancient Magic and Divination 3. Leiden: Brill-Styx.

Scurlock, J. & Anderson, B. R. (2005). *Diagnoses in Assyrian and Babylonian medicine.* Chicago, IL: University of Illinois.

Seal, M. L., Aleman, A. & McGuire, P. K. (2004). Compelling imagery, unanticipated speech and deceptive memory: Neurocognitive models of auditory verbal hallucinations in schizophrenia. *Cognitive Neuropsychiatry,* 9, 43–72.

Seok, J. H., Park, H. J., Chun, H. W., Lee, S. K., Cho, H. S., Kwon, J. S. *et al.* (2007). White matter abnormalities associated with auditory hallucinations in schizophrenia: A combined study of voxel-based analyses of diffusion tensor imaging and structural magnetic resonance imaging. *Psychiatry Research-Neuroimaging,* 156, 93–104.

Shalev, A. Y., Yehuda, R. & McFarlane, A. C. (eds). (2000). *International handbook of human response to trauma*. New York, NY: Plenum.

Shapleske, J., Rossell, S. L., Chitnis, X. A., Suckling, J., Simmons, A., Bullmore, E. T. *et al.* (2002). A computational morphometric MRI study of schizophrenia: Effects of hallucinations. *Cerebral Cortex*, 12, 1331–41.

Shapleske, J., Rossell, S. L., Simmons, A., David, A. S. & Woodruff, P. W. R. (2001). Are auditory hallucinations the consequence of abnormal cerebral lateralization? A morphometric MRI study of the sylvian fissure and planum temporale. *Biological Psychiatry*, 49, 685–93.

Sharfstein, S. S. (2005). Big pharma and American psychiatry: The good, the bad, and the ugly. *Psychiatric News*, 40, 3.

Shawyer, F., Mackinnon, A., Farhall, J., Sims, E., Blaney, S., Yardley, P. *et al.* (2008). Acting on harmful command hallucinations in psychotic disorders: An integrative approach. *Journal of Nervous and Mental Disorder*, 196, 390–8.

Shea, T. L., Sergejew, A. A., Burnham, D., Jones, C., Rossell, S. L., Copolov, D. L. *et al.* (2007). Emotional prosodic processing in auditory hallucinations. *Schizophrenia Research*, 90, 214–20.

Sheikh, A. (2005). Jinn and cross-cultural care. *Journal of the Royal Society of Medicine*, 98, 339–40.

Sher, L. (2000). Neuroimaging, auditory hallucinations, and the bicameral mind. *Journal of Psychiatry & Neuroscience*, 25, 239–40.

Shergill, S. S., Brammer, M. J., Amaro, E., Williams, S. C. R., Murray, R. M. & McGuire, P. K. (2004). Temporal course of auditory hallucinations. *British Journal of Psychiatry*, 185, 516–17.

Shergill, S. S., Brammer, M. J., Fukuda, R., Williams, S. C. R., Murray, R. M. & McGuire, P. K. (2003). Engagement of brain areas implicated in processing inner speech in people with auditory hallucinations. *British Journal of Psychiatry*, 182, 525–31.

Shergill, S. S., Brammer, M. J., Williams, S. C. R., Murray, R. M. & McGuire, P. K. (2000a). Mapping auditory hallucinations in schizophrenia using functional magnetic resonance imaging. *Archives of General Psychiatry*, 57, 1033–8.

Shergill, S. S., Bullmore, E. T., Brammer, M. J., Williams, S. C. R., Murray, R. M. & McGuire, P. K. (2001a). A functional study of auditory verbal imagery. *Psychological Medicine*, 31, 241–53.

Shergill, S. S., Bullmore, E., Simmons, A., Murray, R. & McGuire, P. (2000b). Functional anatomy of auditory verbal imagery in schizophrenic patients with auditory hallucinations. *American Journal of Psychiatry*, 157, 1691–3.

Shergill, S. S., Cameron, L. A., Brammer, M. J., Williams, S. C. R., Murray, R. M. & McGuire, P. K. (2001b). Modality specific neural correlates of auditory and somatic hallucinations. *Journal of Neurology Neurosurgery and Psychiatry*, 71, 688–90.

Shergill, S. S., Kanaan, R. A., Chitnis, X. A., O'Daly, O., Jones, D. K., Frangou, S. *et al.* (2007). A diffusion tensor imaging study of fasciculi in schizophrenia. *American Journal of Psychiatry*, 164, 467–73.

Shergill, S. S., Murray, R. M. & McGuire, P. K. (1998). Auditory hallucinations: a review of psychological treatments. *Schizophrenia Research*, 32, 137–50.

Shevlin, M., Murphy, J., Dorahy, M. J. & Adamson, G. (2007). The distribution of positive psychosis-like symptoms in the population: A latent class analysis of the National Comorbidity Survey. *Schizophrenia Research*, 89, 101–9.

Shin, S. -E., Lee, J. -S., Kang, M. -H., Kim, C. -E., Bae, J. -N. & Jung, G. (2005). Segmented volumes of cerebrum and cerebellum in first episode schizophrenia with auditory hallucinations. *Psychiatry Research: Neuroimaging*, 138, 33–42.

Shorter, J. (1997). *A history of psychiatry: From the era of the asylum to the age of Prozac*. New York, NY: John Wiley & Sons.

Shotter, J. (1981). Vico, moral worlds, accountability and personhood. In P. Heelas & A. Lock (eds), *Indigenous psychologies: The anthropology of the self*. New York, NY: Academic Press.

Sidgwick, H., Johnson, A., Myers, F. W. H., Podmore, F. & Sidgwick, E. M. (1894). Report on the Census of Hallucinations. *Proceedings of the Society for Psychical Research*, 10, 24–422.

Siegel, R. K. (1978). Cocaine hallucinations. *American Journal of Psychiatry*, 135, 309–14.

Silbersweig, D. A., Stern, E., Frith, C., Cahill, C., Holmes, A. & Grootoonk, S. (1995). A functional neuroanatomy of hallucinations in schizophrenia. *Nature*, 378, 176–9.

Simon, B. (2008). Mind and madness in classical antiquity. *History of Psychiatry and Medical Psychology*, 1, 175–97.

Simons, C. J. P., Tracy, D. K., Sanghera, K. K., O'Daly, O., Gilleen, J., Dominguez, M. D. G. *et al.* (2010). Functional magnetic resonance imaging of inner speech in schizophrenia. *Biological Psychiatry*, 67, 232–7.

Simons, J. S., Davis, S. W., Gilbert, S. J., Frith, C. D. & Burgess, P. W. (2006). Discriminating imagined from perceived information engages brain areas implicated in schizophrenia. *Neuroimage*, 32, 696–703.

Simpson, J. (1988). *Touching the void*. London, UK: Cape.

Singer, J. L. (1966). *Daydreaming: An introduction to the experimental study of inner experience*. New York, NY: Random House.

Singer, J. L. & Antrobus, J. S. (1963). A factor-analytic study of daydreaming and conceptually-related cognitive and personality variables. *Perceptual and Motor Skills*, 17, 187–209.

Skirrow, P., Jones, C., Griffiths, R. & Kaney, S. (2002). The impact of current media events on hallucinatory content: The experience of the intensive care unit (ICU) patient. *British Journal of Clinical Psychology*, 41, 87–91.

Slade, P. & Bentall, R. (1988). *Sensory deception: A scientific analysis of hallucination*. London, UK: Croom Helm.

Sluhovsky, M. (2007). *Believe not every spirit: Possession, mysticism, and discernment in early modern Catholicism*. University of Chicago Press.

Smail, D. (2005). *Power, interest and psychology: Elements of a social materialist understanding of distress*. Ross-on-Wye, UK: PCCS Books.

Sommer, I. & Diederen, K. (2009). Language production in the non-dominant hemisphere as a potential source of auditory verbal hallucinations. *Brain*, 132, 1–2.

Sommer, I. E. C., Daalman, K., Rietkerk, T., Diederen, K. M., Bakker, S., Wijkstra, J. *et al.* (2010). Healthy individuals with auditory verbal hallucinations; Who are they? Psychiatric assessments of a selected sample of 103 subjects. *Schizophrenia Bulletin*, 36, 633–41.

Sommer, I. E. C., Diederen, K. M. J., Blom, J. D., Willems, A., Kushan, L., Slotema, K. *et al.* (2008). Auditory verbal hallucinations predominantly activate the right inferior frontal area. *Brain*, 131, 3169–77.

Soppitt R. W. & Birchwood M. (1997). Depression, beliefs, voice content and topography: A cross-sectional study of schizophrenic patients with auditory verbal hallucinations. *Journal of Mental Health*, 6, 525–32.

Spence, S. A., Brooks, D. J., Hirsch, S. R., Liddle, P. F., Meehan, J. & Grasby, P. M. (1997). A PET study of voluntary movement in schizophrenic patients experiencing passivity phenomena (delusions of alien control). *Brain*, 120, 1997–2011.

Spitzer, R. L. (1975). On pseudoscience in science, logic in remission, and psychiatric diagnosis: A critique of Rosenham's 'On being sane in insane places'. *Journal of Abnormal Psychology*, 84, 442–52.

Squire, L. R., Stark, C. E. L. & Clark, R. E. (2004). The medial temporal lobe. *Annual Review of Neuroscience*, 27, 279–306.

Sritharan, A., Line, P., Sergejew, A., Silberhei, R., Egan, G. & Copolov, D. (2005). EEG coherence measures during auditory hallucinations in schizophrenia. *Psychiatry Research*, 136, 189–200.

Stahl, S. M. (2008). *Stahl's essential psychopharmacology: Scientific basis and practical applications*. Cambridge University Press.

Staley, L. (1994). *Margery Kempe's dissenting fictions*. Pennsylvania State University Press.

Steel, C., Fowler, D. & Holmes, E. A. (2005). Trauma related intrusions and psychosis: An information processing account. *Behavioural and Cognitive Psychotherapy*, 33, 139–52.

Stanghellini, G. & Cutting, J. (2003). Auditory verbal hallicinations—breaking the silence of inner dialogue. *Psychopathology*, 36, 120–8.

Stein, D. (2000). Views of mental illness in Morocco: Western medicine meets the traditional symbolic. *Canadian Medical Association Journal*, 163, 1468–70.

Stein, G. (2010). The voices that Ezekiel hears. *British Journal of Psychiatry*, 196, 101.

Steinberg, M. & Siegel, H. D. (2008). Advances in assessment: The differential diagnosis of dissociative identity disorder and schizophrenia. In A. Moskowitz, I. Schafer & M. J. Dorahy (eds), *Psychosis, trauma, and dissociation: Emerging perspectives on severe psychopathology*. Chichester, Sussex: John Wiley & Sons.

Stephane, M., Barton, S. & Boutros, N. N. (2001a). Auditory verbal hallucinations and dysfunctions of the neural substrates of speech. *Schizophrenia Research*, 50, 61–78.

Stephane, M., Polis, I. & Barton, S. M. (2001b). A subtype of auditory verbal hallucinations responds to fleoroxamine. *Journal of Neuropsychiatry and Clinical Neurosciences*, 13, 425–6.

Stephens, G. L. & Graham, G. (2000). *When self-consciousness breaks: Alien voices and inserted thoughts*. Cambridge, MA: MIT Press.

Stewart, K. (1998). On pathologising discourse and psychiatric illness. An interview with Michael White. In M. White (ed.), *Re-authoring lives*. Adelaide, Australia: Dulwich Press.

Stinson, K., Valnaaggia, L. R., Antley, A., Slater, M. & Freeman, D. (2010). Cognitive triggers of auditory hallucinations: An experimental investigation. *Journal of Behavior Therapy and Experimental Psychiatry*, 41, 179–84.

Strassman, R. (2001). *DMT: The spirit molecule. A doctors revolutionary research into the biology of near-death and mystical experiences*. Rochester, VT: Park Street Press.

Straus, E. W. (1958). Aesthesiology and hallucinations (E. W. Straus & B. Morgan, trans.). In *Existence: A new dimension in psychiatry and psychology* (R. May, E. Angel, & H. F. Ellenberger, eds). New York: Simon and Schuster, pp. 139–69.

Strous, R. D. (2010). Psychiatric genocide: Reflections and responsibilities. *Schizophrenia Bulletin*, 36, 208–10.

Suhail, K. & Cochrane, R. (2002). Effect of culture on environment on the phenomenology of delusions and hallucinations. *International Journal of Social Psychiatry*, 48, 126–38.

Sumich, A., Chitnis, X. A., Fannon, D. G., O'Ceallaigh, S., Doku, V. C., Faldrowicz, A. *et al.* (2005). Unreality symptoms and volumetric measures of Heschl's gyrus and planum temporal in first-episode psychosis. *Biological Psychiatry*, 57, 947–50.

Sun, T., Patoine, C., Abu-Khalil, A., Visvader, J., Sum, E., Cherry, T. J. *et al.* (2005). Early asymmetry of gene transcription in embryonic human left and right cerebral cortex. *Science*, 308(5729), 1794–8.

Suzuki, H., Tsukamoto, C., Nakano, Y., Aoki, S. & Kuroda, S. (1998). Delusions and hallucinations in patients with borderline personality disorder. *Psychiatry and Clinical Neurosciences*, 52, 605–10.

Suzuki, M., Yuasa, S., Minabe, Y., Murata, M. & Kurachi, M. (1993). Let superior temporal blood-flow increases in schizophrenia and schizophreniform patients with auditory hallucination – a longitudinal case-study using I-123 SPECT. *European Archives of Psychiatry and Clinical Neuroscience*, 242, 257–61.

Swedenborg, E. (1883 [1746–65]). *The spiritual diary of Emanuel Swedenborg*, trans. G. Bush and J. H. Smithson. London, UK: James Speirs.

Szasz, T. S. (1996). *The meaning of mind: Language, morality and neuroscience*. Westport, CT: Praeger.

(2006). *'My madness saved me': The madness and marriage of Virginia Woolf*. New Brunswick, NJ: Transaction.

Szechtman, H., Woody, E., Bowers, K. S. & Nahmias, C. (1998). Where the imaginal appears real: A positron emission tomography study of auditory hallucinations. *Proceedings of the National Academic of Sciences of the United States of America*, 95, 1956–60.

Takeda, Y., Inoue, Y., Tottori, T. & Mihara, T. (2001). Acute psychosis during intracranial EEG monitoring: Close relationship between psychotic symptoms and discharges in amygdala. *Epilepsia*, 42, 719–24.

Tamburini, A. (1881/1990). A theory of hallucinations. *History of Psychiatry*, 1, 151–6.

Tanabe, H., Sawada, T., Asai, H., Okuda, J. & Shiraishini, J. (1986). Lateralization phenomenon of complex auditory hallucinations. *Acta Psychiatrica Scandinavica*, 74, 178–82.

Tarrier, N., Kinney, C., McCarthy, E., Humphreys, L., Wittkowski, A. & Morris, J. (2000). Two-year follow-up of cognitive – behavioral therapy and supportive counseling in the treatment of persistent symptoms in chronic schizophrenia. *Journal of Consulting and Clinical Psychology*, 68, 917–22.

Tauscher, J., Jones, C., Remington, G., Zipursky, R. B. & Kapur, S. (2002). Significant dissociation of brain and plasma kinetics with antipsychotics. *Molecular Psychiatry*, 7, 317–21.

Taylor, M. (1999). *Imaginary companions and the children who create them.* New York, NY: Oxford University Press.

Thaniel, G. (1973). Lemures and larvae. *The American Journal of Philology*, 94, 182–7.

Tharyan, P. & Adams, C. E. (2005). Electroconvulsive therapy for schizophrenia. *Cochrane Database of Systematic Reviews*, 18, CD000076.

Thirion, B., Pinel, P., Meriaux, S., Roche, A., Dehaene, S. & Poline, J. B. (2007). Analysis of a large fMRI cohort: Statistical and methodological issues for group analyses. *Neuroimage*, 35, 105–20.

Thomas, N., McLeod, H. J. & Brewin, C. R. (2009). Interpersonal complementarity in responses to auditory hallucinations in psychosis. *British Journal of Clinical Psychology*, 48, 411–24.

Thomas, P., Bracken, P. & Leudar, I. (2004). Hearing voices: A phenomenological-hermeneutic approach. *Cognitive Neuropsychiatry*, 9, 13–23.

Thomas, P., Mathur, P., Gottesman, I. I., Nagpal, R., Nimgaonkar, V. L. & Deshpande, S. N. (2007). Correlates of hallucinations in schizophrenia: A cross-cultural evaluation. *Schizophrenia Research*, 92, 41–9.

Thornhill, H., Clare, L. & May, R. (2004). Escape, enlightenment and endurance: Narratives of recovery from psychosis. *Anthropology and Medicine*, 11, 181–99.

Tidey, J. W. & Miczek, K. A. (1996). Social defeat stress selectively alters mesocorticolimbic dopamine release: An in vivo microdialysis study. *Brain Research*, 721, 140–9

Tien, A. Y. (1991). Distributions of hallucination in the population. *Social Psychiatry and Psychiatric Epidemiology*, 26, 287–92.

Toksvig, S. (1948). *Emanuel Swedenborg: Scientist and mystic.* London, UK: Faber & Faber.

Tomoda, A., Sheu, Y., Rabi, K., Suzuki, H., Navalta, C. P., Polcari, A. *et al.* (2011). Exposure to parental verbal abuse is associated with increased gray matter volume in superior temporal gyrus. *Neuroimage*, 54, Suppl. 1, S280–S286.

Tooth, B., Kalyanasundaram, V., Glover, H. & Momenzadah S. (2003). Factors consumers identify as important to recovery from schizophrenia. *Australasian Psychiatry*, 11 Suppl. 1, S70–S77.

Trower, P., Birchwood, M., Meaden, A., Byrne, S., Nelson, A. & Ross, K. (2004). Cognitive therapy for command hallucinations: Randomised controlled trial. *British Journal of Psychiatry*, 184, 312–20.

Twardosz, S. & Lutzker, J. R. (2010). Child maltreatment and the developing brain: A review of neuroscience perspectives. *Aggression and Violent Behavior*, 15, 59–68.

Üçok, A. & Bikmaz, S. (2007). The effects of childhood trauma in patients with first episode schizophrenia. *Acta Psychiatrica Scandinavica*, 116, 371–7.

Underhill, E. (1911). *Mysticism: A study in the nature and development of man's spiritual consciousness*. London, UK: Methuen.

Usher, K. (2001). Taking neuroleptic medications as the treatment for schizophrenia: A phenomenological study. *The Australian and New Zealand Journal of Mental Health Nursing*, 10, 145–55.

Valmaggia, L. R., Van der Gaag, M., Tarrier, N., Pijnenborg, M. & Slooff, C. J. (2005). Cognitive-behavioural therapy for refractory psychotic symptoms of schizophrenia resistant to atypical antipsychotic medication – Randomised controlled trial. *British Journal of Psychiatry*, 186, 324–30.

Van de Ven, V. G., Formisano, E., Roder, C. H., Prvulovic, D., Bittner, R. A., Dietz, M. G. *et al.* (2005). The spatiotemporal pattern of auditory cortical responses during verbal hallucinations. *Neuroimage*, 27, 644–55.

Van Dusen, W. (1972). *The natural depth in man*. New York, NY: Swedenborg Foundation.

Van Harmelen, A., van Tol, M., van der Wee, N. J. A., Veltman, D. J., Aleman, A., Spinhoven, P. *et al.* (2010). Reduced medial prefrontal cortex volume in adults reporting childhood emotional maltreatment. *Biological Psychiatry*, 68, 832–8.

Van Lutterveld, R., Oranje, B., Kemner, C., Abramovic, L., Willems, A. E., Boks, M. P. M. *et al.* (2010). Increased psychophysiological parameters of attention in non-psychotic individuals with auditory verbal hallucinations *Schizophrenia Research*, 121, 153–9.

Van Lutterveld, R., Sommer, I. E. C. & Ford, J. M. (2011). The neurophysiology of auditory hallucinations – a historical and contemporary review. *Frontiers in Psychiatry*, 2, 28.

Van Meer, R. (2003). To listen or not to listen. *British Medical Journal*, 326, 549.

Van Riel, G. (2005). Socrates' daemon: Internalisation of the divine and knowledge of the self. In P. Destrée and N. D. Smith (eds), *Socrates' divine sign: religion, practice and value in Socratic philosophy*. Kelowna, BC: Academic Printing and Publishing.

Varese, F. & Bentall, R. P. (2011). The metacognitive beliefs account of hallucinatory experiences: A literature review and meta-analysis. *Clinical Psychology Review*, 31, 850–64.

Vaughn, C. E., Snyder, K. S., Jones, S., Freeman, W. B. & Falloon, I. R. (1984). Family factors in schizophrenic relapse. Replication in California of British research on expressed emotion. *Archives of General Psychiatry*, 41, 1169–77.

Vercammen, A., de Haan, E. H. F. & Aleman, A. (2008). Hearing a voice in the noise: Auditory hallucinations and speech perception. *Psychological Medicine*, 38, 1177–84.

Vercammen, A., Knegtering, H., Bruggeman, R., Westenbroek, H. M., Jenner, J. A., Slooff, C. J. *et al.* (2009). Effects of bilateral repetitive transcranial magnetic stimulation on treatment resistant auditory-verbal hallucinations in schizophrenia: A randomized controlled trial. *Schizophrenia Research*, 114, 172–9.

Vercammen, A., Knegtering, H., den Boer, J. A., Liemburg, E. J. & Aleman, A. (2010a). Auditory hallucinations in schizophrenia are associated with reduced functional connectivity of the temporo-parietal area. *Biological Psychiatry*, 67, 912–18.

Vercammen, A., Knegtering, H., Liemburg, E. J., Boer, J. A. & Aleman, A. (2010b). Functional connectivity of the temporo-parietal region in schizophrenia: Effects of rTMS treatment of auditory hallucinations. *Journal of Psychiatric Research*, 44, 725–31.

Verdoux, H., Maurice-Tison, S., Gay, B., Van Os, J., Salamon, R. & Bourgeois, M. L. (1998). A survey of delusional ideation in primary-care patients. *Psychological Medicine*, 28, 127–34.

Vernon, A. C., Natesan, S., Modo, M. & Kapur, S. (in press). Effect of chronic antipsychotic treatment on brain structure: A serial magnetic resonance imaging study with ex vivo and postmortem confirmation. *Biological Psychiatry*.

Virkler, M. & Virkler, P. (1986). *Dialogue with God*. Gainesville, FL: Bridge-Logo.

Virtue, D. (2007). *How to hear your angels*. London, UK: Hay House.

Volman, L. & Landeen J. (2007). Uncovering the sexual self in people with schizophrenia. *Journal of Psychiatric and Mental Health Nursing*, 14, 411–17.

Vygotsky, L. S. (1978). In M. Cole, V. John-Steiner, S. Scribner & E. Souberman (eds), *Mind in society: The development of higher mental processes*. Cambridge, MA: Harvard University Press.

Vygotsky, L. S. (1934/1987). *Thinking and speech. The Collected Works of L. S. Vygotsky, Vol. I.* New York, NY: Plenum.

(1934/1986). *Thought and language* (trans. A. Kozulin). Cambridge, MA: MIT Press.

Wachowski, A. & Wachowski, L. (Writers and Directors). (2003). *The Matrix Reloaded (film)*. Burbank, CA: Warner Bros.

Wagner, L. C. & King, M. (2005). Existential needs of people with psychotic disorders in Parto Alegre, Brazil. *British Journal of Psychiatry*, 186, 141–5.

Wahass, S. & Kent, G. (1997a). Coping with auditory hallucinations: A cross-cultural comparison between western (British) and non-western (Saudi Arabian) patients. *Journal of Nervous & Mental Disease*, 185, 664–8.

(1997b). A comparison of public attitudes on Britain and Saudi Arabia towards auditory hallucinations. *International Journal of Social Psychiatry*, 43, 175–83.

(1997c). A cross-cultural study of the attitudes of mental health professionals towards auditory hallucinations. *International Journal of Social Psychiatry*, 43, 184–92.

Wahlbeck, K., Cheine, M. & Essali, M. A. (2000). Clozapine versus typical neuroleptic medication for schizophrenia. *Cochrane Database of Systematic Reviews*, 2, CD000059.

Walker, D. P. (1983). *Unclean spirits. Possession and exorcism in France and England in the late sixteenth and early seventeenth centuries.* London, UK: Scolar Press.

Walsh, J. (2002, 18 March). Is there a link between madness and creativity? *The Independent on Sunday*. Retrieved from www.independent.co.uk/life-style/health-and-families/health-news/is-these-a-link-between-madness-and-creativity-440374.html.

Wang, J., Morales, O. & Hsu, G. (1998). Auditory hallucinations in bilingual immigrants. *Journal of Nervous and Mental Disorder*, 186, 501–3.

Ward, K. (2006). *The Reformation.* Talk given at Gresham College. Retrieved 12 November 2011 from www.gresham.ac.uk/lectures-and-events/the-reformation.

Warner, R. (1985). *Recovery from schizophrenia: Psychiatry and political economy.* London, UK: Routledge & Kegan Paul.

Warren, R. & Bell, P. (2000). An exploratory investigation into the housing preferences of consumers of mental health services. *The Australian and New Zealand Journal of Mental Health Nursing*, 9, 195–202.

Waters, F. A. V., Badcock, J. C. & Maybery, M. T. (2006). The 'who' and 'when' of context memory: Different patterns of association with auditory hallucinations. *Schizophrenia Research*, 82, 271–3.

Waters, F. A. V., Badcock, J. C., Maybery, M. T. & Michie, P. T. (2003). Inhibition in schizophrenia: Association with auditory hallucinations. *Schizophrenia Research*, 62, 275–80.

Waters, F. A. V., Badcock, J. C., Michie, P. T. & Maybery, M. T. (2006). Auditory hallucinations in schizophrenia: Intrusive thoughts and forgotton memories. *Cognitive Neuropsychiatry*, 11, 65–83.

Waters, F. A. V., Maybery, M. T., Badcock, J. C. & Michie, P. T. (2004). Context memory and binding in schizophrenia. *Schizophrenia Research*, 62, 275–80.

Waters, F., Woodward, T., Allen, P., Aleman, A. & Sommer, I. (in press). Self-recognition deficits in schizophrenia patients with auditory hallucinations: A meta-analysis of the literature. Schizophrenia Bulletin.

Watkins, K. & Paus, T. (2004). Modulation of motor excitability during speech perception: The role of Broca'a area. *Journal of Cognitive Neuroscience*, 16, 978–87.

Watson, J. B. (1920). Is thinking merely the action of language mechanisms? *British Journal of Psychology*, 11, 87–104.

Watters, E. (2010). *Crazy like us: The globalization of the American psyche.* New York, NY: Free Press.

Webster, R. (1996). *Why Freud was wrong: Sin, science and psychoanalysis.* New York, NY: Basic Books.

Weckowicz, T. E. & Liebel-Weckowicz, H. P (1990). *A history of great ideas in abnormal psychology.* Amsterdam, Netherlands: Elsevier Science Publishers.

Wegner, D. M. (2002). *The illusion of conscious will.* Cambridge, MA: MIT Press.

Wegner, D. M. & Wheatley, T. (1999). Apparent mental causation: sources of the experience of will. *American Psychologist*, 54, 480–92.

Weinberger, D. R. (1987). Implications of normal brain development for the pathogenesis of schizophrenia. *Archives of General Psychiatry*, 44, 660–9.

Wertsch, J. V. (1980). The significance of dialogue in Vygotsky's account of social, egocentric and inner speech. *Contemporary Educational Psychology*, 5, 150–62.

Wesley, J. (1986[1770]) *The Works of John Wesley*, vol. XXII, *Journals and Diaries, V, 1765–75.* Nashville, TN: Abingdon Press.

West, L. J. (1962). A general theory of hallucinations and dreams. In L. J. West (ed.), *Hallucinations.* New York, NY: Grune & Stratton.

Wiebe, P. H. (2000). Critical reflections on Christic visions. *Journal of Consciousness Studies*, 7, 119–44.

Whitfield-Gabrieli, S., Thermenos, H. W., Milanovic, S., Tsuang, M. T., Faraone, S. V., McCarley, R. W. *et al.* (2009). Hyperactivity and hyperconnectivity of the default network in schizophrenia and in first-degree relatives of persons with schizophrenia. *Proceedings of the National Academy of Sciences*, 106, 1279–84.

WHO (1973). *Report of the international pilot study of schizophrenia.* Geneva: World Health Organization.

(1979). *Schizophrenia. An international follow-up study.* Chichester, UK: John Wiley & Sons.

Wiebe, P. H. (2004). *God and other spirits.* Oxford University Press.

Wilcox, J., Briones, D. & Suess, L. (1991). Auditory hallucinations, posttraumatic stress disorder, and ethnicity. *Comprehensive Psychiatry*, 32, 320–3.

Wilkinson, R. (2005). *The impact of inequality: How to make sick societies healthier.* London, UK: New Press.

Wilkinson, R. & Pickett, K. (2009). *The spirit level: Why more equal societies almost always do better.* London, UK: Allen Lane.

Williams, R. (2003). *Silence and honeycakes: The wisdom of the desert.* Oxford: Lion Publishing.

Wilson, B. (1996). *Wouldn't it be nice: My own story.* London, UK: Bloomsbury.

(2011). *Brian Wilson – A powerful interview.* Retrieved 7 March 2011 from http://abilitymagazine.com/past/brianW/brianw.html.

Winawer, M. R., Ottman, R., Hauser, W. A. & Pedley, T. A. (2000). Autosomal dominant partial epilepsy with auditory features: Defining the phenotype. *Neurology*, 54, 2173–6.

Wing, J. K., Cooper, J. E. & Sartorius, N. (1974). *Measurement and classification of psychiatric symptoms.* Cambridge University Press.

Witte, J. (2007). *The reformation of rights: Law, religion and human rights in early modern Calvinism.* Cambridge University Press.

Wittgenstein, L. (1953). *Philosophical investigations*. Malden, MA: Blackwell.

Woodruff, P., Brammer, M., Mellers, J., Wright, I., Bullmore, E., Williams, S. et al. (1995). Auditory hallucinations and perception of external speech. *Lancet*, 346(8981), 1035–6.

Woodruff, P. W. R. (2004). Auditory halluciantions: Insights and questions from neuroimaging. *Cognitive Neuropsychiatry*, 9, 73–91.

Woodside, H., Schell, L. & Allison-Hedges, J. (2006). Listening for recovery: The vocational success of people living with mental illness. *Canadian Journal of Occupational Therapy*, 73, 36–43.

Wykes, T., Hayward, P., Thomas, N., Green, N., Surguladze, S., Fannon, D. et al. (2005). What are the effects of group cognitive behaviour therapy for voices? A randomised control trial. *Schizophrenia Research*, 77, 201–10.

Yamamoto, J., Okonogi, K., Iwasaki, T. & Yoshimura, S. (1969). Mourning in Japan. *American Journal of Psychiatry*, 125, 1660–5.

Yee, L., Korner, A. J., McSwiggan, S., Meares, R. A. & Stevenson, J. (2005). Persistent hallucinosis in borderline personality disorder. *Comprehensive Psychiatry*, 46, 147–54.

Yomogida, Y., Sugiura, M., Sassa, Y., Wakusawa, K., Sekiguchi, A., Fukushima, A. et al. (2010). The neural basis of agency: An fMRI study. *Neuroimage*, 50, 198–207.

Young, H. E, Bentall, R. P., Slade, P. D. & Dewey, M. (1987). The role of brief instructions and suggestibility in the elicitation of auditory and visual hallucinations in normal and psychiatric subjects. *Journal of Nervous and Mental Disease*, 175, 41–8.

Yung, A. R., Phillips, L. J., Yuen, H. P., Francey, S. M., McFarlane, C. A. Hallgren, M. et al. (2003). Psychosis prediction: 12-month follow up of a high-risk ('prodromal') group. *Schizophrenia Research*, 60, 21–32.

Zimmerman, B. (1910). St. John of the Cross. In *The Catholic Encyclopedia*. New York: Robert Appleton Company. Retrieved 9 June 2009, from New Advent, www.newadvent.org/cathen/08480a.htm.

(1912). St. Teresa of Avila. In *The Catholic Encyclopedia*. New York: Robert Appleton Company. Retrieved 9 June 2009, from New Advent, www. newadvent.org/cathen/14515b.htm.

Zipursky, R. B., Marsh, L., Lim, K. O., Dement, S., Shear, P. K., Sullivan, E. V. et al. (1994). Volumetric MRI assessment of temporal-lobe structures in schizophrenia. *Biological Psychiatry*, 35, 501–16.

Zuckerman, M. (1969). Variables affecting deprivation results. In J. P. Zurek (ed.), *Sensory deprivation: Fifteen years of research* (pp. 47–84). New York, NY: Appleton-Century-Crofts.

Zuravin, S. J. (1989). The ecology of child abuse and neglect: Review of the literature and presentation of data. *Violence and Victims*, 4, 101–20.

Zwerdling, A. (1986). *Virginia Woolf and the real world*. Berkeley, CA: University of California Press.

Index

8583138R00252

Made in the USA
San Bernardino, CA
14 February 2014